JUVENILE
DELINQUENCY

Fourth Edition

JUVENILE DELINQUENCY

Lewis Yablonsky
California State University, Northridge

Martin Haskell
Late, California State University, Long Beach

HarperCollins*Publishers*

Sponsoring Editor: Alan McClare
Project Coordination: Caliber Design Planning, Inc.
Cover Design: Nadja Furlam-Lorbek
Compositor: Keystone Typesetting
Printer and Binder: R. R. Donnelley & Sons Company

Juvenile Delinquency, Fourth Edition

Library of Congress Cataloging-in-Publication Data
Yablonsky, Lewis.
   Juvenile delinquency.

   The late Martin R. Haskell's name appears first on the 3rd ed.
   Includes index.
   1. Juvenile delinquency—United States. 2. Rehabilitation of juvenile delinquents—
United States. I. Haskell, Martin R., 1912–1980.   II. Title.
HV9104.H33   1987   364.3′6′0973   87–25038
ISBN 0- 06–047291–X (pbk.)

90 9 8 7 6 5 4 3

Contents

four

THE CAUSAL CONTEXT OF CRIME AND DELINQUENCY   341

five

THE PREVENTION, TREATMENT, AND CONTROL OF DELINQUENCY   403

Preface

Juvenile misbehavior is a social problem that affects all members of society, young and old, at some time in their lives. This text analyzes delinquent behavior and its causal context. A new delinquency is emerging, and this book studies its major characteristics.

Substance abuse—both drugs and alcohol—have become entwined with delinquent behavior. Almost all delinquents are substance abusers—and various mind-altering substances have become an intrinsic part of the overall delinquency problem.

Attitudes about adolescent sexuality have changed enormously since the 1950s. When I began my work in the field, adolescents, especially girls, were often incarcerated for "incorrigibility" (which was related to "sexual promiscuity"). Incarceration was often ordered for a teenage pregnant girl—and her boyfriend would often become a ward of the court. In recent years these sexual issues have been almost ignored by the juvenile courts because of a generally more liberal view toward teenage sexual behavior.

Another aspect of adolescent sexuality is the specter of AIDS. This is rapidly developing as a major issue in delinquency. Sexual freedom and intravenous drug abuse have become a lethal combination.

Another general trend in the overall delinquency scene is an increase in "senseless violence," often related to drug abuse and reflected in a wilder form of gang violence. Part of this more indiscriminate, "senseless" delinquent violence can be accounted for because of an increase in the use of dangerous drugs, and by the "dealing" of drugs by young people.

Another major change in the field is the burgeoning of middle- and upper-class delinquency, not only in numbers but in patterns of delinquency. This increasing problem is significantly related to the rise in substance and alcohol abuse among all adolescents.

There has been a differential response on the part of middle- and upper-class parents to their teenagers' deviance. These parents, who are often psychologically sophisticated, rescue their children from the juvenile court's administration of justice and place them in mental health facilities. This process has significantly affected the status definitions of delinquency, statistics on delinquency, and led to an increase of mental health facilities and programs for delinquents.

The emergence of a new delinquency has necessitated a complete rewriting of this book. However, this new edition, like its predecessors, benefits from my direct involvement with delinquents as a licensed therapist, as well as my research as a sociologist. It also benefits from the help of many esteemed colleagues. My sponsoring editor at Harper & Row, Alan McClare, brilliantly guided me through the editorial complications of producing this virtually new volume. I am enormously grateful to him for his intelligent guidance. I am also grateful to Joules Gury, an educational therapist who works with delinquents, for her significant contribution to this fourth edition. James Reed was most helpful in researching pertinent data for the book. I remain grateful to my late co-author, Martin Haskell, for his contributions to the first two editions of the book. I further acknowledge my appreciation to the many social scientists, therapists, law enforcement officers, and adolescents who have contributed a variety of research findings, case material, concepts, and treatment methods that are incorporated into this new fourth edition.

Lewis Yablonsky, Ph.D.
Professor of Sociology
California State University
Northridge, California

one

DEFINING DELINQUENCY

chapter 1

The Nature and Extent of Juvenile Delinquency

Juvenile delinquency involves illegal behavior by a person who, in most jurisdictions, is under the age of 18 and has had his or her behavior adjudicated as delinquent in a juvenile court. It encompasses such offenses as homicide, robbery, and theft, acts that if committed by an adult would constitute a crime. Delinquency also includes deviant behavior unique to the juvenile's status in society, such as truancy, curfew violations, running away from home, and "incorrigibility." The latter is a catch-all phrase that usually means that the youth's parents can no longer control their child's behavior.

Juvenile delinquents are treated differently than are criminals in our society, because it is generally assumed that they are less responsible for their deviance and that their illegal behavior has not yet solidified into a more permanent criminal pattern. In brief, we assume that juveniles are less culpable and more responsive to positive behavioral change than adult offenders.

In general, in contemporary law, therefore, the juvenile delinquent is distinguished from the adult criminal by several factors:

1. In most jurisdictions the cutoff point between delinquency and criminality is marked by age, usually 18.
2. Juvenile delinquents are generally considered less responsible for their behavior than adult offenders and hence are considered less culpable.
3. In the administration of justice to a juvenile delinquent, the emphasis is more on the youth's personality and the motivation for the

illegal act than on the offense itself. The opposite is usually true of the adult criminal.

4. In the treatment of juvenile delinquents, the emphasis is more on therapeutic programs than on punishment.
5. The judicial process for a juvenile delinquent originally deemphasized the legal aspects of due process and was geared to a more informal and personalized procedure. Although this is still largely the approach, the trend is toward greater due process in the juvenile court system.

This special treatment of juvenile delinquents is not a recent phenomenon. Throughout recorded history we find evidence of such treatment for young offenders and the recognition that such offenders constitute a special problem. The misbehavior of young people has been regarded as a problem apart from criminality as far back as the Code of Hammurabi in 2270 B.C., which prescribed specific punishments for children who disowned their parents or ran away from home.[1] The Hebrews divided young people into three categories—infant, prepubescent, and adolescent—and established increased penalties as offenders became older. Old English law also indicated special treatment for juvenile offenses by providing less severe punishment for persons under 16. The founding of Hospes St. Michael in Rome for the rehabilitation of young people indicates a concern with this problem by the Vatican as early as the seventeenth century.

Industrialization and urbanization, with their accompanying changes in family structure and function, have resulted in an increased emphasis on juvenile delinquency. Parents working away from home have not been able to fulfill the socialization function (preparation of their children for life in the society) in the same way as was common in prior periods of human history.

The impersonal relationships that accompany urbanization in our society have produced an increased tendency to resort to formal social control of children. Misbehavior traditionally handled by the family and friends in smaller communities now results in complaints to the police and petitions to courts in large urban areas. The juvenile court has become a significant social and legal instrument for defining and controlling juvenile delinquency. In the 1980s, however, there has been a trend toward returning the handling of juvenile delinquents to supervised and sometimes unsupervised community environments.

Another factor that enters into defining "juvenile delinquency" is the recent emergence of a trend in many communities of diverting youths who would formerly have been made wards of the juvenile court into various types of treatment clinics. In this context, they are perceived as individuals with mental disorders, rather than as juvenile delinquents.

---

[1]Albert Kocourek and John H. Wigmore, *Source of Ancient and Primitive Law, Evolution of Law: Select Readings on the Origin and Development of Legal Institutions* (Boston: Little, Brown, 1951), vol. 1.

As I have worked with youths like these in several psychiatric clinics, I have observed that if it had not been for the burgeoning of medical insurance and the growth of treatment clinics, these same youths would be placed in the juvenile court system and defined as juvenile delinquents. Parents who have medical insurance have the possibility of placing their child in a treatment facility, whereas for most other parents the cost is prohibitive. As a consequence of this new development, youths manifesting the same delinquent behavior may arbitrarily be placed in the juvenile court system or a mental hospital.

The delinquency status of a child is also related to the perceptions of parents. For example, one parent may see the smoking of one marijuana cigarette as an horrendous act of juvenile delinquency, whereas another parent may perceive the same act as a normal youthful experiment. The parental perception of certain behavioral acts is critical in determining who is defined as a delinquent by the courts.

Another issue in analyzing delinquency on a national level relates to the fact that norms of conduct vary from state to state, city to city, and neighborhood to neighborhood. Moreover, whether or not these norms are applied to a particular child may depend on the position of his parents in society and the provisions of the law in that community. The community's response is also regulated by the policies and attitudes of community leaders and law enforcement officials.

Legally a "juvenile delinquent" is a youth who has been so adjudged by a juvenile court. Even so, the behavior that leads to a judgment of juvenile delinquency is vaguely defined by the statutes, and the procedures followed by the various juvenile courts are not uniform. In the final analysis, the legal status of "delinquent" tends to depend more on the attitudes of parents, the police, the community, and the juvenile courts than on any specific illegal behavior of a child.

Despite these vagaries and haphazard factors, my observation over the years is that most youths who persistently violate the law end up as delinquents in the juvenile court system and eventually are placed in one of the institutions for delinquents. There are, however, youths who are not committed "delinquents" who acquire this status by chance ("by chance" because they are arrested, whereas another youth who has committed a similar offense is not). Once caught and in the administrative net, the youth may more easily be defined as a juvenile delinquent due to the socialization process inherent in the court system.

Another aspect of defining delinquency is the concept of the *status offender*. The status offender commits offenses that relate to the specific sociocultural status juveniles occupy in the society and the behaviors that accompany their adolescent roles. More specifically, a status offense is one that an adult cannot commit, for example, being a runaway or playing hookey from school.

Not all authorities in the field are in sympathy with softening the delinquency label through the concept of status offender. For example,

Logan and Raush maintain, based on research into the handling of status offenders in a Connecticut program for juveniles, that "When seen in the context of its justifying rationale, [status offender] deinstitutionalizing by itself—without decriminalization and divestiture is an illogical and self-defeating half-measure and therefore pointless."[2]

Ruth Cavan and Theodore Ferdinand cogently delineate various aspects of the status offender:

> Typical laws governing status offenses require obedience to parents' lawful requests, attendance at school and avoidance of immoral situations or persons. These laws are defended as related to the present or future well-being of the child. Status offenders are usually victimless—that is, harmful only to the offender. In the absence of effective control by parents, the court assumes the role of a parent and exercises control traditionally assumed to be the responsibility of parents. It is now recognized that status offenses often indicate deep disturbance in the parental-child relationship and not simply willfulness on the part of the child.

> With these facts in mind, many states now require that delinquents and status offenders be kept separate within the juvenile justice system. Delinquents typically are referred to the juvenile court for a formal hearing, which may result in commitment to a state training school, whereas the status offender is usually placed on informal probation or referred to a social agency or counseling center.[3]

As indicated, the attitudes and actions of parents exercise an important influence on whether or not a child is found to be incorrigible, disobedient, or a runaway. One mother may petition a juvenile court and allege that her son is incorrigible because he does not obey her and have the child declared a juvenile delinquent; another may regard the same behavior as reflecting an independent spirit. Drug abuse, a rampant delinquency problem, is also affected by the parents' reaction to their child's drug use. Some parents take swift legal action, whereas others do not. Consequently, a parent's response to their child's misbehavior has a significant impact on the child's status as a delinquent. This random element of parental response significantly affects the child's status and, therefore, delinquency statistics.

The policies of the police and the attitudes prevailing in the community also influence the action taken. The breaking of store windows on a main street in the course of an encounter of two groups of boys may or may not be classified as delinquency. If the boys are college sophomores "fooling around," the incident is likely to be referred to the college administration for disciplinary action. If the two groups are defined by the police as gangs,

[2]Charles Logan and Sharla Raush, "Why Deinstitutionalizing Status Offenders is Pointless," *Crime and Delinquency* 31 (1985): 514–515.
[3]Ruth S. Cavan and Theodore N. Ferdinand, *Juvenile Delinquency*, 4th ed. (New York: Harper & Row, 1981), p. 18.

the boys are likely to be arrested, taken before a juvenile court, and treated as delinquents.

Another example of the influence of community attitudes is a rape incident at the University of California in Berkeley in 1986. In brief, a number of young male students raped a girl in a dormitory under some absurd guise of "playing around." The youthful offenders were football players. Their punishment involved university censure and "community service." In real life, outside of the university's jurisdiction, they would have, and no doubt should have, received long-term prison sentences.

The attitude of the police is also significant in determining which youths are classified as delinquent. For example, in a tri-city study in Pennsylvania,[4] Nathan Goldman determined that there were great variations in arrest practices on the part of the police. The status of juvenile delinquent depended on police attitudes, the racial background of the child, as well as the time of the day or night that the offense was committed (i.e., a lower-class youth "steals" a car, but a middle-class youth is more likely to be a "borrower" in the view of the police). It is therefore not the behavior alone that results in the label "juvenile delinquent," but also the policies of the police, which often reflect attitudes of the community.

A significant factor, therefore, in the determination of who is delinquent is the element of "labeling." William B. Sanders comments as follows on the process of labeling:

> When we talk about a delinquent, we refer to someone who has been labeled as such by the juvenile justice system. Once a person has been labeled, he is often forced to play the role he has been given even though he may prefer another course. Labeling theory focuses on the interactive aspects of deviance in that it takes into account not only the delinquent activity and performer but also the others who come to define the situation and the actor as delinquent. . . .
>
> For example, if some juveniles are playing in front of a house when a bird flies against a window and breaks it, then flies away, the juveniles are believed to be responsible for the act, the police may be called, and as a consequence of this definition of the situation the juveniles may be labeled delinquents. Now, we might say that they were falsely accused, but the point is that their innocence of the act does not alter the consequences. They have been defined as delinquents; on the basis of this defintion, they are treated as such.[5]

The procedures of the juvenile court also significantly influence the determination of delinquency. The court is more likely to deal unofficially with children whose parents show an interest in them and come to defend them. It must act officially, however, in those cases in which parents present petitions charging their children with delinquency.

Another important determinant of delinquency status is the antisocial

[4]Nathan Goldman, *The Differential Selection of Juvenile Offenders for Court Appearances* (New York: National Council on Crime and Delinquency, 1963).
[5]William B. Sanders, *Juvenile Delinquency* (New York: Praeger, 1976), p. 51.

behavior that is treated by welfare departments and social work agencies. For example, in Washington, D.C., and in New York City, a Central Register of Delinquents is maintained, including the names of all children in the community who are referred to agencies for behavior that could have brought them to the attention of a court.

There are indications that less than half the children known to have committed acts classified as delinquent become part of the recorded statistics. Other studies indicate that similar behavior engaged in by middle-class children does not become known to any agency, public or private. Austin L. Porterfield had students at three colleges in Texas record delinquent behavior they had participated in while attending high school. Forty-three percent reported truancies, and 15 percent reported running away from home. Almost half of the students admitted to petty thefts in their high school days. Porterfield reported that, on the average, each student might have been apprehended and charged with delinquency on at least 11 occasions, yet none of them had ever been charged with an offense. Porterfield compared these student reports with offenses charged against 2,000 ajudicated delinquents who had appeared in the Fort Worth juvenile court. He found that 43 percent of the delinquent boys had been charged as truants and runaways and 27 percent had been charged with theft.[6]

A comparison of the responses of high school boys in Seattle, Washington, with records of boys from that area committed to state training schools also revealed little difference in the type or frequency of delinquent acts.[7]

On the basis of these studies, one may conclude that a large amount of delinquent behavior engaged in by middle-class children goes undetected or unrecorded by enforcement agencies. However, there is considerable evidence to support the conclusion that an even greater amount of lower-class delinquency is not reflected in our statistics. Researchers Wilensky and Lebeaux have noted that

> working class youngsters also commit undetected and unrecorded delinquencies—probably more serious and more frequent. Careful studies of off-the-record delinquency in Passaic [New Jersey], the District of Columbia, and Cambridge-Sommerville (Massachusetts) all show a very large amount of unofficial delinquency among lower class youth. One study of 114 underprivileged boys (40 of whom were official court delinquents) conservatively estimated that they had committed a minimum of 6,416 infractions of law in 5 years—only 95 of which became a matter of official complaint.[8]

[6]Austin L. Porterfield, *Youth in Trouble* (Fort Worth: Leo Potishman Foundation, 1946).
[7]James F. Short, Jr., and F. Ivan Nye, "Extent of Unrecorded Juvenile Delinquency: Tentative Conclusions," *Journal of Criminal Law, Criminology, and Police Science* 49 (July–August 1958): 296–302.
[8]H. L. Wilensky and C. N. Lebeaux, *Industrial Society and Social Welfare* (New York: Macmillan, 1958), p. 190. Reprinted with permission of the Macmillan Publishing Co. Copyright 1958 by Russel Sage Foundation.

While it is difficult to develop a definition of juvenile delinquency based on behavior that would be applicable to persons in all parts of the United States or, for that matter, in any state or city, one definition is clear: A youth is defined as a juvenile delinquent when that status is confirmed upon him by a juvenile court.

A child may also become a delinquency statistic if arrested and charged by the police even when the case is not referred to a court. This type of arrest data provides the basis for FBI statements about the amount of delinquency in the United States. Yet about half the children arrested are never referred to a court, and of those referred even fewer are adjudicated as delinquents.[9]

When a child (any person under 18) is alleged to have committed a serious crime (murder, robbery, etc.), criminal courts can have concurrent jurisdiction with juvenile courts. Prosecuting agencies may have the option of referring to either the criminal court or the juvenile court. Some jurisdictions are required by law to prosecute the child in a criminal court. When this occurs, the criminal court judge may dismiss the case and refer it back to the juvenile court. Therefore, when a serious crime is alleged, we cannot always predict whether the child will be considered a criminal or a juvenile delinquent. The action of a law enforcement agency is often the determining factor. Since juveniles have become increasingly involved with serious offenses, especially violence, the referral of juveniles to adult courts has become more common on a national basis.

Some official organizations have opted for a "get-tough" policy. For example, Alfred Regnery, Director of the United States Office of Juvenile Justice and Delinquency Prevention, advocated in 1986 the implementation of a tougher national policy for handling juveniles. He stated in an article under the heading "Making the Predators Accountable":[10]

> Some of the projects we have undertaken in my office deal with the related problems of juvenile crime—broken families, child abuse, and missing children.
>
> The lion's share of juvenile crime is committed by a relative handful of offenders. A recent study in Philadelphia found that of all teenage boys in the city who were born in one year—about 10,000—only 650 had been arrested more than five times. But those 650 were a nasty group. Among them, they had been arrested more than 5,000 times, and it was estimated that they committed some 50,000 crimes. That 7% of the population committed more than 70% of all serious juvenile crime committed in Philadelphia.
>
> We are meeting that group head on. If that's the way they want to behave, the only way to deal with them is to let them feel the sting of the justice system. My office spent $3.5 million in 1984 to set up special teams of prosecutors in 13 major cities. These projects were funded with the hope that prosecuting habit-

[9]Federal Bureau of Investigation, U.S. Department of Justice, *Uniform Crime Reports for the United States* (Washington, D.C.: U.S. Government Printing Office, 1985).

[10]Alfred Regnery, "A Federal Perspective on Juvenile Justice Reform," *Crime and Delinquency* (1986): 43–44.

ual, serious, and violent juvenile offenders, with specially trained teams who concentrate their efforts solely on these prosecutions, would have a positive impact on juvenile crime. This is a new way of prosecuting juveniles, never tried before. We are very optimistic about its potential success.

Indeed, the result from these efforts in the past few months are worth highlighting. In Philadelphia alone, during the first 3 months of the project, 91 juveniles were accepted for prosecution, representing 550 outstanding cases of robbery, aggravated assault, rape, kidnapping, and sexual assault. Other cities have also had significant results: Cambridge, Massachusetts, has had an intake of 95; Milwaukee, 60; Jacksonville, Florida, 76; and Miami, 50, to mention a few.

Criteria used in targeting juvenile offenders for special prosecution generally require a minimum of three prior serious convictions per offender or one serious prior felony conviction and five pending cases. Based on Philadelphia's intake rate alone, during the two-year project as many as 800 juvenile offenders who are responsible for multiple offenses could be prosecuted.

This "get-tough" approach appears to be a throwback to an earlier era of treating juveniles. Also, Regnery's use of such pejorative terms as "nasty group" and "juvenile crime" rather than "juvenile delinquency" are debatable matters in the field. Yet, the advocacy of this harsher approach is perenially part of the juvenile justice treatment scene. The fluctuation from a policy of "getting tough" to a softer judicial attitude is a pendulum that swings back and forth in the administration of juvenile justice.

I once worked as a criminologist in a juvenile detention facility in Newark, New Jersey, where I observed many cases of the different treatment accorded juvenile and adult offenders. The basic function of the juvenile detention facility is to hold children under 18 years old in custody pending the disposition of the juvenile court. In this case the court was housed in the same building as the juvenile detention facility. This type of jail facility is variously referred to as a juvenile jail, a house of detention, a juvenile hall, or in the past, a parental school. This latter designation implies that the state has taken over the parental role in a situation in which the youth's parents are no longer in effective control of the child.

One of my functions in the custodial facility was intake. One day the police brought in two youths who had been arrested for stealing an automobile. In the arrest process there had been a high-speed chase, which resulted in destruction of the automobile, causing considerable property damage but no physical damage to the boys. Both youths were intoxicated, and when taken into custody they were belligerent with the arresting officers, who had to use maximum force to make their arrest.

Despite the fact that they had no prior serious records, because of their substance abuse and their violent behavior, the juvenile court judge in their preliminary arraignment decided that they should be held in detention and not be released to their families. At the time that they were initially incarcerated, both boys gave their ages as 17.

It came out at the arraignment that one boy, Matt, had given a false name and had lied about his age: He was actually 18 years old. Matt was immediately transferred to the adult city jail. He appeared in court the next day with his lawyer, who plea bargained the case. Matt was found guilty of auto theft, given a suspended sentence, and released.

The 17-year-old, Joe, was treated differently because of his juvenile status. In the parental school Joe saw a social worker daily to deal with the trauma of his incarceration. After a preliminary court appearance in the informal setting of the juvenile court, the judge, who focused more on the juvenile's social and psychological background than the offense, ordered a psychiatric and probation officer workup and report to guide him in the disposition of the case. The probation department was, as is true in most jurisdictions, flooded with casework, and it took three months before Joe, who remained in custody, appeared again before the juvenile court judge. The probation officer's report was quite thorough and revealed a great deal about Joe's emotional condition, his delinquent history, his bad school record, and his disorganized family background. His father was an alcoholic who had physically abused Joe's mother, had sexually abused Joe's sister, and had regularly inflicted beatings on Joe. This difficult family situation was considered responsible for Joe's bellicose attitude and the fact that he was involved in a number of fights while in the detention facility. The judge noted from the probation officer's report that Joe's poor school attendance and record was due to the fact that he had a learning disability. The judge also felt, based on the probation officer's report, that Joe's diagnosed "conduct disorder," which manifested itself in violent behavior, required further analysis before his disposition of the case.

In Joe's interest, the judge ordered a more intense social and psychiatric evaluation for him from the state's diagnostic center. This involved an additional 90 days of custody in the diagnostic center.

Joe reappeared in court after six months of custody and social-psychological analysis. Joe had, by this time, turned 18 and decided that he wanted to join the Army. In lieu of sending Joe to a state training school, the judge accepted Joe's decision to join the Army and the case was dismissed on that basis.

During Joe's incarceration, I had many opportunities to talk with him and counsel him. His friend Matt often visited him and would tease him about the way they were both treated for the same offense. Joe was not impressed by the judicial system's "concern and caring" for his situation. As he told me one day, "I don't understand it. Matt and I were both loaded, stole a car, and tried to kick this cop's ass. He did one day in the joint and I did six months."

The case reveals something of the inequitable system of juvenile justice and criminal justice. The state may perceive its approach as being caring and concerned; the ward of the court may see the same treatment as simply a "doing-time" situation.

TRENDS IN DELINQUENCY

The Federal Bureau of Investigation, beginning with its 1964 Uniform Crime Reports, has annually presented several tables on arrest rates for persons under 18 years of age. Their expansion of these statistics with each succeeding year has proved to be of considerable value to students of juvenile delinquency. The 1985 statistics from the FBI Uniform Crime Reports (Table 1.1) present a perspective on delinquency and age worthy of classroom analysis.

On the issue of age and delinquency, a study by Peter Greenwood concluded:[11]

> The peak ages of criminality fall between the sixteenth and twentieth birthdays, with participation rates falling off rapidly for older age groups. Young men under the age of twenty-one account for half of all felony arrests. However, these arrest figures tend to overestimate the seriousness of the youthful offender crime problem somewhat because their crimes tend to be less serious and are committed in groups. There is a strong and direct connection between juvenile criminal activity and adult criminal careers. Chronic juvenile offenders have a high probability of continuing in crime as adults, while juveniles who were never arrested are unlikely to develop criminal careers as adults. Predictors of chronic juvenile offending include predelinquent deviant or troublesome behavior, physiological deficits associated with abnormal brain development, poor parenting, and evidence of criminal conduct or mental disorder among parents or siblings.

It is important to note that the official FBI statistics only reflect a part of the delinquency problem. As previously indicated, many youths who commit acts of violence or theft, or use illegal drugs are not arrested and are not reflected in the statistics.

A case in point would be the illegal use of marijuana. In the last decade the use of marijuana has steadily risen; however, the community and police increasingly tend to perceive its use as more benign, and the official approach in terms of arrest has been to give users more of a pass. Consequently, the statistics indicate a drop in arrests, despite the fact that the offense is clearly more prevalent.

Since a relatively small percentage of the children who engage in misbehavior are accorded the status of delinquent or become part of our juvenile delinquency statistics, a rise or fall in statistics does not necessarily indicate an increase in antisocial behavior. It often simply reflects changes in family, police, or community responses to children who do not conform to the expectations of their societal sphere.

The fact that families in our urban industrial society have turned more and more to community resources and public authorities for assis-

---

[11]Peter Greenwood, "Differences in Criminal Behavior and Court Responses Among Juvenile and Young Adult Defendants," in *Crime and Justice: An Annual Review of Research*, vol. 7, eds. Michael Tonry and Norval Morris (University of Chicago Press, 1986), p. 86.

tance in performing the family's traditional functions also affects delinquency statistics. Families who perceive various juvenile facilities as responsible for dealing with their misbehaving children tend to relinquish control over their children to these organizations, and this affects delinquency statistics.

Another factor is the changing cultural role of adolescents in our society. Adolescents have attained a high degree of physical maturity, and yet they are usually denied any significant economic or social role. This is especially true of the young male in depressed socioeconomic communities.

He has many of the social, sexual, and material desires of a man, yet without money he tends to be deprived of a legal means for satisfying these wants. He has two alternatives regarding school. He can either continue in school and suppress his desire to drop out, or he can attempt to find employment or some other way of obtaining money. Unemployment, especially among 16- and 17-year-olds who enter the labor market before completing high school, helps to explain the age distribution of arrests for delinquency. Youths quit school not only because of lack of interest in education but also because they need money to obtain material things. The lack of education and skills necessary to obtain worthwhile employment results in further frustration. Many young people fail to obtain employment they consider acceptable; many do not achieve steady employment of any kind. Thus, unemployed and without money, these young people find themselves on the streets with nothing to do. These are the boys who are most likely to engage in delinquent activity, particularly property offenses.

Many had some experience at delinquency when they were 13 and 14, as indicated by the high arrest rates at these ages. While at school, they were occupied part of the time. Once they have dropped out of school, with their need for money not satisfied legitimately, they may, and frequently do, turn to delinquency and, later, to crime.

The greatest incidence of school dropouts appears to coincide with the minimum age at which children can legally leave school. Belton Fleisher notes that this fact tends to confirm a relationship between dropping out of school, unemployment, and delinquency.[12] According to Fleisher's research, a 1-percent increase in unemployment is associated on the average with an increase of approximately 0.15 percent in the rate of delinquency.

The relationship between age and juvenile delinquency is more than a general statistical association. Also involved are the cultural roles of the individual at different age levels and the type of offense. Offenses associated with the cultural role of the younger child, for example, include rock throwing and vandalism. This sort of behavior usually decreases through adolescence. Offenses involving daring and aggression tend to increase in middle adolescence for males, then to decrease in later adolescence as the

[12]Belton M. Fleisher, *The Economics of Delinquency* (Chicago: Quadrangle Books, 1966), pp. 83–84.

Table 1.1   TOTAL ARRESTS, DISTRIBUTION BY AGE, 1985 [11,249 AGENCIES; 1985 ESTIMATED POPULATION 203,035,000]

Offense charged	Total all ages	Ages under 15	Ages under 18	Ages 18 and over
TOTAL	10,289,609	585,745	1,762,539	8,527,070
Percent distribution[1]	100.0	5.7	17.1	82.9
Murder and nonnegligent manslaughter	15,777	165	1,311	14,466
Forcible rape	31,934	1,676	4,830	27,104
Robbery	120,501	7,807	30,154	90,347
Aggravated assault	263,120	11,290	36,257	226,863
Burglary	381,875	54,402	145,254	236,621
Larceny-theft	1,179,066	167,897	386,217	792,849
Motor vehicle theft	115,621	11,026	43,946	71,675
Arson	16,777	4,407	6,906	9,871
Violent crime[2]	431,332	20,938	72,552	358,780
Percent distribution[1]	100.0	4.9	16.8	83.2
Property crime[3]	1,693,339	237,732	582,323	1,111,016
Percent distribution[1]	100.0	14.0	34.4	65.6
Crime Index total[4]	2,124,671	258,670	654,875	1,469,796
Percent distribution[1]	100.0	12.2	30.8	69.2
Other assaults	550,104	31,339	83,411	466,693
Forgery and counterfeiting	75,281	1,247	7,821	67,460
Fraud	286,941	7,252	17,780	269,161
Embezzlement	9,799	116	696	9,103
Stolen property; buying, receiving, possessing	110,415	7,886	27,691	82,724
Vandalism	224,046	52,076	100,353	123,693
Weapons; carrying, possessing, etc.	157,304	7,285	25,863	131,441
Prostitution and commercialized vice	101,167	244	2,447	98,720
Sex offenses (except forcible rape and prostitution)	86,861	6,947	14,836	72,025
Drug abuse violations	702,882	13,138	80,391	622,491
Gambling	28,034	180	754	27,280
Offenses against family and children	48,699	1,175	2,400	46,299
Driving under the influence	1,503,319	611	20,434	1,482,885
Liquor laws	467,149	9,821	117,312	349,837
Drunkenness	834,652	3,031	23,888	810,764
Disorderly conduct	583,532	25,339	83,203	500,329
Vagrancy	29,825	711	2,729	27,096
All other offenses (except traffic)	2,142,121	77,555	281,477	1,860,644
Suspicion	11,229	1,075	2,600	8,629
Curfew and loitering law violations	71,608	20,403	71,608	-------------
Runaways	139,970	59,644	139,970	-------------

[1]Because of rounding, the percentages may not add to total.
[2]Violent crimes are offenses of murder, forcible rape, robbery, and aggravated assault.
[3]Property crimes are offenses of burglary, larceny-theft, motor vehicle theft, and arson.
[4]Includes arson.
Source: "Crime in the United States—*1985 Uniform Crime Reports.*" (Washington, D.C.: U.S. Government Printing Office, 1985).

Age									
Under 10	10–12	13–14	15	16	17	18	19	20	21
47,983 .5	137,146 1.3	400,616 3.9	335,837 3.3	401,239 3.9	439,718 4.3	480,368 4.7	493,216 4.8	494,530 4.8	492,825 4.8
3	18	144	216	391	539	674	755	725	833
85	351	1,240	969	994	1,191	1,289	1,293	1,412	1,469
255	1,480	6,072	6,092	7,634	8,621	8,405	8,142	7,235	6,959
824	2,721	7,745	6,731	8,421	9,815	9,876	10,802	11,454	11,905
4,304	13,034	37,064	29,241	30,432	31,179	29,017	24,842	20,495	18,040
15,604	47,862	104,431	71,438	74,156	72,726	66,126	57,318	49,720	45,033
247	1,376	9,403	10,407	11,633	10,880	8,744	7,562	6,201	5,385
1,236	1,223	1,948	1,012	773	714	667	517	549	505
1,167 .3	4,570 1.1	15,201 3.5	14,008 3.2	17,440 4.0	20,166 4.7	20,244 4.7	20,992 4.9	20,826 4.8	21,166 4.9
21,391 1.3	63,495 3.7	152,846 9.0	112,098 6.6	116,994 6.9	115,499 6.8	104,554 6.2	90,239 5.3	76,965 4.5	68,963 4.1
22,558 1.1	68,065 3.2	168,047 7.9	126,106 5.9	134,434 6.3	135,665 6.4	124,798 5.9	111,231 5.2	97,791 4.6	90,129 4.2
2,545	7,974	20,820	15,538	17,275	19,259	19,430	21,419	23,516	25,576
26	221	1,000	1,414	2,218	2,942	3,728	4,420	4,306	4,121
199	1,418	5,635	5,890	1,706	2,932	5,676	8,280	10,875	12,536
5	31	80	75	182	323	489	472	473	509
358	1,497	6,031	5,649	6,545	7,611	7,998	7,510	6,329	5,839
7,935	15,871	28,270	16,820	16,060	15,397	12,394	10,568	9,577	8,685
258	1,407	5,620	5,177	6,160	7,241	8,108	8,103	7,673	7,733
8	32	204	353	656	1,194	3,375	5,311	5,939	7,437
707	1,728	4,512	2,792	2,526	2,571	2,625	2,816	2,857	3,045
183	1,373	11,582	15,159	22,771	29,323	37,724	41,244	43,009	43,732
11	34	135	123	167	284	427	563	670	737
549	176	450	372	428	425	1,228	1,406	1,635	1,732
152	128	331	905	5,132	13,786	33,338	48,432	59,557	73,610
148	636	9,037	17,239	35,471	54,781	67,609	53,433	43,368	20,537
253	248	2,530	3,986	6,388	10,483	19,530	25,229	28,437	35,262
1,911	5,915	17,513	14,926	19,070	23,868	29,497	31,312	32,980	33,525
79	130	502	456	644	918	1,647	1,582	1,431	1,309
7,110	16,562	53,883	47,354	74,421	82,147	100,255	109,430	113,654	116,310
198	244	633	527	524	474	492	455	453	461
584	3,234	16,585	16,837	18,926	15,442	----------	----------	----------	----------
2,206	10,222	47,216	38,139	29,535	12,652	----------	----------	----------	----------

youth's anxiety about supermasculine identity lessens. Another trend is related to the fact that substance abuse has increased enormously in the late 1980s, and children are starting to abuse drugs at an earlier age.

In general, child and adolescent offense patterns parallel social situations and roles. Offenses of young children are mostly limited to the home, the immediate neighborhood, the school, and a few local institutions accessible to a small child. Adolescents tend to use brute strength or crude weapons, whereas the sophisticated adult criminal depends more on skill and psychological manipulation of victims. Young offenders often combine play with their offenses, whereas the adult criminal is serious and methodical. Young offenders usually do not plan their escapades, but spontaneously seize upon good opportunities for committing offenses, whereas the older offender is more likely to plan his crimes carefully.

PROFILES OF DELINQUENTS

Statistical trends provide some insights into juvenile delinquency, however, the analysis of relevant sociological and psychological characteristics of delinquents are valuable aids to understanding the phenomenon.

Antisocial behavior that results in the status of delinquent correlates highly with certain sociological and psychological factors. For example, the analysis and description of boys and girls committed to the California Youth Authority shown in Table 1.2 provides some guidelines for understanding the "average" juvenile delinquent. The patterns depicted in these profiles agree with data revealed by juvenile court statistics in other states in the United States. Consequently, this profile is useful in more fully understanding the general delinquency problem.

GENDER AND JUVENILE DELINQUENCY: FEMALE DELINQUENTS

In 1985 a total of 1,248,235 boys were arrested as compared to 357,990 girls. Extrapolating from these statistics, about four boys are likely to be arrested for every girl. Delinquency is predominantly a boy's problem for much the same reasons that crime is predominantly a man's problem. As previously indicated, any person's total life organization is determined to a significant extent by the particular subculture in which he or she lives. Thus, male and female role expectations and behavior are strongly influenced by the larger cultural environment and subculture identifications. Since men are expected to be more aggressive, males are more likely to be delinquent than females, who, despite some changes in gender roles, are still expected to adopt a more passive role. Nevertheless, the arrest rate of females is increasing. This may be a consequence of the narrowing of the difference between male and female cultural and occupational roles in recent years. (See Table 1.3.)

The economic and social roles available to women in our society some-

Table 1.2   PROFILES OF FIRST COMMITMENTS

Youth authority males	Youth authority females

Home environment

Fifty percent came from neighborhoods considered below average economically, 44 percent came from average neighborhoods and six percent were from above average neighborhoods.

Forty percent lived in neighborhoods with a high level of delinquency, and 34 percent lived in moderately delinquent neighborhoods. Only seven percent were from neighborhoods considered nondelinquent.

Thirty-two percent came from homes where public assistance funds comprised all or most of the family income.

Family

Seventy-two percent came from broken homes. However, at least one natural parent was present in 92 percent of the homes.

Fifty-two percent had at least one parent, brother, or sister with a delinquent or criminal record.

Less than one percent were married at the time of commitment and five percent had children.

Delinquent behavior

Eighty-six percent had at least one conviction or sustained petition prior to commitment to the Youth Authority, while 23 percent had five or more convictions or sustained petitions prior to commitment. Sixty-eight percent had a previous commitment to a local facility.

Employment/schooling

Of those in the labor force, only seven percent were employed full time while 73 percent were unemployed.

Fifty-five percent were last enrolled in the tenth grade or below. Thirteen percent had reached the 12th grade or had graduated from high school at the time of commitment.

Home environment

Forty percent came from neighborhoods considered below average economically, 49 percent came from average neighborhoods and eleven percent were from above average neighborhoods.

Thirty-four percent lived in neighborhoods with a high level of delinquency, and 30 percent lived in moderately delinquent neighborhoods. Only eight percent were from neighborhoods considered nondelinquent.

Thirty-six percent came from homes where public assistance funds comprised all or most of the family income.

Family

Seventy-five percent came from broken homes. However, at least one natural parent was present in 88 percent of the homes.

Fifty-seven percent had at least one parent, brother, or sister with a delinquent or criminal record.

Less than one percent were married at the time of commitment and 18 percent had children.

Delinquent behavior

Eighty-two percent had at least one conviction or sustained petition prior to commitment to the Youth Authority while 15 percent had five or more convictions or sustained petitions prior to commitment. Forty-two percent had a previous commitment to a local facility.

Employment/schooling

Of those in the labor force 82 percent were unemployed, and three percent were employed full time.

Sixty-six percent were last enrolled in the tenth grade or below. Ten percent had reached the 12th grade or had graduated from high school at the time of commitment.

Source: Biennial Report, California Youth Authority. (Sacramento, CA: California Department of Corrections Publication, 1985).

Table 1.3 TOTAL ARREST TRENDS, SEX, 1984–1985 [9,596 AGENCIES; 1985 ESTIMATED POPULATION 183,022,000]

Offense charged	Males						Females					
	Total			Under 18			Total			Under 18		
	1984	1985	Percent change	1984	1985	Percent change	1984	1985	Percent change	1984	1985	Percent change
Total	7,646,515	7,810,509	+2.1	1,192,495	1,248,235	+4.7	1,544,362	1,639,974	+6.2	336,520	357,990	+6.4
Murder and nonnegligent manslaughter	13,030	12,904	−1.0	1,028	1,124	+9.3	1,975	1,815	−8.1	106	115	+8.5
Forcible rape	28,342	28,865	+1.8	4,343	4,316	−.6	254	303	+19.3	56	80	+42.9
Robbery	105,409	105,401	(¹)	26,627	26,758	+.5	8,189	8,639	+5.5	1,848	1,951	+5.6
Aggravated assault	212,391	211,228	−.5	26,561	28,330	+6.7	33,414	32,926	−1.5	5,311	5,202	−2.1
Burglary	321,370	326,959	+1.7	120,191	124,388	+3.5	25,979	26,753	+3.0	9,511	9,764	+2.7
Larceny-theft	715,767	744,423	+4.0	246,771	255,810	+3.7	309,472	334,053	+7.9	90,654	95,379	+5.2
Motor vehicle theft	88,767	97,835	+10.2	30,695	36,256	+18.1	8,867	10,093	+13.8	3,832	4,619	+20.5
Arson	12,943	13,129	+1.4	5,680	5,671	−.2	1,837	2,003	+9.0	566	609	+7.6
Violent crime²	359,172	358,398	−.2	58,559	60,528	+3.4	43,832	43,683	−.3	7,321	7,348	+.4
Property crime³	1,138,847	1,182,346	+3.8	403,337	422,125	+4.7	346,155	372,902	+7.7	104,563	110,371	+5.6
Crime Index total⁴	1,498,019	1,540,744	+2.9	461,896	482,653	+4.5	389,987	416,585	+6.8	111,884	117,719	+5.2
Other assaults	370,637	416,735	+12.4	52,218	57,280	+9.7	66,033	75,937	+15.0	15,751	17,259	+9.6
Forgery and counterfeiting	45,526	46,286	+1.7	4,723	4,962	+5.1	22,869	23,181	+1.4	2,148	2,302	+7.2
Fraud	140,030	151,773	+8.4	13,375	13,350	−.2	99,846	111,825	+12.0	3,948	3,812	−3.4
Embezzlement	4,821	5,624	+16.7	330	451	+36.7	2,692	3,184	+18.3	171	195	+14.0
Stolen property; buying, receiving, possessing	86,461	89,619	+3.7	20,775	23,032	+10.9	11,334	11,890	+4.9	2,246	2,386	+6.2
Vandalism	173,513	181,600	+4.7	78,451	81,987	+4.5	19,106	20,192	+5.7	7,373	7,730	+4.8
Weapons; carrying, possessing, etc.	129,699	134,210	+3.5	19,766	22,421	+13.4	10,414	10,970	+5.3	1,356	1,628	+20.1

Prostitution and commercialized vice	29,114	29,584	+1.6	754	708	-6.1	65,424	67,592	+3.3	1,723	1,638	-4.9
Sex offenses (except forcible rape and prostitution)	73,808	74,602	+1.1	12,588	12,599	+.1	5,451	6,108	+12.1	883	1,107	+25.4
Drug abuse violations	495,638	562,754	+13.5	57,376	63,255	+10.2	79,677	90,038	+13.0	10,204	10,932	+7.1
Gambling	24,198	21,995	-9.1	628	666	+6.1	3,891	3,879	-.3	67	33	-50.7
Offenses against family and children	34,574	35,553	+2.8	974	1,444	+48.3	4,712	5,086	+7.9	528	804	+52.3
Driving under the influence	1,273,098	1,208,416	-5.1	17,255	16,089	-6.8	166,868	157,131	-5.8	2,768	2,420	-12.6
Liquor laws	325,204	350,942	+7.9	73,886	76,322	+3.3	62,920	67,823	+7.8	25,567	27,483	+7.5
Drunkenness	797,954	726,214	-9.0	19,663	19,112	-2.8	75,473	70,573	-6.5	3,698	3,697	(1)
Disorderly conduct	418,211	435,198	+4.1	57,793	59,944	+3.7	86,449	99,252	+14.8	13,291	14,291	+7.5
Vagrancy	26,207	24,592	-6.2	1,666	2,016	+21.0	2,989	3,001	+.4	399	447	+12.0
All other offenses (except traffic)	1,602,843	1,671,002	+4.3	201,418	206,878	+2.7	287,927	307,269	+6.7	52,215	53,649	+2.7
Suspicion (not included in totals)	12,896	8,502	-34.1	1,702	1,691	-.6	1,881	1,476	-21.5	420	486	+15.7
Curfew and loitering law violations	50,347	49,258	-2.2	50,347	49,258	-2.2	15,603	15,985	+2.4	15,603	15,985	+2.4
Runaways	46,613	53,808	+15.4	46,613	53,808	+15.4	64,697	72,473	+12.0	64,697	72,473	+12.0

[1] Less than one-tenth of 1 percent.
[2] Violent crimes are offenses of murder, forcible rape, robbery, and aggravated assault.
[3] Property crimes are offenses of burglary, larceny-theft, motor vehicle theft, and arson.
[4] Includes arson.
Source: "Crime in the United States—1985" (Washington, D.C.: U.S. Government Printing Office, 1985).

what approximate those available to men. This is particularly true in the big cities. In the 1980s it is no longer unusual for a woman to work outside the home, to be a principal breadwinner, or to share equally with the male members of the household in the major decision-making processes that affect the family. A young girl brought up in such a home, identifying with her mother, tends to consider herself as important as the male members of her family. She further believes herself capable of doing almost anything they can do and feels free to engage in most of the activities that they are involved in—including delinquency.

In one analysis of the equal opportunity-equal crime concept, Josefina Figueira-McDonough concludes that these assumptions about female delinquency have a certain complexity. She states at the conclusion of her analysis: "Our findings suggest that the influx of feminist orientation on illegitimate behavior is far more complex, less linear, and much more tenuous than suggested by some criminologists."[13]

Despite the recent complexity of the gender issue, FBI arrest statistics reveal that between 1960 and 1985, the general crime and delinquency rate for females rose more than six times faster than that for males. The most significant increases were in burglary, armed robbery, and possession of a deadly weapon. To some extent these figures may be magnified by a changing attitude toward females in the courts. Whereas at one time many females, especially those under 18, may not have been formally subjected to the judicial system, they may now be victims of "overkill" in terms of arrest and court decisions by the developing attitude toward women: "You want to be equal. Okay, we will not show you any special courtesy because you are a female."

In an interview for *People* magazine in response to the question, "How big a part does women's liberation play in female criminality?", criminologist Dr. Freda Adler replied,

> The dramatic rise cannot be directly attributed to one factor. The feminist connection is that women are taking on more of the behavior of men. This also means taking on the stress, strain and frustration that males have traditionally dealt with. Many of these women, unskilled and untrained, may turn in desperation to crime. There was a time when a female confined her criminal acts to prostitution and shoplifting. Now she is committing armed robbery, auto theft, and burglary, traditionally male crimes, so that we see a definite change in both the dimension and form of female criminality.[14]

Women now seem to be gravitating toward the center of the action in crime and delinquency. While this is not a positive outgrowth of the women's movement, it does nevertheless show that women are behaving more like men as they increasingly think of themselves as equal to men. The

---

[13]Josefina Figueira-McDonough "Feminism and Delinquency," *The British Journal of Criminology* 24 (1984): 106.

[14]Freda Adler, "In Her Own Words," *People Weekly*, October 13, 1975, pp. 20–22.

general attitudes inherent in women's liberation tend to filter down to adolescent girls—and no doubt are part of the causal backdrop to increased female delinquent behavior.

Not all researchers in the field agree with these assertions about a rise in female delinquency. On this complex issue Daniel Curron comments:

> In recent years, research on the topic of female crime and delinquency has focused on the relationship between the women's liberation movement and increasing female criminal activity. This analysis takes issue with the contention that the women's movement has resulted in a rapid change in both the quantity and quality of female offenses.[15]

After an examination of the Philadelphia family court system, Curron argues that changes in the rate of female delinquent activity as well as in the disposition of youthful offenders are the results of legal and political shifts in orientation. Three significant political-legal periods are identified between 1960 and 1980: (1) a "paternalistic" period (1960–1976), during which female delinquents were harshly treated by the courts "for their own good"; (2) a "due process" era (1968–1976), which reflects the spirit of the Gault decision; and (3) a "law-and-order" phase (1977–1980), during which the court adjusted to the new conservatism of the late seventies.[16]

In a report published by the National Institute of Mental Health, Dr. Rita James Simon, Professor of Sociology at the University of Illinois, referred to statistics that show that the percentage of women arrested for crimes of violence fluctuated between 10 and 13 percent during a 20-year period.[17] Her analysis of female criminality concludes that the increase is not in violence but in property offenses, such as forgery, fraud, and embezzlement. In 1953, one in every 12 persons arrested for a property crime was a woman, and in 1973, one in every five property crimes was committed by a woman. In her report, Simon comments: "It is reasonable to assume that the women's movement has had some effect on the psyche, the consciousness and the self-perceptions of many women in American society. But the extent to which it has motivated those women to act outside the law in order to gain financial rewards, vengeance, or power is still too early to assess." Simon's major hypothesis is that increased participation in the labor force in recent years has given women more opportunities to commit larceny, fraud, embezzlement, and other financial and white-collar crimes. "If the present trends continue, in 20 years women will probably be involved in white collar crimes in a proportion commensurate with their representation in the society. The fact that female arrests have increased for these offenses

---

[15]Daniel J. Curron, "The Myth of the 'New' Female Delinquent," *Crime and Delinquency* 30 (1984): 386.

[16]Ibid.

[17]Rita James Simon, "The Contemporary Woman and Crime," National Institute of Health Publication (Washington, D.C.: U.S. Government Printing Office, September 1975), p. 46.

and not for all offenses is consistent both with the opportunity theory and with the presence of a sizeable women's movement."[18]

Based on a study involving self-reporting by boys and girls by Peter C. Kratcoski and John E. Kratcoski, girls are becoming more involved in delinquent activities that were formerly the province of boys.[19] The researchers studied eleventh and twelfth graders in three high schools, including college preparatory, vocational, and general education students. The students were given a self-reported delinquency questionnaire asking which illegal acts had been committed as well as background questions. For 25 illegal acts males continue to be more aggressive, but in regard to minor delinquent behavior the study revealed few male-female differences, especially for popular activities such as drug use. They concluded that the closeness of the male-female ratio in delinquency "may derive from changing female roles, or from increasing willingness of police to punish illegal acts committed by females, causing more to be reported."

Another factor that may enter into the delinquent female numbers game is the diversion of females. Christine Alder asserts:[20]

> These data suggest that females are disproportionately involved in diversion programs, and that they tend to be referred to programs for minor forms of misconduct. On the basis of this and other evidence that diversion both widens the net of social control and increases later delinquency, it is concluded that the expansion of diversion will mean an increase in the numbers of female youths who experience juvenile justice processing as a consequence of initial non-serious misconduct.

Substance abuse has become one of the most significant problems for young people in American society, and the evidence reveals that it is an activity shared equally by girls and boys. It is also one of the few delinquent behaviors in which females and males are close to being equal participants. Arrest statistics do not confirm this assertion; however, observations at youth gatherings and other research carried out by the author confirm that drug abuse in the late 1980s is more of a unisex activity than is any other type of delinquency.

The increasing problem of females as offenders is accompanied by their unfortunate escalating role as victims of crime. On the theme of females as victims, Rafter and Natalizia make a number of assertions from a "radical-feminist viewpoint" that reflects the viewpoint of an increasing number of social scientists.[21] Their perspective has special significance as it relates to female runaways and prostitutes. They state:

[18]Ibid.

[19]Peter C. Kratcoski and John E. Kratcoski, "Changing Patterns in the Delinquent Activities of Boys and Girls: A Self-Reported Delinquency Analysis," *Adolescence* 10 (Spring 1975): 563–607.

[20]Christine Alder, "Gender Bias in Juvenile Diversion," *Crime and Delinquency* 30 (1984): 400.

[21]N. F. Rafter and E. M. Natalizia, "Marxist Feminism," *Crime and Delinquency* (January 1981): 81–87. Used by permission.

Although women in capitalist society are victimized by the same offenses as are men, some types of victimization are inherently or virtually the domain of women. These include rape, incest, wife abuse, sexual harassment on the job, and prostitution, all of which are rooted in the traditional patriarchal concept of women as sexual chattel. . . .

Rape is an act that symbolizes the political and economic oppression of women in capitalist society. Traditionally, rape has been regarded as a property crime, an offense whose victim is the man whose property (i.e., wife or daughter) has been defiled. This interpretation is reinforced by the fact that, in most jurisdictions, it is legally impossible for a man to rape his wife, for she is his possession and he may demand sexual gratification from her at will. Patriarchal capitalism thus reduces the body and spirit of woman to their property value and then takes from her the control over that property.

Furthermore, the handling of rape cases within the criminal justice system, including very low conviction rates for alleged rapists, reinforces notions of woman as temptress and seducer who, in effect, makes herself vulnerable to sexual attack. Rather than viewing rape as an act of violence in which sex is used as an instrument of oppression, the justice system often regards it as the "natural," though perhaps improper, response of males to seductive women.

From the perspective of Marxist criminology, the traditional "crime" of prostitution is instead another victimization of women, a matter of sexual slavery rather than sexual immorality. The prostitute may be seen, in fact, as the archetype of woman's traditional role of sex partner to man; however, because she performs this role outside the nuclear family model—and does it for profit—she is punished by bourgeois moral codes upholding a double standard of morality for men and women.

An increasing problem of juvenile delinquency is the escalation of teenage prostitution. The problem is increasingly more a function of economic necessity for young [runaway] homeless girls than in the past when young female prostitutes were motivated to prostitution by emotional problems.

What would an alternative, egalitarian system look like in its handling of women as victims? Most important, it would undertake a massive commitment to the female victim, including the following:

1. Mandatory education in public schools in rape, incest, and employment rights. In addition, training of females in self-defense should be offered by the schools.
2. Employment of female staff in all parts of the criminal justice system dealing with female victims.
3. Training of all law enforcement personnel in the problems unique to female victims.
4. Establishment of rape crisis centers and shelters, and of other support systems to encourage bonding among female victims.
5. Encouragement of women who wish to prosecute men who have victimized them, and the provision of legal assistance for these women.

In addition, necessary legal reforms would include the following:

1. Removal of the husband exemption in rape statutes.
2. Making restraining orders against abusive husbands a more effective legal tool for battered women.

3. Recognition of self-defense as a legitimate legal defense for women who retaliate against men who repeatedly batter them.
4. Legalization of prostitution or, at the very least, sanctions directed equally at all parties involved.
5. Adoption of laws criminalizing sexual harassment on the job. Sexual harassment should be established as adequate grounds for leaving a job without forfeiting unemployment compensation.

Rafter and Natalizia present a variety of issues related to gender roles that significantly affect female delinquents. For example, young girls who are sexually abused within their family are much more prone to become runaways. They usually run away to the "combat zones" of large cities where, destitute and with few job skills, they may become victims of male predators. Adult pimps and "tricks" tend to exploit these abused girls as prostitutes. Moreover, they are also more prone, in these onerous circumstances, to act out delinquent patterns like theft and substance abuse. Recent data reveals that substance-abusing mothers give birth to physically and (later) socially defective children. These patterns, among others, contribute to the complicated and burgeoning problem of female delinquency.

MINORITY GROUP FACTORS AND JUVENILE DELINQUENCY

Most of the people who migrated from Europe to the United States in the latter part of the nineteenth century and the first quarter of the twentieth century came in search of economic and social opportunities. By and large they migrated from rural areas in eastern and southern Europe, with well-developed languages and cultures differing from those of the American majority.

Generally, the immigrants were poor, uneducated, honest, and willing and able to work. In the United States these groups tended to settle in areas inhabited by members of their ethnic group where they found others who understood their language and culture. The initial migrations were encouraged by relatives or friends in the United States, and the first residence was usually in or near the homes of these relatives or friends.

This migration pattern resulted in the establishment and expansion of self-segregated populations of Irish, Italian, Jewish, and other ethnic groups in the big cities. These groups, largely because of the basic family structure, experienced a disproportionately high incidence of delinquency in their youths. Many violent and predatory gangs resulted from this condition of family struggles, conflicts, and social disorganization.

The most recent immigrants to United States urban slum areas include blacks, Puerto Ricans, Mexicans, and, to a lesser degree, poor whites from Southern states. These groups have a higher proportionate rate of delinquency than more stable groups in American society. Children of these more recent migrants to urban areas now constitute a large proportion of delinquency cases. Arrests rates and court statistics reveal that the

THE NATURE AND EXTENT OF JUVENILE DELINQUENCY

highest rates of juvenile delinquency in America today are among blacks, Puerto Ricans, Mexican-Americans, and more recent Latin American arrivals to urban areas.

This disproportionately higher incidence of delinquency in relation to their numbers in the general population is revealed in the arrest rates for minority youths, under 18, in statistics compiled by the FBI in the 1985 Uniform Crime Reports. Tables 1.4 and 1.5 contain these statistics, and they are presented here for class discussion.

There are many explanations for the fact that newly arrived immigrant populations tend to have a disproportionately high incidence of delinquency when compared to the general population. Historically, these minority groups were initially restricted, alienated, or excluded from full participation in the social and economic life of American society. With the exception of the American black, minority members speak a foreign language, are expected to integrate into a society with a culture different from their own, and are often regarded as "foreigners" by members of the dominant society. The societal reaction to them as people with different languages, cultural backgrounds, and norms makes it exceedingly difficult for the children of these minority groups to make the adjustments necessary to prepare them for their roles in the dominant social system. They find it difficult to obtain employment other than unskilled labor, partly because of lack of formal education and partly because of discrimination. All of these blockades to full participation in the society tend to coalesce in producing a higher incidence of delinquency.

The family structure of blacks, in particular, appears to be under even greater assault. Four of five white children live in two-parent families; fewer than half of all black children do. Only one white child in thirty-eight lives away from both parents; one in eight black children does. Proportionally, there are far more black children born to unwed teenaged mothers.

On this latter point, a 1985 Census Bureau study reveals some startling facts about delinquency among blacks. More than half of all black babies born in the United States are born to unmarried mothers. In contrast, the Census Bureau study found that white unmarried women accounted for about 18 percent of all out-of-wedlock births. A summary of the 1985 Census Bureau statistics reveals that:

1. Out-of-wedlock births totaled 17.9 percent for all women aged 18–44. The figures revealed 11.7 percent for whites and 54.9 percent for blacks.
2. In the 18–24 group, out-of-wedlock births were 31.1 percent overall, 20.2 percent for white women and 74.5 percent for blacks. These statistics reflect a less favorable circumstance for the family situation of many black children, and this in part accounts for the higher rate of delinquency.

School behavior and its consequences also affects minority group delinquency. For example, school suspension rates for all children have in-

Table 1.4 TOTAL ARRESTS, DISTRIBUTION BY RACE, 1985

Offense charged	Arrests under 18					Percent distribution[1]				
	Total	White	Black	American Indian or Alaskan Native	Asian or Pacific Islander	Total	White	Black	American Indian or Alaskan Native	Asian or Pacific Islander
TOTAL	1,758,753	1,317,806	407,807	15,141	17,999	100.0	74.9	23.2	.9	1.0
Murder and nonnegligent manslaughter	1,305	629	661	3	12	100.0	48.2	50.7	.2	.9
Forcible rape	4,755	2,296	2,406	32	21	100.0	48.3	50.6	.7	.4
Robbery	30,032	9,638	20,060	87	247	100.0	32.1	66.8	.3	.8
Aggravated assault	36,159	20,895	14,716	303	245	100.0	57.8	40.7	.8	.7
Burglary	144,807	109,861	32,582	1,140	1,224	100.0	75.9	22.5	.8	.8
Larceny-theft	385,786	273,127	103,126	4,467	5,066	100.0	70.8	26.7	1.2	1.3
Motor vehicle theft	43,620	30,120	12,601	465	434	100.0	69.1	28.9	1.1	1.0
Arson	6,896	5,841	937	72	46	100.0	84.7	13.6	1.0	.7
Violent crime[2]	72,251	33,458	37,843	425	525	100.0	46.3	52.4	.6	.7
Property crime[3]	581,109	418,949	149,246	6,144	6,770	100.0	72.1	25.7	1.1	1.2
Crime Index total[4]	653,360	452,407	187,089	6,569	7,295	100.0	69.2	28.6	1.0	1.1

Other assaults	83,217	54,295	27,307	649	966	100.0	65.2	32.8	.8	1.2
Forgery and counterfeiting	7,816	6,457	1,249	68	42	100.0	82.6	16.0	.9	.5
Fraud	17,778	9,612	7,868	34	264	100.0	54.1	44.3	.2	1.5
Embezzlement	696	517	165	6	8	100.0	74.3	23.7	.9	1.1
Stolen property; buying, receiving, possessing	27,642	18,150	9,160	154	178	100.0	65.7	33.1	.6	.6
Vandalism	100,226	83,181	15,574	673	798	100.0	83.0	15.5	.7	.8
Weapons; carrying, possessing, etc.	25,805	17,823	7,605	124	253	100.0	69.1	29.5	.5	1.0
Prostitution and commercialized vice	2,435	1,422	984	21	8	100.0	58.4	40.4	.9	.3
Sex offenses (except forcible rape and prostitution)	14,829	10,790	3,873	78	88	100.0	72.8	26.1	.5	.6
Drug abuse violations	79,630	61,288	17,146	361	835	100.0	77.0	21.5	.5	1.0
Gambling	754	184	449	1	120	100.0	24.4	59.5	.1	15.9
Offenses against family and children	2,400	1,835	531	15	19	100.0	76.5	22.1	.6	.8
Driving under the influence	20,307	19,414	544	248	101	100.0	95.6	2.7	1.2	.5
Liquor laws	117,193	111,472	3,318	1,848	555	100.0	95.1	2.8	1.6	.5
Drunkenness	23,853	22,250	1,198	357	48	100.0	93.3	5.0	1.5	.2
Disorderly conduct	83,141	61,616	20,793	467	265	100.0	74.1	25.0	.6	.3
Vagrancy	2,728	2,327	382	11	8	100.0	85.3	14.0	.4	.3
All other offenses (except traffic)	281,057	209,073	66,880	1,523	3,581	100.0	74.4	23.8	.5	1.3
Suspicion	2,600	2,126	442	20	12	100.0	81.8	17.0	.8	.5
Curfew and loitering law violations	71,428	53,055	16,874	627	872	100.0	74.3	23.6	.9	1.2
Runaways	139,858	118,512	18,376	1,287	1,683	100.0	84.7	13.1	.9	1.2

[1]Because of rounding, the percentages may not add to total.
[2]Violent crimes are offenses of murder, forcible rape, robbery, and aggravated assault.
[3]Property crimes are offenses of burglary, larceny-theft, motor vehicle theft, and arson.
[4]Includes arson.

Source: "Crime in the United States—1985 Uniform Crime Reports" (Washington, D.C.: U.S. Government Printing Office, 1985).

Table 1.5 TOTAL ARRESTS, DISTRIBUTION BY ETHNIC ORIGIN, 1985

Offense charged	Under 18 years of age					
	Number of arrests			Percent distribution		
	Total	Hispanic	Non-Hispanic	Total	Hispanic	Non-Hispanic
TOTAL	1,569,251	182,891	1,386,360	100.0	11.7	88.3
Murder and nonnegligent manslaughter	1,144	246	898	100.0	21.5	78.5
Forcible rape	3,981	376	3,605	100.0	9.4	90.6
Robbery	25,505	3,893	21,612	100.0	15.3	84.7
Aggravated assault	30,215	4,289	25,926	100.0	14.2	85.8
Burglary	126,353	16,648	109,705	100.0	13.2	86.8
Larceny-theft	341,982	34,212	307,770	100.0	10.0	90.0
Motor vehicle theft	38,651	4,867	33,784	100.0	12.6	87.4
Arson	6,281	569	5,712	100.0	9.1	90.9
Violent crime[1]	60,845	8,804	52,041	100.0	14.5	85.5
Property crime[2]	513,267	56,296	456,971	100.0	11.0	89.0
Crime Index total[3]	574,112	65,100	509,012	100.0	11.3	88.7

Other assaults	75,503	7,866	67,637	100.0	10.4	89.6
Forgery and counterfeiting	7,225	459	6,766	100.0	6.4	93.6
Fraud	17,275	4,250	13,025	100.0	24.6	75.4
Embezzlement	631	64	567	100.0	10.1	89.9
Stolen property; buying, receiving, possessing	25,395	3,301	22,094	100.0	13.0	87.0
Vandalism	93,134	8,878	84,256	100.0	9.5	90.5
Weapons; carrying, possessing, etc.	23,457	3,760	19,697	100.0	16.0	84.0
Prostitution and commercialized vice	2,186	161	2,025	100.0	7.4	92.6
Sex offenses (except forcible rape and prostitution)	13,458	1,205	12,253	100.0	9.0	91.0
Drug abuse violations	72,261	13,615	58,646	100.0	18.8	81.2
Gambling	641	36	605	100.0	5.6	94.4
Offenses against family and children	2,287	240	2,047	100.0	10.5	89.5
Driving under the influence	19,054	2,161	16,893	100.0	11.3	88.7
Liquor laws	109,758	5,783	103,975	100.0	5.3	94.7
Drunkenness	22,393	5,742	16,651	100.0	25.6	74.4
Disorderly conduct	77,239	8,764	68,475	100.0	11.3	88.7
Vagrancy	2,654	333	2,321	100.0	12.5	87.5
All other offenses (except traffic)	250,728	35,948	214,780	100.0	14.3	85.7
Suspicion	2,343	260	2,083	100.0	11.1	88.9
Curfew and loitering law violations	50,441	5,178	45,263	100.0	10.3	89.7
Runaways	127,076	9,787	117,289	100.0	7.7	92.3

[1]Violent crimes are offenses of murder, forcible rape, robbery, and aggravated assault.
[2]Property crimes are offenses of burglary, larceny-theft, motor vehicle theft, and arson.
[3]Includes arson.

Source: "Crime in the United States—1985 Uniform Crime Reports" (Washington, D.C.: U.S. Government Printing Office, 1985).

creased; however, minority group children are suspended at twice the rate of other children. Minority group elementary and high school pupils are put into programs for the mentally retarded three times more often than white children. For every two black children who graduate from high school, one drops out.

Due to all these factors, minority group children tend to have a disproportionately higher rate of delinquency than the general youth population. The higher rate has little to do with ethnic background or skin color but a great deal to do with the child's socioeconomic situation and lack of opportunity.

More black than white youths are committed to institutional care. This may be due to the juvenile courts' philosophy of earlier state intervention in the case of youths living under conditions of severe poverty, accompanied by family disorganization. Action is taken against blacks more often and for less serious offenses than other groups. Like the immigrants of earlier periods, many black families today are restricted to depressed and obsolescent residential areas, which manifest more forms of social disorganization than most other areas. Vice, crime, and social disorder become traditional in such areas, owing to oppressive negative forces. In many instances blacks move into slum areas abandoned by the poor immigrant groups that preceded them. These groups move up in the system and move out of the inner city to the suburbs. Delinquent groups and gang patterns of behavior are present in these depressed areas and are rapidly transmitted to the new arrivals.

A veiled castelike system accounts in part for the differences between majority and minority group delinquency rates. A subordinate socioeconomic position or lifestyle, with its bitter implications of economic deprivation, overcrowding, substandard housing, and inadequate education, has a tremendous negative impact on the self-concepts and personalities of young children. These factors and others already noted produce a disproportionately high rate of delinquency among minority group children.

SUMMARY: BASIC THEMES FOR CLASS DISCUSSION

1. "Juvenile delinquency" is differentiated from "crime" in a number of ways in American society:
   a. juvenile offenders are usually under 18;
   b. juveniles are generally held to be less culpable and responsible for their offenses;
   c. in the judicial process emphasis in the juvenile court is more likely to be on the youths' personality and social factors than on the alleged offense;
   d. treatment is more likely to be the recommended response to a juvenile than punishment;
   e. an informal court hearing with less emphasis on legal due process is most likely to be the case in the juvenile court.
2. The labeling of a youth as a juvenile delinquent is significantly

affected by police arrest attitudes, community standards of behavior, and parental viewpoints as to what is deviant behavior. It is
also important to note that children and adolescents can become
"status offenders" when they commit behavioral acts such as truancy, run away from home, or their parents find them "incorrigible."

3. Boys are about four times as likely as girls to become delinquents,
largely because deviant behavior has been considered a more masculine than feminine behavioral pattern. However, as gender roles
become more similar, we can expect a narrowing of this statistical
gap.

4. On a percentage basis minority group children are more likely to
receive delinquent status in our society than white youths. This is
due to a continuing pattern in our society of prejudice and discrimination, unequal socioeconomic starting points and opportunities,
a sense of alienation from the larger society by many minority
group children due to language and cultural differences, family
problems related to assimilation into the larger culture, and greater
difficulty in acquiring employment opportunities.

QUESTIONS

1.1. Should we maintain the age factor as the basic delineator between juvenile
delinquency and adult crime?

1.2. What are implications of treating "status offenders" differently from youths
who commit adult types of crime?

1.3. How does the labeling process affect delinquent behavior?

1.4. Delineate and discuss the causal factors for male and female delinquency in
American society.

1.5. What kinds of changes in American society can be implemented to increase the
minority group child's access to equal opportunity in the overall society, with
the result of reducing minority group delinquency?

chapter 2

The Juvenile Court

There are three basic social-psychological perspectives used in defining the *juvenile delinquent*. These include (1) the social perceptions of a juvenile's deviant behavior, (2) the juvenile's self-concept, and (3) the legal definition produced by the juvenile court process. The most definitive perspective is the latter, but the other two viewpoints have real social meaning and consequences.

For example, a youth who is perceived as a delinquent by the community is very likely to experience social and personal consequences, even when he or she is not accorded delinquent status by the juvenile court. One consequence is that the youth develops a delinquent self-concept. As W. I. Thomas, the eminent sociologist, stated: "If people define situations as real, they are real in their consequences."

Following is a brief commentary on each of these perspectives on delinquency, followed by an in-depth analysis of the most definitive perspective on delinquency—adjudication in the juvenile court.

SOCIAL PERCEPTIONS

In many communities a youth may be labeled a "juvenile delinquent" despite the fact that he or she has not been accorded this status by the court. For example, his or her family, neighbors, peers, and teachers may know that he or she has committed acts of theft or violence, or that he or she is a substance abuser. In the case of a female, sexual promiscuity and substance abuse are the primary criteria for delinquency status.

There are different regional and neighborhood ideas of who is a delinquent. In high-delinquency areas, theft, violence, and substance abuse tend to be viewed by the general population as the "normal" behavioral pattern for most youths in the community, whereas in other communities these acts may be perceived as criminal behavior. In certain families, the discovery that a child possesses drugs may be considered a capital offense, whereas in another family parents and children may use drugs together. These varied perceptions have real consequences, since they affect the labeling of youths as delinquents by their respective communities, schools, and families. In response to being unofficially labeled a delinquent by neighbors, relatives, teachers, peers, or family, a youth may or may not develop the self-concept of delinquent; the youth's awareness of being perceived as a delinquent often reinforces his or her deviant behavior.

SELF-CONCEPT

Whether a youth has a delinquent self-concept or not is a subjective matter. Many youths do not define themselves as delinquents, even when their behavior clearly points to this conclusion, and others believe they are "bad" or delinquents based on minor norm violations. At one extreme are young people who engage in deviant acts like robbery, drug abuse, or violence, which by the judgment of most community norms are considered delinquent. At the opposite end of this continuum are youths who commit very few deviant acts, yet believe that they are delinquent. The self-concept of delinquency often does not agree with the objective situation.

Having a delinquent self-concept has a real personal impact. The youth who believes he or she is a delinquent is more apt to confirm the label by acting out further deviant behavior. As one youth put it, "If they think I'm 'bad,' I'll show them how 'bad' I can be." A youth who acknowledges the labeling process as valid tends to feel that he or she has nothing to lose by committing more deviant acts.

Some juvenile delinquents deny their status, and continue their deviant behavior until they are officially defined as juvenile delinquents by the juvenile court's judicial system. Even then, many "convicted" delinquents rationalize or neutralize their deviant behavior by blaming the "system" or their parents or claim that they are victims of discrimination. One of the consequences of this process is that the individual who denies the delinquent label also rejects treatment or change.

For example, a young substance abuser who eschews a delinquent self-concept may rationalize his or her drug addiction and the thefts necessary for supporting the habit. As one youth told me, "I just use drugs for recreation, and I make a little money on the side like everyone else." His denial of his delinquent condition brings to mind the Alcoholics Anonymous philosophy, which states that the first step toward resocialization of an individual is the admission that they are an alcoholic and have a problem. It is likewise necessary for acting-out delinquent youths to stop rationalizing their behavior and in an appropriate measure to accept a delinquent self-concept so that they will be amenable to treatment which might change their behavior.

JUVENILE COURT

The juvenile court is the most central institution in our society for labeling and defining who is delinquent. There are many elements that enter into this process, including the social perceptions and norms of the community, parents, and police. The judgments of these various segments of the society enter into the process and determine which children are propelled into the juvenile justice system in the first place, as well as which children are deemed delinquent by the juvenile court.

In summary, these three perspectives—the community and its norms, the youth's self-concept, and the legal arm of the community (the juvenile court)—all enter into the process of defining who is a delinquent. Of the three, the juvenile court process is the most defined and has the most clarity.

The following analysis of the juvenile court's historical roots—how juveniles become wards of the court; the court's processes; the role of the juvenile court judge; the use of "diversion" programs by the court; and the balance of due process and social welfare in the courts—helps to explain how a youth is officially labeled a juvenile delinquent.

HISTORY OF THE JUVENILE COURT

As recently as the latter part of the nineteenth century, children in both England and the United States were tried for their crimes exclusively in criminal courts. The age of the child was a factor in determining whether or not he or she should be held responsible for delinquent acts, but in most other respects the treatment resembled that accorded an adult charged with a crime. The child was likely to be detained in the same jail as an adult criminal, tried by the same court, and sent to the same correctional facility.

The common law exempted children under 7 years of age from responsibility for criminal behavior, and this rule still generally applies. A child below the age of 7 could not be found guilty of committing a criminal act because of the absence of one essential element: *mens rea*, or criminal intent. But children between the ages of 7 and 14 might be tried and convicted. They were presumed to be incapable of formulating an intent to commit a crime, but this presumption could be overcome by evidence to the contrary presented by the prosecution.

Chancery courts, which had their origin in fifteenth-century England, also dealt with the problems of children. English common law imposed a duty upon parents to provide support, supervision, and care for their children. It also provided that parents had a right to custody of their children unless they defaulted in their duties. Chancery courts were created by the king to protect children in need. If children were left without support as a result of divorce, abandonment, or death of the father, they were often destitute. The chancery court, a court of equity, assumed the duty of seeing that parents, particularly fathers, carried out their obligations to spouses and children. The welfare of the wife and child was the sole and fundamental consideration in actions by this court.

The courts did not normally deal with cases in which misbehavior of children was alleged. They protected children, who would now be referred to as "neglected" or "independent," and were concerned principally with the administration of property or the ordering of financial support for dependents. They acted *in loco parentis* (in place of the parents), taking whatever steps deemed necessary to provide for the child's needs.

In 1825, with the establishment of the House of Refuge in New York City, many states began providing separate correctional facilities for children. The House of Refuge was restricted to children adjudged offenders by a criminal court. By 1860 there were 16 such specialized institutions in the United States, established at the insistence of reformers who objected to having children confined in jails and penitentiaries with adult criminals and subjected to potentially harmful associations and influences.

In 1841, largely owing to the efforts of John Augustus, a Boston shoemaker who helped children in trouble, a form of probation was first tried as a method of treating juvenile offenders outside a correctional institution under the supervision of a criminal court. In 1869, Massachusetts officially established probation for children and provided for the supervision of juvenile delinquents.

By the end of the nineteenth century, as the states provided specialized treatment for children in training schools, the criminal courts began to send children to these schools instead of to prison and to place children on probation for minor offenses. Persons interested in social reform actively sought the establishment of a specialized court for children, organized around objectives significantly different from those of the criminal courts. They wanted a court that would understand the child, diagnose his or her problems, and provide treatment that would restore the child to a constructive role in the community. The welfare of the child was considered more important than the question of guilt or innocence. It is these considerations that led the reformers to seek the establishment of the juvenile court and that continue to motivate its proponents today.

The first statute to define a "delinquent child" and create a juvenile court to deal with dependent, neglected, and delinquent children was enacted in Illinois in 1899. The court established by this statute began operation in Cook County (Chicago) in June of that year. The Latin phrase *parens patriae*, meaning "in place of the parent," best summarizes the legal and social philosophy upon which its policies were based. The establishment of the juvenile court thus came as a logical sequel to the creation and expansion of special and separate treatment facilities for children and the introduction of probation as a method of treatment.

The Children's Bureau, based in the federal government, was created

13 years after the first juvenile court and, under the leadership of social workers, exercised an important influence over the development of juvenile courts throughout the United States. By 1945, every state had passed laws providing for the special treatment of juvenile delinquents.

The juvenile court is not a criminal court, nor is it a chancery court, although, as far as children are concerned, it performs the functions of both. It is a statutory court with powers provided for and limited by statute and procedures fixed by the judge of the court when they are not fixed by law.

Juvenile court statutes do not necessarily create specialized courts completely independent of the criminal or civil court system. In many states, authority over juveniles rests wholly or in part with courts that are primarily engaged in some other function. Often the judge who presides over a juvenile court spends most of his or her time as judge of a criminal court. In most states, especially in large cities, there are completely separate juvenile courts. All states, however, have statutes providing for juvenile courts, specifying or permitting procedures that differ from those required in criminal courts. When a judge normally assigned to a criminal court sits as a juvenile court judge on a particular day of the week, that court becomes a juvenile court for that day, and the procedures followed are those legally prescribed for the juvenile court.

The overall juvenile court justice system has grown enormously in recent years. On a nationwide basis, the juvenile justice system consists of almost 20,000 public and private agencies, with a total budget amounting to hundreds of millions of dollars and over 50,000 employees. Most of the 40,000 police agencies have a juvenile component, and more than 3,000 juvenile courts and about 1,000 juvenile correctional facilities exist throughout the country.[1]

These figures do not take into account the vast numbers of children who are referred to community diversion programs and various psychological treatment facilities. There are thousands of these programs throughout the country, and vast numbers of people are employed in them. This multitude of agencies and people dealing with juvenile delinquency and status offenses has led to the development of an enormous and complex juvenile justice system.

ENTERING THE COURT PROCESS: THE POLICE

Children are brought into the processes of a juvenile court through what is known as a petition. A petition may be initiated by a parent or another adult, but in most cases it is presented by a police officer. Children are often arrested by a regular police officer; however, in some police departments

---

[1]National Council of Juvenile and Family Court Judges, *Directory of Juvenile and Family Court Judges* (Reno: University of Nevada Press, 1985).

officers with special training in handling juveniles, variously known as "youth squads" or "juvenile officers," are assigned to delinquency work. A study by McKeachern and Bauzer concluded that the number of petitions requested for juvenile court varies according to the investigating police officers. They found that police officers handle three out of four apprehended delinquents without reference to court or probation officers.[2]

A study by Malcolm Klein, Susan Rosensweig, and Ronald Bates found juvenile arrest procedures vague and ambiguous.[3] They investigated the uniformity of juvenile arrest definitions and operations, with three issues current in criminology underlying their study: (1) translating legislative intent into efficient and just administrative or operational activities; (2) developing adequate information systems for criminal justice; and (3) reporting and making decisions on the current status and progress of agencies and programs. They attempted empirical documentation of the disparate meanings that the common concept of juvenile arrest has to the various levels of people concerned. They collected data from 49 separate police departments in a large metropolitan county, which included rural, suburban, and urban areas. Generally the stations were asked to report their arrest statistics to the state and federal governments, as well as to their local agencies. They found ambiguous guidelines and dissimilar reporting forms in various police stations. There were different sets of criteria and statistics, making uniformity hard to achieve. Structured interviews with 45 chiefs of police revealed less than 50-percent agreement that "booking" was the critical point in determining arrest. Booking does not correspond to the legal definition of either arrest or recording procedures. The chiefs' lack of knowledge of and interest in this issue seemed to indicate a general tendency for juvenile officers and bureaus to be relatively independent, even in highly structured departments. One hundred and thirty juvenile officers and their supervisors filled out questionnaires, and 77 juvenile officers, one in every station in the county, participated in a structured interview. Consistent with the chiefs' lack of clarity was the variation among juvenile officers in the same and different departments. To some an "arrest" was a field contact; to others it was bringing a suspect to the station; while for others it constituted formal arrest. I can confirm similar findings based on my work with the police in New York and Los Angeles.

In many cases police handle juveniles outside the police station or court in a judicious way—by talking to their parents or by reprimanding or counselling the child. There is, however, considerable evidence that police contact with juveniles, especially in high-delinquency areas, is less than ideal.

[2]A. McKeachern and R. Bauzer, "Factors Related to Disposition in Juvenile Police Contracts," in *Juvenile Gangs in Context*, eds. Malcolm V. Klein and Barbara G. Meyerhoff (Englewood Cliffs, N.J.: Prentice-Hall, 1967), pp. 148–160.

[3]Malcolm W. Klein, Susan Labin Rosensweig, and Ronald Bates, "The Ambiguous Juvenile Arrest," *Criminology* 13, 1 (May 1975): 78–89.

In one analysis Barbara Tomson and Edna R. Fielder characterize police behavior vis-a-vis juveniles as "police pressure" and describe the interaction with juveniles as follows:[4] In "high-delinquency areas" police are continually harassing youth who look delinquent, and therefore police are considered enemies in lower-class neighborhoods. The gang delinquent interprets the effect of this police attitude on his or her life in a way that results in a vicious circle: The delinquent becomes more of a "cop hater" and moves deeper into delinquency, and this causes the police officer to become more of a "delinquent hater."

Based on their analysis of the situation, Tomson and Fielder conclude that when the police apprehend a delinquent, they usually have several choices of action, and the choice they make varies. They delineate five alternatives open to the police: outright release, release and submission of a field interrogation report, official reprimand and release to parents or guardian, petition to the juvenile court, or arrest and confinement in juvenile hall. Treatment of the minor offender depends on the youth's personal characteristics: group affiliation (Is he a gang member?), age, race, grooming, dress, and (most important) demeanor. Tomson and Fielder note a high correlation between cooperative demeanor (exhibited by contriteness, respectfulness, and fearfulness) and police leniency.

Constant police harassment of youths who present a delinquent stereotype results in much negative contact between such youths and the police. As the frequency of contacts increases, the process becomes routine, and youths lose their fear of police. They become indifferent and hostile, attitudes the police often interpret as characteristic of a hardened criminal. The police then tend to treat them severely, reinforcing the youths' hostilities.

Despite these problems, the police officer has more roles, flexibility, and importance in a lower-class neighborhood than in a middle-class neighborhood: He or she intervenes in many crisis situations, including ambulance calls or family fights. Police officers have a more flexible role in lower-class neighborhoods because there is often a greater need for their services in dealing with a variety of human problems, including delinquency. Despite this, some of the negative attitudes about the law and law enforcement in these communities are projected by juveniles onto all officialdom, including the juvenile court and its procedures.

JUVENILE COURT PROCEDURES

The juvenile court was from the outset intended to be primarily rehabilitative and operated in the interest of the child. The juvenile court is a structure for helping "dependent children," "status offenders," or "neglected"

[4]Barbara Tomson and Edna R. Fielder, "Gangs: A Response to the Urban World," in *Gang Delinquency*, eds. Desmond S. Cartwright, Barbara Tomson, and Hershey Schwartz (Monterey, Calif.: Brooks/Cole, 1975), pp. 149–150.

children in need of care and further official attention. One ideal of the court is "individualized justice."

A typical juvenile court act provides for state control as a substitute for parental control and an informal proceeding instead of a trial. In 1920 a United States Children's Bureau publication listed some essential characteristics of the juvenile court that still exist and have validity:

1. Separate hearings for children's cases
2. Informal or chancery procedure
3. Regular probation service
4. Separate detention of children
5. Special court and probation records
6. Provision for mental and physical examination[5]

Official cases in the juvenile court (designated as well as specialized) are initiated by petition. If a child has been arrested by the police, the petitioner may be the police officer, the victim, or a representative of a prosecuting agency. The petition is similar to a complaint against a criminal, in that it alleges a wrongdoing on the part of the child and requests the court to take action. It differs, however, in that it purports to be on behalf of and not against the named child. The intake officer, usually a probation officer, schedules the case for a court hearing. If the child is in court and under arrest when the petition is filed, he or she is arraigned. This means that the child is told the nature of the charge, has the right to secure witnesses, and has a right to counsel.

After arraignment, the case is usually adjourned to permit the probation officer to conduct a social investigation. While awaiting the hearing, the child is normally permitted to return home unless in the opinion of the court he or she (1) might harm himself, (2) might endanger others in the community, (3) is likely to run away, or (4) has violated probation.

Whether a child is released to his or her parents or placed in a detention facility depends on the policy of the court. The social investigation, usually required by law, elicits information about the family living conditions, neighborhood and school relationships, working conditions, health, a psychological profile of the child, and any other information that the probation officer can secure from the child or from any other source. The investigator may refer to any source or interview any person about the child without the knowledge or consent of the child or the family.

The hearing is likely to be held in a private courtroom from which everyone except parents and witnesses are excluded. The proceeding is informal. Most children are not represented by lawyers. Some judges demand proof that the child indeed committed the offense before considering the case and exclude irrelevant, immaterial, and hearsay evidence. These

[5]Evelina Belden, "Courts in the United States Hearing Children's Cases," U.S. Children's Bureau Publication 65 (Washington, D.C.: U.S. Government Printing Office, 1920), pp. 7–10.

judges are in the minority. In most juvenile courts the emphasis is on social-psychological, rather than legal, evidence. This is the case in the juvenile court because the child is not charged with a crime and a finding of juvenile delinquency does not constitute conviction of a crime.

In summary, the procedure followed in a juvenile court may be distinguished from that of a criminal court by the following factors:

1. The hearing is private. Only relevant persons are present.
2. The hearing is informal. The proceeding resembles a conference called to bring forth facts rather than an adversary proceeding in which an attempt is made to prove that someone is guilty of some offense.
3. Juries are not used.
4. The report of a social investigation is often available to the court before the hearing.
5. It is (perhaps too often) assumed that the child committed the act that brought him to the attention of the authorities. The emphasis is on *why* he or she did it. In a criminal trial the accused is presumed innocent, and guilt must be established beyond a reasonable doubt by legal and competent evidence.
6. The disposition, in theory at least, provides for treatment rather than punishment.[6]

At the conclusion of the hearing, the case may be disposed of in any of the following ways:

1. The case may be dismissed. This amounts to a finding of "not guilty."
2. The child may be placed under the supervision of a probation officer.
3. The child may be removed from his or her home and placed in a foster home.
4. The child may be referred to a residential treatment center or hospital for emotionally disturbed children.
5. The child may be sent to a camp or other minimum-security correctional institution.
6. The child may be sent to a state training school.
7. In the case of a serious offense, like an attrocious assault or homicide, the child may be referred to the criminal court system.

To these ways of disposing of a case, we would add another significant vector in juvenile court justice that has become more pronounced in the 1980s—a concern for the victim of the child's offense. In this regard, Judge Lois Forer strongly advocates a greater concern for the victim and the provision of restitution. She discusses the case of a juvenile offender who

---

[6]Paul W. Tappan and Ivan Nicolle, "Juvenile Delinquents and Their Treatment," *Annals of the American Academy of Political and Social Science* 339 (January 1962): 157–170.

blinded his victim by shooting him point-blank in the face. Rather than imprisonment, she advocated that "every penalty must provide for the needs of the victim, society, and the offender.[7] Judge Forer asserts that since most street criminals are young, undereducated, and underemployed or unemployed, the sentencing judge cannot ignore their need for education, employment skills, and a sense of responsibility for their own conduct. She states that it is imperative that sentencing address these needs through the range of penalties available to every trial judge: suspending sentence, fine, restitution, reparation, and probation, as well as imprisonment. For example, in the case cited, the delinquent might be sentenced to a life term of providing some financial restitution to the person who was blinded.

There should indeed be greater flexibility in sentencing procedures in the juvenile court. I agree with Judge Forer that restitution gives the offender a greater awareness of his or her behavior and partially helps the victim of the offense through a form of reparation.

Another factor in juvenile court procedures is the determination of the circumstances under which a juvenile offender should be referred to adjudication by a higher court. Almost all jurisdictions in the United States provide conditions for such referral. In general, a youth who commits a homicide or serious repetitive acts of violence is eligible for referral to the criminal court.

A study by Lee Ann Osbun and Peter A. Rode concluded that the practice of referral to a higher court in most jurisdictions was varied and somewhat capricious.[8] They found that the subjective guidelines under which most courts operate are extremely vague and that the individualized and clinical methods used to determine the desirability of adult prosecution are unreliable. Osbun and Rode note that "Several states recently have established objective criteria that either automatically exclude certain juveniles from juvenile court jurisdiction or create a presumption in favor of exclusion." In 1980 Minnesota enacted a detailed statutory formula to govern its waiver process. The formula combines the variables of age, alleged offense, and prior record to identify juveniles presumed to be unfit for retention in the juvenile system.

Osbun and Rode specifically researched the Minnesota approach and concluded that "Contrary to the claims of its supporters, the objective criteria adopted by the Minnesota legislature have not proven to be an adequate means for selecting juveniles for transfer to adult court. The criteria single out many juveniles whose records do not appear to be very serious and fail to identify many juveniles whose records are characterized by violent, frequent, and persistent delinquent activity."[9] The general conclusion that one can draw is that there are no consistent criteria used in the referral of

---

[7]Lois G. Forer, *Criminals and Victims* (New York: Norton, 1980), p. 136.
[8]Lee Ann Osbun and Peter A. Rode, "Prosecuting Juveniles as Adults" *Criminology*, vol. 22, No. 2, May 1984, p. 87.
[9]Ibid., p. 92.

delinquents to the adult court. In most cases, with the exception of homicide, juveniles are referred to the criminal courts based on the judgments made by the presiding juvenile court judge.

THE JUVENILE COURT JUDGE

The juvenile court judge holds broad powers over delinquent children. These judges are usually the most important decision makers in determining the adjudication process, including whether or not to refer a juvenile to a higher court. The juvenile court judge's powers include the right to depart from legal procedures established for criminal courts and to deny to children and their parents privileges normally accorded defendants in civil court.

The juvenile court judge may, for example, consider evidence that would be inadmissible in both criminal and civil court. There can be no doubt that these powers have at times been exercised in a high-handed manner and that rights of appeal are inadequate. The justification offered for this delegation of power over children is that it is essential if the juvenile court is to determine how best to provide care and rehabilitate the child. The judicial function of the court is often subordinated to the social welfare function. Individuals in tune with the original objectives of the juvenile court recognize the need for specially qualified judges and professional social workers to assist them.

In many jurisdictions the juvenile court judge is expected to perform a judicial function and to administer a probation program and treatment program including diagnostic and rehabilitation services. In most juvenile courts the judge has the following duties and responsibilities.

1. To conduct a judicial proceeding in a fair and equitable manner. If the proceeding is perceived to be arbitrary and unfair by the children who appear in court, the judge may be contributing to disrespect for law and, in a very real sense, to the future delinquencies of children.
2. To decide, after a fair hearing, whether or not the child committed the offense alleged in the petition. The judge also has traditionally had the power to make a finding of delinquency if it is determined that the child committed some infraction other than the one alleged.
3. To protect society. The judge must determine whether or not allowing the child to remain in the community would be dangerous to society or to the child.
4. To determine whether or not the child will remain with his or her family or be taken from the family and:
   a. Placed in a foster home.
   b. Sent to a psychological treatment center.
   c. Sent to a correctional institution.
5. To decide what measures will be taken to rehabilitate the child.

6. If the judge decides to place a child in an institution, he or she must determine the one most appropriate to the needs of the child and the protection of society.
7. In addition to the foregoing, the judge is generally charged with overall supervision of probation and treatment personnel attached to the court.

For a judge to be fully qualified to perform these functions, the standards for juvenile courts specify that the individual should have been admitted to the bar in the state where he or she serves and have had some experience in the practice of law. In order to fulfill the role adequately, a juvenile court judge also needs to have certain humanistic attributes. He or she needs to be:

1. Deeply concerned about the rights of people.
2. Keenly interested in the problems of children and families.
3. Sufficiently aware of the contributions of modern psychology, psychiatry, and social work in order to give due weight to the findings of these sciences and professions.
4. Able to evaluate evidence and situations objectively and to make dispositions uninfluenced by personal concepts of child care.
5. Eager to learn.
6. A good administrator, able to delegate administrative responsibility (applicable to administrative judge).
7. Able to conduct hearings in a kindly manner and to talk to children and adults sympathetically and on their level of understanding without loss of the essential dignity of the court.[10]

These guidelines, set down by the National Probation and Parole Association, basically require that the juvenile court judge have a working knowledge of social casework, child psychology, psychiatry, and the other behavioral sciences.

In recent years juvenile court judges are becoming increasingly and, in my view, properly aware of the need to deal with children in the context of the family system. Judges now often advocate that the child's family should be brought together whenever possible to discuss the child's behavior, along with their feelings about those problems with the judge, in order that he or she may effectively adjudicate the case.

DIVERSION FROM THE JUVENILE COURTS

In the field of juvenile delinquency, the movement to deal with a wide variety of delinquents without referral to courts or other establishment agencies is referred to as "diversion." Diversion for juveniles has come to

[10]Guides for Juvenile Court Judges (New York: National Probation and Parole Association, 1957), p. 125.

mean providing an alternative to the juvenile justice system, most particularly the juvenile court. Prior to or immediately following an arrest, the
young person is often "diverted" to an agency or activity providing services
designed to prevent delinquent behavior. School counseling, family counseling, occupational training, or some other service or therapy may be
provided. Diversion is usually instituted to minimize the negative impacts
of the court process and the labeling of youngsters with a minimal record.
Diversion is used for status offenders. In the late 1980s, psychiatric hospitals have become a prevalent form of diversion.

The arguments presented by advocates of diversion cover a wide
range of concerns. Malcolm Klein suggests that the rationales for diversion
are numerous and sometime conflicting. He describes them as follows:

1. Diversion may override the biases in the juvenile justice system,
   since criteria for releasing or detaining suspects will be explicit and
   applied more equitably.
2. Diversion will decrease the volume of cases in the juvenile justice
   system by handling nonserious cases in alternative ways.
3. Diversion is less expensive than the juvenile court system of processing.
4. Diversion will decrease the stigmatization of youngsters since negative labels such as "delinquent" are not applied.
5. Diversion protects naive young offenders from exposure to more
   hardened offenders.
6. Diversion to alternative treatment agencies may expose the child to
   effective treatment rather than the ineffective programs of some
   juvenile courts.[11]

Klein's description of diversion is commonly held by individuals who
work in diversion projects or who advocate their adoption.

Following are brief descriptions of three noteworthy diversion programs reported by the U.S. Department of Justice:[12]

1. *601 Diversion Project.* The Sacramento County Probation Department created an experimental diversion project designed to give
   family crisis therapy to children on a short-term basis. The name of
   the project, 601 Diversion, is derived from Section 601 of the State
   Welfare and Institutions Code, which deals with juveniles and with
   delinquent problems. Cases generally involve conflict and lack of
   communication between youths and their families. The diversion
   project experimented to determine whether juveniles charged with
   offenses such as refusing to obey their parents or being habitually
   truant could be better handled through short-term family therapy

---

[11]Malcolm Klein et al., "The Explosion in Police Diversion Programs: Evaluating the
Structural Dimensions of a Social Fad," in *The Juvenile Justice System*, ed. Malcolm Klein (Beverly Hills, Calif.: Sage, 1976), p. 106.
[12]U.S. Department of Justice, *Exemplary Projects* (Washington, D.C.: Government
Printing Office, 1978), pp. 19–21.

administered at the intake department by specially trained probation officers than through traditional court procedures. The program identified a particular kind of problem—the problem of children beyond the control of their parents—and provided a referral
service for treatment. When a "601 child" is referred by the police,
school, or parents, the specialized unit of the probation department arranges to see if special counseling can be of assistance.
Thus, instead of the child proceeding through the juvenile court,
the child and the family receive immediate family counseling services.

2. *Los Angeles County Regional Diversion Program.* Since 1974, a regional diversion network has served more than 25,000 troubled
and delinquent youngsters in 64 cities in Los Angeles county. Over
13 diversion programs covering 80 percent of the county work with
law-enforcement agencies, schools probation departments, and
other social-service agencies to identify youngsters and their families who can profit from diversion programs rather than judicial
service. Funds are provided through the Law Enforcement Assistance Administration and the Los Angeles Regional Criminal Justice Planning Board. Both public and private agencies provide the
services, which include crisis intervention, counseling, mental
health programs, legal assistance, and vocational training. Clients
range from troubled youths referred by the schools to hard-core
juvenile offenders.

3. *Bronx Neighborhood Youth Diversion Program.* The Bronx Neighborhood Youth Diversion Program deals with youths between 12 and
15 years of age. It is primarily a community-run program. Cases
are generally referred by probation officers and family court
judges. The program has a staff of counselors and advocates, and it
works on a one-to-one basis. The advocate or counselor directs the
child and supervises his or her overall activities, including work,
school, and home relationships. In addition, the program serves as
a forum, a panel of community residents. The forum deals with
offenses that neighborhood children commit and acts as a resolution group between parents and children.

Programs of this type are increasingly being developed in communities around the United States. They have the general impact of involving
the community in a positive way in dealing with its own unique problems,
saving juveniles from being officially labeled as delinquents, and reducing
the juvenile court load. All of these goals, if realized, lead to positive resolution of a complex problem.

A cogent assessment of diversion was reported by the National Advisory Commission on Criminal Justice. The following statement points out
the positive and negative aspects of diversion programs.

Many programs that are labelled diversion did not originate as formal efforts to
divert people from the criminal justice process but came about through ambigu-
ities in the law or the discretionary practices of individual agents of the justice

system. Real programs of diversion specify objectives, identify a target group, outline means and activities for achieving the goals, implement programs, and produce evidence of a plan to at least attempt to evaluate whether or not the means employed are successful in achieving the goals desired. Because of the variety of diversionary methods, it is essential that the community obtain reliable information concerning their effectiveness in crime control. Information is needed regarding diversion's impact on the justice system, the role diversion plays in crime prevention, and the relative rates of success on cases diverted from the system at different stages as compared with cases subjected to varying degrees of criminalization. Such information is not now available, nor will it be available until records are kept on diversion as well as on cases processed officially. . . .

In the absence of research and experimentation, the assessment of correctional policies is largely a matter of guesswork. But the evidence that does exist suggests that diversion may warrant consideration as the preferred method of control for a far greater number of offenders. Moreover, it appears that diversion plays a significant role in crime prevention and in maintaining the justice system so that it is not swamped by its own activity. . . .

Perhaps the single greatest contribution that diversion can make during the next decade is to make society more conscious and sensitive to the deficiencies of the justice system, and hence to force radical changes within the system so that appropriate offenders are successfully diverted from the system while others are provided with programs within the system that offer social restoration instead of criminal contamination.[13]

THE JUVENILE COURT AND DUE PROCESS: A MAJOR ISSUE

The juvenile court is considered to be a tribunal of civil jurisprudence acting on behalf of children. For that reason the constitutional rights normally guaranteed to persons accused of crimes have not been deemed applicable to children brought before it. This issue has created controversy in the juvenile courts over the years and persists as a basic debatable issue. The basic question is: How does the juvenile court protect and focus on the social welfare of the juvenile and, at the same time, provide a "due-process" legal procedure?

A brief historical review of the due-process issue brings it into focus. In 1955, the U.S. Supreme Court held in the Holmes case that "Since juvenile courts are not criminal courts, the constitutional rights granted to persons accused of crime are not applicable to the children brought before them."[14] The position of the Court was that the state was not seeking to punish Holmes, the defendant, as an offender but to salvage him and safeguard his adolescence.

[13]National Advisory Commission on Criminal Justice and Goals, Corrections (Washington, D.C.: U.S. Government Printing Office, 1978), pp. 93–94.

[14]In re Holmes, 109A, 2d 523 (1955), cert. denied 348 U.S. 973. For discussion, see Paul W. Tappan, *Crime, Justice, and Correction* (New York: McGraw-Hill, 1960), pp. 390–392.

Holmes, a juvenile, was arrested in a stolen car operated by another boy. He was sent to state training school by the municipal court of Philadelphia, acting pursuant to Pennsylvania's juvenile court act. His lawyer, on appeal, contended that (1) Holmes had not been represented by counsel, (2) he had not been informed of the specific charges against him, (3) he was not advised of his rights at his trial, particularly of his right to refuse to testify, (4) the testimony admitted into evidence at his trial was incompetent and inadmissible, and (5) the competent evidence presented at the trial did not link Holmes with any illegal acts.

The reviewing court ruled that all these objections were irrelevant, in other words, that the court was not required to accord the accused the same rights that every person charged with a crime is guaranteed by the Constitution.

Holmes's attorneys appealed the case to the Supreme Court on the grounds that the protections of the Fourteenth Amendment against deprivation of liberty without due process had been violated. The Supreme Court refused to hear the case, and the Holmes verdict was upheld.

In summarizing his opposition to juvenile court practice on the due-process issue, Paul Tappan has stated that

> It has been popular practice to rationalize the abandonment, partial or complete, of even the most basic conceptions of due process of law in the Juvenile Court. These include such matters as: the specific charge; confrontation by adverse witnesses; the right to counsel and appeal; the rejection of prejudicial, irrelevant, and hearsay testimony; adjudication only upon proof or upon a plea of guilt. . . . The presumption is commonly adopted that since the state has determined to protect and save its wards, it will do no injury to them through its diverse officials, so that these children need no due process protections against injury. Several exposures to court; a jail remand of days, weeks, or even months; and a long period in a correctional school with young thieves, muggers, and murderers—these can do no conceivable harm if the state's propose be beneficent and the procedure be "chancery!" Children are adjudicated in this way every day without visible manifestations of due process. They are incarcerated. They become adult criminals, too, in thankless disregard of the state's good intentions as parens patriae.[15]

The 1959 edition of the Standard Juvenile Court Act, perhaps in partial response to critics like Paul Tappan, represented an effort to provide more precision in procedure and greater protection of the legal rights and status of children and their families. The Children's Bureau preferred to differentiate between two parts of the hearing: (1) the findings as to the allegations in the petition, the trial portion in which the judge decides whether or not the child committed the acts alleged, and (2) the disposition,

[15]Paul W. Tappan, *Juvenile Delinquency* (New York: McGraw-Hill, 1949), p. 205. Copyright 1949 by McGraw-Hill Book Company. Used by permission of McGraw-Hill Book Company.

the portion of the proceeding on which the judge bases his determination of the appropriate treatment.[16]

In 1966 the Children's Bureau enlarged its earlier legal position and sought to combine its essential philosophy for handling children's cases, "individualized justice," with the recognition of the need to protect the legal and constitutional rights of parents and children. The court was still to be a "legal tribunal where law and science, especially the science of medicine and those sciences which deal with human behavior, such as biology, sociology, and psychology, work side by side."[17]

The Children's Bureau stated that, for a court to become a fully effective and fair tribunal operating for the general welfare, there must be:

1. A judge and a staff identified with and capable of carrying out a nonpunitive and individualized service.
2. Sufficient facilities available in the court and community to ensure:
   a. That the dispositions of the court are based on the best available knowledge of the needs of the child.
   b. That the child, if he needs care, receives these through facilities adapted to his needs and from persons properly qualified and empowered to give them.
   c. That the community receives adequate protection.
3. Procedures designed to ensure:
   a. That each child and his situation are considered individually.
   b. *That the legal and constitutional rights of both parents and child those of the community are duly considered and protected.*[18] [My emphasis.]

A major development in the battle over due process in the juvenile courts was resolved in 1967 in a landmark case that was finally adjudicated by the United States Supreme Court. The case involved a 15-year-old youth, Gerold Gault, who resided in Arizona. Gault was accused of making lewd and indecent calls to a woman over the phone. He was arrested on June 8, 1964, and placed in custody. Gault's parents were not notified that he was taken into custody; he was not advised of right to counsel; he was not advised that he could remain silent; and no formal notice of the charges were given to Gault or his parents. In spite of considerable debate over whether the Gault boy was guilty, he was sentenced to the State Industrial School "for the period of his minority" or until he was 21. The parents engaged a lawyer who appealed the case up to the United States Supreme Court.

On May 15, 1967, the Supreme Court for the first time considered the constitutional rights of children in juvenile courts by hearing the Gault case. In writing the majority opinion of the Court in their landmark deci-

---

[16]"Standard Juvenile Court Act," *National Probation and Parole Association Journal* 5 (October 1959): 329–391.

[17]William H. Sheridan, Standards for Juvenile and Family Courts, Children's Bureau Publication 437 (Washington, D.C.: U.S. Government Printing Office, 1966), pp. 1–7.

[18]Ibid., p. 2.

sion, which enormously affected later treatment of juveniles in the juvenile court, then Justice Abe Fortas said: "Neither the Fourteenth Amendment nor the Bill of Rights is for adults only. Under our Constitution, the condition of being a boy does not justify a kangaroo court."[19] Although the decision did not give to juveniles all the protections accorded adults charged with crimes, the disenchantment with the juvenile court's lack of due process was explicit and the trend of future opinions on this issue predictable.

The appeal to the U.S. Supreme Court was based on violations of Gault's rights, of which the following were basic:[20]

1. The right to notice of the charges against him
2. The right to counsel
3. The right to face witnesses against him and to cross-examine them
4. The right to refuse to answer questions that might tend to incriminate him
5. The right to a transcript of the proceedings
6. The right to appellate review

The Court reversed the action of the Arizona court on the first four of these grounds. With respect to Arizona's claim that the juvenile proceeding was not a criminal proceeding, the Court said, "For this purpose, at least, commitment is a deprivation of liberty. It is incarceration against one's will, whether is is called 'criminal' or 'civil'. And our Constitution guarantees that no person shall be compelled to be a witness against himself when he is threatened with deprivation of his liberty."[21]

In determining its decision in the Gault case, the Supreme Court discussed the history of the juvenile court and the specialized treatment accorded children. The parens patriae doctrine and the way in which it is applied by the juvenile courts was attacked in far stronger terms by the Supreme Court than those used earlier by Professor Tappan. The Court noted that the early reformers meant to provide "substitute parents" in establishing specialized courts and treatment for children, but these turned out to be, in effect, procedures for sending juveniles to what are, in fact, correctional institutions in which they are confined with other juveniles sent to these institutions for offenses ranging in seriousness from minor juvenile delinquencies to serious crimes. Although the Court did not require that children be granted all the rights that adults charged with crime are guaranteed, a reading of the Gault decision did grant juveniles much more due process in the juvenile courts.

One of the effects of the Gault decision was the more frequent ap-

[19]In re Gault, 387 U.S. 1 (1967).
[20]Alan Neigher, "The Gault Decision: Due Process and the Juvenile Courts," *Federal Probation* 31 (December 1967): 13. This article contains an excellent analysis of the Gault case and the constitutional rights of children after the Supreme Court decision.
[21]Ibid., p. 136.

pearance of lawyers in the juvenile court representing the accused. Before Gault, very few juvenile delinquents were represented by attorneys. In 1974, a survey of judges in 68 of our largest cities revealed that nearly two-thirds reported the presence of defense counsel in 75 percent of the cases involving a felony or serious crime. In nearly half the cities, over 75 percent of the juveniles charged with less serious crimes, not felonies, were represented by counsel. Even in PINS (person in need of supervision—under the New York Family Court Act, a child who has misbehaved repeatedly but not criminally) and neglect cases, nearly half the cities reported that over 75 percent of the juveniles were represented by counsel.[22] This trend has continued into the 1980s.

The more powerful role of the prosecutor and the increased use of defense attorneys makes the juvenile court more and more like an adult court, where an adversary system reigns supreme. This trend, combined with the growing advocacy for adjudicating serious offenders in the adult courts, has somewhat diminished the original concept of social welfare in the juvenile courts. Despite this, most juvenile courts attempt to resocialize rather than punish the youths they define as juvenile delinquents.

SUMMARY: BASIC THEMES FOR CLASS DISCUSSION

1. There are three basic perspectives on defining who is a delinquent. These include
   a. the juvenile court adjudication process;
   b. the social-community perception of the child's behavior; and
   c. the self-concept of youths who commit delinquent acts.
2. The juvenile court often acts in *loco parentis* (in place of the parents of a child) when the parents are not in proper control of their parental responsibilities. The police and parents are the main petitioners for placing a juvenile into the juvenile court system.
3. At its inception the juvenile court system, through its judge, tended to paternalistically dominate and control the juvenile's legal rights. As a result of the Gault decision in 1967, the juvenile court began to operate in terms of greater legal due process for the child. This modified the juvenile court so that the child's legal rights, such as having legal counsel, a possible jury trial, protection against self-incrimination, and the elimination of hearsay evidence, were enhanced.
4. The focus of the juvenile court relies more on the utilization of rehabilitation and social-psychological analysis principles than does the adult criminal court, which rests on the foundation that punishment deters crime.
5. A trend in the juvenile court system is to perceive delinquents as emotionally disturbed, "conduct-disordered" children and to refer them for psychological treatment in a psychiatric facility. Another

[22]M. Marvin Finkelstein et al., *Prosecution in the Juvenile Courts* (Washington, D.C.: Department of Justice, Law Enforcement Assistance Administration, December, 1973), p. 16.

trend is to perceive delinquents as "status offenders," "dependent and neglected children," or "wards of the court."

6. The movement to deal with a wide variety of delinquents by referring them to community agencies other than the juvenile court is referred to as "diversion." The young person who commits deviant acts is often "diverted" to the school counselor, a psychologist, family counselor, or a residential psychiatric clinic or institution. These diversionary processes have lowered overcrowding in the juvenile courts, label fewer children as delinquents, and thus reduce some of the negative impacts of the juvenile court process.

QUESTIONS

2.1. Discuss the various implications of having a delinquent self-concept.

2.2. What changes in procedure would you recommend for modifying the juvenile court system so that it would more effectively serve the functions of protecting and resocializing the child into law-abiding behavior?

2.3. Has the juvenile court become too "legalized"? Should we return to the earlier form of the juvenile court (before the Gault decision), which relied more heavily on the proper selection and administration of the court by a friendly, humanistic judge who had greater power in the process?

2.4. Does punishment deter delinquent behavior? Should the juvenile court become more openly punitive for the purpose of deterring delinquent behavior?

2.5. Some critics of diversion take the position that the process minimizes the child's awareness of the seriousness of their behavior and therefore deters proper control of the delinquent. Agree or disagree with this criticism.

chapter 3

Social-Class Factors and Delinquency

A complex element in defining delinquency is the issue of social class. It is apparent that individuals in the lower socioeconomic strata of our society are often frustrated and blockaded by higher rates of unemployment, prejudice, and discrimination in their quest for the American dream. These blockades to equal opportunity and success tend to produce a high incidence of delinquency in lower socioeconomic groups. This is reflected in the disproportionate number of juveniles from this strata of society who are adjudicated "delinquent" by the juvenile courts. More privileged young deviants are often diverted into other social facilities, or their behavior is absorbed by their family, and they are not accorded delinquent status.

Despite the fact that most youths who appear in juvenile court are from the lower strata of our society, it does not necessarily follow that they comprise the majority of the delinquent population. Research data lead to the conclusion that police biases, legal vulnerability, and parental decisions affect which children wind up in court and are adjudicated delinquent. These factors are related to social-class attitude and power in the society and tend to determine who will be officially defined a delinquent.

Many researchers have explored this issue. Most social-psychological studies that have investigated delinquents and nondelinquents have compared institutionalized delinquents with children who have not been adjudicated delinquent. The assumption is made that those children who had not been judged delinquent by a court had not engaged in delinquent behavior. This assumption may not be totally true. Even though the majority of the children found to be delinquent by courts were from the most socioeconomically deprived segments of our population, and a general appraisal of welfare data reveals that there is a higher incidence of adjudicated delinquents from welfare families, it doesn't necessarily follow that only those youths adjudicated by the courts have committed delinquent acts.

Many "nondelinquent" youths have violated legal norms without being caught or at least without being adjudicated delinquent. Various studies in which anonymous questionnaires were utilized indicate that middle-class children are involved in delinquent behavior similar to that of lower-class adjudicated delinquents.

Class position is a significant, albeit complex, issue in defining who is delinquent. In the following analysis I will examine a wide spectrum of theory, research, and analysis that explores the issues involved in determining social class and in defining delinquency.

SOCIAL CLASS AND DELINQUENCY: THEORY AND RESEARCH

Despite the fact that Karl Marx was not the first social philosopher to analyze the concept of social class, his writings on the subject are predominant in over half the world and have exerted an influence on many economists, psychologists, and sociologists in the United States. Marx defined class in terms of its relationship to the ownership of land and capital. According to Marx there were two basic classes: the bourgeois capitalists, who owned capital and property; and the lower-class masses (the proletariat), who did not possess capital or property. The latter class was the working class, whose members depended on their labor to live. In simplistic terms, he asserted that each class by virtue of its position in the economic order and its relationship to property, had common experiences, economic and political interests, and ways of life. Class conflict, according to Marx, arises when proletarian class consciousness emerges because of the difficulties experienced by the members of the working class.[1] Implicit in Marx's theory was the assumption that the dominated group had less of a stake in the system, and that the lower classes were likely to be more rebellious. This rebellion, according to Marx, often took the form of delinquent and criminal behavior.

In 1916 William A. Bonger, a Dutch sociologist, related Marxist theory in more depth to the crime and delinquency problem.[2] Bonger, building on Marxist theory, asserted that the members of the working class and the unemployed become disproportionately involved in crime because of the economic demands of the capitalist system. This view of society was referred to by Bonger as "economic determinism." Describing people as both altruistic and selfish, Bonger concludes that capitalism stimulates the selfish side of people. People produce for profit rather than for personal

[1]Karl Marx, *Capital*, trans. Ernest Untermann, from 1st German ed. (Chicago: Kerr, 1909), vol. 3.

[2]William Bonger, *Criminality and Economic Conditions* (Boston: Little, Brown, 1916), pp. 401–402.

consumption, and this fact results in, among other things, intense competition between capital and labor for the fruits of labor. Employers try to purchase labor at the lowest possible price; workers try to sell their labor for the highest possible price.

The "selfish *egoistic* competition fostered by the capitalist system," according to Bonger, transforms the businessperson into a "parasite" who lives without working, feels no moral obligation to his fellow human, and regards workers as things to serve and entertain him. Crime and delinquency is by his definition an expression of human selfishness. This selfishness and social irresponsibility causes unemployment, lack of education, and other disabilities of the poor that lead to their commissions of crime.

Richard Quinney, building on the theories of Marx and Bonger, presented in 1974 a contemporary Marxist view of crime control in American society. He maintained that, since 1 percent of the population owns 40 percent of the nation's wealth and nearly all power in American society is concentrated in the hands of a few large corporations, government and business are inseparable. As a capitalist society the United States has two major classes: one which owns and controls, and a working class. Professionals, small businesspeople, office workers, and cultural workers may cut across class lines. However, the ruling class owns and controls the means of production and through its economic power uses the state to dominate the society. The dominant class is the ruling class. Quinney summarizes his position with respect to class and crime as follows:

1. American society is based on an advanced capitalist economy.
2. The state is organized to serve the interests of the dominant economic class, the capitalist ruling class.
3. Criminal law is an instrument of the state and ruling class to maintain and perpetuate the existing social and economic order.
4. Crime control in capitalist society is accomplished through a variety of institutions and agencies established and administered by a governmental elite, representing ruling class interests, for the purpose of establishing domestic order.
5. The contradictions of advanced capitalism—the disjunction between existence and essence—require that the subordinate classes remain oppressed by whatever means necessary, especially through the coercion and violence of the legal system.
6. Only with the collapse of capitalist society and the creating of a new society, based on socialist principles, will there be a solution to the crime problem.[3]

LOWER-CLASS CULTURE AS A GENERATOR OF DELINQUENCY

Applying Bonger's or Quinney's thinking to contemporary conditions, one would conclude that the poor, people on welfare, the unemployed, and

[3]Richard Quinney, "Crime Control in Capitalist Society," in *The Criminologist: Crime and the Criminal*, ed. Charles E. Reasons (Pacific Palisades, Calif.: Goodyear, 1974), pp. 136–143.

workers who consider themselves exploited might favor the commission of crimes against the more privileged and against the economic and political establishment controlled by the wealthy. The underprivileged classes, having little or no voice in their destiny, would be expected to be alienated, hostile, and in favor of retaliatory activities, which would be defined as crimes. In encouraging unrestrained egoism, self-interest, or rugged individualism, a capitalist society inspires attacks on the social organization by those who consider themselves disadvantaged. Because of this situation underprivileged working-class people might be expected to have higher delinquency rates.

Urban slum areas, inhabited by the lower socioeconomic classes, do have the highest rates of juvenile delinquency, the highest arrest rates of young people, the largest number of court referrals, and the largest number of recidivists (repeaters). Also, according to 1987 statistics, these areas produce the largest number of young people who belong to violent gangs and are in custody in correctional institutions. A Juvenile Delinquency Project of the National Education Association, directed by William C. Kvaraceus and Walter B. Miller, published a report delineating how various factors in lower-class culture affected the delinquency problem in the United States. Kvaraceus and Miller's research contrasted lower-class culture with middle-class culture, and described the ways in which lower-class culture contributed to the delinquency of lower-class children.[4] Their report concluded that "the preponderant proportion of our delinquent population consists essentially of normal lower class youngsters."

According to Kvaraceus and Miller, the concerns, values, and characteristic patterns of behavior of the lower socioeconomic class are the products of a well-formed cultural system. It is estimated that between 40 and 60 percent of the total population of the United States share or are significantly influenced by the major outlines of the lower-class cultural system. Many youngsters growing up in these areas are "normally delinquent" if they conform to their culture.

Behavior of those in a given cultural system is said to be motivated by a set of "focal concerns"—concerns that receive special emphasis within that culture. In lower-class society, the following concerns are dominant: trouble, toughness, smartness, excitement, fate, autonomy.

- *Trouble.* A boy or girl may be accorded recognition or prestige by being successfully involved (in trouble) with the authorities (police or school) or for avoiding such involvement (staying out of trouble).
- *Toughness.* Physical prowess, "maculinity," endurance, athletic ability, and strength rank high in the concerns of lower-class adolescents, as is evident in the kinds of heroes they select—tough guy, gangster, tough cop, combat infantryman, "hard" teacher. Boys in

[4]William C. Kvaraceus and Walter B. Miller, *Delinquent Behavior* (Washington, D.C.: National Education Association, 1959), vol. 1, *Culture and the Individual*, pp. 55–75. Copyright 1959 by the National Education Association of the United States. Reprinted with permission.

the streets boast of acts that indicate toughness and belittle those who appear soft.

- *Smartness*. Skill in duping and outsmarting the other guy is admired, as well as the ability to avoid being duped by others. The con man is the hero and model. The victim of a con man is seen as a sucker or fool.
- *Excitement*. The search for thrills and stimulation is a major concern when life is often monotonous and drab.
- *Fate*. Drinking, gambling, and fighting are popular as sources of excitement. Lady Luck is a reigning goddess of lower-class society. Success is attributed to good luck, failure to bad luck. Gambling is viewed as a way of testing one's luck.
- *Autonomy*. Lower-class adolescents say in no uncertain terms that no one is going to boss them. Yet they frequently seek out, through norm-violating behavior, situations in which they will be told what to do, when to do it, how to do it, and whether it is right when done.

There are several class factors that enter into a lower-class child's commission of acts of delinquency.

1. Certain cultural practices that comprise essential elements of the total life pattern of lower-class culture automatically violate certain legal norms.
2. In certain instances, when alternative avenues to valued objectives are available, the law-violating route frequently entails a relatively smaller investment of energy and effort than the law-abiding one.
3. The *demanded* response to certain situations recurrently engendered within lower-class culture calls for the commission of illegal acts.

The lower-class youngster who engages in a long and recurrent series of delinquent acts that are sanctioned by his or her peer group is acting to achieve prestige within this reference system.

Like Kvaraceus and Miller, Albert K. Cohen perceived the delinquency of what he terms "the working-class boy" as a form of rebellion against the middle class and its values. He describes the delinquent subculture as "nonutilitarian, malicious, and negativistic." In addition to such obviously nonutilitarian delinquent acts as vandalism, Cohen contends that even stealing by those involved in the delinquent lower-class subculture is nonutilitarian. He says of this:

> In homelier language, stealing "for the hell of it" and apart from considerations of gain and profit is a valued activity to which attaches glory, prowess and profound satisfaction. There is no accounting in rational and utilitarian terms for the effort expended and the danger run in stealing things which are often discarded, destroyed or casually given away. A group of boys enters a store where each takes a hat, a ball or a light bulb. They then move on to another store where these things are covertly exchanged for like articles. Then they move on to the other stores to continue the game indefinitely. They steal a

basket of peaches, desultorily munch on a few of them and leave the rest to spoil. They steal clothes they cannot wear and toys they will not use. Unquestionably, most delinquents are from the more "needy" and "underprivileged" classes, and unquestionably many things are stolen because they are intrinsically valued. However, a humane and compassionate regard for their economic disabilities should not blind us to the fact that stealing is not merely an alternative means to the acquisition of objects otherwise difficult of attainment.[5]

Cohen concludes that other activities of the lower-class delinquent are even less motivated by rational, utilitarian considerations. He notes that there is a kind of *malice* apparent, an enjoyment in the discomfiture of others, a delight in the defiance against taboos. (This pattern was apparent in news reports of juveniles and adults in lower-class neighborhoods around the country shooting off guns on New Year's Eve, 1986.)

While Kvaraceus and Miller regard the activities of lower-class delinquents as derived from and related to the focal concerns of the adults in their class, Cohen sees the acts of adherents to the delinquent subculture as essentially *negativistic*. He sees an element of active spite in their flouting of rules, defiance of teachers, and misbehavior in school. It is, as Cohen sees it, a revolt against the middle class and its values by the working-class boys. He puts it this way:

All this suggests also the intention of our term *negativistic*. The delinquent subculture is not only a set of rules, a design for living which is different from or indifferent to or even in conflict with the norms of the "respectable" adult society. It would appear at least plausible that it is defined by its "negative polarity" to those norms. That is, the delinquent subculture takes its norms from the larger culture but turns them upside down. The delinquent's conduct is right, by the standards of his subculture, precisely *because* it is wrong by the norms of the larger culture.[6]

Other characteristics of the delinquent subculture noted by Cohen include: *versatility*, demonstrated by a lack of specialization; *short-run hedonism*, evidenced by a lack of planning and absence of long-range goals; and *group autonomy*, expressed through intolerance of restraint except from the informal pressure within the delinquent group. Relations with other groups, he feels, tend to be indifferent, hostile, or rebellious.[7]

The "carriers" of the delinquent subculture, according to Cohen, are lower-class boys. He concludes that juvenile delinquency in general, and the delinquent subculture in particular, are overwhelmingly concentrated in the male, lower-class sector of the juvenile population. Acknowledging that police and court biases may account in part for the correlation between juvenile delinquency and social class, Cohen nevertheless concludes, and

---

[5]Reprinted with permission of The Free Press, a Division of Macmillan, Inc. from *Delinquent Boys* by Albert K. Cohen. Copyright © 1955 by The Free Press, renewed 1983 by Albert K. Cohen.

[6]Ibid., p. 28.

[7]Ibid., pp. 28–32.

almost all statistical analyses of juvenile delinquency agree, that delinquency *in general* is predominantly a working-class phenomenon.

His review of "self-reporting" studies that indicate considerable middle-class delinquent behavior does not lead him to modify this conclusion.[8] As Cohen sees it, working-class children are evaluated in accordance with middle-class standards set by middle-class teachers, social workers, ministers, adults managing settlement houses, etc. Working-class children must come to terms with these norms, which are a tempered version of the Protestant ethic that requires one to strive, by dint of rational, ascetic, self-discplined, and independent activity, *to achieve* in worldly affairs. *Success* is a sign of the exercise of moral qualities. The middle-class norms emphasize control of violence and aggression, respect for property, and constructive use of leisure time.[9]

The working-class boy sees himself as not likely to succeed in school, at work, or anywhere else that middle-class norms are applied. He sees himself at the bottom of the heap. He therefore joins with others like himself in rejecting the middle-class culture and developing a subculture that opposes it. Delinquency then becomes, in a sense, a rebellion against the middle class, a form of class conflict. Frustrated by the fact that his socialization in the working class handicaps him for success in the middle-class status system, he rebels against it and finds a solution in delinquency.[10]

SELF-REPORTING STUDIES, SOCIAL CLASS, AND DELINQUENCY

The explanations offered by Kvaraceus and Miller and by Cohen assume that delinquency is largely a lower-class urban phenomenon. Although this assumption is supported by most available statistics, there is a growing body of research that indicates a growing difference in magnitude between lower-class delinquent behavior and middle-class delinquent behavior. The delinquencies of middle-class children are often not adequately reported because of police bias in making arrests. Some researchers have developed other methods for obtaining this data, one of which is a questionnaire in which young people are asked to report instances of delinquent behavior on a self-reporting basis. Another method is the in-depth interview, granting anonymity to the respondent, in which similar information is elicited.

Using this research methodology in their study of social class and delinquency, Nye, Short, and Olsen obtained their data using anonymous questionnaires. Their research attempted to answer a basic question: Does delinquent behavior occur differentially by socioeconomic status?[11]

[8]Ibid., pp. 36–44.
[9]Ibid., pp. 84–97.
[10]Ibid., pp. 121–137.
[11]Ivan Nye, James F. Short, Jr., and Virgil J. Olson, "Socioeconomic Status and Delinquent Behavior," *American Journal of Sociology* 63 (January 1958): 381–389.

The researchers rejected studies of delinquent behavior based on court records, police files, records maintained by correctional institutions, and other official sources. Such studies, they maintained, might be adequate for an examination of official delinquency but are unreliable as an index of delinquent behavior in the general population. The distinction between the concepts "official delinquency" and "delinquency behavior" was considered important by the researchers. Essentially, from their viewpoint the difference was that delinquent behavior is behavior violating legal norms; it becomes official delinquency only when it results in action by official authority, such as police and courts. Official delinquency in their view represented a *reaction of society* to delinquent behavior.

In general, when sociologists refer to people as members of the lower, middle, or upper class, they base their differentiations on the economic status of the child's family. The occupation of the head of the family, family income, educational attainments, or some combination of the three are generally used as criteria for placing a child in a particular class. In other words, *the class position of the family is ascribed to the child*. In Nye et al., the father's occupation was used to place the child in one of four status groupings: (1) unskilled or semiskilled labor; (2) skilled labor and craftsmen; (3) white-collar workers and small businessmen; and (4) professionals and large businessmen.

The sample for this study was drawn from two sources—selected high schools in several Western and Midwestern communities. The Western sample involved 2,350 boys and girls attending high school in three cities whose populations ranged from 10,000 to 25,000. The Midwestern sample was collected from questionnaires soliciting comparable data from 250 boys and 265 girls in grades nine through twelve in high schools in three communities with populations of under 2,500. No samples were taken from large cities or from large non-Caucasian groups. The young people in the sample were not classified as delinquent; nor were any of the subjects school dropouts.

Delinquent behavior was measured by means of an anonymous delinquency checklist and by a delinquency scale constructed from it. The list was designed to include a broad sampling of juvenile misconduct, although it did not include the more serious types of delinquency, such as rape, breaking and entering, and armed robbery.

In all, 756 differences were tested for, and 33 were found to be significant. That is, 33 significant differences were found in the proportion of acts committed by a particular socioeconomic category. The two middle status groups had the highest proportion of delinquency in four instances; the upper status group in 13 instances; and the lower status group in 16 instances. From this the researchers concluded that either middle-class delinquent behavior is underreported or middle-class parents are more effective in socializing their children and controlling their behavior.

In another study comparing delinquent behavior of boys and girls in different socioeconomic strata, Voss also used self-reported data.[12] The subjects of the study were 620 students in a public intermediate school. Attention was focused primarily on the information provided by 284 male respondents. The data were gathered in Honolulu, a metropolitan center in which the majority of the population is Oriental. Anonymous questionnaires were administered to a 15.5-percent random sample of seventh-grade students. The researcher recorded on a chart the number of times a youth had committed a particular act and the minimum frequency required for the youth to be classified delinquent. Children were placed in four classes based on the socioeconomic position of the father. The four strata were (1) unskilled and semiskilled labor, (2) skilled labor and craftsmen, (3) white-collar workers and small businessmen, and (4) professionals and large businessmen.

The data were subjected to three tests in an attempt to locate significant differences in the incidence of delinquent behavior. In the first test the distribution of most and least delinquent groups of boys and girls by socioeconomic status was tested. The girls in the various status levels were found not to differ significantly. However, for boys, socioeconomic status was found to be significantly related to incidence of delinquent behavior. Boys in the two upper social strata reported more extensive involvement in delinquent activity than did boys in the other two groups. The reported delinquent activity by groups was: Group 1, 29.2 percent; Group 2, 29.9 percent; Group 3, 52.4 percent; and Group 4, 40.0 percent. The second test included only those boys who had reported at least three serious delinquent acts. A slightly larger percentage of the boys in the two higher status levels reported at least three serious delinquent acts, but the difference was not significant. The third test, which was designed to determine differences in specific delinquent acts, was conducted under the assumption that the types of delinquent behavior reported might differ by status level. Of the 18 categories tested, only one significant relationship was observed. The number of those who "purposely damaged or destroyed property" was reported to be higher in the two upper strata.

The researcher concluded that the incidence of admitted illegal behavior of lower-status children did not differ significantly from those of middle- and upper-status children. The fact that boys in the two higher strata reported more property destruction appeared to conflict with Cohen's position. If vandalism is part of the delinquent subculture, as Cohen says it is, one would expect vandalism by the lower-class children to be more frequent.

In another significant study on the issue of social class and delinquency, Erickson and Empey used self-reported data in an attempt to un-

---

[12]Harwin L. Voss, "Socioeconomic Status and Reported Delinquent Behavior," *Social Problems* 13 (Winter 1966): 314–324.

derstand how peer pressure in different strata affects delinquency.[13] They were concerned primarily with studying the child's relationship to peers. They noted that explanations of delinquency are often based on the assumption that the child's class position and exposure or lack of exposure to educational and other socializing activities are directly related to delinquent behavior. Because lower-class children lack the "successes and satisfactions" of upper- and middle-class children, it is believed they are more frequently inclined to become delinquent.

One theory suggested by the authors is that "a lower-class child joins with delinquent peers and participates in delinquent activities because these things represent an alternative means for acquiring many of the social and emotional satisfactions that other children obtain from conventional sources." If their theory is accurate, it would indicate that (1) delinquency is more indicative of the lower class than of the middle or upper classes, (2) peer relations are more predictive of delinquent or nondelinquent behavior than is lower-class position, and (3) children from the lower class are more apt to associate with and have a commitment to delinquents than are children from middle and upper classes.

In testing the validity of these hypotheses, the authors used a sample of white males, aged 15 to 17, selected at random from a county population of 110,000 in Utah. Racial minorities were excluded since they did not represent a numerically significant portion of the population in Utah. Two hundred boys were selected, at random, from groups of boys who had been in prison, boys who had been to court once, boys who were on probation, and boys who had never been to court. The occupation of the guardian or father was used as the basis for defining class level. The lower class included holders of unskilled or semiskilled jobs; the middle class included skilled and white-collar workers and small businessmen; the upper class encompassed most of the professional occupations, corporate positions, and scientists and artists.

Twenty-two delinquent acts were defined by the researchers. Each subject was interviewed personally and asked: (1) had he ever committed such an offense, (2) if so, how many times, and (3) if so, how often had he been caught, arrested, or brought into court. More serious crimes, such as narcotics and arson, were eliminated because they did not play a significant or frequent role in the lives of the youth in the sample.

Erickson and Empey found no significant correlation between class position and delinquency. A slight difference between the classes was explained by a lower amount of delinquency in the upper class rather than a high degree of occurrence in the lower class. The study also indicated that there was much correlation of responses between the lower and middle

[13]Maynard L. Erickson and LaMar T. Empey, "Class Position, Peers, and Delinquency," *Sociology and Social Research* 49 (April 1965): 268–282. Reprinted by permission Sociology and Social Research, University of Southern California, Los Angeles, CA 90089–0032.

classes. In regard to association with delinquents, the results showed that those boys already delinquent were more apt to associate with other delinquents, although this did not necessarily imply identification with the group. All classes responded negatively to "informing on a peer" or "ratting." The authors concluded from their results that social-class position is less predictive of delinquency than is association and identification with delinquent peers.

Erickson and Empey summarized their findings as follows:

1. There was a slight but statistically reliable relationship between social class and delinquency. However, when variance was traced, it was discovered that the correlation was significant more because upper class respondents differed from the other two than because low class respondents differed from the other two. Middle and low class did not differ significantly from each other.

2. The same pattern characterized the relationship of social class to delinquent associates. The upper class group was significantly less inclined than the other two to have delinquent associates. Middle and low class respondents did not differ.

3. The pattern was confirmed even more in the analysis of respondent commitment to peer expectations. Upper class respondents were significantly less committed than others to the expectations of their peers, delinquent or non-delinquent. But, in addition, there was some suggestion that it was the middle rather than the low class group which had the greatest commitment of all.

    The data would definitely not support the notion that peer standards have more importance for the low than the middle class juvenile. In fact, these findings might lead one to hypothesize that because they are departing perhaps even further from the expectations of their parents than low class children, middle class offenders have greater need for peer support than low class offenders.

4. Delinquent associates and peer commitment variables proved to be far more predictive of delinquent behavior than did social class. As a part of an overall pattern, it strongly implied the need to examine more carefully the role of peers, as contrasted to class, in attempting to understand delinquency.[14]

Most self-reported delinquency studies have drawn their samples from small cities and from Caucasian populations. It may very well be that in the small community the differences in behavioral patterns of adolescents in the various social strata are not very pronounced. There appears, however, to be a world of difference in behavioral patterns, performance in school, and style of life when boys who live in urban slums are compared with boys of any social class who live in small cities and suburban areas. Most researchers have indicated an awareness of these differences.

Clark and Wenninger used self-administered questionnaires in a study of differences in delinquent behavior exhibited by members of dif-

[14]Ibid., p. 281.

ferent social classes in four types of communities.[15] A total of 1,154 students drawn from the sixth through twelfth grades of the public school systems of four different types of communities were the subjects. The students responded to a self-administered, anonymous questionnaire given in groups of from 20 to 40 students by the senior researcher, John P. Clark.

Considerable precautions were taken to ensure reliability and validity of responses. The students chosen came from four types of communities:

1. Rural farm (farms and very small villages)
2. Lower-class urban (ghetto-type area of a large metropolis)
3. Industrial city (diffuse, autonomous small industrial city)
4. Upper-class urban (wealthy suburb of a large city)

An inventory of 38 offenses was assembled from delinquency scales, legal statutes, and FBI *Uniform Crime Reports*. No sex offenses were included. Respondents were asked if they had committed any of the listed offenses within the past year and the number of times they had committed each.

To determine whether significant differences existed in the incidence of illegal behavior among the various types of communities, a two-step procedure was followed. First, each community was assigned a rank for each offense on the basis of the percentage of respondents admitting commission of that offense. The resultant numerical total provided a very crude overall measure of the relative degree to which the same population from each community had been involved in illegal behavior during the past year. Second, the communities were arranged in the order given above and the significance of the differences between adjacent pairs was determined. Only comparisons involving either industrial city or lower urban versus upper urban or rural farm resulted in any significant differences.

The findings showed that juveniles from the lower urban community reported significantly more illegal behavior than did the juveniles from the upper urban community and that the two lower-class urban communities— lower urban and industrial city—were quite similar in their high rates of delinquency, while the lower-class rural community was similar to the upper-class urban community in having a much lower rate. On most of the offenses, youths from the lower urban and industrial city communities reported no significant differences. Rural farm youngsters were more prone to commit unsophisticated acts of deviance consonant with rural life. The greatest difference between rates of illegal conduct occurred between the lower urban and upper urban communities. The researchers failed to detect any significant differences in illegal behavior rates among the social classes of rural and small urban areas. However, significant differences were found, both in quantity and quality of illegal acts, among communities

---

[15]Clark and Wenninger, "Socio-economic Class and Area as Correlates of Illegal Behavior among Juveniles," *American Sociological Review* 27 (December 1962): 826–834.

consisting of one predominant socioeconomic class. The lower-class areas had higher delinquency rates, particularly for the more serious offenses.

Clark and Wenninger believe that their research suggests some interesting relationships:

1. The pattern of illegal behavior within small communities or "status areas" of a large metropolitan center is determined by the predominant class of that area.
2. Although juveniles in all communities admit participation in a variety of offenses, serious offenses are more likely to be committed by lower-class urban youth.
3. Present explanations that rely heavily on socioeconomic class as an all-determining factor should be further specified to include data relative to the type of community involved.

Another interesting factor related to social class, community, and delinquency is the idea a majority group has of delinquent behavior. The white majority tends to take it for granted that minority group youngsters are more likely to be delinquent, and they are not as "alarmed" by minority youth delinquency as they are by the delinquent acts of white majority children. A study by psychologists Edward Dietiker and Edlynn Nau supports this perception.[16]

The researchers presented three short profiles like the following to 64 white mothers from a local PTA:

Nine-year-old Jimmy has a personality disorder: he is shy and anxious, plays alone and his teacher says he is afraid to give a book report in class. Randy, too, is a loner who suffers from a conduct disorder: he seems to have been "born angry," swearing at everybody, fighting at the slightest provocation, and hellbent on destruction. Gary can be just as destructive, but, as a social delinquent, he carries out his antisocial acts as a member of a gang known for its truancy, shoplifting and vandalism.

The 64 white mothers read the short profiles on three such boys and then rated the severity of their behavior problem on a scale from one to seven. Some of the children were described as white, some black, and some Chicano. A control group of 16 mothers was given no information about the ethnicity of the three boys they evaluated.

Dietiker and Nau's hypothesis was confirmed. The white mothers tended to underestimate the severity of all three disorders when rating black or Chicano boys as compared with the "problem child," who was described as white. White mothers were most alarmed about deviant behavior when they knew for a fact that the child in question was white rather than a member of a minority group.

Another study—of police officers—by Marcia Garrett and James F. Short tends to support the Dietiker and Nau hypotheses that there are

[16]*Human Behavior* (September 1976).

different perceptions of lower-class delinquents by members of the community.[17] The Garrett and Short study dealt with police attitudes toward delinquents. Data were analyzed to determine police images of delinquency: their estimates of the delinquent involvement of boys from different social-class backgrounds and their predictions, on the basis of first official contacts, of individual boys subsequently repeating. Data were collected in three cities. Ninety-three unstructured interviews of police were conducted; questionnaires were also administered to 453 officers. Officers' predictions about future delinquency were tested over a six-year followup period. Police in widely different settings based their judgments on "street" experience and similar theories of delinquency causation linking social-class background, parental neglect, and delinquent behavior. Police perceived lower-class minority group boys as more likely to be involved in delinquent conduct than boys with "higher" family and social-class backgrounds. The officers' predictions for individual boys proved to be inaccurate when measured by official contact records over the six-year period.

Few studies have focused on the differences and types of delinquency committed by children of different social classes. A study by Empey and Erickson into "hidden delinquency" indicated that important differences do exist.[18] The subjects of the study were 180 white male youths, ages 15 to 17, living in Utah. Fifty of the boys were high school students who had never been to court, 30 had been to court once, 50 were on probation, and 50 were incarcerated offenders. The boys in each of the four categories were selected at random from the respective population of which they were a part.

The method of study was to interview personally each of the 180 boys, questioning him about 22 different offenses which were defined in detail. The respondent was asked if he had ever committed the offense; how many times; if he had ever been caught, arrested, or brought to court for that offense; and if so, how many times. Court records were checked, and it was determined that the respondents were truthful about the offenses. Social status was determined by the occupation of the father. Of the three status levels, 29 percent of the boys were in the lower, 55 percent in the middle, and 16 percent in the upper category.

A tremendous number (in the thousands) of violations were reported. Virtually all respondents had committed not one but a variety of offenses, and 90 percent of these offenses were undetected and unacted upon. In regard to the amount or number of delinquent acts committed, the data provided little support for the notion that there are status differences. Respondents on one status level were neither more nor less delinquent than respondents on another status level (two kinds of statistical analysis were used in order to provide a better comparison). However, there were some

---

[17]Marcia Garrett and James F. Short, "Social Class and Delinquency: Predictions and Outcomes of Police-Juvenile Encounters," *Social Problems* 22 (February 1975): 368–383.

[18]LaMar T. Empey and Maynard L. Erickson, "Hidden Delinquency and Social Status," *Social Forces* 44 (June 1966): 546–554.

hints that there were some differences among status levels with respect to *kinds* of delinquency, especially among the minority of respondents who had been the most delinquent. Of the upper-status delinquents, the major offense was "defying parents." Middle-status delinquency was highest in areas of general traffic violations, theft and forgery, *defying authority*, property violations, and armed robbery. Low-status delinquents were high on the following offenses: driving without a license, stealing (over $50), auto theft, buying alcohol, using narcotics, skipping school, fighting, and assault. The above differences for all three levels held up among incarcerated offenders as well as those not officially defined as delinquent.

CLASS STATUS AND SERIOUS DELINQUENCY

Another study, by Reiss and Rhodes, indicated more serious delinquencies committed by lower-status boys even when based on self-reported delinquencies.[19] In their study involving 9,238 white boys, 12 years old and over, registered in one of the public, private, or parochial junior or senior high schools of Davidson County, Tennessee, during the 1957 school year, Reiss and Rhodes divided the boys into three status groups defined according to the occupation of the head of the household:

1. *Low status*. children of laborers, including farm laborers, operatives, kindred workers, service workers (except protective service workers), peddlers, and door-to-door salesmen.
2. *Middle status*. all craftsmen, foremen, clerical and kindred workers, managers and proprietors of small businesses, sales workers of wholesale and retail stores, and technicians allied to professional services.
3. *High status*. all managers, officials, proprietors, and professional and semiprofessional workers not included in the middle-status category, and sales workers in finance, insurance, and real estate.

Delinquency rates were based on a combined total of official and unofficial cases known to the juvenile court. The researchers concluded that there was no simple relationship between ascribed social status and delinquency. Their data led them to the conclusions that:

1. There is more frequent and serious delinquent deviation in the lower than in the middle stratum when the self-reports of delinquent deviation by boys are examined. This is true for all classes of deviation: career- and peer-oriented delinquents, nonconforming isolates, and conforming nonachievers.
2. *The career-oriented delinquent is found only among lower-class boys*.
3. Peer-oriented delinquency is the most common form of delinquent organization at both status levels.

[19]Albert J. Reiss, Jr. and Albert Lewis Rhodes, "The Distribution of Juvenile Delinquency in the Social Class Structure," *American Sociological Review* 26 (October 1961): 720–732.

4. The major type of lower status boy is a conforming nonachiever, while the conforming achiever is the major type in the middle class.

5. Conformers are more likely to be isolates than are nonconformers. The lone delinquent is infrequent in a population of boys. If it is assumed that in many lower-class areas the pressures of groups are toward nonconforming activities, then at least in these communities isolation from the group may be the price of social conformity. Conforming isolates are more frequent in blue-collar than in white-collar strata. There is much more support for group-organized conventional behavior in middle-class areas.

LIMITATIONS OF SELF-REPORTING

If we accept the various studies based on self-reporting as valid, we must conclude that there is no substantial difference between the amount of delinquent behavior committed by lower-class boys and by middle-class boys. Several reasons for doubting the findings of self-report studies with respect to the relationship between social class and delinquency have been suggested by Hirschi: (1) the self-report measure of delinquency is invalid for this purpose; (2) the samples used in these studies deal only with a restricted class range; (3) the measures of socioeconomic status are invalid; (4) the effects of socioeconomic status are suppressed by the effects of some third variable; and (5) contrary to their assertions, some of the "no-difference" self-report studies do show a relation between socioeconomic status and delinquency.[20]

Furthermore, the acts reported by middle-class youths, although technically illegal, may not be truly comparable with offenses charged against lower-class youths. For example, a 14-year-old middle-class boy, a subject in one self-report study, took a can of beer from his mother's refrigerator without permission and drank it. He reported himself guilty of two delinquent acts: stealing and illegal use of a drug or intoxicant. This offense can hardly be considered comparable with stealing a bicycle and selling it to buy drugs, acts for which a lower-class boy may be found delinquent in court. On some anonymous questionnaires the two respondents would be checking the same boxes. Furthermore, middle-class youths might be considered more likely to exaggerate their "admitted" delinquencies in order to assert their masculinity. It is necessary to take this possibility into consideration when discussing middle-class delinquency. Certainly, the self-image of the youth exerts an influence on his responses to such questionnaires.

In the context of these issues, Fannin and Clinard found important differences in the conception of self as a male held by lower- and middle-class delinquents.[21] Random samples of lower- and middle-class white de-

---

[20]Travis Hirschi, *Causes of Delinquency* (Berkeley: University of California Press, 1969), p. 70.

[21]Leon F. Fannin and Marshall B. Clinard, "Differences in the Conception of Self as a Male among Lower and Middle-Class Delinquents," *Social Problems* 13 (Fall 1965): 205–214.

linquents committed to a training school in a Midwestern state were the subjects of their study. The boys, 16 and 17 years of age, were from urban areas with a population of at least 300,000. Each boy was given a class rank on the basis of his father's or his guardian's level of education and occupation. The most crucial information was elicited through in-depth interviews and the administration of self-conception scales. Official records were used to determine class affiliation and reported delinquent histories. Operationally, self-conception as a male was defined by the relative intensity of specific traits that the delinquent felt characterized him when he was placed, verbally, in varying situations that made him explicitly aware of his sex status. A list of 15 traits was administered three times. The subjects were asked to rank the traits contained in each list according to how they felt the traits actually described them as males (actual self); how they would like to be as males (ideal self); and, last, how they felt other people in general believed them to be as males.

Lower-class boys felt themselves to be (actual self) tougher, more powerful, fierce, fearless, and dangerous than middle-class boys. Middle-class delinquents conceived of themselves as being more loyal, clever, smart, smooth, and bad. Lower-class boys would like to be (ideal self) tougher, harder, and more violent than middle-class boys, while the latter would like to be more loyal, lucky, and firm. Generally speaking, lower-class delinquents felt themselves to be "tough guys," while the middle-class delinquents felt themselves to be "loyal and daring comrades."

The vast majority of lower-class delinquents (84 percent) had committed at least one robbery or assault, compared with 28 percent of middle-class boys. Lower-class delinquents also fought singly and in groups significantly more often than middle-class delinquents. Lower-class boys also carried weapons more frequently than middle-class boys did. Fannin and Clinard concluded that a significant proportion of offenses involving physical violence may be committed by delinquents who stress certain "masculine" traits in their self-conceptions, and this helps to channel and legitimize their violence.

Some of the differences noted in lower-class delinquents may be a consequence of their socialization. Stephen E. Brown summarized his findings as follows:[22]

The relationship between social class and child maltreatment and between maltreatment and delinquency were examined, particular attention being paid to previous deficiencies in the operationalization of maltreatment and class. Maltreatment was operationalized with subscales for physical abuse, emotional abuse, and neglect, while social class was operationalized with multiple indicators. Survey data from 110 high school freshmen were analyzed and revealed the following: (a) a weak but consistent inverse correlation between social class and all forms of child maltreatment, (b) a stronger relationship between social

[22]Stephen E. Brown, "Social Class, Child Maltreatment, and Delinquent Behavior" in *Criminology*, vol. 22, May 1984.

class and maltreatment when lower-class membership was operationalized in a manner consistent with the concept of an underclass, (c) that emotional abuse and neglect were correlated positively with all forms of delinquent behavior examined. . . .

SOME EXPLANATIONS OF MIDDLE-CLASS DELINQUENCY

Although there is ample evidence that the vast majority of young people adjudicated delinquents by our juvenile courts are from lower-socio-economic-class families, there are many whose families are middle class. If we take into consideration research indicating more favorable treatment of middle-class children by the police and the courts, we must conclude that there are probably far more middle-class delinquents than the statistics indicate. Furthermore, the self-report studies suggest that the incidence of delinquent behavior among middle-class boys may be as great as that among lower- or working-class boys. Since we would expect middle-class parents to provide socialization strongly favoring conformity to the law, and since middle-class children have few, if any, economic needs not satisfied by their parents, how can we account for what is claimed to be a large and growing amount of delinquent behavior among middle-class youth? Some efforts to account for this phenomenon will be presented in this section.

Kvaraceus and Miller, who related lower-class delinquency to such focal concerns of the lower class as trouble, toughness, smartness, and autonomy, consider middle-class delinquency in relation to the focal concerns of the middle class. They note that middle-class concerns are centered around:

1. Achievement through directed work effort
2. Deferment of immediate pleasures and gains for future goals
3. Responsibility
4. Maintenance of the solidarity of the nuclear family
5. Child rearing
6. Accumulation of material goods and maintenance of property
7. Education
8. Formal organization
9. Cleanliness
10. Ambition

Kvaraceus and Miller feel that orientation toward these concerns deters middle-class children from delinquency and that the legal codes support the middle-class focal concerns.[23]

The middle-class tradition exerts pressure on children to postpone gratification. Self-denial and impulse control are encouraged. The increase in middle-class delinquency may be attributed, in part, to a weakening of this tradition. Installment buying and buying on impulse, which have in the

[23]Kvaraceus and Miller, *Delinquent Behavior*, Washington, D.C.: National Education Association, 1959. Reprinted with permission.

past been part of the lower-class culture, have spread to the middle class and weakened the idea that success is achieved through deferred gratification, self-discipline, and hard work.

Kvaraceus and Miller have also noted the tendency of lower-class fads and culture to influence middle-class youth through a process of diffusion of the lower-class culture. They also feel that when serious delinquency occurs in middle-class groups, it may be a portent of pathological behavior since it is conduct counter to the definitions of a significant reference group. They point out that "the middle-class youngster who engages in norm-violating behavior may often be viewed more usefully as a 'behavior problem' than as a 'delinquent'."[24]

Albert K. Cohen, who, as previously discussed, sees the delinquent subculture as representing the working-class boy's rebellion against the middle class and its values, also offers an explanation for middle-class delinquency.[25] He describes middle-class standards in much the same way Kvaraceus and Miller describe middle-class focal concerns. Cohen recognizes that the circumstances that give rise to the delinquent subculture may be found in families considered middle class by purely economic criteria. Families that are middle class in terms of income and occupation are usually middle class in terms of culture. However, some families that are middle class in economic terms and live in middle-class neighborhoods may be working class in terms of the experiences they provide their children. For example, a worker brought up in a working-class area and hostile to middle-class values may increase his income to middle-class levels and may even be promoted to a middle-class occupational level without changing his attitudes toward middle-class values. He may move into a suburban middle-class area, resent tax increases, vote Republican, and object to welfare programs in conformity with his new interests and his middle-class neighbors. His children, however, may be rejected by their middle-class neighbors and may never develop any loyalty to the middle-class "focal" concerns with which their middle-class peers have been indoctrinated.

While recognizing the above as a possible explanation of middle-class delinquency, Cohen tends, as do Kvaraceus and Miller, to view middle-class delinquency in terms of personal pathology. He discusses Talcott Parson's view that in our society the mother has the dominant role in socialization. According to this view, the father is preoccupied with his occupational role and is away from the home most of the time. Because of this, as Parsons notes, the child, particularly the middle-class suburban child, is likely to perceive his mother as the principal exemplar of morality, source of discipline, and object of identification.[26] The middle-class delinquent knows it is shameful for a boy to be like a woman and feels constrained to rebel against impulses that suggest femininity and to exaggerate behavior that connotes

---

[24]Kvaraceus and Miller, *Delinquent Behavior*, Washington, D.C.: National Education Association, 1959. Reprinted with permission.

[25]Cohen, *Delinquent Boys*, pp. 88–102.

[26]Talcott Parsons, "Certain Primary Sources and Patterns of Aggression in the Social Structure of the Western World," *Psychiatry* 10 (May 1947): 167–181.

masculinity. "Goodness" represents femininity and "badness" masculinity. Hence, middle-class delinquency may be a form of masculine protest.

Cohen also notes that society fails to give the middle-class boy a meaningful occupational role, and it prolongs his dependence by requiring many years of schooling. These latter considerations, added to sex-role anxieties and masculine protest, Cohen concludes, may provide a basis for boys who share these problems to come together and create a delinquent subculture. Thus, while the working-class delinquent subculture represents a revolt against the middle class, the middle-class delinquent subculture represents a revolt against "femininity" and dependence.[27]

A study by D. Frease, K. Polk, and F. L. Richmond concluded that Cohen's delinquency theory was vulnerable to demonstrations of similar qualities, as well as similar quantities, of delinquency between middle- and working-class groups.[28] In their analyses of questionnaire data from a high school male population, no significant differences in incidence of delinquency emerged between classes. They further concluded that no significant differences obtain between classes of delinquents on items tapping the peer or subcultural dimensions Cohen considers particularly characteristic of working-class delinquency. Lastly, they found that delinquency was shown to be related to academic performance, regardless of class.

Ralph England raises the following objections to Parson's explanation of middle-class delinquency, which Cohen adopted:

A number of objections to this theory can be raised. (a) In the process of "protesting masculinity" why is the trait of adult male responsibility shunned while other presumed traits of the male (loud, aggressive, rambunctious behavior) are adopted? (b) One can imagine middle-class boys who live in dormitory suburbs and large cities having some difficulty picturing their fathers' occupational roles, but this may not be true in smaller cities and in towns where the fathers' places of work are more readily accessible for visits, and where their roles are less likely to be obscured by employment in bureaucratic organizations. (c) How can the participation of girls in the youth culture be explained by Parsons's theory? (d) Are mothers' roles especially ubiquitous in communities where commuting time for the father is not so great that he cannot be with his family meaningfully except on weekends? "Catching the 7:05" each morning before the children are up and returning in the evening shortly before their bedtime is a pattern found only in our largest cities. (e) Is it to be assumed that the seeming increase in middle-class delinquency since the Second World War is the result of a postwar increase in sons' difficulties in identifying with their fathers' roles, in the absence of basic postwar changes in our society's occupation structure?[29]

[27]Reprinted with permission of The Free Press, a Division of Macmillan, Inc. from *Delinquent Boys* by Albert K. Cohen. Copyright © 1955 by The Free Press, renewed 1983 by Albert K. Cohen.

[28]D. Frease, K. Polk, and F. L. Richmond, "Social Class, School Experience, and Delinquency," *Criminology* 44 (December 1974): 84–96.

[29]Ralph W. England, Jr., "A Theory of Middle-Class Juvenile Delinquency," *Journal of Criminal Law, Criminology and Police Science* 50 (March–April 1960): 536. Reprinted by special permission of *The Journal of Criminal Law and Criminology*, © 1960 by Northwestern University School of Law, vol. 50, no. 6.

England sees the emergence of a teenage culture as a result of increased communication among teenagers in recent years. He asserts that the following conditions have influenced the emergence of a teenage culture:

1. The enlargement of a market for teenage goods and services. The wide distribution of such teenage items as rock and roll movies, records, portable phonographs, motor scooters, unusual clothing, and other popular items is contributing to the growth of a nationally shared but age-restricted material culture.
2. Increased reliance on canned material in radio broadcasting has brought into prominence the disc jockey who caters to teenagers.
3. Television programming of teen dance shows and the promulgation by TV of a particular image of teenage life.
4. The growth of teenage magazines with emphasis on hedonistic values, play, and diversion, and not on preparation for responsible adulthood.
5. Public attention given to juvenile problems.[30]

As a result, according to England, a complex of attitudes and values is evolving that tends to control and motivate teenagers in ways consistent with their role as a youthful group having leisure, relatively ample spending money, and few responsibilities. England is, of course, describing middle-class youth, and he sees an emerging culture with increasing institutionalization of immature and irresponsible hedonism. If the teenager's urgent need for status affirmation is met by the teenage culture, it becomes necessary for the adolescent to reject adult influences that threaten it and accept those that give it support. Hard work, thrift, study, and self-denial are values running counter to the short-run hedonism of the teenage culture.

Among the ways in which this teenage culture gives rise to delinquency are:

1. Driving privileges are abused by playing "chicken," drag racing, speeding, and in other ways using a car as a plaything. Also, "borrowing" cars without permission for joyrides.
2. Competitive spirit is applied to fights, car chases, and vandalism as games.
3. Sex and love are redefined as ends in themselves.
4. Alcoholic beverages are used for the hedonistic purpose of intoxication. Drinking parties are held in automobiles, parks, and motels to avoid adult interference.[31]

Thus, middle-class delinquency is largely attributed to the hedonistic pursuits emphasized by the teenage culture and its preoccupation with play.

Scott and Vaz maintain that the bulk of middle-class delinquency occurs in the course of *customary, nondelinquent* activities and falls within the

---

[30]Ibid., pp. 537–538.
[31]Ibid., p. 539.

limits of adolescent group norms.[32] They note that under changing social and economic conditions, the patriarchally controlled family has given way to a more "democratic" family unit in which children shared in the decision-making process. The family atmosphere became more permissive, and achievement goals more difficult to inculcate. The school, too, has become more permissive. As a result, the adolescent role has become vague, and the distinction between right and wrong soft-pedaled. The adolescent is left to define what is "right" conduct. Peer group relationships substitute for ambiguous family relationships and influence the teenager. Comformity to peer group norms is required, and these oppose scholastic effort. Teenage participation is rewarded since even his parents want him to obtain this sort of social approval. A middle-class youth culture similar to the teenage culture described by England has developed, and the middle-class youth cannot jeopardize his status in his peer group. Joyriding, drunkenness, substance abuse, and sexual acting out are variations of conduct patterns that are acceptable. Scott and Vaz describe the process as follows:

> In the course of legitimate, everyday activities and relationships within the middle-class youth culture, "veiled competition" for status leads to varying efforts at innovation. Such innovation covers a wide range of exploratory acts and is likely to be tentative, uncertain, and ambiguous. Yet because there is "mutual exploration and joint elaboration" of behavior among adolescents, such small, almost unobtrusive, acts gradually lead to unanticipated elaboration beyond the limits of legitimacy—into the realm of delinquency and the illegitimate. But since each succeeding exploratory act is so small an increment to the previously acceptable pattern, at no stage in the process need the behavior be perceived as "delinquent." Once these patterns develop and are socially rewarded, they generate their own morality, norms, standards, and rewards. It is in this manner that delinquent behavior gradually emerges . . . within the middle-class culture.[33]

Many of the theories and research findings reported here are of interest in accounting for the middle-class delinquency of the past and, to some extent, for a great deal of the hidden middle-class juvenile delinquency of the present. However, contemporary middle-class delinquency is best explained in relationship to the enormous increase in substance abuse by middle-class juveniles. Drug addiction and alcoholism among middle-class youths is rampant and is a delinquency problem in its own right. It also accounts for a considerable amount of middle-class delinquent behavior, including severe parent-child conflicts, driving under the influence, sexual acting out, family conflict resulting in running away from home, learning problems and truancy, and theft and prostitution to obtain money to support a habit.

[32]Joseph W. Scott and Edmund W. Vaz, "A Perspective of Middle-Class Delinquency," *Canadian Journal of Economics and Political Science* 29 (August 1963): 324–335.
[33]Ibid., pp. 329–330.

In brief, the juvenile social problem of substance abuse, which was formerly mainly a lower-class phenomenon, has become more democratic and now exists among juveniles from all social classes. This factor has contributed enormously to a significant rise in middle-class juvenile delinquency.

CLASS DIFFERENCES AND DELINQUENCY: TWO PORTRAITS

Statistics, various theories, and the social-psychological analysis of class and delinquency provide many insights into the relevant issues. However, case analysis often adds a more illuminating and in-depth understanding of delinquency. The following two cases of a lower-class delinquent substance abuser, Baby Love, and an upper-middle-class female delinquent, Jill, provide more illuminating insights into some of the differences in the sociocultural background of lower-class and upper-middle-class delinquency.

Baby Love

In lower socioeconomic groups drug and alcohol use has become an arch tranquilizer for youths locked into a ghetto or barrio who see little opportunity or hope for their future. Drugs have become an adjunct to poverty and a life of delinquency and, later, crime. The following portrait of Baby Love, derived from an article by James Wilde,[34] reveals the blood and guts social context of lower-class juvenile delinquency:

> Baby Love sits on the stoop, rolling the largest, fattest joint in the world. He wastes little: in go twigs, seeds, everything, until it seems as big as a torpedo. Other joints are tucked over each ear, and more are secreted in plastic bags under his hat. It is Friday night, the night to get high, get drunk and strut. Baby Love's entire wrecking crew is here, sprawled over cars, squatting on the sidewalk, jiving. There is Shistang ("He be cool with dice"), Little Spank, Gugu, Snake Eyes, Shilo, Spider Man, Daddy Rich, Little June, Snatch Pocket Earl and Snootchy Fingers.
>
> "We be in the streets hangin' out an' gettin' high," says Baby Love.[35] He is a very skinny, very small, very lethal 14-year-old. His eyes are slate gray, flashing to blue when he laughs. Mischief is etched across his face as a bittersweet smile. Like his crew, he is dressed in mugger's uniform; designer jeans, T shirt and $45 Pumas, the starched laces neatly untied. A wolf in expensive sneakers, Baby Love is a school dropout, one of more than 800,000 between the ages of 14 and 17 in the U.S.
>
> Baby Love inhabits a world few white folks ever see, a Dickensian hell of cheap thrills, senseless deaths and almost unrelieved hopelessness. He lives in Brooklyn's Bedford Stuyvesant section, one of the oldest black settlements in

[34]Excerpt from "In Brooklyn: A Wolf in $45 Sneakers," *Time*, October 12, 1981, pp. 36–41. Copyright 1981 Time Inc. All rights reserved. Reprinted by permission from TIME.
[35]For an interesting discussion of Baby Love's speech pattern, see J. L. Dillard, *Black English* (New York: Vintage Press, 1973).

the U.S. Unlike the burned and ravaged South Bronx, ten miles to the north, Bedford Stuyvesant does not resemble a war zone; most of its owner-occupied row houses, brownstones and churches are more or less intact. But high unemployment and a 60% dropout rate among black high school students make it a very dangerous place. One Bed-Stuy precinct, the 77th, has the highest murder rate in the city: 86 killings last year.

Baby Love is trapped. He can barely read or write, even though he would have been in the seventh grade this year. Because he is nearly illiterate he could never hold even the meanest job for long. He has been running wild so long now that he may be beyond redemption. Ghetto children today are seduced much earlier by drugs and the street, some of them as young as eight or nine. That is the time they need help. Sinbad Lockwood, a Bed-Stuy street artist who tries to wean boys like Baby Love away from the streets to painting, says, "It be the parents' fault, they gets rid of the kids by sending them to the candy store where they be buying reefer and beer. These kids ain't no monsters—they be raising themselves, that's all."

Baby Love is almost always stoned. He rises late, plays basketball in the park or galactic-warfare games at the pinball arcade all day. If there is any money left over, he and Daddy Rich go to karate movies. He juggles four chicks with Casanova skill, and he makes enough from gambling and stealing to be a real "sportin' man."

For Baby Love, stealing means survival. He is the best goldchain snatcher on the block. "I pretends to be making a phone call when the bus be comin' along," he explains, "so the driver won't warn the passengers. Then when it be by, I's leapin' in the air with my hand through the window and gone befo' anyone sees." He breaks into laughter, slapping skin all around. He has been caught five times this summer for pickpocketing. At Macy's he was caught boosting eight blue Izod Lacoste shirts in his Adidas bag. He has just finished 60 days' probation.

Baby love lives on the fourth floor of a crumbling, turn-of-the-century tenement with his aunt and legal guardian, Cora Lee. He sleeps on a stained mattress in a small room he often shares with his cousins, Butter and Buckeye, and with an army of roaches that waddle fatly across the floor. His two younger sisters, Shantia, 11, and Sarah, 8, are also in Cora Lee's charge. Baby Love's mother, Rose, stays there too. They are all receiving welfare payments.

There have been three bad fires in Baby Love's building in the past couple of years. The fifth floor is gutted. He and his crew now use it as their clubhouse. Baby Love uses the roof as an escape route from police. He jumps across a yawning chasm to the next building, then he is down the stairs and away. "We be doin' this when we drunk," says Baby Love with an impish smile. A born hustler, he is slick at pool and dice. He gambles Friday nights in front of BeeGee's candy store with men who feed him *chiba chiba*, a Puerto Rican expression for an especially potent kind of marijuana, the reefer that zoots you out.

He thinks Bruce Lee is a cool dude, but "Richard Pryor is the Man," says Baby Love. "He's got power." The violence Baby Love sees on the screen is not much different from what he faces on the street. He was 13 when he first saw a man blown away—with a shotgun. He has faced down a few gunslingers himself. He sometimes carries a .25 automatic. "All my friends got guns," he says. "We go and try to shoot birds in the park." Trees are beaten to death in ghetto parks. Youngsters, too get killed on summer evenings when there is disco music in the air. Tough, mean young men shoot it out like Western heroes of old. The dead are dumped in trashed buildings. Some of Baby Love's friends did not live through the summer. A cheeky dude like him risks death or injury every time he steps outside. Being small does not help. He was always getting beaten up until he learned to steal. Now he can bribe would-be assailants with reefer. He sometimes spends $20 a day on the stuff.

On Friday nights the crowds along Fulton and Nostrand avenues ebb and flow like a tide. Dudes are gambling up and down the streets. The sweet smell of reefer is everywhere, and wine bottles are passed around. Up the block, twelve-year-old hookers teeter on high heels, flouncing their boyish hips. There are drunken brawls, skin-and-bone addicts overdosing, police sirens screaming and the rattle of the el in the distance.

A procession of dudes pauses to talk to Baby Love. Most have done hard time. Some push dope, many are boozers. All have bitter wisdom. Crocodile comes by waving a bottle of vodka, his eyes gleaming yellow. He tells Baby Love, "Wait till you do hard time, boy. They'll pat your butt, they'll feel you. You'll come home swishing like a girl." A huge dude, his muscles rippling, speaks in a cool bass: "I got a pair of $600 lizard shoes and I got silk shirts. I'm the Man, boy. I changes my clothes 15 times a day. Learn to hustle girls, and you can wear dark shades and sharkskin suits and ride a big white Caddy." Riff the horn player sniffs in disgust. "You've got to have dignity, boy, you be nothing without dignity. The only way to beat the Man is by going to school. Go back to school, boy."

Baby Love sneers. He stands up. "I'm goin' get all I wants," he says, "and I don't care if I gotta steal to get it. I'm not afraid of doin' time so long as I kin do it fast." Then he goes up to the clubhouse with Daddy Rich. He lies on a mattress puffing on an El Producto cigar hollowed out and filled with *chiba chiba*. There is a bottle of 150-proof Bacardi rum by his side. The cassette player throbs and, for a moment, Baby love is warm and secure, at peace and flying high.

Baby Love's real name is William Andrews. This is the one he uses in family court. "He ain't bad, you understand," says his Aunt Cora. "He just don't like school. And there is no one here he minds." Cora is trying to get Baby Love into a Roman Catholic residential school in upstate New York that specializes in problem children. "But I don't know if he'll stay there. One thing I do know—if he keeps on stealing gold chains he's going to be in a heap of trouble, and that's for sure."

Where did Baby Love go wrong? His mother, Rose, 31, does not deny that she was a drug addict. "I'm an alcoholic too," she adds. She gave up legal custody of her children to Aunt Cora last year. According to Rose, Baby Love's father is an alcoholic, a drug addict and a bisexual. He was doing time at Attica during the prison's 1971 riots, shrugs Rose, and "he flipped his brains. That's why I divorced him." His father beat Baby Love up often with his fists, says Rose, and once he did so with an extension cord. When Baby Love retaliated with a piece of heavy steel pipe, she recalls, his father took him to the police and demanded, futilely, that he be locked up.

Baby Love rebelled against his mother when she started sleeping with other men. He was only five. She says, "My boy steals anything he can get. It is my fault. He saw me steal a woman's pocketbook. It had a lot of money in it. Curtis, he gets high on money now. It's all he wants, that an' reefer."

Despite all the stealing, the drugs, the barely suppressed rage, Baby Love can be polite, almost genteel. He is gracious at table; he learned manners from his grandmother. He can keep house, wash dishes, do the marketing and look after his sisters and baby cousin. He is the only one who can get his mother off the streets when she is drugged and nodding. Once, when she nearly overdosed, he dragged her from the kitchen, poured hot and cold water on her feet and burned her arms with a lighted cigarette to revive her.

Baby Love walks with a slight limp. His mother explains that he had a serious accident while playing ball in the streets when he was four. He was run over by a car and his left leg, right arm and most of his ribs were broken. Rose then did one of the few constructive things she has done in her sad life: she sued the driver and got a settlement of $3,000, which is now in trust. Baby Love will get the money when he turns 21. If he lives that long.

Jill: A Middle-Class Delinquent

In sharp contrast to Baby Love is Jill. She is an attractive, by middle-class standards well-mannered, well-dressed 16-year-old I worked with in my therapy groups over a ten-month period in a psychiatric hospital. Jill's substance abuse and delinquency flowed from a different social-psychological context than Baby Love's. She came from a reasonably affluent family background where any material need she felt was immediately met. While Baby Love had limited or no access to upward mobility in the social system, Jill was already *there* in terms of material success and status. Yet for Jill her status, private room in a large house, and material acquisitions were useless in preventing her incorrigible delinquent behavior.

I first met her after she had been in juvenile court and was remanded for treatment to a psychiatric hospital where I worked. At the time of her entry into the hospital she was suffering from depression, had been addicted to cocaine, alcohol, and a variety of pills for several years, and attempted suicide. Her parents considered her "incorrigible," a common synonym among middle-class children for delinquent. During the ten-month period that I worked with her in the hospital, her treatment included individual psychiatric counseling and group therapy with professional therapists. In particular, I worked directly with her in a drug addict encounter group and a psychodrama group. In addition to these sessions I interviewed her several times on an individual basis for this case analysis.

Jill, an only child, began smoking marijuana at 13—around the time her parents divorced. She lived with her mother. She found her mother cold and unfeeling. According to Jill:

My mother just bored me to death. She never talked to me. When I learned some psychiatric jargon I would say she was catatonic. It was like living with a stone. I missed my father terribly—and saw him rarely—because he was always traveling on business and out making money.

Around the time I was 14 I met Jim. You could say for me he was an older man. He was 25. I realize now it was all bullshit but he had this revolutionary line that got to me. He was always talking against society and how people rip each other off and how bad that was. That's how he justified why he committed a lot of burglaries and robberies. In the meantime, he was really exploiting me. I really thought I was in love with him and he was my one and only. But I found out later I was only one of his girl friends. He was just a terrible liar, and he ripped me off in a lot of ways.

About a year after my parents split my father got married again and I got to go live with him. His new wife, my stepmother, seemed O.K. at first—but turned into a total bitch. I had fooled around with some coke with Jim, but my new stepmother really turned me on to coke. My father didn't know how heavy she was using. All he cared about was that she screwed him whenever he wanted to. She would get stoned and tell me that's how she held on to him.

After my dad went off to work I would have a nice breakfast with my stepmom. She would put out a good spread. It consisted of scrambled eggs, coffee, and several lines of coke. If it wouldn't make me late to school, instead of snorting the coke I would smoke some, crack. For lunch I would smoke a joint; and on other days when it was available I would do some more coke or have a few ludes. This routine went on for a couple of years until I was 15.

My boyfriend Jim and I did lots of drugs, sex, and once in a while I drove the car when he went to rob a house. In my drug haze, I fell madly in love with Jim, and almost worshipped him.

I knew my stepmom was partying and making it with lots of other guys when my Dad was away on his business trips. The bitch was into younger guys and she often flirted openly with Jim. He denied any interest in her. You guessed it. One day I came home early from school and there they were fucking in my father's bed. They hardly stopped when they saw me. I got into a big screaming hassle with the two of them. They tried to calm me down. We all did some coke and they just giggled about what had happened. I was smashed by the incident and felt horrible. But it didn't seem to bother them at all.

Later, when I was alone, I screamed at Jim how I loved him and how could he do this to me. He was totally cold to my feelings. Finally he said, "If you don't like it bitch, get lost."

That night I went over to his house and found out he wasn't home. I told his parents I would just wait on the lawn for him. They must have gone to sleep. So I'm sitting out there in terrible pain full of pills, smoking a joint feeling all alone, sorry for myself and getting more depressed by the minute. The only one I felt I had in the world was Jim and he had abandoned me.

When I came down from my coke highs, I was very depressed. I had thought a lot about suicide around that time. I carried some razor blades in my purse. (They were also good for cutting up hash and lining up coke.) So there I was all alone, depressed, and I decided to do it. I cut my wrists and they were bleeding lightly. I was stoned and actually feeling mellow watching blood ooze out of my wrists. That'll show them all, I thought. Then I got this crazy idea. In my insanity I thought it was logical for me to write Jim a letter in my own blood. I had a pen in my purse and would dip it in my blood. The writing was red and blue from the pen. I talked about my grief, depression, loneliness, what a dick he was, and on and on and on.

His parents must have seen what I was doing through the window. They called the police and my father. They scooped me up and rushed me to the emergency ward. I really hadn't lost that much blood, but I was obviously nuts.

In a way it worked. My father, for the first time in ages, began to talk to me. I told him about his bitch wife and how she had served me cocaine at breakfast time and how she made it with Jim. Well that blew it, for her anyway. My father knew we both had to get some therapy. For me, it was the start of around six drug programs. They were all 60–90-day detoxification programs with a little bullshit group therapy. None of them worked and as soon as I was out the door I would use again.

Along the way, over this year or so when I was in these programs, my Dad divorced the bitch. Then he got himself another one, who was just as bad.

My father became distant again as I wound in and out of these psychiatric hospitals. In a few of them I was able to have friends of mine smuggle in drugs. Jim and I were on again, off again. I still felt I loved him in spite of the fact that he continued to use me. He was always off with other girls—and besides I never forgave him for fucking my stepmom.

Jill, during this period in the hospital, participated in a psychodrama group I directed plus a special drug encounter group for adolescents that I codirected with several recovering ex-addicts who lived in a therapeutic community. In psychodrama she confronted some of the basic underlying issues that she was working on with her psychiatrist. These included her problems with her father, her mother, and Jim, whom she once characterized as a "father substitute because my dad was never around."

The several psychodrama sessions I had with her that related to her father involved the basic theme of feeling emotionally alienated from him and her sense of his lack of real caring for her. "He gave me all the money and things I wanted, but no caring or real love."

In several psychodramas, auxiliary egos played the role of her father. In these dramatic, tearful sessions she would implore this stand-in for her father to please love her, spend some time with her, and make her feel really cared for. She felt especially abandoned by him when she reached puberty.

I recorded her sobbing concluding commentary in one session where she said: "Dad, I was always your special little girl and you adored me. You used to hug me and hold me on your lap and tell me how pretty I was. Then when I was 13 you pushed me off your lap like I was some 'thing.' Our family broke up and you left me with Mom. I love Mom—but she's like a dead person. She never talks or feels anything. You were the important one in my life. When I began to use drugs, it killed the pain of my feeling alone—and it always made me feel better." Drugs became for Jill her self-administered therapy. And the emotional effects were more reliable than her parents.

In various sessions several 14- and 15-year-old girls shared similar feelings of being abandoned by their fathers at puberty. In the group discussions that followed the role playing, several psychological points were made that seemed to fit Jill and many teenage girls. When they make the transition from childhood to adolescence, many teenage girls feel abandoned by their fathers. This is often because their fathers, especially if they are insecure men, like Jill's father, handle some of the normal sexual feeling they might have for them by coldly rejecting their daughters. Of course, this is superior to the problems that ensue from some fathers who act out their feelings either flirtatiously or directly. What is more appropriate is an honest awareness of some sexual feelings that are handled without overreacting and rejecting their daughters. These issues were discussed by the group after Jill's psychodrama, and some insights were acknowledged by her and several others.

Jill learned from several psychodrama sessions and discussions with her psychiatrist on this theme that she had limited control over "getting her father back"; however, she had total control over her response to her intense pain and feeling that her father had rejected her. She further concluded that the onset of her drug problems were related to her feelings of low self-esteem from being rejected by her father, and her self-destructive drug abuse was connected to her conflict and alienation from her father. She said, "I learned from my therapy that I'm not the only girl with these feelings of being abandoned by my Dad. And I also see how I attempted to substitute an older man—Jim—for the father I felt had abandoned me."

Her overall insight was that it was a family problem and she was the "identified patient." This insight relieved some of her sense of being a "bad, sick girl," which had propelled her into becoming a drug addict. The foregoing is only a brief sketch of some of the psychodynamics that were related to Jill's drug abuse symptom syndrome, which were considerably relieved and resolved during her overall therapeutic program. She went back to school, had a more optimistic viewpoint, and at last report was leading a drug-free, relatively happy life.

BABY LOVE AND JILL: AN ANALYSIS

Jill's middle-class perspective on her personal problems and her substance abuse were acquired at first from her friends and relatives. She had read some self-help books on psychology, discussed psychological issues with her friends and family, and was receptive to one of the best treatment systems that society had available to help her resolve her problems. In contrast, Baby Love was on another trip. First of all, he didn't have the financial means or any motivation to have his problems treated in a psychiatric hospital. His "counselers" were streetwise criminal pimps and hustlers who would advise him mainly on how to become a more effective juvenile delinquent. He saw these people as role models and helpers in his battles for "success" on the street scene, the only social ladder available to him for achieving success in our society.

It is also apparent that the social-class, cultural, and economic context that surrounds adolescents like Baby Love and Jill were considerably different. Baby love naturally was attracted to the drugs and hustling behavior that was relatively normal in his environment. Children like Baby Love see little opportunity or hope in their future in the larger society. This partly accounts for their disinterest in school and their gravitation towards becoming like the criminal role models in their neighborhood who have, in their eyes, "made it." Drugs are a pain killer for hopelessness and a commodity for profit in Baby Love's life situation. Drugs and theft are an intrinsic part of this delinquent system. It would be almost impossible for Baby Love's family to have the health insurance or the financial means for him to get any treatment. Inevitably, he will be encarcerated in a state institution where his delinquent value system will be reinforced. In the state facility he will be exposed to other young men much like him, who will collectively rationalize their plight and be eager to learn more in their juvenile apprenticeship for a later life of crime.

In some ways, Jill's delinquency emerged for similar reasons as Baby Love's. They both felt alienated and helpless and turned to drugs for relief from the pain. Their class position in the social system, however, clearly propelled them in different directions. Jill's family's wealth and attitudes about emotional problems motivated them to place her in a psychiatric facility that might help change her behavior. In Baby Love's social-emotional context, the chances of his being resocialized in an appropriate treatment center were slim to none.

The foregoing analysis encompasses some of the central reasons why teenagers from different class backgrounds become delinquent. It is apparent that middle- and upper-class youths like Jill have a greater chance of being resocialized than youths from a lower socioeconomic background. Our state facilities are predominantly filled with Baby Loves and females of similar background, whereas children with Jill's background are rarely encarcerated in state institutions and have greater access to a variety of contemporary treatment facilities in their social orbit.

In brief, delinquency per se has become more democratic and open to youths from all strata of society. The causal social context is different, however, and so are the resocialization systems for treatment. There are two basically different types of delinquency in American society: Baby Love's lower-class delinquency and Jill's upper-class delinquency. Both types will be analyzed and discussed in the balance of this book.

SUMMARY: BASIC THEMES FOR CLASS DISCUSSION

1. There is considerable research evidence that a disproportionate number of juvenile delinquents come from the lower socioeco-

nomic strata of American society. This is partially due to the fact that youths from this class find it more difficult to gain employment, are more likely to be subjected to prejudice, discrimination, police bias, and generally have less power and opportunity in the social system.

2. Some sociologists, like Bonger, perceive class from a Marxist perspective. This viewpoint asserts that working-class individuals often act out economic deprivation and frustrations in the form of crime and delinquency. More contemporary sociologists like Cohen and Walter Miller see class as a social barrier due to middle-class standards being unfairly imposed on working-class youths. They perceive many youngsters growing up in lower socioeconomic areas as being normally delinquent, due to different value systems in high-delinquency areas. Cohen, in particular, perceives delinquency as a form of rebellion against the unfair imposition of middle-class values in school.

3. Self-reporting studies tend to reveal more delinquents among youths from middle-class backgrounds than appear in the juvenile court's official records on adjudicated juvenile delinquents. Police and court bias, according to this finding, reduces the numbers of official delinquency among middle- and upper-class juveniles. Most evidence confirms, however, that children from lower socioeconomic groups act out more offenses of a serious nature than youths from other strata in the society. This is the result of the basic fact that lower-class youths have fewer opportunities to achieve success in our society.

4. A considerable amount of middle-class delinquency is a consequence of the large increase in substance abuse by middle-class youths.

QUESTIONS

3.1. Do you believe that youths from lower socioeconomic groups have less opportunity and more social frustrations than the general juvenile population? Why?

3.2. Do you believe that self-reporting studies effectively get at the statistics on middle- and upper-class delinquency?

3.3. Would delinquency be significantly reduced if the United States became more of a classless society?

3.4. Compare and contrast the differences in lower- and middle-class delinquency as revealed in the cases of Baby Love and Jill. What would happen if Baby Love was treated at a psychiatric hospital and Jill went to a State Reformatory for Girls?

3.5. What are some of the impacts of the increased use of drugs and alcohol on middle-class delinquency?

two

PSYCHOLOGICAL FACTORS IN DELINQUENCY

chapter *4*

Delinquent Personality Types

There is a continuing controversy about whether delinquency is a manifestation of mental illness, the result of negative social factors, such as poverty or depressed socioeconomic factors, a reflection of deviant socialization, or a combination of all of these factors. My own firsthand observation and analysis of relevant research in these areas reveals that all of these forces create a delinquent personality who acts out delinquent behavior.

In the article, "Addressing Inmate Mental Health Problems," Kenneth Adams describes some of the complexity of analyzing mental health issues and delinquency.[1]

> In the early nineteenth century, as scientific approaches to the study of crime were starting to appear psychiatric theories vigorously stressed the notion that mental illness is the major cause of crime. These theories outlined a "medical model" of crime causation which viewed crime as a "disease of the mind" that needed to be "cured." From about the middle of the 19th century to about the middle of the 20th century, psychiatric theories of criminality were widely accepted. Once the proposition that mental illness is the cause of crime was accepted, it followed logically that in order for therapeutic services to be rehabilitative in the penological sense, they must be designed to address mental health problems. From this point of view, there was little to be gained from distinguishing between correctional rehabilitation services and mental health service.

[1]Kenneth Adams, "Addressing Inmate Mental Health Problems," *Federal Probation* (December 1985): 46.

It is apparent to me as a social-psychological criminologist that sociocultural factors influence personality formation. It is of value to research and analyze these sociological factors; however, a better understanding of the general arena of delinquency is fostered by examining the emotional disorders that produce delinquent personality systems.

In brief, I believe it is of great value to comprehend not only the sociological value systems that cause delinquency but the emotional disorders that relate to delinquent behavior. In this regard, before I categorize several basic delinquent personalities, I will here present three aspects of the relationship between emotional disorders and delinquency.

1. A common assumption made by psychotherapists in the field of delinquency is that delinquent behavior is a symptom of some underlying emotional disturbance or disorder. There is no doubt that many delinquent acts are committed by youths who are emotionally disturbed, and that some "normal" people commit criminal acts when under great emotional strain. In brief, some delinquent behavior is a symptomatic acting out of underlying emotional pathology.
2. Behavior considered symptomatic of emotional disturbance is likely to receive more attention when exhibited by one charged with or convicted of an act of delinquency. One conclusion, therefore, is that a certain amount of delinquent behavior is a result of underlying emotional problems; however, because there tends to be a greater focus on the emotional background of a delinquent than on that of the average person, more emotional problems may be attributed to delinquents than to law-abiding youths.

    The deviant behavior may emanate from the emotional disorder, but in some cases there may not be any causal connection between the two. In other words, a delinquent may be emotionally disturbed, but the emotional disorder may not be related to the delinquent behavior.
3. Delinquent behavior may *cause* emotional disorders. What is suggested here is that delinquent youths may develop an induced emotional disturbance as a result of detention, long-term incarceration, or the variety of abnormal social forces involved in the administration of juvenile justice. In some cases normal delinquent youths are hospitalized in psychiatric facilities, where the emotional stress produces personality problems unrelated to their former delinquent behavior. Being a juvenile delinquent is often an exceedingly nerve-wracking occupation or status that can cause emotional problems for the individual involved in this lifestyle. The emotional disorder may be more of a status or occupational disease or a result of a delinquent lifestyle than a causal factor.

Based on my firsthand research in a variety of settings and a review of the relevant research literature, I would group delinquents according to the manner in which their personality types affect their delinquent behavior.

1. *Socialized delinquents.* These are youths who are no more emotionally disturbed than the average person. They become delinquent as a result of the social context within which they learn deviant values. They are more likely to become property violators than violent offenders.
2. *Neurotic delinquents.* These are youths who become delinquents as a result of distortions in their personality and their perception of the world around them. They may have a need to commit delinquent acts to validate the fact that they are not insecure. They may become deviant because of some anxiety or neurotic compulsion. For example, youths who become kleptomaniacs, shoplifters, and pyromaniacs have neurotic compulsions that often result in delinquent behavior.
3. *Psychotic delinquents.* These are youths with severe personality disorders who have a significantly distorted perception of the society and people around them. Unlike socialized offenders, they do not plan their crimes; their distorted view of reality and their delusional thoughts may compel them to commit acts which violate the law. Psychotic offenders are likely to commit acts of violence, including murder. These delinquents are the ones who tend to commit the most bizarre and senseless acts of violence.
4. *Sociopathic Delinquents.* These youths are characterized by an egocentric personality. They have limited or no compassion for others. Because of this character defect, they can easily victimize others with a minimum of anxiety or guilt. The sociopathic element is present in most delinquents, although not all delinquents are clear sociopaths.

These four categories account for most of our delinquent population. It should also be noted, by way of preface to our more detailed analysis of these categories, that there are few pure cases. Many socialized delinquents have sociopathic tendencies, and many murderers manifest a combination of socialized and sociopathic characteristics.

THE SOCIALIZED DELINQUENT

This type of offender is socialized into delinquency. In terms of Edwin Sutherland's causal explanation of "differential association," the socialized delinquent learns a preponderance of values, attitudes, and techniques that make law violation a more desirable way of life than being a law-abiding citizen.[2] The community in which the youth grows up is apt to significantly affect his or her values, ethics, and choices in life. There are high-crime neighborhoods, where becoming a criminal is an attractive choice for a youth growing up with criminal role models. When the neighborhood heroes are "successful" criminals or racketeers, youths (like Baby Love) may

---

[2]Edwin Sutherland, *Criminology* (Philadelphia, Pa.: J. B. Lippincott, 1965), p. 398.

seek to emulate them. Becoming a juvenile delinquent for many youths growing up in this social content is, therefore, paradoxically more a matter of conformity than deviance.

Donald Cressey makes the point that organized crime is a most attractive potential field of endeavor for poor youths growing up in urban ghettos.[3] Cressey asserts that the Cosa Nostra feeds on the urban poor. Of the thousands of people involved in organized crime, the "street men" or street-level commission agents are visible manifestations of a seductive criminal lifestyle, and they exert a primary influence on juvenile delinquency. The agents of organized crime have high status in their neighborhoods and are the idols of young ghetto residents; they are the men who have "made it." In the eyes of many urban youths, the image of success is that of a hustler who promotes his interests by using others.

Cressey takes the position that organized criminals influence the general delinquency rate in the inner city in three ways. First, they demonstrate to the young people that crime does pay. Second, the presence of organized crime exhibits the corruption evident in law enforcement and political organizations. This makes it more difficult for parents to teach their children to achieve in the world by "hard honest labor in service to their family, country, and God." Third, organized crime, through the numbers rackets, prostitution, gambling, and drug dealing, appreciably affects and lowers the economic status of the people in the community; thus the people have less to lose if convicted of crime. Delinquency is therefore more attractive to lower-class youth. Cressey groups his observations into three categories: (1) attraction; (2) corruption; and (3) contamination.

1. *Attraction.* Because of varied forces, according to Cressey, slum boys grow up in an economic and social environment that makes some participation in organized crime attractive, natural, and relatively painless. Cressey cites Irving Spergel, who, in his studies of juvenile delinquents in three different neighborhoods in Chicago, concluded that developing specific social skills is less necessary than learning the point of view or attitudes conducive to the development of organized crime.

   In response to Spergel's question to delinquents, "What is the job of the adult in your neighborhood whom you would want to be like?", eight out of ten responded by naming some aspect of organized crime. Spergel's "Racketville" delinquents believed that connections are the most important quality in getting ahead. Seven out of ten chose education as the least important factor in getting ahead.

   An illustration of this continuing influence and "attraction" to youngsters in a high-crime neighborhood was revealed by the death and burial of a well-known pimp and drug dealer in Oakland, California, in the summer of 1986. The criminal was gunned

---

[3]Donald R. Cressey, "Organized Crime and Inner City Youth," *Crime and Delinquency* (April 1970): 129–138.

down in a prototypical drug war slaying. Over 50,000 people in a paradelike atmosphere witnessed his elaborate hearse rolling down a main street on the way to the cemetery. The funeral reportedly cost over $40,000. Journalists interviewed a number of teenagers who responded with variations on a theme of hero worship: "He was an important man in the neighborhood. He was well liked and I hope I'll be as successful as he was." "Money's the name of the game. I worked for him, and I'll get my share when I get older."

2. *Corruption*. Organized crime, in its alliances with politicians and law-enforcement officials, helps, as Cressey sees it, "to break down the respect for law and order. How can a boy learn to respect authority when that authority figure is known to be on the payroll of criminals?"

3. *Contamination*. Cressey asserts that because the areas of low socioeconomic status are the areas of high delinquency and crime in American cities, it must be concluded that, in some areas, lawlessness has become traditional. He reasons that in poverty-stricken areas the values, social pressures, and norms favorable to crime are strong and constant. The individuals responsible for enforcing these moral systems and concepts are organized criminals. Cressey quotes Dr. Martin Luther King, who once stated that "organized crime flourishes in the ghetto as 'permissive crime' because no one cares particularly about ghetto crime."

Cressey, in his paraphrasing of Sutherland's theory of "differential association," asserts that most people living in low-income or poverty areas are either delinquent or criminal because they are isolated from law-abiding behavior patterns and are in close continuing contact with criminal influences "that affect forces favorable to delinquency." Cressey believes that the "incidence of inner-city delinquency may be reduced by eliminating the behavior patterns spread by organized criminals or by expanding those anticriminal patterns that keep inner-city youth out of trouble."[5]

Cressey concludes his observations by stating:

Keeping vice out of affluent areas while allowing it to flourish in the ghettos, together with corruption that supports the practice, [contributes to] the traditions of delinquency and crime characterizing our inner city areas. In these areas opposition to crime and delinquency is weak because the city is poor, mobile and heterogeneous and people can't act effectively to solve their problems.[4]

The contemporary version of this situation is related to drug dealing. Many urban "socialized delinquents" are making enormous amounts of money, especially in ghetto areas, by dealing drugs, especially crack, a marketable form of cocaine.

[4]Ibid., p. 138.
[5]Ibid., p. 137. Reprinted with permission of the National Council on Crime and Delinquency.

Two Socialized Delinquents

John   John grew up among and was essentially socialized by the criminal forces in the inner city of New York described by Cressey. I became closely acquainted with John in the course of my research on gangs in New York City. The following analysis is based on five lengthy, in-depth taped interviews with John.

John grew up in a delinquent subculture on the West Side of Manhattan. His neighborhood "naturally" socialized him into a delinquent/drug addict lifestyle. The process involved the development of a delinquent mask or macho, tough-guy image that was necessary for survival on the streets.

John was first institutionalized at the age of ten by his parents for being incorrigible. From that time he felt extreme hatred for his parents, especially his father. In the institution, he "always felt a need to protect the underdog in a fight." He had several fights each day and found that the "home" or juvenile detention facility he was periodically in was a "house of horror." He was later sent to a long-term facility for two years and learned all about crime from the older boys.

When he left the institution at about the age of 13, he began running with various youth gangs on the Upper West Side. They were involved in petty theft and destructive acts. He remembered learning to hate his father more and more. "I always stayed out late, and when he would get me at home, he would beat me up pretty badly. Then he would actually sentence me, like a judge. For example, he would give me 'sixty days in the bedroom.' I began my jail time early." John, like many children in his situation, seldom went to school.

During most of his early life, John worshipped older gangsters and criminals; he wanted to be like them. In his neighborhood there were many to imitate. One criminal he especially admired, according to John, "killed a few wrong guys and died in the hot seat at Sing Sing without a whimper."

When John was 14, he took his first fix of heroin. In the course of his delinquent-training apprenticeship, "I used to run dope and deliver packages of heroin to older addicts. One day, out of curiosity, I asked this guy for a little. He fixed me, and that was it. I began using from then on. It's hard to describe my first feelings about heroin. The best way I can describe it is that it's like being under the covers where it's nice and warm on a cold day."

John continued to run the streets, used drugs whenever he could, and received more training for a life of crime. "In my neighborhood, when I was around 13, I was considered a 'cute kid.' The whores liked me, and once in a while, for a gag, they would turn a trick with me. I admired the stand-up guy gangsters. They were my idols. My main hero at that time was the local head of the Mafia family."

John in his teenage years was a thin, baby-faced young fellow. His pale, ascetic face had an almost religious quality. In his neighborhood he became known as "Whitey the Priest." He received this nickname from an addict who was kicking a habit. As John relates it:

> Once, when I was in jail in the Tombs, some Spanish guy who was kicking a bad habit came to for a minute. He saw me and began to scream hysterically in Spanish that I was a priest. Later on, it was picked up by other people who knew me around the city. Some of the whores on Columbus Avenue would even "confess" to me as Whitey the Priest. First I made sure they gave me a good fix of heroin, or money for a fix, and then I would actually listen to their "confession!" They weren't kidding; they were dead serious. After the "confession" took place, usually in some hallway or in a bar, after they poured out their tragic story, I would lay a concept on them. Something like "into each life some rain must fall." I'd bless them and cut out.
>
> I took my first big fall at 14. I was sent to the reformatory at Otisville. I hated everyone there and wanted to kill the director and some of the guards. I was always fighting and spent a lot of time in the hole [solitary confinement]. This gave me a chance to think and plot different ways to kill the guards and the man who ran the joint.

At age 16, John was transferred from Otisville to another reformatory for older boys. Thereafter he spent time in various institutions. These included several trips to Rikers Island Penitentiary, Lexington for a "winder" ("You wind in and out"), Riverside Hospital for youthful addicts, and various New York City jails.

John always considered himself to be a "stand-up guy" (a criminal with ethics), and was determined to become a professional criminal. At one point he tried to learn how to be a safecracker from an old-timer. "Somehow I wasn't very good. I did go on a few jobs, but it wasn't right for me. Whenever I was out of jail, which wasn't too often, I would just use drugs and steal. I became a baby-faced stall for some cannons [pickpockets]. The stall sets up the mark, and the cannon picks his pocket. I made a fair living in this business. I used to like to pick pockets in museums. In fact, I don't know why, but I spent a lot of time walking around museums."

In my lengthy discussions with John, I never determined that the young man had any significant neurotic, psychotic, or sociopathic personality traits. His delinquent lifestyle appeared to result from the "straight-line" learning of delinquent behavior in a neighborhood milieu that stressed delinquency as a correct and logical way of life.

The "socialized delinquent" growing up in a delinquent subculture acquires skills useful in crime and values and attitudes that make a delinquent career attractive. He or she learns to commit burglaries, thefts, and other property offenses as skills and engages in them to earn a livelihood. In later life, young delinquents like John usually develop into what Edwin H. Sutherland has called "the professional criminal."

Sutherland's concept of the professional criminal parallels the sociological model of socialized delinquents. Sutherland's classic theory for "differential association" (grossly oversimplified) states that delinquents learn to become delinquent from association with other offenders. They are trained into delinquent patterns at an early age. Sutherland's "professional thief" is the role that the socialized delinquent will achieve if he or she becomes a specialist in a particular criminal activity. According to Sutherland and Cressey:[6]

> Professional thieves make a regular business of theft. They use techniques which have been developed over a period of centuries and transmitted to them through traditions and personal association. They have codes of behavior, esprit de corps, and consensus. They have a high status among other thieves and in the political and criminal underworld in general. They have differential association in the sense that they associate with each other and not, on the same basis, with outsiders, and also in the sense that they select their colleagues.
>
> Because of this differential association they develop a common language or argot that is relatively unknown to those not in the profession, and they have organization. A thief is a professional when he has these six characteristics: regular work at theft, technical skill, consensus, status, differential association, and organization.
>
> Professional thieves have their group ways of behavior for the principal situations that confront them in their criminal activities. Consequently professional theft is a behavior system and a sociological entity.

This model of the professional criminal characterizes him as resourceful, well-trained, and effective, a member of a profession (albeit illegal) with certain ethics and values that dictate his conduct. In criminal jargon, the professional thief has "class." He would not "rat on his buddies," and even certain victims are proscribed. Assault and violence are used as means to an end, not as ends in themselves.

Jim   Jim, like John, fulfills the criteria for a socialized delinquent. Following is Jim's story as he told it to me:

> When I was sixteen or seventeen I used to hang around a pool hall in our neighborhood a lot. I could shoot pool pretty good and once in a while I would make a couple of bucks. But there were older guys there who were really doing good. They had good reputations in the neighborhood and they always had money, cars, and broads. Me and some kids my age were doing a lot of petty stealing at this time, cars and things from cars, but we didn't know how to make any real money. What we wanted to do was get in with the older guys we admired so we could learn something and make some real money.
>
> One day, I remember, I had just got out of juvenile hall for some petty beef and

[6]Edwin H. Sutherland and Donald R. Cressey, "Developmental Explanation of Criminal Behavior," in *Criminology*, 10th ed. (New York: Harper & Row, 1978), pp. 80–82. Copyright © 1978 by J.B. Lippincott Company. Reprinted by permission of Harper & Row, Publishers, Inc.

one of the older thieves, a guy that was supposed to be one of the slickest safe men around, came over to me and talked to me for a while. This made me feel pretty good. Later one of his friends asked me if I wanted to help him carry a safe out of some office. We worked half a night on that safe and never did get it out of the place. But from then on I was in with this older bunch. Every once in a while one of them would get me to do some little job for him, like "standing point" [lookout] or driving a car or something like that; and once in a while when they had snatched a safe, I would get to help open it. I was learning pretty fast.

By the time I was 18, me and a couple of my buddies had real solid names [reputations] with the older thieves. We were beating a lot of places on our own and we handled ourselves pretty well. But we were still willing to learn more. We used to sit around some coffee shop half the night or ride around in a car listening to a couple of the old hoodlums cut up different scores [crimes]. We would talk about different scores other guys had pulled or scores we had pulled, and we would also talk about how you were supposed to act in certain situations—how to spend your money, how to act when you got arrested. We discussed different trials we knew about, we even talked about San Quentin and Folsom and prisons in other states, because usually the older thieves had done time before in these other places. We talked about the laws, how much time each beef carried, how much time the parole board would give you for each crime. I guess we talked about everything that had anything to do with stealing. Of course we didn't talk about it all the time. Lots of the time we just shot the bull like anyone else. But by the time I was 18 I had a pretty good education in crime.

John and Jim *learned* their criminal behavior in a relatively normal fashion, and it was my opinion that neither of them had any special personality problems. They became criminals as a result of the deviant value system they were exposed to as youths growing up in a neighborhood where becoming a criminal was a "legitimate" and desirable way of life. They were thus socialized into a criminal lifestyle, and can be clearly categorized as "socialized delinquents."

THE NEUROTIC DELINQUENT

The general heading of emotional disorders includes neurotic and psychotic behavior. Neurosis is a less severe form of emotional disorder than psychosis. Neurotic compulsions can cause certain types of delinquent behavior. Youths suffering from a neurosis are typically capable of functioning in everyday life. Unlike the psychotic, the neurotic generally does not perceive sharp distortions of reality. Moreover, neurotics typically are aware that there is something wrong with their thinking and behavior.

The principal symptom of neurosis is anxiety, which involves a visceral sense of fear and personal distress not brought about by any clear stimulus in the environment. In mild cases of neurosis, anxiety may be expressed directly. In some severe cases, a neurotic person may appear to be in a state of panic. According to psychiatrists, anxiety may also be expressed indirectly, showing up as a variety of other problems such as blindness, deafness, exhaustion, inexplicable fear of objects or particular situations, and compulsive activity, including offenses like kleptomania, pyromania, and shoplifting.

Some burglars manifest neurotic tendencies in their modus operandi. One 16-year-old offender, Eric, whom I worked with in a juvenile jail, presented a clear pattern of neurotic compulsion. He was a compulsive house burglar. When he was finally arrested, the police cleared more than 60 burglaries committed over a three-month period.

Eric's burglary pattern always took the following unalterable form: He would locate and break into a house whose residents were on vacation. Once inside the house, he would make himself at home. He would cook himself a meal, read a paper, and then take a nap. Upon awakening he would loot the house of all valuables. Prior to leaving, almost as an afterthought, he would return to the bedroom and defecate on the bed.

I had many lengthy counseling sessions with this neurotic delinquent. We concluded that this last act of defiance and hostility was related to his hostility toward his own parents. He felt that they had never provided him with an adequate home situation, and his delinquency revolved around his unconscious hostility toward people who had "nice homes." Eric's neurotic burglaries and defiant act of defecation were a form of revenge directed at "good homes." He talked further about how he would sometimes walk around for days with an inner feeling of fear and hostility—manifestations of his anxiety. He explained how, when he would act out his compulsions in a burglary, it would relieve his anxiety, and he would feel better for a period of time.

Freud and others have hypothesized that neurotic anxiety is reduced by various *ego defense mechanisms*. Following are several of these basic mechanisms and a discussion of them as they relate to the neurotic delinquent.

1. *Denial of reality*. Protecting self from unpleasant reality by refusal to perceive or face it, often by escapist activities like using drugs or acting out delinquent behavior.
2. *Fantasy*. Gratifying frustrated desires in imaginary achievements. The violent gang in many ways has a pseudoreality component, where youths picture themselves as heroic, embattled individuals fighting a courageous war for their turf.
3. *Projection*. Placing blame for difficulties upon others or attributing one's own unethical desires to others. Gang and other violent youths, often in a paranoid way, project onto others their own violent motivations.
4. *Reaction formation*. Preventing insecure feelings from being expressed by exaggerating opposed attitudes and types of behavior and using them as "barriers." The delinquent boy who is insecure about his power and masculinity acts out in violent and deviant delinquent acts to prove that he is a "powerful man." This is a basic mechanism for violent gang youths.

5. *Displacement.* Discharging pent-up feelings, usually by hostility, on objects less dangerous than those that initially aroused the emotions. Displacement is a common defense mechanism for neurotic delinquents, and it accounts for the violent behavior of many delinquent youths.

In several psychodramas I directed with a 15-year-old violent youth in a psychiatric hospital, this process of displacement was revealed. The young man had enormous feelings of hostility toward his stepfather, which were "displaced" onto the world at large in a series of muggings. As indicated in the ego defense explanation, he found strangers "less dangerous objects" for his hostility and displaced his rage onto these innocent victims.

THE PSYCHOTIC DELINQUENT

Psychosis is a more severe type of mental disorder than neurosis. Individuals diagnosed as psychotic have their own unique version of reality and are usually unable to perform the roles expected of them in everyday life. Consequently, treatment of psychoses commonly involves involuntary confinement.

Psychotics suffer from delusions, hallucinations, deep changes in mood, or an inability to think, speak, or remember. While psychiatrists have found that some psychoses are organic—a result of actual physical damage to the brain or of chemical imbalances in a person's system—they claim that most types of psychosis are caused by defective socialization.

One of the more common psychoses is schizophrenia. This term is applied to people who are extremely withdrawn from their surroundings or who act as if they are living in another world. Schizophrenics' thoughts may appear disorganized and bizarre, their emotions inappropriate to the situation, and their behavior unusual. Various types of schizophrenia have been identified and categorized. Individuals who exhibit delusions of being persecuted by others are called paranoid schizophrenics. Catatonic schizophrenics act in an excessively excited manner or, alternatively, exist in a mute, vegetative state.

When psychotics are in their excited state they can explode into murderous acts of epic proportions. Cases of this sort include the University of Texas rampage of Charles Whitman, the Hillside strangler murders in Los Angeles, the murderous spree of Herbert Mullin, and the "Son of Sam" murders by David Berkowitz that terrorized New York City. These horrendous murders were committed by offenders with psychotic personalities. The following cases of Charles Whitman, Leo Anguiano, and Kenneth Bianchi ("The Hillside Strangler") more graphically and dramatically reveal some of the patterns of psychotic murders.

One August afternoon a blond, husky young man strolled into a hardware store in Austin, Texas, and asked for several boxes of rifle ammunition. As he calmly wrote a check in payment, the clerk inquired with friendly curiosity what all the ammunition was for. "To shoot some pigs," the young man replied. At the time, the answer seemed innocent enough, for wild pigs still abound not far from the capital. The horror of his true intent became obvious a few hours later, when the customer, Charles Joseph Whitman, 25, a student of architectural engineering at the University of Texas, became the perpetrator of one of the worst mass murders in U.S. history.

That morning, Charles Whitman entered two more stores to buy guns before ascending, with his arsenal, to the observation deck of the tower that soars 307 feet above the University of Texas campus. There, from Austin's tallest edifice, he took command of the 232-acre campus. Whitman had visited the tower ten days earlier in the company of a brother and had taken it all in. Today, though, he had no time for the view; he was too intent upon his deadly work.

Methodically, he began shooting everyone in sight. Ranging around the tower's walk at will, he sent his bullets rasping through the flesh and bone of those on the campus below, then of those who walked or stood or rode as far as three blocks away. His victims fell as they went about their various normal tasks. By lingering perhaps a moment too long in a classroom or leaving a moment too soon for lunch, they had unwittingly placed themselves within Whitman's lethal reach. Before he was himself killed by police bullets, Charles Whitman killed 13 people and wounded 31—for a staggering total of 44 casualties. As a prelude to his senseless rampage, it was later discovered, he had also slain his wife and mother, bringing the total dead to 15.

It was later determined that Whitman had emotional problems stemming from early childhood and his relationship to his mother and had sought psychiatric help. He had several counseling sessions, but apparently the depths of his emotional disorder had not been fully revealed.

The following case of Leo, a young psychotic-sociopathic killer, further reveals how family background can create a 12-year-old child-killer.[7]

> When 11-year-old Leo Anguiano would come home from school after getting in another scrap, his grandmother would tell him it is wrong to fight.
>
> But she also would tell him it was all right to defend himself "with whatever he could get hold of."
>
> Leo, whose parents had been murdered, lived with his grandmother, Inez Lara, 48, and her sons; police say the youths have records for gang-related crimes, including assault with a deadly weapon.
>
> Authorities believe that Leo's home environment played a large role in shaping his own violent behavior.
>
> By the time he was 12, Leo had been suspended from school several times for fighting, had killed a boy with a knife and had stabbed another boy with a pencil while in juvenile hall.
>
> "He was the kind of kid who would walk up to some kid and just cold-

[7]Mark Landsbaum, "The Brief History of a Killer at 12," *Los Angeles Times*, February 15, 1982. Copyright 1982, *Los Angeles Times*. Reprinted by permission.

cock him—punch him in the stomach," according to an educator at Sierra Vista Intermediate School where Leo had been suspended. "He didn't know the kid, it was just his way of being macho."

Leo's history of violence peaked on Oct. 9, 1981, just weeks before his 12th birthday, when he stuck a four-inch knife into the heart of James Diaz, 13, during a quarrel.

Many of those who dealt with Leo at school, where he had a reputation for bullying smaller children agreed with teacher Cindy Potts, who said that despite her love for him, she was not surprised that he had committed murder.

"I think Leo was striking out for help," Potts said. "He got some. A little. Maybe as much as the system could give him."

A school psychologist had noted a year before the murder that Leo had "a very short temper and (was) verbally and physically aggressive toward peers and adults."

In an attempt to divert Leo from what seemed an inevitable course of violence, he was counseled, tested, twice evaluated by a psychologist, punished, placed in special classes and referred to other experts for more of the same. . . .

Leo was sentenced . . . to the California Youth Authority for murder and assault with a deadly weapon. He will be closely supervised until age 21, when juvenile court loses jurisdiction, although he could be released on parole sooner.

The following is the history of how those close to Leo dealt with his violence, based on court records and reports by and interviews with educators, counselors, psychologists, probation officers, police, court officials and Leo's relatives.

When Leo was born, his unmarried parents were 15 and 16.

When Leo was 5, his father, who had been in jail and prison for offenses including rape, was shot to death.

When Leo was 8, his mother was stabbed to death.

Both parents had street gang affiliations.

Leo told authorities that when he was 11 he was "jumped into" a street gang by the uncles he lived with at his grandparents' home. . . .

When she testified in Leo's murder trial, Inez Lara was asked if she ever told Leo that "what happened to his mother and father was wrong."

"No," she answered.

"Did you ever tell him not to kill people?" Deputy Dist. Atty. David Evans asked.

"No." . . .

James Diaz lived 46 days in a coma after Leo stabbed him on Oct. 9, 1981. While Diaz lay in a hospital bed, Leo was sentenced to four years in county juvenile facilities in a plea bargained verdict of assault with a deadly weapon. . . .

After Diaz died Nov. 26, the district attorney filed a new charge of murder.

Probation Officer Jerry Wright interviewed Leo for an hour and a half and said he "appeared to be fighting back a smile."

"He did not seem shaken by the offense," Wright reported to the court, "nor did he seem to show any sign of remorse." . . .

On Oct. 10, 1981, his first day in juvenile hall, Leo boasted of his crime, a probation officer reported.

On Dec. 17, 1981, in a Sylmar Juvenile Hall classroom, while awaiting his murder trial, Leo fought with a larger boy, who also had a reputation for picking fights.

The other boy, 13, suffered superficial puncture wounds when Leo stabbed him with a pencil in the neck and stomach.

Probation Officer Nancy Easton said Leo "obviously learned nothing" from the Diaz stabbing, and, in fact, had threatened to shoot juvenile hall counselors "as soon as he gets out of custody."

Many psychotic murderers do not confine their homicidal tendencies to one outburst like Whitman and young Leo. There appears to be an increasing number of serial psychotic murders in the United States. One such notable case involved the so-called Hillside Strangler in Los Angeles, Kenneth Bianchi.[8] (If Leo is set free, he could easily become a murderer like Bianchi since their early life experiences were similar.)

Kenneth Bianchi was responsible for the murders of over 20 young women during a period from September 1977 to February 1978. Almost all the victims were found nude, all were strangled, all were sexually assaulted, all had been handcuffed or bound prior to death, almost all the cases involved sexual intercourse, and all of the bodies were found on hillsides.

After Bianchi's arrest, Dr. John G. Watkins, professor of psychology at the University of Montana, interviewed him and put him under hypnosis. During the time Bianchi was under hypnosis, Dr. Watkins found him to have multiple personalities.

Under hypnosis the personality of "Steve" came to life. Unlike Bianchi, who was polite and courteous most of the time in his sessions with Dr. Watkins, Steve was rude and hostile. Dr. Watkins identified the killer personality as Steve. Steve told Dr. Watkins that he hated Ken because Ken was always nice to people. Steve also said that he made Ken lie and that he liked to hurt anyone who was nice to Ken. Steve related how one night Ken went to his cousin Angelo Buono's house. Angelo had a girl over, and Ken walked in while Angelo was killing the girl. Steve said that he and Angelo talked a lot about killing women. Steve asked Angelo what it was like to kill someone and how many others he had killed. About a week later, Steve and Angelo went out together and picked up a girl. They both had sex with her and then killed her. This was, according to Bianchi, the first of a series of killings that they would commit together.

Steve explained that whenever the murders took place, he was in control of Ken's body, and Ken would have no recollection of what had happened. Bianchi had complained to Dr. Watkins of frequent losses of memory, even before he was put under hypnosis. Steve told Dr. Watkins that he could become sexually aroused only when he knew he was going to

---

[8]This summary of the case of Kenneth Bianchi is based on my collation of numerous articles on the subject as well as court records.

kill a woman. Ken, on the other hand, had a normal sex life with his girlfriend.

Dr. Ralph Allison, a theorist in the field of abnormal psychology, also put Ken into a state of hypnosis. Dr. Allison asked Ken to tell him when he had started to have problems at home. Ken responded by going back to when he was 9 years old. Apparently the Bianchis were having financial problems at this time, and Mrs. Bianchi was constantly upset. Bianchi said she was always yelling at him or hitting him. Ken felt he needed his mother's approval; when she became upset with him, he would run and hide from her. It was at this time that Steve appeared. Steve was at first Ken's imaginary friend. This is a normal occurrence for some children, but most of these imaginary people disappear in time. In this case, however, Steve became the "bad" Ken Bianchi. This enabled Bianchi to defend his "self," so he did not have to accept personal responsibility for his horrendous homicidal behavior. He could displace this negative side of his self onto Steve.

Bianchi was examined for several months by a number of psychiatrists and psychologists. He was diagnosed by several as psychotic with a multiple-personality problem. Several psychiatrists disputed the validity of the Steve personality that appeared under hypnosis. They alleged that Bianchi was faking the Steve personality in order to mount an insanity plea and escape the death penalty. If Steve was real, we can speculate that Bianchi's multiple personality was a complex, defensive psychotic syndrome emanating from an early life that involved severe problems with his mother.

One psychiatrist's analysis related Ken's psychosis to his mother's prostitution. In one interview Bianchi revealed his hostility towards his mother as he lay awake in the next room hearing her having sex with many men. Whether Steve was real, his repressed hostility toward his mother when he was a child was later displaced onto women he perceived as being like her. Part of his psychotic compulsion was to kill women who were or appeared to be prostitutes.

Another aspect of Bianchi's repressed hostility towards his mother was revealed in psychiatric observations made when he was a child. Clinical reports stated that she beat him physically, often without any justifiable reason. In 1984, when he was interviewed and hypnotized by a number of psychiatrists, they videotaped the sessions, and the sessions supplemented the earlier data.

Under hypnosis, Ken described the violent assaults by his mother. His mother, according to Bianchi, "would hit me almost every day. Most of the time she hit me for no reason. I was mad at her all the time—but I would never hit her back. I was fully controlled by her and under her thumb." The psychiatric videotapes revealed that Bianchi repressed all of his enormous hostility toward his mother and avoided any encounters with her. It was during these childhood years that he developed Steve to help him deal with his anger and his feelings towards his mother.

Bianchi's torment and anger were expressed later in life in his ritualistic, torturous, and brutal murders of young women. His homicides can be partially explained as the expression of the rage he felt as a child toward his mother, which was later displaced through the torture and murder perpetrated on his female victims.

In a sense he practiced a kind of role reversal. When he was a child, his mother had all of the power. She was the offender and he was the victim. As an adult, in his ritualistic vengeance against his mother, he had all of the power, and the women he killed (who were often tied up) became the helpless victims of his rage. In this way he seemed to achieve a kind of revenge against his mother.

Many homicidal psychotics like Bianchi develop another personality that is held responsible for their heinous acts. I have encountered several violent delinquents who attribute their darker side to a manufactured "other person" in their body. This other personality, they allege, takes over and commits the horrendous act. This enables the psychotic delinquent to rationalize away their violence, deny responsibility for their deviance, and maintain a self-concept of being a good person. In Kenneth Bianchi's case, Steve was the villain, and Ken remained a good guy. It was, however, the total Kenneth Bianchi who became the vicious Hillside Strangler.

In brief, Whitman, Leo, and Bianchi all became psychotic criminal personalities as a result of defective socialization processes. Their murderous acting out was a reflection of their early childhood problems that festered in their delusionary psychotic personalities.

THE SOCIOPATHIC DELINQUENT

For many years the catch-all label "psychopathic" was applied by psychiatrists to all individuals whose behavior deviated markedly from the normal, yet who could not be clearly categorized as severely neurotic or psychotic. In the last decade, "sociopathic" has been used interchangeably with "psychopathic" to describe individuals who, because of a severe character defect involving a lack of compassion, act out self-destructive and otherwise harmful behavior. In the following analysis I will use the term "sociopath" to describe this personality disorder.

The sociopathic offender is characterized by what has varyingly been called a "moral imbecility" or "character disorder." This type of offender may know right from wrong, but lacks any coherent, appropriate discretionary ability in the realm of compassionate, moral behavior.

A number of sociologists and psychologists have attempted to define this delinquent personality syndrome. Paul Tappan describes the sociopath as follows: "He has a condition of psychological abnormality in which there is neither the overt appearance of psychosis or neurosis, but there is a chronic abnormal response to the environment.[9]

[9]Paul W. Tappan, *Crime, Justice and Correction* (New York: McGraw-Hill, 1960), p. 137.

According to Harrison Gough, the sociopath is "the kind of person who seems insensitive to social demands, who refuses to or cannot cooperate, who is untrustworthy, impulsive, and improvident, who shows poor judgement and shallow emotionality, and who seems unable to appreciate the reactions of others to his behavior."[10]

Albert Rabin succinctly describes the basic trait of a defective social conscience apparent in the sociopathic personality:

There are two major related aspects to this notion of defective conscience. . . . The first aspect is represented in the inability . . . to apply the moral standards of society to his behavior; he cheats, lies, steals, does not keep promises, and so on. He has not absorbed the "thou shalts" and the "thou shalt nots" of his society and cultural milieu. The second aspect is that of absence of guilt. Guilt is an important part of any well-developed conscience. When a normal person violates the moral code he feels guilty; he feels unhappy and blames himself for the transgression. . . .

Guilt is an unknown experience for the personality with no superego. There is none of this automatic self-punishment that goes along with the commission of immoral and unethical acts. The psychopath [sociopath] continues to behave irresponsibly, untruthfully, insincerely, and antisocially without a shred of shame, remorse, or guilt. He may sometime express regret and remorse for the actions and crimes which he may have perpetrated; however, these are usually merely words, spoken for the effect, but not really and sincerely felt.[11]

In the section "Adolescent Disorders" in the American Psychiatric Association's Diagnostic and Statistical Manual of Mental Disorders (DSM III, 1980), juvenile psychopath or sociopath is characterized as a "conduct disorder." The "conduct disorder" syndrome is defined as follows: "The essential feature is a repetitive and persistent pattern of conduct in which either the basic rights of others or major age-appropriate societal norms or rules are violated."[12]

DSM III delineates four specific subtypes of sociopathic conduct disorders: (1) undersocialized aggressive; (2) undersocialized nonaggressive; (3) socialized aggressive; and (4) socialized nonaggressive. These subtypes are based on the presence or absence of adequate social bonds and the presence or absence of a pattern of aggressive antisocial behavior in the delinquent behavior of this type of juvenile.

The category of undersocialized aggressive fits the delinquent sociopath category. In DSM III this youth is described as a person

---

[10]Harrison G. Gough, "A Sociological Theory of Psychopathy," *American Journal of Sociology* 53 (March 1948): 365.

[11]Albert I. Rabin, "Psychopathic (Sociopathic) Personalities," in *Legal and Criminal Psychology*, ed. Hans Toch. (New York: Holt, Rinehart, 1961). Copyright © 1961 by Holt, Rinehart and Winston, Inc. Reprinted by permission of Holt, Rinehart and Winston, Inc.

[12]"Adolescent Disorders," *Diagnostic and Statistical Manual of Mental Disorders III* (New York: American Psychiatric Association, 1980), p. 49.

characterized by a failure to establish a normal degree of affection, empathy, or bond with others. Peer relationships are generally lacking, although the youngster may have superficial relationships with other youngsters. Characteristically the child does not extend himself or herself for others unless there is an obvious immediate advantage. Egocentrism is shown by readiness to manipulate others for favors without any effort to reciprocate. There is generally a lack of concern for the feelings, wishes, and well-being of others, as shown by callous behavior. Appropriate feelings of guilt or remorse are generally absent.[13]

In brief, the sociopathic delinquent has a persistent pattern of deviant behavior characterized by an almost total disregard for the rights and feelings of others. A summary listing of the sociopath's overt personality and behavior traits would include most, if not all, of the following factors: (1) limited social conscience; (2) egocentrism dominating most interaction, "instrumental manipulation" of others for self-advantage (rather than affective relating); (3) inability to forego immediate pleasure for future goals; and (4) a habit of pathological lying to achieve personal advantage.

The Mask of Sanity

Dr. Hervey Cleckley, a psychiatrist who has contributed much to the clarification of the psychiatric terminology on the sociopath, defines the sociopath as follows:

This term refers to chronically antisocial individuals who are always in trouble, profiting neither from experience nor punishment, and maintaining no real loyalties to any person, group, or code. They are frequently callous and hedonistic, showing marked emotional immaturity, with lack of responsibility, lack of judgement, and an ability to rationalize their behavior so that it appears warranted, reasonable, and justified.[14]

In his book, "The Mask of Sanity," Cleckley developed comprehensive criteria for viewing this delinquent personality. Cleckley finds that most psychopaths (sociopaths) manifest the following personality traits:[15]

1. *Superficial charm and good "intelligence."* Typical psychopaths, when first encountered, seem friendly and well adjusted and appear to have many interests. They are also likely to possess superior intelligence.
2. *Absence of delusions and other signs of irrational thinking.* Psychopaths can recognize the physical realities around them, do not "hear voices," and reason logically.

---

[13]"Adolescent Disorders," *Diagnostic and Statistical Manual of Mental Disorders III* (New York: American Psychiatric Association, 1980), p. 52.

[14]Hervey M. Cleckley, "Psychopathic States," in *American Handbook of Psychiatry*, ed. Silvano Arieti (New York: Basic Books, 1959), p. 568.

[15]Summarized by permission from the late Dr. Hervey Cleckley, *The Mask of Sanity*, St. Louis, 1976, The C.V. Mosby Co.

3. *Absence of "nervousness" or psychoneurotic manifestations.* Psychopaths are usually free from minor reactions popularly called "neurotic," and they are typically immune to anxiety and worry such as might be considered normal in disturbing situations.

4. *Unreliability.* Psychopaths, after making substantial gains personally and often financially, will for no predictable reason abruptly throw their gains away in an irresponsible manner.

5. *Untruthfulness and insincerity.* Psychopaths' disregard for truth is remarkable. They seem confident and comfortable when making a solemn promise they will never keep. They will lie recklessly, but with great conviction, to extricate themselves from an accusation.

6. *Lack of remorse or shame.* Psychopaths cannot accept blame for misfortunes that they bring on themselves or others. Although they may claim (insincerely) some responsibility for troubles they have created, this is probably done to elicit confidence and trust from others. Also, they display virtually no sense of shame, even though their lives are filled with immoral exploits.

7. *Inadequately motivated antisocial behavior.* Psychopaths generally follow a course of behavior that is antisocial—cheating, lying, and fighting even when such actions do not serve any purpose.

8. *Poor judgment and failure to learn by experience.* Although more than capable of rationality, psychopaths display terrible judgment about how to get what they want. There is no evidence that they ever learn from their continuing negative experiences. Psychopaths compulsively repeat their failures, even to the point of repeating antisocial behaviors that lead to second or third incarcerations.

9. *Pathologic egocentricity and incapacity for love.* Though psychopaths often manifest the overt signs of affection and love, there is no indication that psychopaths actually experience these emotions in any real sense. They do not form enduring relationships. Despite surface indications of love and compassion, psychopaths are usually callous and destructive toward others.

10. *General poverty in major affective reactions.* Psychopaths display peevishness, spite, and false affection, but they are incapable of experiencing, deeply and truly, such emotions as pride, anger, grief, and joy.

11. *Specific loss of insight.* Psychopaths have limited insight and are apparently not introspective. They cannot see themselves as others do. If they have committed a crime, they assume that the legal penalties do not, or should not apply to them.

12. *Unresponsiveness in general interpersonal relations.* Although they may be superficially courteous in minor matters, psychopaths are incapable of sacrifice or true generosity. They do not demonstrate appreciation when others perform acts of trust or kindness toward them.

13. *Fantastic and uninviting behavior with drink and sometimes without.* Psychopaths typically use alcohol (and drugs) to excess. Unlike most alcoholics, psychopaths under the influence of even a modest amount of alcohol may become extremely irrational and de-

structive. This bizarre behavior can continue even when they are not drinking.

14. *Suicide threats rarely carried out.* Psychopath, or sociopaths, often threaten suicide but rarely carry it out. The lack of real guilt or shame about their behavior does not produce a true motivation for suicide. The threat is used for egocentric immediate personal advantage.

15. *Impersonal, trivial, and poorly integrated sexual activity.* The sexual life of both male and female psychopaths is generally promiscuous and, for the most part, emotionally unfulfilling. The sexual partner is viewed as an object rather than as a person with feelings. Psychopaths often seem to choose sexual exploits solely to put themselves, as well as others, in positions of sharp indignity and distastefulness.

16. *Failure to follow any life plan.* Psychopaths make no steady effort toward reaching any long-range personal goals. One of the remarkable features of psychopaths is their consistent pattern of self-defeat. It is one of their few predictable behavioral characteristics.

By applying Cleckley's criteria, we can distinguish the sociopath from the psychotic (a person whose reasoning is disturbed by delusions and hallucinations) and from the neurotic (a person who suffers from an excess of anxiety and guilt). We can also distinguish the sociopathic personality from the "normal" personalities of career and professional criminals, who are motivated by monetary gain rather than emotional problems. The diagnostic criteria employed by Cleckley clearly illuminates the sociopath as a delinquent personality type.

Two other social scientists, William and Joan McCord, have described the sociopathic syndrome. The McCords' profile of the psychopath (or sociopath) parallels Checkley's categories and may be summarized as follows in further defining the sociopathic delinquent:[16]

1. *Psychopaths are asocial.* No rule, however important, stops them. The professional criminal, the gang criminal, and others may be asocial or antisocial, but they do not share the character structure of the true psychopathic personality. Any adequate study of the psychopath must look beyond asociality.

2. *Psychopaths are driven by uncontrolled desires.* Much of their asociality can be traced to this quest for immediate pleasure. Psychopaths often seem to know no greater pleasure than constant change. They do not seem to receive satisfaction from productive work.

3. *Psychopaths are highly impulsive.* Unlike the normal person, or even the average criminal, psychopaths' adventures often seem purposeless. Even their crimes are rarely planned. They have no stable goals.

[16]William McCord and Joan McCord, *The Psychopath* (Princeton, N.J.: Van Nostrand, 1964).

4. *Psychopaths are aggressive.* Psychopaths characteristically react to frustration with fury. Their uninhibited search for pleasure often clashes with the restrictions of their society. The conflict frequently results in aggressive action.

5. *Psychopaths feel little guilt.* Psychopaths have no conscience in the usual sense. They can commit any act with hardly a twinge of remorse. They show very little anxiety, worry, or inner conflict.

6. *Psychopaths have a warped capacity for love.* They have been characterized by the phrase "lone wolf." They seem cold and compassionless. They treat people as they do objects—as a means for their own pleasure. Either because they are incapable of forming them or because their experience has not shown them how to form them, psychopaths avoid close attachments.

The patterns of the socialized delinquent, who is a relatively well-trained type of offender, differ considerably from those of the sociopathic offender. The following commentary made by a sociopathic youth involved in a brutal gang homicide reveals the compulsive abnormal behavior of the sociopath.

> Momentarily, I started thinking about it inside; I have my mind made up I'm not going to be in no gang. Then I go on inside. Something comes up, then here all my friends coming to me. Like I said before, I'm intelligent and so forth. They be coming to me—then they talk to me about what they gonna do, like kill this guy! Like, "man, I just gotta go with you." Myself, I don't want to go, but when they start talkin' about what they gonna do, I say, "So, he isn't gonna take over my rep, I ain't gonna let him be known more than me." And I go ahead, just for selfishness.[17]

The senseless, other-directed violence of such sociopathic offenders is perpetrated for ego status—for kicks or thrills. The kicks involve a type of emotional euphoria that the sociopathic delinquent maintains "makes me feel good." He does it out of selfishness. The goals of the delinquent are self-oriented in a primary fashion with material gain as a secondary consideration. The socialized delinquent would not place himself in jeopardy for this type of senseless gang-violence offense. He uses violence as an instrument for material gain, not for an emotional charge, which serves to validate his existence.

Violence is often used in a rational way as an instrument in the delinquent activities of the socialized delinquent. The violence of a sociopathic offender, on the other hand, is characterized by the following:

1. There is no evidence of prior contact or interaction between the assailant and the victim.
2. The violent act often occurs in an unpremeditated, generally spontaneous, and impulsive manner.

[17]Lewis Yablonsky, *The Violent Gang*, rev. ed. (Baltimore: Penguin, 1971), p. 256.

3. In some cases (particularly, for example, in gang assault), there is a degree of prior buildup to the act; however, the final consequence (often homicide) is not really anticipated.
4. The offender's expressed reaction to the violent behavior is usually lacking in regret and inappropriate to the act committed.

Causal Factors in the Development
of the Sociopath Delinquent

An adequate social self develops from a consistent pattern of interaction with rational adult parents in a normative socialization process. The parent or adequate adult role model helps a youth learn social feelings of love, compassion, and sympathy. The proper adult role models necessary for adequate socialization are often absent from the social environment of underprivileged youths.

The basic ingredient, missing in the sociopathic delinquent's socialization is a loving parent or adult. Based on extensive analysis of the literature, the McCords state: "Because the rejected child does not love his parents and they do not love him, no identification takes place. Nor does the rejected child feel the loss of love—a love which he never had—when he violates moral restriction. Without love from an adult socializing agent, the psychopath remains asocial."[18]

Dr. Marshall Cherkas, an eminent psychiatrist, has over 15 years of experience as a court psychiatrist and has interviewed several hundred delinquent sociopaths. He has come to similar conclusions about the etiology of the sociopathic delinquent's personality. In the following statement he presents his viewpoint on the causal context of the sociopath's early life experience.[19]

> Children are extremely dependent upon nurturing parents for life's sustenance as well as satisfaction and avoidance of pain. In the earliest phase of life, in their first year, infants maintain a highly narcissistic position in the world. Their sense of security, comfort, reality, and orientation is focused on their own primitive needs with little awareness and reality testing of the external world. As the normal infant develops, its security and comfort is reasonably assured. There occurs a natural attachment, awareness, and interest in "the Other." As the child matures, the dependency upon "the Other," its parents, diminishes, but the strength of the self is enhanced, and the child develops an awareness that its narcissistic needs are met through a cooperative, adaptive, and mutually supportive relationship to its parents and others. In other words, the child recognizes that even though its selfish (narcissistic) needs are extremely important, they can best be served by appropriately relating to other people, especially its parents.

[18]William McCord and Joan McCord, *Origins of Crime* (New York: Columbia University Press, 1959), p. 107.

[19]Adapted from an unpublished paper, "The Sociopathic Delinquent Personality," by permission of the author, Dr. Marshall Cherkas.

This cooperative process is repeated many times in the development of the individual, and there are stages of recapitulation where dependence and narcissistic interest are heightened. There are other stages where the child's sense of social recognition and cooperativeness are greatly increased, with less emphasis upon its own narcissistic needs.

Infants whose needs are not adequately met because of the parents' own exaggerated narcissistic needs develop feelings of mistrust, insecurity, and wariness about the capacities of their provider. In order to protect itself, the child may perform many tasks to gain attention, support, and interest from the parent. The child also begins to feel that it cannot trust others, and that its needs can only be met through self-interest. The child who cannot count on its own parents begins to become egocentric and therefore sociopathic in its behavior.

Megaree and Golden carried out research into this element of causation related to the sociopath. They based their research on the reasoning that the psychopathic offender has a significantly poorer relation with his parents than does either the nondelinquent or the normal [social] delinquent. The purpose of the study was to partially test these formulations by comparing the parental attitudes of psychopathic and subcultural offenders and a nondelinquent group of comparable socioeconomic status.

Megaree and Golden hypothesize that:

1. Psychopathic delinquents' attitudes toward (a) their mothers and (b) their fathers would be significantly more negative than those of nondelinquents.

2. Psychopathic delinquents' attitudes toward (a) their mothers and (b) their fathers would be significantly more negative than those of subcultural delinquents.

3. There would be no noteworthy difference in the subcultural delinquents' and nondelinquents' attitudes toward (a) their mothers and (b) their fathers.[20]

Using various psychological inventories, they cross-compared a sample of identified sociopaths from a federal correctional institution and a matched control group of students attending a technical trade school. Both institutions were located in Tallahassee, Florida. The correctional institution's final sample of 31 was divided into two groups of "subcultural delinquents" and "psychopathic delinquents." (The subcultural delinquents would parallel our described socialized delinquents.)

The delinquent groups (both psychopathic and socialized) were contrasted with the nondelinquents with regard to parental relationships. On the basis of their research, Megaree and Golden came to the following conclusion:

... the nondelinquents expressed the most favorable attitudes toward both their parents, and the psychopathic delinquents the most negative. For these

[20]Edwin I. Megaree and Roy E. Golden, "Parental Attitudes of Psychopathic and Subcultural Delinquents," *Criminology*, vol. 10, no. 4 (February 1973), pp. 427–439. American Society of Criminology, by permission of the publisher, Sage Publications, Beverly Hills.

two groups there was little difference between the ratings for the mother and the father. The subcultural [socialized] delinquents displayed a different pattern, however; their attitude toward mother was as favorable as that of the nondelinquent group, but their attitude toward father was as negative as that of the psychopathic sample. . . .

The data . . . highlighted the important role played by the mother. While the attitude toward the father was the crucial variable separating the delinquents from the nondelinquents, it was the attitude toward the mother that differentiated the subcultural from the psychopathic delinquents. One might speculate that it is this positive relationship with the mother than permits the subcultural delinquent to appear well adjusted and capable of loyalty to his group and adherence to a code of values, albeit a socially deviant code.[21]

The notion of adequate self-emergence through constructive social interaction with others, especially parents, is grounded in the theoretical work of Charles Horton Cooley, later developed by J. L. Moreno and George H. Mead. As Mead developed the theme: "The self arises in conduct when the individual becomes a social object in experience to himself. This takes place when the individual assumes the attitude or uses the gestures which another individual would use and responds to it himself. Through socialization, the child gradually becomes a social being. The self thus has its origin in communication and in taking the role of the other."[22]

Harry Stack Sullivan saw the self as being made up of "reflected appraisals":

The child lacks equipment and experience necessary for a careful and unclouded evaluation of himself. The only guides he has are those of the significant adults or others who take care of him and treat him with compassion. The child thus experiences and appraises himself in accordance with the reactions of parents and others close to him. By facial expressions, gestures, words, and deeds, they convey to him the attitudes they hold toward him, their regard for him or lack of it. A set of positive sympathetic responses, necessary for adequate self-growth, is generally absent in the development of the youth who becomes a sociopath.[23]

In summary, therefore, the sociopathic delinquent is produced by a socialization process that does not include loving role models. Because of this lack of loving role models, the sociopathic delinquent tends to be self-involved, exploitative, and disposed toward violent outbursts. This sociopathic individual lacks social ability, or the ability to assess adequately the role expectations of others. He is characteristically unable to experience the pain or the violence he inflicts on another since he does not have the

[21]Ibid., pp. 433–437.
[22]George H. Mead, "Mind, Self and Society" (Chicago: University of Chicago Press, 1934), p. 236.
[23]Harry Stack Sullivan, "Conceptions of Modern Psychiatry" (Washington, D.C.: William Alanson White Psychiatric Foundation, 1947).

ability to identify or empathize with others. The sociopath is thus capable of committing spontaneous acts of "senseless" violence without feeling concern or guilt.

The sociopathic delinquent is a highly impulsive and explosive youth for whom the moment is a segment of time detached from all other. His actions are unplanned, guided by his whims. The sociopath is aggressive. He has learned few socialized ways of coping with frustration. He feels little if any guilt. He can commit the most appalling acts, yet view them without remorse. The sociopathic delinquent has a warped and limited capacity to love and be compassionate. His emotional relationships, when they exist, are shallow, fleeting, and designed to satisfy his own egocentric desires. Some measure of the negative personality factors found in the prototypical "sociopathic delinquent" are found in all types of delinquents.

A CLASSIC SOCIOPATH: THE CASE OF JOSE

The emergence of the sociopathic delinquent personality is a process that has not been fully explained. Yet there are patterns that recur consistently enough to enable us to identify them as probable causes of the development of the sociopathic personality. As noted earlier, one is the lack of a proper parental role model of love or compassion. By love, we mean the ability to involve oneself with another human being without egocentric designs. Most sociopaths have grown up in a predatory, exploitative, and manipulative social situation. Love and compassion are generally foreign to their lifestyle.

The evolution of the socipath may be seen in the case of a boy we shall call Jose Perez, whom I met during my five-year study of sociopathic gang youths in New York City.[24] Jose had participated in the stabbing and killing of another youth and was convicted of homicide. I had the opportunity to observe his behavior on the streets prior to the murder and to interview him several times in the state reformatory where he was incarcerated after the murder.

Jose migrated from Puerto Rico to New York City with his family when he was 8 years old. Jose's first reaction to New York City was to the cold and dirt. "It's always summer in Puerto Rico," he explained. Although he had lived in a run-down slum called La Perla in San Juan, it was heaven to him compared to the slum he now lived in on Manhattan's Upper West Side. Jose could step out of his shack on the island into sunlight and ocean breezes and the friendly greetings of his neighbors. In New York City he would leave his tenement to enter a cold world of hostile and indifferent strangers.

On the island Jose was somebody. He had an identity. Although they were poor, the Perez name meant something, and Jose sought to live up to it. His family and friends identified him as an individual; he had a position in the community, even though he was still a child. Everyone in the huddle

[24]See Yablonsky, *The Violent Gang* (New York: Macmillan, 1962), p. 136.

of poor shacks where he lived knew everyone else; they all had some concern for one another.

In New York he was shocked to discover that he was considered different. The first time he was called a "dirty spick" at school he became severely upset and angry. His response became aggressive: He retaliated. Finally he began to attack other children without provocation in anticipation of their insults.

Whites and blacks were not his only antagonists. He was often picked on by other Puerto Ricans who had lived longer in New York City. To them he was a foreigner, a "tiger."[25] He embarrassed them because he was a Puerto Rican greenhorn and had not yet become assimilated. Other Puerto Ricans, suffering from self-hatred as a result of their lowered status, took out their resentment on someone they regarded as even more inferior than they.

Jose had a good school record in Puerto Rico, but in New York he hated school and became a habitual truant. His despised identity as a "spick" was accentuated by his inability to speak English. His teacher tried to help but, overwhelmed by a large number of students with various problems, she had limited success. Her students' personal problems, combined with their language difficulties, made teaching any specific subject matter almost impossible.

The one available school guidance counselor (for some thousand students) tried to talk to Jose, but by this time Jose was considered a serious behavior problem. His hatred for school became more intense each time he played hookey. Going back to school seemed increasingly difficult, if not impossible. He spent his days at the movies when he could raise the price of a ticket by petty thievery, or he simply sat and daydreamed. He felt weak, inferior, and alone. His favorite cartoon hero was Mighty Mouse. His comment about his cartoon hero was, "You know he's a mouse—he's dressed up like Superman. He's got little pants—they're red. The shirt is yellow. You know, and then he helps out the mouse. Every time the cats try to get the mouse, Mighty Mouse comes and helps the mouse, just like Superman. He's stronger than he acts. Nothing can hurt him."

Jose alternated now between fantasy and direct acts of violence, increasingly delivered to undeserving and often unsuspecting victims. Lectures and threats to send him to a reformatory meant little to Jose. He already knew from a friend that the state reformatory was "all filled up, and they ain't going to send you there for just playing hookey." Roaming the streets led to other delinquent activities, including petty thievery and vandalism. These, plus a developed pattern of purse snatching, with greater emphasis on violence than on financial gain, helped provide the necessary background for his sentence to the reformatory.

[25]*The Marine Tiger* was one of the ships that carried many Puerto Ricans to New York early in the Puerto Rican migration. The name was shortened and applied to all newly arrived immigrants.

Yet it was not so much what happened to Jose that caused his unfeeling, asocial behavior to grow—it was what was *not* happening. In his world there was a dearth of law-abiding youths and adults from whom he could learn any social feeling toward another person. To Jose, people became things you manipulated to get what you wanted. He discovered that "being nice" was often useful, but only if it helped get what you wanted. When caught stealing, he learned that "sometimes if you hang your head down right and look pitiful, you could avoid punishment."

There were few people in Jose's world who ever considered another person's feelings or welfare, unless they expected to get something in return. Everything Jose saw was a con game. The two most successful types of behavior were manipulation and violence. When one did not work, the other would. Jose found violence and the threat of violence most effective. As his reputation for sudden, unexpected violence grew, others responded by complying with his egocentric needs.

Jose "naturally" learned to manipulate others and to use violence "properly." He never learned to feel affection for anyone, not even the other members of his family. No one ever taught him to express positive emotions or set any example by displaying human feelings. In the hostile and asocial world that surrounded him, he learned the most effective adaptation, and his sociopathic personality became more developed with each day's experience.

Jose's family was of little help to him in New York. His family's rules, language, and appearance were considered old-fashioned and inappropriate. Also, his parents and older brothers were busy battling their own enemies in the cold city. His family was generally not available to fill his needs for humanism and compassion. He sometimes dreamed with fondness about distant pleasant evenings of the past in Puerto Rico with his family. They used to go to a park near their home in the evenings. Mostly the children would play, and the adults would sit around and discuss the day's events. At these times children and adults talked easily with each other. In those days, now gone, Jose had the opportunity to discuss his personal troubles with his parents and older brothers. It was even pleasant to be criticized, since it gave Jose a secure feeling to know that someone was concerned. Not only his own parents, but relatives and other adults had taken an interest in children. One man took the boys swimming; a group of older men from a social club formed a baseball league for the younger boys. Jose belonged to a community.

All of this changed in New York. His father, an unskilled laborer, found it hard to get a job that paid a living wage. Jose's father earned a modest amount when he worked, but he was often unemployed. During these periods, quarrels and conflict developed between his parents, and his father became less and less the man of the house—the role he had clearly occupied in Puerto Rico. Beset with their own overwhelming problems, Jose's parents sometimes attacked their children, who increasingly became a burden to them.

There was no one for Jose to talk to about his feelings. His father began to drink excessively to escape from immediate realities and a sense of inadequacy he could not face. The more he drank, the more violent he became. In his senseless rages, he beat Jose's mother and often attacked Jose for no apparent reason. Senseless violence surrounded Jose and he became indifferent to his family. About his father Jose said, "I'll ask him to take me boat-riding, fishing, or someplace like that, ball game. He'll say no. He don't go no place. The only place where he goes, he goes to the bar. And from the bar, he goes home. Sleep, that's about all he do. I don't talk to my parents a lot of times. I don't hardly talk to them—there's nothing to talk about. There's nothing to discuss about. They can't help me."

Family trouble was compounded by the need for Jose's mother to take a menial job to help support the family. This removed her further from the home. Rents were exorbitant. The family was barred from moving into certain neighborhoods where Puerto Ricans were not welcome. In any case, their erratic income was insufficient for a steady monthly rental in a more stable neighborhood. The family of six continued to live in a rat- and roach-infested two-room hotel apartment. They shared kitchen facilities and an outside toilet with eight other families and paid rent of over $150 a week. Close quarters intensified the family conflict. Jose increasingly resolved his problems outside the home.

Jose became friendly with Juan, an older youth from the neighborhood who took an interest in him and attempted to help him. Juan was a leader in a social gang called the Brave. This group was well organized, participated in sports, ran dances, and belonged to the local community center. The Braves were tough, but they did not go in for "bopping" (gang wars or other violent activity). Although most members of the Braves engaged in occasional fights and petty thievery, they stayed clear of mass rumbles and participated in more socially accepted activities. Juan tried to get Jose into the Braves, but Jose was voted down because the Braves felt he was a "wise punk." He lacked the social ability to be a member.

Then Jose met a violent gang leader called Loco. As his name implies, Loco was thought to be a little crazy, and this did not displease him. His reputation for sudden violence with a knife or a zip gun made him greatly feared. As part of his usual gang-leader activity, Loco was organizing a West Side Dragons division. Jose was accepted without question and was appointed a war counselor after Loco saw him stab a younger boy on a dare.

Jose and the other Dragons enjoyed the exciting stories Loco told about Dragon gang divisions throughout Manhattan. Jose learned, and he began to make brother-gang pacts of his own. Also, as a war counselor for the West Side Dragons, he had what seemed like a good excuse to commit acts of violence every night. His sudden temper and quick use of a blade increased his reputation. With Loco he organized a brother-gang pact with another gang on the Upper West Side called the Egyptian Kings. Membership did not really give Jose a feeling of belonging or provide a comfortable way of life, but the violent gang resolved his anxieties and troubles in the same way alcohol resolves problems for the alcoholic and drugs help the drug addict: It served to destroy him further.

The Kings provided a vehicle for expressing much of the hatred, disillusionment, and aggression that existed in Jose. The group also was compatible with the uncompassionate, unfeeling, and manipulative sociopathic personality he had developed. Violence was expressed at the right opportunity, or opportunities were created. Also, the gang helped minimize feelings of guilt and anxiety about violence at the increasingly rare times such feelings existed in Jose.

Any limited concern about his feelings of worthlessness were diminished by the recognition that there were others like himself. All the Kings were "down cats." "Everyone puts you down" and "Get your kicks now—make it today" were his slogans. "Sounding on people" and "putting them down" were central King activities, and Jose became an expert.

The violent gang gave Jose a feeling of power. He was a core member and accepted the mutually supported gang fantasy that he was now "a leader." In the position of war counselor he enjoyed the gang's violence. He found it gratifying and exciting to strike out at others for whom he had no feeling. Violence was a useful instrument for him, and he was well trained for this activity. Quick, senseless violence gave him a "rep." Success, prestige, and fame were achievable through the quick, unexpected stroke of a knife.

On the night Jose went to Highbridge Park in the Bronx, the trip was just another gang fight. It had all the usual elements of gang activity—mostly talk about violence, about "what we're going to do," "getting even," "being a big shot." Afterward, Jose's comments that "they called me a dirty spick" and "we fought for territory" were rationales. All of Jose's negative social influences converged the night he plunged a bread knife into another boy's back.

ATTEMPTS TO TREAT SOCIOPATHS

Despite the large number of delinquent sociopaths in our institutions, little progress has been made in providing treatment for them. This is partly due to the fact that most experts in the field consider the sociopath to be untreatable. Hervey Cleckley notes that, in spite of the fact that psychoanalysts have reported some success in the treatment of patients regarded as psychopaths, analytic treatment of the psychopathic personality has proven a failure. He notes further that "All other methods available today have been similarly disappointing in well-defined adult cases of this disorder with which I am directly acquainted.[26] He suggests setting up facilities specifically designed to deal with problems of the psychopath and points out that our large state and federal psychiatric institutions are organized for psy-

[26]From "Psychopathic States," by Hervey M. Cleckley, from *American Handbook of Psychiatry*, Volume I., edited by Silvano Arieti. Copyright © 1959 by Basic Books, Inc. Reprinted by permission of the publisher.

chotic patients and are not well adapted to handling the psychopath. Cleckley states further, "Even if no really curative treatment should be discovered, despite organized efforts over the years in institutions specifically adapted to the problems of the psychopath, a great deal might be accomplished through careful supervision and control of destructive activities that today seem to run virtually unchecked."[27]

The National Training School for Boys attempted to evaluate the effect of an action program specifically designed for psychopathic youths in residence. The separation of psychopaths from the general population for treatment purposes was prompted by the same considerations applicable to all correctional institutions. Not only do psychopaths fail to benefit from institutional treatment programs, but their unruly behavior disrupts treatment for the rest of the population. A treatment program for psychopaths was designed with an emphasis on recreational activities providing novelty and excitement. The only therapeutic activity scheduled for the group under study was psychodrama.

Using a diagnostic instrument, it was possible to identify psychopaths within two weeks of admission to the institution. Psychopaths had a higher rate of commitment, a longer rate of stay in the security unit, a higher rate of AWOL, and a higher rate of transfer to more secure institutions. The 20 most recent psychopathic admissions were the "project group." A "contemporary control group" of 21 was set up, consisting of three recent psychopathic admissions plus all psychopaths admitted after the project began. Two other control groups were made up of psychopaths already in the institution. The subjects in the project group and the control groups were matched on the Quay Personality Classification and in race, IQ, and type of commitment. All statistical comparisons of the project youths with the control groups indicated far better adjustment of the project youths. They averaged fewer days in segregation, committed fewer assaultive offenses, provided fewer security problems, and adjusted better to institutional life.[28]

In an attempt to study the effect of the milieu therapy provided at Wiltwyck, a school for emotionally disturbed delinquent boys, McCord and McCord administered a number of personality tests and questionnaires and obtained behavioral ratings of children admitted to the school. The children were tested and then retested a year later, providing before and after measures of change. They found that milieu therapy had a decisively positive effect on the sample of psychopathic boys at Wiltwyck.

The McCords concluded that "Wiltwyck milieu therapy provided an instrument for the treatment of psychopathy. The warm, supportive environment could serve to satisfy the children's dependency needs, which had been frustrated by their families. The consistency, nonpunitiveness,

[27]Ibid., p. 586.
[28]Gilbert Ingram, Roy Grant, Herbert Quay, and Robert Levinson, "An Experimental Program for the Psychopathic Delinquent: Looking in the Correctional Wastebasket," *Journal of Research in Crime and Delinquency* 7 (January 1970): 24–30.

and social controls of the Wiltwyck staff could provide the prerequisites for the establishment of a conscience."[29]

Dr. Raymond J. Corsini reported on the successful use of psychodrama with psychopaths at San Quentin. He also described in detail a psychodrama session with Don, a young inmate of a state school for boys who had been diagnosed by a psychiatrist as a "primary psychopath, with no apparent conception of right or wrong." In explaining why psychodrama was successful in changing this boy's behavior patterns and personality, Corsini stated:

> In summary, it can be said that some people are impervious to certain kinds of symbols. There are, for example, nonreaders who just cannot comprehend written language. Some of these can be taught to read by motor procedure rather than by the ordinary visual procedures. It may well be that much the same is true with that class of people who appear deaf to reason and logic, who are labelled "psychopaths." In the treatment of such cases, actional procedures such as psychodrama do appear effective.[30]

In my book *Psychodrama*, I describe the following case of a young man I successfully treated in several psychodrama sessions. The patient had been diagnosed by the psychiatric staff at Atascadero State Hospital, California, as a psychopath.[31]

> Ralph, at eighteen, was in custody for blacking out of control and attempting to kill his father. He almost succeeded. The verbal interactions he had with various therapists in the hospital about his "past behavior" (which we learned through psychodrama was constantly on his mind) had admittedly been of limited help in reaching him. His immediate therapist had participated in several psychodrama sessions and requested that I direct a session with Ralph to help him explore some of Ralph's psychodynamics in psychodrama. Ralph's therapist was present at all of the sessions and very productively followed the leads we produced in our psychodramas into his private therapeutic verbal sessions with Ralph. In this case, psychodrama became a valuable adjunct to Ralph's individual therapy.
>
> In addition to Ralph's psychopathic potential for violence, another symptom that he manifested was a body tic. When it was active, his body would writhe in an epileptic fashion. The tic usually seemed to appear whenever he felt anger or was under pressure. According to a medical report by a doctor who had examined Ralph, there appeared to be no physiological basis for the tic. In the first psychodrama session I ran with Ralph as the protagonist, I noted that the tic was enacted and accentuated whenever there was reference to his father, or sometimes even when the word father was used.

[29]McCord and McCord, *The Psychopath*, pp. 138–165.

[30]Raymond Corsini, "Psychodrama with a Psychopath," *Group Psychotherapy* 11 (March 1958): 33–39.

[31]Lewis Yablonsky, *Psychodrama* (New York: Basic Books, 1976, and Gardner Press, 1981), pp. 146–151. Reprinted by permission of Gardner Press.

In one session, Ralph led us back to a basic and traumatic scene in his life with his father. He acted out a horrendous situation that occurred when he was eight: his father punished him by tying him up by his hands to a ceiling beam in their cellar—like meat on a hook—and then beat him with a belt.

We determined from several later sessions with Ralph, and my consultations with his therapist, that the traumatic experience of the whipping and other parental atrocities produced his tic, because the tic appeared after this particular beating and, as indicated, there did not seem to be any physiological basis for it. The tic seemed to be a way he controlled striking back at his basic antagonist, his father. In brief, Ralph had two extreme postures that emerged from his father's abuse: one was the tic that incapacitated him from the other reaction of extreme, uncontrolled violence. Other sessions revealed that his rage toward his father was often displaced onto others, especially other children at school.

The father, who had Ralph hospitalized, was obviously the arch object of Ralph's hatred. Ralph could seldom talk to his father in life. He would either manifest the incapacitating tic, run away, or, as he finally did, attempt to kill him.

After several sessions we progressed to a point of his father. In the psychodrama we had progressed to a point where he accepted a male nurse as an auxiliary ego in the role of his father. In the psychodrama scene, Ralph would alternately produce the tic or attempt to attack his "father." There was hardly any verbalization of Ralph's rage—he required an action form to express his emotions—and the time factor was in the psychodramatic "here and now" that included varied time frames.

After Ralph had physically acted out much of his rage, I finally improvised a psychodramatic vehicle that facilitated "a conversation" between Ralph and his auxiliary ego "father." I put a table between him and his "father." At the same time he talked to his father, I gave him the option and the freedom to punch a pillow that he accepted symbolically as his father. This combination of psychodrama devices enabled Ralph to structure in thought and put into words his deep venom for his father. He blurted out much of his long-repressed hatred in a lengthy diatribe. Finally, we removed the props, and after his rage was spent, he fell into his "father's" arms and began to sob, "Why couldn't you love me? I was really a good kid, Dad. Why couldn't you love me?"

In a later session, we had him play the role of his father, and he for the first time began to empathize with the early experiences in his father's life that brutalized him. Ralph's grandfather—who beat his son—was the original culprit and Ralph was indirectly receiving the fallout of his father's anger toward his father, or Ralph's grandfather. When Ralph reversed roles and returned to himself, it diminished his hostility towards his father and he, at least psychodramatically, that day forgave him.

All of the material acted out in the psychodrama sessions was more closely examined in his private sessions with his therapist. Also, I had a number of productive discussions with both Ralph and his therapist on an individual basis. This combination of therapeutic activity seemed to be most effective in helping Ralph reduce his homicidal sociopathic behavior.

In my follow-up of Ralph's case, I learned that he had made a reasonable adjustment after leaving the hospital. He stayed clear of his father because he couldn't fully handle that relationship. The positive results were that he went to work, married at 20, and, according to the reports I received, for the most part adjusted to a law-abiding life.

A central point made by explicating Ralph's extreme psychodrama experience is that the learning-in-action on his part, combined with his private sessions, was effective. Ralph could not just talk about his anger. He required a vehicle like psychodrama, which gave him the opportunity to physically and psychologically reenact the scenarios of the early parental crimes against him in their bizarre details. The total treatment he received at Atascadero, including psychodrama, may have helped him to avert the murderous tragedies that resulted from the criminally sociopathic personalities of individuals like Charles Manson and Kenneth Bianchi. Ralph was provided with some insights into his sociopathic violent nature and was able to overcome his problem sufficiently to function in a law-abiding way in our society.

SUMMARY: BASIC THEMES FOR CLASS DISCUSSION

1. Sociologists tend to focus on the sociocultural forces that produce delinquency, and psychologists concentrate on individual psychological factors. It is apparent that delinquency is a consequence of a combination of both sociological and psychological factors.
2. There are four basic personality prototypes that help to explain different patterns of delinquent behavior.
   a. *The socialized delinquent* becomes delinquent as a result of being educated into a delinquent value system. This type of delinquent is no more emotionally disturbed than youths in the general population. They tend to have criminal role models in their community whom they attempt to emulate. When they grow up they are likely to become professional criminals.
   b. *The neurotic delinquent* has emotional problems which are acted out in delinquent behavior. Their delinquent activities are compulsive efforts at reducing their inner anxiety. When they are violent offenders they often displace their violence onto people other than their parents, who are the real objects of their hostility.
   c. *The psychotic delinquent* is a youth who has a severe emotional disorder which involves a unique perspective on reality. Psychotic delinquents often hallucinate, hear voices, and are driven by their unique perception of the world. Their underlying emotional disorder may motivate them to commit acts of violence, including bizarre forms of murder.
   d. *The sociopathic delinquent* appears normal, however, he or she acts out antisocial acts that reflect an egocentrism and basic lack of compassion for others. They have a limited social conscience, and this facilitates a wide variety of delinquent behavior, including violence. The generally accepted basis for their problem is

that they either were abused by their parents or were unable to identify with them in their early socialization process. As a result, sociopathic delinquents manifest a limited concern for others. They are able to commit atrocious, violent acts on people because they, unlike most people, are unable to experience the pain they inflict on their victims.

QUESTIONS

4.1. In what ways do sociological and psychological factors converge in causing delinquency?

4.2. In what different ways does the emotional disorder factor enter into delinquent behavior?

4.3. Delineate the basic differences between the neurotic delinquent, the psychotic delinquent, and the sociopathic delinquent.

4.4. Why is it so difficult to effectively treat sociopathic delinquents?

4.5. Of what value is it to be able to categorize delinquents in terms of personality types?

4.6. Describe and discuss different types of delinquents you have personally known.

chapter 5

The Family and Delinquency

Our Earth is degenerate . . . children no longer obey their parents.

(Carved in stone 6000 years ago by an Egyptian priest)

The social configuration that exerts the most profound influence on every youth's personality is his or her family. Dislocation in a youth's family, the absence of the family's potentially positive effects, or any severe disturbance in one or both parents that results in the abuse or neglect of a child can produce devastating negative impacts, certainly including juvenile delinquency.

The fundamental meaning of the family is cogently expressed by Robert Bierstedt:

> Of all of the groups that affect the lives of individuals in society none touches them so intimately or so continuously as does the family. From the moment of birth, when young parents gaze with adoration upon their very own creation, to the moment of death, when sons and daughters are summoned to the bedside of a passing patriarch, the family exerts a constant influence. The family is the first social group we encounter in our inchoate experience, and it is the group with which, in one form or another, we shall have the most enduring relationship. Every one of us, with statistically small exceptions, grows up in a family and every one of us, too, with perhaps a few more exceptions, will be a member of a family for the larger part of his life.
>
> The family, almost without question, is the most important of any of the groups that human experience offers. Other groups we join for longer or shorter periods

of time, for the satisfaction of this interest or that. The family, on the contrary, is with us always. Or rather more precisely, we are with it, an identifiable member of some family and an essential unit in its organization. It is the family, in addition, that gives us our principal identity and even our very name, which is the label of this identity, in the larger society of which we are a part.[1]

The family is therefore an important determinant of whether or not a child will become delinquent. The family, as the basic agent of socialization, determines a child's socioeconomic class, and its structure and process is vital in the personality formation of the individual. All of these factors—socialization, class, and dynamics—impinge on the development of either a law-abiding or a delinquent child.

Despite its importance, the decision of which family to be born into is one that the individual will never be able to make. The family into which an individual is born is obviously a condition over which he has no control. In this sense, his destiny has, significantly, already been determined.

This event has determined the social class he will initially, at least, move in, along with the values, advantages, and disadvantages of the class. His class membership will most probably control his economic position, which in turn will select his neighborhood, his friends, his school, the church he will attend, as well as the kind and quality of other community agencies and resources that will be available.

His family's economic resources will also be related to his physical development and the efficiency of biological functioning in terms of dietary standards and access to quality medical care.

His birthright will also set some limits on his intelligence, will probably provide some basic emotional makeup, and will give him a physical appearance that may work to his advantage or disadvantage in a culture where a certain "look" is considered superior.

A child has no control over the actual structure of the family: whether one, two, or no parents are available, and whether or not grandparents are present. The child's family composition of siblings is also not within his or her control.

A child also has limited, if any, control over the family's emotional problems, which may stem from the family's system of relationships. Some children become family scapegoats and are blamed for the family system's problems. A child may become the symptomatic carrier of a family pathology that stems not from the youth's personal problems but from the family's structural problems. Therapists who are appropriately sensitive to a family's dynamics are well aware of the concept of the "identified patient" in a troubled family. This concept posits that, in a pathological family situation, one member is identified as the "sick" one, despite the fact that the overall family is disturbed. Many delinquents are the "identified pa-

[1]Robert Bierstedt, *The Social Order* (New York: McGraw-Hill, 1957) p. 56. Copyright 1957 by McGraw-Hill Book Company. Used with permission of McGraw-Hill Book Company.

tients" in this family situation. For example, emotionally disturbed, substance-abusing parents may blame a child for their problem. They say things like "if it wasn't for you we would all get along, and I would quit drinking. You're the problem in our family." This type of scapegoating, identifying the child as the "sick one," is a projection often used by emotionally disturbed parents to project their problem onto their children. This parental behavior often leads to the child's delinquent behavior.

THE SOCIALIZATION PROCESS

It is important to understand a child's total family system and socialization process to understand his or her delinquent behavior. Socialization refers to the process by which one acquires social skills and learns to participate effectively in society.

This lifelong process may be divided into two stages. The first stage occurs between conception and approximately 5 years of age, when the primary socializing agent is the family. During this time the child must learn and master a number of activities, if his or her later development is to proceed without difficulty. He must master basic motor control and then advance to more complicated skills. He must learn breath control, if language and communication are to develop. The child must develop and understand basic concepts about himself, other people, and the world around him. He must learn that things have names and that events occur together. He must understand a cognitive, aesthetic, and moral value system. Later in the process, he must learn to relate to other people and to the world on a personal basis.

The second stage of the socialization process occurs from the time the child engages in group interaction until his or her death. Throughout an individual's lifetime he or she is constantly forming, evaluating, and refining social skills for effective group interaction.

Gerald Patterson and Thomas Dishion comment on this issue in their article on family impacts on delinquency:[2]

> From a social interactional perspective, delinquent behavior is thought of as the outcome of an extended process characterized by two general stages. The first stage usually begins during preadolescence; it is initiated as a result of a breakdown in family management procedures. This disruption produces both an increase in antisocial child behavior and an impairment in the child's development of social and academic skills. Given that the preadolescent child is exposed to this process, he is placed at risk for rejection by normal peers and eventual academic failure. In the second stage, during adolescence, continued disruptions in the parents' monitoring practices and poor social skills place him further at risk for contact with a deviant peer group. The association with deviant

---

[2]Gerald Patterson and Thomas J. Dishion, "Contributions of Families and Peers to Delinquency" in *Criminology*, 23, 1 (1985): 63–64.

peers, poor parental monitoring of the child, and academic failure during adolescence all contribute directly to the likelihood he will engage in high rates of
delinquent activities.

ERIKSON ON SOCIALIZATION AND DEVELOPMENTAL STAGES

An analysis of Erik Erikson's theories on developmental phases reveals
where family structure and dynamics break down to produce delinquency.
Here we will focus more precisely on the behavioral problems that a child
has to solve, with or without the help of the family, if a healthy adult
personality is to be achieved, using the terms of Erik Erikson's conception
of the socialization process.[3]

Erikson states that there are eight developmental stages in the life of
every individual, which, if properly handled, will produce trust instead of
mistrust, autonomy instead of shame and doubt, initiative instead of guilt,
industry instead of inferiority, identity instead of role diffusion, intimacy
instead of isolation, generativity instead of stagnation, and ego integrity
instead of despair. All of these resolutions are necessary to avoid delinquent
outcomes.

The sense of trust develops in the first year of life and is simply built
upon rewarding experiences and satisfaction of basic needs in the family.
The baby's feelings of hunger are anticipated or closely followed by food;
feelings of uneasiness or anxiety will soon be assuaged by the comfort and
warmth of being held closely and securely. Not only will the baby learn to
trust others, he will learn to trust himself when the reach for an object is
eventually followed by its grasp. He will learn to trust the world when
objects that disappear, like his mother's face, consistently and invariably
reappear. This sense of trust in others, in oneself, and in the world may well
be the most important element in a healthy personality that is not delinquency-prone. Most delinquents are distrustful of adults and authority figures.

According to Erikson, the "sense of autonomy" primarily starts developing when the child is 12 to 15 months old. For the next couple of
years, he will be trying to assert that he has a mind and a will of his own. If
all goes well, he will get the feeling that he is an independent and separate
human being who nevertheless can still depend on the help of his parents
and others in certain situations. This stage is decisive for the proper balance
between love and hate, giving and receiving, and expressing and controlling his feelings. If the child is successful, he will be able to maintain proper
self-control without any loss of self-esteem. If unsuccessful, he will have
doubts about himself and others and feelings of shyness and shame. Donald
R. Peterson and Wesley Becker, speaking from a more classical psychoanalytic framework, tend to support Erikson's concepts when they state that the
four basic childhood needs up to this point are: (1) the security and backing

[3]Erik H. Erikson, *Childhood and Society*, 2d ed. (New York: Norton, 1963), pp. 247–274.

of two present parents; (2) parental love and understanding; (3) an optimum period of gratification for infantile sexual desires; and (4) opportunities to express hostilities, antagonisms, and aggressiveness, so that the child can learn what these feelings are like and how to deal with them. Peterson and Becker list three fears that children in this age group are subject to: (1) fear of being deserted; (2) fear of not being loved; and (3) fear of being mutilated.[4]

A "sense of initiative" is developed, according to Erikson, in the fourth and fifth years. This is a period of experimentation and imagination, or play and fantasy, when the child wants to find out what it can "do." With the arrival of "conscience," the child wants to know the limits of how far he can go without being inhibited by "pangs of guilt." The superego, the censor, says Erikson, must allow the young boy or girl the freedom to "move." A "self-imposed" denial of this freedom often results in a rigid and constricted personality accompanied by resentment, bitterness, and a vindictive attitude against the world. If this occurs, a child would be more prone to be delinquent.

The "sense of industry" begins at around the sixth year and extends over the next five or six years. The slow acquisition of skills and knowledge go on during this period. A child learns fair play and cooperation and the "rules" for becoming a social creature in the larger society. The positive outcome is a sense of duty and personal accomplishment, as opposed to feelings of inadequacy and inferiority. This would relate the adolescent's involvement in a meaningful occupation. Delinquents notoriously resist hard work in a relevant work situation.

A "sense of identity" begins roughly with the onset of adolescence, a period of physiological changes and rapid physical growth. The central question to be answered during this period is, "Who am I?" The adolescent is trying to find out who he is, whether he is a child or an adult, whether he is capable of becoming a husband and father, or wife and mother, how he will make a living, and whether he will be a success in life or a failure. Hopefully, the child will develop an ego identity and an occupational identity that will provide hope and confidence in himself and the future. Some adolescents, according to Erikson, can't seem to "get hold of themselves" or "find themselves"; they don't seem to know who they are or what their place in life really is, and are thus more disposed toward delinquent behavior.

Erikson postulates that a "sense of intimacy" can come only after a sense of personal identity has been established. The individual must have sufficient mastery over mind and body and sufficient ego strength to take the risks involved in personal relationships, close friendships, sexual intimacy, and love. The avoidance of such relationships and experiences due to the fear of ego loss may result in excessive introspection, self-absorption,

---

[4]Donald R. Peterson and Wesley C. Becker, "Family Interaction in Delinquency," in *Juvenile Delinquency: Research and Theory*, ed. Herbert C. Quay (Princeton, N.J.: Van Nostrand, 1965), pp. 36–99.

and a deep sense of isolation and loneliness. Again, this sense of alienation can make a youth more vulnerable to delinquency.

The "sense of generativity" is an adult development: It is the "parental sense" and is characterized by an interest in producing and caring for one's own children, an interest in producing and guiding the next generation.

In summary, it can be inferred from Erikson's stages of development that breakdowns within the frame of the family at any point could lead to delinquent behavior. The effective socialization of the child by the family through these various developmental stages is, therefore, the best insulation from delinquency. Many delinquents come from criminogenic families, which foster their delinquency rather than their proper socialization.

CRIMINOGENIC FAMILIES AND DELINQUENCY

Hiram and Ruth Grogan discuss the criminogenic family's influence on delinquency in a penetrating article.[5] They stress that in families disorganized by unresolved and recurring internal conflicts, the process of socialization, of teaching the child by precept and example, is difficult due to the multitude of attitudes, values, and behavioral patterns. The family that is beset with chronic conflict and tensions labors under a handicap at meeting its socialization reponsibilities effectively. The consequence is a pathological family, or, as the Grogans call it, a "criminogenic family." This type of family produces an inadequately socialized child, one who is ill prepared to face and accept values, standards, and codes of conduct that are socially acceptable. In this regard the Grogans conclude that family disruption lowers the child's resistance to becoming delinquent. A criminogenic family is a family in which significant conflict and tension disrupt the atmosphere conducive to the wholesome personality development of the child by interfering with his socialization patterns of learning. As an inadequately socialized child grows older, the Grogans assert, he may turn away from his family and seek comfort in a clique, or gang, where he eagerly accepts all the antisocial or delinquent values of the group.

The criminogenic family is a phenomenon common to many urban areas. In an article in the *Los Angeles Times*, Joy Horowitz traces the pattern as described by a perceptive police officer. The officer, Tom Corey, on the basis of his extensive analysis of the family and delinquency, proposes a radical and controversial cure—removing children from the criminogenic family.

A Family Tree of Criminal Life
When the case file landed on his desk last fall, Tom Corey figured it was a routine matter. He began to read the arresting officer's report: Two children had been caught shoplifting two plastic toy motorcycles and an orange toy car worth a total of $3.97 from the J. C. Penney store in Pasadena.

[5]Hiram Grogan and Ruth Grogan, "The Criminogenic Family; Does Chronic Tension Trigger Delinquency?" *Crime and Delinquency* 14 (January 1971): 220–225.

It would be up to Corey, a teacher-turned-cop assigned to the Pasadena Police Department's Youth Services Division, to dispose of the case. He carefully reread the report. It indicated that the children—cousins, 8 and 9—had no prior police record and needed "no further counseling."

Corey decided otherwise. On the last page of the report, the name of the children's family—Wilson—popped out at him like a bad omen. "Oh my God," he remembers thinking when he realized the fathers of both children were serving time in prison. "Where will it stop? There's got to be something better for these kids."

Like other local police and probation officers, Corey, an eight-year police veteran, was more than familiar with the activities of the Wilson (a fictitious name) clan—a large, poor family spanning three generations and living adjacent to an area known for its low-income housing and high incidence of drug dealing and other crimes. Police have dubbed the area "The Pit"; the Wilsons call it the ghetto.

Because of the extensive criminal involvement of the Wilson children's grandparents, uncles, aunts, and parents, who have been in and out of jail or prison for offenses including robbery, burglary, assault, larceny and prostitution, the 35-year old police officer was determined to "break the cycle of crime" in the family.

He and his superiors agreed it was time to goad the legal system, to test the court's commitment to preventing crime in the name of protecting children. In this case, Corey reasoned, it could best be done by taking the children from the parents and placing them in foster homes. If not, he believed, "there's a 99% chance these children are going to become criminals."

So Corey initiated court proceedings to remove the third generation of Wilsons from their home, an action that may wind up setting a startling legal precedent, court observers say.

His decision was not based on the home's physical condition ("I've seen a lot worse") or on battering or on lack of adult supervision—all standard criteria for court intervention. "My judgment," Corey explains, "was based on the parents being criminal role models."

In his report, Corey offered a three-generation family tree of the Wilsons—based strictly on their criminal records. "It's the kind of thing we see a lot in police work," he says, rocking back in his desk chair. "The parents are criminals. Their kids are criminals. And the kids' kids are just starting to become criminals. It's a criminal family."[6]

In a precedent-setting decision on April 28, 1981, the Juvenile Court ruled on the "Wilson" case described here. Bill Hazlett reported the decision as follows:

County Takes Custody of Four Children
Juvenile Court authorities Tuesday removed four children from their Pasadena home because their parents and relatives have a history of 400 arrests in the last 10 years.

[6]Joy Horowitz, "A Family Tree of Criminal Life," *Los Angeles Times*, March 25, 1981. Copyright 1981, *Los Angeles Times*. Reprinted by permission.

"The parents—and even the grandparents—have been in and out of jail like a revolving door," Deputy County Counsel Sterling Honea said.

A temporary order making the children, ages 10, 9, 8 and 1½ years, wards of the Juvenile Court was issued by Superior Court Judge Elwood Lui on recommendation of Honea and Pasadena Juvenile Officer Tom Corey.

The four children have three mothers, who are sisters, and share the home with various members of their family group. Two of the fathers of the children are in prison; the whereabouts of the third father is not known.

The children and their mothers are members of a family group that police and juvenile officers call the "Wilsons," though that is not the real name because an effort is being made to protect the youngsters' identities.

The family group lives in a small section of Pasadena called "The Pit."

There is an unusually high rate of drug-related crime in The Pit. But the Wilsons' criminal history is not limited to such offenses. It also includes petty theft, prostitution and other problems.

"These minors," Corey said in one court document, spent their formative years in a family environment in which it was the norm for family members to be arrested and incarcerated. . . .

"Nearly all the adult members of their immediate family have double-digit arrest figures and even their great-aunt was arrested twice this year." Honea said one box of criminal records brought to his office during the investigation of the Wilson clan "weighs about 40 pounds."

Corey, who began investigating the family after two of the children's cousins were caught shoplifting last September, said his goal was to "give these kids a chance to be around some other adults who don't lead a life of crime."[7]

In another research study on the issue of criminogenic families, Raymond R. Crowe of the Department of Psychiatry at the University of Iowa College of Medicine carried out a study to determine whether or not any genetic basis for antisocial behavior emerged from the family.[8] Crowe studied two groups of adoptees—one that included 46 children of convicted female felons (90 percent) and misdemeanants (10 percent) and a control group made up of 46 adoptees specially chosen to parallel the other group demographically.

The offspring of mothers with criminal records had more marks against them socially than did the controls. Seven of then were arrested as adults—all seven had been convicted at least once—some with multiple arrests and convictions. Three were considered felons, and six had spent time incarcerated either as an adult or as a juvenile—one as both. Only one of the control group had been arrested and convicted. In the experimental sample, eight subjects had been referred by the courts, and seven of the eight were treated for antisocial behavior. Although the controls had been treated for antisocial behavior, none had been remanded by the courts, and none had arrest records. This clearly revealed that more of the subjects had

[7]Bill Hazlett, "County Takes Custody of Four Children," *Los Angeles Times*, April 29, 1981. Copyright, 1981, *Los Angeles Times*. Reprinted by permission.
[8]Raymond R. Crowe, Research Report, *Human Behavior* (May, 1975).

antisocial personalities than the controls. Crowe asserts that "the unique finding in the present study is that the unfavorable [family] environment influences were associated with the development of antisocial personality in the subject but not in the controls."[9]

Most children socialized by criminogenic families develop illegal values and become delinquent. There are, however, a small number of youths who overcome many family difficulties and rise above delinquent behavior. Norman Garmezy and Vernon Devine studies these exceptions from the rule. For want of a better term, the labeled these children "the invulnerables." According to Garmezy and Devine: "These are children who have come through. They are the ones who have not just survived but have flourished, despite a variety of genetic, psychological and sociological disadvantages."[10]

Garmezy and Devine offer as an example Todd, who is 11 and lives with an alcoholic father, who sometimes works as a handyman but is usually unemployed. Todd's mother died when he was 3, and he lives in an environment of poverty and unrelieved grimness. By all the usual laws of child development, Todd should be well on his way to juvenile delinquency. Garmezy and Devine noted that Todd is instead cheerful, bright, does well in school, is a natural leader, and is much loved by his friends—as well as by school officials. And there are other Todds, we are learning, everywhere—not just in the ghettos and inner cities, but in suburbia as well.

Garmezy and Devine spent about two years discussing issues, parameters, and theories on invulnerables and another year locating a group of invulnerables to study. They did this by going into the Minneapolis schools and telling principals and social workers that they were looking for children who "when you learned about their background gave you much concern; yet now, when you see them in the halls, you look at them with pleasure."[11] It was an unusual request for school officials, but it was successful. The researchers concluded that out of nearly 400 candidates, about 10 percent turned out to be invulnerables.

The full analysis of what makes these individuals invulnerable has yet to be made, but the researchers suspect that the presence of a role model somewhere provided a positive image for the youngsters. They finally note: "Invulnerables try to find solutions, rather than blame; they test reality, rather than retreat before it; and they learn to make something out of very little. They bounce back. They have a real recovery ability. We don't know why yet, but they do."[12]

FAMILY ISSUES

Shelters, psychiatric hospitals, and various other treatment facilities sometimes serve as surrogate families or as havens from families that produce

[9]Ibid., p. 87.
[10]*Human Behavior* (April 1976), p. 87.
[11]Ibid., p. 88.
[12]Ibid., p. 89.

delinquent children. Most children, however, do stay with their families, and their delinquent behavior is promoted by the roles, rules, and norms in their home.

Rolf Loeber and Magda Stouthhamer-Loeber carried out an extensive analysis of family issues that cause delinquency.[13] They concluded that:

> Analyses of longitudinal data show that socialization variables, such as lack of parental supervision, parental rejection, and parent-child involvement, are among the most powerful predictors of juvenile conduct problems and delinquency. Medium-strength predictors include background variables such as parents' marital relations and parental criminality. Weaker predictors are lack of parental discipline, parental health, and parental absence. The effect of these factors seems to be about the same for boys and for girls. Analyses of concurrent studies comparing delinquents with nondelinquents, and aggressive children with nonaggressive children, largely parallel these findings. Data from concurrent normal samples, however, show less importance for the child's rejection of the parent and the parent's rejection of the child. A small proportion of families produces a disproportionate number of delinquents. The presence of one child with delinquency, aggression, or covert conduct problems increases the probability that other children in the family will exhibit those behaviors. Deficiencies in parenting skills are associated with the seriousness of the child's delinquency. Treatment studies demonstrate that systematic changes in parenting behaviors can lessen the frequency of a child's conduct problems and that of siblings and, to a lesser extent, reduce involvement in delinquent activities.

Since it is through the socialization process that the individual acquires normative prescriptions for behavior, one might anticipate that everyone socialized in a society would conform strictly to the rules. We know, however, that it does not work out that way. All of us deviate from some of the rules. Some deviate to such a degree that society takes action against them. We do not have universal conformity for some or all of the following reasons:

1. There are differences among individuals, accounted for by heredity. People differ from birth.
2. There are differences in rules, supported by socializing agencies. The family may emphasize different sets of rules than do the school or peer groups.
3. There are differences in values, attitudes, and life experiences within each category of socializing agents. Family, school, peer group—each has its own values, born of its own experience.

In the course of his socialization, the child learns his *roles*: what is expected of him by his parents and other adults, by his siblings and other

---

[13]Rolf Loeber and Magda Stouthhamer-Loeber, "Family Factors as Correlates of Juvenile Conduct Problems and Delinquency," in *Crime and Justice, An Annual Review of Research*, vol. 7 (Chicago: The University of Chicago Press, 1986).

peers, and by his school and other institutions of the society. He also learns the *norms* or rules of behavior defined by the socializing agencies and comes to accept their standards of behavior. Knowing his roles helps him to determine what he is supposed to do in a given situation. Knowing the norms helps him select a right way of doing it. When the norms of the three major socializing agencies reinforce each other, his choice of appropriate behavior is relatively simple. It is when they are in conflict that complications arise.

Recent research reveals the changing functions of the family and the increasing influence of other socializing agencies, particularly the peer group. In the predominantly rural society of a century ago, the individual was introduced to virtually all his adult roles in the family. The farm family was a producing as well as a consuming unit. From childhood on, the individual was exposed to the occupational roles that he would be required to perform as an adult. The community was small enough so that by the time he was a youth he knew most of the people in it, their roles (what he could expect them to do), and the behavior expected of him toward everyone else. He was, in effect, socialized in the gestalt of a family and a coherent community.

As we approach the twenty-first century in America, we note that the family is largely a consuming unit and not a cohesive producing unit. Many of its functions have undergone major modifications. Parents simply do not have the necessary training and are not sufficiently familiar with the social and career requirements confronting their children to teach them what they need to know. The child is therefore trained for the performance of occupational and community roles outside the family. The family exerts an influence on the child's acceptance and success in school roles, however. It is in his family that he is motivated to attend school and is prepared for acceptance of school regulations. A child brought up in a middle-class family goes to school better prepared for success than one brought up in a lower-class family. The value placed on education by his parents is a decided advantage to him.

The family also influences the friendship associations of the child, first by selecting the neighborhood he grows up in and then by influencing the choice of friends invited to the home. Failure in school roles frequently leads to delinquency. Failure in friendship roles may be even more damaging. The child may never learn to relate compassionately to others and may become a sociopath. Success in family, school, and friendship roles during childhood may be expected to result in success in family, occupational, and community roles in adulthood.

As the United States changed from a predominantly rural, agricultural society to one that is overwhelmingly urban and industrial, the family became far less effective as a socializing agency. It could still prepare the child for family roles, but it lacked the capability to prepare him for occupational and community roles. The incomplete family, characterized by the absence of one parent, has an additional handicap. A one-parent family, whether as a result of divorce, desertion, or death, usually consists of a mother and children living together. The mother often finds it difficult to provide sustenance and guidance, and the absence of a father leaves the male children without an adult male model. Children born out of wedlock and brought up by their mothers are in much the same position. Whether or not being a member of such a household causes serious emotional disturbances in the child, it adversely affects his socialization.

In summary, therefore, the family may contribute to delinquency in the following ways:

1. **In choice of neighborhood.** Voluntarily or involuntarily, parents pick the location of the home. Locating the home in a high-delinquency area makes it more likely that the child's early associations will be with children adhering to a delinquent subculture.
2. **In failing to influence the friendship patterns of the child.** Maintaining an interest in his associations and rewarding the choice of nondelinquent playmates is believed to influence the child in a nondelinquent direction.
3. **In failing to prepare the child adequately for a successful school experience.**
4. **In failing to influence the child in favor of nondelinquent clubs, play groups, and other interest groups.**

The way in which the child will relate to other socializing agencies is influenced by his family but not totally determined by it. Where the family fails, therefore, other socializing agencies take on increasing importance.

An important aspect of the socialization process and deterrent to delinquency is the quality and process of interaction between parent and child. Lawrence Rosen makes the following observation:[14]

> One important and continuing debate on the relationship between family and delinquency has been the "structure" versus "function" controversy. The structural perspective typically focuses on such factors as parental absence, family size, and birth order, whereas the functional or "quality of family life" position argues for the significance of parent-child interaction, amount and type of discipline, degree of marital happiness.

Robert G. Andry carried out an in-depth study of delinquency and various parental influences.[15] Basically, Andry explored the quality of parental affection and love as it related to youths who become delinquent and nondelinquent. His findings may be summarized as follows:

> Delinquents and nondelinquents were radically differentiated in their feelings as to the adequacy of the affective roles of the parents.
>
> 1. Delinquents tended to feel that their mother loved them most, whereas

[14]Lawrence Rosen, "Family and Delinquency: Structure or Function?" *Criminology*, 23 (3) (1985).

[15]Robert G. Andry, *Delinquency and Parental Pathology* (London: Staples Publications, 1971).

nondelinquents tended to feel loved by both parents—thus the differentiating feature here was the inadequate love given by the father among delinquents.

2. This last statement was reinforced in that delinquents tended to feel that their father should love them more, whereas nondelinquents felt that neither parent should love them more.

3. Delinquent boys tended to feel that their parents (but especially their fathers) were embarrassed to show open affection for them, whereas nondelinquents did not feel this.

4. There was a tendency for delinquents, in contrast to nondelinquents, to feel embarrassment at showing open love for their parents—implying a causal link between parents' inability to show open love and that of the child.

5. There was a tendency for delinquents to feel parental hostility towards them (in terms of nagging), whereas nondelinquents did not feel this.

6. There was a tendency for delinquents to feel that they had their mothers' ways rather than their fathers' ways, whereas nondelinquents tended to feel they had both parents' ways or their fathers' ways—thus indicating delinquents tend less to identify with their fathers than do nondelinquents.

Andry's results indicate that delinquent boys receive less strong and open love from their parents than do nondelinquents, and it is the father's affective role that is (consistently) less satisfactory than the mother's among delinquents, in contrast to a sense of satisfaction with both parents among nondelinquents.

Andry's last point places doubt on the theory that "maternal deprivation" is necessarily the primary determinant of delinquency, at least as far as delinquents who do not come from broken homes are concerned. One can conclude from this study that delinquent boys (suffering neither from mental defects or diseases nor from broken homes) tend to perceive greater defects in their fathers' roles than in their mothers' roles, whereas nondelinquents tend to perceive the roles of both parents as being adequate. Thus, according to Andry's research, the prime differentiating feature between delinquents and nondelinquents, as far as parental role playing is concerned, is the delinquents' negative perception of their fathers' role.[16]

In another study on "affective ties to parents," Eric Linden and James C. Hackler concluded that delinquents may have the same beliefs as do conventional adolescents, but contact with deviant peers might make delinquency involvement more likely among those who have only weak ties to their families.[17]

A study by F. Ivan Nye and his associates of 605 cases involved combinations of parent-child relationships that ranged from mutual acceptance to mutual rejection.[18] Between these extremes were gradations ranging from either the father's or mother's accepting or rejecting a child, or the

[16]Robert G. Andry, "Faulty Paternal and Maternal-Child Relationships, Affection and Delinquency," *British Journal of Delinquency* 1 (1950): 34–48.

[17]Eric Linden and James C. Hackler, "Affective Ties and Delinquency," *Pacific Sociological Review* 16 (January 1973): 27–46.

[18]F. Ivan Nye, *Family Relationships and Delinquent Behavior* (New York: Wiley, 1958).

reverse, to the child's accepting or rejecting either or both of the parents. The children were rank ordered in terms of "delinquent" behavior, from "most delinquent" to "least delinquent." Of the 292 cases of mother-child mutual acceptance, only 14 percent of the children were in the "most delinquent" group, whereas 86 percent were in the "least delinquent" group. Of the 313 cases of mutual mother-child rejection, 48 percent of the children were in the "most delinquent" group, and 52 percent were in the "least delinquent" group. Between these extremes, the percentages of delinquency varied in proportion to the degrees of either acceptance or rejection.

The combinations of father-child acceptance and rejection had similar effects on the children. The data indicated that rejection of the child by the parents closely related to delinquent behavior; acceptance between parent and child was correlated with less chance of juvenile delinquency.

A significant relationship was found between delinquent behavior and the attitudes of boys and girls toward their parents. More emphasis is placed on the rejection of parents by children than the rejection of children by their parents.

Sheldon and Eleanor T. Glueck, in comparing an officially delinquent and a nondelinquent group, made an extensive analysis of the quality of interaction and relationship between boys and their parents as possible factors in delinquency.[19] They studied affectional relations, emotional ties, acceptability for emulation, parental concern for the welfare of their children, and the boys' estimate of parents' concern. They did not attempt to measure or estimate how much of the hostility was the cause or product of delinquency, but their data indicated that there was considerably more hostility and less affection between parents and boys in the delinquency sample than in the nondelinquency group.

More of the boys in the delinquent than in the nondelinquent group regarded their father as unacceptable of emulation. Parents of delinquents seemed to be less concerned about the welfare of their children than were parents of nondelinquents. When the boys sensed this lack of parental concern for their future, it only added to the difficulty.

Although the Glueck's research was carried out in the late 1940s, their findings are still relevant. My own clinical work with several hundred delinquents from 1983–1987 validates most of their observations.

William and Joan McCord, in reexamining the cases of the Cambridge-Sommerville Youth Study, stressed various phases of the relation of the family structure to crime.[20] Their data cover a variety of aspects, but some of the main findings deal with the effects of parents' personality traits as role models; the relative effects of loving, overprotective, and nonliving relations, interpreted of both father and mother; parental discipline (con-

---

[19]Sheldon Glueck and Eleanor T. Glueck, *Unravelling Juvenile Delinquency* (New York: Commonwealth Fund, 1950), chap. 11.

[20]William McCord and Joan McCord, *Origins of Crime* (New York: Columbia University Press, 1959), chap. 5.

sistent, erratically love-oriented, erratically harsh, lax); and the son's position in the family. The McCords found that maternal love is the most important socializing force. Paternal warmth is generally effective as a substitute for maternal love, but if behavior of the parents is deviant, rejection is likely to cause delinquency. In a parallel study Harriett Wilson found that nonloving, inferior parents were a social handicap and contributed to delinquency.[21] Wilson determined in a study of fifty-six families that juvenile delinquency correlated significantly with "social handicaps" and parental criminal record.

In *Cultural Factors in Delinquency*, Gibbens and Ahrenfeldt[22] note that indirect learning plays an important part in the origins of delinquency. Conflict between parents who are demonstrating opposing ideas or a parental pattern of "Don't do as I do; do as I say" may indirectly teach lessons that are completely opposite of what is intended. This form of indirect learning by observing negative parental role models was recognized as an important factor in causing delinquency.

In a study by James F. Alexander, twenty-two "normal" and twenty "delinquent" families were videotape-recorded in a discussion of the "resolution-of-differences" tasks.[23] The interaction data generally supported the hypotheses generated by systems theory and prior small-group research that abnormal families would express high rates of system disintegrating while normal families would express more system-intergrating or supportive communications.

As has been noted in considerable research, disturbed family relations play a very important role in the causes of delinquency. In an investigation of high-delinquency areas in New York City, Craig and Glick found three factors to be related to increased likelihood of delinquency in boys: (1) careless or inadequate supervision by the mother or mother substitute; (2) erratic or overstrict discipline; and (3) lack of cohesiveness of the family unit.[24]

Bandura and Walters came up with somewhat similar findings in a study of 26 delinquent boys and an equal number of nondelinquents from the same social class and IQ range.[25] Both the boys and their parents were interviewed and rated for a variety of psychological variables. The parents of the delinquents were found to be more rejecting and less affectionate than those of the nondelinquents. It is Bandura and Walters' opinion that the boys' relations with their fathers constitute a more important factor in

[21]Harriett Wilson, "Juvenile Delinquency, Parental Criminality and Social Handicap," *British Journal of Criminology* 24 (July 1975): 241–250.

[22]T. C. N. Gibbens and R. H. Ahrenfeldt, eds., *Cultural Factors in Delinquency* (London: Tavistock, 1966), p. 95.

[23]James F. Alexander, "Defensive and Supportive Communication in Normal and Deviant Families," *Journal of Consulting and Clinical Psychology* 14 (April 1973): 223–231.

[24]M. M. Craig and S. J. Glick, *Crime and Delinquency* (New York: New York City Youth Board, 1963), pp. 231–232.

[25]Albert Bandura and R. H. Walters, *Adolescent Aggression* (New York: Ronald, 1959), pp. 153–155.

development than their relationships with their mothers. They noted that the fathers of delinquent boys were prone to ridicule them when they made a mistake and that there was an atmosphere of ill will between father and son. Somewhat similarly, it has been found that the number of criminal convictions was higher among boys whose fathers were rated "cruel" or "neglecting" than among those rated "passive" or "warm." The likelihood of delinquency was also increased if the child was disciplined in an erratic fashion or left undisciplined. A higher number of convictions was also found when the mother was rated as "nonloving" than when she was rated as loving and used consistent discipline.

DISCIPLINE AND DELINQUENCY

Discipline is a significant factor that affects delinquency. Sheldon and Eleanor Glueck found that in most cases of delinquents where the disciplinary attitudes and practices of the fathers of the boys were known, 4.1 percent of the fathers were found to use sound discipline; 26.7 percent fair; and 69.3 percent unsound. The Gluecks defined these discipline practice categories as follows:[26]

> *Sound*—consistent and firm control of the boy by the parent, but not so strict as to arouse fear and antagonism;
>
> *Fair*—control which is indefinite: sometimes strict, sometimes lax;
>
> *Unsound*—extremely lax or extremely rigid control by the parents, which on the one hand gives the boy unrestrained freedom of action and on the other restricts him to the point of rebellion.

Of the delinquent cases in which the disciplinary practices of the mothers were known, 2.5 percent were considered sound, 27.4 percent fair, and 70.1 percent unsound. Discipline practice is therefore a crucial interaction pattern in the background of later delinquent behavior patterns. Discipline is needed if controls are to be adequately internalized into a youth's personality. Situations and appropriate methods of dealing with them must occur regularly enough to let the child develop concepts of conduct and be able to distinguish suitable and unsuitable responses.

Discipline is generally characterized by three variables: consistency, intensity, and quality. *Consistency* pertains to the predictability of the discipline and takes into account the circumstances in which the offense occurred. Discipline that is consistent, rational, and based on explanation is more likely to produce adequate internal controls. *Intensity* is related to the severity and rationality of the punishment. Discipline based on explanation and understanding between parents and child rather than strict, punitive punishment is more likely to produce internalized control from the child. *Quality* is related to the type of punishment, such as physical punishment,

---

[26]Glueck and Glueck, *Unravelling Juvenile Delinquency*.

love withdrawal, nagging, or explanation. Nagging and love withdrawal will produce control by the child based on a fear of losing parental affection, not on an internalized set of standards of behavior. According to Peterson and Becker, "If one endorses the common assumption that capacities for internal control are complexly but closely related to previously imposed external restraints, then parental discipline assumes focal significance as a factor in delinquency."[27]

McCord and McCord concluded in their studies that consistency was more important than the kind of discipline. They reported that consistent love-oriented or punitive discipline by both parents significantly reduced delinquency. Nye, based on his research, reported that 49 percent of both male and female delinquents who reported that their mothers "very often" failed to carry out threats of punishment were found in the "most delinquent" category. This compared to 30 percent of the boys and 22 percent of the girls who reported that their mother "never failed" to implement her threats. The overall relationship is significant for girls but not boys. Nye did show that of the children in his study who considered their father's discipline "always fair," only 30 percent of the boys and 20 percent of the girls fell into his "most delinquent" group. On the other hand, 55 percent of the boys and 44 percent of the girls who felt their father was "unfair" fell into the "most delinquent" group.

Discipline is a highly significant issue not only in the socialization of a child but in the process of "individuating" and discovering a sense of self. When discipline related to family rules are too hard or too soft, deviance is often a resulting behavioral pattern.

FATHERS AND SONS: THE DISCIPLINE FACTOR AND DELINQUENCY

The following analysis, derived in part from my book *Fathers and Sons*, is basically about fathers and sons during the emotional period of the son's adolescent life struggle. The father's disciplinary approach during this period can significantly influence his son's behavior.[28]

The adolescent period is a highly significant emotional time between fathers and sons. A son wants the security of knowing that his father is there for him, yet he has begun to strike out on his own and define his self in his own terms. The normal son begins to strive to become an individual, and he distances himself from his parents and relates more closely to his peers. He also begins to develop a normal rebellious posture.

Many fathers, during this critical phase of their sons' individuation and normal rebellion, behave unwisely and exacerbate a naturally uncomfortable situation into a dreadful one. The father may rhetorically ask: "Where did my acquiescent little boy go? And who is this arrogant mon-

[27]Peterson and Becker, "Family Interaction in Delinquency."
[28]Lewis Yablonsky, *Fathers and Sons* (New York: Simon and Schuster, 1982).

ster?" The son is also at this time beginning to eclipse his father's physical strength.

This phase of a father-son relationship is fraught with seemingly insurmountable problems. If the normal problems that emerge in this phase are not handled properly, the relationship can become a lifelong disaster for both father and son, and can lead to severe delinquent behavior in the son.

This socialization period is characterized by the son's developing sense of his own identity, not only in relation to his father, but toward the world in general. He normally begins to act in a rebellious manner. He becomes belligerent about his ideas and opinions, even when he knows he's wrong. He wants to do everything his way. He begins to feel his own ego power and to begin separating from his father and family, seeking to become a person in his own right. If these normal expressions of rebellion, which reflect his search for identity, are squelched by a severely repressive father, the son's behavior can become recalcitrantly delinquent.

One of the son's major adversaries, or natural enemies, in this phase is his father, because the father is usually the primary carrier of societal norms. A father and son can become engaged in a psychodramatic conflict. In psychodrama terms, the father becomes the son's experimental auxiliary ego or, in some ways, his "punching bag." The auxiliary ego in the form of the father represents all others in his life onto whom the son projects negative and positive emotions. With a compassionate, loving father, the son can try out a variety of outrageous attitudes and behaviors without being hurt by his loving auxiliary-ego father, who absorbs some but not all of his son's punches.

The common sport between father and son of playful physical aggression in a boxing or wrestling match has all the ingredients of the larger loving conflict that centers around social and emotional issues. In a physical encounter, the father is usually bigger, stronger, and a more experienced fighter, and in nonphysical areas he is also more experienced. A loving, understanding father lets his son throw a lot of practice punches to test his strength and ability, both physically and intellectually, without returning a knockout punch. He interprets and explains societal norms, rather than severely squelching his son's natural curiosity.

In contrast, psychopathic-macho fathers may hit their sons with knockout punches because they are stupidly blind to the realities of the jousting. They are unaware that their sons are testing their social and emotional strength, and that they need a safe person—the father—as an auxiliary ego to help socialize them. A son who feels safe with his father can role-test new views and perceptions of the world on him, and in this way learn viable norms of behavior.

In the son's real world of teachers, peers, and school, if he acts experimentally in a rebellious way, there may be harsh reactions of condemnation or ridicule that can have a lasting negative impact on his life. In contrast with a loving father as an auxiliary ego, the young man can test out and experiment with his behavior and attitudes, and an understanding auxiliary-ego father will provide valuable suggestions and nonpunitive feedback to his son.

Immature, macho, or emotionally weak fathers will react as peers and outsiders, often in defense of their own weak egos. With this type of father the adolescent son will receive the same harsh punitive response he is apt to get in the larger community. The effects include inhibiting him, breaking his creative spirit, and not providing him with the needed opportunity to role-test new behavior. This can produce delinquent acting out.

The disciplinary process becomes one of the paramount areas of father-son interaction during this phase. An important dimension of this process is that a son often compares his father's disciplinary response to his behavior with his friends' fathers' approaches. Two fathers may respond entirely differently to the same behavior, based on their own social contexts and values.

An interesting case in point is related to smoking marijuana and the different types of disciplinary response by three fathers from whom I acquired in-depth interviews: One disciplinary extreme involved what I will call a *macho-father*, an alcoholic hypocrite who battered his son unmercifully because his son smoked marijuana. In fact, he kept his son on restriction "under house arrest" for several weeks. During this period he beat the son sporadically. The man used the situation and his son as an outlet for the enormous hostility and rage he had toward life in general, perhaps rationalizing his own drinking problem. The father and son had ferocious debates about the relative destructive effects of marijuana versus alcohol. The father's extreme discpline had little positive effect on the son in dissuading him from marijuana use. In fact, the boy, partly to assuage his increased pain and violent feelings toward his father, graduated to the use of cocaine.

A second father's disciplinary approach was at the opposite extreme. This case involved what I have termed a *buddy-type father*. This father smoked dope regularly with his 15-year-old son. His indulgence of his son, who was totally undisciplined, took a bizarre direction, which manifested itself at a party at their home. After dinner, the father, a successful businessman, came out of his study enraged. He called his son down from his room and raved at him. "You rotten bastard. Don't I give you enough money for dope? I know you've been into my stash—there's a whole lid of grass missing from my desk!" The son shrugged his shoulders and went back to his room. Everyone at the party within earshot of this abysmal father-son situation was embarrassed and tried to act as if it hadn't happened.

A third type of father, one I call a *caring-rational father*, used an approach that was caring but firm. Neither the brutal, macho disciplinarian father nor the indulgent father were effective. A middle-of-the-road approach involving an intelligent discussion between the *caring-rational father* and his son proved to be effective. This third, more rational father set firm

limits, without battering the son or indulging him. This firm but understanding approach was the most effective disciplinary approach.

There are two basic contexts in which father-son discipline occurs.
One is when the father disciplines his son on a family rule. The second
involves a situation where the son has violated a law of the larger society.
The father is not the main disciplinarian, and in many cases may have little
power over his son's fate. A father in this type of situation can sometimes
rescue his son from the pain of the full impact of the larger society's laws,
often to the detriment of his son. This is most likely to happen in the case of
an upper-middle-class youth.

The following case, reported to me by an affluent 40-year-old lawyer,
presents some of the main conflicts and issues that affect a father's response
to society's discipline of his son.

> Bill was sixteen at the time, doing lots of drugs and getting into trouble. I was
> constantly rescuing him from being expelled from school for truancy, bad
> grades—you name it. The final blow came when he was arrested in a depart-
> ment store for shoplifting. He already had a few minor drug arrests on his
> record, so they brought him to the Beverly Hills police station. On the other
> charges, before his trial in the juvenile court, he had been released into my
> custody instead of being taken downtown to the juvenile jail.
>
> The scene at the police station was the same terrible one I had been through
> several times. But this time I decided I was not going to rescue him. I'll never
> forget that painful experience. After a conversation with my son during which he
> told me he would never do it again, the juvenile police officer present asked me
> if I wanted to take him home. I said, "No, do whatever you do with a case like
> this."
>
> My son looked at me in disbelief. "Dad, you mean you're going to let them take
> me to the juvenile jail?" I explained to him as best I could that it would be easier
> for me to take him home, but for his own sake, this time he had to face the real
> consequences of his behavior. He didn't make it easy on me. I told him I wasn't
> doing anything to him; he had done it to himself.
>
> He really didn't believe it was happening, nor did I. I vividly remember him
> looking back at me as they took him away. It was a nightmare for me. The next
> thing I remember I was outside of the police station sitting on the front lawn
> crying like a baby. People, including cops, came by, asking me if I was okay. I
> waved them away and kept on sobbing uncontrollably. My crying must have
> gone on for at least half an hour.
>
> The sight of a 40-year-old attorney, in a business suit, sitting on the lawn in front
> of a police station crying must have been something to see. I've reviewed that
> experience 50 times since in my mind.
>
> What was I crying about? Was it because I was now the father of a juvenile
> delinquent? Or was it because of my compassion for my son? Was I crying for
> him or me? I've since decided it was for both of us.

The family dynamics that produced the son's delinquency were quite
complex. However, focusing on this disciplinary event in reviewing the

incident with this man, who was a brilliant criminal attorney, we both concluded that the following analysis was accurate. This father had logically decided that it was time for his son to confront in full force the realities and consequences of his accelerating delinquent behavior. If the father rescued his son once again from society's discipline he would be doing him a gross disservice. The act of rescue would be more to assuage the father's feelings than to help his son. It was painful for the father to let his son go to jail. When he cried he did so out of pity for himself as a father who had admittedly failed and was experiencing the pain of being the father of a delinquent son; he was also crying out of compassion for the pain his son would experience while being in jail.

The experience turned out to be a success story. The son's encounter with the inevitable disciplinary endpoint of his escalating delinquency brought him up short, opened up communication with his father, and resulted in a positive change of behavior in the son.

Effective fathering often involves biting the bullet and experiencing the personal emotional pain necessary for both father and son to correct dysfunctional behavior. If such behavior is continued, it can be self-destructive to the father's life as well. When a good father states the old platitude before administering discipline, "This is going to hurt me more than it's going to hurt you," he is often stating a fundamental truth.

A nice-guy approach involving a rescue act for his son may take the father off the hook, but it may be bad for the son. Fathers who do this are not fathering effectively and have avoided their responsibilities to the detriment of their sons' proper socialization. To protect a child from the disciplinary consequences of his behavior is to bring him up in an unreal world.

The case I just described had a positive outcome. In a follow-up interview I had with the father and Bill about a year later, the son at one point told his father: "Dad, when you let me go off with that cop to jail I truly hated you, and I felt abandoned. But I now understand you did what you had to do. Being locked up in that dump downtown for three days with those really tough kids was an experience I've never forgotten. It made me think about my life and where I was heading. I decided, never again. I'm glad you did what you did and I thank you." Too many other parents, especially middle-class parents, rescue their children from disciplinary process and in this way reinforce their child's delinquent behavior.

FAMILY STRUCTURE, BROKEN HOMES, AND JUVENILE DELINQUENCY

Broken homes, a child's family position, and family size have been the subjects of considerable research in the field of crime and delinquency. With the enormous increase in divorce—in 1986 one in every two marriages ended in divorce—separations, and working mothers, children are increasingly being entrusted to single parents, day care centers, neighbors, and the television set. One estimate is that 34 percent of mothers with preschool-age children are now working. Child-rearing patterns have thus undergone drastic changes. Interviews with working mothers reveal that the biggest problems they face are:

Finding good care for their infants

Dealing with worry and guilt feelings

Lack of emotional support from relatives, friends, and husbands

Physical and mental exhaustion caused by trying to do two full-time jobs at once.

Over 10 million preschool-age children have working mothers, and only one-sixth of these children can be accommodated in licensed preschools. Many welfare-supported women with too many children in too few rooms have taken in neighbors' children to supplement their income. The result is more overcrowding, less supervision, and less effective socialization of children.

All these forces have resulted in a growing number of "latchkey" children—children who come home to empty houses, where they are unsupervised while they await the return of their parents. The result is increasing runaways, teenage suicides, juvenile teenage parenthood, and delinquency.

A study by Eisenberg of welfare recipients in New York City found that three-quarters of the children did not have a father figure living in the home.[29] These welfare families showed significantly higher rates of juvenile delinquency in a cross-sectional sample of families, both at the beginning of the study and five years later. The effect was more pronounced for long-term than for short-term welfare families. It appears that such high rates are not so much a result of the welfare status itself as absentee parents, emotional illness, poor child-rearing practices, and other handicaps in these one-parent families.

The study cited earlier by Ivan Nye found that proportionately more state training school boys (48.1 percent) came from broken homes than did the "most delinquent" boys in the high schools (23.6 percent). In the high school group (both boys and girls), fewer of the "most delinquent" lived with their original parents than did the "least delinquent," more came from broken homes (mother only, father only, adopted, and other), and more came from unhappy homes. Except for the institutionalized cases, according to Nye, "unhappiness in a home was more significantly related to delinquency than a structurally broken home."[30]

How are children affected when they do not have maternal care? British psychiatrist John Bowlby stressed the importance of the maternal

---

[29]J.G. Eisenberg, "The Welfare Children," in *Research in Community and Mental Health* (Greenwich, Conn.: J.A.I. Publisher, 1979).

[30]Nye, *Family Relationships and Delinquent Behavior*, p. 48.

relationship, particularly for the younger child. He commented about maternal care: "It is this complex, rich, and rewarding relationship with the mother in the early years, varied in countless ways by relations with the father and the siblings, that child psychiatrists and many others now believe to underly the development of character and of mental health.[31]

Bowlby asserts that considerable damage is done to the child by a mother's absence, the amount of damage varying with the age of the child when the absence occurs, the length of the absence, and the quality of the substitute care that is provided. Bowlby related this maternal deprivation to delinquency. In a 1946 study of a group of delinquents, he found significantly more maternal deprivation among the delinquents than among a control group from a child guidance center. He concluded that "on the basis of this varied evidence it appears that there is a very strong case indeed for believing that prolonged separation of a child from his mother (or mother-substitute) during the first five years of life stands foremost among the causes of delinquent character development and persistent misbehavior."

A more recent study by Roland J. Chilton and Gerald E. Markle emphasizes the continuing effects of family disruption on the problem of delinquency.[32] They summarized their findings as follows:

> Employing seriousness of offense as a measure of delinquency, we re-examine the relationship between delinquency referral and family disruption. Information from Juvenile and County Courts of Florida for the first four months of 1969 provided us with uniform delinquency data for 8, 944 children. We compare the family situations of 5,376 of these children with the situations of children in the U.S. population in 1968. The analysis suggests (1) that children charged with delinquency live in disrupted families substantially more often than children in the general population, (2) that children referred for more serious delinquency are more likely to come from incomplete families than juveniles charged with minor offenses, and (3) that family income is a more important factor for understanding the relationship between delinquency referral and family situation than age, sex, or urban-rural residence, but that it may not be more important than race.

In a conclusion on these issues, Chilton and Markle stated based on their analysis of family disruptions:

> Our study provides added empirical support for the conclusions of earlier investigators who have suggested that proportionately more children who come into contact with police agencies and with juvenile courts on delinquency charges live in disrupted families than do children in the general population. In addition,

---

[31]John Bowlby, *Maternal Care and Mental Health* (Geneva: World Health Organization, 1951), p. 11.

[32]Roland J. Chilton and Gerald E. Markle, "Family Disruption, Delinquent Conduct and the Effect of Subclassification," *American Sociological Review* 27 (February 1972): 93–99.

the study suggests that children charged with more serious misconduct more often come from incomplete families than children charged with less serious delinquency.[33]

Most research into family influences on delinquency are derived from studies of boys. There is evidence, however, that similar forces influence female delinquency. Ashley Weeks suggested that the differential impact of the broken home by sex disappeared when one controlled for type of offense.[34] Most girls are arrested for incorrigibility, running away, and sex offenses, while most boys are arrested for vandalism, theft, and assault. (Weeks also concluded that a broken family due to the death of a parent was less consequential than divorce.)

Another interesting study, dealing exclusively with girls, was carried out by K. M. Koller.[35] Koller explored the question of parental loss, deprivation, and delinquency by examining early adverse experiences related to female delinquency in particular and to behavior disturbances in general.

Out of a group of 160 girls at a training school, 121 were chosen at random. The girls were between the ages of 16 and 17 and were designated as belonging to the "unskilled, partly skilled occupations." The girls were committed to the training school for a number of reasons: 44 percent were reported as being exposed to moral danger, 39 percent were uncontrollable, and 12 percent were admitted because of stealing, drugs, and pregnancy. Another group of 101 unmarried girls was chosen randomly from the general population. They were of similar socioeconomic status and age as the delinquent girls.

The following summary of Koller's findings is of significance in understanding both male and female delinquency as related to family impacts. Of the "delinquent" subjects, 61.5 percent experienced parental loss. Most common was the absence of the father or of both parents. Eighty percent of the delinquent subjects who experienced parental deprivation came from broken homes. The delinquent girls came from large families with younger-than-average parents. The intermediate female children were most likely to be affected. It is apparent from these conclusions that the absence of a parental figure can have severe effects on a juvenile of either sex, and result in delinquency.

In another study of the relationship of female delinquency to broken homes, Susan K. Datesman and Frank R. Scarpitti came to some interesting conclusions.[36] In their study of 1,103 adjudicated delinquents, they found

[33]Ibid., p. 98.

[34]Ashley Weeks, "Male and Female Broken Home Rates," *American Sociological Review* 5 (1941): 601–609.

[35]K. M. Koller, "Parental Deprivation, Family Background, and Female Deliquency," *British Journal of Psychiatry* 118 (March 1971): 319–327.

[36]Susan K. Datesman and Frank R. Scarpitti, "Female Delinquency and Broken Homes," *Criminology* 13 (May 1975): 33–56.

that when type of offense was controlled, a higher proportion of broken homes among female delinquents resulted in a greater involvement in "morals" offenses. They further determined that black males arrested for property and person offenses were more likely to come from broken homes than black females. They generally concluded that there appeared to be no unique relationship between broken homes and female delinquency, except for family-related offenses.

It may also be concluded from the variety of research cited that it is not the absence of a parent per se that is associated with delinquency, but rather the kind of relationship that exists between children and the remaining parent. A warm, stable single parent has a much better chance of raising a nondelinquent child than do two parents who are in conflict. Nevertheless, there is very powerful evidence of a direct causal nexus between broken homes and delinquency. The major findings of these well-controlled studies show that the direction of the differences is the same in all comparisons. Broken homes are one and one-half to two times more frequent among delinquents than among nondelinquents.

FAMILY SIZE AND ORDINAL POSITION IN THE FAMILY

The ordinal position that a child occupies in a family has a great effect on his eventual personality and the possibility of his being delinquent. The following assertions are based on a variety of research findings. The first child is born to inexperienced parents and is sometimes called the "trial baby." The child lives the first years of his life as an only child and relates entirely to his parents. He relates easily to adults and is likely to incorporate adult values more rapidly than are later children.

As the size of a family grows, a child is subjected to a number of different relationships: the relationship between the parents, each parent's relationship to the children, the children's relationship to the parents, the relationship among the children, and a particular child's relationship with his siblings. By increasing the number of family members, the number of interpersonal relations is increased. Thus each child's world is different from the world of his siblings. This helps explain the unique personalities that develop in a family and why one child may become delinquent while other members of the family are law-abiding.

The first child, who is more apt to enter the family at a time of greater financial stress, has only five possible interpersonal relationships—between parents, each parent to child, and child to each parent. I. J. Gordon points out that the first child tends to be anxiety-prone, will give up in the face of difficulty, and handles feelings through withdrawal.[37]

The second child arrives into a ready-made family with six interpersonal relations—between parents, each parent to child, child to each parent, and child to older sibling. He can approach his sibling as a peer and

[37]Gordon, *Human Development*, p. 43.

model. The second child tends to be more peer-oriented and more sociable. He seeks more physical affection from his parents and will try to get their attention by approved or unapproved means.

Martin M. Chemers has noted that later-born children are raised in a more complex social environment.[38] The last-born child, for instance, has parents who are by now experienced in child-raising. He has two or more older siblings who function in the capacity of peers and models for imitation and identification. He is more socially oriented and responsive than his siblings, feels secure and adequate in his world, and shows strong desires to establish his own identity.

Lees and Newson studied the differences among delinquents, that might be caused by sibling position and found that intermediaries—children with younger and older siblings—were significantly overrepresented in the delinquent populations studies.[39] The Gluecks in their research found that 60 percent of the delinquents studied were intermediate children, while only 47.8 percent of their nondelinquent control group were. Ivan Nye found that both the youngest siblings and the intermediaries were overrepresented in the "very delinquent" group.

These conclusions tend to explain the overrepresentation of the middle children in delinquency populations. Middle children seem to have the greatest need for attention and affection and are the very ones who are less apt to get it. The parents are apt to devote "realistically" most of their parental time to the youngest child because of his physical and emotional immaturity, while the older sib may claim some "right" by virtue of his age for special attention and consideration.

Nye has speculated that intermediaries get "squeezed out" of the family into gangs because the parents give their attention to younger and older siblings. Although this tendency may exist in some families, one can find many cases of conforming intermediaries in families with both older and younger delinquent siblings.

Researchers have also found some relationship between delinquency and family size. The studies of both Nye and the Gluecks have indicated that delinquents are more apt to come from large families. It is quite possible that parental controls and the familization process are "spread too thin" in large families. A. J. Reiss found that a greater proportion of delinquents from large families had poor superego controls.[40] Again, however, the significant variable is not family size per se, but other pressures characteristic of many large families: poverty and poor educational, economic, and social opportunities.

[38]Martin M. Chemers, "Relationship between Birth Order and Leadership Style," *Journal of Social Psychology* 80 (1970): 243–244.

[39]J. P. Lees and L. J. Newson, "Family or Sibship Position and Some Aspects of Juvenile Delinquency," *British Journal of Delinquency* 5 (1954): 46–65.

[40]A. J. Reiss, "Social Correlates of Psychological Types of Delinquency," *American Sociological Review* 17 (1952): 710–780.

INTERNAL FAMILY DYNAMICS

A considerable amount of research indicates that internal family dynamics are more closely related to social deviance in general and delinquency in particular than are structural elements of the family. It is probably not surprising that gross physical and emotional abuse and outright rejection are closely related to delinquent conduct. It has, nevertheless, been somewhat difficult to assess this area because of the understandable legal and social attitudes regarding the sanctity and privacy of the home. Public behavior is visible and to some extent controllable, but what goes on behind the closed doors of homes is largely invisible and beyond control.

One family variable of considerable importance is the "quality" of marriage existing in the home. The Gluecks found that 31.2 percent of their delinquents came from homes with poor marital relationships, compared with 14.9 percent of the nondelinquent population. In addition, they found that strong family cohesiveness characterized 61.8 percent of the nondelinquent homes but was found in only 16 percent of the delinquent homes. Nye found that 46 percent of the boys and 49 percent of the girls from "unhappy" homes were in his "most delinquent" group, compared with 23 percent of the boys and 22 percent of the girls who reported being from "completely happy" homes.

Lester Jaffe found a correlation between disagreement within the family and a high score on a delinquency-proneness scale.[41] Based on specific case histories and the general results of comprehensive studies by other researchers, the Grogans, in their study of criminogenic families, concluded that excessive conflict and tension in a family interfere with the personality development of a child, with accompanying disruption of his social development.[42] These factors often cause such children to seek social values in a peer group rather than the family environment. The Grogans further concluded that, in a significant number of cases, this seems to be a major contributory factor to the occurrence of criminal or delinquent behavior. All these studies clearly relate delinquency to family variables such as family disagreement and tension.

Lack of affection and rejection also occupy an important causal role in the findings of the Gluecks, Andry, Nye, Slocum and Stone, and McCord and McCord. In another study, Kirson Weinberg says about the parents of delinquents: "Indifference or hostility hindered their children from acquiring positive attitudes towards authority."[43]

In some cases, especially for the violent delinquent, the family influ-

---

[41]Lester D. Jaffe, "Delinquency Proneness and Family Anomie," *Journal of Criminal Law, Criminology and Police Science* 54 (1963): 146–154.

[42]Grogan and Grogan, "Criminogenic Family."

[43]S. Kirson Weinberg, "Sociological Processes and Factors in Juvenile Delinquency," in *Juvenile Delinquency*, ed. Joseph S. Roucek (New York: Philosophical Library, 1958), pp. 126–127.

ence on the child's behavior is not complex. There are situations where the most dreadful act by a child contains a high level of rationality—in the context of family provocations. The following case from a book by Dr. Muriel Gardiner is a classic, and even though the child's behavior is homicidal, it has a degree of rationality.[44]

> "Get that cat out of here, you good-for-nothing son of a bitch," exploded Harry, obviously pleased to have someone on whom to vent his anger.
>
> "I won't let her bother you; I'll keep her in my room," pleaded Tom.
>
> "The hell you will!" cried his uncle, seizing the kitten. And, before Tom's unbelieving eyes, he wrung her neck.
>
> Tom, in a flood of tears, carried the warm little body into his room. He tried in vain to revive it. At last, still weeping, Tom lay down on his bed, stroking and caressing the only thing he had ever loved. . . .
>
> "What's all this mumbo-jumbo?" Harry cried angrily, looking at the patch of earth and the little homemade cross.
>
> "Please, Uncle Harry," implored Tom in terror, "please don't do anything. I just made a little grave for my cat, that's all."
>
> With one great kick, Harry splintered the cross, then stamped on the soft earth of the grave. Turning, he slapped Tom's face with the back of his hand, and strode into the house.
>
> Tom went into the furnace room. He picked up one of his uncle's guns, and, pausing only to make sure it was loaded, went upstairs to where Harry, Bertha, and Catherine were sitting at the breakfast table. Tom raised the gun, and carefully shot his uncle, then his aunt, then Catherine.

The studies of Bandura and Walthers are also relevant to this theme.[45] When the compared a group of aggressive delinquents and their families with a group of nondelinquents and their families, they found that a higher proportion of the parents of the aggressive boys had denied them an opportunity to express their feelings of dependency; rejection, defined in terms of punishment of the boys' striving for gratification of dependency needs, was significantly higher for boys in the delinquent group. It was also concluded that boys whose dependency needs had not been met were less apt to internalize parental standards and values.

If one can assume that parental values generally support conventional behavior and that affectionate parent-child relationships promote such internalization, then affectionate parent-child relationships can serve to insulate the child against delinquency. The opposite, however, can also no doubt be assumed. I recall the case of a 15-year-old delinquent boy in juvenile hall talking to his father on visiting day. The father put his arm around the boy when they met, and both father and son continued to relate

---

[44]Muriel Gardiner, *The Deadly Innocents* (New York: Basic Books, 1976), p. 108.
[45]Bandura and Walthers, *Adolescent Aggression*.

to each other in a very affectionate and friendly manner. The entire conversation was nevertheless restricted to the father's relating his latest physical altercations to the boy. He told his son how he had assaulted a neighbor when the latter had requested that he move his car because it was partially blocking the driveway. The boy's eyes glowed as his father related his macho adventures in great detail. It is of interest that the boy was in juvenile hall for gang activity related to an assault he had committed on a boy who was then in critical condition in the hospital.

On another visiting day I witnessed an incident that concerned a 15-year-old girl incarcerated for "promiscuity." The father greeted his daughter with a "French kiss" that, if portrayed in a film, would be X-rated. He obviously had sexual feelings for his daughter that were probably unconscious and never acted out. However, from the girl's point of view, it appeared that the sexual stimulation of her father was reciprocated on a host of neighborhood boys, and this was why she was in custody.

In Shaw's interesting study of jackrollers, he stated that some neighborhoods encourage crime: "Stealing in the neighborhood was a common practice among children and approved by the parents."[46] Walter Miller has also expressed the opinion that the parents of many lower-class children express values that are conducive to delinquency.[47] To the extent that this view is representative, then, even affectionate parent-child relationships can sometimes result in the internalization of delinquent values if the parent encourages this behavior. Thus a double message on deviance is often given the child.

Sykes and Matza assert: "There is a strong likelihood that the family of the delinquent will agree with respectable society that delinquency is wrong, even though the family may be engaged in a variety of illegal activities."[48]

It may be that certain families tolerate or even encourage the commission of certain offenses but not others. There is also no doubt that many parents covertly encourage their children to commit criminal acts. I am particularly thinking of drug offenses. Parents who depend on drugs, whether they get them illegally or are able to get them legally (as with alcohol), are setting an example that many children no doubt follow. The classic case is the portrait of a parent with a martini in his hand bitterly admonishing his child about the abuse of drugs.

A number of psychiatrists have concentrated their attention on the tendency of some families to encourage delinquency in their children. Adelaide Johnson believes that middle-class parents foster delinquency in their children by projecting their own problems onto the children, suggesting

---

[46]C. R. Shaw, *The Jack-Roller* (Chicago, University of Chicago Press, 1930), p. 54.

[47]Walter B. Miller, "Lower Class Culture as a Generating Milieu of Gang Delinquency," *Journal of Social Issues* 14, 3 (1958): 5–19.

[48]Gresham M. Sykes and David Matza, "Techniques of Neutralization: Theory of Delinquency," *American Sociological Review* 22 (1957): 665.

that the resulting delinquent behavior satisfies unconscious needs of the parents.[49] Ruth S. Eissler also holds this view that the child is the victim of family pathology.[50] David Abrahamsen essentially believes that all delinquents are emotionally disturbed and are produced by tensions and conflicts within the family.[51] Nathan Ackerman holds the view that disturbed individuals almost always come from disturbed families:

> Parents displace onto their children anxieties and hostile urges which belong to their disturbed relations with their own parents and with wider society. Being preoccupied with their own needs, they do not make adequate emotional room for their children's needs. They react to the children's needs as if exorbitant and menacing. They do not love fully or freely. What they give to their children means to them that much less for themselves. Out of a sense of guilt they try to pacify their children, overindulge them inappropriately in material things, and accord them disproportionate power within the home. Out of their own insecurity, doubt, and impotence, parents find themselves governed by their own children. The absence of confidence and natural pleasure in parenthood is expressed in attitudes of rejection, cruelty, overindulgence, anxious overprotection, inconsistent and inappropriate discipline. . . . Precisely because control patterns are weak, erratic and undependable, there is an exaggerated concern with issues of control and discipline. There is a failure to understand that matters of control and discipline cannot be mediated apart from the related issues of basic security, satisfaction, and unity . . . the instability of the family favors implementation of such pathological defenses against anxiety as substitution of aggression for anxiety, scapegoating, magic doing and undoing, projection, isolation, and the tendency to externalize conflict, i.e., to act out. Episodically, these families may turn "delinquent."[52]

Ackerman, in this appraisal, summarizes many of the family dynamics that correlate well with the production of delinquency.

A special case that illustrates many of the structural and dynamic aspects of the family that we have found to be associated with delinquency is seen in some transplanted Mexican-American families. In Mexico, the man takes great pride in being the head of the family, in being the provider and protector of his family, while his wife takes care of the home. The concept of *machismo* or *macho* (pride, manliness, masculinity) is a crucial one in family dynamics and male personal identity. The husband's ability to maintain his macho, as head and chief provider of the family, preserves the paternalistic Mexican family. When the family moves north of the border,

[49]Adelaide M. Johnson, "Sanctions for Super Ego Lacunae of Adolescents," in *Searchlights on Delinquency*, ed. K. R. Eissler et al. (New York: International Universities Press, 1949), pp. 225–246.

[50]Ruth S. Eissler, "Scapegoats of Society," in *Searchlights on Delinquency*, ed. K. R. Eissler et al. (New York: International Universities Press, 1949), pp. 288–305.

[51]David Abrahamsen, *The Psychology of Crime* (New York: Columbia University Press, 1960).

[52]Nathan W. Ackerman, *The Psychodynamics of Family Life: Diagnosis and Treatment of Family Relationships* (New York: Basic Books, 1958), pp. 117–118. Copyright 1958 by Nathan W. Ackerman, Basic Books, Inc., Publishers, New York.

however, it is not unusual for the family and the children to suffer in the new socioeconomic environment.

A "man" is one who takes care of his family, and one who takes care of his family works at a job in which he can have some pride and which pays him sufficient income to meet his family's needs. The sad plight of many fathers unemployed in the United States, however, involves a situation where the man of the house frequently does not have the kind of skills or the educational requirements demanded by a technical, specialized economy. His inability to compete is rapidly translated into inability to support his family, which entails loss of self-respect and of his role as "man" of the house. The family must nevertheless survive and consequently may end up on public assistance, a situation the man may find humiliating. The problem may be exacerbated when his wife, of necessity, seeks and finds employment. This accelerates the corrosion of paternalistic traditions. Marital discord, desertion, and divorce frequently follow. When the man is still physically in the house, he is apt to try to regain his machismo through essentially dysfunctional techniques such as drinking, fighting, and bragging about past exploits. This condition often negatively affects the son and too often leads to delinquency.

FAMILY VIOLENCE, CHILD ABUSE, AND DELINQUENCY

In an article titled "The Family as a Cradle of Violence," Suzanne K. Steinmetz and Murray A. Straus state:[53]

> It would be hard to find a group or institution in American society in which violence is more of an everyday occurrence than it is within the family. Family members physically abuse each other far more often than do nonrelated individuals. Starting with slaps and going on to torture and murder, the family provides a prime setting for every degree of physical violence. So universal is the phenomenon that it is probable that some form of violence will occur in almost every family.

> The most universal type of physical violence is corporal punishment by parents. Studies in England and the United States show that between 84 and 97 percent of all parents use physical punishment at some point in their child's life. Moreover, such use of physical force to maintain parental authority is not confined to early childhood. Data on students in three different regions of the United States show that half of the parents sampled either used or threatened their high school seniors with physical punishment.

> Of course, physical punishment differs significantly from other violence. But it is violence nonetheless. Despite its good intentions, it has some of the same consequences as other forms of violence. Research show that parents who use physical punishment to control the aggressiveness of their children probably

[53]Abridged and adapted from "General Introduction: Social Systems in the Study of Introduction to Family Violence," in *Violence in the Family* by Suzanne K. Steinmetz and Murray A. Straus. Copyright © 1974 by Harper & Row, Publishers, Inc. Reprinted by permission of Harper & Row, Publishers, Inc.

increase rather than decrease their child's aggressive tendencies. Violence begets violence, however peaceful and altruistic the motivation. . . .

A survey conducted for the National Commission on the Cause and Prevention of Violence deals with what violence people would approve. The data showed that one out of four men and one out of six women approve of slapping a wife under certain conditions. As for a wife slapping a husband, 26 percent of the men and 19 percent of the women approve.

Richard Gelles of the University of New Hampshire, who carried out a series of in-depth case studies of a sample of 80 families, found that about 56 percent of the couples used physical force on each other at some time.

According to statistics collated by the National Center on Child Abuse, over one million cases of child abuse were reported in 1986. Based on various studies and my own observations in my work in hospitals and juvenile institutions, it is apparent that most delinquent, emotionally disturbed, or schizophrenic teenagers have been subjected to abusive treatment from the time of birth. Often an adolescent's admission to an institution is occasioned by some bizarre violent retaliatory act the abused teenager perpetrated against his or her parents after many years of being physically abused.

Research reveals that abusive parents are often subject to more severe and frequent life stresses and crises than are nonabusive parents. Prior to the onset of violent behaviors, abusive parents often experience a series of critical events that place an enormous strain on the family, both physically and emotionally. When the stress becomes too great, a child can become the victim of an abusive attack by a parent. Marital difficulties are a primary source of conflict in abusive families. Marital frustrations are often displaced onto an abused child.

The problem is perpetuated among juvenile delinquents through unwanted pregnancies and youthful parenthood. A disproportionately high number of abused children come from homes where the parents are divorced or separated and/or the child is being raised by an unsupported mother.

The abusive family is typically a closed family system characterized by rigidity, inflexibility, authoritarianism, and social isolation. As a result of its isolation, outside services, agencies, and individuals who could help the family and intervene on behalf of the abused child have no access to the family. The family's inability to resolve its own problems can result in frustration, which in turn can produce violent behavior. When violence erupts, the child is typically the most accessible target. In addition, the rigid rules and norms which characterize a closed system are not subject to modification, and when a child violates them, the parent may respond with force to bring the child back into conformity and compliance. The likelihood that violence will be used as a means of control is increased if one or both parents grow up in a family where excessive force was commonly used as a disciplinary method.

In many families of this type, sexual abuse or pedophilia is also a problem. This problem has existed for many years and had an impact on delinquent behavior; however, the problem has become increasingly more visible and actionable in the 1980s. Various dimensions of the problem were revealed in an article by Ursula Vils in the *Los Angeles Times*:

Child Molestation: Causes, Cures, and Penalties

Dixie Bray was 7 when she went to play at a girlfriend's house. The friend wasn't there—but her 19-year-old brother was.

"He enticed me into the bedroom to see some glass figurines," Bray said quietly, looking down at the floor. "I remember pain. . . .

"Then someone in the family came home, and he threw me down the back staircase.

"I did not tell my mother for two years that he had molested me. I had this self-imposed guilt; the guilt a child feels is tremendous. I got an ulcer; I was 9 and weighed only 40 pounds. I could not eat or sleep.

"The school noticed the change and I was sent to a child psychologist. I was in psychiatry off and on until last year.

"I was gregarious as a small child, but I grew up introverted. I am suspicious and cynical, not very trusting.

"It seems almost like it all happened to a separate person. That child is not me. I talk about her as if she were another person."

As Dixie Bray looks at her own daughters, a 3-year-old and a baby 10 months, a tinge of fear—and a determination to protect them—crosses her face.

William Vicary, MD, picked up "Diagnostic and Statistical Manual of Mental Disorders" of the American Psychiatric Assn.—the profession's bible—and read the definition of pedophilia: "The act or fantasy of engaging in sexual activity with prepubertal children."

Vicary, assistant clinical director of County-USC Medical Center's Institute of Psychiatry, Law and Behavioral Science, closed the text, and explained that experts do not agree totally on the characteristics of pedophiles.

"Certain background and personality features, however, seem to be overrepresented," he said, "and exhibitionists, child molesters and rapists have much more in common than differences.

"They tend to be alcoholics and/or drug abusers. They tend to have a passive personality; the majority are very shy. They have a proclivity for impulsive behavioral outbursts.

"The other type—the aggressive—is rare, those given to temper tantrums, to push people around. But some of these are pedophiles, too.

"You'd be astounded at how meek some of these men are. That's why the system finds it difficult to think they could engage in such antisocial sexual behavior." . . .

The pedophile's background often includes a domineering female—wife, mother, perhaps sisters—and he may be impotent with adult females, Vicary said.

"He is only capable of sex with young girls (or boys, if he is homosexual)," Vicary said. "He has low self-esteem, but he has power with a child.

"He also may be a member of the family, a friend or neighbor. It is not uncommon for the molester to be known to the child."

Only 1% of molesters are female, Vicary said, and those women held accountable in such crimes usually are involved with an adult male who is molesting children. The statistic may be somewhat misleading, however, he said.

"Women who have sexual involvement with underaged males are never reported," Vicary said, "or if they are discovered, nothing is done.

"There is a double standard: Girls should be protected, virtuous. Boys are expected to attempt to be or to be involved with peers or older individuals—prostitutes or older women.

"I have interviewed young men who have been molested by older women and traumatized by it. It is not any less damaging for boys than girls, and often the boys molested wind up molesting children."

Vicary said the incidence of child molestation is difficult to determine, "but I agree it is underreported." Recidivism also is difficult to estimate accurately, he said. "The recidivism rate for homosexually oriented pedophilia is from 13% to 28%," he said, "which is twice that for heterosexual pedophilia." (Recidivism for rape is 20%.)

"Keep in mind that it's difficult to get a perfect scientific rate for people who re-offend. The rate may be higher but there is no way of scientifically assessing that.

"But child molesting is a serious form of antisocial conduct; if the person is re-offending, he is very likely to be apprehended."

Vicary's treatment program for sex offenders involves reversing psychological patterns. With pedophiles, he begins by working to extinguish the molesting.

"We use aversive techniques," he said, "coupling painful stimuli with the thought or the fantasy.

"One patient keeps a photo of jail on the visor of his car. If he gets an impulse to molest, he looks at it and it scares him, stops him from acting on impulse. Or we have the molester fantasize that his own child is being molested or harmed.

"The next step is to replace the behavior with pro-social sexual behavior. A third to two-thirds of molesters are impotent with adult females, so we use the Master and Johnson sexual dysfunction treatment.

"Many are quite ignorant about adult sexuality, so we teach sexual behavior. If the patient has a girl-friend or wife, we can use conjoint therapy.

"We also teach social skills. Many are so shy they don't know how to ask for a date, so we teach dating behavior, manners. If he is homosexual, we can do the same thing in terms of relations with adult homosexuals."

Treatment also includes drug- and alcohol-abuse counseling and assertiveness training to combat passivity—and "aggressives can be taught to go the other direction."

Vicary also discussed with his patients their negative experiences with women (or men): "Appreciation of the force in their past defuses its power. We teach them not to relive the past in their relationships."

Often those relationships have been minimal and shallow. "We try to teach them to share their deeper thoughts and feelings and experiences with others," Vicary said. "We show them the warmth and gratification of interacting with other people.

"Some are so uptight, especially about social and sexual behavior. It helps them to find out they're not alone. . . .

"The last part of the treatment involves low self-esteem. We try to increase their self-confidence and self-esteem by focusing on their positive behaviors, by getting them off the 'I'm no good' way of thinking."

Two things are critical in the treatment process, Vicary said.

"The first is rapport between therapist and patient. If there is no rapport, it is very difficult to accomplish anything. There must be trust and respect between patient and doctor.

"The second is confrontation, a coming to grips with the self-destructive, dangerous quality of their sexual behavior."

One tool of confrontation is the peer group of sex offenders, predominantly pedophiles—a rap session among up to a dozen patients and Vicary and, sometimes, a few of their wives or girlfriends.

Their openness is remarkable. Visitors are not only tolerated but welcomed. When one commented to Vicary that the visitor was surprised the group is so open, he commented, "So am I."

Members of the group (whose names have been changed) introduced themselves briefly:

—Nick: "I've been in the group since last October. I molested my step-granddaughters, 9 and 11. I spent 18 months at Patton" (State Hospital).

—Larry: "I molested boys about 13. I've been in the group about six months." . . .

—Marian: "I molested my three children, girls 12 and 8 and a boy 11, from 1973 to 1975. I went to jail for one year and I am on five years' probation. I have been in this group for four years. The force behind my molestating my kids was my common-law husband, an alcoholic—and also a very sick man."

—Louis: "I've been in this group for five or six years. I am an exhibitionist, a child molester and I like to photograph young girls. I spent 71 days in jail. I have a case in court now in which a 23-year-old girl accuses me of rape. We were smoking some grass and she got intimidated by me; she says there was no force. She is into angel dust and kinky sex, and if I had had no past arrests, they wouldn't have arrested me."

—Ricardo: "I am 58. My criminal past is very, very . . . Oh wow! Well . . . I molested my stepson, 12, and my stepdaughter, almost 18. I abused my wife. I was at Atascadero (State Hospital) 4½ years and I have been in treatment here three years. . . . I hate the remorse, the shame of things I have done."

—Ken: "I was charged with two attempted murders and one aggravated sexual assault. The sexual assault was one night in my home, and the unwilling assistant was my sister's boyfriend, who was 18. I do not remember doing anything. . . . I take lithium. . . ."

—Joe: "Charges against me were rape, oral copulation and great bodily harm to a female, 27. I was 19 at the time. I spent four years, four months and 11 days at Patton. I was introduced to Dr. Vicary in 1978. My background is that I was the badass on the street. There was conflict with my mom, a history of assaults."

—Roy: "Child molestation—I had sexual intercourse with my cousin,

13, I spent eight months and 27 days in County Jail. I was molested at 13 by a 26-year-old woman. I've never said this before, but shortly after I was molested I killed a friend of mine. I told him about being molested and he teased me. I shot him. I spent two months in jail and got two years on probation for involuntary manslaughter. I got no psychological help at that time."

—Matt: "Child molestation, 7- and 8-year-old girls. I took pictures, undressing them partially. I got three years' probation. . . . My wife is here (at the group therapy session) for the first time. She didn't find out, but I told her about two weeks ago. . . . If I blow this I blow everything. I have a good job, a lovely wife. . . ."

Hearing that Matt had finally told his wife of his child molesting, Ken jumped in with praise: "Hey, that's a big step right there, Matt."

"I asked my wife," said Joe, the convicted rapist, "What she would have done if I hadn't told her and she said, 'you'd be long gone. If you'd hide this, you'd hide something else.'"

Of the nine in the group this particular evening, five come voluntarily. There are other similarities. Five were themselves molested as children, five had alcohol or drug involvement, three are manic depressives, several take prescribed mood-altering drugs, most are passive (but two, Ken and Joe, are aggressive), some had problems with female relatives.

And some had concern for their victims.

"You never take it out on the person who abused you," said Roy. "You take it out on someone else."

"Doctor," said Ken to Vicary, "I'd like to see the boy I assaulted get some help before he . . . well, you know. Do you have any groups for victims?"

Vicary fixed Ken with a candid stare. "What," he said, "do you think this group is?"[54]

Most offenses of pedophilia are never related. The majority of such hidden offenses involve the sexual abuse of young girls in their family setting. The consequence of the abuse is often regrettably that the victim becomes a female delinquent. A prototypical case in point is Lisa, whose situation is summarized as follows: Lisa, now 18, had one older and one younger brother. Her childhood was spent in the Southwest with her father, a skilled machinist, and her mother, a teacher. Lisa reports that as a child her mother was physically abusive to her, at one point assaulting her in the face and breaking several teeth. Alienated from her mother, she looked to her father for protection. When at the age of 12 he began having sex play with her, she reported she welcomed the attention despite the fact that she felt it "wasn't right." Shortly after this, her parents divorced and her father began living with another woman. Lisa began running away from the mother's home until the courts granted her to the custody of her father, because her mother stated she could not control her.

The sexual play with the father continued when he was granted

[54]Ursula Vils, "Child Molestation: Causes, Cures, and Penalties," *Los Angeles Times*, April 3, 1981. Copyright 1981, *Los Angeles Times*. Reprinted by permission.

custody of her. The father, while drunk, forced Lisa, at age 14, to have intercourse with him. Lisa told her stepmother about the situation, but the stepmother refused to believe her, stating she was misinterpreting his "fatherly affection." Thereafter, intercourse occurred at least monthly for approximately one year, usually when the father was drunk. Lisa sought escape by using drugs. At age 16, she was rescued by being arrested for possession of drugs and put in a juvenile institution.

The problem of pedophilia is not restricted to girls. In a study of sexual abuse focusing on boys rather than girls, M. Dunklee and Mory Spenser found that sexual abuse of boys is much more common than most experts believe.[55] Dunklee and Spenser estimate that as many as 25 percent of all reported childhood sexual molestations involve boys.

The two base their findings on their own small-scale study and reviews of previous medical research reports. Their estimate is much higher than those of other researchers, who have generally estimated that only 9 to 14 percent of reported sexual abuse involves boys. According to Dunklee and Spenser, "It is difficult to estimate the true incidence of sexual abuse in boys, but boys, as well as girls, appear to be at significant risk."

In their research, the two physicians found age-related patterns. "Adolescent boys who are molested are more apt to be molested by strangers. The little boys—ages 2, 3 and 4—are more likely to be neighbors, sons of baby sitters and baby sitters [who molest]."

The American Association for Protecting Children, a division of the American Humane Association in Denver, concur with Dunklee and Spenser. About 22 percent of the 200,000 reported cases of sexual abuse of children in 1984—or 44,000—involved boys.

In their study, Dunklee and Spenser reviewed the medical records of 140 boys, ages 1 to 17, who were treated for sexual abuse at a children's hospital and health center. Among their findings:

Eighty-five percent of the victims were abused by a relative or acquaintance.

Types of abuse reported by victims, whose average age was about 7, ran the gamut, but most common was attempted or actual anal-penile penetration.

Physical evidence (such as bruises and rectal lacerations) was present in 68 percent of the boys.

Multiple assaults, occurring over time periods ranging from a few days to six years, were reported by 53 percent of victims.

According to Dunklee and Spenser boys by nature tend not to disclose sexual abuse. "Boys are not encouraged to be vulnerable and do not envi-

[55]M. Dunklee and Mory Spenser, "The Sexual Abuse of Boys," *Journal of Pediatrics* (October, 1986).

sion themselves as powerless. While girls may 'internalize' an assault and feel guilty, boys are more likely to block it out of their memory."

IMPACT OF CHILD ABUSE ON DELINQUENCY

An important effect of child abuse is that victims invariably develop low self-concepts. In my work in a psychiatric hospital I noted many instances of this. A case in point is that of Alice, who was physically and sexually abused by her father. Partly as a result of her father's treatment, she became one of the girl groupies in a motorcycle gang. Her biker lover would often pass her around to other bikers as a sexual partner.

In one psychodrama session with her, I asked her to have a conversation with the part of her self that was the victim. This victim side of her was role-played by another patient. Alice became furious with the part of herself that was a victim. She began to scream at "herself" and how much she hated this "low-life" person. She was more angry at allowing *herself* to be a victim than at the offenders, and she vowed never to let it happen again.

My research reveals that children who have a low self-concept or self-esteem as a consequence of abusive negative socialization by their parents or others are more likely to become delinquent than children who have a high regard for themselves. Children with low self-esteem often feel they deserve what they get and are more likely to become delinquent because they are accustomed to the role of "loser." (Many delinquents of this type have the "born-to-lose" tatoo emblazoned on their body.)

Verbal, physical, and sexual abuse of children has occurred for a long time. These behaviors have, however, surfaced in recent years with an unprecedented vengeance and properly received considerable attention. These forms of child abuse, which basically involve treating children as objects of adult problems, have an enormously harmful impact on the child. Children who are victims of these forms of abuse have great difficulty recovering from the damage to their egos. And most regrettably these same abused children will most likely act out on their own children.

Children who are abused often develop a familiarity with the acts perpetrated on them and a rage about the powerless position in which they were placed. This may result in their assuming the power role of abuser in their later life. In my clinical work I have observed hundreds of cases that substantiate this "transmission-belt" syndrome, which involves the abused child later becoming the perpetrator of the same delinquent offense of which they were formerly the victim.

One case of this type that I treated in my work with adolescents in a psychiatric hospital involved 15-year-old Fred. When Fred was 6, an older boy of 17 had sodomized him several times at knifepoint and threatened him with further violence if he "told." He finally reported the incidents to his father. His father, who beat him often, told him, "You probably brought it on yourself." Fred's father and mother did not report his abuse to the authorities. Instead they made him feel he was somehow responsible for his own victimization.

This led Fred to believe, on some level, that he was a person who "deserved what he got." Fred developed low self-esteem combined with a deep sense of societal injustice. He was full of rage that was not understood by his parents, and he acted out the consequences of his own victimization on others.

When Fred was 15, out of hostility and a damaged self-concept, he developed his own pattern of sexually abusing children. In several psychodramas it was revealed, among other problems, that he didn't feel able to relate to girls his own age sexually: He was afraid of them. The sessions also revealed that Fred was strongly motivated to overcome his former lowly position as victim and become the transgressor who was now in the offender power position. Consequently, out of his rage about his family's low opinion of him, which validated his low self-esteem, his long familiarity with abusive behavior, and a strong motivation to be in the power position (a position at the other extreme from victim), he became a child molester himself.

Fred is typical of several hundred delinquents whom I worked with in psychodrama and group therapy. Most of these "acting-out" offenders have been victims of child abuse and have low self-esteem. Many of these adolescents turn into hardened adult offenders. I would estimate, based on my clinical experience, that around 80 percent of the criminals and delinquents now doing time in institutions were abused by their families.

FAMILIES THAT PRODUCE RUNAWAYS

An increasingly common reaction to an abusive family is for the child to run away. Becoming a runaway is a "status offense" in our society and automatically defines a child as a delinquent. A conservative estimate is that well over one million children run away from home each year in the United States. Many runaways are girls.

In one study, psychiatrists Donald N. Haupt and David R. Offord analyzed the case histories of 92 runaway children. They found that their average age was 13.[56] Haupt and Offord were immediately struck by the severity of the "social dislocation" that seemed common to such children's lives. Over half had been in at least one foster home, and on the average they had experienced more than four guardianship changes. But their troubles were not limited to being passed around from one set of disappointed parents to the next. Haupt and Offord attempted to come up with a measure for the total problems each child had known, and they developed a "hardship score" based on such factors as number of changes of guardianship, parental physical abuse, and poverty in their early life situation. Runa-

[56]*Human Behavior* (April 1973).

ways scored significantly higher on the "hardship score" than a matched sample of nonrunaways.

Another researcher, Christine Chapman, described what the presence of runaways in such vast numbers revealed about American society.[57] She reported that, although most eventually return home (at least for a time), the act of running away is a statement of a breakdown of communication between child and parent. Chapman reports how one mother, whose returned daughter insisted on and was granted her own rules of behavior, commented, "It is the most frightening thing in the world for parents to feel that if they say or do the wrong thing the child will run away again. Beth held running away over us like a weapon."

What runaways do when they leave home was detailed by several children in a report by a New York State Assembly Committee on Child Care released in 1986. Several young prototypical witnesses, from different class backgrounds, testified about running away from their unhappy, abusive homes. They lived in parks and building hallways, became involved with drugs and prostitution, and were then taken over and controlled by older men.

Diana described her experience when she ran away from home at the age of 13. "My mother used to drink a lot, and every time my mother got drunk she would beat me . . . I had no place to go. I stayed in hallways and in parks with older people. I met this guy who started me prostituting. He was a 42-year-old pimp and he had me on the streets every day. I had to bring in a certain amount of money. If not, he would beat me. He had the drugs I needed."[58]

Sixteen-year-old Nancy testified that she tried to kill herself at age 11 by taking a drug overdose. Her parents were alcoholics, and she tried suicide several times during the next three years. She was committed to a mental institution and ran away. At 14, she began living with a man of 33, who turned her out as a prostitute. "I needed money for drugs and the only time I prostituted was when I absolutely needed the money—once or twice a week. Otherwise I would steal, or go the welfare and lie."[59]

Most runaways are girls, who wind up in the depressed "combat zones"—neon light areas of big cities around the country. Most of them are refugees from physically and sexually abusing families.

One chronic runaway I worked with in a psychiatric hospital was 16-year-old Sally. A closer analysis of her case reveals the plight of the typical female runaway in a more focused perspective.

Sally began running away from home at the age of 12. Her family background involved a more extremely sexually abusive background than most adolescent teenage delinquent runaways; however, in many respects

[57]Christine Chapman, *America's Runaways* (New York: Morrow, 1976).
[58]"Teenage Runaways" (Albany, N.Y.: New York State Assembly Committee on Child Care, September 1986), p. 139.
[59]Ibid.

her case incorporated standard social factors. After a lengthy stay in the psychiatric hospital where she received daily psychotherapy sessions, Sally became quite articulate about analyzing her problem in psychological terms.

> After being here in the hospital for over a year, my mother told me she had been an incest victim like me. Her stepfather abused her sexually. She had very low self-esteem, and she figured she didn't deserve much as a person. So she became involved with around four assholes—stepfathers who "acted" as if they were my father. They all abused me sexually—since I was ten. My mother must have known about these experiences before I told her about them, but she played dumb. And anyway she didn't see anything too wrong with it because, after all, it happened to her too. She knew the territory.
>
> Now that I've been here all this time talking to psychiatrists and here in psycho-drama, I've figured out how terrible those abuses have made me feel about myself. The way I was treated I felt like a piece of meat, or, really, a piece of shit at home. That's why I ran away and became a prostitute to support myself.
>
> The thing I've learned in my therapy is that I have a lot of fear about doing this to my child, like my mother did it to me. Because I feel rotten about myself, and I've seen the way my mother picked these low-life punks, I may do the same thing and wind up with husbands who will do this to my child.
>
> With the help of the therapists here I'm beginning to learn I'm not a bad person, and maybe I'll feel I deserve more than my mother ever got from a man. I've decided it will never happen to any child I have. I'm just not going to let it happen. I think enough of myself so I'll never marry a man who would do to my child what happened to me. I know from my psychiatrist that I have this kind of life-script but I want to rewrite it.

In the year I did therapy with her I learned a great deal about Sally. During her runaway years from 12 to 15, Sally lived most of the time on the streets of Hollywood as a prostitute. Her pattern was typical of many teen-age delinquent girls who turn to prostitution. She had a pimp who treated her both "nice" and "bad." When he was nice, according to Sally, "he was like a good father. He took me places, counseled me, and bought me presents." When he was bad he, of course, abused her like her several step-fathers. Being victim-oriented, she found the abuse and turning tricks a painful yet familiar way of life.

Although she despised the prostitute role, according to Sally it had some advantages: "One thing I liked about being a prostitute was that I was in charge and had power over most of my tricks. In a way I got even with men [her sexually abusing stepfathers] by being mean to these guys, telling them to "hurry up," or sometime stealing their money. My pimp was strong and he would back me. A few times he beat the shit out of a few of my tricks. In a way, it was like getting even with some of my vicious stepfathers."

Sally was luckier than most teenage female runaways because she was able, through a long therapeutic process, to get some insight into her low self-esteem and change her behavior in a positive direction. Most young females simply continue their self-destructive patterns, and their children replicate their behavior.

One development in large urban areas is the proliferation of shelters for runaways. They are often effective in providing short-term counseling, medical aid, and, in some cases, reconnecting the runaways with their parents. Shelters often protect the runaway from developing a more intense delinquent lifestyle. Some, like sociologist Dr. Lois Lee's "Children of The Night" program, are specifically for runaway teenage girls who often become addicts and turn to prostitution to support themselves.

A Los Angeles Children's Hospital study in 1987 showed that, compared to young people who live at home, runaways are four to five times at greater risk to have a disease or a psychological problem, and they are also in recent years at high risk for AIDS.

Shelters, in general, provide runaways with time to find jobs, apartments, and establish independent lifestyles, if they are old enough, or to make other living arrangements. Some shelters help young people reach those goals through educational programs that include workshops on AIDS as well as psychological and occupational counseling.

Most children who run away from their destructive family situations do not find their way into helpful and safe shelters. On the streets of our large cities their delinquency is reinforced and becomes a more integral part of their personality and behavior. After a time many are arrested and placed in traditional, long-term institutions. Placements in foster homes are a temporary diversion from the child's abusive or disorganized families of origin.

In order for the problem to be effectively managed, however, treatment programs are required that do not focus on the delinquent as the "identified patient" but take into account the total family construct. A total-family-system-treatment approach is increasingly recognized as the only logical way to deal with burgeoning family disorganization issues, which clearly affect the delinquency problem.

SUMMARY: BASIC THEMES FOR CLASS DISCUSSION

1. The family is the basic socializing agent in our society. In the family, children and adolescents should learn the basic social skills and values necessary for leading a law-abiding life.
2. When the family, through a parent's neglect or abuse, teaches a child deviant values, they are most prone to become delinquents.
3. Children are most likely to become delinquents when they are socialized in a "criminogenic" family. In this type of family they tend to have parents and relatives who are criminal role models. Due to this condition they learn delinquent values and are in subtle ways encouraged to become delinquents.
4. The proper or improper application of discipline by a child's parents is a significant factor in their socialization and often influences whether or not they will become delinquent. The Glueck

study revealed that (1) "sound discipline" was consistant and firm, (2) "fair discipline" was inconsistent, and (3) "unsound discipline" was extremely rigid or extremely lax. Seventy percent of the delinquents in the Glueck study received "unsound discipline."

5. My own research on fathers and sons and discipline confirmed the Glueck analysis. I found that consistent rules and responses were most effective, whereas strict "macho-fathers" and lax "buddy-type fathers" are not as effective as "compassionate fathers," who are firm but considerate.

6. Most research reveals that a "broken-home" situation does not automatically produce delinquent children. The manner in which the parents separate and their concern for the future of their children are vital factors in averting delinquency. Despite this, juvenile delinquents do have a higher incidence of broken homes in their family backgrounds. Welfare families with only the mother in the home have high rates of delinquency.

7. Violent, child-abusing families create the most problems for their children, and children from this type of family have the highest rates of delinquency. The abusive family is typically a closed-off family system characterized by rigidity, authoritarianism, and social isolation. In families of this type, parents often act out their personal frustrations and hostility on their children. The children in these families become the "identified patients," and this enables the parents to deny their own personal problems. Research about abusive families of this type reveals that in order to solve the delinquent child's problems, the family needs to be perceived and treated as a total system.

8. Children who are sexually and physically abused in their families are vulnerable to becoming delinquents. This is due to the fact that, as a result of their abuse, they develop low self-concepts. When children or adolescents don't care about themselves, they are more prone to commit self-destructive delinquent acts or become drug addicts or alcoholics. Often, because of the rage at being victimized by their parents, they will act out violently and displace the rage felt for their abusing parents onto innocent victims.

9. Victims of child abuse are prone to becoming child molesters themselves. They often become the abuser in order to gain the dominant power position. Their behavior is in part a reaction-formation to try to ensure that they will not become a victim again.

10. Many children who are victims of an abusive family become runaways to avoid their painful family situation. On the streets, without resources or anyone to take proper care of them, they are prone to further abuse and exploitation by predatory adults. Pimps and tricks use young people for their pathological needs, and young runaways are further exploited. In the wake of this growing problem, "safe places" have emerged around the country to attempt to care for the needs of displaced runaway youths. In these shelters an attempt is made to meet the juvenile runaway's food, shelter, health, and educational needs.

QUESTIONS

5.1. Should we develop more foster homes and programs to remove adolescents from criminogenic families? What are the legal and social ramifications of approaching the problem in this way?

5.2. How does discipline enter into the juvenile delinquency equation? What are some of the elements of proper discipline?

5.3. Discuss the "normal" conflicts that exist between parents and adolescents and the most effective way to resolve these battles.

5.4. What can be done in a family broken by death or divorce to help the children in these families avert delinquency?

5.5. How do sexually and physically abusive parents produce delinquent offspring?

5.6. In what way does a delinquent child become the "identified patient" in a family system?

5.7. Discuss how and why a small group of children from family backgrounds might become "invulnerables?"

5.8. What should society do for children who run away from home?

6

The School and Delinquency

Then said a teacher, Speak to us of Teaching.
 And he said:
 No man can reveal to you aught but that which already lies half asleep in the dawning of your knowledge.
 The teacher who walks in the shadow of the temple, among his followers, gives not of his wisdom but rather of his faith and his lovingness.
 If he is indeed wise he does not bid you enter the house of his wisdom, but rather leads you to the threshold of your own mind.

KAHLIL GIBRAN
The Prophet

Once upon a time the rural family assumed almost total responsibility for the socialization of its young. The farm lad of eight or nine would stretch his legs to keep pace with his father as they plowed the field and gathered its crops. This lad had only to follow—literally—in his father's footsteps until the day when he would look back and see the strain of his own son's face as the latter tried to match his stride. The complexities of an occupational identity were reduced to the simplicity of a footprint in the field. The ABCs, learned by the glow of a kerosene lamp as Mom read from the family bible, were about as useful as the shadows hiding in the corners of the room. At Mom's insistence, and given good weather, slow periods on the farm might be interrupted by the kids walking over the hills to a one-room school for a couple of weeks to be with the schoolmaster, who was usually depicted as part devil, part teacher, and part preacher. But when harvest came, the schoolhouse became just part of the landscape as the kids got back to more important things.

In this *Gemeinschaft* setting, the family, usually by direct example, educated the children and taught them whatever they needed to know in preparation for adult roles on a continuing and consistent twenty-four-hour-a-day basis. In an important sense, the family into which one was born was one's destiny. It attempted to meet all of the educational needs of the young—religious, ethical, occupational, academic. There were few if any other resources or alternatives of significance.

The alternatives came, however. With the concentration of capital and industrialization, the family members were recruited to run the mammoth machines of production. Cities sprang up around the industrial centers, and the boy no longer followed the plow but watched the lunch pail come and go. The concept of marriage as a "partnership" arrived with World War II, and the mother also joined the labor force, leaving no more time for bible reading. The home and the family had rather suddenly become something that opened for business at five or so in the evening and closed down at seven or so in the morning. The family reflected the specialization in industry by itself becoming specialized. The educational and developmental functions that used to take place at home during the day had to be contracted out. The public schools got the contract and, in many respects, became the daytime family. This, however, introduces the crucial question: Precisely which functions formerly performed by the rural family were to become the responsibility of the public school system? Were they to provide moral and religious instruction? Were they to administer to the emotional needs of students? Were they only to prepare them for an occupational role or were they also to produce more well-rounded citizens? Were they simply to teach the ABCs? It is my contention that many pressures toward delinquency exist because of no common answer to these questions.

Whatever the goals of the schools, a condition that complicates the educational system is the growing problem of juvenile delinquency. One indicator of this increasing problem is the fact that a nationwide Gallup Poll revealed that delinquency has become one of the top ten problems in American schools. Lack of discipline retained its traditional place in these surveys as a major problem.

In this regard, a well-trained, sensitive elementary school teacher, who taught in a ghetto school in Los Angeles, described the number one problem of discipline in the schools in the following way:

My experiences teaching in Watts have been varied, but the number one problem I confront is discipline and dealing with problem students in violent situations. During my first year of teaching, I went through a period of shock. My students were disrespectful, did not want to learn and did not understand my style of language, nor did I theirs. At least 70 percent of my time was devoted to discipline. My ideals of teaching and education were shattered and I felt like a failure.

During the time I taught in the upper grades, I broke up fights continuously. Once, I used karate in order to keep one of my students from killing another one by bashing his head against the stairs. Another time, I used my arm to prevent a child from being hit in the head by a dictionary thrown by another student. A classic fight in one of my classes was caused by one of my students using another student's chair to stand on in order to change the date. She was half his size. He pushed her off the chair. They exchanged a few words about each other's mothers. As I was trying to get her away from him, he leaped over a few sets of tables. She proceeded to pick up a chair to fight with and he did the same. They started going at each other. At that point, I had the strongest boys in the class hold him down, while I got her out of the classroom. The slightest conflict between students, boys or girls, would bring on a fight. The other students would then gather around and cheer for one or the other side. Ironically, after all of the hostility and anger subsided, the battling participants would later on be the best of friends.

Remedies for dealing with these problem children are hard to come by. Calling or involving a violent child's parent in this situation to rectify their child's behavior can often backfire and lead to a more severe problem. Sometimes, dealing with the parents pours gasoline on the fire. The parents are either disinterested or become defensive and belligerent. In some cases calling a parent can lead to child battering.

After my call, one of my students was beaten with an extension cord by his father. When I found this out, I stopped calling that parent. Another time, after calling home about one of my student's bad behavior, I found out that the child was burned with a hot iron. He appeared with welts all over his arms the next day in class.

As a last resort, I will send a severe discipline problem to the principal. That is often ineffective, due to the school bureaucracy. Most principals are reluctant to suspend a child because every suspension goes on record downtown and reflects negatively on the principal and his school record.

For these varied reasons, discipline problems are tolerated and pushed on from grade to grade. There is limited room for the special problem child to be placed in a special class. Because of their continued presence, the rest of the children suffer and do not acquire the education they are entitled to. Most of a teacher's energies are devoted to the problem kids and the disruptive and violent situations they create in the classroom.[1]

This teacher's dilemma about teaching in the current climate of violence in the schools is representative of the plight of many dedicated teachers. The classroom is besieged by the problems that exist in the children's home and community. Because of these problems, the maintenance of discipline becomes a teacher's major objective, and the teacher's avowed main task of conveying knowledge is subverted.

FUNCTION OF THE SCHOOLS

The discipline problem described by the contemporary teacher is not in accord with the original goals of American education. Over a hundred

[1]Reprinted by permission.

years ago Horace Mann expressed the optimistic notion that education was the "great equalizer of the conditions of men—the balance wheel of the social machinery." Since all men were equally educable, education could provide the poorest child with an equal chance to share in the good life. Mann and his votaries believed that the public school system not only made democracy workable but also guaranteed its prosperity. The "seven cardinal principles of secondary education," formulated in 1918, stressed health, command of the fundamental processes, worthy home membership, vocational preparation, civic education, leisure-time activities, and ethical character as the goals of secondary education. The same objectives appeared in the statements of the Educational Policies Commission from the 1930s onward, especially in *Education for All American Youth* in 1944.[2] These rather exalted conceptions of education are still with us. Based on position statements by the Educational Policies Commission of the National Education Association and other authoritative sources, Schafer and Polk summarize their view regarding the responsibilities of the public schools:

> We assume that all children and youth must be given those skills, attitudes, and values that will enable them to perform adult activities and meet adult obligations. Public education must ensure the maximum development of general knowledge, intellectual competence, psychological stability, social skills, and social awareness so that each new generation will be enlightened, individually strong, yet socially and civically responsible.[3]

So one can see that the role assigned to the public schools far exceeds teaching the ABCs: The school's responsibility also ranges over the psychological and social well-being of its charges. The fact that the school may receive a new student from a dysfunctional or deprived family in no way mitigates the school's responsibility. Robert MacIvar stressed this point at the completion of his five-year juvenile delinquency study in New York: "The school's function is to educate and where the family and the community fail to promote the social adjustment and the psychological development necessary to prepare the young to receive the education the school offers, it must step in to provide it with the area of its capacity."[4]

The school is usually the first institution entrusted with the care of a child away from the protective cloak of his family. As a socializing agency it trains the child to accept rules laid down by strangers and enforced impersonally. At school he learns to read and write and acquires intellectual skills. He also learns to compete with his peers in intellectual and athletic en-

[2]Educational Policies Commission, *Education for All American Youth* (Washington, D.C.: National Education Association, 1944).
[3]W. E. Schafer and Kenneth Polk, "Delinquency and the Schools," in *Task Force Report: Juvenile Delinquency and Youth Crime* (Washington, D.C.: U.S. Government Printing Office, 1967), p. 224.
[4]Robert M. MacIvar, *Final Report: Juvenile Delinquency Evaluation Projects* (New York: The City of New York, 1962).

deavors under the watchful eye of professionals who promulgate and enforce regulations.

As indicated, in predominantly rural and folk societies, children learned to act like adults by observing the behavior of adult members of their families. Occupational roles were learned in the family, a productive as well as a consuming unit. With urbanization and industrialization the schools became more complex, and course content began to include skills related to adult careers. For middle-class children in particular, the school years have become a preparatory phase for professional or business education.

The child is expected by his parents and by society to succeed in life. Neither the family nor the school defines for him what success means in his particular case, what he has to do to achieve it, and how his education will help toward that end. Where the child in the predominantly rural society attained social maturity as soon as he reached biological maturity, the youth in contemporary urban society may find social maturity indefinitely postponed, with no sure way of attaining it. The family frequently cannot and does not socialize the child in adult occupational and community roles. The assumption is that the school will take over this function. Indeed, most of the child's development—physical, personality, and academic—is assumed to rest with the school. The school, however, does not have the resources, personnel, or curriculum to perform these functions adequately. Lower-class children, particularly the dropouts and delinquents, have no well-defined occupational goals and see no connection between what they learn in school and what they will do when they leave it.

Although we have not limited the goal of the schools to the "teaching" of subject matter, Friedenberg has said that this is "simply an accidental by-product which may or may not occur; the real goal of education is something very different."[5] He sees the school system as a sort of screening agency which puts its stamp of approval on its graduates. This "Good Housekeeping seal of approval" is the school system's most important function because it guarantees to future employers and to society that the student so stamped is sufficiently square, naive, and uncreative that he will fit very nicely into the conventional world. He has sufficient lack of character that he will not be upset by the unethical practices of the business world; he has sufficient lack of ability that he will not be able to perform the "official" goals of an agency yet will have enough ability to perform the covert and real goals, which may simply be keeping the internal operation running. The schools thus perform a very clever and valuable service because they can assure society that the candidate has the hidden qualities that society and employers cannot publicly advertise for or admit they value. Friedenberg mentions the examples of social workers who understand the dynamics of social stratification and

[5]Edgar Z. Friedenberg, "Status and Role in Education," in *Crisis in American Institutions*, eds. Jerome H. Skolnick and Elliott Currie (Boston: Little, Brown, 1970), p. 226. This article first appeared in *The Humanist* issue of September/October 1968 and is reprinted by permission.

group work but, more important, are not capable of organizing the poor into an effective political action group, of police officers who "know" the rights of citizens but do not permit this knowledge to interfere with their conception of "doing their job," of teachers who feel a personal or an official commitment to teach their students but would not let this inhibit their more important covert role of controlling the children.

Teaching the children and providing them with real skills is not the point, and employers understand that a diploma is in no way a statement regarding ability. Employers understand and accept that they will have to train the graduate. But what the school has assured them of by conferring the degree is that this person is "trainable": He will be very content advertising a service he cannot provide or selling a product that has obsolescence built into it, or convincing consumers that they "need" a product that has no functional value. He will not make any particular distinctions between manufacturing gasoline or napalm, bow and arrow or bazookas, baby cribs or bombs. He will not be controlled by his own values for the very excellent reason that he has none; he will be controlled by the values previously built into whatever role he assumes in society. If the credential-holder subsequently achieves some position of power in society, the school further guarantees that he will use it to maintain the status quo. Friedenberg states this case:

> Wide acceptance of the value-positions conveyed by the school mystique keeps our social institutions going and reduces conflict; it stabilizes our society. But this is just another way of saying that the schools support the status quo, and, particularly, that the restriction of opportunity to those who come to terms with it virtually ensures that our society, in all its echelons, will be led by people who cannot conceive of better social arrangements or despair of even getting them adopted, and with good reason. This seems to me the final irony—the school, by controlling access to status on terms that perpetuate the characteristics of mass society, while serving simultaneously as the registrar and guarantor of competence, holds competence in escrow. And it does not release it until competence has demonstrated, over a period of years and under a variety of provocations, that its bearer has other qualities that make him unlikely or even unable to direct his competence toward major social change. By placing the school in control of the only legitimate channel to status and power, we virtually ensure that those who gain status and power will use them to perpetuate our difficulties rather to create new and radical solutions.[6]

An additional beauty of this arrangement is that not only is mass society happy, content, and unthreatened, but the credential-holder is also well pleased.

> Those who accept it [the school] well enough to emerge after 16 years with a favorable credential can usually be trusted to have sufficiently conventional

---

[6]Ibid., p. 225.

goals, motives, and anxieties to find the larger social system into which they are released rewarding. To those who have learned to endure and even have fun in a small trap, the big trap built to a similar plan but on a much more lavish scale and with much richer bait looks like freedom. It offers, in any case, all they are likely to have learned to desire or even imagine. "T.V. dinner by the pool! Aren't you glad you finished school?"[7]

One can see, then, that the disadvantaged minority children, with perhaps a natural predilection for social change and the "feeling" that things are not as they should be for them, have great difficulty becoming "certified" by the school system. It is of interest, however, that some of them are able to become certified nowadays. More interesting, however, is how well they learned their lessons and how well they reflect mass society. Many a black defendant without certification who has found himself standing before a black judge or black probation officer can testify to this. Those few minority members who have become certified take it quite seriously and seem to understand their "true" function much better than certified whites.

Jonathan Kozol has a similar conception of the school as an agency of social control that utilizes punitive techniques to keep minority children in their place in society. Those few minorities who do "get ahead" do so in spite of the school system, not because of it.[8]

What exists in many instances, therefore, is a dysfunctional, perhaps single-parent family that does not meet the emotional needs of the children and a school system that cannot meet the emotional needs of the children. Who, then, will meet these emotional needs? Where can the child go to find comfort and support? Since the adult world has made no answer, the youth culture has provided its own answer. It is called "the Egyptian Kings," "the Jesters," "the West Side Dragons," "the Balkans," "the Vultures," "the Crips": It is called the gang.

As mentioned earlier, many executives tend to surround themselves with subordinates who are not argumentative and rebellious because the executives do not have the interpersonal competence to deal with dissent. They prefer the quiet, the passive, the obedient. It is no secret that the public school system in this country is a middle-class system manned by middle-class teachers who, we might add, feel most comfortable with middle-class students who generally react in a predictable, "intelligent," understandable fashion. If the students do get upset, they are likely to suppress the feeling in respectable middle-class fashion and not embarrass anyone. They have self-control. Even under stress they are apt to retain this control and intellectualize their complaints in quite good anti-Ciceronian prose. These are the teachable students, and they are the proper subjects of the educational process. They will go on to college and become lawyers and doctors, politicians and soldiers, and really quite respectable people. Some

---

[7]Ibid., p. 224.
[8]Jonathan Kozol, *Death at an Early Age* (Boston: Houghton Mifflin, 1967).

may even join a Watergate or Iranscam Gang. Whatever they do, they at least will do it with some class. Some will no doubt become teachers, and remembering how conforming and well treated they had been, will not be able to understand some of the loud-mouthed, vulgar, dull students who will slouch in their classrooms. Many middle-class teachers openly reject lower-class students simply because they are "different."

> The teacher is the key person upon whom the educational system depends. His behavior and his attitudes, once he closes the door to the classroom, determine whether learning, indifference to learning, or rejection of learning takes place. Although some teachers, through prejudice and fear, consciously reject youth who are different, most teachers who reject children do so unconsciously, registering distaste and rejection by the nuances and subtleties of their behavior. Refuge behind the classroom walls is not possible if true school-community relationships are to be built.[9]

School Problems and Delinquency

One form of rejection comes out through the attitude that lower-class children, particularly those from minority groups, are simply slow, dull, and intellectually inferior. A New York study concluded that "the major reason why an increasing number of central Harlem pupils fall behind in their grade level is that substandard performance is expected of them."[10] Many "well-meaning" teachers are prejudiced and this attitude comes out in a condescending and embarrassing way. Frank Reissman notes:

> The specific forms of patronization are manifold: The tendency to talk down to the deprived child, to speak his language, to imitate slang and speech inflections; the assumption that these children are lacking intellectual curiosity and conceptual abilities; the lowering of academic standards and the failure to set high goals for the deprived; the too quick taken for granted attitude they are not interested in learning.[11]

The projection of these kinds of attitudes provides the children with a "license for failure." It is quickly communicated to them that they really are not expected to succeed; there really is not much point in trying because they can't make it anyway. Davidson and Lang have pointed out the connections between belief in limited potential and educational failure:

> It is therefore likely that a lower class child, especially if he is not doing well in school, will have a negative perception of his teacher's feelings toward him. These negative perceptions will in turn tend to lower his efforts to achieve in school and/or increase the probability that he will aggravate the negative atti-

[9]Robert S. Fisk, "Task of Educational Administration," in *Administrative Behavior in Education*, eds. R. F. Campbell and R. T. Gregg (New York: Harper & Row, 1957), p. 211.
[10]Kenneth Clark, *Dark Ghetto: Dilemmas of Social Power* (New York: Harper & Row, 1965), p. 139.
[11]Frank Reissman, *The Culturally Deprived Child* (New York: Harper & Row, 1965), p. 139.

tude of his teachers toward him, which in turn will affect his self-confidence and so on.[12]

Expect failure from the children and the children will give you failure. Ravitz quite rightly makes an issue of the self-fulfilling prophecy in the education of culturally deprived children.

> Not infrequently teachers, counselors, principals assigned to the depressed area schools have been people without any real concern for these children and with the common stereotype of them as children of low ability. As a result of this low estimate of potential, the self-fulfilling prophecy went into effect. The children were not encouraged to learn very much; the teacher expended little energy on anything but maintaining order and bemoaning her lot; as a consequence, the children fulfilled the lowest expectations, which in turn enforced the original assumption to prove that the teacher was right.[13]

Damaging attitudes projected by middle-class schools onto lower-class children are often compounded by the fact that an irrelevant and fairy-tale world is presented to the deprived children through the use of essentially middle-class–oriented instructional materials. When the ghetto child walks into the school system, he walks into a middle-class world that may literally shock him. He may be so awed by the mammoth physical facilities and have so little experience in such middle-class settings that he never does find his way around. He may stumble into the right classroom but immediately decide that it is the wrong room for him when confronted with subtle or overt rejection by teacher and middle-class students. His feeling that he is not really wanted here, that he is somehow out of place, will not be changed by the textbook illustration of the ruddy-faced grandfather giving the golden-haired girl in the party dress a piggyback ride in front of the fireplace in the spacious living room with mom and dad holding hands and smiling in the background. The ghetto child's psychological survival may partially hang on the fact that he cannot read the dialogue beneath the picture. He nevertheless knows that he is in a strange world where he does not really belong and is not really wanted. He may have to fall back on, and even exaggerate, "lower-class" patterns of behavior, which are the only acts familiar to him, thus eliciting even more overt forms of rejection from this educational prison to which he has been sentenced until the age of 16. Ralph Tyler has summed up this situation:

> The fact that writers of textbooks and teachers have come from a fairly restricted middle-class environment may account to a great extent for the limiting of content of elementary school reading materials and of the books used in

[12]Helen H. Davidson and Gerhard Lang, "Children's Perceptions of Their Teachers' Feelings Toward Them Related to Self-Perception, School Achievement and Behavior," *Journal of Experimental Education* 29 (December 1960): 114. Reprinted with permission of the Helen Dwight Reid Educational Foundation. Published by Heldref Publications, 4000 Albemarle St., N.W., Washington, D.C. 20016. Copyright © 1960.

[13]Mel Ravitz, "The Role of the School in the Urban Setting," in *Education in Depressed Areas*, ed. A. Harry Passow (New York: Teachers College Press, 1963), p. 19.

other subjects to those aspects of life which are largely middle class in character. Elementary school books do not deal with homes as they are known by a
large percentage of American children. The books in use treat of business,
industry, politics, and the professions usually in the terms of the white-collar
participants rather than in terms of that which would be most understandable to
a large fraction of the children.[14]

Instead of presenting experiences that would tend to foster identification with the school, experiences of alienation are concatenated page after
page, book after book. Schafer and Polk in their excellent work recorded
the response of a former delinquent to educational materials in the public
school:

> It wasn't interesting to me, I liked the science books but I didn't dig that other
> stuff. Dick and Jane went up the hill to fetch a pail of water and all that crap.
> Mary had a little lamb. Spot jumped over the fence. See Spot jump over the
> fence. I mean I got this stuff in the seventh grade too. I got a little book no bigger
> than that. I opened it up. Dick and Jane was in the house. Mom and Dad was
> going to the market. Spot was outside playing with the ball with Sally. I say, ain't
> this the cutest little story. And I took the book one day and shoved it straight
> back to the teacher and said I ain't going to read that stuff.[15]

These kinds of materials are insulting to the intelligence of many culturally
and economically deprived children. It is difficult enough to understand
how middle-class children tolerate them: Apparently such materials don't
contrast as sharply with the middle-class child's real-world experiences as
they do with the "project" child's world. Even for middle-class children,
however, these kinds of books and materials do not prepare them for the
real world. The school presents them with a make-believe world that does
not even introduce, much less wrestle with, the real problems in the world.
What about inflation, and recession, and police brutality, and unemployment, and capital punishment, and prejudice, and parenthood, and love,
and mental illness, and poverty, and conspicuous consumption, and growing old, and marriage, and life and death? What about education? There is
no wonder that middle-class students are shocked and confused and overwhelmed when they leave college, report for their first job at a probation
department or public social service agency, and are confronted by the fact
that nothing they learned seems to have anything to do with the realities of
the work world.

William Kvaraceus and Walter Miller also stressed the infantilism of
the school world:

> Since the high school is careful to skirt and detour around real-life problems and
> controversial issues regarding race relations, alcoholism, materialism, religion,

---

[14]Ralph W. Tyler, "Can Intelligence Tests Be Used to Predict Educability?" in *Intelligence and Cultural Differences: A Study of Cultural Learning and Problem-Solving*, eds. Kenneth
Eells et al. (Chicago: University of Chicago Press, 1951), p. 45.
[15]Schafer and Polk, "Delinquency and the Schools," p. 238.

politics, collectivism, consumer competency, it involves the learner in a type of artificially contrived busy work and shadowboxing that either dulls the adolescent into a stupor or drives him in his resentment out of school to avert agression and resentment. In protecting youths from real-life problems, the school enters into a tragic conspiracy of irresponsible retreat from reality. The perversion of the high school curriculum to neutral and petty purposes emasculates the school program and disintegrates the ego.[16]

The goal of the middle-class school system seems to be the perpetuation of the middle-class lifestyle for middle-class students, particularly the college-bound students. We will not discuss here how successful they are at achieving this limited class goal. The doors are open to lower-class children, but the tone is set by many teachers who expect them to either knock the door down on the way in or not be able to find the handle. The school then responds in a fashion that shows the way out much more clearly than it showed it the way in. Middle-class teachers are largely rational, intellectual beings who have been "trained" by rational, intellectual beings to go underground with their feelings and emotions. Any student (or others) who responds with an emotional outburst is quickly put down for not being reasonable or rational, for "losing control." Many middle-class teachers are not competent in the management of those aspects of interpersonal relationship that involve emotion and feeling: They intellectualize their conflicts. This is essentially a middle-class style, which is significantly reinforced by immersing oneself in middle-class values and surrounding oneself with middle-class people who are essentially the same. Difference cannot be tolerated, particularly the real and fantasized violent kind of acting-out difference attributed to the lower classes. The lower classes consequently get left out, run out, and pushed out of this rejecting, unreal, irrelevant, middle-class setting. Their anger provides the fuel that runs many delinquent and deviant subcultures.

In an article by John P. DeCecco and Arlene K. Richards, some of these issues are analyzed.[17] The article was based on the findings of an 18-month study conducted by the Senate Subcommittee on Juvenile Delinquency and on interviews, conducted by the authors, of 8,500 people, 8,000 of whom were students in more than 60 junior and senior high schools. The conclusion was that there was a serious problem of conflict and anger in most public school systems. They noted that the most popular strategy for dealing with problems of vandalism, serious assaults, and robbery broke down into two patterns of response: avoidance and force. The authors felt that a better pattern of response to the problems would be group interaction between students and faculty.

In a study on problems of delinquency in the schools, D. Boesel found

---

[16]Kvaraceus and Miller, *Delinquent Behavior*, Washington, D.C.: National Education Association, 1959. Reprinted with permission.
[17]John P. DeCecco and Arlene K. Richard, "Civil War in the High Schools," *Psychology Today* (November 1975): 51–56, 120.

various characteristics associated with schools that have a low rate of violence and property loss.[18]

Student violence is lower in:

1. Schools whose attendance areas have low crime rates and few or no fighting gangs.
2. Schools that have a smaller percentage of male students.
3. Schools that are composed of higher grades.
4. Small schools.
5. Schools where students rate classrooms as well disciplined, where rules are strictly enforced, and where the principal is considered strict.
6. Schools where students consider school discipline to be fairly administered.
7. Schools where there are fewer students in each class and where teachers teach fewer different students each week.
8. Schools where students say that classes teach them what they want to learn.
9. Schools whose students consider grades important and plan to go on to college.
10. Schools whose students believe they can influence what happens in their lives by their efforts, rather than feeling that things happen to them that they cannot control.

Property loss is lower in:

1. Schools whose attendance areas have low crime rates.
2. Schools where fewer students live close to the school.
3. Schools that do not have many nonstudents on the campus during the day.
4. Schools where families support school disciplinary policies.
5. Small schools.
6. Schools whose students say that classrooms are well controlled, rules are strictly enforced, and where teachers say they spend more time in non-classroom supervision.
7. Schools where teachers say that the principal works cooperatively with them and is fair and informal in dealing with staff.
8. Schools in which teachers do not express hostile and authoritarian attitudes toward students.
9. Schools whose students value their teachers' opinion of them.
10. Schools where teachers do not lower students' grades for disciplinary reasons.

DRUGS IN THE SCHOOLS

In addition to violence, substance abuse is a horrendous problem in schools today.[19] It affects students and the learning process in a variety of ways:

[18]D. Boesel, "Violent Schools—Safe Schools," National Institute of Education (Washington, D.C.: United States Government Printing Office, 1978).

[19]The overall problem of substance abuse in the community and as it affects learning will be discussed and analyzed in detail in Chapters 9 and 10. Here the substance-abuse problem will be discussed in relationship only to the school situation.

1. Drugs, including alcohol, cloud the mind of the child, and in some cases has long-term deleterious effects on learning skills.
2. Substance abuse produces an amotivational, vegged-out syndrome during a time when the student should be acquiring not only basic knowledge but various skills related to the "learning process" that he or she will require throughout their life (e.g., how to focus or concentrate on a subject, how to gather data, how to collate information, etc.).
3. Substance abuse subverts and diverts the educational process. Students who party with drugs and alcohol have their minds elsewhere, and not on learning, even when they do attend classes. Most students who use drugs and alcohol come to school hung over and unable to learn.
4. A major result of substance abuse is class cutting and truancy.
5. The commercial aspects of acquiring and selling drugs in the schools negatively affects the overall educational process. Dealing drugs often leads to violent forms of delinquent behavior, which has an enormous deleterious impact on a place of learning.

For all of these reasons and others, which will be delineated in Chapters 9 and 10, where I will discuss substance abuse and delinquency in greater detail, drug and alcohol abuse is a significant problem in the schools.

It is difficult to precisely define how widespread substance abuse is in the schools. Obviously, it's a severe problem in certain schools, and less of an issue in others. In brief, it is difficult to generalize about all elementary and high schools in the United States; however, the following case example is, in my view, fairly typical of high schools around the country.

Palisades High School, part of the Unified Los Angeles School System, is located in an idyllic setting overlooking the blue Pacific in Southern California. It was the school that produced the best-seller, *Whatever Happened to the Class of '65?* The area is the home of numerous writers and Hollywood celebrities. President Ronald Reagan maintained a home in the Palisades for almost two decades, before moving to the White House.

The following detailed article provides a dramatic portrait of drug use and abuse in an affluent American high school:[20]

Pali Higher Than Ever

The combo is blasting at 9 p.m. and the first beer drinkers around the keg are starting to get sick. The bouncers muscle out six guys who heard about the party at school and don't want to pay the $4 to join in. Most of the gang is standing around, washed in flashing colored light, too "blazed" to dance or even talk much. The well-to-do 16–17 years olds toke up on Hawaiian gold

[20]Nina Kidd, "Pali Higher Than Ever," in *Palisades Previews* (P.O. Box 1076, Pacific Palisades, Calif. 90272), February 1981. Reprinted by permission. Copyright Santa Monica Bay Printing and Publishing Company DBA L.A. WEST (formerly Palisades Previews).

(high potency marijuana, "you're gone in two hits") or, on special occasions, snort coke, their favored high.

The usual cops arrive to break things up, called by neighbors because of the noise. Then groups leave the Palisades home, and go party elsewhere. By 10:30 or 11:00 at another house, most of the druggers are getting into beer; though some have warned their buddies about getting ill mixing (drugs and alcohol). The drivers finally manage to deliver their spaced passengers to their homes and another Pali party night is over. It's not until the following night that Mom and Dad come home.

This scenario or something similar is repeated twice a week on the average in Pacific Palisades. This is an "open" Pali party, including up to 100 guests who pay the tab for music and keg beer and bring their own smokes. Parents, according to participating kids, would rather allow these functions and have their kids at home than risk their children getting in trouble by being caught somewhere else. . . .

Since the dismaying arrest of 18 youths for selling drugs at Pali High one year ago the main change in students seems to be more wariness about new kids, more antagonism to the LAPD undercover School Buy Program, and . . . more drugs.

According to Detective John Weinbeck of LA Police Juvenile Narcotics Division, drug sales in LA high schools are on the increase. There are more arrests for dealing made every year. Undercover officers at Pali attribute the higher figures to better detection but also to more drug activity on campus. (The reason we don't hear of arrests regularly is that an officer works a school for 14 or 15 weeks, then rounds up a group of suspects toward the end of the semester. Also, at present there are only about 12 trained officers available for the undercover job, and 42 Los Angeles schools to cover.)

Drug use and regulation is a regular subject in the Pali student newspaper, and the latest student poll, published Nov. 7, 1980, placed students in five categories—from recreational drug-user to peer-pressure user. The non-user "seems to be gaining strength at Pali," says the article, but in a sampling of 562 students (out of 2300 in the student body) most had at least tried drugs.

Poll of 562 Pali Students

Tried	
Alcohol	96%
Marijuana	84%
Cocaine	41%
Mushrooms	32%
Hashish	28%
Quaaludes	19%
Acid	15%
Valium	1.4%
Speed	1%
Heroin	.03%

And these substances aren't cheap. According to student dealers, prices as of last December 4 on campus are as follows:

Drug Prices

Marijuana (seedless)	$7–10/gram
Cocaine	1 gram/$150 and up
'Shrooms'	$5–10/gram
Hashish	$10/gram
Quaaludes	$5 each
Acid	$5–10/hit

(Not all prices were available.)

Last December 8, a Superior Court judge upheld the right of Los Angeles police officers to pose as students in high school classrooms to arrest narcotic dealers. The "School Buy" program has been severely limited by budget and manpower, but it is the only active force on campus combating the drug traffic. Pali Principal James Mercer reports that there is no staff at the school available to deal with the drug problem and the school security officer is needed for other tasks. Besides, he says, it is too dangerous for someone within the school to deal with. Detection and removal of dealers is left to the undercover police agents, the "Narc's." . . .

[According to the Pali undercover officer] "The kids at Pali are sharp, good students and goal oriented, but they're sharp when it comes to drugs too. They have the 'good' stuff, the pot with the higher THC levels (stronger), the cocaine; and they know how to deal for a profit."

How many drug dealers did you find at Pali?

"I figure I identified 25% to 50% of the dealers when I was there." (Fall, 1979).

That would make the number of dealers on the Pali campus?

"I'd estimate fifty."

What happens to the students arrested?

"It varies with the offense, but many are simply taken out of Pali and sent to University High School in West L.A. . . . and the Uni dealers come to Pali."

And many walk right into kids' homes under the parents' noses. The undercover "buy" officer at Pali says he walked into Palisades homes with kids looking really "bad" and wasn't questioned by parents.

The narc's have an impact other than on just the students arrested, don't they?

"Well, it's harder to get to the dealers once some arrests have been made. Pali had been worked in '76; and when I came in late '79 the kids and faculty were still referring to it. The first school I was in had never had an undercover officer, and it was quite easy to get to the right people. One of my suspects at Pali had been suspected by the kids of being a 'narc' and had a bad time socially for quite a while. The students get more careful knowing there might be undercover officers around."

According to an officer at Pali most drugs don't come across town. He bought some heroin just a couple of blocks from the school and it was coming from adults in a home right here. School narcotics officers sometimes get to their sources through the high school suspects but their main job is to find dealers at the schools.

There are drug users among both local students and bussed students. Undercover officers say there are also more pills, "whites" and "reds," at Pali than at other schools and that the black students are increasingly using PCP. Also LSD is unfortunately on the increase here according to the police.

While Principal Mercer speaks for the school administration in endorsing the activities of undercover narcotics agents, neither students nor faculty wholeheartedly agree. Students feel that narcs violate their privacy and they claim that new students have a very hard time. "You can't trust anybody," they say. Articles in their Tideline [the Palisades High newspaper] talk of entrapment and the ultimate futility of the undercover program in wiping out drug traffic.

Some faculty members object to the idea of a police officer in their classes. Pali's school buy officer heard that the teachers feared reports on their teaching techniques or class discipline. One teacher spoke to this interviewer about faculty objecting to a bogus student with "dummy" papers to correct. We heard of a letter sent from some faculty to the principal during the last school year objecting to the undercover police and asking that none be assigned to their classes. However, either the letter was withdrawn or suppressed, for the copies could not be located and Principal Mercer said he had received no such communication.

According to the principal, even he does not know the identity of the undercover officer, though he knows when one is assigned to the school. He counters complaints about the school buy program with requests for a better way to handle the problem. "They haven't come up with one yet," he says.

Depending on demand, one dealer says he sells $100 to $1000 of drugs per week there. If all fifty drug dealers on campus have a "good" week the amount of money changing hands is staggering. And it happengs all over the campus, "even in the classroom," according to students.

Students now are reportedly more sophisticated about drug use than in the '60s and early '70s. "Everyone takes care of everyone," they say; and the once familiar sight of the paramedics retrieving an unconscious youngster is now uncommon. Perhaps the medical findings on effects of drugs are becoming known, but maybe not . . . because if they really understood the risks, Pali kids wouldn't be spending thousands of dollars monthly to fry their brain cells and blacken their lungs.

A variety of programs, many with federal grants, have been implemented around the country to combat substance abuse in the schools. The basic forms these programs have taken include the following: (1) education about the deleterious effects of drugs; (2) sloganish programs like, "Just say no!" combined with a pep talk on the evils of drug abuse; (3) group support programs, including role-playing skits which attempt to show students how to resist peer pressure; and (4) repressive police programs, where youthful-looking police officers go undercover in a high school and attempt to arrest dealers and users.

Hard research evidence about the effectiveness of these varied programs is currently unavailable. Preliminary data, however, reveals the following: Educational programs about drugs seems to cut both ways. Some children are deterred from using drugs, others seem to become intrigued by the information and choose to experiment. The sloganish programs involving "say no" seem to have little effect unless they are backed up with auxiliary group pressure discussions. The undercover police efforts are difficult to assess. They create a climate of fear in the school where police become part of the student body, which probably deters some juveniles. On the other hand, police "school-buy" programs often arrest first-time users, since the more sophisticated delinquent dealers in the school are more adept at identifying police officers. Having police in the schools also tends to have a negative affect on the overall educational process.

The most effective programs appear to be those which involve group therapy combined with the substance-abuser attending teen support groups like Alcoholics Anonymous, Narcotics Anonymous, and Cocaine Anonymous. In these varied groups the juvenile substance abuser tends to learn more about why he or she uses drugs, and abusers are supported by their peers in their effort to stay drug-free. (This therapeutic process is more extensively discussed in Part V, "The Prevention, Treatment, and Control of Delinquency.")

LABELING JUVENILE DELINQUENCY IN SCHOOL

As I delineated earlier, labeling a person delinquent is often more related to the "social perception" of the labeler rather than through the juvenile courts' adjudication process. Labeling students should be done cautiously, particularly so when the labels are negative ones. The dangers can be seen simply by looking up the term or label juvenile delinquent in the *Dictionary of Education*: "Any child or youth whose conduct deviates sufficiently from normal social usage to warrant his being considered a menace to himself, to his future interests, or to society itself."[21] This calls for a judgment, and suppose this judgment takes place in the middle-class school setting where the conduct of the lower-class child is apt to deviate significantly from that of the middle classes just on the basis of class and cultural differences. Are all these deviations going to be labeled delinquent? I would suggest that difference superimposed on a background of expected middle-class behavior frequently is labeled delinquent when it constitutes behavior considered unacceptable by a particular teacher.

Deviant behavior does not refer to some intrinsic quality of a specific act, rather is external to the act; it is a property conferred upon some form of behavior by observers. Howard Becker states this case as follows:

> Social groups create deviance by making the rules whose infraction constitutes deviance, and by applying these rules to particular people and labeling them outsiders. From this point of view, deviance is not a quality of the act of the person commits, but rather a consequence of the application by others of rules

and sanctions to an "offender." The deviant is one to whom that label has successfully been applied; deviant behavior is behavior that people so label.[22]

Although there is no doubt that deviant behavior is behavior that people so label, most of us would say that there are certain kinds of behavior that are intrinsically deviant. It nevertheless appears that much of what Becker is saying is applicable to the school system. Cavan has similarly conceptualized delinquency as a matter of "public tolerance, intolerance or outright condemnation."[23] Backing up the public school system is a middle-class system that demands conformity to middle-class modes of dressing, looking, speaking, and behaving. One of the ways in which it attempts to induce conformity is through the labeling process, through the induction of guilt and the manipulation of the child's need to be loved and to belong. As Fromm says, control is no longer maintained through overt authority but through anonymous authority masquerading as the best interest of the child.

> While the teacher of the past said to Johnny, "You must do this. If you don't I'll punish you"; today's teacher says, "I'm sure you'll 'like' to do this." Here, the sanction for disobedience is not corporal punishment, but the suffering face of the parent (or teacher), or what is worse, conveying the feeling of not being "adjusted," of not acting as the crowd acts. Overt authority used physical force; anonymous authority employs psychic manipulation.[24]

So, in the attempts to induce "respectable" middle-class behavior and to control "difficult" behavior, many students will be mislabeled as bad or troublemakers on the basis of traits, qualities, and characteristics that really do not refer to any genuinely "bad" act. The labeling process may actually be only a function of the teacher's conscious and unconscious attitudes toward class and race. The danger of the labeling process is that the kind of label and the manner in which it is applied will determine (1) the kind of self-image the student develops, (2) the kind of response to the person who applies the label and to the system that person represents, and (3) the kind of reputation the student might get and the responses of others to that reputation.

Walter Reckless has found that one of the important variables determining an adolescent's commitment to delinquency is his self-image. Delinquents whom Reckless has examined consistently held a bad self-image as opposed to the approved self-images of nondelinquents.[25] In accordance

[22]Howard S. Becker, *Outsiders: Studies in the Sociology of Deviance* (New York: Free Press, 1963), p. 9.
[23]Ruth Shonle Cavan, *Juvenile Delinquency* (Philadelphia: Lippincott, 1969), p. 28.
[24]Erich Fromm in the introduction of A. S. Neill, *Summerhill* (New York: Hart, 1960), p. x.
[25]Walter C. Reckless, *The Crime Problem* (New York: Appleton-Century-Crofts, 1960).

with Cooley's "looking-glass self,"[26] the boy is apt to start seeing himself as others see him and begin acting accordingly or to increase his slightly deviant behavior to where it fits or exceeds his developing poor self-image. If this evaluative process goes on publicly, which it most probably does, the impact on the youth can be psychologically as well as educationally devastating. It may not take many such public shamings to turn the youth totally against teachers, schools, authority, and respectable society, particularly if he already has the strong sense of injustice that many lower-class boys have. It is also quite possible that a boy's alleged bad reputation can be reduced to one bad interaction with one teacher (such as the boy with the beard in a former example). Yet that one teacher, facilitated by the "will to believe" manifested by the other teachers, can spread that reputation throughout the school during one break in the faculty lunchroom. In the student's other classes and in upper grades, teachers will be more apt to react to his "rep" than to him. This kind of boy may soon decide that he just can't adjust to the school setting and drop out.

The reaction of the school personnel is crucial to the future course the student might take.

> One of the factors affecting the chances that misconduct in the school will be reduced or will be repeated and extended to include misbehavior in the community is the character and effect of the school's sanctioning system. On one hand, the school can prevent behavior problems from re-occurring by imposing firm sanctions, while at the same time involving the student in the legitimate system, rewarding him for conforming behavior, and developing academic and social competencies. On the other hand, the school can inadvertently push the student toward illegitimate commitments by imposing overly-punitive sanctions in a degrading way; by locking the individual out of the legitimate system through such mechanisms as expulsion, suspension, withdrawal of extracurricular privileges, and placement in a special classroom for the "emotionally disturbed," a child may be pushed further into delinquent behavior.[27]

SCHOOL AND THE DELINQUENT CHILD

The child from a poor family going to school encounters many special difficulties, some attributable to his early experiences in the family, the consequences of heavy drug problems in his community, and others resulting from deficiencies in the school system. The fact that almost every delinquent has a record of poor achievement, truancy, or both suggests a serious failure of the school to meet his needs. As Kvaraceus points out:

---

[26]Richard Dewery, "Charles Horton Cooley: Pioneer in Psychosociology," in *An Introduction to the History of Sociology*, ed. Harry Elmer Barnes (Chicago: University of Chicago Press, 1948).

[27]Schafer and Polk, "Delinquency and the Schools," p. 234.

Literature in the field of juvenile delinquency reveals, on the whole, rather unsatisfactory school adjustments for most children who fall into difficulty with the law. Retardation is usually high, low school achievement and poor marks predominate, truancy is frequent, dislike for school and teachers is the rule rather than the exception, and early school leaving is very often the delinquent's own solution of an unsatisfactory situation.[28]

Kvaraceus found that in a sample of 761 children being handled by the Children's Bureau of Passaic, New Jersey, very few went on to finish high school, 52 percent never completed junior high school, and 7 percent left even before completion of seventh grade. Their school grades were so low that marks of excellent, very good, and good had to be combined in one group before Kvaraceus could work with them statistically. The truancy rate of the delinquents was found to be 34 percent, as compared with 6.8 for the general population of schoolchildren.

Kvaraceus asserts that these factors cause the child to feel inferior and often frustrated. A child who is kept back a grade is usually the biggest and oldest child in the class. Since he cannot show his superiority academically, he often finds some other way to establish high status. The pattern is usually one frowned on by both teachers and parents.

William S. Amoss found evidence that further supports the relationship between low school performance and delinquency.[29] He selected 76 male and 52 female grade school students by using the criterion that the child had a "demonstrated need for supervision by the juvenile court." He then matched them to "normal" kids, scanning the school records of each, taking into account factors such as age, race, changes in family residence, intelligence, the number of parents at home, and the kinds of ratings they had compiled in social attitudes and work habits.

The records of the group with the eyes of the court upon them were different from those of the less troublesome youngsters. Delinquent girls had more unstable home conditions and were older than their academic peers, while the boys with bad reports had low grade-point averages and poor attitudes and work habits.

Possibly, delinquent girls got the same grades and department ratings as their nondelinquent sisters because these ratings are usually made by female teachers. Amoss suggests that there may be "a psychological conflict for the male delinquent with female standards of behavior in the classroom." Since the unstable home conditions of the girls usually meant an absent father, they could be having problems with "psychosexual development." As far as their comparatively advanced age was concerned, Amoss speculated that the delinquent girls might have been seeking older peers outside of school by whom they were negatively influenced.

[28]William C. Kvaraceus, *Juvenile Delinquency and the School* (Yonkers, N.Y.: World, 1945), p. 135.
[29]As quoted in a report on William S. Amoss in *Human Behavior* (March 1976).

The delinquent pattern for boys as a group seems to be more concretely connected to school matters; however, clues that point toward delinquency can be found in the school records of both sexes.

My research reveals that there is a link between juvenile delinquency and learning disabilities. In most cases juvenile delinquents have a history of poor performance in reading, writing, and verbal communication in their predelinquent behavior. The learning-disabled child and the juvenile delinquent have similar characteristics—"both develop a negative self-concept and low frustration tolerance."

In an effort to cope with learning disabilities and educationally handicapped delinquents, the Federal Government in 1975 passed Public Law 94–142. The law provided funds to enrich programs for learning-disabled children. In 1986 they extended the discretionary programs authorized under the 1975 Education of the Handicapped Act through the fiscal year 1989. The Congress in many instances specified that particular attention be accorded special groups of handicapped children and youth. With respect to minorities, the report accompanying the extension of the law states:

> Individual discretionary programs under the Act have periodically supported projects and activities aimed at minority populations. Notable in this regard is the personnel preparation program whose projects include historically Black institutions as well as projects preparing personnel for limited English proficient, bilingual, American Indian, Asian/Pacific Islander and migrant children and youth.

Under these laws, delinquent handicapped youths are eligible for a free and appropriate education under the Education for All Handicapped Children Act of 1975. Many of these incarcerated youth, however, are not receiving the education services to which they are entitled under federal and state mandates, doubtlessly due in part to the problematic nature of providing services to the diverse and highly transitory juvenile institution populations.

The *highest priority* of these laws is to serve the most severely educationally handicapped "underserved" population. Targeting these groups is one issue, while determining the relative severity of the individual's handicapped condition is a more difficult assessment. The dilemma is further confounded by governance realities. Laws addressing the education of incarcerated youth vary nationwide, and in many states legislation regulating education applies only to the school districts, not to social service agencies or juvenile court authorities.

Incarcerated educationally handicapped children pose a special problem in relation to delinquency. Over 150,000 children and youths under the age of 22 are currently confined in the juvenile and adult correctional institutions of this country. Facilities for adults house approximately 117,000 of these juveniles, or about 20 percent of the adult inmate population, while more than 33,000 children and adolescents reside in juvenile facilities. Furthermore, an additional 300,000 juveniles are committed each year to pretrial detention centers and jails.

According to Donna M. Murphy, "Although reports of the prevalence of handicapping conditions among juvenile delinquents vary greatly, rapidly accumulating evidence indicates that a disproportionate percentage of that population, as compared to nondelinquents, are [educationally] handicapped."[30]

A major problem in the problem of the educationally handicapped child (incarcerated or not) is his or her difficulty with reading. Reading deficiencies clearly set up a blockade to learning. There has been a considerable amount of research on this issue. In one significant study, focusing on reading as a predictor of delinquency, Thomas J. Taglianetti observed that the problem of reading failure affects about one-third of our nation's students.[31] The subjects of the study were 1,200 elementary school children (tested at normal intelligence) and 200 former residents of juvenile detention facilities. Among the delinquents Taglianetti found that failure to read caused "general school failure, and constituted a possible contributing basis for delinquency."

For the delinquent, then, "school and the process of learning may be an extension of the distortion he finds everywhere else. The normal school may emphasize his difference from the 'in group' or become a battlefield for home-originated hostility."[32] The learning process may seem unreal to him either because of his personal problems or because he sees no relation between what he learns in school and life as he knows it in his home and community.

The result has been cogently stated by Milton L. Barron: "The insistence of schools teaching children subjects in which they cannot succeed often damages self-confidence, leads to rejection by teachers and classmates, and makes them vulnerable to neurotic and delinquent behavior."[33] Children start to wonder why they are in school and what good it is actually doing them. When they do not get good marks, they are made to feel like failures, when actually they may have other, nonacademic assets worth development.

In this context, different types of delinquents described react differently: (1) The "neurotic delinquent" often in conflict with himself and society develops anxiety; (2) the "socialized delinquent" may view the teacher's values as alien to his own; (3) the "sociopath delinquent" doesn't care and employs his own "situation ethics"; and (4) the "psychotic delin-

---

[30]Donna M. Murphy, "The Prevalence of Handicapping Conditions Among Juvenile Delinquents," *Remedial and Special Education Journal* 7 (June 1986): 26.

[31]Thomas J. Taglianetti, "Reading Failure: A Predictor of Delinquency," *Crime Prevention Review* 2 (April 1975): 24–30.

[32]Benneta B. Washington, *Youth in Conflict* (Chicago: Science Research Associates, 1963), p. 177.

[33]Milton L. Barron, *The Juvenile in Delinquent Society* (New York: Knopf, 1960), p. 177.

quent" is usually excluded from school because he is not in communication with the reality of the school situation.

Other negative factors often operating in the schools include textbooks too difficult for use or understanding by children from underprivileged families and areas, teachers excessively permissive or excessively rigid in control or inconsistent in discipline, and careless gossip among teachers about children who have been in trouble or whose families are in difficulty.[34]

The question arises as to whether or not it is advisable to require a child to go to school until he is 16 years old. If a child is doing poorly in school, does not wish to continue, and is physically able and anxious to get a job, should we compel him to stay in school? If we do, perhaps the school curriculum should be adapted to his perceived needs.

Several school programs have been developed to help prepare young people for occupational roles. One is the New York School to Employment Program for boys 15 years of age and over who show signs of being able to succeed in a job despite poor school records. The boys go through a modified school program, attending regular and select classes in the morning and then working at jobs in the afternoon, for which they can receive school credit. The Detroit Job Up-Grading, designed for boys 16 to 20, attempts to get high school dropouts back in school long enough to train for a job and get placed in one. Counseling continues for six months after the end of the course. The Chicago Double E (Education and Employment) Program is designed for dropouts selected by counselors. After a preemployment session, the boys start to work in a department store that sponsors the program along with the Chicago Board of Education. They attend classes concurrently with their jobs. With a working knowledge of the operations of such a store, they can get jobs upon completion of school. Other companies are also becoming interested in this type of program.

This idea of school-to-employment adjustment is summed up by James B. Conant: "*I submit that in a heavily urbanized and industrialized free society the educational experiences of youth should fit their subsequent employment. There should be a smooth transition from full-time schooling to a full-time job, whether that transition be after grade ten or after graduation from high school, college, or university.*"[35]

The schools should not just propel delinquents or problem children out their front doors; they should make efforts to help them. School is the first testing ground away from the protective atmosphere of the family. The school should be able to detect early misbehavior and to help the child while he is still young and more receptive to treatment than he will be later. There is no better place to detect negative behavior than the school, and it

[34]Bernice Milburn Moore, "The Schools and the Problems of Delinquency: Research Studies and Findings," *Crime and Delinquency* 7 (March 1961): 201–212.

[35]James B. Conant, *Slums and Suburbs* (New York: McGraw-Hill, 1961), p. 41.

should be able to serve a very useful purpose in preventing delinquency. There are several failures in the school system that are believed to contribute to delinquency. These include:

1. *Providing frustrating experiences.* If the child experiences failure at school every day, he not only learns little, but becomes frustrated and unhappy. Curricula that do not provide a reasonable opportunity for *every* child to experience success in some areas may therefore be said to contribute to delinquency.
2. *Failing to maintain interest.* Teaching without in some way relating the subject matter to the needs and aspirations of the student leaves him uninvolved. There is little or no effort in most schools to develop curricula specifically of interest to the students.
3. *Failing to provide a feeling of satisfaction among children.* To many lower-class children, school is a prison. They find little or no activity designed to give them pleasure. They are seldom asked what they would really like to learn and then given the opportunity to do so.
4. *Failing to provide satisfying personal relationships between students and teachers.* Many classes are too large and impersonal to permit any warm relationships to develop. A child who fails to develop warm relationships with parents and relatives is unlikely to find such relationships in the impersonal school.[36]

The child is required each day to spend more waking hours in school than in any other place, with the possible exception of his home. In his first few years at school, the child is likely to be assigned to one teacher, who becomes, in effect, a parent substitute. Under these conditions he may very well spend more time under the teacher's direction than under parental supervision, especially if his mother is employed outside the home. Thus, whatever the reason for his leaving school, the child who does not adjust and drops out is deprived of the socializing influence of an adult who could influence his conformity to the law. The absence of such influence makes it more likely that he will become delinquent. That delinquency and school adjustment are related is evidenced by the fact that approximately 61 percent of the delinquents between the ages of 8 and 17 are not in school.

Children who find school traumatic tend to stay away. Repeated truancy may become defined as delinquency. In any case, children are more likely to learn and engage in delinquent behavior on the streets than they would if they stayed in school. As a result of frequent absences, the child falls behind in his work. Most delinquents are about two years behind others of their age in their schoolwork, particularly in reading. Retardation makes further attendance at school even more difficult, and many such

[36]For a detailed analysis of these issues, see Bernice Milburn Moore, *Juvenile Delinquency* (Washington, D.C.: National Education Association, 1958); and William C. Kvaraceus and William E. Ulrich, *Delinquent Behavior: Principles and Practices* (Washington, D.C.: National Education Association, 1959).

children drop out of school entirely. The school truant is more likely to engage in delinquent behavior than the youth who remains in school. In an article on the relationship of truancy to delinquency, Claire Berman describes how a prototypical truant spends his time on the streets of New York City:

> The 15-year-old boy pointed to his signature "Dune 1"—an artfully spray-painted nom de graffitti in bold, 4-foot letters on the concrete wall of a school playground. "Everybody knows my name," he said proudly, "I painted it all over the city."
>
> His proclamations notwithstanding, Dune 1 is a nobody to a city school system that lost track of him more than two years ago. He is one of possibly 90,000 youngsters listed by the board of Education as long-term absentees—and frequently referred to as "ghosts."
>
> Instead of going to school, they crowd department stores, the Port Authority bus terminal, the Bronx Zoo, Central Park, Coney Island. They wander the hallways of other schools. They join gangs. They spend hours on the subways, their transistor radios blaring. Many like Dune 1 have learned to decorate the trains, using cans of spray paint "lifted" from the shelves of local stores. They commit petty crimes and some of them get into trouble—known to the law if not to the schools.[37]

The next step for a habitual truant is to totally drop out of school and become more involved in delinquent behavior.

THE SCHOOL DROPOUT AND DELINQUENCY

The term dropout has generally been applied to describe a student who leaves school without completing his or her education. The lower-class, frustrated child is most likely to drop out. On the streets and unemployed, the dropout is a high-risk candidate for delinquent behavior. On this issue a study by Terence Thornberry, Melanie Moore, and R.L. Christensen, "The Effect of Dropping Out of High School on Subsequent Criminal Behavior," reveals the impact of dropping out on delinquency and, later, crime. In their article they state:[38]

> The relationship between school failure and criminal behavior is a recurrent theme in theories of delinquency. Eventual dropouts have been found to have considerably higher rates of delinquency during high school than do graduates, a finding consistent both with conventional wisdom and most theories of delinquency. However, what is not clear either theoretically or empirically is the effect that dropping out of high school has on subsequent criminal behavior.

[37]Clair Berman, "The 90,000 Ghosts Who Haunt the Schools," *The New York Times*, November 14, 1976. Copyright © 1976 by the New York Times Company. Reprinted by permission.

[38]Terrence P. Thornberry, Melanie Moore, and R. L. Christensen, "The Effect of Dropping Out of High School on Subsequent Criminal Behavior," *Criminology* 23, 1 (February 1985): 56.

Indeed, for this relationship two basic models of delinquency, strain theory and social control theory, offer rather divergent predictions.

Based on their extensive study the researchers conclude:

Dropping out of school has a long-term effect on later criminal behavior. Throughout the early twenties dropouts have consistently higher rates of arrests than do graduates and it is not until the mid-twenties that the rates for the two groups begin to converge. These findings are also observed for minority group subjects and those from blue-collar backgrounds, the groups of particular interest to strain theory. Finally, dropout status was also found to have a significant positive effect on crime when the postschool experiences of marriage and employment are controlled. In general, therefore, results of this analysis are quite consistent with the theoretical expectations of social control theory; dropping out has a positive effect on subsequent arrest even when age and postschool experiences are controlled.

. . . Although control theory appears to be more accurate than strain theory in assessing the role that dropping out of school plays in the genesis of delinquency, these results cannot be interpreted as providing general support for a control perspective versus a strain perspective. The present analysis has focused exclusively on one behavioral area—dropping out of school—while the theories are concerned with a much wider array of behavioral issues—family, peers beliefs, and so forth. Nevertheless, with respect to dropping out of school, where the theories do offer contradictory predictions, the evidence from this study is quite clear: dropping out is significantly and positively related to subsequent criminal involvement as predicted by social control theory.[39]

DEHUMANIZATION IN THE SCHOOLS AND DELINQUENCY

The general problem of dehumanization often found in the school derives from the larger social context. The products of this system have been identified as robopaths.[40] The term *robopath*, simply defined, relates to the pathology of robot behavior.

Many schools (at all levels) are large, bureaucratic, human teaching machines that place no emphasis on people relating to people. In some cases, actual mechanical teaching machines have replaced human beings in interaction. In other cases, the teachers are as mechanistic in their approach as the machines. As Charles E. Silberman (among many other observers) suggests in his book *Crisis in the Classroom*, routine, order, and discipline have become more important than humanistic education, and teachers are more concerned with routine and order than education.

In fact, youngsters who display spontaneity are referred to by human teaching machines as "hyperactives." In many cases the normal and healthy

---

[39]Ibid., p. 58.

[40]Lewis Yablonsky, *Robopaths: People as Machines* (Baltimore: Penguin, 1972), pp. 40–41.

exuberance of childhood is viewed as an emotional problem. Increasingly, in many schools around the country, such children who "act out" too much are sedated with various kinds of drugs to calm them down. These drugs are, of course, legally administered by the "system." Later in life, in their teenage years, when these same young people take drugs outside the established order in a kind of self-administered therapy for changing their emotional state, they may be arrested and labeled "criminal." The point is that spontaneity is suspect and is too often placed under rigid controls by a social-machine educational system.

One of the social philosophers who envisioned these problems was J. L. Moreno, who in the mid-1920s attempted to develop an innovative "impromptu school" that would counterattack the educational social-machine impact of overconformity. His rationale was:

> Children are endowed with the gift of spontaneous expression up to the age of five, while they are still in an unconscious creative state, unhampered by the laws and customs laid down by a long succession of preceding generations. After that they fall heir to accepted methods of expression; they become imitative, turn into automatons and in a large measure are deprived of natural outlets of volitional creation. . . .

> Until a certain age all children's learning is spontaneously acquired. . . . Soon, however, the adult begins to introduce into the child's world subjects unrelated to its needs. The little victim from then on is pressed by many adult sophistries into learning poems, lessons, facts, songs, and so on, all of which remain like a foreign substance in an organism. The child begins to accept as superior that which is taught him and to distrust his own creative life. So very early in the life of the individual there is a tendency to mar and divert creative impulses. . . .

> Here the impromptu comes to the rescue. It offers a school of training which can be practiced in the small or large group or within the family circle itself. The impromptu method concerns itself with mental and emotional states. We do things and learn things because we are in certain states—states of fear, of love, of excitement, aspiration, etc. These states may be directly affected through stimulation and control of imagination and emotion. When the impromptu instructor recognizes the pupil to be lacking in a certain state, e.g., courage, joy, etc., he places him in a specific situation in which the lacking state will be emphasized. The pupil "plays" that situation, dramatizing the state impromptu. In other words, if lacking in courage, he "plays" courage until he learns to be courageous.[41]

In summary, the "natural" press of socialization by parents, friends, and school in machine societies often tends to make children grow into robopathic adults. Many children, however, are able to incorporate the rules, roles, expectations, and aspirations of the society into their personality and maintain their spontaneous, creative, and compassionate abilities and capacities. Children caught in the press of a heavy social-machine

[41]J. L. Moreno, M.D., *Theatre of Spontaneity* (Beacon, N.Y.: Beacon House, 1947), pp. 105–106. Reprinted by permission.

society do not become self-actualized in the Maslow sense; they tend to become robopathic role players and thus help perpetuate the social-machine system. Another fallout of this behavior is a disposition to violence from frustration and the child's limited compassion.

Robopathic students are members of an impersonal school system in which they are treated impersonally; the net result is often a feeling of alienation. Durkheim,[42] Merton,[43] Cloward and Ohlin,[44] and others have documented the destructive effects of this lack of integration into society and significant groups. Tönnies[45] and a long line of successors have stressed the impersonalization that accompanies the complexities of city life.

What is happening in the schools must be viewed against the conceptual background of alienation and robopathology. Teachers and administrators must be cogently aware of the cost in morale of a bureaucratic, impersonal approach to campus problems, especially in high schools. It appears that a caste system has developed in schools, with a we-they differentiation of students and their teachers/administrators. Administration has become the "enemy" who issues orders from above but is silent on communications from below. The effect of this breakdown in communications is to render the students impotent; they are victims in a system over which they have no control. The importance of "feelings of efficacy"[46] in life situations has certainly been well documented but is no doubt generalizable to all people, including students. We like to feel that we have some part in determining the conditions of our life. Even if determinism is an illusion, it is a grand illusion that most of us have a need to maintain.

In 1965, a conference of adolescents met in California to discuss problems of youth concerning schools. Unanimous recommendations were: (1) students be given more responsibility in student affairs; (2) students be involved in setting school standards and rules through youth councils; (3) school and youth organizations be encouraged to involve students more actively in problems concerning the community. Every effort should therefore be made to involve students in decision making, particularly in decisions that affect their lives in important ways. If this is not accomplished, if the communication block remains intact, students will continue to act out more dramatic ways of communicating.

Many pressures toward delinquency derive from a conflict regarding the goals of the public school system. Although society has said that the schools have the multiple goals of responding positively to the academic, occupational, emotional, and social needs of students, especially of culturally deprived children, it is my thesis that many of these goals do not get implemented at the classroom level. The goals that are not realized are

---

[42]Emile Durkheim, *Le Suicide*, Paris, 1897.

[43]R. K. Merton, *Social Theory and Social Structure* (Glencoe, Ill.: Free Press, 1957).

[44]Richard A. Cloward and Lloyd E. Ohlin, *Delinquency and Opportunity* (New York: Free Press of Glencoe, 1960).

[45]Tönnies, *Community and Society*.

[46]Lewis Yablonsky, *The Violent Gang* (New York: Macmillan, 1962).

precisely those that require warmth, understanding, insight (into self as well as others), patience—in short, those that require good interpersonal skills. Robopathic, impersonal school systems do not have the kind of personnel that respond to the emotional needs of children. Many of them are rigid, anxiety-ridden people who can barely handle their own emotional lives. They consequently retreat into an intellectual area where they feel more comfortable and more competent—the straight teaching of academic materials.

Glasser has noted that the importance of personal contact in teaching has been receiving less attention as the emphasis on methods, objective testing, and classification of students has increased. The prevailing attitude is to "remain objective and detached, don't get involved"; but teaching *should* be personal. Treating children as objects rather than people who desperately need involvement only compounds the problem.[47]

Glasser develops his reality-therapy approach more fully in his book *Schools Without Failure*.[48] In this book Glasser notes that most schools in the central areas of cities process children for failure because their educational programs are "irrelevant and do not provide methods for effectively involving children in the educational process." Children react to this failure with withdrawal and, often, delinquent behavior. Glasser's central thesis is that "if a child, no matter what his background, can succeed in school he has an excellent chance for success in life." He asserts that teachers should in effect become reality therapists—"offer friendship, understanding, and get involved with helping children overcome their emotional problems." To accomplish this he recommends that every subject taught should be related to something the child acts out in his day-to-day life inside and outside of school.

In the same context, psychodrama, related to both curriculum and personal problems, is a method that can involve children more effectively than most discussion techniques. Psychodrama relevantly applied in the classroom situation can counterattack the conditions that produce the emotional problems that emerge later in life.

Psychodrama and Group Methods in the Classroom: Combatting Robopathic Behavior and Delinquency

Psychodrama has been utilized at every level of the educational system—from kindergarten to the postgraduate seminar.[49] The sessions have not only been related to subject matter but to current social events," character development," and preventing delinquency.

[47]William Glasser, *Reality Therapy* (New York: Harper & Row, 1965), p. 165.
[48]William Glasser, *Schools Without Failure* (New York: Harper & Row, 1968).
[49]The following analysis on psychodrama as a theory-methodology for humanizing the school situation and preventing delinquency is derived from Lewis Yablonsky, *Psychodrama: Resolving Emotional Problems Through Role Playing* (New York: Gardner, 1981).

The debate over a teacher's dealing with a child's emotional state in class—beyond the curriculum—still goes on in many school systems, but despite this, the application of role playing that relates to emotional and deviance problems has become an established practice in the classroom. Psychodrama is utilized in the classroom for both the child's emotional growth and for curriculum purposes on subject matter. In connection with transmitting information, many teachers use a wide array of role-playing techniques to involve delinquency-prone children in learning more effectively.

Many teachers have role-playing sessions where children (after being informed on a subject) psychodramatically assume the role of an inanimate or animate object they are studying. To understand the subject or role on a deeper level a child may become a tree or an animal or assume the role of police officer, judge, lawyer, or attendance officer. (In this latter context a child playing the role of his attendance officer invariably asks himself, "Why do you play hookey?" This often produces a meaningful discussion of why kids do not attend school.) We would suggest that the literature and the characters be acted out in a free style that facilitates the student's development of spontaneity and gives him a broad range for interpretation. For example, consider the possibilities of the "To be or not to be" scene from Hamlet. In a session one of the authors ran with high school–age students, it kicked off an exciting and useful examination of the social problems and implications of suicide, violence, and homicide. It was noted that the youths most prone to this behavior were the students most involved in the sessions.

History can be made exciting and interesting through role playing that goes beyond the surface into emotional issues. Portraits of significant periods and episodes in history tend to personally and emotionally stimulate student involvement. For example, in examining patriotic emotions, it might be useful in lieu of saluting the flag to have a different child, each day, role-play "the flag" and talk about such issues as how he (as the flag) came into existence and what he stands for. Dialogue with the "student flag" should, of course, be encouraged. This type of psychodramatic interaction would breathe some life into a role ritual that no longer has much meaning for most children. It fosters a discussion by many delinquency-prone children into the meaning and values of laws and the Constitution.

In a deeper historical context, a student can play George Washington, Abraham Lincoln, John F. Kennedy, or Ronald Reagan and present each president's speeches. Have students (black and white) play blacks of that era and militants of today as the audience to the speech. Properly done, this type of session will veer into a psychodrama on contemporary race relations between students, racial militancy, and the role of presidents and politicians, and reveal some of the emotions young people have about these issues.

On a more direct emotional level, psychodrama sessions in the classroom can encompass such subjects as dating, meeting new people, envying others, not having lots of clothes (or the right clothes), getting low grades, being embarrassed to speak in front of the class, getting high grades on tests, making a mistake in front of the class, being complimented, having money stolen, cheating on tests, gossiping, running for school office, taking drugs, "sexual promiscuity," vandalism, losing in a contest, being absent from school frequently, losing one's possessions, forgetting things, not completing assignments, and fair and unfair discipline by teachers.

The psychodrama sessions can utilize the following order of action:

1. Have students select and discuss a problem as a warm-up.
2. Assign roles according to the problem situation.
3. Enact a specific situation or situation involving tensions and conflict.
4. Analyze patterns of conflict which appear in the role playing.
5. Replay for better relationships and improved role performance.

One inner-city teacher's report on her role playing in the classroom reveals the broad range of subjects covered and the practice involved.

With the younger pre-school children my "games" are painless "let's pretend" although I do like to ask the children the whys of the profession they choose and also to try to have the significant others present (i.e., doctors and nurses, football players and spectators or coaches, teachers and, of course, students). In all these role-playing experiences I feel the children are being creative; however with the primary grade children I go one step further. Instead of just "playing" roles I have them reverse roles. One that seems to be the favorite is that boys are girls and girls are boys, or children from different ethnic or racial groups reverse roles. When the children are finished at playing each other I ask them to share what it *felt* like. I like to know if they would like to always be a boy (girl), black (white), parent (child), teacher (student), or if they were glad it was a game. Most indicate they like their real role.

It was really helpful to use this technique in disciplinary action. If a child is really making a lot of disturbance or is hurting another child I use role reversal with the child and myself or let the two children do it. Of course this involves a short explanation of the theory and method, but I try to let them confront each other as soon as possible in role-playing after the fight.

I have often thought that when I am having a particular crabby day it would be good for me to let one of the children reverse roles with me, but my courage has not permitted this as yet. If by using these techniques I am able to encourage humanness in my children then the rewards are self-evident.

The potential of the use of psychodrama in schools among those children who are having learning and social problems is illustrated by a group psychodrama experiment I conducted in a New York school with a class of 18 so-called maladjusted delinquent boys. Of the 18 boys, 10 were confirmed truants, and most had been involved in petty theft or vandalism. All the boys were aggressive, and many were prone to acting out violence.

All the boys were performing well below standards in school, were discouraged easily in school, and then either cut school, lost their tempers, fought, or stole. All the boys in the study tended to be disruptive and undisciplined in school. Whenever they ran up against a situation they could not handle, they became antagonistic and quarrelsome, sulked, walked around the room, and generally interefered with other children who were working.

Applying psychodrama to their learning situations was not merely a matter of getting a selfish boy to play a generous role or a cowardly child a heroic role, although this appeared to have value, but rather of presenting the children with situations in their daily lives which trouble them and to which they responded inadequately. It was recognized that positive change in these boys could not be achieved in just one session. As a consequence of many psychodrama sessions, there were improved social responses in the various situations these boys confronted daily in their home, family, and school life. In five weeks some remarkable changes were noted in the behavior of most of the boys. By the end of the school term they showed better attitudes, developed improved relationships with classmates, and had greater self-discipline, and class attendance and work all showed a marked improvement.

Using psychodrama with problem children in school is much more effective if the children's parents can be involved. In this regard, as part of a delinquency prevention program I ran in New York, I introduced this approach with positive results.

The project took place at P.S. 93 in Manhattan—a school located in an urban area beset by the many complex and extreme problems of contemporary society. I selected the parents we would work with simply by having teachers select the 20 most difficult problem children in the school. Who these students were was determined by having the principal and a panel of ten teachers list their "top 20 troublemakers." There was a remarkable consensus—interestingly—in identifying these students, and most of these students had been to juvenile court. The principal then invited the parents to "become part of a group exploring children's problems in school."

The group met one night a week for a six-month period. Most of the parents (fathers and mothers) attended regularly. We moved into role-playing situations about disciplining children, good and bad teachers, and a range of personal-family problems. A report was written at the end of the program that summarized the following "therapeutic effects":

1. Parents felt free to "blast" the school within the group. Some catharsis was observed as well as some understanding about the fact that they were in many cases projecting onto the school their own limitations as parents.
2. Parents seemed to benefit from the knowledge that other parents had problems similar to theirs.
3. Parents found they could help each other to understand and resolve

conflict situations by acting out and discussing their experiences in the group. They agreed that more dimensions of a problem were brought to light in the role playing than in their discussions. Moreover, the discussion parts of the session were more dynamic after role playing.

4. Many recommendations and suggestions about methods and techniques for positively dealing with their children emerged in the group as a result of the role playing, and the group gave its support to those parents who wanted to try them out.

5. The group established parent behavior norms. Permissive and punitive disciplinary approaches were acted out with the extremes tending to give way to more moderate approaches.

I have often effectively used psychodrama in my college classrooms. It is a valuable tool for having students understand delinquency on a more personal and profound level. For example, after exploring a concept, such as "the violent sociopath," in a delinquency course, we would have a student come forward and play the role. The class would ask the "student sociopath" a variety of interesting and self-revealing questions. In exploring crime causation we often get a student as a protagonist who is courageous enough to admit to a delinquent act from his past. In one session, at the height of "an act of burglary as a teenager," we had a student protagonist freeze in the moment of the role and soliloquize his motivations. We then had other volunteer students double with his soliloquy. It is interesting to note that almost a third of the students in classes where this type of psychodrama was presented come forward one by one and soliloquize a parallel act—and their motivations. The process seems to make the subject more interesting, but more important, it provides an opportunity for a student to personally and emotionally identify with the subject.

Over the years I have taught courses on the subject of psychodrama, crime, and delinquency almost every semester. The course always involves actual sessions with students. The discussion of sociological concepts is invariably enriched by a psychodrama session. For example, it seems arid to present a lecture on role theory without actually involving students in some scene in their life that related to communication, empathy, or the socialization process. When all these concepts are taught, various psychodramatic techniques seem to be intrinsic vehicles to help the student to understand basic concepts. In exploring role theory, for example, the Charles Horton Cooley concept of the "looking-glass self" or the G. H. Mead theory of empathy or "taking" the role of the other is actualized and explicated when a student psychodramatically reverses roles, doubles, or becomes an auxiliary ego. The method is especially helpful to students who plan to become teachers, work in the field of delinquency prevention, or in a juvenile institutional setting.

In brief, the use of a range of psychodramatic concepts and group methods in education at all levels helps to resolve regular and complex educational problems, can serve as an aid to transmitting standard educational material, and can enliven the day-to-day procedures of the classroom so that it becomes a more attractive and enjoyable human situation. These groups can also be relevant in the treatment of children in the schools to combat substance abuse and delinquent behavior.

SUMMARY: BASIC THEMES FOR CLASS DISCUSSION

1. In earlier periods, especially in rural America, the family was a more dominant force and exercised a more significant role in educating children. In contemporary society the schools, in terms of their function, have a more significant influence in both educating and socializing children. As a consequence, educational institutions have a more significant role in providing children with their values and preventing delinquency.

2. Children who come from families beset by conflicts and emotional problems tend to bring these problems into the classroom. This has the effect of producing delinquent problems in the classroom, or in some cases leads to a child dropping out of school and becoming delinquent.

3. Too often all school means to some children is a diploma that enables them to get a job. School can be a more meaningful situation in providing a child with positive rather than negative values.

4. Minority children tend too often to find schools a place where their language, culture, and values collide with what they have been taught by their family in their community. This conflict often produces rebelliousness, and in some cases deviant behavior. This conflict of values and rebelliousness can often lead to a child dropping out of school and a later life of delinquency.

5. The federal government has passed legislation to provide special funds to help children with special learning problems. These funds are earmarked for both public schools and schools where delinquents are in custody.

6. Too many children are labeled in schools as "bad" or "deviant," when in fact their behavior is more a manifestation of their family and community values than delinquent behavior. Despite this, however, some of the consequences of this labeling results in adjudicated delinquency.

7. Substance abuse has become a major problem in the schools. It negatively affects the substance-abusing student in a variety of ways, including their ability to learn, and drugs in the schools negatively affect the proper climate of the educational process.

8. Teachers who are more aware of these various issues and the special problems of learning disabled and minority children can become a vital force in preventing delinquency.

9. Some schools have become dehumanized places where the learning process has become too machinelike and "robopathic." In these situations group approaches, including psychodrama, can relieve the boredom and make school more attractive. In this context, any

approach that makes the school situation more desirable and keeps students learning and in school serves as a deterrent to juvenile delinquency.

QUESTIONS

6.1. Why does the contemporary school situation have a more profound role in the education and socializing of a child than it did in the past?

6.2. Why do family problems produce school problems? What are the social and psychological dynamics of this family-school situation?

6.3. Why do minority children tend to have more school problems than students in the general population?

6.4. What are the issues involved in the assertion that school problems lead to delinquent and criminal behavior?

6.5. How does substance abuse affect the educational process? Design a model program for treating substance abuse in the schools.

6.6. You are given unlimited funds to "humanize" a school system so that it becomes a more attractive learning and socializing system for all students and has the effect of preventing and controlling delinquency. Design a model plan that would operationalize and achieve these goals.

three

SIGNIFICANT PROBLEMS: VIOLENCE AND DRUGS

chapter 7

The Juvenile in a Violent Society

Albert Camus, in *The Rebel*, his philosophical essay on the meanings of rebellion and revolution, had this to say about the contemporary violence that engulfs all citizens and has its special effect on juveniles:

> The poets themselves, confronted with the murder of their fellow men, proudly declare that their hands are clean. The whole world absentmindedly turns its back on these crimes; the victims have reached the extremity of their disgrace: they are a bore. In ancient times the blood of murder at least produced a religious horror and in this way sanctified the value of life. The real condemnation of the period we live in is, on the contrary, that it leads us to think that it is not bloodthirsty enough. Blood is no longer visible; it does not bespatter the faces of our pharisees visibly enough. This is the extreme of nihilism; blind and savage murder becomes an oasis, and the imbecile criminal seems positively refreshing in comparison with our highly intelligent executioners.

THE SOCIOCULTURAL CLIMATE OF VIOLENCE

There are still types of senseless violence and homicide that produce emotional reactions in the mass mind. The highly intelligent and socially ingrained executions of war, starvation, pollution, and disease no longer seem to stir the general population beyond a murmur of tacit recognition. These phenomena are almost unreal, since they are mainly experienced secondhand on television, in the newspapers, or on the movie screen. This blurring of reality is most evident in today's children. For many of them, the violence shown in a real-war report on the TV news is not too different from the fictionalized war of a dramatic program, and in the late 1980s the ultimate in chain-saw murders, mad-killer revenge rampages, Rambo mayhem, and violent abuses of people (especially women) has found its young audiences in neighborhood movie houses and on records like "Psychokiller."

In many films, violence is presented as an effective way of handling problems, not only for ordinary people, but for "heroes" and for representatives of the state, police officers, and people in authority. If we accept the available data on the relationship between viewing violence on television and increased aggressive behavior in children, we could conclude that watching violent films is likely to increase violent crime. The individual, particularly the very young boy, watching movie stars perform the violent "hero" role is likely to consider violence as an approved way of asserting his masculinity and of solving life's problems. This is particularly true for children who have emotional problems.

In the 1980s violence was raised in film to a higher and bloodier level. Such films as *The Texas Chainsaw Massacre, Halloween,* and *Friday the Thirteenth* involved sociopathic killers out on a rampage. In the film, *My Bloody Valentine,* people's hearts were cut out and sent in a bloody mess to potential victims. We can only speculate about how these grotesque portraits of violence affect young people. We can say, however, with great assurance that these images of bloody mayhem and death by knife and gun provide a clear framework of violence for our children. A steady diet of this violent poison negatively affects many people in our society and may cause young people to be indifferent to its horrendous quality.

There is increasing evidence that some young people become more and more inured to violence because of the constant bombardment of the mass media. A case in point is the response of one relatively normal 16-year-old youth who witnessed an actual homicide. His father, a psychologist, related the story of his son's response to the murder and his own reaction to his son's response as follows:[1]

The movies I saw during my childhood years contained simple human stories and had very little violence. Today the movies are full of mutilations, grisly murders and outrageous horror scenarios.

My son is an afficionado of these modern horror films, and I detest them. He thinks they are fun and exciting, and I think they are crass examples of the product of the typical banal, mercenary Hollywood mind. He sees them all, and I see only a few for purely psychological interest in understanding modern tastes.

In this context, my son recently had what would have been a horrendous emotional experience for me. The experience and his reaction to it reveal something about the conflict of perceptions in this generation gap. During the

[1]Lewis Yablonsky, *Fathers and Sons* (New York: Simon and Schuster, 1982), pp. 109–110.

summer he became friends with a young man—I will call him Jim—a twenty-five-year-old who seemed more like sixteen, my son's age at the time. The "man" was quite immature and had the basic personality of the standard Hollywood hustler who had no special talent yet was trying to break into the film and music business. He would do anything but work for his glorified and exorbitant goals. He did not have to work because he had a wealthy father who sent him a sizeable allowance. My son would tell me about his friend's escapades with dope and prostitutes.

Jim's story is rather complex, but the bottom line is that one day he got into an altercation (in my son's presence) with a man who lived near his apartment. Apparently Jim owed him money for drugs and refused to pay up. The man assaulted Jim. Jim went into his apartment, got a gun he had bought that day and shot his adversary in the head, killing him.

My son was an eyewitness to this horrible event. He was interrogated by the police for several hours. Knowing something about the psychological impact of such bizarre emotional events, when I saw my son after the police interrogation, I pressed him to open up and freely discuss his deeper emotional feelings about his dreadful experience. He ran through it one time, and in response to my continuing concern about how it affected him personally, he finally said in an exasperated voice: "Dad, I know what you're getting at. But it really doesn't bother me that much. I've seen plenty of killings on the tube and in the movies. It really is okay. You don't have to worry about me."

Alienation, mass media, and the cultural climate of violence often converge into bizarre acts of violence seen on a movie screen and replicated in real life. For example, John Hinckley's attempt to assassinate President Reagan flowed from this composite of emotional ingredients that was ignited by a movie, *Taxi Driver*, a film in which the alienated "hero" planned the assassination of a political figure.

The film, *Taxi Driver*, dramatized Hinckley's sense of alienation of loneliness. In it, the taxi driver hero is a person who moves through the alienated crowd: jostled, brushed, ignored or abused, hassled or pandered to, but somehow utterly untouched by any of it because of his own secret world of fantasy and his inability to communicate with his fellow humans. In brief a lonely man, aching to be noticed, recognized, and loved, but unable to attain it. At the end of the film the taxi driver goes on a brutal, senseless mass murder spree, claiming at least five lives. The character was someone Hinckley could identify with; and his later acting out made sense in these terms.

This brand of dehumanized violence, found in film, was clearly linked to Hinckley's reality. The rambling aimlessness of the taxi driver was absorbed into Hinckley's real life. He patterned his violent fantasies into his attempted assassination of President Ronald Reagan.

The literary image of the taxi driver had its impact on Hinckley, but it is by no means a random cause-and-effect phenomenon; young sociopaths often seek out literary and historical materials in the violent larger society that synthesize the violent fantasies they already harbor in their minds.

The Nazi model for violent behavior is often easily adopted by sociopathic youths. A prototypical case of this sociopathic syndrome is revealed in the following case history of a boy who, like Hinckley, read many books on Nazis shortly before he killed his parents.

Greg Sanders, 15, of Mountainside, New Jersey, killed his parents with an ax and then threw himself to his death from a water tower. He seemed to be a likable youth. His teachers liked him and his neighbors thought him thoughtful and courteous.

In dozens of interviews with his friends, his teachers, his physicians, and law-enforcement officials that were conducted after the suicide-murders, another picture of Greg emerged—that of an adolescent tormented by unattained and secret aspirations, who sought solace in a secret room and in secret dreams.

On Tuesday, January 14, the day Greg killed his parents and himself, Paul Gleason, Greg's German teacher, recalled that during class discussion he had asked Greg what he had been doing the night before.

"I read Shirer's *The Rise and Fall of the Third Reich*," the boy answered. In a secret room in his attic there were a mattress, a lamp, books, empty liquor bottles, and canteens of water. There were also a number of Nazi emblems and insignia. It was the fifth time he had read the book.

Sanders and Hinckley were like many youths whose inner thoughts are in disparity with their external behavior.

It would be logical to speculate that a youth growing up in a nonviolent social system would be less inclined to be violent than a youth growing up in a sociocultural climate of violence. War, parental violence (overt and covert), institutionalized violence by political leaders, mass media presentations of violence—all are factors that produce this violent ethos for today's youth.

My basic hypothesis on this issue is that the violent nature of a society affects the degree of violence committed by young people in the same society. Obviously, in a nonviolent social system most people would not ordinarily commit acts of aggression. The opposite would also hold true. Within the violent climate of Nazi Germany, for example, it would be expected that youth growing up would be most amenable to violent behavior, as they were goaded into becoming murderers by a violent sociopathic leader like Adolf Hitler (a general hypothesis that was affirmed by the facts of the resulting holocaust involving the mass murder). In this context a person (young or old) in Nazi Germany would be more likely to follow orders and commit brutal acts than people in more humanistic societies.

In the following analysis I am essentially concerned with the predisposition of Americans to commit acts of violence. Information on this general societal theme can provide some clues to the violence of young delinquents that often stems from the violent characteristics of their adult role models in American society. One set of experiments that fits into this analytic category was the research of psychologist Stanley Milgram at Yale University.[2]

In his studies Milgram was concerned with the conditions under which people would be obedient or disobedient to authority. In his overall project, which extended over a period of several years, almost a thousand individuals were subjects of his research. He investigated a variety of experimental settings and variable modifications. The results, however, were frighteningly uniform. On the basis of his research, Milgram concluded that a majority of "good people," who in their everyday lives were responsible and decent, could be made to perform "callous and severe" violent acts upon other people when they were placed in situations that had the "trappings of authority."

The "harsh acts" included giving electric shocks to another individual who might have just died of a heart attack. The following detailed description of one of Milgram's projects more clearly illustrates the general research approach that was used.

The subjects in this prototype example of the Milgram experiments on obedience were a random sample of New Haven adult males who came to Milgram's Yale Research Center in response to a newspaper advertisement. They were paid by the hour and individually brought to a laboratory and introduced to their partners who were, in reality, members of the research team. Each subject was told that he was going to participate in a learning experiment with his partner. One of them was to be the "teacher" and the other the "learner." It was contrived that the subject always wound up as the teacher, and the research assistant always became the learner. The subject was then told, incorrectly, that the research was being conducted to determine the effects of punishment on learning.

The subject, now the teacher, witnessed the standard procedure by which the learner (in reality a member of the research staff) was strapped into a chair that apparently had electrical connections. The subject was then taken into another room and told to ask the learner certain questions from a questionnaire he was given. The teacher was told to administer electric shocks every time the learner gave a wrong answer. (In some cases, before the learner was strapped into his *electric chair*, he would comment, "Take it easy on me, I have a heart condition.")

In the room with the teacher was another member of the research team who served as an authority figure and as a provocateur. He was present to make sure that the subject administered the proper shocks for incorrect answers.

The subject was told by the authority figure to give progressively stronger shocks to the learner when the latter's answers were incorrect. In front of the subject was an elaborate electric board that, as far as the subject

[2]Stanley Milgram, "Some Conditions of Obedience and Disobedience to Authority," *Human Relations* 18 (1965): 57–76.

knew, controlled shock levels from 15 to 450 volts in 15-volt gradations. The last two switches were ominously labeled XXX.

The researcher in the room would admonish the subject to increase the shock for each incorrect answer. In a short time the subject was repeatedly, as far as he knew, giving shocks of up to 450 volts to another person in the next room. The "victim" would often dramatically pound the wall and shout "Stop it, you're killing me!" Some subjects balked at continuing but proceeded on the orders of the authority figure, who would simply say, "Continue the experiment."

At a certain point the "victim," after pounding on the wall, would "play dead," or act as if he passed out and make no sound. The researcher in the room would instruct the subject to count "no response" as an incorrect answer. He would then order him to continue to shock an apparently inert or dead body with heavy electric shocks.

In several cases, when the subject refused to act out his robopathic behavior of continuing to shock the victim because "Christ, I don't hear him anymore, maybe I killed him! You know he said he had a bad heart," the researcher would say, "Go on with the experiment." The authoritative voice of the Yale researcher caused more than half of the subjects to continue to robopathically shock what might very well have been a dead body!

In a part of the experiment, some subjects refused to go on. The researcher would tell the subject to continue, and say, "Go ahead, I'll be responsible for what happens to the 'learner'." When this was done, the subject would usually say, "O.K., I'll continue. Remember you're responsible, not me!"

One of Milgram's experiments, conducted with 40 subjects, is typical of those overall experiments carried out with almost a thousand people. All 40 subjects complied by shocking their "victims" with up to 300 volts. Fourteen stopped at that point or at slightly higher levels. But the majority—26 subjects—continued to administer increasingly severe shocks until they reached 450 volts. This was beyond the switch marked *Danger: Severe Shock*. Thus 65 percent of this representative sample of "good people," paid a few dollars an hour, conformed to the dictates of an experimental authority situation to the point that they supposedly inflicted severe pain or possible death on another human being.

Essentially the research validated the assumption that people would conform to dictates of people in authority even when they knew they were inflicting severe harm on another person up to and beyond homicide. Authority, in a legitimate social context, thus produced obedience and conformity to inhuman goals—even in America.

It would be difficult to measure the degree of violent components in an individual and perhaps even more difficult to estimate the number of such individuals in a society. (A wild speculation, in accord with the Milgram experiment, would be more than half of the population.) Perhaps even more difficult is the measurement of the number of what Jules Feiffer calls "little murders," which people "just doing their job" inflict on others in everyday life.

Another reason for the contemporary climate of violence that effects violence in juveniles is the growing alienation of people in a machinelike social system. One observer of the scene, Lynn B. Iglitzin, comments:

> By far the most potent source of violence is the ubiquity of feelings of alienation and anomie which plague so many human beings in modern society. Feelings of normlessness and meaninglessness, of estrangement from one's self and from others are generally accepted characteristics of alienation. The alienated person is out of touch with himself and with other persons; he is at the mercy of his technological creations, a "thing" dependent on unknown powerful forces.[3]

R. D. Laing, the British psychoanalyst, defines alienation in his poignant description of the human condition, particularly of the white European and North American, as a sense of "being at an end: of being only half alive in the fibrillating heartland of a senescent civilization."[4] This pervasive condition of estrangement from ourselves and from the human community provides a setting in which people have perpetrated incredible acts of violence upon each other and have been able to rationalize such behavior as "normality." According to psychiatrists such as Laing and Erich Fromm, it has become "normal" to be alienated, and the more one thus behaves like everyone else—that is, treating others as commodities rather than as human beings—the more one is taken to be sane. It is Laing's belief that those who are considered sick in an alienated world might be the healthiest of all. Laing conceptualizes that "the condition of alienation, of being asleep, of being unconscious, of being out of one's mind, is the condition of the normal man." As support for this premise, he notes that "normal men have killed perhaps 100,000,000 of their fellow normal men in the last fifty years."[5]

In this context, although limited research has been carried out, we can speculate that the shadow of ultimate nuclear annihilation by the bombs which are now in place is another significant factor in the climate of contemporary violence. Many delinquents I have interviewed blame this Sword of Damocles hanging over our world for their indifferent attitude toward violent behavior.

One researcher, Henry De Young, accounted for an upsurge in adolescent violence as follows.

> First of all, and perhaps most relevant, there is television which contributes immensely to the "unreality" of death and the generally low value ascribed to

---

[3]Lynne B. Iglitzin, *Violent Conflict in American Society* (San Francisco: Chandler, 1972), p. 97.

[4]R. D. Laing, *The Politics of Experience* (New York: Pantheon, 1967), p. xiii.
[5]Ibid., p. 12.

human life. Every night of the week, children may see as many as two dozen shootings, hangings, knifings, poisonings, assaults with clubs and automobiles and countless other forms of mayhem. Furthermore, such assaults on life are rarely depicted as wrong, or even objectionable; they're perpetrated, often as not, by the good guys—police officers, cowboys and cowgirls, private eyes, cartoon characters—against the bad guys, or those who are perceived to be bad. To further confuse the young and undiscriminating mind, the victims of this senseless violence never seem to be really dead; an actor who "dies" on "The Rookies" at 7:30 P.M. is often magically resurrected to appear, unharmed and little the worse off for his ordeal, an hour later on "S.W.A.T." Dying in TV-land is also a nice, clean way of departing this life. There's rarely any blood, and never an honest depiction of what violent death is really like.

"If every kid under 10 could see what a gunshot does to people in real life," observes a Chicago police officer, "I have little doubt that our homicide rate would be cut in half. It's an ugly sight."[6]

In an article on delinquent murder, "What Can Be Done about Juvenile Homicide?" James Sorrells, Jr., delineates the sociopathic personality of children who kill in the following way:

These juveniles see other people solely in terms of their own needs—to be used if useful, to be eliminated if presenting an obstacle or threat. The question, "How will that person feel if you harm him?" has little meaning and almost no relevance to this group of juveniles. It never occurs to them that other people have a right to life and feelings, too. They lack the capacity to experience empathy or identification with, or compassion for, other human beings.[7]

In brief, they are sociopaths who have no concern for their victims.

The availability of guns, a much-debated subject, has become in my view a significant factor in fostering a climate of violence and contributes to specific violent offenses. A prototypical example of this problem is revealed in the following report on two homicidal teenagers and their bloody rampage with handguns.

They started walking at dusk, two teen-agers casually spreading the message that the streets of West Los Angeles were no longer safe. First they stopped Phillip Lerner and demanded money. Lerner had no cash, only his infant in a stroller. They let him pass and kept walking. They hailed Arkady and Rachel Muskin at a nearby intersection. The couple quickly handed over $8 and two wristwatches, and gratefully fled. Next the boys intercepted two elderly Chinese women and pulled out a pistol. When one woman tried to push the gun out of her face, ten bullets blazed out, killing both. The boys kept walking. They came upon a trio of friends out for an evening stroll. They took a watch and a few

[6]Henry De Young, "Homicide (Children's Division)," *Human Behavior* (February 1976): 89. Copyright © 1976 *Human Behavior* magazine. Reprinted by permission.
[7]Reprinted, with permission of the National Council on Crime and Delinquency, from James Sorrels, Jr., "What Can Be Done about Juvenile Homicide?" *Crime & Delinquency* (April 1980): 156–157.

dollars and, without so much as a word, killed one of the three, a Frenchman visiting Los Angeles for the first time. The boys kept walking. At last they reached a drive-in restaurant where they found 76-year-old Leo Ocon walking on the sidewalk. They argued with him for less than a minute and then shot him down. Their evening over, they climed into an old sedan and then, much as they had started, calmly went off into the night.

In the year that mainstream America rediscovered violent crime, that Sunday-night massacre was the paradigmatic act. The four killings were in plain view and without cause in a neighborhood where murder is not a fact of life. All the dead were strangers to the killers. The police couldn't interrupt the slaughter—they didn't hear about the carnage until the last bullets had landed. It was, in short, the urban nightmare come to life.[8]

In 1985, 64 percent of all homicides known to the police as reported in the Uniform Crime Report of the FBI were committed through the use of firearms. The ready availability of handguns is blamed by many criminologists and law enforcement authorities for the increase in such violent crime as murder and robbery. Around 20,000 Americans are killed with guns each year, including homicides, suicides, and accidents.

The homicide rate per capita in the United States is reported to be 35 times higher than the rate in Germany or in England, yet a substantial portion of the American population, especially the National Rifle Association, supports the view that everyone should be entitled to own a gun. A law has been passed in California requiring prison sentences for criminals who use firearms in committing serious crimes, ranging from robbery to attempted murder. A small community in Illinois passed a gun control law in 1982 and spurred consideration of similar action by many other communities. In another American community, a radical gun advocate was attempting to pass a law making it mandatory for every family to have a gun.

The British do not subscribe to the view held by many in the United States that every citizen is entitled to own a gun. They control the use of guns in the following ways:

Under Britain's firearms control laws, no one may own a firearm without a police certificate, except for antique weapons and certain types of airguns.

To get a certificate, the applicant must have a "good reason" which in the vast majority of cases is the desire to have a weapon for hunting or sport shooting. Membership in a gun or hunting club is usually the way to get the certificate.

"The gun clubs," Russell said, "are mindful of the danger of a person joining for the purpose of getting a certificate that might otherwise be withheld."

"We have worried about that," he said. "That's why virtually all clubs have a six-month probationary period for new members which enables the club's officers to find out if the new member is really interested in sport shooting."

The certificates are issued for periods of up to three years. Police are not required to state a reason for rejecting an application, unless the applicant challenges the rejection in court. Aside from the "good reason" requirement, the applicant must show, usually through completion of a safety course, that he knows how to handle a firearm properly . . . The minimum legal age for possession of a firearm is 17.

There are especially heavy penalties for possession of a firearm, whether used or not in the commission of a crime, and the intended use of a fake gun in the commission of a crime carries a maximum penalty of 14 years in prison. This is only one of 80 different offenses linked to the illegal possession of firearms. . . .

As a result, firearms play a relatively small role in British crime. . . .

Since 1965, 10 police officers have been killed in shootings.

British police generally are not armed and there are no Wild West shootouts. . . .

British police may use firearms, but, as a government statement put it, "only when necessary to protect the life of the police officer or some other person.

"The responsibility for using the weapon rests with the police officer; unnecessary use of firearms might constitute a criminal offense."[9]

Why is there so much opposition to gun control in the United States? For one thing, the manufacture and sale of firearms is a very big business, with gun owners spending an estimated $2 billion a year on guns. Gun and ammunition manufacturers, retail gun dealers, gun-magazine publishers, and hunting-resort owners make a great deal of money from the sale and distribution of weapons. They also spend a good deal of money in the form of contributions to the political campaigns of congressional and state legislative candidates. The National Rifle Association, probably the most effective lobby in Washington, carries on a continuous campaign against gun-control legislation. Its officials have boasted that they can get their million members to send at least half a million letters to Congress on 72-hour notice.

In an article in *Psychology Today*,[10] psychologist Leonard Berkowitz directs our attention to a phenomenon he calls "the weapons effect." He says past and present research reveals that weapons have an aggressive effect on our behavior. In his studies and those of others, he notes that the sight of a weapon increases any aggressiveness that one is already experiencing. In a study done in Sweden, it was found that the weapons effect occurred even without previous frustration being introduced. Still other studies have shown that children, when given toy guns to play with, will act more aggressively than when they play with other toys.

[9]Harry Trimborn, "Britain Dismayed by U.S. 'Myth'—Right to Own Guns," *Los Angeles Times*, September 25, 1975. Copyright, 1975, *Los Angeles Times*. Reprinted by permission.
[10]Leonard Berkowitz, "How Guns Control Us," *Psychology Today* (June 1981): 11–12.

Berkowitz offers two theories as to why the weapons effect occurs:

1. Weapons function as a conditioned stimulus eliciting associated responses.
2. Guns might remind people of earlier occasions when they have seen aggression rewarded (as on TV and in movies).

He feels it is this increase of aggression when a gun is present that leads to the "trigger pulling the finger."

The easy availability of guns is clearly part of the problem in the escalation of "senseless" teenage violence. Pete Hamill, writing for *The New York Times*, emotionally clarifies the problem in the following article:

Why Must Guns Be So Available?

Go ahead: Sell the kid a gun. What the hell, he's white, isn't he? He's got the money, he gets a gun. A Luger. A .357 Magnum. A .38 Smith and Wesson police special. Sure are beautiful, aren't they? Nice weight, beautiful finish.

Why buy just one, kid? Here, buy two. They're on sale. And have some extra ammo. Where you going, kid? Washington, huh? Hey, I hear it's pretty there this time of year, with the cherry blossoms and all that. Well, have a good time, kid. All right, who's next?

John Warnock Hinckley, Jr. came to Washington with at least one gun. But he was carrying a lot of extra baggage with him. There was his unrequited love for Jody Foster, the star of a blood-and-guns movie called Taxi Driver. He had photographs of her. He wrote letters to her in the corrupted language of the fan magazine. He didn't know her, of course, any more than he knew Ronald Reagan. He never met the real Jody Foster, a person of flesh and blood, no doubt burdened with the usual ration of human frailties and folly. She was part of his baggage anyway, a shimmering illusion glimpsed in a darkened theater, shaped by the deceptions of art.

But when the art was over, when the men who made this movie were finished splattering phony blood around their celluloid world, someone yelled "cut" and the actors got up and went to a bar.

Last Monday, in the drizzle of T Street in Washington, nobody yelled "cut" over James Brady; a real bullet had carved a real tunnel through his real brain. Timothy Delahanty did not go to a bar, and neither did the President of the United States. They all had real bullets slammed into their real bodies. They had bullets in their bodies . . . because someone sold guns to a young man named John Warnock Hinckley, Jr.[11]

THE IMPACT OF VIOLENCE

In research I carried out with victims of violence in New York City, I noted that violence often resulted in lifelong fear and emotional damage. Most victims suffer tremendously from a violent assault—far beyond the immediate situation in which they are harmed.

[11]Pete Hamill, "Why Must Guns Be So Available?" *The New York Times*, April 5, 1981. Copyright © 1981 by The New York Times Company. Reprinted by permission.

A Gallup poll published in *Newsweek* reported the following findings on the impact of crime, especially violence:[12]

Is there any area within a mile of your home where you would be afraid to walk alone at night:	
Yes	53%
No	46%
Don't know	1%
Which of the following have happened to you in the past twelve months?	
Property vandalized	20%
Money or property stolen	21%
House broken into or attempt made	14%
Assaulted or mugged	3%
Car stolen	3%
Which of these precautions against crime have you taken?	
Try not to go out alone at night	64%
Never carry very much cash	79%
Avoid certain areas even during the day	60%
Avoid wearing expensive jewelry	64%
Keep a gun or other weapon	31%
Keep a dog for protection	44%

American society has always had a large amount of the brand of violence that is popularly called "senseless violence." Notable in American history are the following cases: the assassinations of John F. Kennedy, Martin Luther King, and Robert Kennedy; the serial killing of eight student nurses by Richard Speck in Chicago; the mass killing of nine people in a home in Victorville, California; the brutal ritualistic murders of Charles Manson's "family"; the murder of over 25 migrant farm workers by Juan Corona; the Hillside Strangler Murders; and the brutal homicides of more than 28 teenagers over a three-year period in Houston, Texas, by Wayne Henley, David Brooks, and Dean Corll. These last grisly murders were described by Brooks in his statement to the police:[13]

In all, I guess there were between 25 and 30 boys killed, and they were buried in three different places. I was present and helped bury many of them but not all of them. . . . On the first one at Sam Rayburn [Reservoir] I helped bury him, and then the next one we took to Sam Rayburn. When we got there, Dean and Wayne found that the first one had come to the surface and either a foot or a hand was above the ground. When they buried this one the second time, they put some type of rock sheet on top of him to keep him down.

A bizarre characteristic of a considerable amount of recent violence is the fact that many grisly killings are committed by two or more killers in concert, in what might be termed a "buddy-killer" form. In the past, the killers would serve as checks on each other's extreme and horrendous acts. Recently it appears that anything goes when it comes to murder, especially in a small gang of partners in murder.

The so-called "Los Angeles Freeway Murders" are a case in point. Although several other individuals were involved in the Freeway Murders in Los Angeles, there were two principals—Vernon Butts and William Bonin. Their 21 teenage victims, most alleged to be homosexuals, were sodomized, tortured (several with ice picks through their ears), and then killed. The following article provides some of the bizarre psychological characteristics of the new breed of pathological "buddy-killers."

> When Vernon Butts kept telling his co-workers that he slept in a coffin, they thought he was putting them on.
>
> But now that he is accused of being an accomplice to "Freeway Killer" suspect William Bonin, they aren't so sure.
>
> What is for sure, investigators say, is that Butts had two coffins in the Norwalk apartment he occupied until last January. One was used as a coffee table and the other was rigged up as a telephone booth.
>
> Bonin, a 33-year-old convicted sex offender, has been accused of killing 21 victims with assistance from Butts in at least six of the slayings, which authorities said involved torture and homosexual acts. The victims, mostly teen-age boys, were picked up while hitchhiking and their bodies dumped near freeways throughout southern California, giving rise to the "Freeway Killer" label. . . .[14]

Is is easier to comprehend how a psychotic or sociopathic individual, for example the Boston Strangler, could kill because of his individual pathology. However, with buddy-murderers we have two pathological minds operating in concert.

There has been no intensive research to date on buddy-murderers. Some of the questions raised are: Do the two killers set each other off psychologically? What do they talk about during and after their buddy-murders? How does one dominate the other(s)? Isn't there any kind of superego or moral quotient that surfaces between the two to stop their horrendous spree? Are buddy-murderers individuals whose pathological backgrounds have similarities?

Another bizarre form of contemporary murder that is increasing is the "serial killer." In an article on serial killers, Ronald Holmes and James DeBurger comment on their characteristics:[15]

> The majority of serial killers appear to share certain characteristics. First of all, most are white and are in the age group of 25 to 34 years of age. They are

---

[14]From "Murder Suspect Described as 'Weirdo'" by Bill Farr and Kristina Lindgren. Published July 31, 1980. Copyright, 1980, *Los Angeles Times*. Reprinted by permission.

[15]Ronald Holmes and James DeBurger "Profiles in Terror: The Serial Murder" in Federal Probation, September 1985.

intelligent or at least "street smart." They are charming and charismatic; and many of them are psychopathic. . . .

Many of the known serial murderers were born out of wedlock. As children many were physically, sexually, or emotionally abused. These killers tend to abuse alcohol or drugs, and often this abuse exacerbated their sadistic fantasies. For example, their interest in media would lie more in the area of sadistic porn or other depictions of violence. Many are intimately involved with women who have no knowledge of their partner's homicidal activities. Sexual relationships with these women are often characterized by sadistic behavior.

Richard Ramirez, known as "the nighstalker," is a prime example of a serial murderer. In 1985 he was alleged to have killed more than 15 people in a murder spree in California.

Although buddy-murderers and serial murderers tend to be in their twenties, many of their victims are emotionally disturbed teenagers—often runaways engaged in "hustling" and prostitution. A July 1985 report, titled "Runaways in the United States," from the United States Department of Justice reveals that a disproportionate number of adolescents are violence-prone victims. The report states that teenagers are more than twice as likely as adults to be victims of rape, robbery, and assault. The study revealed that more than 60 of every 1,000 teenagers are victims of violent crime each year, compared to just 27 of every 1,000 adults.

The study also found that teenagers were nearly twice as likely as adults to be victimized by theft. The teenage victim rate for theft was 123 per 1,000 teenagers compared to 65 per 1,000 for adults.

The report also stated that victims of violent teen crime usually know their assailant and that more than 60 percent of such violent teen crimes are committed by offenders under age 18.

The report further revealed that offenses against teenagers show up less than crimes against adults. Two-thirds of the violent crime against teenagers from ages 12 to 15 were never reported to the police. Also unreported were nearly 60 percent of the violent crimes against 16- to 19-year-olds. In contrast, more than half of the violent crimes against adults were reported to police. Teenage violence is more prevalent than it appears in official records, and other teenagers are most likely to become victims of this violence.

DELINQUENT SUICIDAL TENDENCIES: VIOLATOR OR VICTIM?

In my research into violent gangs and other forms of juvenile violence I would conclude that a considerable amount of violence by juveniles has an interactional quality where the aggressor who initiates the violence winds up as the ultimate victim. A child who comes home crying about being hit or beaten up may have a perceptive parent raise the question, "What did you do to provoke being hit?" The victim of violence is often a participant in his own injury.

This pattern of "victim-precipitated violence" was first analyzed in Hans von Hentig's classic work, *The Criminal and His Victim*.[16] Von Hentig's concept was further developed and researched by Marvin Wolfgang. The concept of victim-precipitated violence is relevant to the analysis of violent juveniles and why juveniles are disproportionately likely to be victims of violence.

Wolfgang initially researched the pattern of victim-precipitated homicide in a study of over 588 consecutive homicides committed in Philadelphia in a four-year period. Wolfgang concluded that 150 cases, or 26 percent, fit the model of victim-precipitated homicide. Wolfgang explains the concept this way. (Although Wolfgang and Von Hentig refer mainly to the ultimate violence of murder, the concept is also relevant to explaining lesser forms of assault and violence.)

In many crimes, especially in criminal homicide, the victim is often a major contributor to the criminal act. Except in cases in which the victim is an innocent bystander and is killed in lieu of an intended victim, or in cases in which a pure accident is involved, the victim may be one of the major precipitating causes of his own demise.

Various theories of social interaction, particularly in social psychology, have established the framework for the present discussion. In criminological literature, however, probably von Hentig, in "The Criminal and His Victim," provided the most useful theoretical base for analysis of the victim-offender relationship. In Chapter XII, entitled "The Contribution of the Victim to the Genesis of Crime," the author discussed this "duet frame of crime" and suggests that homicide is particularly amenable to analysis. In "Penal Philosophy," Tarde frequently attacks the "legislative mistake" of concentrating too much on premeditation and paying too little attention to motives, which indicate an important interrelationship between victim and offender. And in one of his satirical essays, "On Murder Considered as One of the Fine Arts," Thomas De Quincey shows cognizance of the idea that sometimes the victim is a would-be murderer. Garofalo, too, noted that the victim may provoke another individual into attack, and though the provocation be slight, if perceived by an egoistic attacker it may be sufficient to result in homicide.

The role of the victim is characterized by his having been the first in the homicide drama to use physical force directed against his subsequent slayer. The victim-precipitated cases are those in which the victim was the first to show and use a deadly weapon, to strike a blow in an altercation—in short, the first to commence the interplay or resort to physical violence.[17]

Von Hentig's and Wolfgang's interactional hypothesis has been developed further in an analysis by Dr. David Abrahamsen.

[16]Hans von Hentig, *The Criminal and His Victim* (New Haven: Yale University Press, 1948), pp. 383–385.
[17]Marvin E. Wolfgang, "Victim-Precipitated Criminal Homicide," *Journal of Criminal Law, Criminology and Police Science* 48 (June 1957): 1. Reprinted by special permission of *The Journal of Criminal Law and Criminology*, © 1957 by Northwestern University School of Law, vol. 48, no. 1.

The relationship between criminal and victim is much more complicated than the law would care to acknowledge. The criminal and his victim work on each other unconsciously. We can say that as the criminal shapes the victim, the victim also shapes the criminal. While the law looks upon this relationship from an objective, nonemotional viewpoint, the psychological attitude of the participants is quite different. The law differentiates distinctly between the attacker and the victim. But their relationship may be, and often is, quite close, so that their roles are reversed and the victim becomes the determining person, while the victimizer in the end becomes his own victim. . . .

Trapped and helpless, and beset by inner conflicts, the murderer encounters his victim, who also is full of conflicts. Through the foreplay—comparable to foreplay preceding sexual intercourse—and interplay between attacker and victim, intentions and motivations may be spelled out, because the protagonists do not understand themselves. Instead they act out what they harbor in their mind. There is a victimizer and a victim; and the border between them during the victimization is as blurred as their self-image. Intertwined with each other, they represent on every level of the conscious and unconscious mind a stream of fluid and transitory emotions than can hardly be deciphered.[18]

The pattern of victim-precipitated violence is often acted out by youths who have a chip on their shoulder. Such youths, by their demeanor, provoke violence. For example, it might be impossible to ascertain the victim-proneness of the 28 or so youths killed by the mass slayers in Houston, Texas, yet we can speculate with a degree of rationality that a number of them placed themselves in jeopardy by joining gangs, or attending the "sex parties" reputedly run by the killer and his cohorts.

The victim-precipitated crime hypothesis can explain a considerable amount of youth violence. Many runaways and teenage prostitutes (male and female) are, as has been indicated, youths with low self-esteem. Many of them have attempted suicide or have suicidal tendencies, which makes them more vulnerable when they place themselves in dangerous situations that the average emotionally healthy adolescent would clearly avoid.

In this context, youths who place themselves in vulnerable situations tend to be suicidal. Researchers at the United States Centers for Disease Control estimated that about 50,000 young people committed suicide in the 1970s. Around 62 percent of these suicides were carried out with firearms.

There has been a dramatic increase in suicide by young people in the past 30 years. In 1950 the rate was 4.5 suicides per 100,000 population; and in 1985 there were around 12 suicides per 100,000 population.

Suicide is a form of violent homicide turned on one's self. In young people a simplistic analysis reveals that suicide generally results from a state of depression complicated by a sense of hopelessness. In recent years the situation has been complicated by the enormous phenomenon of substance abuse by adolescents. Many youths, male and female, commit suicide by

---

[18]David Abrahamsen, *The Murdering Mind* (New York: Harper & Row, 1973), p. 35.

overdosing on drugs or place themselves in vulnerable positions because of their drug behavior and suicidal tendencies.

In my work with delinquents in several psychiatric hospitals using group psychotherapy and psychodrama I find that more than half of these incarcerated youths have attempted suicide at least once. This leads me to the speculation that a considerable amount of contemporary youth violence reflects the victim-precipitated interactional thesis: Many youths start out as the perpetrators of violence, not caring what happens to them, and often end up as the victims.

My extensive research into violent gangs, in particular, confirms a low self-esteem–suicide hypothesis, which explains a considerable amount of violent behavior among juveniles. Many gang youths I have interviewed believe as one told me: "I don't give a f--- about myself, so when our gang gets into a fight I don't care who goes down, even me. What do I have to live for? Who gives a f---. You may be right, I don't care if I get it or I kill someone else."

This suicidal attitude in many youths, not only in violent gang members, but in young people behind the wheels of automobiles, stoned on intense mind-altering drugs, or committing a mugging, may account for a large amount of contemporary delinquent violence.

In summary, my "suicidal tendency and violence" hypothesis has the following elements:

1. The youth who has low self-esteem, feels despondent, and doesn't see much to live for is suicidal or has suicidal tendencies. He or she doesn't highly value their life.
2. Consequently, they are more apt to place themselves in "death-defying" violent situations than are youths who value their life. Delinquent adolescents who are violence-prone are more contentious and will commit violent acts which endanger their lives. This is especially true of both male and female delinquent runaways, who chose to live in more dangerous, high-violence areas of the city.
3. These young people live in and participate more in a "life in the fast lane" climate of violence. Drug abuse contributes to their vulnerability and suicidal tendencies. Because of their suicidal tendencies these youths are much more prone to be both victims and perpetrators of violence. A considerable amount of the aggressive behavior these adolescents participate in has the quality of senseless violence.

SENSELESS VIOLENCE

What factors delineate "logical" from "senseless" violence? One context for analysis is the viewpoint on violence of the dominant segment of the society. In my view four categories encompass almost all patterns of violence:

1. *Legal, sanctioned, rational violence.* Many violent acts are supported in law. The soldier is rewarded as a hero for the intensity of his violent action. In fact, a nonviolent soldier may, under certain conditions, be court-martialed and executed. Police officers enact another role that is supported by legal violence. Other legally justified violence is found in certain aggressive sports (football, boxing) and in certain acts of self-defense.

2. *Illegal, rational, socially sanctioned violence.* A significant factor in any analysis of violence is its degree of social sanction or support. No one would argue that an assault committed by a deceived spouse on an adulterer was not illegal, but many would sanction this violence. Even when homicide is the result, the "unwritten law" has wide support. Other examples of violence that are illegal yet sanctioned and considered rational would include violent responses to insults or an attack upon one's honor. This pattern accounts for a considerable amount of youth gang violence.

    Violence, even when it is illegal, has varying degrees of acceptance within different segments of American society. Dr. S. J. Ball-Rokeach cogently comments on the issue of what he terms "social violence," a pattern that fits into this category:

    [If] we define violence as primarily goal-oriented and therefore rational human behavior, then it permits exploration of "normal" social processes and "functioning" personal and social systems as possible causes of violence. The issue becomes not whether violence is prescribed, but how violence is incorporated into everyday systems of social action. Violence caused by "normal" social and personal processes may be called "social" violence to distinguish it from "asocial" violence caused by "abnormal" or deficit states. Asocial violence thus becomes a residual category of acts that are caused by such abnormal or deficit states as psychopathology, biochemical disorder (e.g., certain drugs or blood sugar levels), neurological, hormonal or genetic malfunction, or acute breakdown of reasoning faculties (e.g., drunken rage or panic). Acts of violence would certainly vary in the extent to which they are or are not perceived by their perpetrators to fit the present definition of social violence.[19]

3. *Illegal, nonsanctioned, rational violence.* Some violent acts that are neither legal nor sanctioned are still considered rational in a delinquent context. A most prevalent form of delinquent act, violence for financial gain, would fit into this category. Robbery and assault upon a person or the commission of violence within the framework of a drug deal would be considered rational behavior to a delinquent.

4. *Illegal, nonsanctioned, irrational violence.* This category, popularly referred to as "senseless violence," includes such crimes as Bonin's "freeway murders," Whitman's shooting and killing of 15 people (and the wounding of 31) from a university tower, the "kill-for-kicks" assault by three youths on an elderly man who was whistling

---

[19]S. J. Ball-Rokeach, "Normative and Deviant Violence from a Conflict Perspective." © 1980 by The Society for the Study of Social Problems, Inc. Reprinted from *Social Problems*, Vol. 28, No. 1, October 1980, pp. 45–62, by permission.

a tune they didn't like, and the stabbing and bludgeoning to death of a 15-year-old polio victim by a teenage gang. This kind of violence outrageously defies the law, social sanction, and rationality and fulfills the criteria of "senseless violence."

Many psychotic delinquent youths who are paranoid and have delusions of being persecuted will have hallucinations and fantasize that people are out to get them and retaliate with violence. In this context the paranoid juvenile assaults or kills his imagined enemy before they can harm him.

A considerable proportion of acts of senseless violence by juveniles can also be accounted for by the previously described sociopathic delinquent personality. An aspect of the sociopathic youth's breakthrough into senseless violence may be termed "existential validation." When a youth with this personality syndrome feels constantly alienated from other human beings, he begins to lose the sense of his own humanity and requires increasingly heavier dosages of bizarre and extreme behavior to validate the fact that he really exists. The extreme violent behavior gives the sociopathic youth a glimmer of emotional feeling when nothing else does. As one gang killer of this type told me in an interview: "When I stabbed him once, I did it again and again, because it really made me feel alive for the first time in my life.[20]

The noted playwright Arthur Miller, drawing upon a study he made of gangs in a gang neighborhood in New York City, described this pattern of sociopathic "senseless violence" as stemming, in part, from the malaise of boredom:

> The boredom of the delinquent is remarkable mainly because it is so little compensated for, as it may be among the middle classes and the rich who can fly down to the Caribbean or to Europe, or refurnish the house, or have an affair, or at least go shopping. The delinquent is stuck with his boredom, stuck inside it, stuck to it, until for two or three minutes he "lives"; he goes on a violent raid around the corner and feels the thrill of risking his skin or his life as he smashes a bottle filled with gasoline on some other kid's head. In a sense, it is his trip to Miami. It makes his day. It is his shopping tour. It gives him something to talk about for a week. It is life. Standing around with nothing coming up is as close to dying as you can get. Unless one grasps the power of boredom, the threat of it to one's existence, it is impossible to "place" the delinquent as a member of the human race.[21]

The commission of a violent murder is obviously not the equivalent of a vacation from boredom, however, many violent acts are committed to give the perpetrator a sense "of being," or as I have described it "existential validation." An act or murder committed by the central character in Albert Camus' novel *The Stranger* is justified in part on the basis that it made the

---

[20]This concept is detailed in Lewis Yablonsky's, *The Violent Gang*, rev. ed. (Baltimore: Penguin, 1971).

[21]Arthur Miller, "The Bored and the Violent," *Harpers Magazine* (November 1962): 51.

murderer feel some emotion where none existed. Many acts of youth violence are committed for the purpose of this bizarre type of "high" experience. Young people play "chicken," involving two cars headed for a head-on collision. They dare each other to commit senseless, potentially suicidal acts, fight with each other, and go out on "gang bangs" out of the ennui described by Miller, and explained by my concept of "existential validation."

The case history of an adolescent murder committed in Milpitas, California, delineates this type of senseless violence in its many facets. The bizarre murder became a type of existential spectator event when the young murderer, who killed his girlfriend in 1981, brought his friends to witness the dead victim's body.

In an extensive article based on her research into this senseless murder, Elizabeth Kaye described some of the forces at work in this illegal, irrational senseless murder, and its even more bizarre aftermath.[22]

At moments in history, events occur that mirror society in so fundamental a way that they become metaphorical and reveal us to ourselves with the indisputable clarity of a traffic signal. An event such as this gave rise to the notoriety of Milpitas, a Northern California town.

November 3, 1981, was a Tuesday, and on that day a sixteen year old named Jacques Broussard cut school with a fourteen year old named Marcy Conrad. This, in itself, was unexceptional. Jacques and Marcy were stoners. Stoners smoke a lot of pot and cut school often. They are also given, as are many children nowadays, to the utterly unchildish apprehension that life is not necessarily getting better, for they are part of the first generation of Americans raised by parents who no longer have reason to believe the sustaining tenet of the American dream: that the reward for hard work and sacrifice is the privilege of making one's children's lives far better than one's own. As members of that generation, they view the world through the tarnished prism of their parents' disappointment and conclude that they may as well live for today since being young may very well be the best thing that will ever happen to them.

So it may have been in the name of living for today that Jacques and Marcy cut school and eventually went to his house, a one-story, dark green house six blocks from hers, with a BEWARE OF THE DOG sign on the door, in the sort of neighborhood where houses are neatly centered between tiny front and back yards and where the color television is, as a rule, the focal point of the living room. Homes such as these were once a mere rung on the American ladder of acquisition and success, but in this era of diminished prospects they simultaneously constitute the end of the line and the apogee of a certain level of middle-class attainment.

Jacques's family had lived in this house for many years, and it was here that his mother had died. His mother's death was one of two things that set Jacques apart from everyone. The other was that he was black, while all his friends were white. Of these two things, his mother's death was the more significant by far.

[22]Elizabeth Kaye, "Growing Up Stoned," *California* (April 1982). Excerpted with permission from the April issue of *California*. Copyright 1982 by *California*.

Gloria Broussard died when her son was eight years old. Jacques was the one who found her body, so the impact of her death transcended grief and became one of abject horror. On what was an otherwise ordinary day Jacques came home from school, and the harbinger that something was dreadfully wrong was the living room rug, which was sodden with water. When he heard the shower running he treaded his way to the bathroom door, opened it, made his way through the water-soaked room, and drew back the shower curtain. He saw his mother's naked body. She had died of natural causes a few hours earlier.

Jacques never quite recovered from that day, and all his friends knew it, which is why it was understood among them that they never breathed a word to Jacques about his mother. But Marcy Conrad dispensed with this crucial amenity, it seems, and said something about her, something truly mean. Or so Jacques told his friends. He also told them that is why he killed her.

Marcy became a corpse on Jacques's living room couch. The corpse was half naked, and this was because before Marcy died Jacques either made love to her or raped her. Were stoners at all interested in irony or observation, Jacques might have been taken by the fact that the corpse was clad in nothing but a tank top with the words SPOILED ROTTEN on it and a necklace decorated with a gold marijuana leaf-shape charm.

Once Marcy was dead Jacques was confronted with a succession of practical considerations, to which he apparently responded quite methodically. First he went outside, backed his pickup truck into the garage, and set about gathering up Marcy's purse, jeans, and schoolbooks. He then lifted her body from the couch and began the formidable task of getting it out of the house. Jacques weighed 280 pounds and stood six foot four, and Marcy was just a little girl, but she was dead weight now. Jacques would later tell his friends that he had one hell of a time moving her. But finally he got the body into the back of his truck. The white truck was an unlikely hearse, with its KOME and KSJO stickers that appear on the cars of most stoners, letters that also appear as patches on their jeans and as decals on their schoolbooks. They are the call letters of two rock stations. The only thing the average stoner likes as well as weed is fine rock music. . . .

Jacques drove on to Old Marsh Road, and then the scenery abruptly changed, and the trees and grass beside the road became as sensuously moist as those in the center of a rain-soaked forest. This spot is a gathering place for many young people in Milpitas, and the pungent blanket of fallen leaves and bright green clover that covers the earth shares its space with empty, crushed beer cans and shards of broken wine bottles.

It is here that Jacques scattered Marcy's purse, jeans, shoes, and schoolbooks. Then he drove on, a half mile or so, to where Old Marsh Road merges again with the sun, and where the land to the south of the road slants down sharply to a barbwire fence. . . .

This place was selected by Jacques Broussard as his final destination. He stopped the truck and took the half-naked corpse from it. He carried it down the incline and pushed it beneath the barbwire fence. The body rolled and was stopped by the thick trunk of the oak tree. There it remained for the next two days, in the sun and the wind and the cold and the dark, face down.

In the days that followed, the murder of Marcy Conrad assumed its allegorical significance and ultimately became that rare event of equal interest to news-paper reporters and to poets. It is at this stage in the narrative that the focus shifts and both the murderer and victim become oddly peripheral to its telling. Events center instead on nine young people, all of whom are self-described stoners.

In retrospect, it seemed inevitable that others be drawn into it. It was not all that likely that a sixteen year old could indefinitely keep to himself the amazing fact that he has just become a killer. So it was, on the day following the murder, that three teenage boys were told of it by Jacques Broussard himself. They did not believe him, so he took them up the hill and showed them what all the horror movies and all the televised violence they had ever seen could not have con-ceivably prepared them for, just as they had hardened them to it.

There was no requiem at the oak tree. There was only gazing. And there was this thought in the mind of one of the boys: "Jacques is in real trouble now."

The hours that followed were extraordinary only for their ordinariness, only for the ways the three boys managed to proceed as if nothing had occurred that was in the least unusual. One fell asleep in his room listening to the radio and did not wake up for dinner. Another would later say he thought the body was a mannequin and didn't think anymore about it. The third was met at his door by his mother, who told him not to come in. She had discovered he had stolen her marijuana. This was something that had happened before; he had been warned that he would not be welcome in the house if it happened again.

The boy's name is John Hanson. He went out into the night and later met up with a friend named Robby Engle. He told Engle about the corpse, and when Engle wanted to see it, Hanson said he would show it to him the next day since it was now too dark to see anything. Instead they walked to Engle's house, went to his room to smoke some dope, and fell asleep. The night air was cool. In the hills where Marcy Conrad's body lay it was even cooler. Both boys slept dream-lessly.

All the next morning at Milpitas High, the huge bulk of Jacques Broussard traversed the grassy campus, telling students that he had killed Marcy and conveying that information with the reckless resolve of a man committing sui-cide because he is afraid of dying. Among the students, many of whom knew Marcy, though she had been enrolled at another school, the consensus was that Jacques couldn't have killed her, that he was simply "bragging" about it. Students at Milpitas High do not place too high a premium on the subtleties of words, which may be why the thought that bragging about a murder is kind of a contradiction in terms did not seem to occur to any of them.

Later in the day, Jacques, perhaps resenting that the most significant thing he had ever done had proven too significant to seem feasible, took a young girl and two boys up the hill so they might make witness to his claim, and having done so they, too, joined the circle of silence, increasing its number to six.

And now the passive silence was augmented by an action, when one of the boys aided Broussard in covering the corpse with a plastic bag and a scattering of leaves. Eventually he would be charged as an accessory after the fact, sentenced to three years at a county ranch for delinquent boys, and his exis-tence would become a study in the curious way an entire life can be irrevocably altered in a single moment.

After lunch hour at the high school, John Hanson made a second sojourn to Old Marsh Road. He took Engle and two other friends, Mike Irvin and Dave Leffler, with him. Hanson was low on dope that day, so he bet Irvin a joint that the human form at the foot of the giant tree was an actual corpse. All right, he was told, but if it isn't, you give me your shoes and socks and walk home barefoot. It was on this note that they began to drive up the hill. They parked the car just as the oak tree became discernible. They scrambled down the incline. They stopped when they saw what they had come to see.

The four young men stared down at Marcy Conrad's earthly remains. Moments passed; nothing was said. The only sound was the insistent yammering of a few distant birds. Then Hanson wanted to collect on his bet. Leffler said, "This is no time to smoke," but they climbed up the incline and smoked anyway.

On the way down the hill Mike Irvin said he was going to the police. Hanson and Engle wanted to go back to class. "As far as we're concerned," Engle said, "the body doesn't exist." All Hanson could think of was that he had seen the corpse the day before and not reported it and that if he got involved at this point he might be arrested as an accessory. And he thought of how he had hated the time he once spent in juvenile hall after committing a burglary. And he thought of one of the terms of his parole, which was that he not associate with Mike Irvin, his alleged partner in that crime, the same young man who wanted to go to the police at this moment.

So Hanson and Engle went back to class, and Irvin and Leffler drove to the Milpitas police station. Leffler waited in the car. It was left to Irvin to walk alone up the sidewalk and open the thick glass door and, once inside, tell of the incredible thing he had seen in the hills, so that 48 hours after the murder of Marcy Conrad, the silence of the young people who knew she had died would be forever broken.

While Mike Irvin was in the office of the Milpitas police, Sergeant Garry Meeker was driving on Interstate 680. Meeker is the homicide and assaults investigator for Santa Clara County. . . . He takes a cop's pride in being tough and when he is summoned to view a corpse tries to regard it not as a body but as a piece of evidence. He often apologizes for the coldness of that attitude but has never doubted that if he's going to do his job, that's the way to do it.

It was two-thirty in the afternoon when he got the radio dispatch about the body up on Old Marsh Road. Meeker knew the area well. For one thing, it was something of a dump ground for corpses. . . .

When Meeker got to the oak tree, five of his colleagues were already there, men who were also paid to think of Marcy Conrad as a juvenile female, deceased. Before they left, two or three cars came up the hill and turned around when they drew near the police. Meeker did not give it much thought at the time; an hour or so would pass before he would learn of Broussard's boasts and the young people who had not reported the murder, and then he figured that the cars must have been those of young kids coming to see for themselves whether or not Broussard was lying.

The Milpitas police picked up Jacques Broussard later that evening. Shortly afterward Meeker questioned the young people who had gone up the hill to see Marcy's body. It had been an unsettling experience, though it was not the murder that was troubling. Meeker had seen a lot of murder victims, and murder itself was as old as dirt. There was really nothing else you could say about it. But this case was different, and what made it so was the silence of the young- sters. "They were supposedly normal people," Meeker said. "But people who see dead bodies get shook. It bothers them. It still bothers me if you want to know the truth. But these kids . . . it didn't seem to bother them."

The silence of the children was the issue. The silence was the metaphor. And the only question of pertinence was, metaphor for what? "That's a moral break- through somewhere," Meeker concluded. "That's what this thing represents. And it's not the kids' fault. The kids are a product of what we made them."

The murder was shocking in and of itself, but not nearly as unsettling as the circle of young people who knew what happened and maintained their silence for 48 hours. It wasn't "reefer madness" that produced their response. Smoking marijuana does not usually produce the extreme indif- ference noted in this case. It may be, however, that a steady day-to-day diet in our violent society of smoking dope, dropping pills, watching horren- dous acts of violence on the television and in the movies, and the continuing nonuse of intellectual capacities lead to a cool boredom that produces this indifference to human life and breeds senseless violence.

The gloomy prediction of Albert Camus on violence that "the whole world turns its back on these crimes; the victims have reached the extremity of their disgrace; they have become a bore," may have become a social reality that characterizes the type of senseless violence that has become rampant in recent years in American society.[23]

VANDALISM AS VIOLENCE

Most of the violence heretofore discussed has involved people against peo- ple. Violence is often expressed in an attack on inanimate objects. Vandal- ism involves a violent act of this type and is an expression of inner rage. Vandalism is often construed as senseless violence, yet a closer analysis of the delinquent act of vandalism reveals some definitive motivation. It is often motivated by a desire to commit violence on a person displaced onto an inanimate object.

One researcher in this area, British criminologist Stanley Cohen, maintains that despite the fact that most people view vandalism as "mind- less, random action there are meanings and motives that surround various forms of vandalism." Cohen asserts, after careful study, that vandalism has more structure to it than most people believe. He states:

Vandalism—the illegal and deliberate destruction or defacement of property— might be labeled differently according to circumstances and might not always be considered a crime. Some groups are given a sort of collective license to commit vandalism. Much routine property damage (such as graffiti) becomes

---

[23] Albert Camus, *The Rebel*, trans. by Anthony Bowker (New York: Knopf, 1954), p. 279.

accepted or condoned, and there are forms of official vandalism such as the destruction of buildings of architectural merit in the name of urban "renewal."

From the outset the words "wanton," "senseless," "malicious" and so on used by social scientists, the mass media and the public to describe vandalism have obscured any real attempt to understand what such behavior is all about.

In property-oriented soceites such as ours, it is incomprehensible that someone could destroy property without any apparent gain. Theft is easy to understand in straightforward economic terms; even personal violence usually seems intelligible. But for most people the only way to make sense of vandalism is to assume that it does not make sense—that it is mindless, random action.

Research in England and America suggests that there are clear clusters of meanings and motives around the various forms of vandalism. There is:

- Acquisitive vandalism: Damage to acquire money or property: breaking open telephone coin boxes, stealing material from construction sites.
- Tactical vandalism: Damage as a conscious tactic used to advance some other end: breaking a window to be arrested and get a bed in prison, jamming a machine in a factory to gain a rest period.
- Ideological vandalism: Similar to some tactical vandalism, but carried out to further an explicit ideological cause or to deliver a message: breaking embassy windows during a demonstration, chalking slogans on walls.
- Vindictive vandalism: Damage done to gain revenge: breaking windows of a school to settle a grudge against a teacher.
- Play vandalism: Damage done as part of a game: who can break the most windows of a house, who can shoot out the most street lamps.
- Malicious vandalism: Damage as an expression of rage or frustration, often directed at symbolic middle class property. It is this type that has the vicious and apparently senseless facade that many find so difficult to understand.[24]

A central proposition of Cohen's analysis is that vandalism—or, restated, violence against property—is more apt to flourish against an anonymous enemy—"them."

This study is supported by my observations and research when I directed a delinquency-prevention program for several years on the Upper West Side of Manhattan. The program was largely sponsored by Columbia University.

The vast gray edifices of Columbia were adjacent to a highly deprived ghetto that contained violence of all types, especially muggings and gang violence. Many young people, bored, deprived, and full of hostility, would choose Columbia University as a fitting target for their frustrations. They would often ventilate their aggression by breaking expensive windows and generally vandalizing the property. One youth told me how he always felt better after he destroyed something at Columbia. To him, the anonymous

---

[24]Stanley Cohen, "Vandalism," *Los Angeles Times*, October 5, 1973. See also Stanley Cohen, "The Politics of Vandalism," *The Nation*, November 11, 1968, pp. 497–500; "The Future of Vandalism," *The Nation*, August 13, 1973, pp. 110–113; and chapters by Stanley Cohen in *Vandalism*, ed. Colin Ward (London: Architectural Press, 1973).

gray buildings were inhabited by enemies who, he felt, "took care of rich kids—not me."

Over a period of several years, I set up a delinquency-prevention program that helped provide access for several hundred poor, minority gang youths to facilities in Columbia. The gymnasium, swimming pool, and baseball fields were opened up for use by neighborhood youths under controlled conditions. The results—unsurprisingly—were that vandalism in and on the buildings was sharply reduced. The cold, anonymous "them" became part of the juveniles' real community, and they saw no point in destroying property that, in part, now belonged to the youngsters in the neighborhood. The program broke down their formerly aggressive "we-they" stance.

A research project by Richard A. Berk and Howard E. Aldrich confirmes my observations on the Columbia University project that vandalism against property by youths is often a displaced act of aggression against a particular person or class of people.[25] They conclude, based on their research that:

> . . . patterns of attack during civil disorders strongly imply choices by some rioters. Civil disorders cannot accurately be described as "irrational" or "mindless" destruction. We are not arguing that the overall events were planned, but rather that individual participants appear to have been selecting many of their targets. . . . Apparently some believe consumer goods are distributed unfairly, label the villains and take collective action against them.[26]

A novel view of juvenile vandalism is revealed in *Crime as Play* by Richards, Berk, and Foster. The book presents the results of an extensive questionnaire study, in which almost 3,000 teenagers, ranging from fifth graders to high school students, told the investigators about their habits concerning vandalism, drugs, theft, and other forms of deviant behavior. Basically the authors assume that shoplifting or vandalism can be explained as a choice that, to the "delinquent," produces a maximum return on his or her investment of time and energy. They state: "As is the case with other economic choices, the returns consist of capital formation (in this case, the learning of skills), commodity production (the stolen or destroyed goods), and consumption (enjoyment, fun).[27]

Another facet of vandalism is its relationship to a youth's participation in a gang or peer group. Andrew L. Wade makes the point that vandalism is one means of producing group solidarity among alienated youngsters. Wade thus views aggressive juvenile vandalism as a "social act" of fraternity, despite the fact that the results may be destructive.

[25]Richard A. Berk and Howard E. Aldrich, "Patterns of Vandalism during Civil Disorders as an Indicator of Selection of Targets," *American Sociological Review* 37 (October 1972): 533–547.

[26]Ibid., p. 545.

[27]Pamela Richards, Richard Berk, and Brenda Foster, *Crime as Play: Delinquency in a Middle Class Suburb* (Cambridge, Mass.: Bollinger, 1979).

The act of vandalism functions as a means of ensuring group solidarity. Conformity to the peer group occurs because involvement tends to satisfy the adolescent's need dispositions for status, recognition, and response. Identification with societal property norms becomes subordinate to the demands of the peer group. The adolescent will thus participate in acts of property destruction in order not to appear "chicken." In other words, he can through his involvement maintain a satisfying self-definition and avoid becoming a marginal member of the group. Even though he may recognize the act to be "wrong" or "delinquent," he finds some comfort through the guilt-assuaging rationalizations present in the subculture of the peer group.[28]

In another context Wade comes closer to my "senseless violence" hypothesis of vandalism when he states:

Some property destruction appears to function for the adolescent as a protest against his ill-defined social role and ambiguous status in the social structure. Other meanings are more specific. If a boy has suffered frustration, he may express his resentment by a revengeful act of destruction:

"Well, he accused us of stealing some stuff out of his joint. He didn't come right out and say it was us, but the way he talked he made it sound like it, particularly us. We were kidding him about an old rifle he had in there, about ninety years old. And he wanted $15 for it, and the stock on it was all cracked up and everything. And we kept kidding his mother—she's in there [the store] with him—and we kept kidding her. And old Gay [the store owner] himself came over there and started raising the devil, blowing off steam and everything. We didn't like it too well. We left and came back later. I told him [his companion], 'Let's go down and break those windows.' He said, 'Okay,' and we went down there and picked up some rocks along the way. We got down there and stood in front of the place till there weren't any cars very close to us, and we threw the rocks and ran."[29]

In another case Wade uses an example that describes the previously cited theme of vandalism as displaced aggression toward a person:

I know of some friends of mine who went over to school and we decided to break some of Mr. X's windows for the simple reason that we absolutely despise this teacher. There were about four or five of us. . . .

Many windows are broken in our school. In one room in particular in which one unpopular teacher holds classes, about twenty-five panes a year have to be replaced. The vandals believe that this is a way to "get back at" a teacher.[30]

---

[28]From *Criminal Behavior Systems: A Typology* by Marshall B. Clinard and Richard Quinney. Copyright © 1967 by Holt, Rinehart and Winston, Inc. Reprinted by permission of Holt, Rinehart and Winston.

[29]Ibid., pp. 177–178.

[30]Andrew L. Wade, "Social Processes in the Act of Vandalism," in *Criminal Behavior Systems*, eds., Marshall B. Clinard and Richard Quinney (New York: Holt, Rinehart and Winston, 1967), pp. 168–182.

CHILD ABUSE AS VIOLENCE

The general sociocultural violent aspects of a society have their impact in creating violent delinquent behavior. On a more specific level, the way in which a child is socialized has a profound affect on the child's self-concept and later violent behavior. This facet of the problem of child abuse was discussed in Chapter 5. In this chapter I will discuss a variety of aspects of child abuse as violence that generally impacts on society.

Prior to 1960, the issue of child abuse was not as widely recognized or discussed as it is today. Recently, however, various articles have generated considerable concern and numerous studies on child abuse. The problem has become familiar not only to individuals working in the medical, the helping professions, social service, and law enforcement agencies, but to the general public as well.

From a general legal standpoint, "child abuse" is viewed as any "harm that is done to a person under the age of 18, whether it is done by the child's parents, a relative, a guardian, or caretaker, or by a total stranger." Nonlegal definitions typically regard abuse as a physical injury requiring medical attention or, more generally, as an intentional infliction of harm to a child, usually by a parent or other caretaker.

One definition of child abuse by Everstine and Everstine incorporates both acts of commission (which are more frequently considered to represent child abuse) and acts of omission (which are often alternatively referred to as "negligence"): "Abuse of children is the *intentional* non-accidental use of force or *intentional* non-accidental acts of omission on the part of the parent or caretaker interacting with the child in his care, aimed at hurting or destroying the child."[31]

A California Penal Code defines child abuse as follows:

> "Child abuse" means a physical injury which is inflicted by other than accidental means on a child by another person. "Child abuse" also means the sexual assault of a child or omission . . . (willful cruelty or unjustifiable punishment of a child . . . or . . . corporal punishment or injury). "Child abuse" also means the neglect of a child or abuse in out-of-home care. . . .

Dr. Frederic Wertham calls child abuse "the maltreatment syndrome":

> The syndrome itself, in all its aspects, is the most important symptom of our time. It is a link in the documentation of my theses that the spirit of violence is rampant in our society. It is a matter not only of the occurrence of these heartless cruelties against defenseless children but of the inadequacy of the steps taken so far to prevent them. Physicians, legislators, and child-care agencies have taken up the question belatedly. Even now no proper solution has been found. This is one of those forms of violence which society calls "incredible"

---

[31]D. Everstine and L. Everstine, *People in Crisis* (New York: Bruner/Mazel, 1983).

and is unequipped to deal with. Why in an orderly society, should this be such a baffling medical, social, and legal problem?[32]

Another researcher in the field, Dr. Vincent Fontana (a medical doctor specializing in pediatrics), has concluded that child abuse is a more widespread practice than we are willing to admit.

According to Dr. Fontana: "It is a myth that in this nation we love our children." He estimates that each year at least 700 American children are killed by their parents or parent surrogates. Fontana maintains "that some 10,000 are severely battered every year; 50,000 to 75,000 are sexually abused; 100,000 are emotionally neglected; and another 100,000 are physically, morally, and educationally neglected."[33] The tragic stories behind these appalling statistics are related by Fontana in his book, and his profiles of James Earl Ray, Arthur Bremer, and other convicted violent criminals illustrate the fate of some of yesterday's violently battered children—who retaliated in kind against society.

Many child-battering cases end up in murder. An extensive study by social worker David Kaplun and psychiatrist Robert Reich reveals many interesting and significant dynamics of the relationship of child abuse to murder.[34]

Kaplun and Reich studied the records of the chief medical examiner in New York City and found, in a one-year period, 140 cases of apparent homicide of children under the age of 15. They reviewed the postmortem reports and police inquiries for the 112 victims who could be identified. They also examined the case reports of the city's public assistance and child welfare agencies for 66 of the victims' families.

Poverty seemed to be a strong factor in the child murderer's background. Seventy percent of the victims' families lived in areas of extreme poverty. Many of the murderers in these families were involved in alcoholism, narcotics use, criminal activity, or assault other than child abuse. Most of the victims were infants; over half were under a year old.

According to Kaplun and Reich's study, the murderers usually killed out of rage—beating and kicking the child to death. One mother of three, estranged from her husband, was described by her social worker as "a sweet-tempered, affectionate young woman overburdened with home responsibilities." A short time later her 3-year-old son was hospitalized with bruises, burns, and a leg fracture caused, said the mother, by a fall from a crib against a hot radiator. Because the mother was so attentive and affectionate toward her child, the hospital and social worker decided she was not to blame. A year later the boy was killed. The mother again attributed his injuries to an accident, an accident that police investigation disclosed could

[32]Frederic Wertham, *A Sign for Cain* (New York: Macmillan, 1973), p. 1.

[33]Vincent Fontana, *Somewhere a Child Is Crying* (New York: Macmillan, 1973), p. 1.

[34]David Kaplun and Robert Reich, "Child Battering and Murder," *American Journal of Psychiatry* 133, 7 (September 1975): 87–99.

not have happened. She was not charged, but her two other children were taken from her.

In the search for the causes of various patterns of violent behavior in delinquents, many studies reveal a correlation between brutal parents and violent children. In brief, as has been indicated in earlier chapters, the use of harsh discipline or abuse to discipline children in their family may be a significant factor in producing violent people.

A cross-cultural study by psychiatrist Leopold Bellak and psychologist Maxine Antell suggests that child abuse varies from society to society and appears to be linked to the socialization of violent offenders.[35] Bellak and Antell note that "the Nazis who goosestepped their way across Europe in the 1940s may have begun their training as toddlers on the playgrounds of Germany, and the child rearing practices that produced Hitler's war criminals may still be creating violence." Bellak and Antell, who analyzed their biographies, concluded that nearly all of the Nazi leaders were cruelly abused as children. As he was wandering through playgrounds in Frankfurt and on the banks of the Main River, Bellak was struck by the violence both in the play of the children and in the handling of children by their parents. Over a period of several hours, he saw children throw knives dangerously close to one another, pelt one another with rocks, and twist each other's arms. On a similar stroll through playgrounds in Copenhagen, the psychiatrist did not see a single aggressive act. These observations motivated his systematic comparison of aggressive behavior on the playgrounds of different nations.

Two German, two Italian, and two Danish psychologists were asked to choose playgrounds in similar neighborhoods in their respective countries. Each team observed six different groups of children at play. They were not told the nature of the study; they were only told that they were to record everything that took place. The transcripts were then sent to two American graduate students, who also were in the dark about the hypothesis being tested but were asked to score the severity and number of violent acts racked up by the children and parents in each account. In Italy and Denmark, they found not a single act of aggression by parents against children but in Germany the adults hit a score of 73. In turn, German children were rated significantly more aggressive toward one another than were Italian or Danish children.

The notion that German culture is *kinderfeindlich* (hostile to children) is widely accepted even by Germans themselves, according to Bellak and Antell. A recent poll in West Germany found that 60 percent of the parents believe in "beating, not slapping or spanking, but beating their children," quotes Bellak. He also quotes Munich psychologist Rolf Luckert as saying, "We beat our children dumb in this nation." Adult aggressive outlets, including auto accidents, suicides, and self-inflicted injuries and homicides, occurred at much higher rates in Frankfurt than in Florence or Copenha-

[35]*Human Behavior* (March 1975).

gen, Bellak notes, perhaps further supporting the notion that people who are abused as children are more likely to abuse others and themselves as adults. Bellak and Antell comment: "The fact seems to be that German treatment of children, as still practiced today and consistent with what is known of past German attitudes toward child rearing, is strongly correlated with cruelty exhibited by these children and likely to be related to behavior of adult Germans in everyday life."[35]

Rather than reproaching only the Germans for their violent child-rearing practices, the researchers question whether parents in other countries are also guilty of such aggression. "Are there certain ethnic or social groups in the United States, for instance, whose methods of discipline and harsh handling of their children are creating people who as adults will be easily prone to express hatred, aggression and prejudiced attitudes toward others or toward other groups?"

Child abuse is violence in its own right—yet its impact on producing violent delinquents is highly significant. In my research in working with various delinquents (over 5,000 in the past 35 years) I would conclude that about 80 percent of those who act out violent behavior were abused or neglected by one or both parents.

In brief, my conclusions about the dynamic process involved in child abuse and violence are as follows:

1. Being a victim of child abuse produces humiliation, low self-esteem and *rage* in a youth.
2. The abused delinquent youth develops a low threshhold for violence, low impulse control, and is apt to "go off" violently when even slightly provoked. In many cases abused children attempt to create situations where he or she can act out or displace an inner, often unconscious, violent rage.
3. Most violent youths do not attack the child-abusing creators or provocateurs of their rage, because they fear the wrath of these offenders, many of whom are alcoholics or substance abusers.
4. As a consequence of their fear of being "hit back" by the person who has abused them, they displace their rage and act out against victims who are weaker targets.

THE MASS MEDIA AND JUVENILE VIOLENCE: RESEARCH FINDINGS

In this overall analysis of the juvenile in a violent society, I have alluded a number of times to the impact of the mass media on delinquent violence. Over the past 20 years there has been a considerable amount of research into the effects of television on children. The findings have been varied. Some assert that watching television negatively influences adolescent behavior; other research concludes that television has a minimal impact on the average psychologically healthy child. Following is a compendium of various research, which may enable students to come to their own conclusions about the impact of mass media on juvenile violence.

Children see a lot of violence on television. A Nielsen survey reports that preschoolers watch an average of 54 hours of television a week. And according to the "Violence Profile" of the Annenberg Institute of Communications, children's programs contain violence as standard content.

Two psychologists, Ronald S. Drabman and Margaret Hanratty Thomas, studied the relationship between television violence and violence in real life.[36] They specifically analyzed to what extent exposure to televised aggression makes children more tolerant to the real thing.

One of their experiments involved 40 fifth-graders from a white, lower-middle-class parochial school. Each child watched either a 15-minute segment from a television detective series that contained several shootings and other acts of violence or a 15-minute segment of a baseball game. Then the experimenter said he had to leave for a while and asked each child to keep an eye on two kindergarteners playing nearby. The child was told that the toddlers were being filmed by a camera and could be watched on the television screen. If anything went wrong, the fifth-grader was to get help. Actually, what the child saw was a staged videotaped sequence in which the kindergarteners became more and more unruly, screaming and fighting until they apparently knocked over the camera and the monitor went blank. The researchers were interested in how long it would take the fifth-grader to seek help after seeing this real-life violence.

The children who had watched the detective show took much longer to respond than did the baseball watchers. Five children in the aggressive film group (two boys and three girls) never went for help at all, as opposed to only one girl in the control group.

In another research experiment Drabman and Thomas studied third- and fourth-graders. Half the children saw a violent Hopalong Cassidy film on a movie screen, while the rest saw no film at all. Fifty-eight percent of the control children ran to get help before the kindergarteners began slugging it out. It took a lot more aggression to stir the children who had seen the film; 83 percent of them waited until the kindergarteners physically battled before they sought help.

Thomas and Drabman suggested two possible reasons for the apathy of the test group. Perhaps violence on television teaches children that aggression is a way of life, not to be taken seriously. Or perhaps real-life aggression simply seems bland when compared to the vicious violence on television.

There is insufficient research to conclude firmly that media violence does or does not cause violent behavior in children. Despite the inconclusiveness of the evidence, however, occasionally events occur that produce simplistic cause-effect observations, and demonstrate that fictionalized vio-

---

[36]Ronald S. Drabman and Margaret Hanratty Thomas, "Television Violence," *Pediatrics Journal* (September 1975): 36–43.

lence in the mass media is sometimes replicated in real life. For example, on October 10, 1973, the film *Fuzz* was aired over network television. In the film, teenage boys are shown setting fire to skid-row bums along Boston's waterfront. Two nights later, a woman was burned to death by a group of young blacks in Boston. The woman, Evelyn Wagler, a Swiss divorcée, had moved to Boston only five days earlier and was living in a small commune in the city's Roxbury ghetto with another white and four black women. While she was on her way home from a job-hunting trip, her car ran out of gasoline in the center of Roxbury's business district. Returning to her car with a two-gallon refill can from a service station, the young woman was forced into a trash-filled backyard along Blue Hill Avenue by six black teenagers, beaten, and ordered to douse herself with the fuel. After the terrified victim complied, one of them set her afire with a match. Before dying five hours later, she told the police that three of her assailants had been part of a black group that had called her a "honky" the previous day and warned her that whites were unwelcome in Roxbury. Thus a combination of racism and television influence may have caused this atrocious homicide.

Since 1969, the Surgeon General's Scientific Advisory Committee on Television and Social Behavior has subsidized over 23 independent research projects to study (1) the characteristics of television program content, (2) the characteristics of the audience (Who watches what? For how long?), and (3) the potential impact of televised violence on the attitudes, values, and behavior of the viewers. The advisory committee received 60 reports and papers, and published a summary report and five volumes of research reports.[37] Following is a summary of some of this mass of data, combined with the author's observations.

Television program content includes an enormous amount of violence. Programs designed for children contain by far the most violence. One researcher is quoted as concluding that "of all 95 cartoon plays analyzed during the three annual study periods, only two did not contain violence." In this study violent episodes occurred at the rate of five per play or eight episodes per hour, with eight out of ten plays containing some form of violence. Another study reported that during one season, *71 percent of all segments* had at least one instance of human violence and three out of ten dramatic segments were saturated with violence. About 70 percent of all leading characters studied were involved in some violence, and the odds were two to one in favor of the leading character being a killer, and seven to one that the killer would not be killed in return. Children are the heaviest viewers and they prefer the type of cartoons and situation comedies described.

---

[37]Television and Growing Up: The Impact of Televised Violence," Report to the Surgeon General, U.S. Public Health Service, from the Surgeon General's Scientific Advisory Committee on Television and Social Behavior, HEW Publication HSM72-9090 (Washington, D.C.: U.S. Government Printing Office, 1972).

Another aspect of violence on television is that killing someone is an approved method of solving problems. What does the hero do when he encounters the villain? He draws a weapon and kills him. No action is taken against him. This may very well influence the young viewer into seeking similar solutions to his problems. He can be a hero and resolve his problems by killing somebody.

The study also involved the relationship between TV violence and aggression in children. The study examined the TV habits of a large group of children over a 10-year period. The subjects were 427 teenagers of an original group of 875 children who had participated in a study of third-grade children. The original 875 constituted the entire third-grade population of a semirural county in New York. The 427 subjects were those of the 875 who could be located and interviewed 10 years later. The third-grade children were rated on their aggressiveness by their peers, and their preferences for violent television were obtained. All programs mentioned were rated either violent or nonviolent.

In the follow-up 10 years later, each subject reported his four favorite TV programs, and these were categorized as violent or nonviolent. The subjects were also rated by their peers using the same aggression criteria. Two hundred eleven of the subjects were male and 216 were female, the model age being 19 at the end of the study. The males scored higher on aggression than the females, and those females scoring higher than other females were significantly more masculine in interests and attitudes.

There was a high correlation between a boy's television preferences in the third grade and peer-rated aggression. Also there was a significant relation between a boy's preferences for violent TV programs in the third grade and aggression 10 years later. An analysis of the findings in this study led to the conclusion that watching violent television programs in early years influenced aggressive behavior later on in life.

A number of other studies point to the conclusion that viewing televised violence caused the viewer to become more aggressive. The advisory committee indicated in general that "there is a convergence of the fairly substantial experimental evidence for *short-run* causation of aggression by viewing violence on the screen and the much less certain evidence from field studies that extensive violence viewing precedes some *long-run* manifestations of aggressive behavior."

Another study that attempted to discover the impact of media violence on people was carried out by psychologist Leonard Berkowitz at the University of Wisconsin. The results of Berkowitz's research can be summarized as follows:[38]

Aristotle wrote that watching drama could "accomplish a purgation of . . . emotions," and apologists for the excessive violence in some movies and television shows have taken this concept of catharsis to mean that the physical violence

[38]"Pictures of Violence," *Newsweek*, February 24, 1964, p. 91. Copyright 1964 by Newsweek, Inc. All rights reserved. Reprinted by permission.

portrayed can be good for the psyche. There hasn't been any scientific evidence to the contrary—until now. . . .

For his experiments, Berkowitz used student volunteers and told them he was simply interested in physiological responses to a variety of stimuli. He even took blood-pressure readings to strengthen his camouflage. In reality, he was after something quite different.

Each experiment involved two subjects, one of them actually Berkowitz's assistant. The first task presented was an intelligence test. Berkowitz's conspirator always finished first, whereupon he would lean over to the subject and with a sly smile make a remark such as, "You're certainly taking a long time with that." This was usually enough for the subject to develop a dislike for his coworker.

Then both subjects were shown a seven-minute film sequence taken from the movie *Champion*, in which Kirk Douglas is reduced to a bloody, battered mess. The last test involved the floor plan for a house, which the conspirator had supposedly drawn up. The subject was to indicate his degree of disapproval of the plan by pressing a button that he was told would administer electric shocks to his coworker.

In this way, Berkowitz attempted to create a situation mirroring real life when someone nursing some new anger happens to attend a movie depicting physical violence. Soon afterward, he is given the opportunity to vent his feelings. The test results were illuminating.

In the cases where Berkowitz's conspirator refrained from making any insulting remarks during the intelligence test, or when peaceful travel scenes were used instead of the fight sequence, he received fewer shocks during the floor-plan experiment. But he felt a veritable barrage when the subjects were treated to the full course of insults and the violent boxing sequence.

The research also showed that so-called "justified aggression" triggers the greatest violence. In briefing his subjects on the overall plot of the movie, Berkowitz told some that Douglas was an "unprincipled scoundrel." Others were told he was about to go straight. Those who watched what they believed was the bad guy getting beaten almost always delivered more shocks. In other words, Berkowitz writes: "If it was all right for the movie villain to be injured aggressively . . . then perhaps it was all right for them to attack the villain in their own lives."

Still, Berkowitz does not believe movies can make a delinquent out of a model teen-ager. "The effect of filmed violence is temporary," he said in an interview last week. "But by the same token, a normal average citizen who is angry about something and then sees a case of justified aggression is more likely to attack, apparently because what he has seen has weakened his normal inhibitions against committing aggression."

Another noteworthy study that focuses more precisely on the effects of TV violence on children was carried out by psychologist Albert Bandura.[39] For Bandura, the basic issue was what happens to a child who watches violence on television. He designed a series of experiments to

---

[39]Albert Bandura, "What TV Violence Can Do to Your Child," *Look*, October 22, 1963, pp. 46–48.

determine the extent to which children will copy the aggressive patterns of behavior of adult models in real life, as real people on film, and as cartoon characters on film.

A first group observed real adults. The children were brought into a room, one by one. In one corner, each child found a set of play materials; in another corner was an adult sitting quietly with a set of toys including an inflated plastic Bobo doll and a mallet. Soon after the child started to play in his corner, the adult began attacking the Bobo doll ferociously—sitting on it, punching it on the nose, pounding it with the mallet, tossing it up in the air, and kicking it, while saying things like "Sock him in the nose!" "Hit him down!" "Throw him in the air!" "Kick him!"

A second group of children saw a movie of the adult attacking the Bobo doll. A third group watched a movie, through a television set, in which an adult attacked the doll while dressed as a cartoon cat. A fourth group served as a control group, did not see any aggressive behavior, and allowed comparison with the actions of the first three groups.

At the end of ten minutes, each child was taken to an "observation room" where the youngster was watched through a one-way mirror. The child had access to "aggressive toys" and "nonaggressive toys" for a 20-minute period. According to a team of psychologists-observers, those youngsters who had previously been exposed to the aggressive model showed almost twice as much aggression in the observation room as did the children in the control group.

From this Bandura reached two important conclusions about the effect of the aggressive models on a child:

1. The experience tends to reduce the child's inhibitions against acting in a violent, aggressive manner.
2. The experience helps to shape the form of the child's aggressive behavior. Most of the children from the first three groups sat on the Bobo doll and punched its nose, beat it on the head with a mallet, tossed it into the air and kicked it around the room. And they used the familiar hostile remarks, "Hit him down!" "Kick him!" and so forth. This kind of conduct was rare among the children in the control group.[40]

Bandura's findings led him to a third, and highly significant, conclusion. He noticed that a person who behaved violently on film is as influential as one who behaves violently in real life. The children were not too interested in imitating the cartoon character, but many children copied precisely the actions of both real-life and film models. From these observations, Bandura concluded that televised models are influential sources of social behavior whose impact on personality development can no longer be ignored. He points out that as audiovisual technology improves, television will become even more influential.

[40]Ibid., p. 48.

In another study on the relation between movies and violence, Dr. Richard Walters at the University of Toronto asked a group of adult men and adolescent boys to assist in a study of the effects of punishment on learning.[41] (This research seemed to parallel the earlier cited research of Dr. Stanley Milgram.) The subjects could give an electric shock to a "learner" each time he made a mistake on a test. Subjects were permitted to vary the length and intensity of the shock. Before beginning the test, each participant received a few shocks to become familiar with the various levels of pain.

The "learner" then made intentional mistakes, and Dr. Walters measured the length and strength of the shocks he was given. (Unknown to the participants, the electrodes were disconnected, and the learner felt no pain.)

In the second step of the study, half the subjects were shown the switchblade knife scene from the film *Rebel Without a Cause*, while the other half were shown a short film about picture making. All then repeated the shock-administration test.

Those subjects who had seen the picture-making film administered relatively weak shocks. Those who had seen *Rebel* gave longer, more powerful shocks, which would have caused considerable pain if the electrodes had been connected. Moreover, this latter group exhibited a pronounced increase in aggressiveness and hostility on an objective personality test.

The data presented on the relation between viewing violence on television and increased aggressive behavior on the part of children, although not conclusive, does indicate that the mass media have their effect on increasing violence in juveniles. Individuals, particularly very young boys, who watch film stars perform violent "hero" roles like Rambo are likely to consider violence as an approved way of asserting masculinity and of solving problems.

George Gerbner, a professor of communications, assessed an effort to curb the negative effects of violence on children by what became known as "the family hour."[42] Gerbner notes that the concept of a "family viewing" period arose in late 1974. It was a result of congressional prodding. Somebody had to do something to follow up the conclusion former Surgeon General Jesse L. Steinfeld reached, on the basis of extensive investigations, before the Pastore Senate Subcommittee. "It is clear to me," Steinfeld said, "that the causal relationship between televised violence and antisocial behavior is sufficient to warrant appropriate and remedial action."

The concept was eventually expressed as an addition to the Code of the National Association of Broadcasters: "Entertainment programming inappropriate for viewing by a general family audience should not be broadcast

[41]Cited in ibid., p. 52.

[42]George Gerbner, "Assessing Television's Try for a Non-Combat Hour," *Human Behavior* (November 1976): 43–49. Copyright © 1976 *Human Behavior* magazine. Reprinted by permission.

during the first hour of network entertainment programming in prime time and in the immediately preceding hour." The rule, riddled with exceptions and embroiled in controversy, went into effect in late 1975. Gerbner concluded:

> Our results to date show that violence in video (as in any storytelling) demonstrates how power works in society: who can—and who cannot—get away with what. Experience in the world of TV drama teaches regular viewers many of their assumptions about the relative risks in life. When you see a fight on television, you do not call the police or an ambulance; you absorb and confirm a sense of relative powers, and risks.
>
> Obviously, a few points' difference on the Violence Index does not necessarily transform the structure of symbolic action. In fact, our measures of the structure, called Risk Ratios, proved to be remarkably stable over the years. For example, for every violent male, there were 1.19 male victims. For every violent female, there were 1.32 female victims; for every young woman, there were 1.67 young women victims. Old, poor and black women mostly appeared as victims. Clearly, the structure of dramatic action on television is rooted in —and thus perpetuates—the pecking order of society. A change in the rate of victimization may be even more significant than a dip in the Violence Index.
>
> The Family Hour should be seen as a gesture of recognition by both broadcasters and the FCC of the growing citizen and congressional concern about the video's power and accountability.[43]

Most research, including the family-hour effort, results in debatable conclusions about the effects of television violence on aggressive behavior. A comprehensive study by two psychology professors, Robert M. Kaplan and Robert D. Singer, concluded that there was no justification for censorship of television programming because of the violence it portrays.[44]

Kaplan and Singer reviewed more than 120 studies of television violence and concluded that "the accumulated research does not show aggressive behavior. Too much of the research that draws a correlation between television violence and aggressive behavior is conducted in an unrealistic laboratory setting." According to Kaplan and Singer:

> The lab setting doesn't seem to generalize to the real world. We're trying to argue that research should meet certain criteria before it is used to justify changes in public policy. When you look closely at the [past] research, television doesn't show potent effects on aggressive behavior.
>
> It is fascinating that so many hours of research and so much money has been spent and directed at the possible effect of TV violence on aggressive behavior, when it is most likely that television is not a significant cause of human aggression. Instead of castigating the networks it may be more useful to ask why the public is so fascinated by programs portraying violence.

[43]Ibid., p. 51.
[44]"Television Violence," *Los Angeles Times*, January 7, 1972.

The professors suggested that researchers "could turn their attention to economic, developmental, social and cultural factors" in an attempt to find the major causes of violence. However, they added, further research into television would be useful, especially if it focused on the probability that television is a major influence in promoting aggression in a natural setting. A more natural setting, according to Kaplan and Singer, would include social sanctions against aggression which are lacking in a lab setting, and a broader sample of subjects and long-term viewing by subjects.

Other observations made by Professors Kaplan and Singer were that:

1. Violent television programming has not been shown to have the effect of reducing aggressive behavior by allowing a person to "drain off" his aggressive tendencies while watching violence on television.
2. There still remains the possibility that violence on television may contribute to violent behavior by "disturbed" viewers. "Unfortunately, the literature and current methodology does not permit us to evaluate such possibilities," the professors said.
3. There is a difference in the influences of fantasy violence and real violence—as portrayed on news shows—on aggressive behavior.

They concluded: "As in so many other areas of juvenile delinquency, we have to conclude, based on many studies, that a clear causal connection between mass media violence and actual violent behavior is still inconclusive. Yet it is our observation that several studies indicate a degree of brutalization occurs from certain types of programs." This latter statement is a position that I am in agreement with on the basis of my own analysis of relevant research. I would, however, add one factor to this conclusion. The psychological state of the observer of mass media violence is a significant factor. For example, many people saw the film *Taxi Driver*, but no one else reacted to the film in the same way as John Hinckley.

In order to combat the negative influences of violence in the mass media I would recommend the psychodrama approach. The psychodrama approach would involve the dramatization of actual instances of violence, but instead of glamorizing delinquent acts as sometimes is the case in the mass media, the sessions would emphasize the "causes" or reasons for the violent behavior. Such reasons would invariably turn out to indicate some weakness in the personality of the violent individual or in his social relationships.

I have directed psychodramas of this type in my university classrooms. For example, I have set up role-playing conversations for the class with other students playing the role of "The Hillside Strangler," "Kenneth Bianchi," or "Charles Manson." In this exercise a student would play the role of this violent offender and would in response to other students questions defend his violent behavior on the basis of his causal family context of abuse and abandonment as a child. This would lead to a heated discussion of the causes of violent behavior and its meaning in the larger, sociocultural context of violence. The sessions are invariably illuminating and cause the students to try to better understand violence in our society. In this type of psychodrama context, violence is not glamorized. It is explored with the class so they can better understand their own real feelings on the subject.

A greater understanding of the social dynamics and rationales for violence described here, combined with the actual participation of young people (live and on film), might produce some valuable forces for counterattacking the growing problems of violence by juveniles in a society that seems to perpetuate the climate of violence.

SUMMARY: BASIC THEMES FOR CLASS DISCUSSION

1. The sociocultural climate of violence that pervades our society has its impact on and contributes to the violent behavior of juveniles. The sociocultural violence factors range from the persistent threat of a nuclear holocaust to the violent gore and mayhem witnessed by children and adolescents on TV and in the movies.

2. A partial indicator of the ability of the average person to commit acts of violence "under orders" is revealed by the Milgram research, which leads to the conclusion that most people will commit acts of violence if ordered to do so in the correct societal context.

3. The Hinckley assassination attempt on President Reagan's life is significant in that it depicts a prototypical contemporary situation, where an alienated, emotionally disordered person, somewhat influenced by the mass media, acts out his fantasies by perpetrating a real act of violence. Hinckley's case was notorious because of the status of his victim in our society; however, it is representative of many lesser-known acts of juvenile violence.

4. The presence and adulation of guns in our society contributes to the climate and acting out of violence in American society. The easy availability of guns is significantly related to the fact that the United States is one of the most violent societies in the world.

5. Although "buddy-murders" and "serial killings" have always existed in our society, there is evidence that these bizarre forms of violence are escalating in American society. There is also evidence that juveniles increasingly commit many so-called senseless acts of violence, and that they become victims of violence in disproportionately high rates.

6. A partial explanation for this increased violence is found in the Hans Von Hentig hypotheses of the "duet frame of reference." In "victim-precipitated violence" it is difficult to ascertain who will be the "offender" and who will be the "victim." There are violent scenarios which are often the consequence of low self-esteem and an increasing ethos of "suicidal tendencies" among juveniles.

7. Most juveniles who are perpetrators or victims of violence have a sense of low self-esteem due to the fact that they were abused or

neglected by their parents in the socialization process. These abused children, are more vulnerable to committing or becoming victims of violence. These complex social forces produce an increase in what has been termed "senseless violence."

8. Another form of violence by juveniles is involved in vandalism. Here inner rage and hostility is displaced from human victims onto property.

9. There is evidence that the gory and bizarre violence depicted in the mass media of film and TV is on the rise. This socio-cultural ethos of violence is most likely to affect juveniles who, due to a pre-existing state of emotional disorder, are more prone to act-out violent behavior. In brief, the violent mass-media has an affect on juvenile violent behavior; however, some youths are more violence-prone than others to commit actual violent acts.

QUESTIONS

7.1. Discuss some of the factors that affect the contemporary sociocultural ethos of violence.

7.2. Why are some juveniles more likely to become perpetrators or victims of violence than others?

7.3. How does the mass media affect violent behavior?

7.4. Define and discuss how and why juveniles who are abused and neglected in their socialization process have a greater tendency to participate in violent behavior.

chapter 8

Juvenile Gangs

Juvenile gangs, like the gangs of the Old West, have become part of American reality and folklore. They have become a persistent part of the delinquency problem in the depressed socioeconomic areas of America's large cities and in the late 1980s have taken form in some measure in more affluent suburban areas.

Gangs are both denounced and glorified in contemporary society. In the black ghettos and Hispanic barrios of most large American cities, gangs are perceived by civic-minded people and law enforcement leaders as a cancer that must be eliminated from the community. In contrast, in the community itself and in the mass media, gangs are often romantically depicted as a haven for distressed youths growing up under adverse socioeconomic conditions. Both viewpoints have validity.

My firsthand research into juvenile gang structure and function over the past 35 years reveals that many descriptions of gangs in the press and pop culture have debatable characteristics.[1] For example: (1) Gangs are not all the same with regard to violence and delinquency. There are relatively law-abiding social peer group gangs. (2) Some violent gangs have a cohesive and coherent structure; however, most violent juvenile gangs have an incoherent amorphous structure. (3) Most gang leaders do not have leadership talents. They are usually violent sociopaths who become "leaders" because of their reckless and indiscriminate violent behavior.

In the late 1980s a new term, "gang-related" homicide, came into

---

[1]Lewis Yablonsky, *The Violent Gang* (New York: Macmillan, 1962; New York: Penguin, 1966; New York: Irvington Press, 1982).

vogue and is used almost daily in the big city newspapers, usually in relationship to a story about a gang murder. Often this police-developed description has nothing to do with an actual gang homicide. A "gang-related" murder may simply mean that a psychotic or sociopathic murderer, who has some tenuous gang affiliation, has committed a senseless act of homicide. Most victims of so-called "gang-related" murders (about 60 percent) are ordinary citizens of all ages who happen to innocently and tragically find themselves in the line of fire of an emotionally disordered sociopath. The "gang-related" murder may have very little connection to gang retaliation and more to do with a disturbed sociopath's paranoia acted out in murder. In brief, many emotionally disturbed individuals' violent behavior is erroneously characterized as gang-related violence.

Despite a number of debatable issues on violent gangs, it is clear that the phenomenon has become a permanent sociocultural fixture on the American scene even though the "gang problem" in urban ghettos has been cyclical. Violent gangs were very prevalent in the post-World War II era, became less visible in the 1960s, then resurfaced with a vengeance in the 1970s, and the gang problem has persisted into the late 1980s.

Based on a study funded by the Federal Law Enforcement Assistance Administration, Dr. Walter Miller of the Harvard Law School's Center for Criminal Justice concluded that gang members tend to be males between the ages of 12 and 21, living predominantly in low-income ghettos. According to Miller, the weaponry of gangs have escalated: "The prevalence, use, quality, and sophistication of weaponry in the gang far surpasses anything known in the past. Murder by firearms or other weapons, the central and most dangerous form of gang-member violence, in all probability stands today at the highest level it has reached in the history of the nation."[2] My own research reveals that in the late 1980s the lethal use of guns in "gang-related" violence has risen sharply.

Apart from weaponry and increased violence, there is evidence that in recent years the age level of gang members has gone down to encompass younger and younger children in urban ghettos. Desmond S. Cartwright, Barbara Tomson, and Hershey Schwartz report:

> Some cities saw substantial decreases in gang fighting during the 1960's with as much as 40% fewer conflict incidents reported. This decrease may have been due only to a change to less visible activities, but, in any case, there has been a resurgence in gang activity in the 1970s. Youth-gang violence has flared up in Chicago, New York, Los Angeles, and Philadelphia; 700 gangs are said to "retain their identity" in Chicago alone. In Philadelphia, 160 killings in four years have been attributed to street gangs. Recent reports from Los Angeles, Boston, San Francisco, and rural Montana indicate that many violent gangs of 8-to-12-year-olds are creating "mousepack" mayhem.[3]

[2]Walter Miller, *Los Angeles Times*, May 14, 1976.
[3]Desmond S. Cartwright, Barbara Tomson, and Hershey Schwartz, *Gang Delinquency* (Monterey, Calif.: Brooks/Cole, 1975), p. vii.

Another pattern of gang activity is a growing shift from pedestrian violent activity to a mechanized form of assault and murder from a passing automobile. This is illustrated by a growing number of homicides that take the following prototypical form where an individual, often a nongang member, is shot from a passing car.

It was dusk Tuesday when Pastor Joshua Jeffries saw 12-year-old Patricia Jefferson and her girlfriend waiting at the bus stop outside his church in Watts.

There was no bus in sight, and the pastor thought to himself that this was no place for two young girls to be at that hour. So he came out to ask them in to use the church's phone to call someone for a ride.

The words were barely out of his mouth when three youths, evidently aiming at a rival gang member, rode by and opened fire, hitting Jefferson twice in the back.

The apparent intended victim, 16-year-old Charles Duncan, was shot twice in the leg as he walked near the group, in front of the Pentecostal Temple Church of God in Christ, at 301 E. 120th St. He was treated at Martin Luther King Hospital and released.

But Jefferson, who lived a few blocks from the church, at 244 E. 119th St., died later while undergoing surgery at Martin Luther King Hospital.

Jeffries, and Jefferson's companion, a 14-year-old school friend, also escaped injury. Although the small, neat, white adobe church was hit by some of the bullets, the 10 or 15 persons attending the service inside all escaped injury as well.

Los Angeles police officers early yesterday arrested three young males—one a juvenile—and booked them on suspicion of murder: Gregory Rivers, 22, of Compton, who allegedly fired the shots; Lonel Bell, 19; and a 16-year-old youth, who reportedly drove the moped two of the assailants were riding. The third was on a 10-speed bike, witnesses said.

Lt. Don Benton, of the LAPD's South Bureau CRASH (Community Resources Against Street Hoodlums) said four to six shots were fired as the youths rode by.

"It was another stupid gang shooting," Benton said. "A stupid, useless, pointless gang shooting. Old ladies and young women can't even walk the streets anymore. Maybe this will get enough people excited to do something," he said, but his voice sounded like he didn't believe it.

"I can't get over it. I have a 12-year-old daughter myself," said another officer, Mike Mejia, one of the detectives handling the case. "It's unreal once it sinks in."

Benton refused to name the gang involved, saying it would only glorify them. He would say that it was the 10th known gang-related homicide so far this year in the LAPD's four South Bureau divisions: Southeast, 77th Street, Southwest and Harbor.[4]

Another general pattern of increasing concern related to violent

[4]Patricia Klein, *Los Angeles Herald Examiner*, April 30, 1981. Reprinted by permission.

gangs is the manner in which the mayhem has moved out of the ghetto and into the larger community. The old saw "we only kill each other," first stated by Benjamin (Bugsy) Siegel, a chief of one of the earliest and deadliest criminal gangs, New York's Murder, Inc., is no longer as true today as it was in the past. Gang violence increasingly has been transplanted to the suburbs and downtown areas of our major cities. A prototypical example of this phenomenon is the rash of gang violence in downtown areas that has plagued many large cities.

For example, in one report on this issue from Detroit, the then police chief Philip G. Tannian was given an ultimatum by the city council to bring Detroit's youth gang violence under control or be replaced. The ultimatum was related to violence that began at a concert at Cobo Hall in downtown Detroit by two rock groups—the Average White Band and Kool and the Gang. It later spilled over into the area around the hall. When the concert started, a group of about 80 youths belonging to two of the city's black gangs stormed the stage and began to throw chairs at the audience. Some of the audience were robbed and beaten, and gang members blocked exits to prevent patrons from leaving. The same type of situation at one of their prior concerts in 1986 caused a concert by a rock group, Run DMC, to be cancelled in Los Angeles.

Another general issue related to gang phenomena is the role of drugs in their violent behavior. The phenomenon of substance abuse and gangs has changed over the years. Marijuana has always been a drug used by gang members. In Los Angeles, one notorious graffiti-advertised gang that has been around for most of the 1980s is named V-13. (Thirteen is derived from M for marijuana, the thirteenth letter in the alphabet.)

In my early research into gangs in the 1950s and 1960s I noted that heroin, then the major drug of choice for some gang members, tended to break up violent gangs. When a gang member started using heroin, I noticed that the pursuit of the drug was all-consuming. Heroin addiction is a "loner" activity that requires daily forays into the community involving thefts, burglary, and muggings for the purpose of supporting the expensive habit. Several gangs I was working with at that time were broken up because a number of members became heroin addicts.

In the late 1980s the development of an inexpensive form of cocaine, known as rock cocaine or "crack," has had a similar disorganizing impact on violent gangs. Many sociopathic gang members have given up the "high" they obtained from violence to become crack cocaine addicts. Some gang youths not only became cocaine addicts, but entrepreneurs in the drug trade. In this context, violence made more sense than their former senseless gang-related violence. The dealing of drugs, a most profitable enterprise, created "turf" or territorial disputes, and the enforcement of a profitable position often involved a more logical brand of violence. In effect, the drug wars dramatized by the "Miami Vice" TV show are played out in a less glamorized version on the streets of large cities around the country. One news report on this issue states: "There has been a 20.2% upsurge in the first half of the year in major youth gang violence in Los Angeles, most of it related to narcotics street sales and the territorial struggles that go along with them, police officials said Wednesday."[5]

The delinquent gang phenomenon has persisted in American society for almost 100 years with some variations on gang structure and function. One constant in the American gang phenomenon is that there has always been a variety of juvenile gangs available to youths growing up in socioeconomically depressed urban areas. Some comprise youths in a close, friendly association, as in athletic clubs. At the other extreme are delinquent and violent gangs. Gangs of this type are extremely negative socializing agents that train youths into delinquent and violent patterns of behavior.

This negative pattern is illustrated by a homicidal assault by the Egyptian Kings, a particularly extremist violent gang, on two boys in a New York City park. Here is a description of the assault given by some of the gang members and by one of the victims, Roger McShane, who, although badly stabbed, survived the attack.[6] The other boy, Michael Farmer, who was a polio victim, was killed.

> MCSHANE: It was ten-thirty when we entered the park. We saw couples on the benches, in the back of the pool, and they all stared at us, and I guess they must've saw the gang there—I don't think they were fifty or sixty feet away. When we reached the front of the stairs, we looked up and there was two of their gang members on top of the stairs. They were two smaller ones, and they had garrison belts wrapped around their hands. They didn't say nothin' to us, they looked kind of scared.
>
> FIRST EGYPTIAN KING: I was scared. I knew they were gonna jump 'em an everythin', and I was scared. When they were comin' up, they all were separatin' and everythin' like that.
>
> MCSHANE: I saw the main body of the gang slowly walk out of the bushes, on my right. I turned around fast, to see what Michael was going to do, and this kid came runnin' at me with the belts. Then I ran, myself, and told Michael to run.
>
> SECOND EGYPTIAN KING: He couldn't run anyway, 'cause we were all

---

[5]*Los Angeles Times,* July 17, 1986.
[6]Derived in part from Lewis Yablonsky, *The Violent Gang.*

around him. So then I said, "You're a Jester," and he said, "Yeah," and I punched him in the face. And then somebody hit him with a bat over the head. And then I kept punchin' him. Some of them were too scared to do anything. They were just standin' there, lookin'.

THIRD EGYPTIAN KING: I was watchin' him, I didn't wanna hit him, at first. Then I kicked him twice. He was layin' on the ground, lookin' up at us. I kicked him on the jaw, or someplace; then I kicked him in the stomach. That was the least I could do, was kick 'im.

FOURTH EGYPTIAN KING: I was aimin' to hit him, but didn't get a chance to hit him. There were so many guys on him—I got scared when I saw the knife go into the guy, and I ran right there. After everybody ran, this guy stayed, and started hittin' him with a machete.

FIRST EGYPTIAN KING: Somebody yelled out, "Grab him. He's a Jester." So then they grabbed him. Magician grabbed him, he turned around and stabbed him in the back. I was . . . I was stunned. I couldn't do nothin'. And then Magician—he went like that he pulled . . . he had a switchblade and he said, "You're gonna hit him with that bat or I'll stab you." So I just hit him lightly with the bat.

SECOND EGYPTIAN KING: Magician stabbed him and the guy, he . . . like hunched over. He's standin' up and I knock him down. Then he was down on the ground, everybody was kickin' him, stompin' him, punchin' him, stabbin' him, so he tried to get back up and I knock him down again. Then the guy stabbed him in the back with a bread knife.

THIRD EGYPTIAN KING: I just went like that, and I stabbed him with the bread knife. You know, I was drunk, so I just stabbed him. (Laughs) He was screamin' like a dog. He was screamin' there. And then I took the knife out and I told the other guys to run. So I ran and then the rest of the guys ran with me. They wanted to stay there and keep on doin' it.

FOURTH EGYPTIAN KING: The guy that stabbed him in the back with

> the bread knife, he told me that when he took the knife out o' his back, he said, "Thank you."
>
> MCSHANE: They got up fast right after they stabbed me. And I just lay there on my stomach and there was five of them as they walked away. And as they walked away . . . this other big kid came down with a machete or some large knife of some sort, and he wanted to stab me too with it. And they told him, "No, come on. We got him. We messed him up already. Come on." And they took off up the hill and they all walked up the hill and right after that they all of 'em turned their heads and looked back at me. I got up and staggered into the street to get a cab. And I got in a taxi and asked him to take me to the Medical Center and get my friend and I blacked out.

The coroner's report reveals the intensity of the violence:

I found a fifteen-year-old white boy, five feet and a half inches in length, scale weight 138 pounds, the face showing an ecchymosis . . . [a] hemorrhage beneath the skin. . . . You would compare it to a black-and-blue mark.

There was an ecchymosis of the outer aspect of the right eye, with a superimposed superficial abrasion. . . . There was an incised wound . . . one made with a very sharp implement . . . situated over the bridge of the nose and [extending] . . . . over the right eyebrow.

He had found wounds and abrasions on the knuckles and hands, the doctor said, which seemed to indicate that Michael Farmer had raised his hands to protect himself against the blows being rained upon him. The doctor had also found an incised wound beneath the left armpit, but that one had not penetrated deeper than the epidermis. A wound on the right thigh had been deeper: "It measured one and a half inches in length with a gap that was slightly less than three-quarters of an inch . . . a gaping wound with sharp edges. . . ."

On the left side was another penetrating stab wound, lower and more deadly. This one "went through the entire back into the pleural cavity" and "severed a vein and a nerve." This wound, four inches deep, had caused Farmer's death.

A BRIEF HISTORY OF GANGS IN AMERICA

The violent gang, such as the Egyptian Kings, is a comparatively recent phenomenon. Earlier gangs used violence, but they were more cohesive than contemporary gangs, and there was more camaraderie among their members.

Significant sociological appraisals of gangs first appear in the early writings (1920 to 1940) of sociologists associated with what was termed the *Chicago school*. This group, which included such pioneers as Frederic M. Thrasher, Frank Tannenbaum, Clifford R. Shaw, Henry D. McKay, and William F. Whyte, relied heavily on firsthand research data collected directly from the boys in the gangs. In general, their assessments of the problem of gang causation were tied to theories of the slum community and the disorganized "interstitial" area. Ganging and delinquent activity were considered essentially a result of what Edwin H. Sutherland later termed *differential association*.

The Chicago School and Gangs

During the late twenties and the depression era of the thirties, a group of sociologists at the University of Chicago focused upon various social problems that they attributed to urban social disorganization. Thrasher, Shaw, and McKay, in particular, instituted several delinquency research projects that produced data that remain the backbone of many current conceptions of delinquency and gangs. Their research and writing were heavily based upon case-history material and personal documents obtained from offenders both in institutions and in the open community.

Thrasher's gang's   Frederic M. Thrasher may be credited with the first extensive sociological study of gangs. His findings were presented in a classic volume appropriately called *The Gang*. On the basis of his study of 1,313 cases, he defined the gang as "an interstitial group originally formed spontaneously and then integrated through conflict," and characterized by "meeting face to face, milling, movement through space as a unit, conflict, and planning." The result of this behavior is the development of a "tradition, unreflective internal structure, *esprit de corps*, solidarity, morale, group awareness, and attachment to a local territory."[7] Thrasher's definition has been the basis for most current conceptions of the gang.[8]

The Chicago Area Project   The Chicago Area Project, instituted in the early thirties and currently operating out of the Juvenile Division of the Illinois Department of Corrections, has contributed some of the most significant theories, research, and correction programs that have evolved in the field of American criminology. Early in its career the project was described by its originators as a program that sought to discover by demon-

---

[7]Frederic M. Thrasher, *The Gang* (Chicago: University of Chicago Press, 1926). © 1926, 1954 by The University of Chicago. Reprinted by permission.

[8]Currently some of the most widely used college textbooks on criminology base their discussions of gangs on Thrasher's appraisal.

stration and measurement a procedure for the treatment of delinquents and the prevention of delinquency in those Chicago neighborhoods that sent disproportionately large numbers of boys to the Cook County Juvenile Court. Residents of the neighborhoods were encouraged to aid in planning and operating the program. An effort was made to effect changes in the social environment of the neighborhoods by providing residents with facilities and professional guidance for the development of their own programs of child welfare.[9]

Clifford Shaw and Henry McKay were the prime movers of the Chicago Project. Their work over several decades, with the aid of many able assistants, revealed a conception of delinquency that remains currently of major significance. Their basic working assumptions were that delinquency was normal in the slum ("interstitial") neighborhood, that most offenses (about 95 percent) were committed in association with others in gangs, and that most boys were trained into criminal careers by other offenders in the neighborhood; in short, that the average offender evolved in the normal course of events as a product of his social training.

In the early stages of the delinquent's development, according to Shaw and McKay, robbery was a playful act in a kind of game:

> When we were shoplifting we always made a game of it. For example, we might gamble on who could steal the most caps in a day, or who could steal caps from the largest number of stores in a day, or who could steal in the presence of a detective and then get away. We were always daring each other that way and thinking up new schemes. This was the best part of the game. I would go into a store to steal a cap, by trying one on and when the clerk was not watching walk out of the store leaving the old cap. With the new cap on my head I would go into another store, do the same thing as in other store, getting a new hat and leaving the one I had taken from the other place. I might do this all day and have one hat at night. It was the fun I wanted, not the hat. I kept this up for months and then began to sell the things to a man on the west side. It was at this time that I began to steal for gain.[10]

After the initial gang play activity, stealing would become a more serious business. In the late 1930s Tannenbaum described the gang boy's graduation to more serious crimes. The youth went from shoplifting to rolling bums. Then came pickpocketing, car-stealing, holdups, and sometimes murder. All these activities were carried out in company with other members of the gang. It was a collective enterprise that had the approval of

[9]Ernest W. Burgess, Joseph D. Lohman, and Clifford R. Shaw, "The Chicago Area Project," in N.P.P.A *Yearbook* (Washington, D.C.: National Probation and Parole Association, 1937), pp. 8–28. See also Anthony C. Sorrentino, "Chicago Area Project After 25 Years," *Federal Probation* 23 (June 1959): 40–43.

[10]Clifford R. Shaw and Henry D. McKay, "Social Factors in Juvenile Delinquency," in *Report on the Causes of Crime*, National Commission on Law Observance and Enforcement report 13 (Washington, D.C.: U.S. Government Printing Office, 1931).

the group. The play group became the criminal gang by slow differentiation and habituation.[11]

Delinquent-trained youths tend to become further pulled into the
gang as they begin to conflict with some elements of the community. The
gang seems to develop almost according to the Toynbee scheme of "challenge and response." Its increased cohesion is a function of the response it
meets in the community. According to Thrasher, it does not become a gang
until it begins to "excite disapproval and opposition." The opposition could
come from another gang or from any adult representatives of the community; the cops begin to "shag" it (chase it), or some representative of the
community steps in and tries to break it up. This is the real beginning of the
gang, for now it begins to draw itself more closely together as it becomes a
conflict group.[12]

Tannenbaum broadens Thrasher's conception of delinquent gang
formation to include the youth's conflict with additional elements of the
"out-group" law-abiding community. These forces, he contends, help to
sharpen the gang youth's delinquent self-conception. In his conflict with
the community there develop two opposing definitions of the situation. For
the young delinquent it may be a form of play, adventure, excitement,
interest, mischief, fun. "Breaking windows, annoying people, running
around porches, climbing over roofs, stealing from pushcarts, playing truant—all are items of play, adventure, excitement."[13] To the community,
however, these activities take on a form of "nuisance, evil, delinquency,
with the demand for control, admonition, chastisement, punishment, police court, truant school."[14] The conflict arises out of a divergence of values.
As the problem develops, the situation gradually becomes redefined and
the community attitude demands suppression. Under these conditions of
conflict, the gang becomes more developed and cohesive. The delinquent
gang wins out against more socially acceptable forces not because of its
inherent attraction but because the positive sociocultural forces that might
train a youth into socially acceptable behavior patterns are weak.

The Chicago school gave heavy weight to family disorganization in
the production of the delinquent. It saw the disorganized family as a family
whose potential positive social force did not fulfill its function.

Street-corner society The Chicago school spurred other studies of street
gangs. A major participant-observation study by William Whyte[15] tended to
confirm many of the speculations of the earlier Chicago studies. Whyte

[11]Frank Tannenbaum, *Crime and the Community* (New York: Columbia University Press, 1939).
[12]Thrasher, *The Gang*, p. 30.
[13]Tannenbaum, *Crime and the Community*, pp. 9–10.
[14]Ibid.
[15]William F. Whyte, *Street Corner Society* (Chicago: University of Chicago Press, 1955). Whyte's analysis of criminal influence and politics was also a major contribution of this book; however, this theme is not discussed here in any detail, since the focus is on youth gangs.

moved into the Italian neighborhood of a large Eastern city near Boston, which he called "Cornerville." He learned Italian and hung out with the "Norton Street Gang," the focus of his study. For three years he participated in the activities of the gang, developed friendly relations with the leaders, and, with their cooperation, studied the group's structure.

A central fact about the Norton Street Gang was that it was a product of the Depression. Most of the members were in their twenties and normally would have been working if jobs had been available. The gang, according to Whyte, emerged because the boys could accomplish more together than separately. The gang gave its members a feeling of solidarity or belonging. They participated in constructive activities, engaged in athletics, helped each other financially (when they could), and discussed mutual problems. The Norton Street Gang was a cooperative group, beneficial to its members.

This pattern of essentially constructive interaction is in considerable contrast to the mutual hostility, aggression, and violence found among contemporary violent gangs. In addition to a high degree of cooperative action and esprit de corps, Whyte found permanence and cohesion in the corner gangs he studied:

> The corner-gang structure arises out of the habitual association of the members over a long period of time. The nuclei of most gangs can be traced back to early boyhood, when living close together provided the first opportunities for social contacts. . . . The gangs grew up on the corner and remained there with remarkable persistence from early boyhood until the members reached their late twenties or early thirties.
>
> The stable composition of the group and the lack of social assurance on the part of its members contribute toward producing a very high rate of social interaction within the group. The group structure is a product of these interactions.
>
> Out of such interaction, there arises a system of mutual obligations which is fundamental to group cohesion.[16]

Whyte's comments on gang leadership further support an image of the Norton Street Gang as a constructive organization:

> The leader is the man who acts when the situation requires action. He is more resourceful than his followers. Past events have shown that his ideas were right. In this sense "right" simply means satisfactory to the members. He is the most independent in judgment. While his followers are undecided as to a course of action or upon the character of a newcomer, the leader makes up his mind.
>
> When he gives his word to one of the boys, he keeps it. The followers look to him for advice and encouragement, and he receives more of their confidence than any other man.
>
> The leader is respected for his fair-mindedness.[17]

---

[16]Ibid., p. 255.

Not only did Whyte's studies support the earlier images of the Chicago school; they also fostered conceptions of the gangs dealt with in the postwar era of the 1940s and 1950s.

Youth Board "Bopping Gangs"

About 1946 New York City was struck by the emergence of violent youth gangs that committed a number of seemingly senseless and vicious homicides. Workers were sent into the streets to deal with them in a special project that became known as the "detached-worker program." The mayor later developed a permanent social agency called the New York City Youth Board to carry out work along these lines with the gangs. In a series of manuals and books based on its work, the Youth Board developed a concept of the gang that has become an accepted diagnostic image for many similar programs in urban areas throughout the country:

> The gangs with which we worked were surprisingly well organized, on both a formal and informal level. Each club was divided into several divisions, usually on the basis of age. These divisions were called the Tiny Tims, Kids, Cubs, Midgets, Juniors, and Seniors. Nine- to 13-year-old boys usually belonged to the Tiny Tims, while young men over 20 were members of the Seniors division. These divisions regarded themselves as autonomous groups; at the same time they had a strong feeling of kinship with each other. As the boys grew older they "graduated" from one division to another—a feeding process which insured the continued life of each club. The divisions were in a hierarchical relationship to each other, the older groups having more power, status, and influence than the younger groups. . . .
>
> Each division had its own officers including a president, vice-president, war counsellor, and "light-up" man. The gang president played a central role in coordinating the group's activities, in exerting discipline, and in determining club goals. In addition, he frequently represented his group in its dealings with other clubs. The war counsellor contacted enemy gangs with whom fights were to take place; he arranged the time and place for these "rumbles" and the weapons to be used. He also planned strategy and tactics.[18]

The Youth Board seemed to accept fully the stories of gang organization and leadership operation presented to them by gang members. An appraisal of Youth Board publications reveals their conceptual view. According to the Youth Board, the gangs with which they worked generally possessed the following characteristics: (1) their behavior was "normal" for youths; (2) the gangs had a high degree of cohesion, esprit de corps, and organization; (3) gang size or membership was measurable; (4) the gang's role patterns were clearly defined; (5) gangs possessed a consistent set of norms and expectations clearly understood by all members; (6) they had a

[17]Ibid., p. 256.
[18]*Working with Teenage Gangs: A Report on the Central Harlem Street Clubs Project* (New York: Welfare Council of New York City, 1950).

group of clearly defined leaders who were respected by gang members, distinctly specified, and vested with a direct flow of authority; and (7) they had a coherent organization for gang warfare. The Youth Board's image of the modern "bopping gang" was apparently greatly influenced by the earlier work of Thrasher, Shaw, McKay, and Whyte.

GANG THEORY AND RESEARCH IN THE FIFTIES AND SIXTIES

More recent research has added additional perspectives to our understanding of the structure and process of gangs. Two studies, one by Albert Cohen and the other by Richard Cloward and Lloyd Ohlin, are seminal works not only with regard to gang theory but also with regard to a more general theory of juvenile delinquency. These studies will be discussed briefly here in terms of their perspective on gangs and then more fully in Chapters 11 and 12, which deal with the causes of crime and delinquency.

Value Conflicts

Cohen, in his book *Delinquent Boys*, emphasizes that gang youths have a different value system than do youths in the general population.[19] However, gang members are negatively judged by middle-class values in schools and in other settings. This, Cohen asserts, leads to a "status frustration" that is acted out in a "nonutilitarian, negativistic" fashion through the vehicle of the gang. In Cohen's context, the gang is a subculture for striking back at an unjust social system.

Carl Werthman and Irving Piliavin noted this subcultural conflict, in this case between gang members and the police, as representatives of middle-class American society:

> From the front seat of a moving patrol car, street life in a typical Negro ghetto is perceived as an uninterrupted sequence of suspicious scenes. Every well-dressed man or woman standing aimlessly on the street during hours when most people are at work is carefully scrutinized for signs of an illegal source of income; every boy wearing boots, black pants, long hair, and a club jacket is viewed as potentially responsible for some item on the list of muggings, broken windows, and petty thefts that still remain to be cleared; and every hostile glance directed at the passing patrolman is read as a sign of possible guilt.
>
> The residents of these neighborhoods regard this kind of surveillance as the deepest of insults. As soon as a patrolman begins to interrogate, the suspect can easily see that his moral identity is being challenged because of his dress, his hair style, his skin color, and his presence in the ghetto itself.
>
> Negro gang members are constantly singled out for interrogation by the police, and the boys develop their own techniques of retaliation. They taunt the police

[19]Albert K. Cohen, *Delinquent Boys: The Culture of the Gang* (New York: Macmillan, 1955).

with jibes and threaten their authority with gestures of insolence, as if daring the police to become bigots and bullies in order to defend their honor. Moreover, these techniques of retaliation often do succeed in provoking this response. When suspect after suspect becomes hostile and surly, the police begin to see themselves as representing the law among a people that lack proper respect for it. They, too, begin to feel maligned, and they soon become defensively cynical and aggressively moralistic. From the point of view of a patrolman, night sticks are only used upon sufficient provocation, and arrests are only made with just cause.[20]

Gang Subcultures and Urbanism

Irving Spergel explores three different styles of delinquency in three different lower-class areas of a large Eastern city.[21] He recorded his data as a field worker in New York City. Spergel's study is based on firsthand field study interviews and is liberally sprinkled with the verbatim responses of gang youths.

Spergel's fundamental assumption is that delinquent subcultures are created and thrive under the impetus of socially unacceptable opportunities available to youths for achieving acceptable, culturally induced success goals. He found three major types of such delinquent youth subcultures; one characterized by racket activities, another by violence and conflict, and a third by theft. These patterns depend on the interaction of conventional and criminal opportunities. Drug addiction in these neighborhoods, Spergel states, develops "mainly as a variant and transitional pattern for older adolescents and young adults, many of whom have been participants in the major delinquent-youth subcultures."[22]

It is readily apparent that Spergel's working hypotheses are derived from the Cloward and Ohlin schema in *Delinquency and Opportunity*.[23] One departure from the Cloward and Ohlin system is to further subdivide their category of criminal subculture into two different subcultures: racket and theft. The study also deviates in another major respect from the Cloward-Ohlin formulation. Spergel states the following about Cloward and Ohlin's retreatist subculture of addiction:

> The patterns of retreatists, or drug-users, have not been regarded as sufficiently distinct to comprise a special delinquent subculture. The delinquent behavior, norms, and values of drug-users and drug addicts were found to be more like than unlike the respective modes of the delinquents in each of the three types of lower class neighborhoods. Therefore, the drug-use delinquent

---

[20]Carl Werthman and Irving Piliavin, "Gang Members and the Police," in *The Police*, ed. David J. Bordua (New York: Wiley, 1967), p. 46. Reprinted by permission of John Wiley & Sons, Inc.

[21]Irvin Spergel, *Racketville, Slumtown, Haulburg: An Exploratory Study of Delinquent Subcultures* (Chicago: University of Chicago Press, 1964).

[22]Ibid., p. xv.

[23]Richard A. Cloward and Lloyd E. Ohlin, *Delinquency and Opportunity: A Theory of Delinquent Gangs* (New York: Free Press, 1960).

pattern is viewed as a variant or subcategory of each of the three forms of delinquent subcultures. It was observed to be primarily a late-teenage and young-adult phenomenon.[24]

Despite this departure, Spergel closely adheres to the Cloward and Ohlin notion that "when legitimate or conventional means of achieving common success-goals are not available, delinquency or crime may become an alternate way of reaching them." Spergel further points out that even criminal careers may not be equally available to youths in different lower-class neighborhoods. Possession of special skills, a minimal store of criminal knowledge, appropriate attitudes, and access to a complex criminal organization or to "connections" may be essential for the achievement of success by criminal means.

A later analysis by Barbara Tomson and Edna R. Fielder tends to support Spergel's general assumption that gang membership is often a response to the urban scene.[25] Their research dealt with the gang member's response to the urban structure, the political structure, and the mass media—institutions in which they are unlikely to have formalized individual contacts. In this context, gangs provide a positive identity for their individual members.

1. The urban setting in which gangs thrive reduces varied pressures: the need to deal successfully with strangers, the need to deal with a money-based economy, loneliness, and lack of privacy. The delinquent responds to these pressures by identifying with the gang, which offers him symbols of identity, activities, and helps him obtain money, companionship, and friends.
2. The purpose of the political machinery is to provide services and resolve conflicts for members of the society. Delinquents assess the political situation correctly by concluding that they do not belong to society and are not wanted. They can, however, identify with and be understood by a gang.
3. Mass media teach slum-dwelling youngsters by default. Possessions are emphasized in the mass media, and filmed aggression has a longer-lasting influence on delinquents than on other members of society. The delinquent's response is to agree with the mass media's use of aggression; gang members successfully use aggression to get what they want.

Aleatory Nature of Gangs

In Chicago during the late fifties and early sixties, James F. Short, Jr., carried out extensive research into gangs. Among the conclusions of his

[24]Spergel, *Racketville, Slumtown, Haulburg*, pp. xii–xiii.
[25]Barbara Tomson and Edna R. Fielder, "Gangs: A Response to the Urban World," in *Gang Delinquency*, eds. Barbara Tomson and Edna Fielder (Monterey, Calif.: Brooks/Cole, 1975), p. 83.

varied studies was that aleatory (or chance) elements play a considerable part in gang behavior. Gang activities, whether for fun or profit, usually involve a degree of risk. Most of the time these activities are engaged in without serious consequences, but sometimes something happens and the outcome is calamitous. Writing with Fred L. Strodtbeck, Short discusses the implication of these aleatory risks, particularly in relation to the gang's seemingly hedonistic impulses:

> . . . our use of the term *aleatory* did not restrict it to events which are independent of the actions of the persons involved. It was incidentally true that the events in question were not, for this stratum, punished by society. However, we now wish to be beyond this feature and direct the argument to instances of serious aggression in which the outcome is not desired either by the boys or the community, and for which serious consequence, like imprisonment, may result from the response by the larger society. We do not say that all cases of serious aggression result from action with such an aleatory element, but that, etiologically, those which do should be distinguished from cases in which serious injury is the clear intent of the actor.
>
> Specifically, it is our hypothesis that much of what has previously been described as short-run hedonism, may, under closer scrutiny, be revealed to be a rational balancing, from the actor's perspective, of the near certainty of *immediate* loss of status in the group against the remote possibility of punishment by the larger society *if* the most serious outcome eventuates. Viewed in this way, one does not hold that punishable behavior occurs because the youngsters are blind to the possibility of unfortunate consequences.[26]

In a later study based on Short's Chicago research, Short, Rivera, and Tennyson[27] attempted to apply certain aspects of Cloward and Ohlin's opportunity-structure paradigm in a study of delinquent gangs in Chicago. Negro and white lower-class gang boys were compared with lower-class nongang boys from the same neighborhood, and with middle-class boys of the same race. They found that the ranking of the six race-by-class-by-gang-status groups on official delinquency rates corresponded more closely to ranking on perceptions of legitimate opportunities than to ranking on perceptions of illegitimate opportunities, which is consistent with the assumption that illegitimate opportunities intervene after legitimate opportunities have been appraised and found wanting. Gang members, lower-class boys, and Negro youth perceived legitimate opportunities to be less available than did nongang boys, middle-class boys, and white youth. Differences in perceptions of illegitimate opportunities were in the reverse direction, as expected.

Another series of significant studies was carried out by Malcolm Klein

---

[26]Fred L. Strodtbeck and James F. Short, Jr., "Aleatory Risks Versus Short-Run Hedonism in Explanation of Gang Behavior." © 1964 by The Society for the Study of Social Problems 1964. Reprinted from *Social Problems*, Vol. 12, No. 2, Fall 1964, pp. 127–140, by permission.

[27]James F. Short, Jr., Ramon Rivera, and Ray A. Tennyson, "Perceived Opportunities, Gang Membership, and Delinquency," *American Sociological Review* 30 (February 1965): 56–67.

and associates over a five-year period (1962–1967) of field research with Negro and Mexican-American gangs in Los Angeles.[28] The report was primarily an exposition of observations and speculations for the purpose of updating delinquency studies. A detached worker was assigned to all the gangs under observation.

Based on the findings, Klein concluded that leadership is not a position, as many have theorized, but is rather a collection of functions. Leadership varies with the activity, such as fighting, athletics, girls, etc. Most leaders are not sociopaths. The leaders are often difficult to pick out except by the reactions of other members. Age is an influence in leadership. Structure and function are part of the same phenomenon. Leadership is often "hesitant." Many leaders are ambivalent and will back away from leadership in a crucial situation.

Also, according to Klein's findings, gang boys portray a caricature of adolescence. They behave and react in excess, and they definitely overplay roles. Gang boys have little confidence in themselves and are insecure with respect to their own abilities and social relationships. These feelings of inadequacy often result in a dependence on the peer group and, consequently, on arrest-provoking behavior. Adolescents float together as they reject and are rejected by their community. Thus the gang is a cluster of youths held together by their individual incapacities rather than common goals or interests. It serves a need satisfaction and leads to delinquency only secondarily.

Short, in a later study, attempted to reexamine his earlier study of gangs in Chicago in the 1960s.[29] In his more recent research Short attempted to utilize as subjects the same gang members and detached social workers with whom he had worked in his research in the 1960s. He determined that the changes attributed to gang behavior in the past decade are more a product of the attitude of legitimate society toward gangs than the gangs themselves. Despite attempts on the part of detached social workers to involve youth in civil rights and other political issues, the gangs participated as more or less "innocent bystanders." They did not get involved in the political ideologies but merely responded to the pressures placed on them from outside. According to Short, the supergangs that emerged in the 1960s as a result of community support were not independent and were not capable of understanding or integrating into a political framework. Some of the surface political activities undertaken by these groups were simply reactions to police harassment and the actions of the GIU (Gang Intelligence Unit). Finally, attempts on the part of legitimate society to involve youth gangs in business and other endeavors, in some cases, actually caused an increase in criminal behavior due to the inability of these groups to appropriate funds and pursue legitimate activities. Short concluded that "what

[28]Malcolm W. Klein, "Impressions of Juvenile Gang Members," *Adolescence* 3 (Spring 1968): 53–76.
[29]James F. Short, Jr., "Youth, Gangs and Society: Micro- and Macrosociological Processes," *Sociological Quarterly* 36 (Winter 1974): 3–19.

changed, more than the behavior of youngsters, most of whom still meet on corners to pass the time away, was the behavior of adults, particularly the agents and agencies of 'respectable society'."

Many former gang members who were recruited during the 1970s for gang-prevention programs, of the type Short alludes to, performed admirably and effectively. There were many cases, however, where an ex-gang member exploited the system or, in gang parlance, "blew his cool." One example of this was the case of a former Los Angeles gang member who, while serving in a city-sponsored project, shot a member of a "rival gang."[30]

Official In Gang Project Facing Assault Charges

A gang member serving as coordinator for a city-sponsored project to combat gang violence is facing assault charges for an alleged shotgun attack on rival gang members at the project's headquarters, the district attorney's office disclosed Monday.

Bennie R. Simpson, 22, the No. 2 man in a city-financed program called Project Longtable and a member of the so-called Crips gang, was charged with five counts of assault with a deadly weapon stemming from an Oct. 18 incident at the project's Broadway and 46th St. headquarters.

Five other young men affiliated with the Crips and Project Longtable were named as codefendants with Simpson in a 13-count criminal indictment filed last week by Dep. Dist. Atty. Richard Jenkins.

Jenkins said the Oct. 18 confrontation reportedly occurred when members of the Brims, another South-Central Los Angeles gang, came to the project's offices seeking funds to finance a funeral for Jimmy Celestin, a 19-year-old Brim gunned down two days earlier by assailants on bicycles.

As the Brims departed from the successful negotiations, they reportedly were attacked with shotguns and wooden clubs.

Four other felony charges were filed against Simpson for alleged efforts to shake down nongang youths for money and guns last July. Two counts of extortion, one count of attempted extortion and one count of kidnapping were charged against Simpson in connection with these alleged events.

In one of the alleged extortion incidents, Simpson and others reportedly abducted a youth in his own car, forced him to sign over the pink slip.

TOWARD A DEFINITION OF GANGS

Emile Durkheim exhorts the sociologist to "emancipate himself from the fallacious ideas that dominate the mind of the layman; he must throw off, once and for all, the yoke of these empirical categories which from long continued habit have become tyrannical."[31]

Not only is a freedom from preconception urged; Durkheim's second canon is the necessity of being explicit:

---

[30]William Farr, "Official in Gang Project Facing Assault Charges," *Los Angeles Times*, January 4, 1977. Copyright (1977), *Los Angeles Times*. Reprinted by permission.

[31]Emile Durkheim, *The Rules of Sociological Method*, 8th ed. (Glencoe, Ill.: Free Press, 1950), p. 32.

Every scientific investigation is directed toward a limited class of phenomena, included in the same definition. The first step of the sociologist, then, ought to be to define the things he treats, in order that his subject matter may be known. This is the first and most indispensable condition of all proofs and verifications. A theory, indeed, can be checked only if we know how to recognize the facts of which it is intended to give an account.[32]

A Classification of Gangs

Three types of gangs appear most persistently in "gang neighborhoods": (1) social gangs; (2) delinquent gangs; and (3) violent gangs. Although these prototypes seldom appear in pure form, the structure and behavior of the ideal type may be described: The *social gang* is a social group comprised of tough youths who band together because they find their individual goals of a socially constructive nature can most adequately be achieved through a gang pattern; the *delinquent gang* is characterized by delinquent patterns of activity, such as stealing or assault, with material profit as the essential objective; the *violent gang* is characterized by sociopathic themes of spontaneous prestige-seeking violence, with psychic gratification (kicks) as the goal. There are, of course, some youths who belong to more than one type of gang during their gang careers, and some youths who belong to several simultaneously. (See Figure 8.1.)

Social Gangs   The social gang is a relatively permanent organization that centers around a specific location, such as a candy store or clubhouse. All members are intimately known to one another and there is a strong sense of comradeship. Members are the in-group; all others are outsiders. Members may wear club jackets or sweaters with insignia that identify them to the external community.

Activities are socially dominated and require a high degree of responsible social interaction in the group: organized athletics, personal discussions, dances, and other socially acceptable activities characteristic of youths. Membership is not based upon self-protection (as in the violent gang) or on athletic prowess (as on an athletic team) but upon feelings of mutual attraction. Cohesiveness is based on the feeling that through the group the individual can lead a fuller life. Members are willing to submerge individualistic interests to group activities. Leadership is based upon popularity and constructive leadership qualities and generally operates informally. The leader is apt to be the idealized group member.

This type of gang seldom participates in delinquent behavior, gang warfare, or petty thievery except under unusual circumstances. Members may become involved in minor gang clashes, but only under pressure. The social gang has considerable permanence. Its members often grow up to-

[32]Ibid., pp. 34–35.

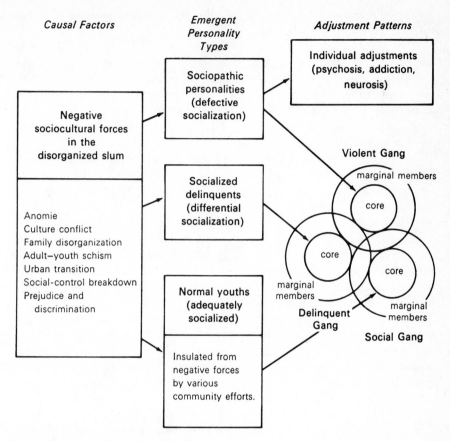

Figure 8.1   Gang patterns of slum youths

gether on the same block and develop permanent lifelong friendships that continue when they leave the "corner" and move into adult life patterns.

The social gang is closely associated with and acts in accordance with the values of the larger society. It draws its membership from the most emotionally stable and socially effective youths in the neighborhood—those most closely influenced by and involved with the norms and values of the more inclusive society. Thus, of all gang types, the social gang is the one least dissociated from the overall society.

Delinquent Gangs   The delinquent gang is primarily organized to carry out various illegal acts. The social interaction of the members is a secondary factor. Prominent among the delinquent gang's activities are burglary, petty thievery, mugging, assault for profit—not simply kicks—and other illegal acts directed at "raising bread." It is generally a tight clique, a small mobile gang that can steal and escape with minimum risk. It would lose its cohesive quality and the intimate cooperation required for success in illegal ventures if it became too large. Membership is not easily achieved and must generally be approved by all gang members.

The delinquent gang has a tight primary-group structure. The members know each other and rely heavily upon each other for cooperation in their illegal enterprises. The group has some duration and lasting structure. This usually continues in action until interrupted by arrest or imprisonment. Members lost in this way are usually replaced. The leader is usually the most effective thief, the best organizer and planner of delinquent activities.

Often members of these cliques also participate in the activities of violent or social gangs, but such participation is only a sideline; their basic allegiance is to the delinquent gang, with its opportunities to act out their impulses for fun and profit.

With some exceptions, delinquent gang members are emotionally stable youths. Their delinquency is more likely to result from being socialized in delinquent behavior patterns than from emotional disturbance. The emotionally disturbed delinquent is more likely to steal or assault on his own in a bizarre way. He does not usually have the social ability required to belong to the organized delinquent gang.

In summary, the delinquent gang is comprised of a cohesive group of emotionally stable youths trained into illegal patterns of behavior. Violence may be employed as a means toward the end of acquiring material and financial rewards, but it is rarely an end in itself since the activities of the gang are profit-oriented. The delinquent gang accepts the materialistic success goals of the society but rejects the normative ways of achievement.

Although the criminal gangs studied by the Chicago school are similar in structure to the current delinquent gangs, there are some differences. Chief among them is the lack of a criminal hierarchy in which the young offender may rise. The delinquent gang member is restricted to present-oriented delinquent "success." The only criminal future he may look forward to is the possibility of learning a good criminal trade (safecracker, policy-number writer). Generally, however, the delinquent gang member from a disorganized slum does not concern himself with the future. He accepts his later criminal life as it develops without any significant planning.

Violent Gangs   In contrast with the other gang types, the violent gang is primarily organized for emotional gratification, and violence is the theme around which all activities center. Sports, social, even delinquent activities are side issues to its primary assaultive pattern. The violent gang's organization and membership are constantly shifting in accord with the emotional needs of its members. Membership size is exaggerated as a psychological weapon for influencing other gangs and for self-aggrandizement. Small arsenals of weapons are discussed and, whenever possible, accumulated. These caches include switchblades and hunting knives, homemade zip guns, standard guns, pipes, blackjacks, and discarded U.S. Army bayonets and machetes. The violent gang is thus essentially organized around gang-war activities, although occasionally certain youths will form delinquent cliques or subgroups within the overall violent gang.

Membership characteristics are unclear in the violent gang's structure. Leaders are characterized by megalomania, a strong need to control, and an emotionally distorted picture of the gang's organization. The image of the leader is often exaggerated and glorified by gang members to enhance their own self-concepts. Strong power drives in the violent gang are demonstrated by attempts to control territory. Territorial disputes are constant sources of conflict between gangs.

Because of the unclarified nature of its structure, the violent gang has a chameleonlike quality. Its organization shifts with the needs of its members and is always in a state of flux. Conflicts with other groups go on constantly either in discussion or in actuality. Other gangs are allies one day and enemies the next, according to the whims of disturbed gang members and leaders.

A considerable amount of the gang boys' time is spent "sounding," a pattern of needling, ridiculing, or fighting with other members; consequently a great deal of their social participation is of a negative nature. The underlying theme of these street-corner sounding sessions is an attempt to prove oneself and to disprove and disparage others. Verbal and physical attack and defense are almost constant. In most discussions the underlying theme is one of hostility and aggression.

The expression of violence by the group appears to be more acceptable than individual violent behavior. The consensus factor of the group seems to permit a wider range of "legitimate" abnormal behavior. A disturbed youth may therefore cloak his pathology in the group image, which simultaneously aggrandizes him and lends him anonymity.

Many gang leaders appear to be involved in an attempt to redefine earlier years when they were disturbed, insecure, and unhappy. At this later period in their lives (approximately between the ages of 18 and 25), they act out the powerful role they could not achieve when they were younger.

Gang warfare usually has no clear purpose or consensus of definition for all participants. For many gang members it is an opportunity to channel personal aggressions and hostilities. Many gang wars originate over trivia. Territory, a "bad look," an exaggerated argument over a girl, or a nasty remark may stir up a large collection of youths into gang warfare. Such surface provocations give disturbed youths a *cause célèbre* and a banner under which they can vent hostilities related to other issues. The gang members' emotions are fanned through interaction and produce a group contagion. What starts out as a "bad look" from one youth toward another can thus develop into a major battle. Each youth who becomes involved can project into the battle whatever angers or hostilities he has toward school, his family, the neighborhood, the Man, or any other problems he may be living through at the time.

An important facet of the mass gang war is the negotiation and manipulation of alliances and affiliations as demonstrations of strength. Many agreements and contracts are made in the process of putting on the rumble. These are generally pseudobargains, which mobilize the gang members to flex muscles they are unsure they have.

At the actual gang-war event, most youths on hand have little or no idea why they are there or what they are expected to do, except to assault someone. Leaders, gang members, citizens, and sometimes the police and the press are caught up in the fallout of gang-war hysteria. Although violent gang members may not be clear about their motives or their gang's organization, the gang war can result in homicide—a very clear situation indeed. In fact, the confused nature of the gang and its fantasies helps to make it a highly destructive instrument of violence.

Thus gang violence results from a set of interrelated circumstances:

1. Varied negative sociocultural dislocations exist in the disorganized, rapidly changing urban slum area.
2. These dislocations produce dysfunctional gaps in the socialization process that would ordinarily train the child for normative social roles.
3. Children not adequately socialized may develop asocial or sociopathic personalities.
4. The resulting sociopathic personalities are essentially characterized by (a) a lack of social conscience; (b) a limited ability to relate, identify, or empathize with others except for egocentric objectives; and (c) impulsive, aggressive, and socially destructive behavior when impulsive, immediate needs are not satisfied.
5. Because of his personality deficiencies, the sociopathic individual cannot relate adequately to more socially demanding groups (including delinquent and social gangs).
6. Individualized emotional outbursts are more stigmatized, are considered more bizarre, and to some extent are more unrewarding than group pathological expressions. In the context of the violent gang, such individualistic expression becomes socially "legitimate."
7. The malleable nature of the violent gang makes it a compatible and legitimate vehicle for adjusting the emotional needs of the sociopathic youth, who cannot relate adequately in more demanding social groups.

THE PSEUDOCOMMUNITY OF THE VIOLENT GANG

Normal groups are constellations of roles defining prescribed ways in which members may interact effectively and harmoniously. The normal group may be viewed partially as a projected model for behavior toward the accomplishment of the mutually agreed-upon goals of its members. A dominant characteristic of such a group is the fact that most members are in consensual agreement about the important norms and reciprocal expectations that regulate and determine each group's members' behavior. Thus essential elements in a normal group are its members' agreement upon and ability to fulfill certain prescribed norms or standards of behavior.

According to Norman Cameron, a group makes certain demands upon the individual, and in the normative pattern of life the individual gives of himself to group demands. This the normal individual finds satisfying. On the daily level of group interaction, relevant "others" validate the individual's group participation at a minimum level of social expectation. However, "under certain circumstances individuals with socially inadequate development fail progressively to maintain such a level, with the result that they become socially disarticulated and very often have to be set aside from the rest of their community to live under artificially simplified conditions."[33] The violent gang serves the sociopathic youth as a "simplified" refuge from the more demanding community.

The person who requires this forced or voluntary dissociation from the general community has sociopathic characteristics. His essential limitation is his inability to take the role of another, except for egocentric purposes. He lacks a social conscience. To oversimplify, this type of individual tends to become paranoid and to have interchangeable delusions of persecution and excessive grandeur. These emotions result from an essentially correct assessment of his personal and social disability—a disability developed in a vacuum of effective socializing agents and processes. The paranoid's reactions of delusion and persecution are useful in enabling him to fool himself into believing that he is powerful and at the same time to blame his social disability upon a world that unfairly persecutes him. Both paranoid devices (grandeur and persecution) tend temporarily to relieve his already battered ineffectual self of blame for his problems.

The delusional process is at first internal and on the level of personal thought; however, in time it tends to become projected onto and involved with the surrounding community. According to Cameron:

The paranoid person, because of poorly developed role-taking ability, which may have been derived from defective social learning in earlier life, faces his real or fancied slights and discriminations without adequate give-and-take in his communication with others and without competence in the social interpretation of motives and intentions.[34]

This type of person, whose role-taking skills are impaired, lacks the ability adequately to assess the "other" in interaction. He begins to take everything the wrong way, and because of his inability to think as others do, he becomes increasingly alienated and dissociated from the real world. His delusional fantasies become hardened, and he begins to see and experience things not consensually validated or similarly felt by others. As Cameron specifies, he "becomes prejudiced with regard to his social environment." His responses tend first to select reactions from his surroundings that fit into his personal interpretation and then to reshape in retrospect things

[33]Norman Cameron, "The Paranoid Pseudo-Community," *American Journal of Sociology* 49 (July 1943): 32–38, published by The University of Chicago Press.
[34]Ibid., p. 33.

that seemed innocent enough when they occurred, until they support the trend of his suspicions. Because of his already incipient disturbance, and particularly if the individual is evolving in a defective socializing community (for example, the disorganized slum), he is unable to get relevant responses from others to counteract a developing reaction formation that finally hardens into what Cameron has termed a *paranoid pseudocommunity*.

As he begins attributing to others the attitudes he has toward himself, he unintentionally organizes these others into a functional community, a group unified in its supposed reactions, attitudes, and plans with respect to him. In this way he organizes individuals, some of whom are actual persons and some only inferred or imagined, into a whole that satisfies for the time being his immediate need for explanation but which brings no reassurance with it and usually serves to increase his tensions. The community he forms not only fails to correspond to any organization shared by others but actually contradicts the consensus. More than this, these others do not actually perform the actions or maintain the attitudes he ascribes to them; they are united in no common undertaking against him. What he takes to be a functional community is only a pseudocommunity created by his own unskilled attempts at interpretation, anticipation, and validation of social behavior.

This pseudocommunity of attitude and intent that he succeeds in thus setting up organizes his own responses still further in the direction they have been taking; and these responses in turn lead to greater and greater systematization of his surroundings. The pseudocommunity grows until it seems to constitute so grave a threat to the individual's integrity or to his life that, often after clumsy attempts to get at the root of things indirectly, he bursts into directly defensive or vengeful activity. This brings out into the open a whole system of organized responses to a supposed functional community of detractors or persecutors which he has been rehearsing in private. The real community, which cannot share in his attitudes and reactions, counters his actions with forcible restraint or retaliation.[35]

The real community's response and retaliation only serve to strengthen the individual's suspicions and distorted interpretations. He sees this as further evidence of the unfair discrimination to which he is being subjected. "The reactions of the real community in now uniting against him are precisely those which he has been anticipating on the basis of his delusional beliefs."[36] The pseudocommunity calcifies, becomes more articulate and real to him. He begins after a while to live in his delusional realm almost to the exclusion of other social alternatives.

The processes through which an individual becomes enmeshed in a paranoid pseudocommunity closely parallel the processes that hook a sociopathic youth into the violent gang. The sociopathic youth growing up in

[35]Ibid., p. 35
[36]Ibid.

the disorganized slum has a personality syndrome that easily interlocks with the paranoid pseudocommunity of the violent gang.

Development of a Pseudocommunity

The pseudocommunity processes as they apply to the violent gang show the following sequential pattern of development:

1. *Defective socialization.* The socialization vacuum of the disorganized slum, with its many inconsistencies, produces sociopathic youths with limited social conscience or ability to relate. This asocial milieu is fertile for negative conditioning.
2. *Alienation and dissociation.* Owing to their sociopathic tendencies, these youths are further disconnected and alienated from the more consensually real and constructive community. Their negative feelings of "difference," social ineffectiveness, and rejection become reinforced and hardened by the disorganized and callous world to which they are exposed.
3. *Paranoid reactions.* Two paranoid patterns, delusions of grandeur and delusions of persecution, emerge in reaction to the world around the defectively socialized youth. These patterns become functional in shifting the responsibility from himself to others and take the pressure off an already weak and suffering self. Gang leadership, control of "large divisions," being part of a "vast gang army," and a reputation for violence give the depressed youth some illusionary ego strength. Indications of persecution—enemy gangs, getting kicked out of school, and so on—are seized upon and enable the sociopathic youth to shift the responsibility from himself to society. His prejudice toward the community hardens, and he selectively perceives the outside world's behavior to fit his emotional needs.
4. *The pseudocommunity of the violent gang.* For this type of youth, the violent gang becomes a convenient pseudocommunity, one that is functional in at least temporarily alleviating his personal inadequacies and problems. The structure of the violent gang, with its flexibility of size, power roles, and delusionary possibilities, makes it a most convenient and socially acceptable escape hatch for the sociopathic youth.

The "Legitimate" Quality of Violent Gang Structure

The worship of the hoodlum as a hero and the acceptance of violent gang behavior as normal by the larger society help to harden the gang's arteries. Most pathological behavior is stigmatized and/or sympathized with; not so the activities of the violent gang. The general community response of intrigue, and in some fashion covert aggrandizement, reinforces the violent gang as a most desirable, stigma-free pseudocommunity for the sociopathic youth. The community's almost positive response to this pattern of pathology may be partially accounted for by a traditional American worship of aggressive, adventuresome, two-gun heroes who go it alone, unencumbered by social restraints or conscience.[37]

Another possible explanation of the seeming public acceptance of the violent gang syndrome may be found in an assumption that pathological behavior is restricted to individuals; that is, if one individual commits a bizarre act, he is considered disturbed, but the same act committed by 50 youths together achieves a sort of legitimacy that gives the individual a degree of immunity to the stigma of pathology. The appraisal of collective behavior patterns gives some clue to this element of group legitimization and sanction for bizarre and pathological group action. Lang and Lang make this point in a discussion of crowds. They comment that certain aspects of a group situation help to make pathological acts and emotions acceptable.

> The principle that expressions of impulses and sentiments are validated by the social support they attract extends to collective expressions generally. The mere fact that an idea is held by a multitude of people tends to give it credence.
>
> The feeling of being anonymous sets further limits to the sentiment of responsibility. The individual in the crowd or mass is often unrecognized; hence, there is a partial loss of critical self-control and the inhibitions it places on precipitate action. There is less incentive to adhere to normative standards when it appears to the individual that his behavior is not likely to provoke sanctions against him personally. . . . Each person sees himself acting as part of a larger collectivity which, by inference, shares his motives and sentiments and thereby sanctions the collective action. In this sense the crowd is an excuse for people all going crazy together.[38]

When all the boys in a violent gang go crazy together, their behavior tends, at least in the public view, to have greater rationality. Gang legitimacy therefore partially derives from the fact that group behavior, however irrational, is generally not considered truly bizarre. Although society may disapprove, the gang remains as a rational social group in the public mind. Thus, public agencies give recognition to the violent gang and try to

---

[37]To some extent the competitive, aggressive salesman, unencumbered by conscience, serves as a positive role model. Other sociopathic heroes include many mass media leading men, such as Marlon Brando as the motorcycle gang leader in *The Wild One*, George Raft as the archetypical hood, Warren Beatty as Clyde Barrow. See Lewis Yablonsky, *George Raft* (New York: McGraw-Hill, 1974). In the criminal tradition, John Dillinger, Al Capone, and Frank Costello have served as idealized figures for many youths. (Costello was once mobbed by a crowd of autograph-hunting hero worshipers of all ages when he was released from prison.)

[38]Kurt Lang and Gladys Engel Lang, *Collective Dynamics* (New York: Crowell, 1961), p. 35.

redirect it as an entity. (In "detached street gang worker" projects, for example, the violent gang is viewed as a legitimate, nonpathological entity suffering only from misguided efforts that need to be redirected into "constructive channels.")

Another clue to the legitimation of gang violence may lie in its uncomfortable closeness to the behavior of the overall society. The warfare of the violent gang and its paramilitary structure are bizarre replicas of current structures of international violence. In the social context of the current international scene, violent gang machinations do not appear too pathological. Although many gang adjustments require closer examination, the violent gang interestingly caricatures many patterns of the larger world. The gang president (even if he doesn't really lead), drafting new soldiers (even if they are not really members), forging grand alliances (even if its members do not fully cooperate), and attending summit peace meetings (even if they are only for propaganda and solve nothing), bears a striking resemblance to men whose names are internationally known.

The gang thus emerges as a desirable pseudocommunity reaction for many sociopathic youths. Various degrees of membership participation meet the individual's momentary emotional needs. The gang leader and the core gang member are more closely identified with the violent-gang paranoid pseudocommunity than are more marginal members. Of considerable significance is the fact that the nature of the violent gang's pathological membership produces an unusual pattern of group structuring quite different from the structure usually found in normal groups.

THE VIOLENT GANG AS A NEAR-GROUP

The organization of human collectives may be viewed as a continuum of organization factors. At one extreme, an organized, cohesive collection of persons interacting around shared functions and goals for some period of time forms a normal group. At the other extreme of human organization, a loose collection of individuals, generally characterized by anonymity and spontaneous leadership, motivated and ruled by momentary emotions, forms a mob or crowd. Although the term *mob* fits a youth riot and *group* fits a cohesive delinquent gang, neither group nor mob seems especially appropriate to describe violent gang structure.

Groups that emerge midway on a continuum of organization are distorted in one direction or the other by most perceivers. It appears as though there is a psychological (autistic) need to consolidate one's view of the world. Violent gangs, therefore, despite considerable evidence to the contrary, are often mistakenly perceived by observers as cohesive groups, and in some youth riots no organization is seen despite the fact that in most cases a degree of organization exists.

Because no existing group conceptions seem suitable for describing the violent gang, it may be referred to as a near-group.[39] The near-group stands midway on the continuum from mob to group. (See Figure 8.2.) It is differentiated from other collectivities that are temporarily midway because it has some degree of permanence or homeostasis. A cohesive group may be partially disorganized for a period of time, but it is in a state of becoming either organized or disorganized.

The violent gang as an ideal-type near-group structure includes most of the following characteristics:

1. Participants in the violent gang near-group are generally sociopathic personalities. The most sociopathic are core participants or leaders.
2. To these individuals the near-group gang is a compensatory paranoid pseudocommunity, which serves as a more socially desirable adjustment pattern than other pathological syndromes available in the community.
3. Individualized roles are defined to fit the emotional needs of the participants.
4. The definition of membership is diffuse and varies for each participant.
5. Behavior is essentially emotion-motivated within loosely defined boundaries.
6. Group cohesiveness decreases as one moves from the center of the collectivity to the periphery.
7. Membership requires only limited responsibility and social ability.
8. Leadership is self-appointed and sociopathic.
9. There is a limited consensus among participants in the collectivity as to its functions or goals.
10. There is a shifting and personalized stratification system.
11. Membership is in flux.

Figure 8.2   Collective structures

[39]One of the authors carried out extensive research during a five-year period in New York City (1953–1958) from which he developed a theory of gangs based on group structure. The theory was originally presented in an article by Lewis Yablonsky, "The Delinquent Gang as a Near-Group," *Social Problems* 7 (Fall 1959): 108–117, and was later expanded into the book *The Violent Gang* (New York: Macmillan, 1962; rev. ed., Penguin, 1970). Since that time, numbers of researchers have confirmed the near-group concept. In 1966 and 1980, the author again studied several gangs and concluded that the original thesis of the near-group continues to be a valid system for understanding violent gang structure and process.

12. Fantasy membership is included in the size of the collective.
13. There is a limited consensus of normative expectations for behavior.
14. Norms and behavior patterns are often in conflict with the inclusive social system's prescriptions.
15. Interaction within the collectivity and toward the outer community is hostile and aggressive, with spontaneous outbursts of violence to achieve impulsively felt goals.

Validation of Near-Group Therapy

After the appearance of near-group theory in 1959, Howard and Barbara Myerhoff[40] and other researchers carried out extensive empirical and theoretical research into the near-group thesis. These later findings affirmed the validity of the concept for illuminating the structure of many cases of lower-class and middle-class gangs. Myerhoff and Myerhoff summarize these findings:

> The sociological literature about gangs contains at least two sharply conflicting descriptions of the extent of gang structure and the nature of their values. In the most prevalent view, the gang is seen as a kind of primary group, highly structured, relatively permanent and autonomous, possessing a well-developed delinquent subculture which is transmitted to new members. . . .

> Cohen has identified the primary needs met by the gang as those of resolving status frustration for lower-class boys, and providing an expression of masculine identification for middle-class boys. Parsons has also emphasized the achievement of sexual identity as a problem dealt with by delinquent behavior. Cloward and Ohlin, following Merton's conception, have specified the discrepancy between aspirations toward success goals and opportunities for achieving them as the problem giving rise to gang behavior. Kvaraceus and Miller have stressed the inherent conflict between lower and middle-class values and the delinquent's predisposition to the former in explaining gang behavior. Eisenstadt and Bloch and Niederhoffer have pointed to the gang as a collective response to the adolescent's striving toward the attainment of adulthood and the frustrations attendant on the transition from one age status to another. These authors identify different components of the gang subculture according to their interpretation of its function, but implicit or explicit in all these positions is the view of the gang as an integrated and relatively cohesive group.

> A strikingly different interpretation of the structure of gangs describes them as informal, short lived, secondary groups without a clear cut, stable delinquent structure. Lewis Yablonsky has suggested a conceptualization of the gang as a "near-group," specifying the following definitive characteristics: diffuse role definitions, limited cohesion, impermanence, minimal consensus on norms, shifting membership, emotionally disturbed leaders, and limited definition of mem-

---

[40]Howard L. Myerhoff and Barbara G. Myerhoff, "Field Observations of Middle-Class Gangs," *Social Forces* 42 (March 1964): 328–336.

bership expectations. On a continuum of the extent of social organization, Yablonsky locates the gang midway between the mob at one end and the group at the other.[41]

The authors go on to explicate near-group theory, noting some views on the theory:

James F. Short, Jr. objects to Yablonsky's description of the gang as a near-group on the grounds that he has overstated the case, but agrees, nevertheless, that gangs do not have "the stability of membership, the tightly knit organization and rigid hierarchical structure which is sometimes attributed to them." Most of the groups he has observed have the kind of shifting membership which Yablonsky described.[42]

The Meyerhoffs expand on this in a footnote:

In a recent article Pfautz raised the question of whether Yablonsky's "near-group" concept is necessary. He suggests that Yablonsky's findings could be more productively recast into the theoretical traditions of collective behavior in general and social movements in particular. Certainly, Pfautz's point that this would widen the theoretical relevance of Yablonsky's findings is well taken. There are two reasons for the authors' preference for the near-group concept rather than a collective behavior orientation: first, an immediate concern with indicating the point by point similarity between these observations and those reported by Yablonsky, regardless of the conceptual framework he uses in describing them, and second, the authors' feeling that in view of the fragmented and discontinuous state of the literature on the subject, it is at present more important to compare and relate studies of adolescent collective deviant activities to one another than to more general sociological issues and concepts.[43]

They then present another conceptualization:

The supervisor of a large, long-lived detached worker program in Los Angeles, with many years of gang experience there and in Harlem, has given a description much like that of Yablonsky. He observed that delinquent gangs seldom act as a corporate group and that most of their antisocial activities are committed in groups of two's or three's, or by a single person. He found communication between members to be meager and sporadic, reflecting the same limitations in social abilities that Yablonsky identified.[44]

In summary, the Myerhoffs note: "There is a coincidence of opinion based on three sets of observations (Yablonsky's, the supervisor of a de-

[41]Reprinted from *Social Forces* 42 (March 1964). "Field Observations of Middle-Class Gangs" by Howard L. Myerhoff and Barbara G. Myerhoff. Copyright © The University of North Carolina Press.
[42]Ibid., p. 329.
[43]Ibid.
[44]Ibid., pp. 329–330.

tached worker program in Los Angeles, and those reported in this paper) suggesting that the common conception of the gang as a highly organized primary group is not always accurate."[45] Regarding the gangs they studied and their appraisal of gang literature, the Myerhoffs concluded that "the groups described here manifest all but one of the characteristics (disturbed leadership) described by Yablonsky as those of a near-group."[46]

THE VIOLENT GANG AND MINORITY YOUTHS

In the modern disorganized slum, the violent gang has been for many minority group youths their only source of identity, status, and emotional satisfaction. Ill-trained to participate with any degree of success in the dominant white middle-class world of rigid ideas, community centers, and adult demands, they construct their own community. They set goals that are achievable; they build an empire, partly real and partly fantasy, that helps them live through the confusion of adolescence.

For youngsters growing up in places like Los Angeles, Chicago's South Side, the East Bronz, or Harlem, the schools, community centers, and government projects are often foreign domains with values and expectations that are not compatible with the residents' perception of the world. The demands of scheduled activities, forms, dues, and middle-class skills can be all but incomprehensible to a youth who has grown up in the ghetto.

The demands for performance and responsibility in the violent gang, however, are readily adapted to the personal needs of these youths. Usually the criteria for membership are vague. In many gangs, a youth can say he belongs one day and quit the next without necessarily telling any other gang member. Some boys say that the gang is organized for protection and that one role of a gang member is to fight. For others, the standard violent gang still provides the company that misery seeks. Among the "sanctioned" opportunities the gang provides a youth in his confused search for "success" are robbery and intimidation. Other ways to Nirvana include alcohol, drug addiction, and kicks based on assault and violence. If only in caricature, he can become a "success" and at the same time strike back at society.

In the violent gang, ghetto youth can become president or war lord, control vast domains, and generally act out a powerful even though sometimes fantasized success image. The boys can mutually expand their shared and highly valued success by reinforcing each other's fantasies of power. The unwritten contractual agreement is "Don't call my bluff and I won't call yours"; "I'll support your big-man gang image if you'll support mine." This lends prestige to all involved in the charade. Aside from real addiction, common among deprived minority group youths, the violent gang can serve as a social narcotic.

In most respects Chicano, black, and Puerto Rican gangs parallel each

[45]Ibid., p. 335.
[46]Ibid.

other. In one study into the social context in which gang violence occurs studied the norms of Mexican-American gangs.[47] Based on their research, they conclude that gang violence arises in situations where one party impugns the honor of his adversary. This sort of conduct violates the norms of interpersonal etiquette and constitutes a violation of "personal space." Horowitz and Schwartz focused on the normative processes whereby acts and complex structures of action "were built, elaborated and transformed into violence."

In a study, *Homeboys*, by Joan W. Moore in East Los Angeles, she delineates the structure and nature of Mexican gangs in the barrio and in prison. She points out that the Chicano youth gang is a significant structure in a large proportion of poor urban Chicano barrios, not only in Los Angeles but in El Paso, San Antonio, and perhaps in other large cities as well. The gangs in these cities, she asserts, share some common features.

> First, the gang is territorially based. This is a truism in most gang studies, because young male peer groups all tend to be based in some local network. For Chicano gang members the word for gang and for neighborhood is identical. *"Mi barrio"* refers equally to "my gang" and "my neighborhood." This complete intermingling of peer group and neighborhood identity is a core characteristic of the Chicano gang, and extends even to the gang member who resides in a different barrio.

> Second, Chicano gangs are age graded, with a new klika, or cohort, forming every two years or so. Regardless of the degree of discipline and cohesiveness of any given klika, their origin lies in interbarrio conflicts between teenage boys in school or in sports.

> The gang and the klika remain salient lifelong membership and reference groups for some, but not all, members of the gang. During the peak years of barrio-based participation, a meaningful source of cohesiveness appears to lie in fighting. During adulthood, the primary loyalty may be reinforced by experiences in Juvenile Hall, prison, and other institutional structures outside the barrio, confrontations with active racism, and experiences in the illegal economy.[48]

Moore further states that all Chicano gangs are fighting gangs—and most, if not all, use drugs. In fact, the gang is the principal context for both use and marketing of heroin. This combination of fighting and drugs is unique to Chicano gangs. She writes:

> The gang is a quasi-institution in many Chicano communities, and it is best understood as such, rather than as a specialized juvenile phenomenon whose main feature is the production of delinquent acts. It is intertwined into the adult world, and thus cannot be understood outside the whole barrio and the ethnic

[47]Ruth Horowitz and Gary Schwartz, "Honor, Normative Ambiguity and Gang Violence," *American Sociological Review* 39 (April 1974): 238–251.

[48]Joan W. Moore, *Homeboys: Gangs, Drugs, and Prison in the Barrios of Los Angeles* (Philadelphia: Temple University Press, 1978) pp. 35–36.

context. At the same time the youth gang is a specialized structure of the barrio, and like any other specialized structure (such as the neighborhood church), it develops a specialized subculture, a set of values, norms, and specialized traditions, and sources of status honor. These gain special significance when it is remembered that the adolescent gang is a semisecret organization of adolescents and that gang cliques are organizations that in later life may be involved in illegal economic activities. . . .

Participation by Mexican-American youth gangs inside the barrio and in prison has a gloomy future. Barrio-based norms are also a significant source of inmate status. "You are known" from the barrio streets, and your reputation follows you into prison. In addition, the prisoners from each barrio are expected to help out others from that barrio. The ability to help and to provide resources becomes an asset in prison. These resources may grow from a position attained in the prison resource network, from particular skills, or from access to outside resources.

Status-related behavior in the prison is also related to the crime pattern. For example, the very few professional criminals among Chicanos rarely mix with the Chicano population. The professionals tend largely to keep to themselves, doing their time "with the least amount of suffering and the greatest amount of comfort." For prisoners with some prestige in the world of organized crime, prison is a time for laying low, for avoiding attention from the authorities, and for spending energy on getting out.

In contrast to the relatively petty scale of their typical crimes, the state-raised youth tend to assume a high visibility in the prison world. They wheel and deal. They dress better (because they care about appearance and have prison connections to get better clothes) and they may have a cluster of younger men who do their bidding without apparent question.

But these men have little to hope for on the outside. Their youth has been spent learning to optimize their environment inside the camps, youth facilities, and prisons but nowhere else. This optimizing is very visible; to the outsider, they appear to be "influentials." But the barrio-based norms continue, and the ultimate grim fate of the state-raised youth is underscored in a series of sayings in Spanish that emphasize the implacability of the prison destiny.[49]

The exploits and involvement of an effective barrio gang worker, Leo Cortez, provide other insights into the dynamics of Chicano gangs, which have become a fixed part of Los Angeles culture and history.

East L.A. Gangs: Youth Worker Struggles For Peace in Barrio
The night before, a youth with a sawed-off shotgun had shot a middle-aged mother who was picnicking with several small children in an East Los Angeles park. And now, although the woman's sons and their friends were probably plotting a bloody gang revenge at this very minute, Leo Cortez found himself sitting inside a small county office while assorted law officers and social workers drank coffee, ate doughnuts and wondered what to do about the youth gang problem in East Los Angeles. At times such as these,

[49]Ibid., pp. 35–36.

Leo Cortez, 37, a county youth worker and one-time gang member, wonders why he isn't out on the streets working with those he understands so well.

So well, in fact, that many residents of that small 8.36-square-mile enclave known as unincorporated East Los Angeles, population about 140,000, are convinced that Leo Cortez has probably averted more gang wars and saved more lives than all the sheriff's deputies combined. . . .

Cortez drove directly to County-USC General Hospital where he made his way through the maze of corridors to her room, a crowded ward on the ninth floor.

Momentarily, he stood at the bedside, silently surveying the damage.

Her bruised body was riddled with at least 50 shotgun pellets, two of them only a fraction away from her right eye.

Gently, he touched her shoulder, and, once her dazed eyes focused, she smiled, almost brightly.

But her thoughts were confused, her mind as baffled as a child's.

Because she was an East Los Angeles mother, she understood gangs. Her two sons belonged to one of the roughest gangs in the area. And, she whispered, with weary acceptance, "they only try to kill each other. . . ."

So, why her?

Cortez only shrugged, perhaps thinking of the long day ahead, a day of shuttling back and forth among half a dozen barrios, trying to keep the peace.

And as she read his mind, the woman's clouded eyes momentarily cleared, filled with sudden, sharp alarm.

"Leo," she said, her voice beseeching, as she raised a battered arm toward him. "The boys . . . Don't let them go for revenge? Make them stay home?"

[Cortez meets with the gang.]

"Man, tonight we'll go down there and kill a couple of those vatos (bad dudes)," declared one skinny youth of 14. The only problem was that, though they all suspected the assailant had come from one particular rival gang, nobody was sure.

"But I tell you something!" shouted another boy of 18 whose nickname was "Little Boy" and whose eyes were glazed over by something much stronger than liquor.

"When we go, we'll be cool. We won't go around shooting women and kids. We'll kill the vato who did it."

Patiently, in soft Spanish, Cortez urged them all to leave the park. Getting arrested wouldn't help anything. Better yet, why not visit the hospital?

With surprising passivity, like small, uncertain children, most quickly agreed.

Even Little Boy, who was reeling so badly he could hardly walk.

And so Cortez gave him a lift home, not knowing, when he let the boy out that in two days Little Boy would be dead himself—shot to death by youths from another barrio. . . .

Leo Cortez seems to know not only the names of almost every youth in East Los Angeles but also the names of their friends and their enemies.

He also knows which kids are hard-core murderers, which ones can be influenced to kill, which ones never could, and, finally, which youths are "locos"—crazy enough to be altogether unpredictable.

Whatever he doesn't already know, his grapevine apparently tells him. Indeed, it sometimes appears that Leo Cortez knows about most gang crimes before they even happen—in time to head them off.

So when he cruised into a strange barrio, "just to see what's happening," it seemed likely that Cortez at least suspected which gang was to blame for the shooting. Perhaps he even knew the identity of the assailant.

"What most people don't understand is that the kids out here, the gang members, don't consider themselves criminals," Cortez said.

"Here, even when they kill, national standards just don't apply. Because, here, a gang member regards himself as a soldier, you understand? Even if he's only patrolling a few square blocks. No matter how small his turf is, he still regards himself as a patriot . . . protecting his homeland. Because that's all he's got, all he's ever had. . . .

East Lost Angeles Sheriff's Administrative Lt. Hayden Finley, who calls the entire area "a damned war zone," documented the increasing violence. In 1975, he said, a total of 333 "gang-related incidents," including 17 murders, were reported—compared to 319 "incidents," including 13 murders, during only the first six months of 1976.

And, he said, "those are only the reported crimes. The actual figures are probably much higher, because most people are too afraid of retaliation out here to report anything to us."

Even so, to local workers like Leo Cortez, the statistical increase in crimes isn't nearly so frightening as the changing nature of those crimes.

"Sometimes it really scares me," said Cortez, "because too many kids nowadays aren't following any of the old rules."

In the old days, Cortez added almost sadly, gang members made certain that when they went on a retaliatory raid, they hit their enemy.

But, now, he said, they often are sloppy, or heedless, simply speeding by an enemy house at night and spraying it with bullets, regardless of who's inside.

Likewise, Cortez continued, there was a time when small children weren't allowed to even associate with gang members.

"But now I see little kids, 10 or 12 years old, wandering around with guns . . . and, now, too, even 8-year-old kids are sniffing glue, paint, Angel Dust (an animal tranquilizer) . . . and even doing hard stuff."

"Actually," Cortez concluded, "I think that's why there's more violence here now . . . they've got no future, nothing but their barrio and their 'home-boys.' So, they can only prove their manhood by standing up and getting killed, or killing."[50]

VIOLENT GANGS IN THE EIGHTIES: A SUMMARY

For a time during the 1960s and early 1970s there was a decrease in violent gang activities. This decrease in violence is difficult to account for. Perhaps it occurred because of a sense of hope that positive social change might take

---

[50]Bella Stumbo, "East L.A. Gangs: Youth Worker Struggles for Peace in Barrios," *Los Angeles Times*, September 19, 1976. Copyright, 1976, *Los Angeles Times*. Reprinted by permission.

place, and perhaps because potential violent gang members were involved in the then-vibrant civil rights movement. But as apathy and despair reappeared in the ghetto, violent gangs reemerged as vehicles for venting anger and frustration.

The symptom of violent gangs is often an overt reflection of deeper disorders in a society. The violent gang can be a counterattack against the overall society and ultimately lead to a positive revolutionary change in the system. Historically, many total societies have been changed by politically oriented violent gangs.

The resurgent violent gangs of the 1980s do not have any clear-cut political characteristics. Our observations indicate that the new violent urban gangs are very similar to the gangs researched mainly in the 1950s. This genre of violent gang was, for thousands of young people living under the oppression of the American urban ghetto, a viable alternative way of life. The violence had a seemingly senseless quality. It was not turned against any oppressor or the society at large. The pattern fits the model "we only kill each other."

Gang forms, as described in the 1960s, were modified. Violence was used as a vehicle for social change. For example, during the Watts riots, black gangs that had previously fought each other joined forces against their common enemy—Whitey. Many ghetto youngsters who, in the fifties, would almost automatically join a "senseless" violent gang became members of quasi-political militant groups like the Black Panthers or the Brown Berets. Their violence was no longer senseless: It appeared to have purpose.

The extravagant faith in these varied minority group militant organizations has clearly diminished. Intensive leadership battles, ego trips, selling out to impotent bureaucratic programs seem to have taken their toll, and many of these organizations have become unattractive or defunct. As these vehicles for social change diminish, the despair, alienation, and hopelessness of many young people are now being rechanneled into structures that parallel the violent gangs of the fifties.

A sense of despair and alienation produces this type of violent gang. For an individual who sees little hope or opportunity for achievement in the overall society, the violent gang becomes an acceptable substitute. In it, the youth has identity and an extravagant hope for "stardom" in a success- and power-oriented society. With one stroke of a knife or bullet from a gun, the individual can achieve status among his peers and, in a perverted way, in the larger society.

The youth most susceptible to violent gang membership emerges from a social milieu that trains him inadequately for assuming constructive social roles. In fact, the defective socialization process to which he is subjected fosters a lack of humanistic feelings. At hardly any point is he trained to have feelings of compassion or responsibility for other people.

In a technological society that values machines over people there are large pockets of deprived people who become egocentric, hedonistic, frustrated, and, consequently, violent. Violent gangs become a standard cultural form when there are thousands of young people with limited compassion. In a machine system people are dehumanized and unable to experience the pain of the violence they may inflict on others, since they have a limited ability to identify or empathize with others. They are capable, therefore, of committing spontaneous acts of "senseless" violence without feeling concern or guilt. The classic sociopathic comment of a gang member who had killed another boy aptly describes this pattern of feeling: "What was I thinking about when I stabbed him? Man, are you crazy? I was thinking about whether to do it again!"

The selection of violence by gang youths is not difficult to understand. Violent behavior requires limited training, personal ability, or even physical strength. (As one gang boy stated, "A knife or a gun makes you ten feet tall.") Because violence is a demonstration of easily achieved power, it becomes the paramount value of the gang. Violence requires characteristics that gang boys have in quantity: limited social ability and training, considerable resentment and aggression, and a motivation to retaliate against others and the system. Violence serves as a quick and sure means for upward social mobility within the violent gang and, to some extent, in the overall society.

The very fact that it is "senseless" rather than "rational" violence that appeals to the gang boy tells us a great deal about the meaning of violence to him. It is an easy, quick, almost magical way of achieving power and prestige. In a single act of unpremeditated intensity, he established a sense of his own identity and impresses this existence on others. No special ability is required to commit this brand of violence—not even a plan—and the guilt connected with it is minimized by the gang code of approval, especially if the violence fulfills the gang's idealized standards of a swift, sudden, and senseless outbreak.

An aspect of senseless violence is related to a concept we would term *existential validation*, the validation of one's existence. This basically involves the individual's sense of alienation from human feeling or meaning. People increasingly have a more limited awareness of their personal human value in a vast, technological, dehumanized society. Many people feel a social death. Extremist violence is one way of establishing identity and experiencing some feeling of existence.

Most people have a sense of identity and existence in their everyday activities. They do not require intense emotional excitement to know they are alive, that they exist. In contrast, many people, including the sociopath, do need such arousal; indeed, their sense of being ahuman and unfeeling requires increasingly heavier dosages of bizarre and extreme behavior to validate the fact that they really exist. Extreme, violent behavior is one pattern that gives the sociopath a glimmer of feeling. Existential validation through violence (or other extremist bizarre behavior involving, say, sex or drugs) gives the socially dead person some feeling. As one gang killer reported, "When I stabbed him once, it felt good. I did it again and again because it made me feel alive for the first time in my life."

Violence is not exclusively the prestige symbol of the gang. The larger society covertly approves of, or is at least intrigued by, the outrageous as depicted in literature, television, movies, and other mass media. On the surface most members of society condemn violence; however, on a covert level there is a tendency to aggrandize and give recognition to violent people. The sociopathic personality who commits intense acts of violence is the "hero" of many plays and stories portrayed in the contemporary mass media.

The continuance in the 1980s of "senseless" violent gangs in conjunction with the increased use of enormously self-destructive drugs is an indicator of the deep despair and alienation experienced by many minority and ghetto youths. This phenomenon is strong evidence that many significant social dislocations persist in American society.

SUMMARY: BASIC THEMES FOR CLASS DISCUSSION

1. Violent gangs are not as cohesive and coherent in their behavior as generally reported. This factor is often reflected in reports where over 50 percent of gang victims have nothing to do with gangs, and the violent act is nevertheless referred to by police and the press as "gang-related."

2. Historically, gangs in early America were comprised of older members and had a greater cohesiveness and camaraderie. Their violent behavior was more rationally connected to illegal, profit-making goals.

3. The violent juvenile gangs of the post-World War II era are characterized by: a violent ethos; territorial or "turf" claims or perogatives; sociopathic leaders; and vague definitions of membership. These characteristics enabled emotionally disordered youngsters to act out their problems in the context of the violent gang.

4. In research for my book *The Violent Gang*, I determined that there are three types of juvenile gangs. (1) Social gangs are more structurally cohesive and function mainly within the boundaries of the law. They tend to be dominantly engaged in socially approved activities like sports and other sociable functions. (2) Delinquent gangs are comprised of a small tight-knit unit. They will utilize violence in furtherance of their illegal profit-making motives of theft or robbery. (3) Violent gangs are characterized by violent behavior directed at emotional gratification and prestige-seeking violence.

5. The violent gang is a "near-group." It is not a coherent group with specific identifiable members and coherent goals, nor is it a mob comprised of disparate members; it falls somewhere between these two collectivities.

6. I would predict that contemporary violent gangs will exist into the twenty-first century, because the violent gang fulfills the needs of many juveniles growing up in depressed socioeconomic conditions. Unless society changes to provide a role for these adolescents in the

larger society, they will continue to produce pseudocommunities like the violent gang to fulfill their "macho," supermasculine needs which are satisfied in some measure by their senseless violent activities.

QUESTIONS

8.1. Describe the basic structures, goals, and behavior of violent gangs, social gangs, and delinquent gangs.

8.2. Delineate and discuss the functions and ego gratification that each type of gang provides for its members.

8.3. Given the violent gang's behavior and structure, design a treatment program for effectively dealing with the problems created by these *near-groups*.

8.4. Have the students discuss the group or groups they were members of when they were adolescents. How were these groups like or unlike the gangs discussed in this chapter?

chapter 9

Growing Up in a Substance-Abusing Society

Boy, 11, Sentenced for Selling Drugs
Pasadena—An 11-year-old boy was sentenced Wednesday in Pasadena Juvenile Court for selling $20 worth of rock cocaine to an undercover police officer.

Commissioner Virginia Chernak ordered the youth removed from the custody of his parents, who live in Pasadena, and placed in either a county boys' home or a foster home for up to five years.

The boy, whose identity was withheld because he is a minor, was arrested October 8 after he sold a small amount of the drug on a street corner near the Kings Village housing project in Pasadena, Deputy District Attorney Jodi Rafkin said.

Los Angeles Daily News, *February 7, 1987*

The substance-abuse problem has reached awesome proportions in the United States and on an international level. The problem not only affects the self-destructive abuser and his or her family but has insidiously intruded into the political relationships of nations. From the countries who supply the drugs (and have their own share of addicts) to the major nations who illegally import the various drug poisons into their country, the problem is increasingly part of everyone's life. As major political powers agonize and attempt to develop flimsy blockades for preventing the flow of drugs into their society, too often they lose sight of the simple fact that if there were no consumer there would be no problem. Moreover, most drug consumers begin using at a younger and younger age, thus ensuring later adult substance abuse.

Some relevant statistics collated by The National Institute of Drug

Abuse reveal that in 1986 there were 5 million regular cocaine users; 20–24 million people tried cocaine; there were 563 cocaine-related deaths; 30 percent of all college students had tried cocaine by their fourth year; 42 percent of all college students had tried marijuana; and there are about 500,000 hard-core heroin users. Over 80 percent of high school students have used some illegal substance.

Despite the variety of efforts to combat the problem on all levels, there has been an increase in the number of substance abusers in the United States. Not only has the number of addicts increased, the problem has become more "democratic" and widespread. Formerly, severe addiction was primarily restricted to the lower socioeconomic segments of society. Today, the problem is found among people in all walks of life. People of all ages, in high schools, universities, sports, publishing, entertainment, corporations, and industry, have become addicted to drugs and alcohol. The current problem has affected people with high and low statuses in these different social organizations. Consequently, the crippling affects of substance abuse have had a profound negative impact on all major social institutions in American society.

The best statistics we have indicate that today's drug problem tends to begin at an earlier age. Young addicts are found in the elementary schools; however, high schools tend to be infested with the problem. In high schools around the country it is estimated that over 80 percent of the students have tried some illegal substance, and that many are addicts.

In the early 1940s less than 3 percent of the high school student population experimented with drugs. Today the statistics are almost reversed. The fact that over 8 out of 10 adolescents have used some kind of drug during their teenage years sets up a pattern of substance abuse that too often continues into the person's adult life.

The abuse of drugs in high school is often referred to by teenage users as "recreational drug use." In my view the popular phrase "recreational drug use" is a misnomer that attempts to deny and obfuscate the seriousness of their addiction problem. This casual attitude about the substance-abuse problem is often carried by adolescents into their adult life, and this exacerbates the overall problem.

Another factor related to the general substance-abuse problem in the United States is the proliferation of a *variety* of drugs in the illicit marketplace. The former staples of substance abuse such as alcohol, marijuana, and heroin have been joined by PCP, "ecstacy," "designer" drugs, cocaine (in various forms, including "crack"), and an increasingly larger selection of addictive pills.

Also, along the way certain drugs, which were formerly perceived as "fun and games" by many people, have turned out to have long-term and even lethal consequences in their affect on the user's personality and life. Notable in this context are marijuana and especially cocaine.

Individuals who began smoking marijuana several years ago for "fun" discover too late that they have become amotivational, "vegged-out," and strongly psychologically dependent on the drug. Cocaine, formerly a rich person's party drug, has in a more marketable form known as "crack" penetrated into usage in all segments of society and has had the impact of destructively affecting many user's lives. In particular, a number of well-known athletes, men in perfect physical condition, have died from heart failure shortly after using cocaine. On the contemporary substance-abuse scene, adolescents are heavily into the use of crack, and are susceptible to its short- and long-term lethal consequences.

Another cataclysmic problem related to substance abuse, especially for delinquents, is the dark disease clouds forming around the complex relationship that exists between intravenous use of drugs and AIDS. In one recent research report from New York, it was determined that 50 percent of intravenous drug users had the AIDS virus.[1] Delinquents, especially teenage runaways of both genders involved in prostitution, are especially vulnerable and susceptible to participating in this new drug scene that has the real developing possibility of killing them and all those with whom they have sex. Many alienated delinquents relate sexually and through intravenous drug use to this contemporary complex and lethal world of crime.

DEFINING THE SUBSTANCE ABUSER

The melange of more widespread drug abuse and the variety and combination of drug abuse in all segments of the society has somewhat clouded the question: Who is a substance abuser?

This point is, of course, a significant variable in determining the validity of any supposed trends or statistics on addiction. The question of when a person is truly addicted and the form of help needed is a very complex issue. In most cases, when a user's family and friends perceive the person as addicted to a drug or alcohol, the "addict" denies his addiction. Because of self-deception and denial, the addicted person refuses to take the basic first step in treatment: admitting he or she is a substance abuser.

Based on my research and observation of young substance abusers over the past 35 years on the street and in therapeutic settings, I would delineate the following five elements as present in defining the complex issue of who is a substance abuser.

Overwhelming Need (I)

Substance abusers have an intense conscious desire for their drug of choice—or a variety of drugs. They have a mental set where acquiring and using drugs becomes the paramount fixation or concern in the person's life.

The need or motivation to use drugs emanates from a number of

---

[1]Don C. Des Jarlais and Samuel R. Friedman, "A.I.D.S. and Intravenous Drug Use," a paper presented at the 15th Institute on Drug Abuse in Amsterdam, The Netherlands, April 1986.

complex situations in the substance abuser's social-psychological sphere. These needs or motivation come from one or several of the following forces:[2]

1. *Self-medication.* This involves the use of a drug to relieve some specific emotional or physiological pain.
2. *Addictive-continuance.* After an individual has become addicted they need to continue to use an addictive substance to relieve the potential pain of withdrawal.
3. *"Recreational."* This form involves an effort to temporarily alter one's mood and "have fun" under the influence of the drug.
4. *Peer pressure and conformity.* Adolescents (of all ages) are often motivated to use drugs or alcohol in order to conform with the substance-abuse behavior of their friends and peer groups.
5. *Hallucinogenic use.* Here the user is attempting to alter his or her state of consciousness to a higher level of awareness.
6. *Releasing inhibitions.* In this context the user has a need to attempt to remove mental blockades in order to enact behavior he or she wouldn't ordinarily **act** out. A drug is sometimes used, in this context, to remove **sexual** inhibitions or attempt to perform more effectively on an intellectual level.

These are only some of the modalities that motivate substance abuse. For some adolescents, peer pressure is a primary motivation. Others take drugs as a way of self-medicating their emotional problems. For most, however, their need for drugs is motivated by a complex of these forces.

Controlled by Substance (II)

The Alcoholics Anonymous first-step issue, that the substance has taken power over the person and their life has "become unmanageable," is another significant criterion in determining who is a substance abuser.

Self-deception and Denial (III)

Almost all substance abusers in the early phase, and even in later phases of the addictive process, when confronted about their addiction, practice self-deception and denial. This takes the form of lying to others and themselves about the amount of drugs they use, the degree they are dominated by their drug habit, the fact that the drug has become an integral part of their day-to-day behavior, and that their use of drugs has negatively affected their personal relationships. (In regard to denial about the amount of drugs used, I have developed in my work with adolescent groups what I have termed the "Yablonsky principle." This principle basically asserts that the

---

[2]These six categories of motivation or drug needs are derived and summarized from James Reed, "Patterns of Drug Abuse," an unpublished paper.

amount of drugs or alcohol the substance abuser admits to when first asked the question—how much, and what kinds of drugs or alcohol do you use and how often?—can be immediately doubled. (In groups I have directed, where I interviewed over 1,000 substance abusers, the interviewee, 100% of the time, will, upon further probing, admit to *at least twice* the amount of his initial response.)

The substance abuser's favorite defensive denial platitude, in one form or another is: "You're crazy. I can quit any time I want to." Somehow, they do not, unless some strong outside pressure is brought to bear on them.

Periodic Abstinence (IV)

Most addicts occasionally become drug-free for a period of time when their habit becomes too onerous. They often quit for a brief period to prove to themselves that their platitude and self-delusion, "I can quit anytime I want to," is true. The period of abstinence is usually very short compared to the length of their overall abuse syndrome.

The Addict Self-image and Primary Group Relationship (V)

After a period of time as a user, the addict's substance abuse becomes a central focus of his or her behavior and in many cases represents their identity. The addict no longer denies being an addict after he has tried to quit a number of times and failed. The true addict now begins to feel most at ease with peers, "friends," and cohorts who have the same drug problem they have, and these "friends" more and more comprise their primary group. They increasingly become alienated from people, friends, and family who are not drug abusers. They become identified by others, even if they don't accept the applied label as being, for example, a "pillhead," an alcoholic, a "junkie," a "cokehead," a "pothead," or, in high schools, the generic "stoner."

The perceptions and the response of others tends to have a self-fulfilling prophecy affect that begins to sink into the addict's self-concept. This perception by other people reinforces the addict's self-image and identity as a drug abuser. The delinquent now has developed a firm self-concept of being part of a substance-abusing ("stoner") subculture, and this perpetuates his or her addiction.

PATTERNS AND TRENDS IN DELINQUENT SUBSTANCE ABUSE

It is of value to review the historical background and basic trends in substance abuse by delinquents, and analyze the sociocultural and adult context in which adolescents become substance abusers.

Drug abuse has been a problem since the beginning of recorded history. The bible cites cases of the use of substances that were no doubt antecedents of modern drugs. In the past century, most societies have had serious problems with the abuse of alcohol, morphine, opium, heroin (a derivative of morphine), cocaine, and marijuana.

The 1960s was a peak period in the use of drugs by adolescents around the world. Beginning in early 1960s with Timothy Leary and Richard Alpert's experiments with hallucinogenic drugs, there was a major decade of experimentation with such drugs as marijuana, LSD, and later methamphetamines, or "speed." Leary's early pop-culture admonition to America's youth to "turn on" (use psychedelic substances); "tune in" (explore your inner emotional world through "consciousness-raising" drugs), and "drop out" (quit bureaucratic game playing) was followed by a major explosion of psychedelic substance abuse by young people around the country. The so-called "hippies" of that era, many of whom are the parents of today's generation, set an ethos of embracing drugs as a way of exploring one's inner world and raising a person's level of consciousness. This attitude was carried over and is prevalent in the 1980s and affects our contemporary drug problem.[3]

Traditionally, the opiate drugs, especially heroin, have been used to block out an onerous social environment, to attempt to resolve personal problems, and to escape into a state of pleasant reverie. Heroin, especially among lower socioeconomic groups, has posed a persistant drug abuse problem since the 1930s in American society. Although heroin has been used to some extent by young people in the middle and upper segments of society, it has been and remains a predominantly lower-class phenomenon.

In recent years cocaine has become one of the most widely abused drugs by young people in an inexpensive form known as "rock cocaine" or "crack." The drug is usually smoked, rather than snorted, as was the case when it was expensive and in powder form.

In brief, an analysis of adolescent substance abuse in the United States over the past 50 years reveals the following five evolutionary phases:

1. In the 1940s very few youths used illegal substances. Some used alcohol, however, the alcoholic problem among teenagers was moderate. Marijuana in general, and heroin in particular, were part of the juvenile drug scene in the ghettos of large cities. Cocaine was restricted to the welathy and some jazz musicians.
2. In the 1950s, combined with the advent of rock-and-roll concerts, marijuana and alcohol became more widely used by adolescents. Heroine and marijuana increasingly became a problem among minority youths growing up in depressed socioeconomic conditions.
3. In the 1960s, with the "greening" of America, on a philosophical pretext of raising consciousness and mind expansion, a variety of psychedelic substances were advocated and used by a large number of adolescents. Most teenage, and young adult dropouts used psy-

[3]See Lewis Yablonsky, *The Hippie Trip* (New York: Pegasus, 1968; New York: Penguin, 1969).

chedelic substances (e.g., LSD, mescaline, "mushrooms," etc.) in the context of a new sociocultural awakening—free from the "heavy trips" of the larger society. In the "hippie" orbit marijuana was the "black-bread staple" drug used on a daily basis by millions of young people to maintain their plateau of being and staying high. They referred to this process as *"maintaining."* LSD and other psychedelics became part of this social-exploration scene. Toward the late 1960s many youths began to "crash" and run into serious emotional problems from substance abuse. Also methamphetamine, "crystal," or speed began to intrude on this fading social movement of young people.

In the depressed socioeconomic areas of the city marijuana and heroin continued as the drugs of choice to achieve euphoric highs that would block out a sense of hopelessness and lack of opportunities in the overall society.

4. The 1970s was a period of increased acceptance and varied drug use by many people who had been part of the "psychedelic revolution" and had now moved back into the mainstream of society. The more accepting attitude towards marijuana made it an easily accessible drug tacitly condoned by parents, many of whom had been into the hippie scene in the sixties. Some of these parents used drugs with their children, partly to rationalize their own substance abuse as acceptable behavior.

5. The 1980s, especially since 1986, has been strongly impacted by the commercialization of cocaine in the form of crack. A consumer can easily purchase a readily available $10–$50 of rock in a "rock house," on the streets, or in the business section of large cities during the noon lunch break. In this period drug use and abuse has reached grotesque proportions and caused the federal government to declare "war" on this severe national problem that has pervaded all segments of society. Youths growing up under these conditions have become heavily involved in substance abuse. Although crack came particularly into vogue, all other substances continued to be used.

The impact of the general substance-abuse pattern has had a profound impact on the delinquency problem. I would estimate that over 90 percent of all delinquents have used illegal substances, and most of this group has, or has had a serious substance-abuse problem. In contemporary society, therefore, substance abuse has become an integral and significant part of the overall juvenile delinquency problem in the United States.

The Sociocultural Context of Adolescent Substance Abuse

A major influence in the creation of the burgeoning adolescent drug problem emanates from the sociocultural context of adult substance abuse in the United States, with special emphasis on parents as negative role models. This issue is revealed in the apocryphal and sometimes real story of parents ferociously admonishing their son or daughter on the evils of drug abuse with a tinkling fifth martini in their shaky hands.

This parental-child drug syndrome was especially the case in the late 1960s and early 1970s. I believe the attitudes and behavior with drugs during that time set the stage for an explosion of drug abuse by adolescents in the 1980s.

In this regard, there is increasing research data which supports the theory that the children of substance-abusing parents, especially alcoholic parents, are most likely to become substance abusers. There are several assumptions about the link between parental substance abuse and its impact on children: (1) The parent may influence the child to become an abuser because of their substance-abuse role modeling; (2) nonusing but severely disciplinarian parents may cause their children to rebel against their harsh norms, and the rebellion may include substance abuse; (3) substance-abusing parents may genetically or physiologically transmit the problem to their children. In this regard, there is clear evidence that the children of addicted mothers are often born addicted to the same drug their mother was abusing; (4) in some cases a parent clearly and directly influences the child's drug use by using drugs with them. Each of these assumptions will be dealt with in the course of my overall analysis of the sociocultural impact of a substance-abusing society on adolescent substance abuse.

Many parent-child links on the subject are debatable, however, the most clear-cut case of the parent-child substance-abuse connection is revealed in situations where parents and children use drugs together. This connection was cogently described in an article, "The Parent as Drug Supplier," by Mike Granberry.[4]

> Bob is 41. His daughter, Melissa, is 16. They first "did drugs together" when she was 11. Their basic high? Marijuana.
>
> "I never considered marijuana a drug," he said. "I thought it a sacrament—a religious experience. I actually quit drinking before I quit using marijuana."
>
> Melissa says that her mother, Doris, 39, also used drugs. By the time she was 15, Melissa was smoking marijuana, drinking, "doing crystal and coke, LSD, mushrooms. . . . The way I got into drugs was totally through the family," she said. "They were so [screwed] up, I had to start using, just to fit in."
>
> Once, in front of friends at a birthday party, Melissa was given a "giant joint" [marijuana] tied with a bow and ribbon—Mom's gift to her. "Thought it was so cool," Melissa said, "I think back on it now and realize how bizarre it really was."
>
> Today, Bob and family appear to be normal middle-class Americans, living in the San Diego suburb of Chula Vista. They agreed to be interviewed as long as their real names were not used. They are "recovering drug addicts and alcoholics," under the care of a program for the children of alcoholics in San Diego.

[4]Mike Granberry, *Los Angeles Times*, March 17, 1986. Copyright (1986), *Los Angeles Times*. Reprinted by permission.

They chose to share their story, hoping it might give some insights to parents giving drugs to children. At the end of the interview Bob remarked, "I can't smoke one joint, and I can't drink one beer. If I do, I lose my entire sobriety. My chief symptom was denial—even to giving drugs to my kid. Denial is what keeps you going. It can keep you going for a very long time."

He glanced at the floor, then at his daughter's face. "Wow," he said. "I could have killed her."

In another case of this type, Debbie, the 16-year-old daughter of parents who continue to abuse drugs, has heard talk about the horrible influence of peers, school, and MTV (the rock video channel on cable television) on the teenage drug problem. She disputes this by stating: "MTV wasn't my problem. My dad was my problem. He's the one who first . . . gave me drugs."[4]

In my own work I have encountered many situations of the type described in the foregoing article. In one case, a 14-year-old girl in a drug-treatment group I directed revealed that she had been turned on to the drugs by her grandfather. Many children who become serious substance abusers's first use of a substance that sets them off involves alcohol or marijuana they get from their parents' bar or stash in their own home.

A Society of Pill-Users as It Affects Adolescents

In the overall sociocultural context of substance abuse in the United States, adult mind-altering pill popping has had an enormous impact on the adolescent substance-abuse problem. In addition to their parents' use of mind-altering pills, children are inundated by television and other advertisements for nonprescription headache and sleeping pills: "A little pill will do you." These set the tone for the belief that emotional problems are easily cured by ingesting pills. The model in a complex way influences children and adolescents to cure their personal emotional problems with mind-altering drugs in the sociocultural context of a pill-popping society.

In 1986 over 400 prescriptions were written by physicians for psychoactive drugs, such as amphetamines and barbiturates. These drugs were essentially used by "right-thinking," generally conservative, middle- and upper-class people who had no reason to have a criminal self-concept. This use, however, indirectly facilitates juvenile use because it demonstrates to children that drug use is an acceptable way to cope with the stresses and strains of living. The paradox is that when an adolescent turns to drugs to solve his problems, he may find himself labeled "juvenile delinquent."

In a penetrating article, Drs. Lennard, Epstein, Bernstein, and Ransom make a devastating comment on this pattern of drug abuse.[5] They allege that the pharmaceutical companies are engaged in promoting drug

[5]Henry L. Lennard, Leon J. Epstein, Arnold Bernstein, and Donald C. Ransom, "Hazards Implicit in Prescribing Psychoactive Drugs," *Science* 169 (July 31, 1970): 438–441. Copyright 1970 by the American Association for the Advancement of Science.

use: "In order to extend the potential market for its product, the pharmaceutical industry, in its communications to physicians, all too often practices mystification in relabeling an increasing number of human and personal problems as medical problems."[6]

They continue by elucidating their meaning of *mystification*:

It is apparent that the pharmaceutical industry is redefining and relabeling as medical problems calling for drug intervention a wide range of human behaviors which, in the past, have been viewed as falling within the bounds of the normal trials and tribulations of human existence. Much evidence for this position is to be found in the advertisements of drug companies, both in medical journals and in direct mailings to physicians.

A series of examples will be sufficient to illustrate this point. The first involves the potential personal conflict a young woman may experience when first going off to college.

On the inside front cover of one journal [*Journal of the American College Health Association*] an advertisement states: "A Whole New World . . . of Anxiety" . . . "to help free her of excessive anxiety . . . adjunctive Librium." Accompanying the bold print is a full-page picture of an attractive, worried-looking young woman, standing with an armful of books. In captions surrounding her, the potential problems of a new college student are foretold: "Exposure to new friends and other influences may force her to reevaluate herself and her goals." . . . "Hew newly stimulated intellectual curiosity may make her more sensitive to and apprehensive about unstable national and world conditions." The text suggests that Librium (chlordiazepoxide HC1), together with counseling and reassurance "can help the anxious student to handle the primary problem and to 'get her back on her feet.'" Thus, the normal problems and conflicts associated with the status change and personal growth that accompany the college experience are relabeled medical-psychiatric problems, and as such are subject to amelioration through Librium.

Another journal has an advertisement that advises a physician on how he can help deal with such everyday anxieties of childhood as school and dental visits. This advertisement, in the *American Journal of Diseases of Children*, portrays a tearful little girl, and in large type appear the words: "School, the dark, separation, dental visits, 'monsters.'" On the subsequent page the physician is told in bold print that "The everyday anxieties of childhood sometimes get out of hand." In small print below he reads that "A child can usually deal with his anxieties. But sometimes the anxieties overpower the child. Then, he needs your help.

"Your help may include Vistaril (hydroxyzine pamoate)."

The advertisement, in effect, presents an oversimplified conception of behavior and behavior change. Potential anxiety engendered by new and different situations is defined as undesirable, as constituting a medical and psychiatric problem which requires the intervention of a physician and, most particularly, intervention through the prescription of a psychoactive drug.

Physicians and parents with low tolerance for anxiety, or those with limited

[6]Ibid., p. 428.

ability to meet the demands of even a temporarily troubled child, are more prone to believe that the child is disturbed and in need of drug treatment.

There is, however, no substantial evidence for the proposition that the prescribed drug does indeed facilitate children's participation in school situations. *What is especially disturbing about advertisements such as this is that they tend to enlist the help of physicians to introduce children to a pattern of psychoactive drug use. Paradoxically, such drug use, at a later date, without a physician's prescription, is deplored both by the medical profession and the community at large.*[7]

Psychoactive drugs, according to Lennard and his colleagues, play an important role in many parent-child relationships. The authors describe an ad on a box of physicians' samples of Tofranil (imipramine hydrochloride), a psychic energizer used to combat depression:

On the box is a picture of an adolescent girl. Above the picture in bold print is the legend, "Missing, Kathy Miller." Below the picture we read, "$500 reward for information concerning her whereabouts." Alongside in white print we read the plea, "Kathy, please come home!" Inside the box is a letter entitled, "Kathy, We love you. . . . Please come home." We quote: "Dear Doctor: For parents, inability to communicate with their children is a significant loss. The 'What did I do wrong?' lament of the parent may be accompanied by feelings of incapacity, inferiority, guilt and unworthiness. Many may, in fact, be suffering from symptoms of pathological depression. What can Tofranil, imipramine hydrochloride, do for your depressed patient?"[8]

The advertisement then goes on to describe how Tofranil can relieve these symptoms.

The drug manufacturer thus suggests a fascinating method of handling a delinquent runaway: First remove the delinquency problem from the realm of family dynamics, then convert it into a medical problem that can be "cured" by drugs. The parents, rather than dealing with the behavioral situation, are encouraged to allay their fears and anxieties with a drug. In this way, the authors point out, drug use is set up as a model for the false resolution of an intrafamily problem. The authors comment:

Thus, when a physician prescribes a drug for the control or solution (or both) of personal problems of living, he does more than merely relieve the discomfort caused by the problem. He simultaneously communicates a model for an acceptable and useful way of dealing with personal and interpersonal problems. The implications attached to this model and its long-term effects are what concern us.[9]

A gross error in rationality is also emphasized by these advertisements of the pharmaceutical establishment. Promotion pieces describe specific

[7]Ibid., pp. 438–439. Emphasis added.
[8]Ibid., p. 438.
[9]Ibid., p. 439.

psychotropic drugs as altering specific emotional states and effecting specific psychological processes—this even though it has been clearly established that any agent produces not a single effect but a diffusion of effects. In other words, the manufacturer singles out the desired effects of a drug's impact and labels them "main effects"; all other changes are labeled "side effects," regardless of whether they are positive or negative, merely uncomfortable or highly dangerous. Using this philosophy, an advertisement for heroin could read: "Here is the solution to all your problems. Relief is just a fix away. Warning: may be addictive." Essentially this statement is true. But it is totally misleading because it fails to mention that the addictive "side effects" are so horrendous that they negate any positive benefits of the drug.

"Mystification" in legal drug use is a complex matter that undoubtedly influences the way people perceive their personal and interpersonal problems. Lennard and his colleagues conclude:

> Drug giving and drug taking represent all too brittle and undiscriminating responses, and ultimately, in our view, they will breed only more frustration and more alienation. Changing the human environment is a monumental undertaking. While seeking to change cognitive shapes through chemical means is more convenient and economical, the drug solution has already become another technological Trojan horse.

> The ultimate task is to alter the shapes of human relatedness and social arrangements that determine the context and the substance of our existence. To maintain, as do significant groups within the pharmaceutical industry, the medical profession, and the youth culture, that this can be accomplished merely through chemical means is indeed to have fallen victim to mystification.[10]

There is little doubt that this adult concept of the power of psychoactive drugs affects the patterns of drug use of youth. The concept of drug use to alter and resolve human problems has in the past decade been a central theme of youth movements. The tremendous growth of drug use among young people stems in part from the tremendous affirmation of its use by adults in "legal form." Allen Geller and Maxwell Boas describe succinctly the adult influence on juvenile drug use:

> Today's teenagers entered a world in which mood-changing substances were a fact of existence; sleeping pills, stimulants, tranquilizers, depressants and many other varieties of mind-altering chemical compounds had long been absorbed into the nation's pharmacopoeia, and copping pills, swallowing capsules and downing tablets were a national habit. Our youngsters' indulgence in drugs can hardly be blamed on some sinister outside influence; they witnessed firsthand the tranquilizer-amphetamine-barbiturate boom of the fifties as their own parents took eagerly to psychic delights. They grew up regarding chemicals as tools to be used to manipulate the inner mind. Some youngsters were even recipients of these drugs; until the dangers were clearly delineated, it was not

[10]Ibid., p. 441.

uncommon for parents to dose their children with half of a barbituate tablet so that they would be sure to go to sleep.[11]

Physicians, who are often referred to as "Dr. Feelgoods," have become dealers in the growing pill-popping development of the 1980s. The pattern was described by George Reasons and Mike Goodman in a fascinating article in the *Los Angeles Times:*

California's New Drug Pushers

The president of the state's Division of Medical Quality estimates there are "Between 500 and 1,000 of these drug-pusher doctors" in California.

They are illegally giving out close to a million pills a day, and they do it by writing prescriptions for anyone who can pay their fees. They operate in almost every community. Many doctors know who they are but will not expose them, said Dr. Eugene Feldman, president of the Division of Medical Quality. "It's the brotherhood code: turn your back or get sued," he told The Times.

Although it is estimated that less than 2% of the state's doctors are involved, narcotics agents say, the doctors now illegally supply about 90% of all pharmaceutical drugs on the street. Some of these doctors earn $1,000 a day writing illegal prescriptions for anybody who can pay the $10 to $20 fee, preferably in cash. . . . "A doctor with a pencil and prescription pad has a ticket to a fortune," one narcotics agent said. "He works great hours and makes no house calls, doesn't need medical equipment or medical employees."

The drugs they deal in are powerful narcotics that can transform young men and women into helpless addicts whose drug tolerance grows along with their drug dependence. . . . The Physicians Desk Reference, the drug manual for members of the medical profession, warns over and over of the danger to patients who use the drugs without careful supervision. The most sought after pills on the high school and college campuses across the nation all carry warnings [as to their danger]. . . .

Many are swallowed by the handful, but often they are dissolved and injected into the bloodstream with hypodermic needle and syringe, known as "outfits."

The outfits sometimes are supplied by pharmacists who work with the "scrip" doctors, cashing thousands of their prescriptions a week for up to 100% profits. There are dozens of these pharmacies in Los Angeles. . . .

There is evidence of more than 100 doctors who have been writing "scrips" for several hundred thousand dangerous pills a day. . . .

As a rule scrip doctors run assembly-line operations. Waiting rooms are jammed with addicts, pushers and teenagers. Long lines spill out into the street, like a line "waiting to see 'Star Wars,'" one agent reported.

Some doctors pass around a sign-up sheet and take people in numerical order. There's a desperate scramble because more people are waiting than the doctor can see in a day. . . .

[11]From *The Drug Beat* by Allen Geller and Maxwell Boas (New York: McGraw-Hill, 1971), p. xvi.

The doctor's office becomes a meeting place for the drug culture. Those awaiting their turn—often an all-day vigil—make their wait a social event by swapping information on new scrip doctors and "easy" pharmacies, trading prescriptions and pills and selling marijuana and sometimes heroin.

The doctor's waiting room was a second home to Dennis, who told The Times he worked his way through UCLA by selling narcotics and dangerous pills supplied to him by numerous local physicians.

"I was living off the doctors. A lot of my friends were, too," recalled the 25-year-old-son of a Los Angeles area executive.

The doctors, Dennis said, also helped him become a junkie. They kept him well supplied with the powerful narcotic pain-killer Dilaudid, knowing that he was shooting it up and selling it. . . .

He said he could carry his "outfit" (syringe, needle and drugs) in his backpack with his books.

Dennis said that when he needed a fix, about every two hours, he headed for a special campus bathroom where the toilet stall doors closed tightly so no one could see him "tie off" his arm with cord to make the veins stand out.

"I would crush the tablet, drop the powder into the spoon, put some water on top, fire underneath, cook it, draw it and fix. It took four or five minutes."

Then once a week Dennis performed this all-important ritual of visiting his main "Dilaudid doctor," a Los Angeles area physician now under indictment on drug charges.

"I was getting 18 to 20 (Dilaudid) tabs a day from the doctor," Dennis said. What tabs he didn't shoot he sold for $10 apiece on the street, he said.

A prescription for 50 Dilaudid cost only about $12 from the pharmacy, and Dennis' doctor charged another $20 for writing it.

"He knew I was selling it. A lot of people made some fortunes," said Dennis, "particularly if they weren't addicts and didn't shoot up the profits. Any junkie feels it's just as good as heroin."

Every few weeks Dennis would visit four or five other doctors for a variety of other pills such as "black beauties" (uppers), and downers such as Qualudes, reds (Seconal)" and "rainbows (Tuinal)."

At one point, Dennis said, he was getting 700 to 800 pills a month from the doctors.

"If I wasn't into using them they were easy to sell. Sometimes I'd make $800 a month plus keeping my habit."

Dennis said that his drug habit grew until it was all he thought about. It consumed his life. He said he didn't care about eating and lost 40 pounds. . . .

One doctor's impact [in this new illicit market] can be staggering, according to court records which show pills prescribed here sometimes wind up in the hands of large-scale dealers in Las Vegas, Seattle, Chicago, New York and Miami.

- A Los Angeles doctor working with a criminal syndicate wrote prescriptions for more than a million pills, delivered to his confederates by the boxload.
- Nearly 200,000 pills were seized in the office of an Oakland doctor who confessed to "indiscriminately and recklessly dispensing huge quantities of dangerous drugs" over 2½ years.

- A San Francisco doctor was caught driving a panel truck loaded with 1.7 million amphetamines destined for the street.
- A west Los Angeles doctor sold thousands of prescription blanks to a dealer who filled them out, got the drugs and sold them to criminal syndicates in Las Vegas and New York.
- A second San Francisco doctor wrote 5,017 prescriptions for 130,442 pills in a 90-day period, according to a federal study of 13 San Francisco pharmacies.[12]

There is evidence that the enormous usage of these "Dr. Feelgood" drugs is indirectly facilitated by large pharmaceutical companies. This form of quasilegal drug dealing was researched by one of the authors. He interviewed a number of individuals who worked for large pharmaceutical corporations that were involved in this form of white-collar crime. Needless to say, these sources preferred to be anonymous.

Several of the companies have no real concern about the potential users of their products or the fact that their customers might become addicted—a classic case of profit values taking precedence over human values. As described above, in their advertising to their doctor-dealers they emphasize one affect of the drug and conveniently deemphasize the deleterious impacts of addiction. (*I'm Dancing as Fast as I Can*, a book by Barbara Gordon, who became addicted to Valium, was made into a film with the same name. The pharmaceutical company-manufacturer attempted to ban the showing of the film because they felt it depicted their product in a negative light.)

A student told me the following story about the large pharmaceutical firm he worked for:

> My company doesn't care who uses their drugs or who gets addicted. They are only involved with sales and profits. In one case they received an order and shipped a staggering amount of amphetamines to a drugstore in a small town in Mexico. I would estimate that the shipment would keep every man, woman, and child in that town loaded for 50 years!
>
> Our executives knew it was a crooked deal, and that those drugs would be sold back across the border, probably in San Diego and Los Angeles in the illegal drug market, and that California high school kids would be using those drugs. But they didn't see that part of it as their problem. They were and are in business to sell drugs.

The impact of this sociocultural situation is staggering in terms of its impact, especially on the addiction of women. Some of these issues, as well as a promising treatment approach for pill poppers, are incorporated in the following article by Ann Japenga.

---

[12]From "California's New Drug Pushers" by George Reasons and Mike Goodman. *Los Angeles Times*, March 2, 1978. Copyright, 1978, *Los Angeles Times*. Reprinted by permission.

Wingspread Clinic: For Women Hooked on Legal Drugs

Barbara Wessel, a 38-year-old medical technician, got off drugs the hard way. She just stopped.

The first days without Dalmane, a sedative her doctor had first prescribed for sleeplessness, were bad—anxiety, the shakes. But on the seventh day she lost control of her muscles. To survive the following weeks, she clung to a scrap of paper on which she'd written "This is withdrawal. You're not crazy."

Some people think of drugs like Dalmane and the tranquilizer Valium as the choice of housewives and lightweights. "Wimpy" drugs. What they don't know, and what the women who take them (67% of prescriptions for psychoactive drugs go to women, according to the National Institute on Drug Abuse) don't know, is that the withdrawals can be more terrifying than anything experienced by a street-drug junkie.

Soon after Wessel's ordeal, Wingspread opened in her hometown of Santa Cruz. It is, as far as founder Dr. Josette Mondanaro knows, the only facility of its kind in the country: a detoxification center providing both medical care and counseling for women addicted to prescription drugs.

In her career, Mondanaro, a general practitioner has gravitated to serving minorities, the poor and "anyone who can't buy into the system."

"When you work with oppressed people it's almost impossible not to work with chemicals," she said. "They're used in the *barrios* to keep minorities down. They're used in old age homes to keep senior citizens in place. And in houses and apartments, they're used to keep women down."

While serving as director of the state Division of Substance Abuse in 1976–78 . . . Mondanaro said she learned that established detox programs weren't being used by women because the services are geared to the male street-drug addict (although 10 times as many people are dependent on prescription drugs as are addicted to heroin). They are staffed with men. And most are unequipped to handle withdrawal from prescription drugs—a long-term project.

There's another reason women aren't using the programs: image. *A woman who talks, thinks and looks like the mainstream of society has a hard time going to a place reserved for junkies, said Mondanaro. She doesn't think of herself as an addict and she's not easily identified as one. The only clue that something is wrong may be recurring backaches, migraines or insomnia.* [My emphasis.]

Mondanaro's plan was to open a center where women could go for non-drug-related complaints. Because Wingspread operates as a women's clinic, a woman with a drug problem can walk in for a routine exam without losing face. (Wingspread's drug program is funded by the National Institute for Drug Abuse as well as the proceeds from the clinic operations.)

During her intake interview, she may be paired with ex-addict Barbara Wessel, who now works at Wingspread. The moment of enlightenment often comes, Mondanaro said, when a patient answers the routine questions, "What drugs are you taking and for how long?"

Mary is one who didn't believe drugs were her problem until she came to Wingspread. "I thought I was crazy on the natch," she said. "My mother had a medicine cabinet full of drugs. If anything was out of whack, you took a pill."

Contrasting with the Santa Cruz casual look, Mary (not her real name) dresses expensively, furs complementing her silver-gray hair. At 41, she's 20 years older than the average client in a street-drug program. Like most of the women at Wingspread, she's been addicted more than 15 years.

Her doctor prescribed diet pills when she was 15. Later, she was in a traffic accident and another doctor gave her an open prescription for Codeine and Dalmane for neck pain.

This month she's celebrating a year of sobriety. Over the slow course of recovery at Wingspread, she said she's been able to admit to part of her problem: she's an alcoholic, but her self-image won't allow her to identify with pill-heads. "The drug addict part I still really have a problem with. And none of my family (she has two teenage children) believes I've ever been an alcoholic or drug addict."

While a woman is dependent on a drug like Valium, her nervous system is depressed and during a cold turkey withdrawal, it rebounds with a fury, Mondanaro said. "There's a real feeling of imminent death," said an ex-addict. "In addition to psychological symptoms, muscles twitch. The patient jerks violently in her sleep. She sweats, has a bad taste in her mouth and a constant headache. Some have seizures."

"These are all the kinds of symptoms that make people think they're crazy," said Mondanaro. "They don't think the drugs are driving them crazy. They don't realize it's the withdrawal they're experiencing." Because the effects of some prescription drug withdrawals often don't appear until seven days after stopping the drug, many patients don't associate the withdrawal with the symptoms, she said.

Mondanaro said some patients come into the center saying: "I've flushed all my drugs down the toilet. I want to go cold turkey." In those cases, the doctor tells the patient something she doesn't want to hear: "It's taken you 10 years to get like this. It's going to take two to get better."

The pills to which the patient is addicted are doled out in decreasing dosages a day at a time. The actual detox process takes from six to eight weeks—and then begins the long haul to recovery. In a year the former addict will begin to regain her memory and physical capacities. ("I still don't know what it's like to feel hungry," said Wessel, two years after the detox.) In another year she'll begin to get back on her feet emotionally.

Many clients continue coming to Wingspread. One patient said being in an ongoing group with other ex-addicts was "proof I wouldn't die. It could be done."

Wingspread, for that first shaky year, becomes a sanctuary. "There aren't a lot of places that feel safe," said Wessel. "This is one of them."[13]

The widespread and insidious problems created by the enormous sociocultural impact of quasilegal pill production and use in its impact on adolescent substance abuse may be summarized as follows:

1. There are valid reasons for a person to use some form of physician-prescribed tranquilizer to get through a life crisis or in a therapeutic situation.

---

[13]Ann Japenga, "Wingspread Clinic: for Women Hooked on Legal Drugs," *Los Angeles Times*, February 18, 1982. Copyright, 1982, *Los Angeles Times*. Reprinted by permission.

2. Despite this legitimate use, the wide acceptance and use of psycho-active substances tends to relabel "human problems" as "medical problems." It sets up an ethos where drugs are used in an attempt to solve human problems, which might be better solved by intro-spection or therapeutic counseling.

3. An ironic situation is created where it is legitimate for a doctor to give an adolescent drugs; however, if a juvenile administers a drug to himself on his own he is violating the law and may be adjudi-cated as a delinquent.

4. The supplying of psychoactive drugs to adolescents may be more beneficial for the parents and doctors who give them the drugs than it is for the juvenile. An adolescent under the influence of a psychoactive drug is sedated and not usually belligerent or argu-mentive. As in Huxley's *Brave New World*, where the soma pill tranquilized people, the adolescent may become more malleable in their sedated state.

5. When proponents advocate the extensive use of modern "soma pills," or tranquilizers, they tend to emphasize only the immediate positive effects and not the longer-term negative side effects. For example, a good case can be made for the powerful energy one achieves on cocaine or amphetamines; however, the downside, longer-term consequences can be addiction and depression when the user stops using the drug.

6. Finally, the use of psychoactive substances which tranquilize peo-ple and oversimplify their problems may sidetrack them from get-ting effective long-term psychotherapy or counseling, which over the long run would be more beneficial to their emotional health and life situation.

Female Substance Abuse

In the overall sociocultural context of American society, both adolescent females and males have achieved equality as substance abusers. There are, however, some special issues and hazards related to female substance abuse that are worthy of attention: (1) Substance-abusing pregnant women can deleteriously affect their fetus and their progeny; and (2) mothers are most likely to be the primary socializing agent to their children. Following is an analysis of some noteworthy issues related to the female substance abusers.

How do most females become substance abusers? There is consider-able research evidence that suggests that many young women are first turned on to drugs by male companions. Research by Lee Bowker suggests that girls' use of alcohol and marijuana is influenced more by their boy-friends than by their girlfriends.[14] For boys, he notes, peer influences ap-pear to be "homosocial" (that is, boy influencing boy), whereas for girls, peer influences appear to be "heterosocial" (boy influencing girl). It ap-

[14]Lee H. Bowker, *Women, Crime and the Criminal Justice System* (Lexington, Mass.: Lex-ington Books, Heath), p. 90. Copyright 1978, D.C. Heath and Company.

pears that drug use spreads more from males to females than from females to other females. There is a good deal of evidence that males provide illicit drugs and receive sexual favors in return. Bowker has summarized the situation as follows:

> The combination of biological and social pressure may lead to ambivalence about sex among females. For males the pressures are all toward engaging in sexual behavior. As a result, males try to get their girlfriends to agree to partici-pate in sexual intercourse. Females are socialized to please males (on dates and everywhere else), yet expected to avoid pleasing them so much that they ruin their reputations. A reasonable solution to this double-bind dilemma is for females to join their boyfriends in recreational drug use and use it as an excuse for participation in initial and subsequent drug seduction (I'm not that kind of girl, but I was just so drunk. . . .").

In recent years this phenomenon is referred to by adolescents as the "coke-whore syndrome." This relates to the sexual favors which are ac-corded men who supply a female with cocaine. It is a form of what I would term "soft-prostitution."

A special aspect of females and substance abuse is that many women support their habits through the "coke-whore syndrome" or in more clear-cut forms of prostitution. Paula, was a New York prostitute and drug addict for many years. Her story provides a prototypical case history of the path travelled by many women who become substance-abusing prostitutes.

> Before I was nine or ten, I was a problem child. I was put into a problem child's institution at a very early age. I think I was a year or a year and a half old when I was placed. I progressed from there to different institutions until I was sixteen. The last reformatory I was in was a so-called treatment center. Here I got my final street education.
>
> Most of the kids there, including myself, were considered incorrigible. Most of the guys had criminal records. Some of the girls had been runaways and whores from the age of 12. The guys were violent and some were accomplished thieves and con men. I absorbed all of their teachings readily. I enjoyed it.
>
> I think I always knew I was going to use drugs. I used my first form of drugs when I was twelve. There were two guys who lived in the same apartment house with my family. I admired and looked up to them. They were about seventeen or eighteen at the time. I was allowed home visits once or twice a year for a weekend (when my behavior, in the institution I was in at the time, was good enough).
>
> Whenever I did manage a home visit, I looked forward to hanging out a night in front of the house with these guys. They seemed to know I was hurting inside and tolerated me. One summer night I saw them going to the roof of the house, and I followed them. They were smoking marijuana. It smelled good to me, and I asked for a drag. I turned on. I remember that I felt it was the most beautiful thing that ever happened to me. I was very happy and started to imitate all the

singers I like. The guys gave me lots of approval for my singing. From then on, I was one of them and got all the pot I could use.

After that year, I was introduced to cocaine by the same two guys, and horned it whenever the opportunity arose. For fourteen years I enjoyed all the drugs I ever used. Heroin crept up on me. I normally weighed 125 pounds. There was a period when I was badly strung out [addicted] on heroin and weighed 90 pounds. I thought my clothes had stretched!

I had a six-year period of using every form of narcotic and everything that went with it. Maybe if I describe the average life of an addict in New York City, you will get an idea of what my life was life. . . .

My hours were from six to six. That is, six in the evening to six in the morning. . . .I'd get up as late as possible, because the sun hurt my eyes. I didn't want people to look at me.

You know something's terribly wrong. You're different. Squares are scurrying around, bumping up against each other. They look insane to you. Addicts talk a lot about how crazy squares are.

You get dressed, and if you happen to have some drugs you take your morning fix. From there on in, you begin to scramble for bread [money] and drugs, and anything goes. I would buy or sell drugs. Most pushers are addicts. They're not the big-time people you read about with beautiful apartments. The heavier pushers [those with large quantities of drugs] are usually addicts too. That's the reason they're pushing. It's a simple matter of economics. You buy a quantity. You cut the drugs yourself. You sell a little bit. You make a little money to buy more dope.

Most of the time you're broke, so you use your wiles. You'll use anything you've learned. You con, and being female you have a few tools that guys don't have. I did a few nasty things in my time. I turned out as a whore. I participated in many degrading acts. If you check Krafft-Ebbing, you will find a pretty good catalog of what I had to do to make my money.

If you get drugs that are pretty strong, you can go along on them for a few hours. But usually drugs are so weak and cut down, you have to fix [inject the drugs] six or eight times a day to feel normal. When you have a real habit going, you don't really get loaded like you see acted out in the movies or read about. You need the drug to feel normal.

After the first few months of addiction, the stuff takes over. The demand builds higher and higher and the supply is never enough. You need more and more drugs and money. I spent as much for myself as I did for my old man. (You would call him a pimp—I didn't think he was.) If I made $200 a day, it would be spent on drugs.

Paula could have become the mother of Maria, a 13-year-old crack-cocaine addict-prostitute. Maria lived with her prostitute-addict mother, turned tricks, and used drugs with her in San Francisco.

Maria was torn between two worlds when she cleaned up her habit in a drug rehabilitation therapeutic community. Her mother often called begging her to return to their life on the streets. According to Maria, "the most important lesson I've learned in the program is that I'm worth something." Maria at 13 looks twice her age. A small "12" tattooed on her hand betrays her past. It was tattooed there one night after she did 12 lines of cocaine. Now, it reminds her of the 12 stages of her drug-abuse recovery program.

Maria's family background is prototypical. When she was five, her drug addict parents left her to be raised near Oakland by her grandmother. She was seven when she began experimenting with marijuana and PCP. At 11, she went to live with her mother and joined her world of sex and drugs. She turned to prostitution when her habit reached $200 a day. She returned to her grandmother the following year, but soon she ran away. She was raped twice and arrested for heroin use, and even when she moved back to her grandmother's house, she continued using crack. One night last January she returned home intoxicated and high on PCP. "I walked into the house, then I fell on the floor and started kicking and screaming, telling my grandmother to kill me." Instead her grandmother enrolled her in the drug-treatment program. "It was the first time I was strong enough to say, 'That's it.'"

The beginning was difficult. She was hard to reach—cold and distant. "I don't always trust others with my feelings." Soon, however, she was talking openly in groups which emphasized the discussed family problems along with detoxification. The program taught Maria that she will probably never be free of the urge to use drugs or the pressures of the world outside. Despite her problems Maria was learning to live one positive, drug-free day at a time in the therapeutic community. Maria is prototypical of many teenage addict-prostitutes who have been resocialized in recent years in "therapeutic community." (This type of program will be more fully discussed in the section on treatment programs.)

The social-cultural forces that produced Paula and Maria's substance-abuse problems emanated from a lower socioeconomic class situation. The contemporary substance-abuse scene for adolescent females appears at all levels of society. The following case depicts this situation.[15]

> Andrea had it all. She was a cheerleader in suburban Atlanta, a member of the homecoming queen's court and an honor student who thought that taking drugs was dumb. But Andrea did an abrupt about-face when she was suspended from the cheerleader squad for putting on lipstick during class. She bleached her hair white and cut it in a Mohawk. As her mother, Jan, remembers, "She went from preppy to punk in seven months."
>
> No longer in the teenage social elite, Andrea sought acceptance in the school's drug culture. "I just wanted to be 'it' again, and I was, with another group," she says. Soon her grades dropped to F's, she couldn't wake up in the morning, and she had screaming fights with her divorced mother. 'I was strung out on coke, acid—everything I could put into my body," Andrea recalls. Jan suspected drugs, but when she broached the subject, Andrea ran away. Friends found her a sanctuary in a rundown Atlanta neighborhood called Cabbagetown and intro-

[15]Excerpted from "Kids and Crack," *Newsweek*, March 17, 1986.

duced her to free-based cocaine. Andrea called an old school friend, giving her a phone number "in case anything happens to me." The call probably saved her life.

The friend finally betrayed Andrea's secret to Andrea's frantic parents. Two juvenile officers plucked her from a seedy apartment about 4 a.m. and later that day, she was committed to Charter Brook Hospital, a drug-rehabilitation center for youths. "She was screaming and carrying on," Jan says. But shortly after admission, Andrea grew determined to come clean. "I wanted help." she said. "I was about dead."

Andrea's most vivid memory of treatment was being able to see colors again. In the depths of her addiction, she saw everything in shades of black and gray. She stayed in the locked inpatient program for seven months, then attended public school part-time for five months. In January she was released to the third phase of the program—called aftercare—and still attends Narcotics Anonymous meetings every night. She changed schools to avoid her old drug-based friendships and has to fight temptation constantly. "Most everyone in high school uses in some way or other—even if it's just drinking on the weekends," she says. But Andrea is determined to stay off drugs. "Look at what staying clean has done for me. I'm going to go for it." She is earning straight A's. She hopes to attend college after graduation and is living in a far happier household with a new stepfather who has taken an active role in her recovery. "Now, I tell my mother I love her—more than once a day," Andrea says. "It's been a miracle."

Two psychologists, Frederic Suffet and Richard Brotman, draw a number of relevant conclusions about female addicts from their analysis of several studies.[16] When they reviewed the findings on female drug use, Suffet and Brotman found that whether the drug is marijuana or heroin or cocaine, women are usually initiated into the scene by men. One study pointed out that marriage to a male addict is associated with a wife later getting hooked on heroin, while men who marry addicts are more likely to stay clean. In a study of needle sharing, it appeared that most men (68 percent) but few women (29 percent) "hit" themselves. The data imply, say Suffet and Brotman, that it is a man who puts the first needle in a woman's vein.

Most studies of drugs for "recreational and pleasure-oriented use" indicate that males tend to be the regular users, although among the very young and bohemian that sex gap narrows. While females are still more likely than males to spurn illicit drugs, they are the major consumers of "psychotherapeutics" (e.g., barbiturates and other sedatives, tranquilizers, antidepressants, and amphetamines). When persons were asked what they use to cope with life, more men reported they hit the bottle while women said they popped pills. When addicts were asked why they first dabbled in drugs, women were more likely than men to cite "relief of personal disturbance." Suffet and Brotman also found that female addicts held conven-

[16]"Research Report," *Human Behavior* (August 1976): 326–327.

tional values, despite the fact that over 50 percent of them turned to prostitution to support their habits.

Although Suffet and Brotman, based on their research, admit that "social forecasting is a notoriously risky business," they ventured some predictions about the future of female drug use. Since "recreational" drugs are linked with liberated lifestyles, more and more females will use drugs in the future. According to these researchers, "as women take their rightful place in the work world, they will be subject to the same pressures men experience. They may continue to pop pills or they may turn to booze to forget the strains of the office."

It is apparent from various statistics, the foregoing analysis, and the cases cited that women, especially minor teenage girls, are increasingly becoming serious substance abusers. This creates a special problem related to female pregnancies, and future generation.

A especially serious and significant problem for women is related to transmitting their substance-abuse problem to their child at birth. There is increasing research evidence that a substance-abusing pregnant mother has a drug-induced physical impact on her child at birth.

A prototypical case of the addicted mother is Mary. She was a 12-year-old girl on her way to becoming a delinquent when a teenage boyfriend shot her up with heroin for the first time. "I liked the way it felt, and I wasn't thinking then about babies. But when she first became pregnant three years later and tried, cold turkey, to kick what had become an addiction to heroin and cocaine, the consequences were devastating. Her severe physiological withdrawal killed the fetus.

After that, Mary gave birth to two children during a period when she used "speed" and cocaine. She was using a considerable amount of cocaine while she carried her first child, a son. The boy was born premature, was brain-damaged, and exhibited the irritability, jitteriness, and slow development that is characteristic of children who are born addicted to cocaine.

When her second child was born, Mary went into premature labor after injecting herself with her drug of choice at the time, crystal methamphetamine (or "speed"). Her daughter nearly died at birth. The infant spent three weeks in intensive care and was then placed by social workers in a foster home.

Mary's case raises a number of questions. When and how should society intervene to protect a substance-exposed baby from its addicted parent? Should a pregnant mother be held legally accountable for not following sound medical advice during pregnancy?

"Eight out of every 1,000 infants born in New York City are born as drug addicts," according to the latest City Health Department estimate. This figure is up from 1.5 per 1,000 in the mid 1960s.

Heroin was at one time the drug that most affected births. In recent years in hospitals around the country, cocaine is the drug that most negatively affects newborn infants. A recent study found that stillborns and fetal deaths occur twice as often among cocaine-exposed babies as among infants exposed to other drugs. Often, physicians say, the placenta tears away from the mother's uterus prematurely, leaving the fetus without a life-support system.

In this same context, alcohol abuse also remains a major danger. Research reveals that about 6,000 children annually are born with fetal alcohol syndrome. This malady is characterized by distinctive facial and body malformations, mental retardation, and inhibited growth. Another 36,000 infants are born each year with more subtle forms of alcohol-related damage.

The response to maternal drug abuse is in disarray in most communities. There is a lack of money and understanding to provide needed prevention, intervention, and rehabilitation programs—from detoxification, counseling, and social work for pregnant drug users to special nursery care and developmental follow-up for drug-affected newborns. The increasing numbers of teenage addicted mothers exacerbates the problem.

The horrendous behavior of adult substance abusers is having a profound influence on the next generation of potential substance abusers. In summary, the following sociocultural factors profoundly influence the substance abuse patterns of juveniles:

1. The direct influence of parents who use drugs with their children.
2. Negative adult-parental role models who implicitly say "do as I say, not as I do."
3. A pill-popping philosophy that erroneously states that human problems can be resolved with psychoactive drugs.
4. And Substance-abusing mothers who directly transmit addictive problems to their child.

All of these factors converge to significantly affect the enormous and widespread substance-abuse attitudes and behavior of children and adolescents in contemporary society.

SUMMARY: BASIC THEMES FOR CLASS DISCUSSION

1. Substance abuse, which includes alcoholism, is a major problem that has been on the rise in the past decade in American society.
2. The substance-abuse problem was formerly an issue mainly in depressed socioeconomic areas. It has recently become a behavioral problem for people of all ages in all positions and occupations in American society.
3. Adolescent substance abuse is a significant problem in its own right. It also, however, has become inextricably bound up with all delinquent behavior. Over 90 percent of delinquents are substance abusers.
4. Defined substance abusers tend to manifest all of the following characteristics: (1) They have an overwhelming need for the drug; (2) they are controlled by the substances they abuse; (3) they usu-

ally practice self-deception and denial about their addiction; (4) they abstain periodically; and (5) they become associated with a substance-abusing subculture, and after a period of time develop an addict self-image.

5. Parents and other adult role models have a profound negative or positive influence on juvenile substance abusers. In extreme cases parents actually use drugs with their children. Drug-addict mothers often give birth to fetally damaged or addicted newborn infants.

6. The society has become infested with the overt and covert advocacy for using drugs for emotional problems. In this context, the use of psychoactive, mind-altering drugs has become an integral part of American culture. Pill popping by adults has a profound affect on the overall substance-abuse practices of juveniles. The false thesis advertised is that all human problems can be resolved through some kind of drug, and this too often deters people from resolving their personal problems without drugs.

7. Female substance abusers have special problems with drugs. Most female substance abusers are at first turned on to drugs by males. Many turn to prostitution to support their habit. Substance-abusing mothers, in addition to their own problems, negatively affect their offspring through transmitting their addiction to their newborn infant, and are likely to be irresponsible mothers in the socialization of their children.

QUESTIONS

9.1. What accounts for the enormous increase in substance abuse in the United States?

9.2. Delineate and discuss the factors that define who is a substance abuser.

9.3. How do parents and other adult role models encourage or facilitate substance abuse in adolescents?

9.4. Delineate the special problems experienced by female substance abusers. How can society ameliorate these problems?

9.5. Discuss the various sociocultural factors that exist in American society that cause adolescents to use harmful substances.

chapter *10*

Basic Substances Abused by Juveniles and Their Social-Psychological Effects

In the following analysis I will examine in detail the basic substances abused by juveniles. Emphasis will be placed on the emotional effects of the psychoactive substance, the context in which the drugs are used, and how substance abuse is related to the overall delinquency problem.

ALCOHOL

The use of alcohol by an adolescent is a "status" delinquent offense in the sense that it is illegal for a juvenile to drink alcohol, and alcohol is probably the substance most abused by teenagers in the United States. Alcoholism has been defined as "a chronic behavioral disorder manifested by repeated drinking of alcoholic beverages in excess of the dietary and social uses of the community and to an extent that interferes with the drinker's health or his social or economic functioning."[1] According to the National Institute on Alcoholic Abuse, in 1986 there were 12 million alcoholics in the United States. Alcoholism is considered the nation's fourth greatest health problem, and since it results in serious economic consequences to the alcoholic and his family, its prevalence contributes substantially to crime and delinquency.

    The National Council on Alcoholism reports that the proportion of high school students who drink more than doubled from 1969 to 1986 and

---

[1]Mark Keller, "Alcoholism: Nature and Extent of the Problem," *Annals of the American Academy of Political and Social Science* 315 (January 1958).

that in the same period the age of the youngest alcoholic dropped from age 14 to 12.

According to Wright and Kitchens, in an earlier study of adolescent alcoholism:

> The drinking patterns of children tend to model those of their parents and the immediate sociocultural milieu. . . . Like father, like son is true in many areas, and as a result boys are more likely to drink than girls. The children of Catholic and Jewish parents are more likely to drink than their Protestant or Mormon peers.[2]

A 1981 nationwide study carried out by the Research Triangle Institute for the National Institute of Drug Abuse resulted in some interesting conclusions about teenage alcoholism. The study found that most American teenagers drink alcoholic beverages and that one-third of the nation's high school students are "problem drinkers." Drinking among girls is increasing. The study showed that, despite laws against minors purchasing alcohol, seven of ten high school students said they could "usually" or "always" obtain it.

Probably because drinking alcoholic beverages is a source of pleasure for about half the population, the person addicted to alcohol is not rejected by society to the same extent as other addicts. There is an increasing tendency to regard alcoholism as a disease that requires hospitalization and treatment. Evidence to support this position is based on physiological and psychological data.

Medical experts maintain that excessive use of alcohol results in such physical complications as malnutrition, cirrhosis of the liver, polyneuritis, and gastrointestinal bleeding. Psychologists and psychiatrists note the compulsive nature and self-destructive characteristics of the alcoholic's drinking patterns. The actions of the alcoholic so closely approximate those of an emotionally sick individual that alcoholism is increasingly viewed as a disease.

Every state has a law against drunken driving, and this is a common way in which juveniles acquire delinquent status. Drunken drivers account for a disproportionate share of automobile accidents and death on the highways.

The use of alcohol affects delinquency in two ways:

1. Directly, in that the use of alcohol by a minor is a "status offense." Also, drunkenness that interferes with others is forbidden in most states. Where state laws do not provide penalties for such behavior, county, municipal, or other local laws usually do.
2. Indirectly, when the excessive use of alcohol contributes to the

[2]Jack Wright and James Kitchens, *Social Problems in America* (Columbus, Ohio: Merrill, 1976), p. 97.

commission of serious delinquent acts. Many delinquents admit that they have committed serious delinquent acts under the influence of alcohol.

In this regard, Grace Barnes concluded, based upon her research that:

> Adolescent alcohol abuse is a complex issue which has been shown in this work to be related to other problem behaviors as well as to other general socialization factors such as parental nurturance. It is clear from this study that heavier drinkers have more specific alcohol-related problems and a greater prevalence of problem drinking in general than do infrequent to moderate users of alcohol. A profile of adolescent problem drinkers emerges from this study. Problem drinkers have a variety of other problem behavior or problems in living. They are characterized as having negative attitudes toward school, receiving poor grades in school, having poor interactions with parents, and placing little value on parental advice in decision making. In addition, there is a strong relationship between heavy drinking and various other deviant behaviors, including staying out later than parents allow, running away from home, skipping school, and using marijuana.[3]

Alcohol is a drug that seems to be back in vogue with youths in the late 1980s, after being put down to some degree during the 1960s. Despite the fact that alcohol remains illegal in most jurisdictions for young people under 18, drinking alcoholic beverages appears to be a growing pattern of accepted behavior in juvenile peer groups. Most youths drink because of the positive immediate effects it has on their personality. Drinking tends to mask feelings of inadequacy, gives some youths a sense of power, provides euphoric feelings, and in some instances is used to overcome inhibitions.

A number of sociologists see adolescent drinking as a form of rebellion. Robert F. Bales reasons that abstinence norms may actually encourage the use of alcohol as a symbol of aggression against authority. He writes:

> The breaking of the taboo becomes an ideal way of expressing dissent and aggression, especially where the original solidarity of the group is weak and aggression is strong. This total prohibition sometimes overshoots the mark and encourages the very thing it is designed to prevent. This situation is frequently found among individual alcoholics whose parents were firm teetotalers and absolutely forbade their sons to drink.[4]

Based on a study of the drinking patterns of 1,410 high school students, C. Norman Alexander, Jr., affirmed Bales's observations:

[3]Grace M. Barnes, "Adolescent Alcohol Abuse and Other Behaviors," *Journal of Youths and Adolescence* 13 (4) (1984): 36.
[4]Robert F. Bales, "Cultural Differences in Rates of Alcoholism," in *Drinking and Intoxication*, ed. Raymond G. McCarthy (New York: Free Press of Glencoe, 1959), pp. 263–267.

It has been shown that the likelihood of drinking and of legitimating the use of alcohol (in opposition to parental expectations) is inversely related to the closeness of the adolescent to an abstinent father. Furthermore, among drinkers who lack peer support for alcohol use, rejection of father is associated with frequent disobedience of parental authority in order to "get even" with them. And, when positive peer influence to drink is lacking, the rejection of parental authority (negative affect and frequent disobedience) is associated with frequent drinking, excessive drinking leading to extreme intoxication, and drinking for psychological rather than social reasons—all of these early drinking patterns being common in histories of problem-drinking, when not due to positive pressures to drink, is a negative response, an expression of rebellion against the paternal authority figure.[5]

Further support for the parent-child-rebellion alcohol thesis, especially in relationship to fathers and sons, is reported by psychiatrists Henri Begleiter, Bernice Joyesc, Bernard Bithari, and Benjamin Kissin. Based on their research they assert:

Genetic factors may be involved in the development of alcoholism. Sons of alcoholic fathers represent a special group at high risk for developing alcoholism even when they are separated from their biological parents soon after birth. Studies of male adoptees indicate that the biological rather than the adoptive parent is predictive of later drinking problems. Further evidence for a genetic predisposition comes from twin studies indicating that the concordance rate for alcohol abuse among identical twins is almost double the rate for fraternal twins; patterns of alcohol consumption are also highly concordant among identical twins. This evidence suggests that a genetic factor may be involved in the presence of natal pathophysiology associated with alcohol abuse.[6]

G. Lawson, J. Peterson, and A. Lawson have identified four parent types associated with the development of alcoholism in children.[7] According to these researchers, alcoholics typically have one or both parents in one or more of the following categories:

1. *The alcoholic parent*: While alcoholic parents encourage development of alcoholism in their offspring in many ways, the most important way is through role modeling. Thus, if the child's parent deals with problems by drinking, so too will the child.
2. *The teetotaler parent*: In general, teetotaler parents provide their children with rigid rules and expectations which are unrealistic and inconsistent with basic human needs. In response, the child of a teetotaler parent may display his or her contempt for such unrea-

[5]C. Norman Alexander, "Alcohol and Adolescent Rebellion," *Social Forces* 45 (June 1967): 548.
[6]Henri Begleiter, Bernice Porjesz, Bernard Bihari, and Benjamin Kissin, "Event-Related Brain Potentials in Boys at Risk for Alcoholism" in *Science* 225 (September 1984): 280. Copyright 1984 by the American Association for the Advancement of Science.
[7]G. Lawson, J. Peterson, and A. Lawson, *Alcoholism and The Family* (New York: Aspen Publishers, 1983).

sonable expectations by abusing alcohol, typically during adolescence or early adulthood.

3. *The overdemanding parent*: The high expectations of overdemanding parents make it impossible for the child to develop a positive self-image. In response, such children may turn to alcohol, drug abuse, or become mentally ill.

4. *The overly protective parent*: As a result of being overly protected, children of these parents have been deprived of opportunities to develop self-confidence or feelings of self-worth or to learn how to deal with life's problems. Thus, such children may respond to problems by drinking.

Another significant aspect of alcohol abuse and delinquency of significance is that it is often a "stepping stone" to the use and abuse of other illegal substances. A study by John W. Welte and Grace Barnes summarizes their findings as follows:

> The "stepping-stone" theory of progression into drug use was examined, based on the alcohol and other drug use of over 27,000 seventh- through eighth-grade students in New York State. The data show that students do not use illicit drugs unless they also use alcohol. White, black and Hispanic students all tend to initiate the use of drugs in the following order—alcohol, marijuana, pill, and "hard" drugs. Among blacks and Hispanics, pills are not as important a transition between marijuana and hard drugs as they are among whites. Cigarettes form an important step between alcohol and marijuana use for younger students, particularly for females. Since alcohol serves as the gateway to all other drug use, prevention approaches that control and limit alcohol use among adolescents may be warranted. . . .

> While a great deal of emphasis on the stepping-stone theory has centered around marijuana use, it is critically important to note that alcohol precedes marijuana in the developmental sequence and that alcohol serves as the gateway to other drug use. Stated simply, use precedes all other drug use. These results tend to justify a jaundiced view of the use of alcohol by adolescents.[8]

MARIJUANA

According to the National Institute for Drug Abuse, there were 22 million marijuana smokers in the United States in 1986. Marijuana is an intoxicant used daily by many adolescents and most delinquents in the United States. "Grass" is plentiful; usually the only questions raised about it concern its strength. It is generally used by juveniles without question, without guilt, and with little self-examination.

Although marijuana remains an illegal drug, because of the increasing acceptance of its usage the laws against its use are now seldom enforced. This situation is reflected in a somewhat absurd but factual statistic re-

---

[8]John W. Welte and Grace M. Barnes "Alcohol: The Gateway to Other Drug Use Among Secondary-School Students," *Journal of Youth and Adolescence* 14 (6) (1985): 228.

ported in a Criminal Justice Data Profile report prepared by the California Youth Authority in 1985. The statistics are that there were fewer juvenile arrests for marijuana use in California in 1985 than in 1975. There is ample evidence that, if anything, marijuana use significantly escalated between 1975 and 1985; however, due to the fact that the attitude of the general public on marijuana use has softened, the police in recent years seldom arrest users. They usually let them go completely or give them a citation that carries a small fine. It portends the possibility that marijuana use may be further decriminalized, and might even become legalized in the 1990s.

There are mixed opinions on the deleterious affects of marijuana on users; however, in recent years it is increasingly perceived as a harmful drug—particularly for juveniles.

One researcher, Constandinos J. Miras, who studied chronic users in Greece, where marijuana is quite strong, defines a chronic user as one who has smoked at least two marijuana cigarettes a day for two years. Dr. Miras alleges that chronic users have "slowed speech, lethargy, and lowered inhibitions." Some become "suddenly violent without any apparent provocation." Dr. Miras's most serious charge is that prolonged marijuana use produces brain damage. His studies with THC (a chemical known as tetrahydrocannabinol, found in all parts of the marijuana plant) have shown that the substance passes through the brain very quickly. Chronic users, according to Dr. Miras, are prone to anemia, eye inflammations, and respiratory infections; and there is also good evidence of abnormal brain-wave readings.[9] It is important to remember that Dr. Miras's research was with the Greek population. There is evidence that the marijuana used in Greece is somewhat different in nature and strength from the type used in the United States and northern Europe, although it should be noted that research carried out in 1987 reveals that marijuana used in the United States has steadily increased in toxicity.

In an interesting discussion of the pharmacologic effects of marijuana, noted pharmacologist Frederick H. Meyer concluded that:

> The effects of marijuana, both operationally and in its mechanism of action, correspond exactly to those of other sedatives and anesthetics, especially alcohol. The apparent distinctiveness of marijuana is due mostly to the use of a route of administration that permits the rapid dvelopment of an effect and to properties of the active components that lead to rapid decrease in the effects. One is driven to the conclusion that the differences between the dominant attitudes and consequent laws toward marijuana and alcohol are unrelated to the pharmacologic effects of the drugs but are due to a conflict between the mores of the dominant and one or more of the subcultures in this country.[10]

Dr. Norman Zinberg carried out an extensive survey of several major areas of concern about marijuana, including its emotional syndrome, possi-

[9]From a lecture by Constandinos J. Miras given at UCLA, March 1966.
[10]Frederick H. Myer, "Pharmacologic Effects of Marijuana," in *The New Social Drug*, ed. David E. Smith (Englewood Cliffs, N.J.: Prentice-Hall, 1972), p. 87.

ble psychosis, brain damage, chromosome damage, marijuana as a stepping stone to heroin, sex impairment, and its general health hazards. On the basis of all the evidence on both sides of the subject, Zinberg summarized his conclusions in this way:

> Obviously there are areas of concern. Drawing any hot substance into the lungs cannot be good for anyone, but we should remember that no marijuana smoker in this country uses as many cigarettes a day as tobacco smokers do. Also, marijuana is an intoxicant; and despite the research showing that someone high on marijuana does better on a driving simulator than someone high on alcohol, driving under the influence of any intoxicant must be considered a real danger. Finally, it is my absolute conviction that adolescents below the age of 18 should not use intoxicants of any kind, whether nicotine, alcohol, or marijuana. The 14-, 15-, or 16-year-old struggling to develop in this complex society needs as clear a head as possible. One argument made some years ago for the legalization of illicit substances was based on the possibility that parents and other authorities could more readily control above-ground use of licit substances than they could control the under ground use of illicit substances. . . .
>
> In the end, after all this work and all these words, I still find myself echoing the remark made by Dr. Daniel S. Freedman of the University of Chicago, after a Drug Abuse Council conference on marijuana. "Nobody can tell you it's harmless. Each person must decide for himself what he wants to do."[11]

In a televised news report on ABC network news, Dr. Robert DuPont, former director of the National Institute on Drug Abuse, stated in 1979, "In all of history, no young people have ever before used marijuana regularly on a large scale. Therefore our youngsters are, in effect, making themselves guinea pigs in a tragic national experiment. Thus far, our research clearly suggests that we will see horrendous results."

There is increasing evidence that Dr. DuPont's general predictive comments are being scientifically confirmed in recent years. A study in 1981 by Dr. Robert Heath of the Tulane University School of Medicine[12] reported that regular marijuana smoking may, in the long run, widen the gaps (synapses) between nerve endings in vital parts of the brain. Dr. Heath administered marijuana smoke and its active ingredient, THC, to rhesus monkeys over a period of six to eight months. At doses that are comparable to those inhaled by a moderate-to-heavy smoker, THC caused structural changes, widening synapses by 35 percent. The most marked effects occurred in the septal region (associated with emotions), the hippocampus (concerned with memory formation), and the amygdala (responsible for certain behavioral functions).

A study that also confirms Dr. DuPont's dire prediction was carried out by the Institute of Medicine of the National Academy of Science in 1980. Their research produced data indicating that persistent marijuana

---

[11]Norman E. Zinberg, "The War Over Marijuana," *Psychology Today* (December 1976): 46.

[12]Robert Heath, "The Effects of Marijuana," *Science Digest* (October 1981): 221.

usage can produce severe health problems. Their research revealed that over 25 million Americans spent some $24 billion in 1980 for the illegal privilege of regularly smoking marijuana. Another 25 million have tried the drug at least once, making it the most widely used illegal substance in the country.

This study determined that the principal active element in marijuana, tetrahydrocannabinol (THC), like alcohol, impairs motor coordination, the ability to follow a moving object, and to detect a flash of light. Since these functions are necessary for safe driving, among other activities, impairment "may suggest a substance risk." The effects may last four to eight hours after the time the user feels a "high," unlike alcohol, which is more quickly metabolized. Marijuana hampers short-term memory, slows learning, and produces distortions of judgment, including reactions of panic and confusion.

There is special concern about marijuana use since much of the heavy use of marijuana "takes place within the school setting." Charles O'Brien, a professor of psychiatry at the University of Pennsylvania School of Medicine and a member of the committee, stated in the report, *"There's no way a student's brain can function normally when he uses marijuana daily. . ."* [My emphasis].

Perspectives on Marijuana Research and Use—1987

Following are my conclusions based on various research, including my own, on marijuana use.

Marijuana for some time in the 1930s and 1940s was perceived as the "killer weed." From about 1950 to 1980 marijuana use became the "hip," "in" drug of choice. It has been used by people of all ages, social statuses, in all occupations, with a general sense that smoking marijuana was a recreational activity, useful as a relaxant or aphrodisiac with minimal deleterious effect. Over the years an old film, *Reefer Madness*, has been seen by many young people as a campy joke.

In recent years, due in part to the increased strength of the marijuana used and the accumulation of research evidence that marijuana has a variety of negative effects on users, the pendulum is swinging back to a perception of marijuana as a clearly serious and destructive drug.

In the 1960s and 1970s most of the marijuana smoked in the United States came from northern Mexico. The potency was relatively low. The crackdown on smuggling drugs from northern Mexico was effective, and more potent marijuana from southern Mexico, Colombia, and Thailand began to flow into the country. A further war on drug smuggling caused an increase in home-grown marijuana production, especially in California. Domestic marijuana growers and some of the foreign suppliers have developed the "art" of growing stronger marijuana.

One long-time researcher in the field, Sidney Cohen of UCLA recently estimated that tetrahydrocannabinol (THC), the active ingredient in marijuana, now comprises about 7 to 14 percent of the content. In contrast, ten years ago the content was from .5 to 2 percent. Researchers who have tested the potency of the marijuana smoked in the United States in recent years estimate that it is now about *ten times* stronger than it was a few short years ago. Dr. Cohen asserts that the current marijuana in use is almost a different drug. Dr. Cohen and other researchers assert that the new stronger marijuana has some of the following deleterious effects:

> THC causes changes in the reproductive systems of test animals.
>
> Marijuana smoking among pregnant women can adversely affect fetal development.
>
> Extensive lung damage has been documented in chronic marijuana smokers.
>
> THC has impaired the immune system in test animals and decreased resistance to infections.
>
> The already critical problem of drunken driving is exacerbated by marijuana smoking.

While some research has been conducted using marijuana with extremely high THC contents, drug clinics are beginning to see these effects. Darryl Inaba, director of the Haight-Ashbury Drug Clinic in San Francisco, noted in 1986 that since the potent California marijuana became prevalent in the early 1980s, he has begun treating patients suffering from "acute anxiety reactions." At first those at the clinic assumed the marijuana was laced with PCP, but it was just high-grade pot. The patients who smoke too much strong marijuana too fast, he said, "require talk-down treatment, just like we treat a bad LSD trip."

"Ten years ago people would have laughed at the idea that marijuana could cause such an adverse reaction or that users would have a difficult time giving up smoking pot." But now, he said, "several patients a month check into the detoxification clinic because they cannot quit smoking this potent pot."

Doctors recently have been reporting a new phenomenon among pregnant women who smoke marijuana. Some are now giving birth to children who have symptoms similar to the fetal alcohol syndrome. The syndrome, previously only associated with pregnant women who were alcoholics, causes a number of abnormalities, such as an unusual facial appearance, deficient fetal growth, reduced central nervous functioning, mental deficiency, and an increased frequency of other major abnormalities.

Studies conducted during the past two years on these issues have also revealed that marijuana use is associated with lower infant birth weight and length and a higher incidence of premature births. In a study in 1986 at Brigham and Women's Hospital in Boston, the children of mothers who smoked marijuana had five types of malformations, including congenital heart disease and spinal problems, at a rate twice as high as a control group.

Although the overall rate of all malformations was only slightly higher in the study—which surveyed about 12,000 women, 1,200 of whom smoked marijuana—the association between marijuana usage and major malformations is "suggestive" and "merits further investigation," the study concluded.

Recent drug testing for marijuana reveals that THC stays in the person's system from three to five weeks. Many researchers and medical experts maintain it is significant that marijuana smokers retain the drug in the system for so long. Cocaine and heroin are water-soluble, quickly metabolized, and usually cannot be detected by urine tests after 48 hours. But marijuana, which is fat-soluble, lodges in the body's fat deposits and can be detected in chronic smokers up to 40 days after use.

Dr. Forest Tenant, director of Community Health Care Projects Inc., a string of Los Angeles-based drug abuse clinics, commented in a lecture: "It's scary to think that any drug is floating around in your system that long. The question is what is it doing? We can only conjecture that the health implications are not good."

Many doctors are concerned about the effect of stronger strains of marijuana on people's reproductive systems. Recent primate research has revealed that THC induces decreases in the female sex hormones, estrogen and progesterone, interfering with ovulation and other hormone-related functions.

Marijuana use is also associated with a reduction of the male sex hormone testosterone. The administration of THC to male mice in one study for as little as five days resulted in a reduction of sperm production and in abnormal sperm forms.

Although some of these changes are reversible when marijuana use is halted, many questions remain about long-term use. These findings have serious implications for adolescents who are still maturing.

According to Dr. Sidney Cohen of UCLA, in one of his lectures, "animal studies have indicated that THC interferes with the immune system. In tests with guinea pigs, the drug was shown to decrease resistance to herpes simplex virus. And other studies have shown that THC appears to inhibit the production of lymphocytes, which are important in the synthesis of antibodies."

On the issue of marijuana's effect on the lungs, Dr. Donald Tashkin, a professor at UCLA Medical School, who has been studying the effects of marijuana smoking since 1972, concludes that chronic marijuana smokers face a greater risk of developing lung cancer than cigarette smokers. In a study of 74 subjects, Tashkin found that "even smoking one joint a day for at least two years causes abnormality of air passages and increases the effort necessary to breathe by 25 percent. One marijuana cigarette is as deleterious as 20 tobacco cigarettes."

Tashkin recently completed another study of about 275 marijuana smokers who have smoked at least two marijuana cigarettes a day for several years.[13] About half of the group also smoked tobacco. He conducted bronchoscope studies, which allowed him to view and biopsy samples of lung tissue.

"The marijuana smokers who didn't smoke cigarettes had extensive lung changes—things you wouldn't expect to see in young individuals. They were the kinds of changes you see only in older, long-term cigarette smokers. Some of the changes could be considered precursors of lung cancer. . . . Every marijuana smoker had some kind of abnormality."

Because marijuana is smoked in a different fashion than cigarettes— marijuana is inhaled deeply and held in the lungs longer—those in the test group had damaged different parts of the throat and lungs. As a result, according to Tashkin, they could run a greater risk of lung cancer and cancer of the larynx than tobacco smokers, even though they smoke much less. Tobacco smoking further exacerbates the problem. Tashkin concluded that "Marijuana smoking now is where cigarette smoking was in the 1940s. With something like smoking, you've got a precancerous smoldering and it takes decades for the cancer to develop."

On the issue of marijuana and death on the highway, a study published last year by the Insurance Institute for Highway Safety conducted autopsies on 440 southern California males who had died in traffic accidents. Thirty-seven percent had recently smoked marijuana and many of them had also consumed alcohol. The men were between the ages of 15 and 34—an age group responsible for more than half of all fatal accidents.

The recent research reports on the negative consequences of marijuana use are not restricted to the United States. Studies reporting on the problem by other countries at the 15th International Institute on The Prevention and Treatment of Drug Dependence in Amsterdam in April 1986, which I attended, revealed similar findings. Notable among the many papers on this subject was one by K. Tunving, J. Risberg, O. Thulin, and S. Warkentin of the University of Lund, Sweden on the "Long-Term Effects of Cannabis Use."

In their paper they reported in a summary: "During recent years an increasing number of young male patients with a heavy abuse of cannabis have been referred to one of the Drug Dependence Units in Stockholm and to the Detoxification Unit at St. Lars Hospital in Lund. . . . A few of the patients are 'pure' cannabis users; they abandon all other psychotropic drugs including alcohol and stick to a very strong hashish. When they come to treatment they seem to have in common a general bluntness of feelings and intellectual functions."

The Socialization Process, Marijuana Use, and Delinquency

All of these recent studies by researchers point to the highly harmful social, physiological, and psychological consequences from smoking marijuana. I

---

[13]News report, *Los Angeles Times*, October 15, 1986.

am in agreement with the dire negative effects of marijuana revealed by the recent research. There are, however, other negative consequences which I found in my own research into marijuana usage as it affects young users. These additional horrendous effects relate to the defective socialization of children, adolescents, and young adults. The harm I perceive is related to two significant aspects of the social development process: (1) the loss of learning basic social and educational data and skills during a significant developmental period of life; and (2) the amotivational syndrome. These factors are interrelated.

The following observations on these two issues and their interrelationships are based on my study of over 500 adolescent marijuana users. All of these young males and females smoked marijuana almost daily for a period of from 18 months to five years. Although many of the youths in this sample also used other drugs like alcohol, cocaine, and LSD, their primary constant drug of choice was marijuana.

Social and Educational Deficits About 90 percent of these marijuana users had educational problems. These took the form of excessive truancy and a dull-ineffectual learning ability. This resulted in missing out in learning educational processing techniques and the subject matter that is acquired by most relatively normal adolescents. This deficit learning is cumulative and results in an increasingly alienated posture towards school and working.

About 90 percent of the sample studied presented a flat, listless personality in their social relationships. They were often alone or in the presence of peers who shared their retreatist posture of low-level social interaction. Basic human interaction in their lives was not only blockaded by their "stoned" condition but made almost impossible by a continuing intrusive diet of loud blasting music or television watching. Their speech patterns were curt and minimal. There were limited or no signs of any intellectual curiosity or concern.

Almost all of these youths had family problems. It was difficult to ascertain, using the "Which came first, the chicken or the egg?" homily, whether family problems caused the marijuana-abuse syndrome or their drugged behavior created a problem between the abuser and his or her parents. In some cases it appeared that abusing or neglectful parents caused the use of marijuana in their adolescents. The adolescents used the drug to cope with or block out the emotional pain that resulted from their pathological and emotionally painful family situation. In some cases in the family's dynamics, the drug abuser was the "identified patient" and smoked marijuana as a self-administered therapeutic sedative. In other family configurations it appeared that the family was reasonably healthy and the use of marijuana by the youth created a rational concern and disruption in the family situation.

Whatever the specific cause, it was my observation in about 90 percent of the cases that the long-term, almost daily, use of marijuana (from one to five years) produced a deficit in learning basic social skills required for effective participation in society. Marijuana abuse interfered with or blockaded the youth from going through the normal developmental phases required for proper socialization. As a consequence, as stated, 90 percent of these youths had deficits in their educational and social abilities.

The Amotivational Syndrome That Results from Marijuana Use The complex of social-psychological problems caused by marijuana use results in what may be termed an "amotivational syndrome." In this regard I am not describing the immediate "listless, withdrawal" effects of marijuana intoxication. The "amotivational syndrome" refers to the long-term personality consequences of the abuse of marijuana.

The "amotivational syndrome" creates a person who: (1) has limited ability to concentrate on any subject for any length of time; (2) does not learn any new data brought to their attention commensurate with their basic intelligence; (3) has difficulty relating to others and carrying on a normal social conversation; (4) has difficulty acquiring employment because of deficits in their attention span and occupational ability; (5) has a high level of apathy and boredom in relationship to subjects that go beyond his immediate life situation (a form of sociopathic egocentrism); and (6) in general has difficulty in relating on a meaningful and intimate level to other people.

The "amotivational syndrome" that results from marijuana use, in more common parlance, refers to an alienated, bored, "vegged-out, and self-centered adolescent. Apart from the fact that the adolescent marijuana abuser is already delinquent due to the buying and use of an illegal substance, long-term abuse renders the user susceptible to other kinds of self-destructive deviance.

Abusers are more prone to lie, cheat, or commit acts of theft to support their habit and get their parents off their back. They are often in relationships with an illegal underworld in the process of acquiring their drug. Both males and females are more prone to participate in irresponsible sexual acts with partners they would not select if not under the influence. They are also less likely to take precautions to avoid unwanted pregnancies. In the context of the contemporary proliferation of sexually transmitted diseases, especially AIDS, unsafe, irresponsible sex can be enormously self-destructive or lead to death. In brief, marijuana abusers are more prone to commit self-destructive acts of delinquency than nonabusers.

It should be noted that there are some marijuana users who acquire good grades in school, relate well to their family, have healthy personalities, are sociable, and enter their adult life phase with no special social deficits. These "invulnerables" are the small exceptions who validate the rule. Most marijuana users, about 90 percent, have family, school, and personal problems, and are victims of self-destructive behavior and the emotionally crippling amotivational syndrome.

HALLUCINOGENICS

The use of hallucinogenics such as LSD, peyote, various "magic mush-rooms," and other hallucinogenic drugs did not begin with the psychedelic revolution, but their usage was accelerated by the "hippie," "countercul-ture," consciousness-raising movement of the 1960s. Among the various hallucinogenics, the use of LSD is widespread, and it remains a drug of choice and popularity for adolescents in the 1980s. We shall concentrate on the use and abuse of LSD, or acid, in the following discussion because its social context of use and its effect is similar to other hallucinogenic drugs.

Although LSD (lysergic acid diethylamide) is much abused, the men-tal distortions produced by the chemical have an emotional impact that often meshes with the user's search for emotional liberation or conscious-ness raising. Despite its misuse for fun and highs, the LSD trip sometimes, under proper circumstances, appears to be a deep and meaningful spiritual experience.

Compared with the opium derivatives, LSD is a very recent discov-ery.[14] The ergot alkaloids are a group of drugs obtained from the fungus ergot, which grows on rye and gives rise to a great number of medically useful compounds, such as ergonovine and ergotamine. These latter com-pounds are used to contract the uterus after childbirth and to treat mi-graine headaches. LSD was first synthesized in 1938 as an intermediate stage leading to the synthesis of ergonovine. Its profound psychological effects were completely unknown at that time.

In 1943, Dr. Albert Hoffman was one of the people involved in the original synthesis of LSD. At the time he was seeking a stimulant using lysergic acid (the base of all the ergot alkaloids) in combination with a chemical similar in structure to nikethamide, a central nervous system stim-ulant. One day, while working with these drugs, Dr. Hoffman began to experience some peculiar psychological effects, which he later described:

> On the afternoon of April 16, 1943, when I was working with these drugs and had ingested some I was seized by a peculiar sensation of vertigo and restless-ness. Objects, as well as the shape of my associates in the laboratory, ap-peared to undergo optical changes. I was unable to concentrate on my work. In a dreamlike state I left for home, where an irresistible urge to lie down overcame me. I drew the curtains and immediately fell into a peculiar state similar to drunkenness, characterized by an exaggerated imagination. With my eyes closed, fantastic pictures of extraordinary plasticity and intensive color seemed to surge toward me. After two hours this state gradually wore off.

When a person ingests an average dose of LSD (150–250 micro-grams), nothing happens for the first 30 or 45 minutes. The first thing the

---

[14]With the permission of David E. Smith and the Journal, the following commentary is derived from his excellent article, "Lysergic Acid Diethylamide: An Historical Perspective," *Journal of Psychedelic Drugs* 1:1 (Summer 1967): 1–5.

individual usually notices is a change in the way he perceives things. The walls and other objects may become a bit wavy or seem to move. Then he might notice that colors are much brighter than usual. As time goes on, colors can seem exquisitely more intense and beautiful than ever before. It is also common to see a halo or rainbow around white lights.

Hallucinations, or false sensory perceptions without any basis in external reality, are rather rare with LSD. More common are what may be called pseudohallucinations. The individual may see something out of the ordinary, but at the same time he usually knows his perception has no basis in external reality; if he sees dancing geometric forms or brilliantly colored pulsating shapes, he realizes that they don't really exist out there.

There is another kind of rather remarkable perceptual change referred to as synesthesia—a translation of one type of sensory experience into another. If the LSD user is listening to music, for example, he can sometimes feel the vibrations of the music surging through his body; or he may see the actual notes moving or colors beating in rhythm with the music.

A third kind of change is in the area of cognitive functioning, or ordinary thinking. When someone is under the influence of LSD there is no loss of awareness. The tripper is fully conscious and usually remembers most of the experience. Thoughts move much more rapidly than usual. One doesn't necessarily think in a logical way or on the basis of causal relationships. Things that are ordinarily thought of as opposites can now exist together in harmony, and in fact become indistinguishable; black and white or good and bad are equal. A person can feel heavy and light at the same time. There is a kind of breakdown of logical thinking; but if the tripper is asked to perform some ordinary task—write his name or take a psychological test—he can usually do it, although he will resent the interruption of his drug-induced experience.

The time sense is frequently affected. Past, present, and future get mixed up. Strange bodily sensations may occur. A tripper's body may seem to lose its solidity and distinctness, and to blend into the universe. Sometimes hands seem to flicker and become disconnected from the body. The LSD user may feel his neck elongate, and experience other Alice-In-Wonderland phenomena.

The effects of LSD are largely psychological and can be divided into acute immediate effects and chronic aftereffects. When a person takes LSD, he may feel that he has lost control of himself—as indeed he may have done. Under this circumstance, some people panic. In their desperation to escape from this powerless state, they sometimes literally run away in blind terror. If they do not run away, they may become excessively fearful and suspicious of the people who are with them. Convinced that their companions are trying to harm them, they lash out at them first.

In other ways, too, people under the influence of LSD often show very poor judgment. More than one person on a trip has jumped out of a window under the impression that he could fly. There have been reports that LSD users have actually walked out of windows or committed suicide by strolling into the ocean, feeling they were "simply part of the universe." Many people have experienced feelings of invincibility and omnipotence, have stepped confidently into the paths of cars and trains, and never stepped anywhere again.

Further adverse effects sometimes occur after the acute effects of the drug have apparently worn off. Some people have had prolonged psychotic reactions to their drugged experience. These psychotic consequences do not appear to be totally irreversible, but in some cases the emotional disorders have lasted for many months, and in a few cases involved long-term hospitalization.

The adverse side effect known as the "flashback" involves a recurrence of the acute effects of the drug many days and sometimes weeks or months after the individual has taken it. This recurrence of symptoms can have a frightening impact. The person may feel he is losing his mind. The flashback phenomenon is relatively rare but seems to occur more frequently to individuals who take the drug regularly.

The "crash" or self-destruct condition that has emerged for many young psychedelic drug users is a personality pattern that defies description. It is hard to know in many cases whether the hallucinogenic drug-induced personality is a traditional psychosis, or a flashback phenomenological consequence of the extended period of drug abuse.

The LSD-induced hallucinogenic experience seems to produce personality reactions that shatter older modes of definition. Some individuals who take LSD as part of a goal of a religious experience or consciousness raising may wind up in a psychotic state in a psychiatric hospital. One case of this type that I studied involved a 16-year-old boy who claimed to have been on a "religious trip." He had taken LSD around 40 times and "smoked pot as a daily religious sacrament." He was taken to a psychiatric hospital by his parents because he claimed he had, and could still, on occasion, talk to God. Shortly after he was admitted, we had the following conversation, which is summarily reported here:

LY: How old are you?

BOY: You obviously want to know my chronological age. In your terms I am 16. However, in *my reality* I have lived for 4,000 years. (Long dialogue about reincarnation and the cosmic view of life.)

LY: Tell me about your family.

BOY: You are obviously referring to my mother, father, and two sisters. However, my real family is in a commune in northern California. That's where my spiritual heart is. (Long dialogue about the Family of Man and Nature).

LY: Do you believe in God?

BOY: I am God. God is in me. When I have had some good acid (LSD) I am tuned into the Universe. I can now tune into God and communicate with him without drugs. I can meditate and reproduce the acid experience. Acid helped get me to this point, but I can achieve this state without drugs now.

Is this young man deeply religious or spiritual? Or is he a psychotic having a flashback experience? These are questions for which there are no simple answers. All of these roles, emotions, and states of being tend to be parallel and overlap.

One of the primary characteristics of most psychoses is a belief in a fantasy world that supersedes the reality felt by the majority of people. Many hallucinogenic drug-induced "psychotics" can balance several worlds adequately. They are not usually blocked from communicating with anyone in terms of the "real" world; and yet many appear to be on their own cosmic trip. The fact that people in this condition can communicate on a simple "everyday" reality level tends to minimize the likelihood that they are clinically psychotic.

The confusion of the usual psychological categories by the impact of psychedelic drugs has produced many problems for standard psychotherapeutic practitioners. The new clients often view the "headshrinker" forced upon them by their parents with mingled feelings of spiritual superiority, condescension, and even pity. They have no self-concept of having a problem or any pathology.

The use of LSD and other hallucinogenics in the 1960s was an integral part of the "hippie" consciousness-raising movement.[15] The powerful drug is still used in the 1980s but more in a context of recreational use.

Another type of drug in the hallucinogenic category is a variety of so-called designer drugs. Many were developed in laboratores to avoid restrictions imposed by the United States Drug Enforcement Administration. Some have dire and dangerous consequences. In this category of hallucinogenic substances MDMA, or "Ecstacy," was placed on the Administration's dangerous drug list in 1986. At this time, these hallucinogenics are not widely used by adolescents.

PCP: "Angel Dust"

A drug that has become a devastating problem in urban areas around the nation is PCP, or "angel dust."[16] PCP is a potent hallucinogenic anesthetic agent. Exhibiting high potency with almost no respiratory depressant effect, it seemed to fulfill the promise of the long-sought "perfect" anesthetic. It is currently dealt on the streets with names like "angel dust," "crystal," "hog," "key-jay," and "rocket fuel." Often, because of its extreme potency, it may be misrepresented as a "consciousness-altering" drug, like cocaine, LSD, mescaline, or psilocybin. It is easy to make in a kitchen lab, and it is

[15]See Lewis Yablonsky, *The Hippie Trip* (N.Y.: Pegasus, 1968).
[16]The following discussion of PCP is derived in part from George Gay, Richard Rappolt, and R. David Farris, "PCP Intoxication," *Clinical Toxology* 14 (4): 509–529. Reprinted by courtesy of Marcel Dekker, Inc.

therefore cheap. One gram of PCP, ranging in purity from 10 to 100 percent, may retail on the street for $60 to 75. For comparison, a dosage of highest grade marijuana might retail for $15, and the same amount of "high-grade" PCP would retail for $3.75. With the price of Hawaiian marijuana (kona gold) currently around $1,000 per pound, PCP's incursion into the marijuana market in socially depressed areas is understandable.

The most favored route among chronic abusers of PCP is that of smoking, usually rolled into a joint of marijuana or tobacco leaves. This and snorting ("horning," "snarfing") permit the user to titrate to some degree his level of intoxication. The onset is rapid, and profoundly incapacitating symptoms occur at relatively light levels of anesthesia. Oral ingestion of PCP is now rare for the sophisticated drug user, although this method may be employed in a suicide attempt.

Even the mildly intoxicated PCP user presents a bizarre clinical picture. One description of a PCP user by an observer in an emergency ward is typical:

> The PCP patient is sometimes "zombielike" but quite often "combative and hostile." . . . An orderly said that a lot of patients come in after they punched out a window or something and that they liked to make animal sounds . . . barking, growling, and gorilla-like snorting. . . . They seem to gain enormous strength, crazy strength. It takes a lot of people to hold them down. . . . You can hit them in the face, break their noses, and that would stop anyone. On PCP it might just agitate them.

Disorientation, hallucination, extreme agitation, loss of motor control, drooling, and vomiting create a frightening emergency room experience for the uninitiated health professional. The mildly intoxicated patient who is still upright will exhibit a slow, awkward, stiff-legged, lurching gait.

PCP has emerged in the public consciousness as the newest "drug threat" to the youth of our nation. Yet the development of effective medical management of PCP overdoses has lagged behind the lurid headline articles, remaining at best piecemeal and inexact, largely empiric, and often lacking in sound sociologic and psychopharmacologic bases.

Drs. Rappolt, Gay, and Farris depict the symptoms of PCP in the following case history:

> Dr. Gay called to see a young person who had smoked a "duster" at a Led Zeppelin rock concert (one of 13 people so seen that day). The patient was a 13-year-old Chicano from the South San Francisco Bay area. She was of slight habitus, and reportedly had just inhaled "only a few tokes." History available indicated that she was not new to this form of recreational drug use.

> The patient arrived by stretcher to a medical field tent. She was comatose, and her posture was a board-stiff extensor rigidity. Her extremities showed a tonic-clonic spasticity, accentuated by stimulus (movement of the stretcher, loud noises). Her eyes were open and staring, nonblinking.

She was moved to a quiet area, and counselors proceeded to gently talk to her and to massage the muscles of her legs, upper back, and arms. At 15 min. her muscle spasms appeared much improved, but she was still unresponsive to voice. . . .

At 30 min. she appeared visibly more relaxed, and responded to voice. Within an additional 15 min. she was sitting up, appeared weak but with voluntary muscular control, and was sipping water and conversing.

One hour after admission she was released to the care of her friends, and walked out unassisted. Several hours later she was seen in the crowd, animated and enjoying the music.[17]

At this time PCP is an attractive drug to inner-urban ghetto dwellers, but a spillover is to be seen in almost every drug-pseudosophisticated social sphere. PCP is, interestingly, a drug that is used without pride. As one user comments: "People who smoke PCP all the time are ashamed, man. You talk to them when they're ashamed. They don't want anyone to know that they're burning up their brains."

Heroin

Heroin, since the early 1940s has been a drug primarily used in the urban ghettos of American cities. The drug has essentially been used by delinquents to escape from the oppressive conditions of poverty and racial discrimination. For these youngsters, heroin provides a horrendous way to blank out a dim future of limited opportunity and little hope. A dramatic portrait of the meaning of heroin to a ghetto youth is almost poetically provided by Piri Thomas, a former addict himself, in his perceptive book on Spanish Harlem:

Heroin does a lot for one—and it's all bad. It becomes your whole life once you allow it to sink its white teeth in your blood stream. . . . Yet there is something about dogie—heroin—it's a super-duper tranquilizer. All your troubles become a bunch of bleary blurred memories when you're in a nod of your own special dimension. Ant it was only when my messed-up system became a screaming want for the next fix did I really know just how short an escape from reality it really brought. The shivering, nose-running, crawling damp, ice-cold skin it produced were just the next worst step of—like my guts were gonna blow up and muscles in my body becoming so tight I could almost hear them snapping.[18]

Heroin abuse is cyclical but appears to be on the rise in the 1980s, along with cocaine and the steady use of marijuana. In the 1970s in the United States there were peaks and valleys in the use of heroin. Between

---

[17]Ibid., p. 528.
[18]Piri Thomas, *Down These Mean Streets* (New York: Knopf, 1967), pp. 200–201. © 1967 by Alfred A. Knopf, Inc. Reprinted by permission.

1969 and 1971, a virtual epidemic of heroin abuse hit the United States. Whether through the intevention of drug-treatment centers or more effective law enforcement (including the disruption of the famous French-Corsican Connection), heroin use declined sharply in major U.S. cities in 1972 and 1973. What appeared to be a decisive victory, however, was apparently no more than an extended time out.

Heroin use in the 1980s is again on the rise, judging from the increase in heroin-positive urine samples collected from arrestees and the growing number of people entering addiction programs. According the the U.S. Public Health Service, the recent higher incidence coincides with an upward trend in the purity of street heroin, an increase in heroin overdose deaths and a rise in property crimes. Many middle-class youngsters who were introduced to drugs in the psychedelic scene of the 1960s stayed on to become heroin addicts, and the use of heroin by some persists in the late 1980s. About this trend in heroin use, Dr. George Gay and Ann Gay state:

It is no longer buried in Black and Puerto Rican ghettos; no longer confined to the "ignorant" poor. Heroin is in the suburbs, and White parents are beginning to know the impotent range of fear and despair that Black parents have lived with for decades; the call from school, from the police, from some hospital somewhere, the call that rips you from complacency and tells you the cold, mean, street-corner truth: your kid has been arrested; your kid is a junkie.

Your daughter, the lovely, clear-eyed child who was going to marry a nice attractive, sensible, hard-working young man, who was going to give you grandchildren and comfort your old age—well . . . she ran off with a greasy slob on a motorcycle. When he got tired of fucking her, he split, so now she is turning tricks on the street, hustling for enough bread to cop a balloon [a bag of heroin actually sold in a rubber balloon].[19]

Recent research indicates that heroin is increasingly more widely used by members of the middle class as an arch tranquilizer for their problems. Although it remains a drug of choice among poor people in the depressed socioeconomic areas of large cities, more and more affluent people are using the drug. The more widespread heroin addiction problem is delineated in the following article:[20]

To exploit the boom, dealers use what one drug-treatment specialist calls "sophisticated marketing techniques, like the ones used to sell soap." To help buyers find the potency they can tolerate, for example, dealers are labeling their packages with colored tape (red for a "dynamite high"). Another ploy: starting new users on high-purity heroin at bargain prices, which builds up need quickly;

[19]Anne C. Gay and George R. Gay, "Evolution of a Drug Culture in a Decade of Mendacity," in *"It's So Good, Don't Even Try It Once"—Heroin in Perspective*, eds. David E. Smith and George R. Gay. © 1972. Reprinted by permission of Prentice-Hall, Inc., Englewood Cliffs, N.J.

[20]"Middle-Class Junkies," *Newsweek*, August 10, 1981. Copyright 1981, by Newsweek, Inc. All Rights Reserved. Reprinted by Permission.

then diluting the dose once the customer is hooked, so that he must buy more to meet his needs—at higher prices.

One of the early signs that heroin trade was no longer off limits to middle-class shoppers came in September 1979, when David Kennedy, a son of the late Sen. Robert Kennedy, reported that he had been beaten and robbed in a Harlem hotel that police said was a notorious heroin "shooting gallery." Since then, some dealers have relocated to less dangerous "transitional" neighborhoods. And a few are even providing their own security patrols to ensure safe conduct for their clientele.

When the Asian heroin first appeared, a generation of potential users was seemingly waiting for it, prepared by decades of casual pill-popping and, more recently, cocaine chic. "If you're into recreational drug use," says Frank Mc-Gurk, director of Manhattan's Greenwich House treatment center, "whatever good and new comes along gets tired out." Dr. Robert Millman, an addiction specialist at New York's Payne-Whitney Clinic, agrees that cocaine opened the doors to the harder drug. "The same people who would have run out of the room at the mention of heroin a few years ago are buying it intermittently and using it," Millman observes. "It's become another white powder to them, and they don't have to inject it or cop it on the street. Where you used to go to someone's house and he'd say, 'Do you want some cocaine?' you now hear, 'Would you like some Uptown [cocaine] or Downtown [heroin]?'"

But there may be a more compelling connection between the two drugs. Because cocaine produces a swift, surging high, users often need something to "come down" with, once the initial euphoria wears off. As a result, drug connoiseurs often take cocaine and heroin together—a potent mixture called a "speedball"—or in alternating doses. "When people have been using a stimulant drug like cocaine, they tend to end up with a sedative drug like heroin," says Yale psychiatry professor Herbert Kleber, who runs a New Haven, Conn., drug-treatment program that includes the children of business and political leaders among its patients.

Although some drug counselors insist that heroin addiction is not a novelty among the middle class—it has always cut across socioeconomic lines, they argue—the phenomenon is clearly spreading. One rehabilitation expert, Edward Flowers of Washington's Second Genesis center, is convinced that the drug has become "deeply rooted" in middle-class society. The number of middle-class patients at Second Genesis has doubled in the past three years, Flower says. And while heroin arrests are actually down in many cities, some authorities believe the figures are meaningless. "These are not the sort of people who get arrested," says Rick Tibor of Los Angeles's Do It Now Foundation. "They don't have to steal toasters and TV sets to support their habits."

Indeed, one difference in middle-class addicts may be that they do their stealing at home. One patient at New York's Daytop Village says that to pay for his heroin he was looting his father's business. "Once I got $50 from my grandmother to buy some clothes, and I went out and spent it on heroin," says Kathy of San Francisco. But other than "writing some bad checks to Safeway for a while," she adds, she has never had to steal, "because somebody's always got money." . . .

No one knows why heroin has become so widespread among the middle class.

Answers range from the specific influence of the rock culture to the general breakdown of middle-class values. But some experts believe that many people seem no longer able, or willing, to handle stress without a palliative drug. "They are refusing to accept pain," says Donald Russakoff, a regional director of the Therapeutic Communities of America. "Youngsters are growing up that way. They are being told they don't have to deal with pain in any sense, from headaches to anything that's bothering you. It's hard to say whose fault it is, but it happened." In fact, the use of all drugs continues to rise among all classes of people—from alcohol and over-the-counter potions through prescription drugs like Valium to hard drugs like heroin. Authorities fear that this is more than a problem of individual addiction. They now worry about the graver threat of an addictive society.

Despite the fact that heroin is now used at every level of society, it is most widely used in the ghettos, by the poor. It has become so integrated into city life that it is now packaged, advertised, and sold with identifying brand names.

In a study that took place from 1978 to 1981, Paul Goldstein and co-workers reserached the marketing process developed by New York City vendors.[21] According to the researchers, in recent years the distribution of illicit narcotics in New York City has taken on a new character. Merchandising techniques that would delight a Madison Avenue executive are being used with increasing regularity. One law-enforcement official was quoted as saying, "They're doing everything but advertising on television."

Illicit drugs (chiefly heroin) are being distinctively packaged prior to sale. The labeling of street heroin entails stamping, writing, or pasting a name, symbol, or number, usually in a specific color, on the bag containing the drugs. The bag may then be sealed with colored tape. The colored tape alone may serve as the identifying marking.

According to Goldstein, to properly understand the utilization of heroin labels, it is necessary to be aware of the "copping" or purchasing behavior of heroin users. Heroin users always try to purchase the most powerful heroin that is available. They express little fear of overdose in this regard. If word gets out on the street that somebody has overdosed from a specific dealer's wares, that heroin will be eagerly sought. This fact is expressed in such labels as BLACK DEATH, BLACK OUT, DEATH, DEATH WISH, DOA, KILLER, KISS OF DEATH, NOT RESPONSIBLE, O.D., SUICIDE, and SUPER CLEAR (SOMETIMES COULD BE FATAL). Experienced heroin users may reminisce about great "dope" or great "highs" of the past in a fashion similar to ball players recalling an important home run or poker players recalling a spectacular pot. The positive side of heroin highs is expressed in such labels as A-1, CAN'T GET ENOUGH THAT FUNKY STUFF, DYNAMITE, EVENINGS DELIGHT, FEEL LIKE DYNAMITE, FIRST CLASS, HEAVEN, IT'S NICE, LIBERATION, MAGIC,

[21]Excerpted from Paul Goldstein, "The Marketing of Street Heroin in New York City," *Journal of Drug Issues* (Fall 1983): 46. Used by permission.

MAGIC BAG, 100 PROOF, PEACE, RED HOT, SATISFACTION GUARANTEED, SUPER-STAR, and TOP SHELF.

The actual variability in the quality of heroin currently being sold on the streets is rather problematic. Most informed sources say that, in general, the purity has ranged from two to five percent throughout the late 1970s and early 1980s. This range is considered poor by heroin users, and many older addicts fondly recall the 1950s and early 1960s when the heroin was allegedly much more potent. One addict interviewed by Goldstein stated: "Years ago we used to get a bag and on that bag seven of us used to get straight. On that five dollar bag. Now you have to shoot 3, 4, 5 bags to feel as high. It's a lot of money that you have to get and it may not be worth it. Sometimes it's garbage, and it's hard. . . . People don't appreciate that."

Goldstein notes that most street addicts "trust" their dealers. They usually don't experiment with other dealers. But if word gets out that a particular dealer has "dynamite stuff" they may pursue him. One woman addict described her copping procedure as follows:

> I don't know how the word gets around which is the best, but the word gets out. If you're going up to the bar on 116th and Eighth its "get the red and black tape." Or "today it's the yellow" or whatever, and that's how you get off. When I used to go uptown, I'd usually talk to the people outside the bar, who's got what and what is it. I don't know how the word gets out that morning, but it does.

Seen in this context, heroin users' responses to the question of why heroin bags are labeled seem quite reasonable:

- If you try different kinds of dope, and some are better, you can go back and buy the good stuff.
- There are so many different people selling a dealer's stuff you have to be able to identify it.
- People mark bags to sell their product.
- Say you've got 50 people out there selling narcotics and you don't know who's who. And you hear the name THE JOINT, well, this is the best. And you hear somebody on the street saying RED TAPE. So you say, "Nah, I heard RED TAPE ain't nothing. Let's try THE JOINT. It's supposed to be better."
- Marked bags identify who the dealer is. It gives people an idea of which is the best stuff.
- Sometimes the name or sound of something can turn your head to a particular product.
- If your dope was the best dope, people would always look for your marker.
- If the person liked it, they'd come back and ask for that one. They'd always come back and get that one. That particular one.
- [Dealers] . . . have their own kind of style. I guess for people to know whether its theirs or not.
- So that it will sell. So they can let them know they've got the best thing out there. Any time something new would come out there,

somebody would jump on the new thing. Cause that would be better than something out there from last month.

The social realities confronting heroin purchasers may be summarized as follows: Most have limited capital to expend on heroin. There are a multitude of street dealers to choose from. Getting beat on a herion purchase (i.e., being sold "dummy" bags) or buying inferior quality heroin is an omnipresent risk. The quality of heroin that is commonly available is poor. Heroin users have either experienced or heard reminiscences of the superior dope of yesteryear and may have occasionally encountered highly potent heroin themselves in more recent years.

Heroin is a lethal drug. In 1985, a form of potent heroin known as "black tar" from Mexico resulted in over 224 overdose deaths in Los Angeles County alone. The heroin problem, despite the fact that it remains a widely used drug by people of all ages and socioeconomic strata, has been dwarfed by the enormous increase in cocaine abuse and the social problems caused by the use of this lethal drug.

Cocaine

Cocaine was in its earlier use pattern considered to be the Rolls-Royce of drugs, only used by a select number of affluent people and musicians. Recently it has become a drug abused by people of all ages, in all strata of society. The drug has been snorted in powder form, smoked and inhaled in a "freebase" form, "slammed" (injected intravenously), and smoked in a pipe in the form of "crack" or "rock."

Originally the coca leaf was believed to be a gift to the Incan people from Manco Capac, son of the Sun god, bestowed as a token of esteem and sympathy for their suffering labor. Coca served as a stimulating tonic to those working in the thin mountain air of the Andes. Further, anthropologic documentation indicates that the higly sophisticated surgical procedure of trephination was repeatedly successful in this era, as the operating surgeon allowed coca-drenched saliva to drip from his mouth onto the surgical wound, thus providing adequate (and very real) anesthesia. This permitted the operation to proceed efficiently in relative quiet.

The coca boom began in Europe when, in 1884, a cocaine "kit" was delivered to Dr. Sigmund Freud in Vienna. Ever the visionary experimenter, Freud was shortly using coca in the treatment of various medical and psychologic disorders. Between 1884 and 1887, he wrote five papers extolling coca as a wonder drug. His "coca euphoria" subsided abruptly, however, and he subsequently deleted these laudatory writings from the collected papers of his autobiography when he began to experience the devastating negative side effect of addiction.

When coke entered the drug-using consciousness of middle America, the earlier historical pattern of injection was largely supplanted (in a needle-fearing society) by the inhalation route, in which a "line" of coke was "horned" or snorted. This was often done by self-styled elite users through a Federal Reserve note of high denomination (to denote affluence), or through a red, white, and blue sipping straw. In some cases users bought various expensive instruments sold in boutiques.

A side effect of this nasal method of ingestion of cocaine is septal perforation due to intense and repeated vasoconstriction. Snorters are also prone to infection of the nasal mucosa and upper respiratory tract due to chronic local irritation. Smoking "crack" cocaine, or "freebasing," has introduced a much more expensive habit and a method whereby a much greater quantity of substance is introduced per unit time (being almost equivalent to the rate of intravenous use) with a concomitant increase in euphoria, leading to dysphoria, toxicity, and, in some cases, death.

Prolonged or chronic use of cocaine may lead to an irrational effect not unlike paranoid schizophrenia. Plagued with the dark shadows of increasing nervousness, inability to concentrate, and disturbed sleep patterns, the chronic user is increasingly prone to violence. Because of these paranoia-producing qualities, coupled with the very real heavy legal sanctions involved in the possession of cocaine, the user will seldom be seen in offices or emergency rooms of traditional medical facilities.

A recent case pointing up the ravages of cocaine use is that of John Phillips, the musician, and his daughter, actress Mackenzie Phillips: They recently admitted in the national media that they had both become addicted to cocaine and that it had almost killed them.

Richard Pryor, the comedian, almost died of burns from an explosion while "freebasing" the drug. This method of cocaine use, adopted by many users, is exceedingly dangerous. The purified cocaine base is smoked in a water pipe or sprinkled on a tobacco or marijuana cigarette for a sudden and intense high. The substance reaches the brain within a few seconds. However, the euphoria quickly subsides into a feeling of restlessness, irritability, and depression. The freebase posthigh is so uncomfortable that, to maintain the original high and to avoid crashing (coming down), smokers often continue smoking until they are either exhausted, pass out, or have run out of cocaine.

Smoking cocaine is much more serious than snorting the drug. An enormous craving results from the rapid high-low shifts, and the smoker tends to become compulsive and less able to control the amounts of the drug used. Consequently, dosage and frequency of use tend to increase rapidly, so that cocaine smokers are likely to develop extreme dependency.

Adolescents and Cocaine

From a historical perspective the cocaine problem in the United States has increased enormously. The most significant aspect of the problem may be related to the degree to which "rock" or "crack" cocaine has pervaded the lives of adolescents in all strata of society.

In "Kids and Crack," published by *Newsweek* magazine, the problem is graphically described in its many facets.[22]

The federal government's failed attempts to interdict smuggling from Central and South America has allowed a flood tide of cocaine to reach consumers of all ages in this country: prices are down, purity is up and The Man doesn't care if you're under 21. "There are two trends in cocaine use," says Frank LaVecchia, a former high-school guidance counselor who runs a drug-treatment center in suburban Miami. "Younger and younger and more and more. . . ."

The plain fact is that coke is widely available at low prices—within the financial reach of the young. And the plain fact is that coke is now being sold and used in an especially destructive new form. The new coke goes by many names on the street, but it is usually called "crack" or "rock." It is smoked, not snorted, and the resulting intoxication is far more intense than that of snorted cocaine—much quicker, much more addictive. "Crack is the most addictive drug known to man right now," says Arnold Washton, a psychopharmacologist at Fair Oaks Hospital in Summit, N.J. "It is almost instantaneous addiction, whereas if you snort coke it can take two to five years before addiction sets in. There is no such thing as the 'recreational use' of crack."

Crack is simply a variant on "freebasing," which is the conversion of sniffable cocaine crystals into a smokable "base" form of the drug. Most Americans heard about freebasing for the first time in 1980, when comedian Richard Pryor sustained third-degree burns when he accidentally ignited a container of ether, a flammable solvent then used in the conversion process. But ether is no longer needed to make base cocaine—and the conversion process is so simple it can be performed in any kitchen. Dealers make crack by mixing cocaine with common baking soda and water, creating a paste that is usually at least 75 percent cocaine. The paste hardens and is cut into chips that resemble soap or whitish gravel. A small piece, sometimes called "a quarter rock," produces a 20- to 30-minute high. It is usually smoked in water pipes.

Crack is not widely used in many areas of the country—but that may only be a matter of time. It is already creating social havoc in the ghettos of Los Angeles, New York and other large cities, and it is rapidly spreading into the suburbs on both coasts. It is probably a major reason that cocaine abuse among the young is on the rise, although the available national surveys do not distinguish between cocaine in its usual form and crack. "Right now, we don't know the answer," says Edgar Adams, acting director of epidemiology and statistical analysis at the National Institute on Drug Abuse (NIDA). "Is crack responsible for the increase or is the increase responsible for crack? We do know that cocaine use has gone up among high-school seniors, and we have been hearing about crack for eight months or so. I think it's entirely feasible that as the price has gone down you've had more people able to try it."

Adams' stress on "unit-dose distribution" is a cautious way of saying that crack is a drug dealer's dream. It is easy to prepare, easy to use, easy to hide—and a single dose sells for as little as $10 to $15. "Crack itself is a marketing effort," says Washton. Like fast food, it's a quick-sale product. Because it transforms the occasional cocaine user into an addictive user, it is much more likely to yield

22"Kids and Crack," *Newsweek*, March 17, 1986.

a repeat customer." Though the dealer himself may be an adult, crack is widely peddled by juvenile front men—primarily because teenagers, under the law in most states, normally do not face heavy penalties when arrested. According to NIDA sociologist Michael Backenheimer, crack "is an extremely dangerous precedent because the distribution level now includes the kids. It's a form that is terribly pure and a form that is smoked. In certain cities they have 'crack houses' where it is totally possible to buy a 'rock' for $10. I was even told that an ice-cream truck in one city was actually peddling this stuff. If that's true, it scares the hell out of me."

In New York, eager buyers queue up outside crack houses like movie fans outside a theater—and the lines, according to one drug agent, "are loaded with kids. There are white kids, black kids, Hispanic kids—kids from the ghetto and kids from the suburbs." Austin Muldoon, a New York City police officer, remembers a recent crackhouse bust in upper Manhattan. Muldoon was stationed in an alley while his partners broke through the apartment door. The dealer dumped the evidence—a plastic bag containing several hundred vials of crack—out a window. Muldoon soon found himself mobbed by "a crowd of people, including young kids" begging for free drugs. The mob engulfed him, and Muldoon was forced to run. Breaking tackles and clutching the plastic bag in his arms, he escaped from the alleyway with his dignity—and the evidence— barely intact. It was just another day in the war against cocaine.

"We have lost the cocaine battle," Los Angeles police detective Frank Goldberg says flatly. Goldberg is a juvenile-narcotics officer who works L.A.'s south central black ghetto—an area where rock is epidemic and where the dealers, many of them in their teens, have taken over. Like some other big-city ghettos, south central L.A. is infested with rock houses; also known as crack houses or base houses, they are centers of the new cocaine trade. Typically, a rock house is a rented apartment or bungalow with a reinforced steel door. The dealer sits inside with his drugs, taking money and doling out doses of crack through a slot in the door. The door prevents ripoffs by the customers, and it slows down the cops: by the time a police raiding party breaks in, the dealer can flush his coke stash down the toilet. Some rock houses have a room for customers as well: typically, it contains a mattress, a TV set and a water pipe. In many respects, crack houses are the modern-day equivalent of opium dens—and their clientele includes young people from the suburbs as well as the city and from virtually every level of society.

Crack, with its enormous profits and violent crime, has transformed the ghetto. To a striking degree, the coke boom is a youth phenomenon: in both L.A. and New York, crack houses are protected by armed teenagers. Other teens hawk crack on street corners, and in some cities dealers ply their trade from cars: in Atlanta, where suburban teens have begun driving into the city to make quick curbside purchases, it's known as "stop-and-cop." ("To cop" is junkie slang for buying drugs.) "The size of the cocaine market is beyond description," says Lt. Joe Kunkel of the Houston police. "It's everywhere. You could stand on any street corner in town and say, 'I want a toot' and three people will try to sell it to you." And in Camden County, N.J., where police have sent undercover agents into local high schools, prosecutor Samuel Asbell is convinced that the city's contagion has already spread to suburbia.

Police in Houston and Los Angeles estimate that hundreds of rock houses are operating in their cities at any given time, and the same statement could be made about New York, where Police Commissioner Benjamin Ward has declared crack to be the top-priority drug-enforcement problem of 1986. "They're like fast-food franchises," Kunkel says of Houston's rock houses. "They rent a location, bring in a crew of kids to work it, and if those kids get busted the middleman just gets another crew." For a ghetto teenager, working in a crack house means big money. "When a 16-year-old can sit in a rock house for six or seven hours and earn $300 a day just for taking the chance of getting busted, he sees that as a good tradeoff," says Sgt. Michael Jennings of the Houston P.D. L.A.P.D. detective Steven Havel says the kids "are living a 'Miami Vice' fantasy—heavy gold chains, $200 sweat suits, 500SEC Mercedeses and $160 Porsche sunglasses. Their aspiration is to be a successful supplier with a string of condos."

The side effect is violence—and even hardened street cops are shocked by the viciousness of the cocaine wars now raging in big cities. The dealers are armed heavily—pistols are commonplace and automatic carbines are de rigueur—and their teenage guards carry weapons as well. Rubouts and ripoffs are frequent, and law-abiding neighbors are cowed. Over the past three years, 57 persons have been killed in drug-related violence in Oakland, Calif., and a community leader in south L.A. compared her neighborhood to "Beirut, without the tanks." But that was a year ago: since then, the L.A.P.D. has escalated the cocaine-war arms race by deploying a six-ton truck with a 14-foot battering ram to punch through the rock houses' steel doors. . . .

Cocaine in all its forms is seeping into the nation's schools. An annual survey conducted by the Institute of Social Research at the University of Michigan in 1986 shows the percentage of high-school seniors who have ever tried cocaine has nearly doubled in the past 10 years, from 9 percent to 17.3 percent. The use of all other drugs—marijuana, stimulants, depressants and so on—has leveled off or declined in recent years, although researchers now fear the decline has ended. Overall, marijuana remains the most widely used illicit drug among high-school seniors: 49.6 percent say they have used it within the past year. It is followed by stimulants (15.8 percent) and cocaine (13.1 percent). Predictably, because of the pattern of cocaine distribution from South America, school-age cocaine abuse is higher on the East and West coasts—but it has also increased significantly in all areas of the country.

The reality of school-age drug abuse in any given community cannot, of course, be inferred from national surveys—just as the presence of drugs in a given school does not predict that any individual student will use them. And it is still broadly true that the vast majority of American high-school students will pass through the turmoils of adolescence without succumbing to addiction. But it is also true, according to Lloyd Johnston, program director of the Institute for Social Research, that "there is no other industrialized country in the world that has a comparable proportion of young people involved with illicit drugs." Cocaine abuse by school-age children is growing rapidly.

Cocaine's increasing availability, its glamour and its undeserved reputation as a low-risk high have combined to expand its appeal to teenagers. Over the past 10 years, the Michigan survey has recorded a steady increase in the percentage of high-school students who say cocaine is available to them: the latest figure, for 1985, is 49 percent. At the same time, he says, the survey shows that

> "a great number of high-school seniors see a great risk in being regular mari-
> juana users—but very few see experimenting with cocaine as a great risk."
>
> There are three ways for a teenage user to support a habit, and none of them is
> legal. There is theft, there is prostitution and there is dealing drugs. In one case
> in the San Fernando Valley: a boy drove a $14,000 Toyota pickup and wore a
> beeper to keep in touch with his supplier. He sold $600 worth of rock before
> police made the arrest. . . ."

My research and study of the adolescent cocaine-crack problem reveals that crack is intensely addictive. Recent research on cocaine is changing the definition of addiction itself. According to many researchers, the
traditional emphasis on physiological dependence must be broadened to
include the much subtler psychological compulsion that drives most juveniles back to drugs like cocaine and marijuana again and again. In addition
to the widespread abuse, the habit is difficult to treat, especially with adolescents.

TREATMENT ISSUES IN RESOCIALIZING JUVENILE SUBSTANCE ABUSERS

It is difficult in treatment to convince adolescents that the euphoria of
drugs will be ultimately self-destructive. At the time they are using, the
hedonistic fun-and-games pleasure of the drug far outweighs the pain and
problems they will have to face in the future. In my group treatment work
with adolescent abusers, I include recovering substance-abuse veterans who
were once in the teenagers' position. They can often convey the fact to
adolescents that drug abuse involves deficit emotional spending, and that
eventually they will pay a high price of future pain for their current euphoric lifestyle.

In the later section (especially Chapter 15) on treatment, I will describe and discuss a variety of specific treatment approaches, including
Alcoholics Anonymous, Narcotics Anonymous, Cocaine Anonymous, and
the development of the "therapeutic-community" concept for treating adolescent substance abusers. It is relevant here, however, to delineate a number of issues generally related to juvenile substance abusers that need to be
assessed and resolved if they are to recover from their self-destructive problem. These eight issues, based on my research and treatment experience,
reveal some of the inherent problems in changing the delinquent substance
abuser's self-destructive behavior.

Addict-Alcoholic Self-Concept (I)

"*I am an addict or an alcoholic.*" Even after an addict has entered treatment
and has evidence that he is an "addict" or an "alcoholic," he continually
attempts to deceive himself about this fact. An encounter-group process is
vital in order to constantly remind the potentially self-destructive addicts

about their problem. The delinquents' self-delusion in this area can lead them right back into their former lifestyle.

The "Co-Addict" or "Enabler" Issue (II)

A considerable amount of research has established the fact that a family's sociometry and psychodynamics can reinforce addiction in a youth. A mother's admonition to her addicted teenager, "It's OK for you to drink at home, but don't smoke marijuana or use cocaine," is a simplistic example of the way some co-addicts' family members facilitate the addict-alcoholics' return to their self-destructive poison. In their treatment it often requires extreme language and harshness to communicate to young addicts the way in which their families might reinforce their habit at the time or some time in the future. Juvenile substance-abusers need to understand how their families may subtly push them toward drugs. They need to be eternally vigilant so they can assess when a "loved one" or "friend" is unconsciously facilitating their slide back to drug abuse. In many cases, as described, substance abuse is reinforced or facilitated because the addict's mother or father is a substance abuser.

"Friends" or "Peers" (III)

A teenager in an encounter group I directed remarked: "My best friend offered me some 'crack' yesterday when I was at school, and he knows I'm trying to quit drugs." It takes an extreme amount of energy and discussion in the group to prove to a substance abuser that "No one who uses drugs or offers you drugs is a 'friend.'"

Addict: "But I've known him for ten years."

Group: "He is not a 'friend,' if you want to stop using drugs." Peer pressure is a most significant factor in delinquent substance abuse. It is enormously difficult to extricate a youth from his or her substance-abusing peer group and involve him or her in an antidrug support group.

Projected Despair: A Life Without Drugs or Alcohol (IV)

One of the most difficult issues a young substance abuser must confront is the research-established fact that they can never "use" again. For most addicts or alcoholics, this issue in their life produces an emotional feeling of gloom and despair, "You mean, later on I can't have one drink or smoke one joint without falling back into my habit? That's really depressing." Most young addict-alcoholics who want to stop using continue to harbor a covert self-deceptive idea that some day after they're drug-free X period of time they can successfully "use again or 'party' on a recreational basis." The treatment group has to hammer away at this self-deceptive, self-destructive notion over and over again in an encounter group. The Alcoholics Anonymous concept of staying drug-free "one day at a time" is often a helpful slogan for the recovering person to keep in mind.

Are Drugs "Fun" or Self-destructive? (V)

The fact that drugs are in reality quite pleasurable in the short-run is another issue that requires repetitive group discussion and attack in order to point to the long-term negative self-destructive effects of substance abuse. Many recovering alcoholic-addicts believe on a deep emotional level that giving up drugs will take away their main or *only* source of fun, recreation, and enjoyment. The recovering substance abuser fights this issue in a variety of ways. He or she tends to remember the pleasurable aspects of drug abuse more readily than the long-term negative effects the habit has had on his or her life. The recovering substance abuser needs to be constantly reminded of the real long-term impacts and consequences of his or her drug-use. This requires continuing extremist verbal tactics as well as education.

Slippage-Regression (VI)

Another primary issue for young substance abusers is related to the fact that many slip at some point in their recovery process. This is one situation in the psychodynamics of drug abuse where *verbal punishment deters*, when properly administered in an encounter-group process. Individuals who have regressed or "slipped" should know that if they use a drug, they can expect to be *verbally* brutalized by the indignant group of holier-than-thou addicts who comprise their support group. For the violator, a group attack can prove most humiliating, when the group pours out its righteous indignation at the "offender." The fear of this flood of wrath from their support group often serves as a valid deterrent when temptation appears.

In this context, I recall a youth commenting to his fellow group members, "When I weighed it up against what you guys would do to me when I copped-out in this group—something I would have to do—it wasn't worth it."

Painkiller and/or Social Lubricant (VII)

"Why do I use drugs?" is a topic that is repeatedly discussed by recovering addicts. Two of the most common responses by addict-alcoholics to this question (beyond deeper psychodynamic reasons) include variations on: "It helps kill the pain of my personal problems"; and "It's the only way I feel a sense of belonging in a group." What, of course, is pointed out to the drug abuser is: "It's difficult, but the only way you'll resolve your problems is to encounter them head on, without submerging or complicating them with drugs."

Substance abuse as a psychological painkiller issue is an area where it is valuable to have some awareness of the relationships issue that affects the addict's "pain."

The group's answer to the fact that drugs do provide a short-term "sense of belonging" and assuage feelings of alienation is "that it is necessary for the abuser to learn how to relate and communicate with people drug-free." It is difficult for the recovering addict-alcoholic to learn how to confront day-to-day life situations without drugs as their arch "painkiller" (for depression) or "social lubricant." The addict and the alcoholic, in their using life-situations, had "friends" and social scenes (e.g., the corner, the party, etc.) where their addiction identity was validated and rewarded. They often resist giving up this past identity because of a fear of having to relate drug-free to another set of friends in a drug-free social setting.

The Life-and-Death Factor in Drug Abuse

An allegation often hurled at an addict in an encounter drug-treatment group is: "You are committing suicide with drugs." This forces the youth to assess what Albert Camus has referred to "not as a philosophical question but the *only* question: life or death." This is a critical and often dismal subject for a substance abuser to discuss in a group because many group members are forced to confront the fact that on some level their drug use *is* suicidal behavior.

In an adolescent group I directed, a 15-year-old girl revealed how she immediately went back to drugs when she left the group. She talked about her despair of ever stopping: "I have no self-control." Because of her openness and vulnerability, the group was very supportive. One group member, trying to pull her out of her abject state of depression, asked her to "tell us about some of your positive fantasies." She responded, "I do have one positive fantasy." The group members eagerly awaited her response, hoping that her comment about something positive would cheer her up. They asked, "What's that?" She replied, "My positive fantasy is being dead and free from my depression and pain."

It is obviously difficult for an addict to confront the fact that his or her drug use may constitute an unconscious suicidal tendency. Yet it is a bottom-line issue that must be encountered by all addict-alcoholics. The life-death issue in substance abuse leads to a basic premise about the delinquent abuser: On some level their behavior is related to a self-destructive pattern, which in its extreme form is short- or long-term suicidal behavior.

SUMMARY: BASIC THEMES FOR CLASS DISCUSSION

1. Different substances have different social and emotional impacts on the adolescent substance abuser. In general, drugs like alcohol, LSD, and marijuana are perceived by adolescents as less dangerous than PCP, heroin, or cocaine.

2. *Alcohol*. Most adolescents sporadically drink alcohol without becoming alcoholics. It is generally perceived as a recreational substance used for the purpose of "partying." It is a delinquent status offense and sometimes leads to more serious deviant behavior; and for some alcohol is a stepping stone to more severe substance abuse.

3. *Marijuana*. For many years marijuana use has been considered a relatively harmless form of substance abuse. In recent years in the United States the strength of marijuana has increased enormously. Research reveals that the consequences of this new potent form of marijuana use includes: (1) lung damage; (2) brain damage effects; (3) changes in the reproductive organs of test animals; (4) adverse effects on the fetus of pregnant women; (5) impairment of a user's immune system; (6) impairment of the ability to drive safely; (7) deficits in educational and social skills; and (8) in general, over a long period of abuse an "amotivational syndrome".

4. *Hallucinogenics*. These substances, like LSD, peyote, and other psychedelic drugs were first used extensively in the 1960s for spiritual effects, self-exploration, and consciousness raising. These drugs helped create a generation of individuals who had a casual perception of drug abuse. Many people from the psychedelic generation are now the parents of adolescent substance abusers. In some respects the attitudes and widespread use of psychedelic drugs in the 1960s has produced the devastating substance-abuse problem among adolescents that exists in contemporary society.

5. *PCP*. PCP is an hallucinogenic and anesthetic drug that has caused many delinquent problems. Youths who use this drug often explode into serious violent and combative behavior which becomes self- and other destructive.

6. *Heroin*. Heroin is an arch tranquilizer which has seduced many adolescents, especially those living in depressed socioeconomic areas, into becoming severely addicted. Heroin addicts notoriously require large sums of money to support their habits. As a consequence, a considerable amount of crime and delinquency is acted out to acquire money to support a heroin habit. In recent years many adolescents from the middle and upper classes have become heroin addicts. Another extremely deleterious side effect of heroin addiction is that it involves intravenous injection, which increases the danger of contracting the AIDS virus.

7. *Cocaine*. In its earlier use pattern, cocaine was perceived as a highly pleasurable drug that had limited deleterious effects. It was used by people of wealth and position for fun and recreation. In recent years, especially in the form of "rock cocaine," which is freebased and smoked, it has become extremely harmful and an occasionally lethal drug. In its new forms, it has become a highly commercial drug, and some of the side effects of its distribution system involve increasingly violent behavior. It has become an extremely widespread and harmful form of substance abuse, especially for adolescents.

8. It is difficult to effectively treat delinquent substance abusers for a

variety of reasons. These include: (1) they are reluctant to admit they are addicted; (2) family and "friends" tend to facilitate the adolescent's substance-abuse behavior; and (3) many adolescents feel enormous despair when confronted with the fact that they must *totally*, for life, give up the use of any and all drugs if they are to quit their addiction. The various substances used by adolescents often help them to deal with their psychological pain and in a way facilitate their social interaction. Because of these factors, it is difficult for the adolescent substance abuser to quit his or her habit.

QUESTIONS

10.1. Discuss the *various* substances abused by teenagers in regard to their (1) emotional effects and (2) their impact on delinquent behavior.

10.2. List and discuss the various reasons why it is so difficult to successfully treat adolescent substance abusers.

10.3. Structure a plan which you believe would be effective for preventing adolescent addiction.

10.4. Set up a circle in the classroom. Have each student discuss (1) his or her past or present substance use, (2) why he or she used (or didn't use) drugs; and (3) how this chapter's analysis of substance abuse has influenced his or her future substance use.

four

THE CAUSAL CONTEXT
OF CRIME AND
DELINQUENCY

chapter *11*

Causal Theories
Emphasis on the Individual

A fundamental pursuit of criminology and the study of delinquency is the search for causes. The endeavor to understand the causal context or background of crime and delinquency has historically challenged the best minds of all civilized societies. In examining the variety of causal explanations of crime and delinquency, we must keep in mind several concepts and issues as guides to their scientific validity:

1. A relationship of factors is not necessarily a causal nexus. The fact that a preponderance of criminals and delinquents come from broken homes does not necessarily mean a broken home must cause delinquency and crime.
2. No single theory explains all crime and delinquency. Different patterns of crime and delinquency require different causal explanations. The sexual psychopath, the burglar, and the violent gang youth would not tend to emerge from the same causal context.
3. Primary and secondary causes should not be confused. The lack of social workers and poor school facilities are not primary causes of delinquency; however, a broken home *may* be a primary causal factor.
4. One cannot logically isolate one single cause of crime or delinquency. Causation is a multifactored condition. The relative weight of each factor is difficult to determine.
5. In examining causal explanations based on research with offenders, we have the problem of separating the causal force from the impacts of the administration of justice (arrest, jail, courts, prison).

These factors and others make the issue of causation a complex matter for analysis. The following analysis makes it clear that a search for a theory inclusive enough to explain all criminality would be uproductive.

> A skid-row drunk lying in a gutter is a crime. So is the killing of an unfaithful mate. A Cosa Nostra conspiracy to bribe public officials is crime. So is a strong-arm robbery by a 15-year-old boy. The embezzlement of a corporation's funds by an executive is crime. So is the possession of marijuana cigarettes by a student. These crimes can no more be lumped together for purposes of analysis than can measles and schizophrenia, or lung cancer and a broken ankle. As with disease, so with crime; if causes are to be understood, if risks are to be evaluated, and if preventive or remedial actions are to be taken, each kind must be looked at separately.[1]

Although traditional crime and delinquency, organized crime, white-collar crime, and political crime may have some elements in common, the differences are so great that some theories explaining criminal behavior are likely to be more relevant to one than to another.

In this analysis I have divided what I consider to be significant causal theories into two broad categories:

1. Those theories that attempt to explain the criminal or delinquent behavior of people who are given the status of criminal or delinquent. An assumption basic to all these theories is that the cause or causes of criminality can be attributed to some characteristic or characteristics of the offender or the subculture with which he is identified. Constitutional, psychological, and subcultural deviance theories, grouped into this broad category, will be delineated in this chapter.
2. Those theories that seek to explain criminality or delinquency as a response to some societal attribute or policies. Some of the questions these theories deal with are: Why does a society have a high incidence of crime and delinquency? Why is there a high incidence of a particular type of crime? Why do some subgroups in the society have higher crime or delinquency rates than others? These theories, most of which may be regarded as macrosociological, will be delineated in Chapter 12.

The inclusion of a causal "theory" or concept in this section does not necessarily mean that I agree with the causal viewpoint. It does mean that the concept cited has had a significant influence on thinking about delinquency at some historical period, and that the viewpoint currently has an influence on society's perception of delinquents, the administration of justice, and treatment strategies.

[1]The Challenge of Crime in a Free Society: A Report by the President's Commission on Law Enforcement and the Administration of Justice (Washington, D.C.: U.S. Government Printing Office, 1967), p. 3.

DEMONOLOGY

The demon theory, or some modification of it, has been presented as an explanation of crime and juvenile delinquency for a long period of recorded history. This fundamentalist religious viewpoint posits that people who fail to follow the basic norms of the group are possessed by demons. From this viewpoint, there is little or no distinction between crime and sin, and the offender is regarded as an antagonist to both the group and the gods. The offender's criminal action in this context is caused by evil spirits, who take possession of the person's soul and force him to perform their evil will. During the Middle Ages, when Christianity dominated the life of Western man, the theory of possession by the devil tended to merge with the Christian concept of original sin.

The influence of theories of demonology and "natural depravity" upon the legal codes and the practices of the courts is evidenced by the fact that as late as the nineteenth century, a formal indictment in England accused the criminal of "being prompted and instigated by the devil." In the United States as late as 1862, a state supreme court declared that "to know the right, and still the wrong pursue, proceeds from a perverse will brought about by the seduction of the evil one."[2] Even in contemporary society, people will remark that a delinquent "is full of the devil," or say "I'm going to shake the devil out of you."

In an address to 6,000 people at his weekly public audience in Rome on November 29, 1972, Pope Paul VI said that the devil is dominating "communities and entire societies" through sex, narcotics, and doctrinal errors. His address included the following references to the devil: "We are all under obscure domination. It is by Satan, the prince of this world, the No. 1 enemy." He criticized those who question the existence of the devil, saying: "This obscure and disturbing being does exist."

The concept of demonology is generally believed to be of no value to most criminologists. However, the pronouncements of many clergymen, some judges, and the popularity of a concept of the devil makes it a meaningful aspect of treating delinquents in many communities—even in contemporary twentieth-century society.

THE CLASSICAL SCHOOL OF CRIMINOLOGY

A significant effort to explain crime in a philosophical manner was made by Cesare Beccaria, the founder of what is now known as the classical school of criminology. Beccaria's theory postulated that only conduct dangerous to the state or to other people should be prohibited and that punishment should be no more severe than deemed necessary to deter persons from committing such crimes. The importance of knowing in advance the

---

[2]"Pope Blames Devil For Sex and Drug Evils," *Los Angeles Times*, Dec. 1, 1972.

amount of punishment to be administered led to the adoption of the fixed or "determinate" sentence.

Accepting the Christian doctrine of free will, the classical school postulated that man could choose between good and evil alternatives. The explanation of crime included the notion that man was essentially hedonistic, desiring a maximum of pleasure and the avoidance of pain. A man committed a crime because the pleasure anticipated from the criminal act was greater than the subsequent pain that might be expected.

A major proponent of the classical explanation was Jeremy Bentham. In 1825 he published a book called *An Introduction to the Principles of Morals and Legislation*, in which he proposed a "penal pharmacy" where definitely prescribed punishments were to be applied for specific crimes. The assumption was that men had free will and would decide whether or not it was personally profitable to commit a crime. It was assumed that if the punishment or pain was always more than the pleasure or benefit from a crime, the potential offender would be rational and be deterred from committing the offense.

The classical philosophical and judicial view of crime is still held by many contemporary courts. The counterpoint position to the classical view is determinism. This position asserts almost no free will. It postulates that the socialization process and all the social factors that impinge on an individual determine his personality. In this framework an individual has no free will or individual choice. He is propelled by social forces and other conditions beyond his control. The controversy over the contradictory positions of free will and social determinism is still discussed in contemporary society.[3]

PHYSIOLOGICAL EXPLANATIONS OF CRIMINALITY

The Italian Positivist School

Cesare Lombroso, an Italian medical doctor, on the basis of research with military personnel and inmates of Italian military prisons, developed a theory that challenged Beccaria and the classical school. His chief investigative work was done between 1864 and 1878. Lombroso and his followers became known as "the positive school of criminology," essentially because they attempted to base their conclusions on objective firsthand empirical data.

Lombroso's major early conclusions were that criminal tendencies were hereditary and that "born criminals" were characterized by physical stigmata. To Lombroso the born criminal was an *atavist*, a throwback to an earlier, more primitive species. Lombroso concluded that:

1. Criminals are at birth a distinct type.

[3]The argument was revived in a probing analysis by David Matza. See *Delinquency and Drift* (New York: Wiley, 1966).

2. They can be recognized by certain stigmata (e.g., "long lower jaw, scanty beard, low sensitivity to pain").

3. These stigmata or physical characteristics do not cause crime, but enable identification of criminal types.

4. Only through severe social intervention can born criminals be restrained from criminal behavior.

After his initial studies, Lombroso greatly modified his theories. A central error in his early studies was that he neglected to note that most of the criminals in the Italian army were Sicilians and thus were a distinct physical type. They did not, however, commit more crimes than the general population because of their *physical typology*, as Lombroso alleged, but because they came from a culture that was more criminally oriented. Lombroso and his followers in the Italian school—Ferri, Garofalo, and others—later included more social factors in their analyses of criminality.

Although Lombroso was obviously wrong about his born-criminal thesis, he did make significant contributions to the field of criminology. His research (1) caused a focus on the firsthand study of criminals and moved the field from a philosophical posture of analysis to empirical research; (2) broadened the discussion of crime causation; (3) produced a school of criminology that attracted many distinguished students to the field; and (4) produced a reform of the Beccaria-Bentham classical school.

Enrico Ferri described the impact of the new "positivist school" on the classical school:

The general opinion of classic criminalists and of the people at large is that crime involves a moral guilt, because it is due to the free will of the individual who leaves the path of virtue and chooses the path of crime, and therefore it must be suppressed by meeting it with a proportionate quantity of punishment. This is to this day the current conception of crime. And the illusion of a free human will (the only miraculous factor in the eternal ocean of cause and effect) leads to the assumption that one can choose freely between virtue and vice. How can you still believe in the existence of a free will when modern psychology, armed with all the instruments of positive modern research, denies that there is any free will and demonstrates that every act of a human being is the result of an interaction between the personality and the environment of man?

It has continued in the nineteenth century to look upon crime in the same way that the Middle Ages did: "Whoever commits murder or theft is alone the absolute arbiter to decide whether he wants to commit the crime or not." This remains the foundation of the classic school of criminology. This explains why it could travel on its way more rapidly than the positive school of criminology. And yet, it took half a century from the time of Beccaria before the penal codes showed signs of the reformatory influence of the classic school of criminology. So that it has also taken quite a long time to establish it so well that it became accepted by general consent, as it is today. The positive school of criminology was born in 1878, and although it does not stand for a mere reform of the methods of criminal justice itself, it has already gone quite a distance and made considerable conquests which begin to show in our country. It is a fact that the penal code now in force in this country represents a compromise, so far as the theory of personal responsibility is concerned, between the old theory of free will and the conclusions of the positive school which denies this free will.[4]

Later Studies of Genetics, Physical Types, and Delinquency

In 1901 Dr. Charles B. Goring, an English prison official, tested Lombroso's theory by measuring 3,000 criminals and comparing these measurements with those of 1,000 students at Cambridge University. He found no significant differences in physical types between criminals and noncriminals.[5] Later studies by Hooton and Kretschmer on physical types and crime postulated a degree of support for Lombroso's original thesis.[6] A close appraisal of their research methods, however, tends to make their conclusions suspect.

In the 1940s William Sheldon also concluded that there was a relationship between certain physical characteristics and temperamental characteristics.[7] Sheldon divided human beings into four physical types, based upon body measurements: *endomorphs*, who tend to be fat; *mesomorphs*, who tend to be muscular with large bones and athletic build; *ectomorphs*, who are inclined to be thin and fragile; and *balanced types*, a "combination category," composed of people who showed no marked dominance of any single type.

Each body type, according to Sheldon, was characterized by a distinctive temperament. *Endomorphs* were described as viscerotonic, submissive, and little interested in physical activity or adventure. *Mesomorphs* were described as somatotonic, physically active, self-assertive, and daring. *Ectomorphs* were categorized as cerebrotonic, inhibited, and introverted.

Sheldon attributed the various body types and their characteristics to heredity, maintaining that they were genetically determined. In a study of 200 juvenile delinquents, he found that about 60 percent were mesomorphs. Since most police officers, army officers, football players, and other energetic leaders of our society are also likely to be mesomorphic, this correlation between mesomorphy and delinquency was not considered to be a causal explanation of delinquency.

In a review of Sheldon's work in the *American Sociological Review*, Sutherland virtually demolished his conclusions. Here are some of Sutherland's criticisms:

1. Sheldon defines delinquency in terms of "disappointingness" and not in terms of violation of the law.
2. His method of scoring delinquents is subjective and unreliable. For example,

[4]Enrico Ferri, *Criminal Sociology* (Boston: Little, Brown, 1901).
[5]Charles Goring, *The English Convict* (London: His Majesty's Stationery Office, 1913).
[6]Earnest A. Hooton, *Crime and the Man* (Cambridge, Mass.: Harvard University Press, 1939); Ernest Kretschmer, *Physique and Character* (London: Kegan Paul, Trench, Trubner, 1936).
[7]William H. Sheldon, *The Varieties of Delinquent Youth* (New York: Harper, 1949).

he defines "first-order psychopathy" in terms of subjectively determined interference with adjustment, apparently the same as "disappointingness."

3. The varieties of delinquent youth he presents are overlapping and inconsistent. They do not differ significantly from each other in their somatotypes or psychiatric indices.

4. The relationship of the psychiatric indices to social fitness is not made clear.[8]

Sheldon and Eleanor Glueck revived interest in William Sheldon's somatotypes in the 1950s. They found that 60.1 percent of the delinquents they studied were mesomorphs, as against 30.7 percent of the nondelinquents. They were cautious in their interpretation of these findings, concluding that "there is no 'delinquent personality' in the sense of a constant and stable combination of physique, character, and temperament which determines that a certain individual would become delinquent."[9]

Although no causal relationship has been established between any physical characteristic and criminal behavior, there is some evidence that the muscular mesomorphic child is more likely to become delinquent than children with other body types, *all other things being equal.* The mesomorph, who is by definition muscular, active, and relatively uninhibited, may be more likely than others to take action defined as delinquent by society when confronted with favorable social environment. Research exploring the possibility of using body types as a predictive device has been going on for many years. The conclusions so far have been inconclusive, if not outright specious.

A recent book by James Q. Wilson and Richard J. Hernstein revives the assessment of biological and genetic factors in looking at crime and delinquency.[10] In their book, *Crime and Human Nature,* they assert that to understand street crime we must redirect attention away from an excessive concern with social and economic factors and focus instead on differences among individual people. These often reflect biological and genetic differences. Different types of family upbringing also play a role. They state, "One way or another bad families produce bad children. The interplay of genes and environment creates, in some people but not in others, the kind of personality likely to commit crime."

In another assessment of the biological connection to crime, Sarnoff A. Mednick and William F. Gabriella report in an article in *Science*:[11] "We conclude that some factor transmitted by criminal parents increases the likelihood that their [biological] children will engage in criminal behavior.

[8]Edwin H. Sutherland, "Critique of Sheldon's *Varieties of Delinquent Youth*," *American Sociological Review* 16 (February 1951): 10–13.

[9]Sheldon Glueck and Eleanor Glueck, *Unraveling Juvenile Delinquency* (New York: Commonwealth Fund, 1950), p. 221.

[10]James Q. Wilson and Richard J. Hernstein, *Crime and Human Nature* (New York: Simon and Schuster, 1984).

[11]Sarnoff A. Mednick and William F. Gabriella, "Genetic Influences in Criminal Convictions: Evidence from a Adoption Cohort," *Science* 224, 25 (May 1984): 891–894. Copyright 1984 by the American Association for the Advancement of Science.

This claim holds especially for chronic criminality. The findings imply that biological predispositions are involved on the etiology of at least some criminal behavior."

Chromosomes and Criminality

Studies of chromosomal deviation have attempted to show a correlation between criminal behavior and males possessing an extra male chromosome, called the Y gonosome; that is, they are XYY, rather than the normal XY. In spite of the varied and conflicting results of the various studies, there are some suggestive consistencies of behavior and traits that appear to be evolved from the research. In general, they include the fact that, among criminals, the chance of possessing an extra Y gonosome is up to 60 times greater than it is among the general population; also, a higher frequency of aggressive and disturbed behavior and higher rates of violent crime were found among those having an extra Y gonosome.

One theory holds that the criminal act itself is biologically and hereditarily determined; that is, there is a direct relationship between the biological structure and the behavior that is supposedly determined by it. A second theory is that what is genetically transmitted is a general tendency to maladjustment and that, given certain environmental pressures, this disposition leads to criminal behavior. Inherent in this theory is the supposition that crime is just one of many possible outcomes of a defective physiological structure.

If criminality is inherited, then noncriminality or conforming behavior must also be inherited. If we accept the premise that the factors determining criminal behavior already exist at birth, then it follows that the influence of environment is not very important. If, however, criminal behavior is frequently found among persons lacking genetic defects, or if biological defects are found among a great many noncriminals, then the genetic theory of crime becomes questionable. Before we can reach any conclusions on the relationship between chromosomes and criminality, we would need to know what proportion of criminals do not have genetic or biological defects. If the number is large, the theory is defective.[12]

In the journal *Science* in 1976, Herman Witkin (a research psychologist with the Educational Testing Service) and his colleagues commented on earlier studies: First, the search for XYY men has often been conducted in selected groups presumed to be likely to contain them, such as institutionalized men and tall men. Second, a number of reports now in the literature are based on observations of a single case or just a few cases. Third, many studies of XYYs have not included control XYs; in those that did, comparisons were often made without knowledge of the genotype of the individuals being evaluated. The control groups used have varied in

---

[12]Menachim Amir and Yitzcham Berman, "Chromosomal Deviation and Crime," *Federal Probation* 34 (June 1970): 55–62. See also Robert W. Stock, "The XXY and the Criminal," *The New York Times Magazine*, October 20, 1968, p. 30.

nature, and comparison of results from different studies has therefore been difficult. There has been a dearth of psychological, somatic, and social data obtained for the same individual XYY men. Finally, there do not yet exist adequate prevalence data for the XYY genotype in the general adult population with which the XYY yield of any particular study may be compared.[13]

To avoid these problems, Witkin and his colleagues chose to gather data in Denmark by using social records that were available for a sample of the general population. They then compared normal males with males having different patterns of chromosomal abnormalities and attempted to identify the possible intervening factors that might account for any predominance of abnormalities among inmates or among men with criminal records. Out of a sample of 4,139 men, they found 12 XYY cases, sixteen XXY cases, and 13 XY cases that had other chromosomal anomalies. Of the 12 XYY cases, five (42 percent) were found to have been convicted of one or more offenses, as compared to three of the 16 XXY cases (19 percent) and nine of the 13 abnormal XY cases. There did appear to be an inordinately high probability that XYY men would have criminal records. However, there were 389 men with records, and only five of them were XYY cases. The abnormality is so rare that it cannot account for very much criminal activity.

Further analysis by Witkin et al. yielded no evidence that XYY males are more prone to violent crimes than XY males. The elevated crime rate reflected property crimes, not aggressive acts against persons. The XYY males were found to have lower scores on intelligence tests and to be taller than XY males. However, even with these differences in intelligence and height taken into account, there was still a difference between XYY and XY cases. The researchers suggested that chromosomal anomalies may have pervasive developmental consequences, but there is no evidence that aggression against persons is one of them.

MODERN POSITIVISM: FREE WILL AND DETERMINISM

The classical and the positivistic conceptions of crime and delinquency continue as central subjects for discussion. Each view projects its own image of people and their motivation. The classical school of criminology (Bentham, Beccaria) sketched people as essentially having free will, implying that a person who chooses to violate the law can be restrained from this impulse by a proper measure of punishment. In counterpoint, the positivists believed in what is today more often called determinism. They viewed the criminal as something of a billiard ball, propelled by conditions outside his control.

As early as 1906 Ferri stated these opposing views most succinctly:

---

[13]Herman Witkin, "Criminality in XYY and XXY Men," *Science* 193 (August 1976): 547–555.

"Whoever commits murder or theft is alone the absolute arbiter to decide whether he wants to commit the crime or not." This remains the foundation of the classic school of criminology. . . . The positive school of criminology maintains, on the contrary, that it is not the criminal who wills; in order to be a criminal it is rather necessary that the individual should find himself permanently or transitorily in such personal, physical, and moral conditions, and live in such an environment, which become for him a chain of cause and effect, externally and internally, that disposes him toward crime. This is our conclusion, which I anticipate, and it constitutes the vastly different and opposite method, which the positive school of criminology employs as compared to the leading principle of the classic school of criminal science.[14]

Matza, after closely reviewing each of these conceptions in depth, presents a more middle-of-the-road viewpoint. He first points to the danger of being overdeterministic. Using the juvenile court concept as an example of overdeterminism, he comments:

To philosophically attribute fault to underlying conditions, but to actually hold the immediate agent responsible is an invitation to distrust. And to refer to penal sanction as protective care is to compound the distrust. Thus, by its insistence on a philosophy of child welfare and its addiction to word magic, the juvenile court systematically interferes with its alleged program. By its own hypocrisy perceived and real, it prepares the way for the delinquent's withdrawal of legitimacy. Without the grant of legitimacy, the court's lofty aspirations cannot be effectively pursued.

Thus, the ideology of child welfare supports the delinquent's viewpoint in two ways. It confirms his conception of irresponsibility, and it feeds his sense of injustice. Both support the processes by which the moral bind of law is neutralized. Both facilitate the drift into delinquency.[15]

Matza believes that contemporary theorists in the field of criminology have gone too far in the direction of positivism. Although he does not attempt fully to revive the classical viewpoint, he does attempt to incorporate "some modified versions of the classical viewpoint into the current framework of positive criminology." Matza posits what he refers to as "soft determinism" in discussing his basic concept of delinquency and drift. He contends that man is neither wholly free nor wholly constrained, but somewhere midway between the two. The delinquent is never totally a law-breaker. He *drifts* into delinquency.

The image of the delinquent I wish to convey is one of drift; an actor neither compelled nor committed to deeds nor freely choosing them; neither different in any simple or fundamental sense from the law abiding, nor the same; conforming to certain traditions in American life while partially unreceptive to other more conventional traditions; and finally, an actor whose motivational system may be

[14]Enrico Ferri, *The Positive School of Criminology* (Chicago: Kerr, 1906), p. 23.
[15]Matza, *Delinquency and Drift*, pp. 97–98.

explored along lines explicitly commended by classical criminology—his peculiar relation to legal institutions. . . . The delinquent transiently exists in a limbo between convention and crime, responding in turn to the demands of each, flirting now with one, now the other, but postponing commitment, evading decision. Thus, he drifts between criminal and conventional action.[16]

One argument against this theory of drift preceded Matza. Ferri stated back in 1906:

It is evident that the idea of accident, applied to physical nature, is unscientific. Every physical phenomenon is the necessary effect of the causes that determined it beforehand. If those causes are known to us, we have the conviction that the phenomenon is necessary, is fate, and, if we do not know them, we think it is accidental. The same is true of human phenomena. But since we do not know the internal and external causes in the majority of cases, we pretend that they are free phenomena, that is to say, that they are not determined necessarily by their causes.[17]

Matza believes that most delinquents are drifters is stated as follows: "The delinquent as drifter more approximates the substantial majority of juvenile delinquents who do not become adult criminals than the minority who do." To Matza, delinquency is seldom a youth's total career. Most delinquents, he believes, participate in juvenile delinquency as a part-time enterprise.

Sykes and Matza describe five ways in which delinquents deny that their behavior is bad. These techniques tend to neutralize their responsibility for delinquent activity:

1. *The denial of personal responsibility.* Here the delinquent uses a kind of social word play. "Of course I'm delinquent. Who wouldn't be, coming from my background?" He then can neutralize personal responsibility by detailing the background of a broken home, lack of love, and a host of other factors.
2. *The denial of harm to anyone.* In this pattern of neutralization, stealing a car is only borrowing it; truancy harms no one; and drug use "doesn't hurt anyone but me."
3. *The delinquent denies that the person injured or wronged is really a victim.* "The (assaulted) teacher was unfair"; the victim of a mugging "was only a queer"; and the gang youth assaulted was "out to get me."
4. *The delinquent condemns the condemners.* "Society is much more corrupt than I am."
5. *Delinquent group or gang loyalties supersede loyalty to the norms of an impersonal society.* "When I stabbed him I was only defending my turf." The youth places his gang or delinquent group and its values (even if delinquent) above the law, the school, and society.[18]

---

[16]Ibid., p. 28.

[17]Ferri, *Positive School of Criminology*, pp. 35–36.

[18]Gresham Sykes and David Matza, "Techniques of Neutralization: A Theory of Delinquency," *American Sociological Review* 22 (December 1957): 665–666.

All these factors tend to neutralize the delinquent's belief that he is delinquent or has done anything wrong. These rationalizations enable him to deny any real personal responsibility for delinquent behavior.

In any case, according to Matza, most delinquents are really not delinquent, but are acting out the "subterranean values" of the society. Who can deny that the mass public admires and respects a smart operator, even if his actions are illegal? The delinquent may in his own self-concept merely be acting out the norms he sees beneath the surface of the law. In some respects, the delinquent may see himself as a lower-class white-collar criminal. He feels there is really nothing wrong with his behavior. In fact, he feels he is being unfairly treated by being punished for what society does not really condemn.

By adapting concepts found in the large society, the delinquent rationally negates his own offense. Since the law supports self-defense as a justification for violent action, it is easy for the delinquent to justify in his own mind the use of violence to defend his gang turf. The delinquent also uses the concept of insanity ("I went crazy") to negate his offense, and he widens the extenuating circumstance of "accident" to include recklessness. The sense of injustice found in the delinquent subculture is thus reinforced by the vagaries of many societal laws and norms. Many of society's irrational prescriptions weaken prohibitions of certain actions by the juvenile and facilitate the drift to juvenile delinquency and, in time, into a criminal career.

THE PSYCHOANALYTIC VIEW OF CRIME AND DELINQUENCY

Psychoanalytic theory, as originally formulated by Sigmund Freud, has been offered as an explanation of delinquent and criminal behavior. According to psychoanalytic theory, the individual begins life with two basic instincts or urges: Eros, the life or love instinct, and Thanatos, the death or hate instinct. The personality of the normal adult is composed of the id, the ego, and the superego. At birth there is only the id, the reservoir of both the life and the death instincts. The id seeks immediate gratification and is concerned with striving after pleasure. It is governed by the pleasure principle, seeking the maximization of pleasure and the avoidance of pain. It has no idea of time or reality.

In the first few years of life the individual develops an ego and a superego. The *ego* is the part of the self in closest contact with the social reality. It directs behavior toward the satisfaction of urges consistent with a knowledge of social and physical reality. In living out the *reality principle* through the ego, the individual may postpone immediate gratification; he does not abandon it.

Morality, remorse, and feelings of guilt arise with the development of the *superego*, the chief force in the socialization of the individual. The superego is sociologically or culturally conditioned. It includes the development of a *conscience* and an *ego ideal*. The ego ideal represents what we *should* do and the conscience gives us guilt feelings when we do "wrong."

The following oversimplified model serves to illustrate the operation of the Freudian id, ego, and superego: A child sees cookies on the table. His id demands immediate gratification, and he is governed by the pleasure principle. He grabs a cookie. His mother slaps his hand and takes the cookie away from him. When he has developed an ego, he waits for his mother to leave before taking a cookie, or he asks for one and coaxes if it is denied him. In either case he has applied the reality principle and postponed gratification. When he has developed a superego, he will not take the cookie if it is defined as wrong for him to do so. If he does take the cookie without being observed, he feels guilty.

Psychoanalytic theory tends to attribute delinquency or criminality to any of the following causes:

1. Inability to control criminal drives (id) because of a deficiency in ego or superego development. Because of faulty development, the delinquent or criminal is believed to possess little capacity for repressing instinctual (criminal) impulses. The individual who is dominated by his id is consequently criminal.
2. Antisocial character formation resulting from a disturbed ego development. This occurs during the first three years of life.
3. An overdeveloped superego, which makes no provision for the satisfaction of the demands of the id. Offenders of this type are considered neurotic.

Freudians, neo-Freudians, and other psychoanalytic schools attribute criminality to inner conflicts, emotional problems, unconscious feelings of insecurity, inadequacy, and inferiority. They regard criminal behavior and delinquencies as symptoms of underlying emotional problems. Psychoanalytic theory does not explain the criminal acts of the "normal" criminal, who simply learns to be criminal from differential association with criminal teachers. Psychoanalysis offers an explanation for the impulsive behavior of the psychotic, the neurotic, and the psychopath. This behavior, in psychoanalytic terms, would generally be id-dominated behavior evidencing ego deficiency, the inability to control criminal impulses.[19]

For criminologists the most important assertion of psychoanalytic theory is that to understand criminality we must understand unconscious motivation. In this context everyone is basically, in his id, a criminal. Freud further asserts that if this is true, we must condemn in others the criminal thrust that lurks in all of us. This accounts for the psychoanalytic assumption that *the public demands severe punishment for certain crimes because the*

[19]For a detailed presentation of the psychoanalytic explanation of criminality and delinquency, see Kate Friedlander, *The Psychoanalytic Approach to Juvenile Delinquency* (New York: International Universities Press, 1947), and Walter Bromberg, *Crime and the Mind* (Philadelphia: Lippincott, 1948).

offender has acted as the rest of us would like to act ourselves. Another philosopher put it this way: "We stamp out in others the evil we dimly perceive in ourselves."

The classical Freudian view of the interplay of crime and punishment has been most comprehensively and cogently presented in Alexander and Staub's *The Criminal, the Judge, and the Public.* Several of its central themes are worth pondering for the light they cast on past and present attitudes toward offenders:

1. *Psychodynamically, all people are born criminals.* The human being enters the world as a criminal, i.e., socially not adjusted. During the first years of his life he preserves his criminality to the fullest degree, concerned only with achieving pleasure and avoiding pain. Between the ages of four and six the development of the criminal begins to differentiate itself from that of the normal. During this period (the latency period), which ends at puberty, the future normal individual partially succeeds in repressing his genuine criminal instinctive drives and stops their actual expression. He converts or transforms these criminal libidinal drives into socially acceptable forms. The future criminal fails to accomplish this adjustment.

   The criminal carries out in his actions his natural unbridled instinctual drives. He acts as the child would act if it only could. The repressed and therefore unconscious criminality of the normal man finds a few socially harmless outlets, such as dream and fantasy life, neurotic symptoms, and also some transitional forms of behavior that are less harmless, like dueling, boxing, bullfights, and occasionally the free expression of criminality in war. According to Alexander and Staub, "The universal criminality of the man of today demands violent, purely physical outlets."[20]

2. *The Oedipus complex is a fundamental psychodynamic fact that produces criminality unless it is successfully resolved.* The Freudian doctrine of the Oedipus complex asserts that all boys have a natural hostility toward their fathers and a love for their mothers that encompasses sexual desire. The guilt and anxiety aroused by these feelings must be resolved, according to Freud, if the youth is to grow up to become a psychologically healthy man. Alexander and Staub are extreme and dogmatic about the "fact" of the Oedipal condition:

   It took two decades of psychoanalytical research to prove conclusively that the Oedipus complex presented the chief unconscious psychological content of neurotic symptoms. It was found that all those psychological undercurrents which the adult person usually represses are affectively connected with the Oedipus situation of early childhood; these psychic currents, after they are repressed, continue in the unconscious, tied as with a navel cord to the infantile Oedipus complex.[21]

---

[20]Franz Alexander and Hugo Staub, *The Criminal, the Judge, and the Public* (Glencoe, Ill.: Free Press, 1956), p. 52.
[21]Ibid., p. 73.

A major concomitant of the Oedipus complex is the assumption that a youth who represses his hostility toward his father will displace his aggression elsewhere. For the Freudian psychoanalyst, this accounts for much of the violent behavior (including homicide) of delinquent youths. The Freudian asserts that when the Oedipal situation is resolved through psychoanalysis, the analysand, now aware of the real object of his aggression, can curb his hostility.

3. *Uncovering unconscious motives is the fundamental task of criminology.* Alexander and Staub state:

> Theoretically speaking, every human being's responsibility is limited, because no human act is performed under the full control of the conscious ego. We must, therefore, always evaluate the quantitative distribution of conscious and unconscious motivations of every given act. Only such evaluation will provide us with definite criteria for purposes of diagnosis, or of sentencing or of any other measure which we might consider necessary to take in regard to a given act. The task of the judge of the future will be the establishment of such a psychological diagnosis; the measures resulting from such a diagnosis will, therefore, be founded on the psychological understanding of the criminal.[22]

Among those who take the extreme psychoanalytic view, certain criminal patterns are symbolic reflections of unconscious motivation. For example, the use of a gun by an armed robber is considered a reaction formation to a sense of male impotence. The gun is considered a symbol of male potency, and without attempting to be facetious, some extremists of the psychoanalytic school contend that when the armed robber says, "Stick 'em up," he is symbolically trying to adjust his unconscious sense of impotence. Similarly, the crime of breaking-entering and theft is considered to be displaced unconscious rape. These are the things the courts must understand, according to Alexander and Staub, before taking any "measures" against offenders.

4. *The first rebellious act or crime is committed in early childhood and is an important determinant of one's sense of justice.* "The first crime which all humans, without exception, sooner or later commit is the violation of the prescription for cleanliness. Under the rule of this penal code of the nursery, man for the first time becomes acquainted with the punishment which the world metes out to the individual transgressors."[23]

Therefore, according to Alexander and Staub, Ferenczi is right when he speaks of "sphincter morality" as the beginning and the foundation of adult human morality.[24] A refractory criminal who persists in his spiteful rejection of social demands is like "a

---

[22]Ibid., p. 85.
[23]Ibid., p. 55.
[24]Sandor Ferenczi, "Psychoanalysis of Sexual Habits," in *Sex in Psychoanalysis*, trans. Ernest Jones (New York: Basic Books, 1950).

baby sitting on its little chamber pot persistently rejecting any demands coming from the outside; it sits in this sovereign position and feels superior to the grown-ups."[25]

Alexander and Staub allege that the moment when the child begins to impose inhibitions on the demands of his own sphincter, he makes the first decisive step toward adjustment to the outside world, because at that moment he creates an inhibitory agency within his own personality. In brief, the child begins to develop internal reference points for conduct and a sense of justice or injustice from his toilet training. The justice (or lack of it) of this training becomes a prototype of future restrictions on the child's instinctual life, and a disturbance during this phase of development may naturally serve as a cause of future disturbance in one's social adjustment.

Freudian psychoanalytic theory remains a prevalent construct among social workers and psychiatrists treating offenders, but criminologists today tend to a greater inclusion of social factors and the societal framework in their search for an understanding of the causes of crime and delinquency.

REINFORCEMENT THEORY AND DELINQUENCY

A widely accepted psychological theory that explains the learning process is called *reinforcement theory.* Fundamental to this theoretical approach is the idea that learning does not take place unless there is some sort of reinforcement, some equivalent of reward or punishment. Gordon Trasler applies this theory in an effort to determine *how a person learns not to be a criminal.* The basic assumption of the theory—still in the development stage—is that *the individual learns not to become a criminal by a training procedure.* He learns to inhibit certain kinds of behavior, some of which are defined as criminal. Trasler tested his assumption in an experiment with rats, using *passive avoidance conditioning.*

In this experiment, the rat first learned how to obtain food by depressing a lever. An electric shock was then substituted for the food. The rat learned to avoid depressing the lever, even though the original drive, hunger, remained. Even when the unpleasant stimulus was removed, the rat would not touch the lever. The researchers concluded that it was in this way that the rat acquired "anxiety." An individual's aversion to criminality is believed to develop in the same way. The individual is conditioned to feel anxiety in anticipation of punishment, even though the punishment originally used to condition him is no longer present.

According to this theory, the degree of anxiety is in direct proportion

[25]Alexander and Staub, *The Criminal, the Judge, and the Public,* p. 55.

to the amount of punishment meted out during one's early conditioning or socialization process. The intensity of the anxiety is a function of the severity of fear stimulated at the time of conditioning. The theory alleges that persons predisposed to criminal behavior have not been adequately punished for criminal acts during childhood. No anxiety is aroused by contemplating a criminal act because there was little or no fear-producing punishment.

Trasler lists the following as points of importance in adequate social conditioning:

1. The effectiveness of social conditioning will depend upon the strength of the unconditioned reaction (anxiety) with which it is associated.
2. Where there is a strong dependent relationship between a child and his parents, the sanction of withdrawal of approval will evoke intense anxiety.
3. The relationship between a child and his parents is likely to be one of dependence if it is (a) exclusive, (b) affectionate, and (c) reliable.[26]

Differences in conditioning methods, differences in sensitivity and family attitudes toward crime, and differences in class attitudes toward crime determine whether or not an individual will be predisposed to criminal behavior.

DIFFERENTIAL ASSOCIATION AND CRIME

A noted French scholar, Gabriel Tarde, was among the first to contend that patterns of delinquency and crime are learned in much the same manner as any other occupation. Learning, according to Tarde, occurs by imitation and in association with others. Imitation, as Tarde conceived it, involves more than simply emulating the behavior of another. The process is similar to that of *identification,* as the term is used in modern psychology. The individual is assumed to have selected a role model and fashioned his behavior after that model. To Tarde, crime is not a characteristic that the individual inherits or a disease he contracts; it is an occupation that he learns from others. The only difference between crime and any lawful occupation is in the content of what is learned.[27]

A more systematic explanation of the way criminal behavior patterns are acquired was developed by Edwin Sutherland and later elaborated upon by Donald Cressey, his student and collaborator. The central thesis of the theory, known as differential association, is that "criminal behavior is learned through interaction with others in intimate personal groups. The learning includes techniques of committing criminal acts, plus the motives,

[26]Gordon Trasler, *The Explanation of Criminality* (London: Routledge & Kegan Paul, 1962).

[27]Gabriel Tarde, *Penal Philosophy* (Boston: Little, Brown, 1912).

drives, rationalizations, and attitudes favorable to the commission of crime."[28] The basic principles of differential association are stated as follows:

1. *Criminal behavior is learned.* Negatively, this means that criminal behavior is not inherited, as such; also, the person who is not already trained in crime does not invent criminal behavior, just as a person does not make mechanical inventions unless he has had training in mechanics.

2. *Criminal behavior is learned in interaction with other persons in a process of communication.* This communication is verbal in many respects but includes "the communication of gestures."

3. The principal part of the learning of criminal behavior occurs within *intimate personal groups.* Negatively, this means that the impersonal agencies of communication, such as movies and newspapers, play a relatively unimportant part in the genesis of criminal behavior.

4. When criminal behavior is learned, the learning includes *(a) techniques of committing the crime,* which are sometimes very complicated, sometimes very simple; *(b) the specific direction of motives, drives, rationalizations, and attitudes.*

5. The specific direction of motives and drives is *learned from definitions of the legal codes as favorable or unfavorable.* In some societies an individual is surrounded by persons who invariably define the legal codes as rules to be observed, while in others he is surrounded by persons whose definitions are favorable to the violation of the legal codes. In our American society these definitions are almost always mixed, with the consequence that we have culture conflict in relation to the legal codes.

6. *A person becomes delinquent because of an excess of definitions favorable to violation of law over definitions unfavorable to violation of law.* This is the principle of differential association. It refers to both criminal and anti-criminal associations and has to do with counteracting forces. When persons become criminal, *they do so because of contacts with criminal patterns* and also because of isolation from anti-criminal patterns. Any person inevitably assimilates the surrounding culture unless other patterns are in conflict; a Southerner does not pronounce "r" because other Southerners do not pronounce "r." Negatively, this proposition of differential association means that associations which are neutral so far as crime is concerned have little or no effect on the genesis of criminal behavior. Much of the experience of a person is neutral in this sense, e.g., learning to brush one's teeth. This behavior has no negative or positive effect on criminal behavior except as it may be related to associations which are concerned with the legal codes. This neutral behavior is important especially as an occupier of the time of a child so that he is not in contact with criminal behavior during the time he is so engaged in the neutral behavior.

7. *Differential associations may vary in frequency, duration, priority, and intensity.* This means that associations with criminal behavior and also associations with anti-criminal behavior vary in those respects. "Frequency" and "duration" as modalities of associations are obvious and need no explana-

[28]Edwin H. Sutherland and Donald R. Cressey, *Criminology*, 8th ed., 1970, p. 75. By permission of the publishers, J. B. Lippincott Company, and the author.

tion. "Priority" is assumed to be important in the sense that lawful behavior developed in early childhood may persist throughout life, and also that delinquent behavior developed in early childhood may persist throughout life. This tendency, however, has not been adequately demonstrated, and priority seems to be important principally through its selective influence. "Intensity" is not precisely defined but it has to do with such things as the prestige of the source of the criminal or anti-criminal pattern and with emotional reactions related to the associations. In a precise description of the criminal behavior of a person these modalities would be stated in quantitative form and a mathematical ratio be reached. A formula in this sense has not been developed, and the development of such a formula would be extremely difficult.

8. The process of learning criminal behavior by association with criminal and anti-criminal patterns involves all of the mechanisms that are involved in any other learning. Negatively, this means that the learning of criminal behavior is not restricted to the process of imitation. A person who is seduced, for instance, *learns criminal behavior by association,* but this process would not ordinarily be described as imitation.

9. While criminal behavior is an expression of general needs and values, it is not explained by those general needs and values since non-criminal behavior is an expression of the same needs and values. Thieves generally steal in order to secure money, but likewise honest laborers work in order to secure money. The attempts by many scholars to explain criminal behavior by general drives and values, such as the happiness principle, striving for social status, the money motive, or frustration, have been and must continue to be futile since they explain lawful behavior as completely as they explain criminal behavior. They are similar to respiration, which is necessary for any behavior but which does not differentiate criminal from non-criminal behavior.[29]

This theory does not explain why some people associate with those who approve of violation of the law while others do not, nor does it explain why some individuals become intensely committed to definitions favorable to the law while others with similar associations do not. It remains significant, however, because most current theorists have adopted the emphasis that differential association places on social learning through interaction in intimate groups as the principal method of the transmission of criminal values.

The impact of Sutherland's theory on criminology was detailed by Cressey in an article in *Social Problems.* Sutherland's theory has had such a profound impact on the field of criminology in the United States that it is pertinent to present most of Cressey's remarks on the origin and development of the theory of differential association:

The first formal statement of Edwin H. Sutherland's theory of differential association appeared in the third edition of his *Principles of Criminology*, in 1939.

[29]Ibid., pp. 77–79.

Sutherland later pointed out that the idea of differential association was stated in an earlier edition of the text, and he confessed that he was unaware that this statement was a general theory of criminal behavior. At the insistence of his colleagues, he drew up a formal set of propositions based on this earlier notion and appended it to the 1939 edition of the textbook.

In one sense, this first formal statement of the theory of differential association was short lived. For reasons which never have been clear, the statement of the theory was qualified so that it pertained only to "systematic criminal behavior," rather than to the more general category, "criminal behavior." Further, the statement was redundant, for it proposed generally that individual criminality is learned in a process of differential association with criminal and anti-criminal behavior patterns, but then went on to use "consistency" of association with the two kinds of patterns as one of the conditions affecting the impact of differential association on individuals. Thus, "consistency" of behavior patterns presented was used as a general explanation of criminality, but "consistency" also was used to describe the process by which differential association takes place. . . .

He also deleted the word "systematic," principally because it led to errors of interpretation. He believed that "systematic criminal behavior" included almost all criminal behavior, while his readers, colleagues, and students considered only a very small proportion of criminal behavior to be "systematic." The theory now refers to all criminal behavior.

The current statement of the theory of differential association holds, in essence, that "criminal behavior is learned in interaction with persons in a pattern of communication," and that the specific direction of motives, drives, rationalizations, and attitudes—whether in the direction of anti-criminality or criminality— is learned from persons who define the codes as rules to be observed and from persons whose attitudes are favorable to violation of legal codes. "A person becomes delinquent because of an excess of definitions favorable to violation of law over definitions unfavorable to violations of law." In any society, the two kinds of definitions of what is desirable in reference to legal codes exist side by side, and a person might present contradictory definitions to another person at different times and in different situations. Sutherland called the process of receiving these definitions "differential association," because the content of what is learned in association with criminal behavior patterns differs from the content of what is learned in association with anti-criminal behavior patterns. "When persons become criminals, they do so because of contacts with criminal behavior patterns and also because of isolation from anti-criminal patterns." These contacts, however, "may vary in frequency, duration, priority, and intensity."

When this idea is applied to a nation, a city, or a group, it becomes a sociological theory, rather than a social psychological theory, for it deals with differential rates of crime and delinquency. For example, a high crime rate in urban areas, as compared to rural areas, can be considered an end product of a situation in which a relatively large proportion of persons are presented with an excess of criminal behavior patterns. Similarly, the fact that the rate for all crimes is not higher in some urban areas than it is in some rural areas can be attributed to differences in probabilities of exposure to criminal behavior patterns. The important general point is that in a multi-group type of social organization, alternative and inconsistent standards of conduct are possessed by various groups, so that individuals who are members of one group have a higher probability of learning to use legal means for achieving success, or of learning to deny the importance of success, while individuals in other groups learn to accept the importance of success and to achieve it by illegal means. Stated in another way, there are alternative educational processes in operation, varying with groups, so that a person may be educated in either conventional or criminal means of achieving success. Sutherland called this situation "differential social organization" or "differential group organization," and he proposed that "differential group organization should explain the crime rate, while differential association should explain the criminal behavior of a person. The two explanations must be consistent with each other."

Sutherland's theory has had an important effect on sociological thought about criminality and crime, if only because it has become the center of controversy. Strangely, it seems to have received more discussion, comment, and research attention in the last five years than in the first fifteen years of its existence. Also, there rapidly is developing a situation in which probation, parole, and prison workers have at least heard of the theory, even if they are barely beginning to try using it for prevention of crime and rehabilitation of criminals. A social worker has recently written, "The hallmark of this new departure (in delinquency prevention) is the recognition that delinquency is not primarily a psychological problem of neuroses but a social problem of differential values. Essentially most delinquent behavior arises from the fact that core concepts of what is right and wrong, what is worth striving for and what is attainable, are not transmitted with equal force and clarity throughout the community."[30]

SOCIAL ALIENATION AND CRIMINALITY

Clarence R. Jeffery proposes a theory of social alienation to explain criminality. He points out that the concept of crime must exist before the concept of the criminal is possible. Antisocial behavior is not criminal behavior until a system of criminal law emerges. He states that all of the theories of crime now put forth in criminology are theories of criminal behavior, attempting to explain the behavior of the criminal. Regardless of the adequacy of the theories of behavior, they do not explain why the behavior is regarded as criminal. This is why Jeffery feels that criminologists need a theory of crime that explains the origin and development of criminal law in terms of the institutional structure of society.

A Theory of the Development of Law

Law came into existence at a time when the tribal system was disintegrating and social cohesion was no longer available as a means of social control.

[30]Donald R. Cressey, "The Theory of Differential Association: An Introduction." © 1960 by The Society for the Study of Social Problems. Reprinted from *Social Problems*, Vol. 8, No. 1, Summer 1960, pp. 2–6, by permission.

Primitive law is custom enforced by the kinship group and based on the cohesiveness of the group. It is private and personal in nature and in operation.

Law is a product of impersonalization and the decline in social cohesion. It is a product of urbanization. Law emerges in a society whenever intimate, personal relationships are no longer efficient as agents of social control.[31]

Jeffery groups explanations of criminal behavior into two schools: the psychological and the sociological.

The *psychological* school is based on the proposition that criminals differ from noncriminals in terms of personality traits that are expressed in some form of antisocial behavior. Criminal behavior is caused by emotional or mental conflict. The most damaging criticism raised against the psychological school is the observation that few neurotics are criminals and that most criminals are neither neurotic nor psychotic.

Jeffery chose Sutherland, with his theory of differential association, to represent the *sociological* school. Jeffery describes it as basically a theory of learning and states that criminal behavior is learned from contact with those who maintain criminal attitudes and practices. Criminal behavior is learned by association with criminal and antisocial patterns. He points out the following criticisms of the theory of differential association:

1. The theory does not explain the origin of criminality.
2. It does not explain crimes of passion or accident.
3. The theory does not explain crimes by those with no prior contact with criminal attitudes.
4. It does not explain the noncriminal living in a criminal environment.
5. The theory does not differentiate between criminal and noncriminal behavior.
6. It does not take into account motivation or "differential response patterns." People respond differently to similar situations.
7. The theory does not account for the differential rate of crime associated with age, sex, urban areas, and minority groups.[32]

Jeffery advanced a *theory of social alienation* in an attempt to integrate the psychological and sociological concepts of criminality. His theory states that crime rates are highest in groups where social interaction is characterized by isolation, anonymity, impersonalization, and anomie.

According to this theory, the criminal is one who lacks interpersonal relationships and suffers from interpersonal failure. The typical criminal has failed to achieve satisfactory interpersonal relations with others; he is lonely and emotionally isolated; he lacks membership in lawful primary groups, is insecure, hostile, aggressive; he feels unloved and unwanted, and

[31]Clarence R. Jeffery, "An Integrated Theory of Crime and Criminal Behavior," *Journal of Criminal Law, Criminology and Police Science* 50 (March 1959): 533–552. Summary on p. 536.
[32]Ibid., p. 537.

has an inadequate sense of belonging. He is the product of social imperson-alization.

The theory of social alienation is in essential agreement with the psy-chological thinking that places emphasis on such concepts as feelings of rejection, emotional starvation, psychological isolation from others, and so forth.

Jeffery's theory is in agreement with Sutherland's theory in that both emphasize the importance of social interaction that occurs in the primary group. It differs from differential association in the following respects: (1) It explains sudden crimes of passion. (2) It explains why an individual can live in a delinquent subculture and yet isolate himself from delinquent patterns. (3) It explains why a person with no history of association with criminals can commit criminal acts. (4) It explains the origin of criminal behavior in the first place by suggesting that high crime rates exist in areas characterized by anonymous, impersonal relationships. The theory of social alienation represents an attempt to integrate the sociological and psycho-logical schools. It retains emphasis on social interaction while emphasizing the emotional content of human interaction.

In support of his theory, Jeffery points to the fact that crime rates are high for young adult males who live in urban slum areas, who are from lower-socioeconomic groups, and who are members of minority groups. In these areas one also finds social isolation, a preponderance of impersonal relationships, and anonymity.

Types of Alienation

Jeffery divided social alienation into three types. First there is *individual alienation*. The individual is alienated and isolated from interpersonal rela-tions. This person is often characterized as a sociopath. He does not accept the values of the society.

The second type is *group alienation*. The group to which the person belongs is alienated and isolated from the larger community. The individ-ual who identifies with such a group is often characterized as a cultural deviate or a dyssocial person. A lack of integration of the various segments of society produces alienation of the segments.

The third type is *legal alienation*. The inequitable treatment of Ne-groes and whites, and of lower-class and upper-class individuals, in courts of law illustrates the fact that different social groups have differential access to justice. In a large, complex society, government by representation re-places government by direct citizen participation. The function and pro-cesses of government are removed from the people and placed in the hands of a corps of professional politicians and lobbyists. A type of alienation exists between legal values and those expressed in other institutions of our society.[33]

[33]Jeffery, "An Integrated Theory of Crime and Criminal Behavior," pp. 550–551.

CONTAINMENT THEORY

To explain the way in which criminal behavior is influenced by a variety of factors, Walter Reckless offers the containment theory:

1. At the top of a vertical arrangement impinging on an individual is a layer of *social pressures*. Pressure factors include adverse living conditions and economic conditions, minority group status, lack of opportunities, and family conflicts.
2. The pressures include what Reckless refers to as *pull factors*. These draw the individual away from the accepted norms. They include bad companions, delinquent or criminal subculture, and deviant groups.
3. In the situation immediately surrounding the individual is the structure of effective or ineffective *external containment*. This structure consists of effective family living and supportive groups.
4. The next layer is the *inner containment* within the individual. It is a product of good or poor internalization. When external containment is weak, inner containment must be additionally strong to withstand the pushes from within and the pulls and pressures from without.
5. The bottom layer consists of the *pushes*. These include inner tensions, hostility, aggressiveness, strong feelings of inadequacy and inferiority, and organic impairments.[34]

Reckless uses outer containment and inner containment as intervening variables. The individual may be pressured into criminality by unfavorable economic conditions or pulled into it by association with a delinquent subculture if his outer containment is deficient. The lack of outer containment is evidenced by the lack of well-defined limits to behavior, the breakdown of rules, the absence of definite roles for adolescents to play, and the failure of family life to present adequate limits and roles to the youth.

Reckless contends that a boy in a high-delinquency area where outer containment is weak may remain nondelinquent if inner containment is good. Inner containment consists of good ego strength, self-control, good self-conceptualization, and strong resistance against diversions.

Containment theory does have the advantage of merging the psychological and the sociological viewpoints of crime causation. It facilitates an analysis of the inner personal forces that propel a person to commit a crime, and at the same time permits an examination of the sociocultural forces that shape his motivation and personality.

SELF-CONCEPT AND DELINQUENCY: THE YABLONSKY CAUSAL THEORY

It has been my observation, based on almost four decades of research and observation, that a significant causal factor in delinquency is a youth's self-

---

[34]Walter C. Reckless, *The Crime Problem* (New York: Appleton-Century-Crofts, 1961), pp. 355–356.

concept.[35] This factor has several roots and implications. Youths who are physically and emotionally abused, mainly by their parents, develop low self-esteem and are more apt to commit delinquent acts. They also denigrate themselves, feel worthless, and are less likely to care about what happens to them. These social-psychological forces push these juveniles toward self-destructive behavior involving drugs and violence. Their "suicidal tendencies" make them prone to commit senseless, destructive delinquent acts which are as harmful to themselves as they are to their victims.

In my work with delinquents, especially in psychiatric facilities, I have observed the impact of self-concept on delinquent behavior in thousands of youths who are the end result of their negative socialization process. One example is 14-year-old Andy. He was emotionally and physically abused, from the age of four, three to five times a week by his alcoholic father. The physical beatings and verbal abuse administered by his father often had little relationship to Andy's behavior. He would be beaten or verbally abused for such offenses as poor school grades, not keeping his room clean, or being suspected of smoking marijuana, and he would also be beaten whenever his alcoholic father had a need to act out his personal frustrations on his son. According to Andy, "He would hit me or scream at me at times when I deserved it. Like I knew I did something wrong. He would also beat the shit out of me for no reason—just because he was loaded [drunk] and mad at the world. I've always felt like a punching bag, or maybe more like a piece of shit."

There were several consequences of Andy's father's irrational and indiscriminate behavior. The beatings and verbal abuse had the effect of producing low self-esteem in the youth. He felt humiliated and worthless. As a result he felt he was a "loser" and was not a worthwhile person. He was demeaned by the most significant person in his life, his father. As Andy stated in a moment of self-revelation, "If my own father thinks I'm a punk and a loser, maybe that's what I am."

The result of these feelings of *low self-esteem* are often acted out in self-destructive, delinquent behavior that involves violence. For example, with regard to violent gang youths, some researchers and reporters misperceived gang youths as "fighting for their turf," and committing Rambolike acts of violence in a coherent defense of their comrades-in-arms. A more accurate perspective on their violent behavior is that they are, because of their underlying low self-esteem, acting out self-destructive behavior because they don't care whether they live or die.

Low self-concept is one consequence of abuse; another is extreme rage. The *rage* in the child created by the physical and emotional abuse of his parents is a significant facet of the causal theory of delinquency and self-concept. In this context, I recall a 15-year-old member of a gang I worked with in New York who accounted for his being wild in the streets in this way: "My father always beat me up since I was a little kid. When I hit 14 we

---

[35]This is a theory I have developed to account for and explain a large proportion of delinquent behavior in contemporary society.

would wrestle and fight even. Sometimes I would beat him up—but mostly he won. Our fights would totally piss me off, and when I hit the streets I was looking for trouble. I had fights every day, and when our gang would go bopping I was always up in the front line I never cared what happened to me or anyone else." A considerable amount of displaced, so-called senseless violence by delinquents in gang fights, muggings, or armed robbery is cooked up in the cauldron of family violence that involves the physical and emotional abuse of the youth.

Substance abuse is another consequence of the abuse–low-self-concept syndrome. Substance abuse and alcoholism are ways of ameliorating the painful feelings of having low self-esteem. Substance abuse is also a form of self-destructive behavior.

As a case in point, one female juvenile drug abuser, Jane, whom I worked with in a therapy group in a psychiatric hospital, had been sexually abused by her stepfather for three years. In addition to her drug problem, one of the fallouts from her sexual traumas was the practice of self-mutilation. She would slash herself with razor blades and almost died on several occasions. She very obviously had a low self-concept, considerable rage, and didn't care what happened to her.

In one encounter-group therapy session I directed, I delivered a diatribe about the deadly destructive effects of drug abuse and remarked, "Drug addiction is a form of slow suicide." As I said this, I noticed Jane's eyes light up. I later asked her about her response and she said, "You're absolutely right. Now I know why I do drugs. I feel like a worthless piece of shit and if I had enough courage I would kill myself. I often feel, especially when I smoke crack, maybe I'll die painlessly and suddenly from the coke like those two football players."

Child abuse, low self-esteem, a delinquent self-concept, and suicidal tendencies are all entwined factors in the cases of most juvenile delinquents. In some respects, teenage suicide is the opposite side of homicide. One delinquent youth, 16-year-old Pete, was in the hospital for stabbing himself in the chest with a hunting knife. He almost died from this self-inflicted wound. Although he was in the hospital for attempted suicide, he had a long delinquent career that included drug addiction and robbery. In a psychodrama session I had him act out the specific dramatic episode that involved his suicide attempt. A number of dimensions of his feelings about his father, delinquent behavior, and self-concept as a delinquent emerged in the session.

In Pete's psychodrama, a key dramatic episode involved a screaming battle with his father. In the core dialogue with his father, Pete screamed at him as he brandished a rolled-up magazine, which represented the knife he had actually held in his hand during the real fight:

> PETE: (to his father) You drunken M-F you've been beating on me since I was a little kid. I'll never forget that day you threw me up

against the wall when I was 10. And, I really
didn't do anything.

AUXILIARY-EGO IN THE ROLE

OF PETE'S FATHER: You deserved every beating I gave you.

PETE: Bullshit. No kid deserves the things you did
to me. I'm going to end this pain now. I'm
going to kill you!

I intervened in the psychodrama at this point and used a psychodramatic technique known as a soliloquy.

L.Y.: Pete, I want you to hold off your next move. Here
you are in this terrible situation. Like Hamlet just
say your inner thoughts out loud.

PETE'S SOLILOQUY: I hate this man. He's never been a father to me. He
doesn't deserve to live. With one move of this knife
[the rolled-up magazine in his hand] I can wipe
him out of my life, and get rid of all my pain. . . .
It's either him or me. (Begins to cry.) But there
were times when he was good to me. We went to
ball games and fishing. I guess I love him, and
maybe he's right about me. I'm no fucking good.
I'm everything he's accused me of. I'm just worthless. It's never going to work out, and I can't stand
it anymore.

Sobbing, Pete stabs himself in the chest with the symbolic knife in the
psychodrama. This was the behavioral act he had committed in *reality*,
which resulted in his placement in the psychiatric hospital.

The session was a classic representation of many delinquent youths
who have these conflicting emotional vectors at work in their life. They
have low self-esteem because they have been physically and emotionally
abused. They are full of rage toward the perpetrator of the abuse, in Pete's
case his father. They *displace* a lot of their aggression onto people other
than the primary object of their hostility, and this accounts for their violent
delinquent behavior. Yet on some level their low self-esteem persists and is
reflected in self-destructive behavior. In Pete's case, it resulted in his horrendous self-inflicted wound. In brief, it was almost a toss up between
killing his father or himself. Pete believed that either act, killing his father
or himself in the context of Pete's twisted desperate life, would end his
emotional pain.

Another factor that produces a delinquent self-concept and perpetuates delinquent behavior is related to having a *criminogenic* family background that fosters the adoption of deviant values. As a case in point, a
young man, Bill, whom I worked with in juvenile detention, had a father
who was a "biker." All his life Bill was surrounded by a biker culture, which
included drugs, violence, and sexual acting out. These behavioral patterns

constituted a normal part of his family's day-to-day life situation. When he went to school he began to notice that he came from what he later termed "a criminal family." Others in the community, including his teachers and neighbors, perceived Bill as being delinquent, and in time Bill's family background tended to reinforce his self-image as a delinquent. His deviant behavior, which involved drug abuse and violence, was reinforced by his self-concept and the deviant values he learned from his family.

Society finally places the stamp of delinquency on a youth in the juvenile court. Being labeled a delinquent by the juvenile court validates a delinquent's self-concept and the delinquent behavior that emanates from this self-description. Following is a case in point of this dynamic factor in defining delinquency. I recall escorting a youth, George, who was 14 at the time, into juvenile court when I worked in a juvenile detention institution in Newark, New Jersey. Prior to this court appearance, George had been involved in various thefts, gang fighting, and drug abuse. Despite several court appearances for these varied offenses, he had managed to avoid being sent to the state reformatory. In our conversation prior to George's court appearance he was concerned, and revealed a great deal of anxiety about his behavior, his parents' reactions, and what was going to happen to him in court. The judge determined that probation was no longer feasible and that he should be sent to the state reformatory for 18 months.

When George and I left the court to return to the detention facility to prepare him for his transfer to the state reformatory his earlier attitude of concern and anxiety was radically changed. He seemed angry, swaggered, and had a determined look on his face. On the way to the detention facility I vividly recall his looking up at me with a snickering smile and flatly stating, "I guess I am now a juvenile delinquent."

George now had the self-concept of "delinquent" officially conferred upon him by the courts. In further probing as to his feelings and attitudes, he revealed that this meant he had more status in his gang and that from here on "nobody cares and I may as well do anything I want."

This youth's attitude was typical of many who, when defined as a delinquent by the courts, define themselves in this way more definitively and take on the attitudes and behavior of a delinquent. The label becomes more of a fact. In brief, the definitiveness of a delinquent self-concept tends to reinforce further delinquent behavior as a prelude to later adult criminal behavior.

Walter Reckless, Simon Dinitz, and Ellwyn Murray, based on their research, state:

> The concept of self as a delinquent may work negatively. To attribute certain abstract characteristics and predictions of delinquency to certain individuals or groups could possibly influence persons to accept the ascribed roles, a self-fulfilling prophecy. Applying labels and epithets such as "juvenile delinquent" and "young criminal" does not help anyone to think well of himself. Active, aggressive, impetuous, sometimes violent and irrational behavior does not au-

tomatically mean that a child is a junior public enemy. Equating healthy defiance with delinquency may encourage a child to think of himself as a delinquent.[36]

In summary, child abuse and neglect and their impact on a juvenile's
self-concept affects delinquent behavior. The basic propositions that I
would posit on this issue of self-concept to help explain most (but not all)
delinquency has several related characteristics: (1) The child (male or female) is abused (sexually or physically) or neglected by his or her primary
socializing agents—the parents. (2) Because he or she is treated in negative
ways with limited respect, the child feels humiliated, demeaned, and unworthy. As a consequence of this pattern of socialization the child develops
a low self-concept, and feels self-hatred. He or she thinks on some deeper
emotional level; "If these important, powerful people in my life think that I
am stupid, inadequate and unworthy of love and respect, I must be a
terrible person." (3) Mixed in with low self-esteem, the child develops a rage
against the people—the parents—who have abused or neglected him or
her, and this rage is often displaced onto people in the general society. (4)
The juvenile court reflects society's viewpoint and puts the final stamp of
"delinquent" on the juvenile.

Children with delinquent self-concepts tend to care little about what
happens to them. They not only do not value themselves, it carries over into
their attitude towards other people in their world. Their "I don't give a
damn about anything" attitude, mixed with the rage that derives from
being abused, creates a youth who is apt to be violent and has a disrespect
for the rights of others. In brief, this type of juvenile, who has little regard
for self or for others, is most likely to be delinquency-prone. The emotional
pain which results from the abuse and consequential low self-concept facilitates law-violating behavior. A significant facet of this low self-esteem involves a "suicidal tendency" that is characteristically acted out in the delinquent behavior of violence and substance abuse.

SUMMARY: BASIC THEMES FOR CLASS DISCUSSION

1. As a prelude to analyzing various causal theories it should be noted
that (1) a relationship of factors does not necessarily imply a causal
connection between the factors; (2) no single theory explains all
delinquent behavior; (3) there are primary and secondary causes of
delinquency; (4) causation is a multifactor situation; and (5) it is
often difficult to isolate out the impact of the administration of
justice on delinquent behavior.
2. *Demonology* posits a fundamentalist religious viewpoint on crime,
which asserts that there is a devil responsible for causing evil behavior, including delinquency.

[36]Walter C. Reckless, Simon Dinitz, and Ellwyn Murray, "Self-Concept as an Insulator
Against Delinquency," *American Sociological Review* 21 (December 1956): 744–746.

3. *The classical school* of causal theory rests on the basic assumption that there is free will to commit delinquent acts, which can be controlled by a clear and present punitive response by society.

4. The *modern positivistic* viewpoint of David Matza asserts that people are not totally free or wholly constrained, and that many juveniles "drift" into delinquent behavior.

5. The *psychoanalytic viewpoint* contends, in part, that delinquency results from a defective superego or conscience, and that the best way to understand delinquency is to study the "unconscious" motivations of the adolescent.

6. *Reinforcement theory* posits a behavioral viewpoint that delinquency is a behavior that is reinforced when it accrues positive rewards, and that delinquency is extinguished by proper punishment.

7. *Differential association* is a causal theory first presented by Edwin Sutherland and later further developed by Donald Cressey. The theory asserts that delinquent behavior is learned in association with criminal individuals in interaction in small primary groups, and the learning includes criminal techniques, rationalizations, and values and attitudes favorable to the commission of crimes.

8. *Containment theory*, developed by Walter Reckless, maintains that delinquent behavior is caused by greater pressures or "push factors" to commit delinquent acts than strong "inner-containment" factors that deter delinquency.

9. *Child abuse and a delinquent self-concept*, a theory I have developed, asserts that youths are most likely to become delinquent when they are abused or neglected as children. The abuse creates a low self-concept in the child, creates rage, and makes him or her predisposed to act out violent or self-destructive behavior. This behavior includes delinquent acts like assault, theft, robbery, and substance abuse. The child's low self-esteem is finally validated when he or she is defined as a juvenile delinquent by the juvenile court.

QUESTIONS

11.1. Discuss the concept of "causation" in relationship to human behavior in general.

11.2. Select the three causal theories on delinquency you believe are most falacious and critically analyze their defects.

11.3. Select the three causal theories you find most useful for understanding delinquent behavior and discuss their attributes.

11.4. Relate different causal theories to the delinquent behavior they tend to explain. For example, which theories best explain violence against the person as compared to property offenses.

11.5. Select three theories of causation and discuss the implications of these theories for preventing, treating, and controlling delinquency.

chapter 12

Causal Theories
Emphasis on the Group and Society

The noted French sociologist Emile Durkheim considered crime an integral part of all societies. Having defined crime as an act that is punished, he expressed the view that a society exempt from crime was utterly impossible. The dominant group in the society invariably defines certain behavior as undesirable and punishable. It is this societal definition that confers criminal character upon the act, and not the intrinsic quality of the act. According to Durkheim:

> Crime is present . . . in all societies of all types. Its form changes; the acts thus characterized are not the same everywhere; but, everywhere and always, there have been men who have behaved in such a way as to draw upon themselves penal repression. If, in proportion as societies pass from the lower to the higher types, the rate of criminality . . . tended to decline, it might be believed that crime, while still normal, is tending to lose this character of normality. [Actually] it has everywhere increased. . . . There is, then, no phenomenon that presents more indisputably all the symptoms of normality, since it appears closely connected with the conditions of all collective life.[1]

Durkheim did recognize that some criminal behavior was pathological and was made punishable with the complete consensus of the society—murder, for example. With respect to other behavior classified as criminal there is less general agreement.

In a society that permits individuals to differ more or less from the

[1]Emile Durkheim, *The Rules of Sociological Method*, 8th ed., trans. Sarah A. Solvag and John H. Mueller (Glencoe, Ill.: Free Press, 1950), pp. 65–66.

collective type, it is inevitable that some acts are criminal. However, since nothing is "good" indefinitely and to an unlimited extent, people must be free to deviate; otherwise, social change would be impossible.

As Durkheim saw it, if progress is to be made, individual originality must be able to express itself. For the originality of the idealist to find expression it is necessary that the originality of the criminal also be expressible. It would never have been possible to establish the freedom of thought we now enjoy if the regulations prohibiting it had not been violated by people who were at one time classified as criminals. It should be remembered that the founding fathers of the United States were at first considered legally criminals in the context of the British Empire. Crime is thus sometimes a valuable force for social change.

Anomie, as first presented by Emile Durkheim in his search for the cause of suicide and later elaborated upon by Robert K. Merton and others, is characterized as a condition in which an individual feels a loss of orientation; he is without outside controls he can trust or believe in. For such an individual, little is real or meaningful; he cannot relate to society wholly, and its norms and values are without meaning to him. He is free of the restrictions imposed on those belonging to society and, free, he is lost.[2]

In his treatise on anomic suicide, Durkheim points out the dangers of such freedom from acceptable restraint. "Those who have only empty space above them are almost inevitably lost in it, if no force restrains them."[3]

Durkheim points out that "no living being can be happy or even exist unless his needs are sufficiently proportioned to his means."[4] Society limits the means available to him. Society also sets goals appropriate to each category of people in it. There may be some flexibility, but there are also limits. "To pursue a goal which is by definition unattainable is to condemn oneself to a state of perpetual unhappiness."[5] Yet, in our society, as in the France of Durkheim's time, all classes contend among themselves because no established classification any longer exists. Society, according to Durkheim, is the only agency that is acceptable to people as a regulator of the desires of men. It is the only agency recognized as superior to the individual, with the acknowledged right to make demands and impose restrictions. Yet ". . . discipline can be useful only if considered just by the peoples subject to it. When it is maintained only by custom and force, peace and harmony are illusory; the spirit of unrest and discontent are latent; appetites superficially restrained are ready for revolt."[6]

Merton relates crime to anomie through the four following concepts:

1. Society, in the United States, places an emphasis on success as

---

[2]Emile Durkheim, *Suicide*, trans. John A. Spaulding and George Simpson (Glencoe, Ill.: Free Press, 1951).

[3]Ibid., p. 257.

[4]Ibid., p. 246.

[5]Ibid., p. 248.

[6]Ibid., p. 251.

represented by possessions and their consumption, and at the same time, for some people, blocks legitimate paths to the achievement of that goal. Success is assumed to be achievable by all.

2. The access to legitimate means of achievement are effectively denied to many members of the lower classes and to members of minority groups.

3. The conflict thus established is often resolved by resorting to illegal means of achievement of acceptable goals.

4. On the other hand, an individual may deny the value of the goal and act out that denial in the destruction of property.

Resorting to either illegitimate means or destruction of the goal is anomie. It is an inability to correlate the ends of action and the action to the values of society. Since legitimate means and shared goals become contradictory, the individual must relieve his anxiety and frustration by denying the one or the other as meaningful. As distance grows between institutional means and cultural goals, anomie grows more prevalent.[7]

Some people, for whatever reason, come to reject the goals defined by the society as appropriate and the means defined as legitimate. If they seek to substitute other means and other goals for those dictated by the society, they may move toward rebellion. A solution does not come easily. It may require a reorganization of society. This seems to be the solution some are striving for on a national level by peaceful means. Effective civil rights legislation and the chance of equal opportunity for all can effectively reduce the disparity between goal and means for many people. The attempt to reduce the wide differences in income may be helpful to others. Unless these objectives are attained, we can, by applying this theoretical position, predict increased criminality and/or increased rebellion.

CRIME AND DISLOCATIONS IN THE SOCIAL SYSTEM

In his focus on anomie, Robert K. Merton examined the way in which the social structure exerts definite pressure upon some persons to engage in nonconformist behavior. He asserts that deviant behavior results from discrepancies between culturally defined goals and the socially structured means of achieving them.

According to Merton, American society defines success as a goal for everyone. Some of the socially approved means of achieving success are hard work, education, and thrift. The emphasis in our society, he points out, is on the goals—winning the game—not on the means—how you do it. Since some people do not have equal access to approved means, they have a more limited chance to achieve the goals of the society unless they deviate.

Merton describes five basic modes of adaptation to the goals and means of the society:

[7]Robert K. Merton, *Social Theory and Social Structure* (Glencoe, Ill.: Free Press, 1957), pp. 131–160.

- *Adaptation I:* Conformity to both culture goals and means. This is the most commonly used adaptation in every society.
- *Adaptation II:* Innovation, the acceptance of the cultural emphasis on success goals without equally internalizing the morally prescribed norms governing the means for their attainment. The individual accepts the goals of wealth and power, but does not accept work as means. The innovator may choose illegal means and become a criminal. This choice is particularly attractive to the person who concludes that he does not have access to approved means of achieving his goals.
- *Adaptation III:* Ritualism, the rejection of culturally defined goals with conformity to the mores defining the means. The ritualistic individual does not try to get ahead; he is overly involved with the ritualistic means of success.
- *Adaptation IV:* Retreatism, the rejection of both the culturally defined goals and the institutionalized means. The individual escapes by becoming a drug addict, an alcoholic, a psychotic, or by some other method.
- *Adaptation V:* Rebellion, the rejection of both the goals and the means of attaining them. The rebel attempts to introduce a "new social order."[8]

I would like to add another adaptation to those described by Merton:

- *Adaptation VI:* Dropping out, the rejection of both the culturally defined goals and the institutionalized means by taking no action to effectuate change. The "dropout" simply waits for something to happen. While waiting, to keep alive and to relieve boredom he engages in behavior defined as criminal by the society whenever he finds such behavior appropriate.

In general Merton's fundamental explanation of the tendency to criminality is that the emphasis on goals rather than on the means of attaining them causes many people, who cannot achieve material success goals through legitimate means, to resort to any means, including crime. Merton's point of reference for accounting for criminality is found in the analysis of social dislocations. This is the fundamental direction taken by many recent sociological theorists of crime causation.

ECONOMIC DETERMINISM

The Dutch criminologist William A. Bonger, a Marxist, was an early proponent of a theory of economic causation of crime. Bonger attributed criminal acts, particularly crimes against property, directly to the poverty of the proletariat in a competitive capitalistic system. Poverty, which resulted from unsuccessful economic competition, led to personal disorganization and was an inherent part of a capitalist society. The solution to crime, according to this theory, could be achieved only through the reorganization of the

---

[8]Merton, *Social Theory and Social Structure*, pp. 141–156.

means of production and the development of a classless society. Bonger described this viewpoint this way:

> The egoistic tendency does not by itself make a man criminal. For this something else is necessary. . . . For example, a man who is enriched by the exploitation of children may nevertheless remain all his life an honest man from the legal point of view. He does not think of stealing, because he has a surer and more lucrative means of getting wealth, although he lacks the moral sense which would prevent him from committing a crime if the thought of it occurred to him. . . . As a consequence of the present environment, man has become very egoistic and hence more capable of crime, than if the environment had developed the germs of altruism.

> The present economic system is based upon exchange. . . . Such a mode of production cannot fail to have an egoistic character. A society based upon exchange isolates the individuals by weakening the bond that unites them. When it is a question of exchange the two parties interested think only of their own advantage even to the detriment of the other party. . . .

> No commerce without trickery is a proverbial expression (among consumers), and with the ancients Mercury, the god of commerce, was also the god of thieves. This is true, that the merchant and the thief are alike in taking account exclusively of their own interest to the detriment of those with whom they have to do.[9]

There has been sufficient evidence since Bonger wrote to indicate that poverty alone does not cause crime and that most poor people are not criminals. Most Western societies, however, have assumed greater responsibility for care of the unemployed and the poor than they did in Bonger's time. A commentary of Bonger's that still appears to hold true in his observation that conspicuous consumption tends indirectly to set goals impossible of legitimate achievement by people in the lower strata of society. Bonger's postulate of the discrepancy between culturally approved goals and institutionalized means of achieving them as a cause of crime has been incorporated into the theoretical positions of many recent sociologists.

Economic determinism as part of a contemporary radical criminology has been supported by the work of Gordon and others.[10] According to this view, capitalist societies depend on basically competitive forms of social and economic interaction and upon substantial inequalities in the allocation of social resources. Without competition and a competitive ideology, workers might not be expected to struggle to improve their relative income and status in society by working harder. Although property rights are protected, capitalist societies do not guarantee economic security to most individual members. *Driven by fear of economic insecurity and by a competitive desire*

---

[9]William A. Bonger, *Criminality and Economic Conditions* (Boston: Little, Brown, 1916), pp. 401–402.

[10]David M. Gordon, "Capitalism, Class and Crime in America," *Crime and Delinquency* (April 1973): 163–186.

to gain some of the goods unequally distributed throughout the society, many individuals will eventually become "criminals."

The following three different kinds of crime in the United States provide examples of functionally similar rationality:

1. *Ghetto crime.* The legitimate jobs open to many young ghetto residents typically pay low wages, offer relatively demeaning assignments, and carry constant risk of layoff. Many types of "crimes" available in the ghetto offer higher monetary return, higher status, and often low risk of arrest and punishment.
2. *Organized crime.* Activities like gambling, prostitution, and drug distribution are illegal for various reasons, but there is a demand for these activities. Opportunities for monetary rewards are great, and the risks of arrest and punishment low.
3. *Corporate crime.* Corporations exist to protect and augment the capital of their owners. If it becomes difficult to do this lawfully, corporate officials will try to do it another way.

Gordon also points out that current patterns of crime and punishment in the United States support the capitalist system in three ways:

1. The pervasive patterns of selective law enforcement reinforce a prevalent ideology in the society that *individuals rather than institutions are to blame for social problems.*
2. The patterns of crime and punishment manage "legitimately" to neutralize the potential opposition to the system of many oppressed citizens. The cycle of crime, imprisonment, parole, and recidivism denies to the poor, particularly the black poor, meaningful participation in a society, denies them decent employment opportunities, and keeps them on the run.
3. By treating criminals as animals and misfits, as enemies of the state, we are permitted to continue to avoid some basic questions about the dehumanizing effects of our social institutions.

A critical theory of criminal law that generally supports Gordon's position is stated by Quinney in the following terms:

1. American society is based on an advanced capitalist economy.
2. The state is organized to serve the interests of the dominant economic class, the capitalist ruling class.
3. Criminal law is an instrument of the state and ruling class to maintain and perpetuate the existing social and economic order.
4. Crime control in capitalist society is accomplished through a variety of institutions and agencies established and administered by a governmental elite, representing ruling class interests, for the purpose of establishing domestic order.
5. The contradictions of advanced capitalism—the disjunction between existence and essence—require that the subordinate classes remain oppressed by whatever means necessary, especially through the coercion and violence of the legal system.

6. Only with the collapse of capitalist society and the creation of a new society, based on socialist principles, will there be a solution to the crime problem.

As capitalist society is further threatened by its own contradictions, criminal law is increasingly used in the attempt to maintain domestic order. The underclass, the class that must remain oppressed for the triumph of the dominant economic class, will continue to be the object of criminal law as long as the dominant class seeks to perpetuate itself.[11]

Radical theorists like Quinney draw heavily on economic and Marxist theory. They argue that delinquency is the product of the perpetual class struggle in capitalist societies. The ruling class creates the conditions out of which delinquency arises, and nothing short of revolution will alter the situation. Such theorists tend to see delinquency as a result of the *marginalization of youth*. Capitalism is viewed as a "criminogenic" system that perpetuates inequities based on age, sex, race, and occupation. Thus, merely "tinkering" with the system by investing time and resources into rehabilitation, diversion, or prevention will not rectify the delinquency problem. They assert that when children are freed from the evils of class struggles and reintegrated into the mainstream of life, the cooperative instincts of the young will become dominant, and a society free of crime and delinquency will emerge. The prescriptions for this revolution are stated by Quinney as follows:

Our task as students is to consider the alternatives to the capitalist legal order. Further study of crime and justice in America must be devoted to the contradictions of the existing system. At this advanced stage of capitalist development, law is little more than a repressive instrument of manipulation and control. We must make others aware of the current meaning of crime and justice in America. The objective is to move beyond the existing order. And this means ultimately that we engage in socialist revolution.[12]

Most of the theories expressed by Gordon and Quinney focus on male delinquency. A body of Marxist theory and research being developed by feminists asserts that "the special oppression of women by . . . [the criminal justice] system is not isolated or arbitrary, but rather is rooted in systematic sexist practices and ideologies which can only be fully understood by analyzing the position of women in capitalist society."[13]

The relationship among capitalism, sexism, and crime is interestingly stated by Rafter and Natalizia.[14] On various aspects of this issue, they write:

Capitalism and sexism are intimately related, and it is this relationship that accounts for the inferior status traditionally given to women by the American

---

[11]Richard Quinney, *Criminal Justice in America* (Boston: Little, Brown, 1974), p. 24.

[12]Ibid., p. 25.

[13]Dorie Klein and June Kress, "Any Woman's Blues: A Critical Overview of Women, Crime, and the Criminal Justice System," *Crime and Social Justice* (Spring/Summer 1976): 45.

[14]Nicole Rafter and Elena Natalizia, "Marxist Feminism: Implications for Criminal Justice," *Crime and Delinquency* (January 1981): 81–87. Used by permission.

criminal justice system. Sexism is not merely the prejudice of individuals; it is embedded in the very economic, legal, and social framework of life in the United States. The criminal justice system, as one part of that institutional framework, reflects the same sexist underpinning that is evidenced throughout capitalist society.

Capitalism relies upon the traditional structure of monogamy and the nuclear family to fulfill its economic potential. The division of labor essential to the capitalist system is one that cuts off those who produce from control over the means of production. And it dictates that men shall be the chief producers of goods, while women shall function primarily as nurturers of the next generation of producers.

Legal policy and structures evolve in response to the particular system of morals prevalent in a given society. This means that, in a capitalist system, law reflects a bourgeois moral code which restricts women to specific roles within the economic scheme. Women are properly chattel of the dominant men in their lives (husbands, fathers, lovers, pimps), and women's work is defined as unworthy of significant remuneration. Violations of the moral code defining women's proper role are labeled deviant and punished by stringent sanctions. Law becomes an instrument of social control over women and a means of preserving the economic status quo.

Historically, the entire justice system in America has been dominated by men. Our legal framework has been codified by male legislators, enforced by male police officers, and interpreted by male judges. Rehabilitation programs have been administered by males. The prison system has been managed by men, primarily for men.

Chivalrous motives are the ostensible grounds for a particularly discriminatory instrument for the oppression of female juveniles—status offense statutes. These statutes specify that juveniles can be prosecuted for behaviors or conditions that would not be illegal if committed or manifested by an adult, such as running away, incorrigibility, and being in danger of falling into vice. Although theoretically applying to juveniles of both sexes and all economic levels, these laws reflect efforts to uphold bourgois standards of feminity—standards glorifying submissiveness, docility, and sexual purity. That these statutes function with sexual bias is borne out by studies revealing that the prosecution rate for status offenses is much higher among girls than among boys, and that female status offenders are punished more severely than are boys who commit more serious property or violent offenses. And, as in the case of their adult counterparts, low-income and minority girls bear most of the burden of such sanctions. At an early age therefore, these girls learn that deviance from economically based sex role patterns will result in legal sanctions, despite the chivalrous intent of our justice system.

The second way in which the legal system oppresses women is through its almost total failure to respond to issues of concern to women. Wife abuse, sexual harassment, incest, rape, production of unsafe methods of birth control, forced sterilization for eugenic purposes—these are critically important problems to women, whose needs the legal system has either failed to consider or has glossed over with token, ad hoc efforts. Such problems, moreover, have the greatest significance for poor and working-class women, indicating that class is at least as critical as sex in the struggle to obtain legal equality for women.

Rafter and Natalizia have a point, but are overstating their indictment of the system as it currently oppresses women. In effect there is considerable awareness of the conditions they focus on, and recently efforts are being made to remedy the problems cited.

SOCIAL DISORGANIZATION AND CRIME: SOCIAL ECOLOGY

Social ecologists are involved in establishing relationships between residential areas and the natural groups that inhabit them. The urban industrial community may be described as consisting of five successive zones:

I. The central business district tends in American cities to be at once the retail, financial, recreational, civic, and political centers. By day the skyscrapers and canyon-like streets of the downtown district are thronged with shoppers, clerks and office workers. . . . The central business district has few inhabitants. . . .
II. The zone in transition . . . [is] an interstitial area in the throes of change from residence to business and industry. Here are to be found the slum or semi-slum districts. . . .
III. The zone of workingmen's homes . . . [lies] beyond the factory belt surrounding the central business district, which is still accessible, often within walking distance to the workers. . . .
IV. The better residential zone is inhabited chiefly by the families engaged in professional and clerical pursuits who have high school if not college education. . . . This is the home of the great middle class. . . .
V. The commuter's zone comprises the suburban districts.[15]

These descriptive categories were based on observations of Chicago. While many urban communities do not follow this explicit pattern, residential areas surrounding industrial centers in the great majority of our cities are comparable "zones in transition."

Burgess noted that Zone II, in transition from workingmen's homes to business and industry, was the area in which social disorganization was greatest. Clifford R. Shaw and other students of Burgess conducted extensive studies of Chicago and 21 other cities, dividing the urban population into mile-square areas and quantifying the deterioration, and found support for Burgess' viewpoint.

Shaw concentrated upon the distribution of juvenile delinquency. He found that the highest delinquency rates occurred in Zone I and that there was a progressive slope in rates downward away from Zone I. The results were the same for such other indicia of social disorganization as crime rates, rates of mental disorder, and truancy rates. (See Table 12.1).

Shaw found that the greatest concentration of delinquents occurred in areas of marked social disorganization and described the process as follows:

[15]Robert E. Park, Ernest W. Burgess, and R. D. McKenzie, *The City* (Chicago: University of Chicago Press, 1925), p. 50.

Table 12.1   SOCIAL DATA BY ZONES

	Zones				
Community problems	I	II	III	IV	V
Rates of delinquents, 1927–1933	9.8	6.7	4.5	2.5	1.8
Rates of truants, 1927–1933	4.4	3.1	1.7	1.0	0.7
Boys' court rates, 1938	6.3	5.9	3.9	2.6	1.6
Rates of infant mortality, 1923–1933	86.7	67.5	54.7	45.9	41.3
Rates of tuberculosis, 1931–1937	33.5	25.0	18.4	12.5	9.2
Rates of mental disorder, 1922–1934	32.0	18.8	13.2	110.1	8.4
Rates of adult criminals, 1920	2.2	1.6	0.8	0.6	0.4

Source: Clifford R. Shaw and Henry McKay, *Juvenile Delinquency and Urban Areas* (Chicago: University of Chicago Press, 1942), p. 158, Table 1. © 1942 by the University of Chicago.

In the process of city growth, the neighborhood organizations, cultural institutions and social standards in practically all of the areas adjacent to the central business district and the major industrial centers are subject to rapid change and disorganization. The gradual invasion of these areas by industry and commerce, the continuous movement of the older residents out of the area and the influx of newer groups, the confusion of many divergent cultural standards, the economic insecurity of the families, all combine to render difficult the development of a stable and efficient neighborhood organization for the education and control of the child and the suppression of lawlessness.[16]

In the slum area, delinquent traditions were transmitted to the new arrival. There were adult criminal gangs engaged in theft and the sale of stolen goods. Children were exposed to a variety of contradictory standards and forms of behavior. They were often found guilty in the courts for behavior that was approved by the neighborhood in which they lived. High-delinquency areas developed social values and patterns of behavior that conflicted with the values of the larger society. Thus behavior that was considered "correct" by the norms of the slum neighborhood was considered delinquent and criminal by the norms and laws of the larger society. This condition of social disorganization is often referred to as "culture conflict."

CULTURAL ELEMENTS OF CRIMINALITY

Social Theory of Crime

Donald R. Taft and Ralph W. England, Jr., formulated a social theory that attempts to explain the high rate of crime in the United States and other Western societies. They see criminality resulting from a combination of the following aspects of the culture:[17]

[16]National Commission on Law Observance and Enforcement, *Report on the Causes of Crime*, vol. 2, no. 13 (Washington, D.C.: U.S. Government Printing Office, 1931), p. 387.
[17]Donald R. Taft and Ralph W. England, Jr., *Criminology* (New York: Macmillan, 1964), pp. 27–31.

1. *American culture is dynamic.* Our standards are constantly changing. "The wrong of yesterday is the right of today."
2. *American culture is complex.* According to Taft, crime is the product of culture conflict, and culture conflict is widespread as a result of immigration and internal migration.
3. *American culture is materialistic.* "Speaking generally, the underprivileged and unsuccessful accept the same values as the successful and aspire to imitate their success." It is apparent that the underprivileged have a more difficult time achieving success goals than the privileged.
4. *American social relations are increasingly impersonal.* Primary relationships in the family and neighborhood have declined. Anonymity breeds alienation and a greater impetus to crime and delinquency.
5. *American culture fosters restricted group loyalties.* "Preference for men, not wholly because of their personal qualities, but because they are natives, neighbors, Masons, or of our race, class, or creed, is widespread and not essentially different in quality from gang loyalty." This leaves people out, produces conflict, hostility, and crime.
6. *Survival of frontier values.* Among frontier values that have survived into the present are the tradition of extreme individualism and the tendency of some groups within our society to take the law into their own hands.

All these factors in American culture, according to Taft and England, "normally" produce a high incidence of crime.

The Criminogenic Society

Barron presents a detailed analysis of the criminogenic aspects of the American society and culture.[18] He discusses several official and unofficial American values which are likely to encourage norm-violating and illegal behavior. These are:

1. *Success.* There is an emphasis in our culture on the importance of succeeding and asserting one's self. The well-known quotation of football coach Lombardi is cited. "Winning isn't everything, it is the only thing." Americans hate to admit failure. They feel frustrated if they do not achieve success. There is also a very high value placed on moving up, going higher on the scale toward ultimate success. When people realize that they are not going to succeed and are not moving up through hard work, thrift, study, etc., many turn to crime and delinquency as ways of achieving success.
2. *Status and power ascendance.* The answer to the question "How far can I get?" is found in terms of social status. Evidence of higher status is provided by high grades, expensive cars, expensive clothes, jewelry,

[18]Milton L. Barron, "The Criminogenic Society: Social Values and Deviance," in *Current Perspectives on Criminal Behavior*, ed. Abraham S. Blumberg (New York: Knopf, 1974), pp. 68–86.

etc. Dollars provide the power. Money and material goods have become values in themselves. People who cannot obtain them lawfully may violate laws to get them.

3. *Resistance to authority.* Independence, individuality, and nonconformity are encouraged. All these involve resistance to authority. Americans tend to ridicule literal observance and strict conformity. This tendency applies to observance of laws. The Caspar Milquetoast is an object of ridicule.

4. *Toughness.* There are class differences in the emphasis on toughness. However, in every subculture people are encouraged to fight back. Violence is celebrated in crime and gangster programs, on TV, in films, in magazines, etc.

5. *Dupery.* People are rewarded for getting the better of others. The observation of P. T. Barnum that "there's a sucker born every minute" meets with general agreement if not approval. Official norms and laws are violated with the tacit acceptance of the society or group as long as violations are concealed. People are proud of getting the better of others.

6. *American culture is dynamic.* Changes in norms are so rapid that differences between right and wrong are weakened.

7. *American culture offers alternative and conflicting values and norms.* Behavior that is defined as illegal in the American society may not necessarily be "wrong" in the subcultures of some groups.

8. *Social relations in the American society have become increasingly impersonal.* Urban living, in which one hardly knows one's neighbor, does not provide the informal controls of rural society.

9. *A multigroup society fosters a duality of loyalty and ethics.* Many people apply one code of ethics in their relations with members of their ingroup and a different code with outgroup members.

Barron tempers the impact of criminogenic theory by acknowledging that widespread crime and corruption existed at other times in history and occur in other places than the United States. Nevertheless, although these factors are not unique to American society, they are part of the problem.

Subculture of Delinquency

Albert Cohen views delinquent youths as comprising a subculture with a value system different from the dominant one found in the inclusive American culture. Lower-class children, according to Cohen, use the delinquent subculture as a mode of reaction and adjustment to a dominant middle-class society that indirectly discriminates against them because of their lower-class position. Lower-class youths, trained in a different value system, are not adequately socialized to fulfill the status requirements of middle-class society. Despite this differential socialization, they are unfairly exposed to the middle-class aspirations and judgments they cannot fulfill.

This conflict produces in the lower-class youths what Cohen has termed "status frustration." In reaction, they manifest a delinquent adjustment, acting out their status frustrations in "non-utilitarian, malicious, negativistic" forms of delinquency.

In such settings as the school and community center, the lower-class youth finds himself exposed to generally middle-class agents of the society (teachers and social workers). Their efforts to impose on him their middleclass values of orderliness, cleanliness, responsibility, and ambitions are met with sharp negativism.

Cohen lists nine middle-class values that are specifically rejected by the lower-class child: (1) ambition; (2) responsibility; (3) the cultivation of skills and tangible achievement; (4) postponement of immediate satisfactions and self-indulgence in the interest of long-term goals; (5) rationality, in the sense of forethought, planning, and budgeting of time; (6) the rational cultivation of manners, courtesy, personality; (7) the need to control physical aggression and violence; (8) the need for wholesome recreation; and (9) respect for property and its proper care.

The lower-class child, in reaction against these unfair impositions, substitutes norms that reverse those of the larger society: "The delinquent subculture takes its norms from the larger subculture, but turns them upside down. The delinquent's conduct is right by the standards of his subculture precisely because it is wrong by the norms of the larger culture."[19] The dominant theme of the delinquent subculture is the explicit and wholesale repudiation of middle-class standards and the adoption of their very antitheses. In this negative polarity of "just for the hell of it" vandalism and violence, lower-class youths attempt to adjust their status frustration and hostility toward the larger society's unfair imposition of middle-class values upon them; and the gang is the vehicle for their delinquencies. The individual delinquent is "the exception rather than the rule."[20]

Cohen's position on the gang's relation to the community and the family parallels the conceptions of the early Chicago school.

> Relations with gang members tend to be intensely solidary and imperious. Relations with other groups tend to be indifferent, hostile or rebellious. Gang members are unusually resistant to the efforts of home, school and other agencies to regulate, not only their delinquent activities, but any activities carried on within the group, and to efforts to compete with the gang for the time and other resources of its members. It may be argued that the resistance of gang members to the authority of the home may not be a result of their membership in gangs but that membership in gangs, on the contrary, is a result of ineffective family supervision, the breakdown of parental authority and the hostility of the child toward the parents; in short, that the delinquent gang recruits members who have already achieved autonomy. Certainly a previous breakdown in fam-

[19]Reprinted with permission of The Macmillan Company from *Delinquent Boys* by Albert K. Cohen, p. 19. © The Free Press, a Corporation, 1955.
[20]Ibid., p. 46.

ily controls facilitates recruitment into delinquent gangs. But we are not speaking of the autonomy, the emancipation of individuals. It is not the individual delinquent but the gang that is autonomous. For many of our subcultural delinquents the claims of the home are very real and very compelling. The point is that the gang is a separate, distinct and often irresistible focus of attraction, loyalty, and solidarity.[21]

In summary, the delinquent subculture described by Cohen represents a collective effort on the part of the youths to resolve adjustment problems produced by dislocations in the larger society. In the gang the norms of the larger society are reversed so that nonutilitarian deviant behavior (especially violence) becomes a legitimized activity. The gang thus serves lower-class boys as a legitimate opportunity structure for striking back at a larger society that produces their status-frustration problems.

Delinquent Opportunity System

In their analysis of delinquency causation, Cloward and Ohlin "attempt to explore two questions: (1) Why do delinquent 'norms,' or rules of conduct, develop? (2) What are the conditions which account for the distinctive content of various systems of delinquent norms—such as those prescribing violence or theft or drug-use?"[22]

Cloward and Ohlin rely heavily on the concept of the delinquent subculture. In their view, "A delinquent subculture is one in which certain forms of delinquent activity are essential requirements for the performance of the dominant roles supported by the subculture. It is the central position accorded to specifically delinquent activity that distinguishes the delinquent subculture from other deviant subcultures."[23]

They define three dominant kinds of delinquent subculture—the "criminal," the "conflict," and the "retreatist." Cloward and Ohlin recognize that the extent to which the norms of the delinquent subculture control behavior will vary from one member to another. Their description of each subculture is therefore stated in terms of the fully doctrinated member rather than the average member: The "criminal" subculture is devoted to theft, extortion, and other illegal means of securing an income; some of its members may graduate into the ranks of organized or professional crime. The "conflict" group commits acts of violence as an important means of securing status. The "retreatist" group stresses drug use, and addiction is prevalent.

Their central explanation for the emergence of delinquent subcultures is derived from the theories of Durkheim and Merton. Their basic view is "that pressures toward the formation of delinquent subcultures

[21]Ibid.
[22]Reprinted with permission of The Macmillan Company from *Delinquency and Opportunity* by Richard A. Cloward and Lloyd E. Ohlin. © The Free Press, a Corporation, 1960.
[23]Ibid., p. 7.

originate in marked discrepancies between culturally induced aspirations among lower class youth and the possibilities of achieving them by legitimate means."[24]

Cultural goals become an important aspect of Cloward and Ohlin's thesis. In describing two categories of need, physical and social, Durkheim makes the point that physical needs are satiable, whereas social gratification is "an insatiable and bottomless abyss." Given this condition, Cloward and Ohlin state that when men's goals become unlimited, their actions can no longer be controlled by norms, and a state of normlessness or anomie exists.

Cloward and Ohlin turn to Merton's elaboration of Durkheim's basic postulate to account for the various patterns of deviant behavior. In Merton's view, anomie (normlessness) and the breakdown of social control emerge not because of insatiable goals alone but because of a lack of fit between the goals and the legitimate means for attaining them. As Merton specifies, "Aberrant behavior may be regarded sociologically as a symptom of dissociation between culturally prescribed aspirations and socially structured avenues of realizing these aspirations."[25]

Merton's formulation, according to Cloward and Ohlin, helps to explain the existence of a large proportion of law violators among lower-class youths. Because they are denied equal access to normative social opportunity, they experience a greater pull toward deviance.

> The ideology of common success-goals and equal opportunity may become an empty myth for those who find themselves cut off from legitimate pathways upward. We may predict, then, that the pressure to engage in deviant behavior will be greatest in the lower levels of the society.
>
> Our hypothesis can be summarized as follows: The disparity between what lower class youth are led to want and what is actually available to them is the source of a major problem of adjustment. Adolescents who form delinquent subcultures, we suggest, have internalized an emphasis upon conventional goals. Faced with limitations on legitimate avenues of access to these goals, and unable to revise their aspirations downward, they experience intense frustrations; the exploration of nonconformist alternatives may be the result.[26]

Cloward and Ohlin view the gang as one of the "nonconformist alternatives" these boys may explore. Alienated youths band together in the collectivity of the gang in an effort to resolve their mutual problems. The same theme is used to explain the normative patterning of gangs; the conflict, criminal, and retreatist. A youth's selection of one type of subcultural adjustment over another is related to the degree of availability of these illegitimate "opportunity structures" in various sociocultural settings.

[24]Ibid., p. 36.

[25]Merton, *Social Theory and Social Structure*, p. 134.

[26]Reprinted with permission of The Free Press, a Division of Macmillan, Inc. from *Delinquency and Opportunity* by Richard E. Cloward and Lloyd E. Ohlin. Copyright © 1960 by The Free Press.

We believe that the way in which these problems are resolved may depend upon the kind of support for one or another type of illegitimate activity that is given at different points in the social structure. If, in a given social location, illegal or criminal means are not readily available, then we should not expect a criminal subculture to develop among adolescents. By the same logic, we should expect the manipulation of violence to become a primary avenue to higher status only in areas where the means of violence are not denied to the young. To give a third example, drug addiction and participation in subcultures organized around the consumption of drugs presuppose that persons can secure access to drugs and knowledge about how to use them. In some parts of the social structure, this would be very difficult; in others, very easy. In short, there are marked differences from one part of the social structure to another in the types of illegitimate adaptation that are available to persons in search of solutions to problems of adjustment arising from the restricted availability of legitimate means. In this sense, then, we can think of individuals as being located in two opportunity structures—one legitimate, the other illegitimate. Given limited access to success-goals by legitimate means, the nature of the delinquent response that may result will vary according to the availability of various illegitimate means.[27]

Cloward and Ohlin tend to minimize the importance of individual personality factors and characteristics. "The social milieu affects the nature of the deviant response whatever the motivation and social position (i.e., age, sex, socioeconomic level) of the participants in the delinquent subculture."[28]

Criminal subcultures, according to Cloward and Ohlin, are most likely to occur in the somewhat stable slum neighborhoods that provide a hierarchy of criminal opportunity. In some conflict with Cohen's description of delinquency as "malicious, negativistic, and nonutilitarian," Cloward and Ohlin argue that for many youths in this type of neighborhood, the desire to move up in the neighborhood criminal hierarchy may cause them to overconform to delinquent values and behavior to show off their criminal ability. Such criminal overconformity, Cloward and Ohlin maintain, accounts for rash, nonutilitarian delinquent acts.

The criminal subculture is likely to arise in a neighborhood milieu characterized by close bonds between different age-levels of offender, and between criminal and conventional elements. As a consequence of these integrative relationships, a new opportunity structure emerges which provides alternative avenues to success-goals. Hence the pressures generated by restrictions on legitimate access to success-goals are drained off. Social controls over the conduct of the young are effectively exercised, limiting expressive behavior and constraining the discontented to adopt instrumental, if criminalistic, styles of life.[29]

Conflict subcultures, according to Cloward and Ohlin, tend to arise in

[27]Ibid., pp. 151–152.
[28]Ibid., p. 160.
[29]Ibid., p. 171.

disorganized slums that provide no organized hierarchy for criminal development. These slums, with their high degree of disorganization and their orientation toward the present, offer limited legitimate and illegitimate opportunity structures. The social disorganization of such slums contributes to the breakdown of social control.

> The young in such areas are also exposed to acute frustrations, arising from conditions in which access to success-goals is blocked by the absence of any institutionalized channels, legitimate or illegitimate. They are deprived not only of conventional opportunity but also of criminal routes to the "big money." In other words, precisely when frustrations are maximized, social controls are weakened. Social controls and channels to success-goals are generally related: where opportunities exist, patterns of control will be found; where opportunities are absent, patterns of social control are likely to be absent too. The association of these two features of social organization is a logical implication of our theory.[30]

The lack of opportunity in these areas causes such youths to seek it in other ways. "Adolescents turn to violence in search of status. Violence comes to be ascendant, in short, under conditions of relative detachment from all institutionalized systems of opportunity and social control."[31]

The *retreatist subculture* emerges, according to Cloward and Ohlin, as an adjustment pattern for those lower-class youths who have failed to find a position in the criminal or conflict subculture and have also failed to use either legitimate or illegitimate opportunity structures. "Persons who experience this 'double failure' are likely to move into a retreatist pattern of behavior."[32]

Some youths who either drop out of other types of subcultures or find the conflict or criminal subculture no longer functional may also resort to the retreatist pattern. Cloward and Ohlin conclude that limitations on both legitimate and illegitimate opportunity structures produce intense pressures toward retreatist behavior. All three types of delinquent behavior are viewed by Cloward and Ohlin as adjustment patterns that utilize the most available opportunity structure provided by the anomic social system.

Lower-Class Culture and "Normal" Delinquency

Using cultural concepts in a somewhat different fashion, Walter Miller projects a lower-class adolescent theory of gangs. He maintains (in a fashion somewhat similar to Cohen's position) that the values of lower-class culture produce deviance because they are "naturally" in discord with middle-class values. The youth who heavily conforms to lower-class values is thus automatically delinquent. Miller lists a set of characteristics of lower-class cul-

[30]Ibid., pp. 174–175.
[31]Ibid., p. 178.
[32]Ibid., p. 181.

ture that tend to foster delinquent behavior. These include such focal concerns as trouble, toughness, "smartness" (ability to con), and excitement (kicks).

According to Miller, gang activity is, in part, a striving to prove masculinity. Females are exploited by tough gang hoods in the "normal" process of relating. Girls are "conquest objects" utilized to prove and boost the masculinity of the street-corner male.

Miller further theorizes that the gap between levels of aspiration of lower-class youths and their general ability to achieve produces distinct types of lower-class categories, which reveal the degree of delinquency proneness of a youth:

1. *"Stable" lower class.* This group consists of youngsters who, for all practical purposes, do not aspire to higher status or who have no realistic possibility of achieving such aspiration.
2. *Aspiring but conflicted lower class.* This group represents those for whom family or other community influences have produced a desire to elevate their status, but who lack the necessary personal attributes or cultural "equipment" to make the grade, or for whom cultural pressures effectively inhibit aspirations.
3. *Successfully aspiring lower class.* This group, popularly assumed to be the most prevalent, includes those who have both the will and the capability to elevate their status.[33]

Miller emphasizes the fact that lower-class youths who are confronted with the largest gap between aspirations and possibilities for achievement are most delinquency-prone. Such youths are apt to utilize heavily the normal range of lower-class delinquent patterns in an effort to achieve prestige and status:

... toughness, physical prowess, skill, fearlessness, bravery, ability to con people, gaining money by wits, shrewdness, adroitness, smart repartee, seeking and finding thrills, risk, danger, freedom from external constraint, and freedom from superordinate authority. These are the explicit values of the most important and essential reference group of many delinquent youngsters. These are the things he respects and strives to attain. The lower class youngster who engages in a long and recurrent series of delinquent behaviors that are sanctioned by his peer group is acting so as to achieve prestige within his reference system.[34]

The Adolescent Striving for Manhood

Bloch and Niederhoffer, in a somewhat different interpretation, view delinquent behavior as a universal and normal adolescent striving for adult

---

[33]William C. Kvaraceus and Walter B. Miller, *Delinquent Behavior* (Washington, D.C.: National Education Association, 1959), vol. 1, *Culture and the Individual*, p. 72. Copyright 1959 by the National Education Association of the United States. Reprinted with permission.

[34]Kvaraceus and Miller, *Delinquent Behavior*, p. 69. Copyright 1959 by the National Education Association of the United States. Reprinted with permission.

status. Their hypothesis is reached by the utilization of considerable cross-cultural material that attempts to reveal the differences and similarities of the adolescent condition in a variety of societies. Their basic position is presented in the following concise statement:

> The adolescent period in all cultures, visualized as a phase of striving for the attainment of adult status, produces experiences which are much the same for all youths, and certain common dynamisms for expressing reaction to such subjectively held experience. The intensity of the adolescent experience and the vehemence of external expression depend on a variety of factors, including the general societal attitudes toward adolescence, the duration of the adolescent period itself, and the degree to which the society tends to facilitate entrance into adulthood by virtue of institutionalized patterns, ceremonials, rites and rituals, and socially supported emotional and intellectual preparation. When a society does not make adequate preparation, formal or otherwise, for the induction of its adolescents to the adult status, equivalent forms of behavior arise spontaneously among adolescents themselves, reinforced by their own group structure, which seemingly provide the same psychological content and function as the more formalized rituals found in other societies. This the gang structure appears to do in American society, apparently satisfying deep-seated needs experienced by adolescents in all cultures. Such, very briefly, is our hypothesis.[35]

In their analysis they attempt to assess the effects of such cultural patterns as puberty rites, self-decoration, and circumcision on adolescent behavior. Gang behavior, with its symbolic evidence of the "urge for manhood," is seen as an American equivalent of the puberty rites of other cultures. The gang is thus viewed as a vehicle for accomplishing the assumed highly desired status of manhood.

According to Bloch and Niederhoffer, gang structure has a high degree of stability. In their criticism of those investigators who attribute characteristics of flux and "movement" to gang organization, they argue:

> Observations of gang behavior in various neighborhoods of New York City, for example, seem to reveal just the opposite to be true. In fact, one of the outstanding characteristics of numerous gangs which have been observed appears to be their highly non-mobile and stationary nature, a fact to which many exasperated shopkeepers and building custodians, as well as the police, can amply testify. Gangs, thus, might just as well be characterized by an absence of movement since, for the most part, they frequent the same corner or candy store for hours on end, every day of the week.[36]

Bloch and Niederhoffer strongly emphasize the highly controversial point that delinquency is a "characteristic of all adolescent groups" and that the organizational structures of all adolescent groups (delinquent or not) are similar:

[35]Herbert A. Bloch and Arthur Niederhoffer, *The Gang* (New York: Philosophical Library, 1958), p. 17. Reprinted by permission.
[36]Ibid., pp. 6–7.

In respect to the type of organizational structure, there is little to distinguish, in one sense, between middle and lower class adolescent groups. Although middle class groups of teenagers are not as apt to have the formal, almost military, structure characteristic of certain lower class "war gangs" . . . they do have similar and well-defined informal patterns of leadership and control. Even here, however, the distinctions become blurred and, upon occasion, almost indistinguishable when one recalls the ceremonial designations and ritualistic roles performed by college functionaries.[37]

Using data about adolescents from such diverse groups as the Mundugumor of New Guinea, the Manus of the Admiralty Islands, the Kaffirs of South Africa, the Comanche and Plains Indians, and a tightly knit delinquent New York gang, Bloch and Niederhoffer attempt to draw the inference that the ganging process provides symbolic evidence of the urge to manhood. They conclude:

1. Adolescent gangs may be profitably studied by using as a frame of reference the theory of power.
2. The gang's attempt to gain status and power through the domination and manipulation of persons and events is a collective representation of the individual gang member's guiding fiction, which is "to prove he is man." In passing it is worthy of note that Alfred Adler's system of psychology is "tailor made" for the analysis of the gang since it is principally concerned with the struggle for power and the "masculine protest."
3. The presence of the gang, real, constructive or symbolic, gives the individual member ego support and courage. He gains a psychological sense of power and manhood which he does not possess at all when he is on his own.
4. If single gangs can pose a threat to the peace and safety of the community— and they certainly do so—then the well-meaning efforts to organize several gangs into a confederation may be a very grave error. Without significant changes in behavior and values on the part of such gangs, this maneuver may only multiply to extremely dangerous proportions the looming menace which even now we find difficult to control.[38]

LABELING THEORY

A person convicted of a crime is given the status of criminal. The term *criminal* may, therefore, be viewed as a stigmatizing label. Once given the stigmatizing label the individual may be subjected to isolation, segregation, degradation, incarceration, and chemical or psychological treatment. These things can happen to him if he is found guilty of a crime and labeled criminal *whether or not he actually committed the crime.* In a sense, we may view all this punishment as the result of the labeling rather than of the behavior.

Becker, a leading exponent of labeling theory, put it this way:

[37]Ibid., p. 9.
[38]Ibid., p. 217.

Social groups create deviance by making the rules whose infraction con-stitutes deviance, and by applying those rules to particular people and labeling them as outsiders. From this point of view, deviance is not a quality of the act the person commits, but rather a consequence of the application by others of rules and sanctions to an "offender." The deviant is one to whom that label has successfully been applied; deviant behavior is behavior that people so label.[39]

It is clear from the above that the labeling theorist does not consider criminality a property inherent in certain types of behavior, but rather a status conferred upon a person who is found to have engaged in the be-havior.

Another implication of this theory is that the process of labeling is itself a critical determinant of the subsequent deviant or conforming career of the individual. For example, Tannenbaum says:

The young delinquent becomes bad because he is defined as bad and because he is not believed if he is good. . . .

The person becomes the thing he is described as being. Nor does it seem to matter whether the valuation is made by those who would punish or those who would reform. . . . Their [police, courts, parents, etc.] very enthusiasm defeats their aim. The harder they work to reform the evil, the greater the evil grows under their hands.[40]

One of the institutions most often guilty of labeling juveniles is the school. The school is in a position to be the greatest influence upon the lives of juveniles—particularly toward career orientation. If the student is la-beled negatively in the school, he will likely come to regard himself as inferior and is unlikely to succeed at school or elsewhere. The student who is given failing grades seldom makes a comeback. He tends to view himself as a failure and drops out of school.

A third implication of this theoretical position is that one of the factors determining whether deviancy will be reduced, repeated, or even broad-ened to include a wider range of acts is the nature of the reactions of the group to the initial act.[41] The reactions may have several possible effects. On the one hand, if the reprimanding institution wisely and discreetly imposes firm sanctions on the individual and attempts to involve the indi-vidual in acceptable activities, the chances are good that the individual will conform to the acceptable ways of the society and will develop a good self-image. On the other hand, if the sanctions are harsh, degrading, public—particularly if the actor is forced to leave the acceptable mainstream of society—chances of future deviancy may be heightened. It is possible that institutions contribute highly to delinquency by reacting to misbehaving

[39]Howard S. Becker, *Outsiders* (New York: Free Press, 1963), p. 9.
[40]Frank Tannenbaum, *Crime and the Community* (New York: McGraw-Hill, 1951), p. 18.
[41]Albert K. Cohen, "The Sociology of the Deviant Act: Anomie Theory and Beyond," *American Sociological Review* 30 (February 1965): 5–14. For the effect of sanctions, see John Delamater, "On the Nature of Deviance," *Social Forces* 46 (June 1968): 445–455.

juveniles in such a way that they are pushed away, excluded, further alienated from more responsible persons and standards, rather than pulled back in and rescued. In other words, there seems to be a tendency to shut out rather than open up opportunities for a juvenile to become involved in a legitimate, acceptable, conforming-to-the-norm situation. The person labeled is excluded even more.

Labeling theory raises serious questions about the advisability of recklessly stigmatizing people with labels like "criminal" and "delinquent" when the objective is principally to deter the behavior. When we attach the stigmatizing label, we may actually contribute to an increase in the undesirable behavior by seriously handicapping the individual's efforts to secure employment, training, licenses, etc. Labeling theory does little to explain delinquent or criminal behavior. It does a great deal, however, to emphasize the damage that can be done by attaching stigmatizing labels. The creation of the juvenile court and the introduction of specialized judicial detention and treatment services for children was intended to avoid giving them the stigmatizing label of criminal. Now that the term "juvenile delinquent" has become a stigmatizing label it may be time to reexamine the entire juvenile justice system.

All sorts of data acquired in the course of the delinquency- and criminality-labeling process are now in computers. Niederhoffer points out that the arrest, which places the stigma of criminal on an individual, is the culmination of a systematic labeling process. The labeling process begins with suspicion, with the suspect being known only to the police or some other investigatory agency. Eventually the courts certify the label of the defendant's criminality. The data are then computerized. The tremendous increase in the use of computers means that the label attached to a person as a result of his arrest and, later on, his conviction becomes a matter of permanent record available to law enforcement agencies and others throughout the country. Recently there are hardly any modern effective law-enforcement agencies without computer services. Stigmatizing data often go to data banks of the Federal Bureau of Investigation and the National Crime Information Center. The availability of these data to persons who might misuse them constitutes a threat to freedom and privacy. Regarding this, Niederhoffer states:

> The other side of computer technology is that it constitutes a threat to democracy—to privacy and freedom to dissent. Inevitably computerized information systems will place everyone in America from the age of fourteen to seventy into the category of possible suspect. And there is no statute of limitation on tapes, disks, and memory banks; they can be held thirty, forty, and fifty years, or in perpetuity. Moreover, not only state and federal law enforcement agencies, but also the Pentagon, the Army, the Navy, and the Air Force, have gathered data on millions of citizens. They, too, are interested in "troublemakers." The C.I.A. and the State Department have their computerized card files. The Civil Service Commission has millions of names listed in its security files. And how many other governmental agencies are quietly amassing their own computer banks of

data on "persons of interest"? In addition, the federal agencies intermesh with private agencies and organizations that collect information on credit risks, peace demonstrators, welfare recipients, radicals, liberals, intellectuals, and writers and speakers critical of the government's policies.

It is disheartening to contemplate that every "person of interest" may now be shadowed from birth to grave by a web of computers. With computers as master, we are a nation in which the citizens are under control and under suspicion. In fact, a campaign is under way to assign a "universal identifier" code number to each person in America, so that any scrap of information collected anytime and anyplace can be easily assembled.[42]

The possibility of a future "Senator Joseph McCarthy" using stigmatizing data contained in computers is raised by Niederhoffer in the following terms:

In a series of speeches in early 1950, McCarthy ominously waved a paper alleged to contain a list of 205 (then 81, and finally 57) Communists holding government positions. The source of the information was reputed to be files supplied by the State Department. In testimony before the Tydings Committee in the Senate, McCarthy ranted:

I am not making charges. I am giving the committee information of individuals who appear by all the rules of common sense as being very bad security risks.

Armed with a few incomplete dossiers, McCarthy terrorized the nation's leaders, demolished reputations, and devastated countless lives.

What would happen today if someone like Senator McCarthy could produce, not a spurious piece of paper, but an awe-inspiring computer printout of thousands or perhaps millions of names of people singled out as security risks because they had taken part in a demonstration against the Vietnam War? What would result if he arbitrarily demanded that they be dismissed immediately from their jobs in government or universities? The computer and all its ramifications just discussed constitute an electronic straitjacket, constraining freedom of thought and restricting even politically neutral activity, let alone dissent.

Furthermore, the typical victim of computer accusations is virtually helpless. He may never be able to pinpoint or prove the source of error in the computer record that damns him. And the very features of the computer that induce a paralysis of will in its victims generate in the minds of its masters a peculiar faith in its infallibility that nurtures bureaucratic arrogance.[43]

The following incident appears to justify Niederhoffer's fears:

In October 1970 an assault charge against a defendant in a Washington, D.C. court was dropped by the prosecutor because the arrest was obviously an error.

---

[42]Arthur Niederhoffer, "Criminal Justice by Dossier: Law Enforcement, Labeling, and Liberty," in *Current Perspectives on Criminal Behavior*, ed. Abraham S. Blumberg (New York: Knopf, 1974), pp. 47–67.
[43]Ibid., p. 60.

Soon after, at the request of the defendant, the Washington, D.C., police department destroyed the arrest records, the mug shots, and the fingerprints. However, in accordance with standard operating procedure, it had already forwarded copies of the records and the fingerprints to the central office of the F.B.I. Following its usual procedures, the F.B.I. refused outright to invalidate or destroy this criminal history, although the case was unfounded.[44]

CONFLICT THEORY OF CRIMINAL BEHAVIOR

The explanation of criminality as a form of deviant behavior must deal with at least two problems:

1. The process by which individuals come to commit acts that are defined by society as crimes.
2. The kinds of groups and areas that produce certain kinds of criminality.

Those criminologists who seek to explain why certain behavior is defined as criminal tend toward a conflict theory explanation. What becomes defined as a crime is related to the power of some groups in the society to include in the criminal law their values and interests. The same power structure, or one closely related to it, by its enforcement of the law imposes a variation of the same values and interests.

This point of view leads to the conclusion that the passage of virtually all criminal laws, the policies of nearly all law-enforcement agencies, and the operation of the criminal justice system are in some way influenced by political pressures of competing interest groups. Economic interest groups exercise a predominant influence on the governmental system, including the legislative, enforcement, and criminal justice systems.

Culture Conflict and Crime

The criminal law is a body of rules or norms of conduct that prohibit specific forms of conduct and provide for punishment for them. The type of conduct prohibited often depends upon the character and interests of the groups that influence legislation.[45] Everyone is required to obey the rules set forth by the state, as described in the penal code. Some people, however, belong to groups that have sets of rules or norms of conduct different from those required by the overall society's criminal law. Culture conflict arises when an individual is committed to rules that are contrary to those of the overall society. Whether behavior is criminal or noncriminal depends upon which conduct norms are applied.

Culture conflict is a common experience among immigrants to the

---

[44]Ibid., p. 63.
[45]Thorsten Sellin, *Culture Conflict and Crime* (New York: Social Science Research Council, 1938), p. 21.

United States. They come with many customs and traditions that are not acceptable in this country. Prior to World War II, when American influence was less pervasive than it is now, the problem was even more acute. Consider the Oriental tradition of "family honor." Under this system, if a woman committed adultery, it was the duty of either her elder brother or her father to kill her. This was not something that he *might* do; he was *obligated* to do it. If a man were to kill his daughter for that or for any other reason in this country, he would be convicted of murder.

There are still many conduct norms of foreign countries that clash with those found in the United States and lead immigrants into trouble with the law. When culture conflict arises in this way, it is referred to as *primary* culture conflict.[46]

Another type of culture conflict arises when people are committed to a subculture within the country that differs in some respects from the norms of the overall society. This sort of conflict is experienced by a person migrating from a rural area to an urban center—the Puerto Rican migrating from the island to New York City or a Negro family moving from the rural south to the urban north.[47] When culture conflict arises as a result of conflicting conduct norms within the society, it is referred to as *secondary* culture conflict.

The overall society has defined the "right ways" of doing things. "The hallmark of the delinquent subculture is the explicit and wholesale repudiation of middle class standards and the adoption of their very antithesis."[48]

Whether we regard the delinquent subculture as a repudiation of middle-class standard or simply a way of conforming to lower-class standards, it contains rules of behavior at variance from those of the overall culture of our society, and often leads to behavior that is legally viewed as delinquent.

Group-Conflict Theory as Explanation of Crime

In developing a group-conflict theory, Vold began with assumptions long established in sociology: first, that man is always involved in groups and, second, that action within groups and between groups is influenced by opposing individual and group interests. Society is a collection of such groups in equilibrium; that is, opposing group interests are in some way balanced or reconciled. There is a continuous struggle within and between groups to improve relative status. Groups come into conflict when the interests and purposes they serve tend to overlap and become competitive. As conflict between groups intensifies, loyalties to groups intensify. The outcome of group conflict is either victory for one side and defeat for the other or some form of compromise. Politics is primarily a way of finding

[46]Ibid., p. 6.
[47]Ibid., p. 70.
[48]Cohen, *Delinquent Boys*, p. 3.

practical compromises between antagonistic groups.[49] In a democracy, a struggle between conflicting groups often culminates in legislation trans- lating compromise into law. Those who produce legislative majorities domi- nate policies that decide who is likely to be involved in violation of the law. Crime, then, may be seen as minority group behavior.[50] Some of those whose actions have become illegal as a result of legislation violate the law as individuals. Many of those who belong to groups that oppose the law react as a group—a conflict group. The juvenile gang, in this sense, would be an example of a "minority group" in opposition to the rules of the dominant "majority."

In a group-centered conflict, "criminal" behavior occurs when action is based on the principle that *"the end justifies the means"* and *the end object is the maintenance of the group position.*[51] This principle is the rationalization offered to justify the actions of a juvenile gang, of organized crime running gambling operations, of the white-collar criminals who fixed prices in the steel and electric conspiracies, and of the people involved in Watergate. Whenever there is genuine conflict between groups and interpretations, correctness is decided by the exercise of power and/or persuasion.

Richard Quinney has developed a comprehensive group-conflict the- ory which he calls the *social reality of crime.* As he sees it, the legal order gives reality to the crime problem in the United States.

The theory of the social reality of crime, as formulated, contains six propositions and a number of statements within each. These may be sum- marized as follows:[52]

1. The official definition of crime. *Crime as a legal definition of human conduct is created by agents of the dominant class in a politically organized society.* Crime, as *officially* determined, is a definition of behavior that is conferred on some people by those in power. Legislators, police, prosecutors, judges, and other agents of the law are respon- sible for formulating and administering criminal law. Upon formu- lation and application of these definitions of crime, persons and behaviors become criminal. The greater the number of definitions of crime that are formulated and applied, the greater the amount of crime.

2. Formulating definitions of crime. *Definitions of crime are composed of behaviors that conflict with the interests of the dominant class.* Definitions of crime are formulated, and ultimately incorporated into the crim- inal law, according to the interests of those who have the power to translate their interests into public policy. The definitions of crime change as the interests of the dominant class change. From the

---

[49]George B. Vold, "Group Conflict Theory as Explanation of Crime," in *Deviance, Conflict and Criminality*, eds. R. Serge Denisoff and Charles H. McCaghy (Chicago: Rand McNally, 1973), pp. 77–88.

[50]Ibid., p. 81.

[51]Ibid., p. 84.

[52]This revised version of the theory is contained in: Richard Quinney, *Criminology* (Boston: Little, Brown, 1975), pp. 37–41.

initial defintions of crime to the subsequent procedures, correctional and penal programs, and police for controlling and preventing crime, those who have the power regulate the behavior of those without power.

3. Applying definitions of crime. *Definitions of crime are applied by the class that has the power to shape the enforcement and administration of criminal law.* The dominant interests intervene in all the stages at which definitions of crime are created and operate where the definitions of crime reach the *application* stage. Those whose interests conflict with the ones represented in the law must either change their behavior or possibly find it defined as criminal. Law-enforcement efforts and judicial activity are likely to increase when the interests of the dominant class are threatened. The criminal law is not applied directly by those in power; its enforcement and administration are delegated to authorized *legal agents.* As legal agents evaluate more behaviors and persons as worthy of being defined as crime, the probability that definitions of crime will be applied grows.

4. How behavior patterns develop in relation to definitions of crime. *Behavior patterns are structured in relation to definitions of crime, and within this context people engage in actions that have relative probabilities of being defined as criminal.* The probability that persons will develop action patterns with a high potential for being defined as criminal depends on structured opportunities, learning experiences, interpersonal associations and identifications, and self-conceptions. Personal action patterns develop among those defined as criminal because they are so defined. Those who have been defined as criminal begin to conceive of themselves as criminal, adjust to the definitions imposed upon them, and learn to play the criminal role.

5. Constructing an ideology of crime. *An ideology of crime is constructed and diffused by the dominant class to secure its hegemony.* An ideology which includes ideas about the nature of crime, the relevance of crime, offenders' characteristics, appropriate reactions to crime, and the relation of crime to the social order is diffused throughout the society in personal and mass communication. The President's Commission on Law Enforcement and Administration of Justice is the best contemporary example of the state's role in shaping an ideology of crime. Official policy on crime has been established in a crime bill, the Omnibus Crime Control and Safe Streets Act of 1968. This bill, a reaction to the growing fears of class conflict in American society, creates an image of a severe crime problem and, in so doing, threatens to negate some of our basic constitutional guarantees in the name of controlling crime. The conceptions that are most critical in actually formulating and applying the definitions of crime are those held by the dominant class. These conceptions are certain to be incorporated into the social reality of crime.

6. Constructing the social reality of crime. *The social reality of crime is constructed by the formulation and application of definitions of crime, the development of behavior patterns in relation to these definitions, and the construction of an ideology of crime.*

APPLICATION OF THEORY TO AN UNDERSTANDING OF CRIME AND CRIMINALITY

An examination of the theories discussed in this and the preceding chapter clearly indicates that some theories contribute more than others to an understanding of particular types of crime and criminals. For example, psychoanalytic theory, reinforcement theory, containment theory, and theories related to self-concept all contribute to an understanding of the emotionally disordered delinquent drug addict, a sex offender, a violent offender, or a sociopath. The activities of socialized delinquents may best be explained by such theories as differential association, anomie (Durkheim and Merton), social alienation, and reference-group theory. The high incidence of juvenile delinquency in the United States is best explained by such theories as modern positivism, the cultural dimension (Taft), economic determinism, social disorganization, culture conflict, and group-conflict theories. Other theories which help to explain the socialized delinquent include group theory, the subculture of delinquency (Cohen), the adolescent striving for manhood (Bloch and Niederhoffer), delinquency and opportunity (Cloward and Ohlin), and lower-class culture (Miller and Kvaraceus).

The various theories presented, therefore, may be more useful in explaining certain specific types of delinquency. As yet, no single causal theory has been developed that explain all forms of juvenile delinquency.

Another reason for studying causal theories is related to the proposition that understanding a theory can logically lead to programs and policies for effectively treating delinquent behavior. For example, if one believes that there is a degree of validity to the proposition that poverty causes delinquency, then we should implement programs for creating jobs for the unemployed and work out a more equitable distribution of the society's wealth. In this same context, if the negative self-concept problem is ameliorated in the family, this can result in reducing delinquency. In the following part we will present and analyze a variety of institutional programs, therapies, and intervention strategies for preventing and controlling delinquency.

SUMMARY: BASIC THEMES FOR CLASS DISCUSSION

1. *Anomie and Delinquency.* Durkheim originated the theory of anomie for explaining crime and deviance. Merton later developed the theory to explain crime and delinquency in terms of the following two basic points: (1) In most societies, including the United States, a great emphasis is placed on success goals. (2) When certain segments of the society are blockaded from achieving these goals through the legitimate normative means, a higher proportion of these people will use illegal means to achieve the success goals held out by the society. This concept explains why delinquency is higher in certain areas and among particular populations in our social system.

2. *Economic Determinism*. William Bonger was a leading proponent of an economic causal theory. He attributed the higher crime and delinquency rate among the poorer people in our society to a capitalist system where they were denied equal access to wealth. In response to this denial, according to Bonger, "the proletariat would fight back" by committing acts of crime and delinquency.

3. *Social Disorganization*. According to Clifford Shaw, Ernest Burgess, and other sociologists in the "Chicago School," crime and delinquency is higher in socially disorganized neighborhoods than in other areas of the city. Patterns of delinquency become embedded in these neighborhoods, and these patterns are transmitted from one generation to the next.

4. *The Criminogenic Society*. Milton Barron, like Merton and others, asserted that American society is dominated by a "win any way you can" philosophy. This makes the individual more likely to commit acts of delinquency in order to win in a success-dominated society.

5. *The Delinquent Subculture*. According to Albert Cohen, a delinquent subculture, often in the form of a gang, arises in socioeconomically depressed areas to cope with a society that indirectly discriminates against lower-class youths. In response to their being unfairly judged by middle-class standards, especially in school, they respond in "nonmalicious, negativistic forms of delinquency."

6. *Delinquent Opportunity Theory*. According to Richard Cloward and Lloyd Ohlin, who build on Durkheim and Merton's theory of anomie, the delinquent gang is formed to cope with the fact that lower-class youths are blocked from achievement in the society through normative means. They state in their central thesis: "Pressures towards the formation of delinquent subcultures originate in marked discrepancies between culturally induced aspirations among lower class youth and the possibility of achieving them by legitimate means."

7. *"Normal" Delinquency in Lower-Class Culture*. Walter Miller asserts that the value system of lower-class culture generates delinquency. The list of factors that generates delinquency among lower-class youths includes such focal concerns as: toughness, the ability to "con" or be "smart," and excitement for "kicks." Because these and other forces are often in conflict with the law, according to Miller, lower-class youths are "normally" delinquent.

8. *Adolescent Striving for Manhood and Delinquency*. Herbert Block and Arthur Niederhoffer, after examining the "adolescent striving for manhood" in various cultures, concluded that this was a significant factor in inducing juveniles to violate the law in American society. They found that delinquency during the adolescent period of life was a normal pattern for many youths. The gang and its concomitant violence is seen as a way for a juvenile "to prove that he is a man." Many black and Hispanic gangs in urban areas validate this macho premise.

9. *Group-Conflict Theory and Labeling*. Richard Quinney and others assert that crime and delinquency is a lower-class battle with rules of the dominant class in the society. They maintain that the laws of a

social system are created by the "ruling class" to maintain power; and that crime and delinquency is a way of fighting back against the dominant society's power.

QUESTIONS

12.1. What are some of the common elements of most group-oriented theories of crime and delinquency causation?

12.2. What is the value of studying theories of causation?

12.3. Delineate and critically analyze the three causal theories in this chapter that you find most useful for understanding delinquency.

12.4. Select several theories of crime and delinquency causation; then discuss the treatment or policy approach implied by these theories.

12.5. Do you believe that providing more opportunity for certain segments of the population would reduce delinquency? Why?

five

THE PREVENTION, TREATMENT, AND CONTROL OF DELINQUENCY

chapter *13*

Treatment Methods and Strategies

The origination of the juvenile justice system in 1899 was the foundation for the development of a variety of treatment methods and strategies for resocializing juvenile delinquents. In this section I will delineate a variety of the basic methods and issues that impact on the therapeutic process in different types of institutional and community facilities for preventing, treating, and controlling juvenile delinquency. These methods and treatment strategies are incorporated and utilized, more or less, in the various overall programs of juvenile reformatories, camps, halfway houses, mental hospitals, "therapeutic communities," and probation and parole programs. I will describe and analyze their uses in the context of these various institutions in the later chapters on community approaches and institutional programs for delinquents.

INDIVIDUAL COUNSELING AND THERAPY

A basic approach to treating delinquents involves individual counseling. Parents, teachers, and professional therapists utilize individual counseling approaches in the home, school, office settings, and institutions for delinquents. In professional therapeutic or therapy counseling, there are two persons present—the therapist or counselor and the patient or counselee. What occurs in the course of the counseling depends largely on the philosophy, training, and ability of the therapist. For example, if the therapist or counselor is a psychologist, probation officer, or other person trained in transactional analysis, the session will include an analysis of the "games" the delinquent is playing. Similarly, the psychodramatist, the reality therapist, and the gestalt therapist will utilize their systems in a therapeutic effort to gain an understanding of the juvenile and to increase his understanding of himself and of his reality.

Dr. Richard R. Korn, an eminent criminologist and therapist, shows in the following individual counseling session the unique problems posed in individual therapy when dealing with a recalcitrant sociopathic delinquent in an institutional setting. The session took place in an office in a custodial institution. Dr. Korn opens the session by asking the youth why he had come to see him.

> INMATE: Well, I've been talking to a few of the guys. . . . They said it might be a good idea.
>
> COUNSELOR: Why?
>
> INMATE (in a fairly convincing attempt to appear reticent): Well— they said it did them good. . . . They said a guy needs somebody he can talk to around here . . . somebody he can trust. A . . . a friend.
>
> COUNSELOR: And the reason you asked to see me was that you felt that I might be a friend? Why did you feel this?
>
> INMATE (a little defensively): Because they told me, I guess. Aren't you supposed to be a friend to the guys?
>
> COUNSELOR: Well, let's see now. What is a friend supposed to do? (Inmate looks puzzled.) Let's take your best buddy, for example. Why do you consider him a friend?
>
> INMATE (puzzled and a little more aggressive): I dunno . . . we help each other, I guess. We do things for each other.
>
> COUNSELOR: And friends are people who do things for each other?
>
> INMATE: Yes.
>
> COUNSELOR: Fine, Now as my friend, what is it you feel you'd like to do for me?
>
> INMATE (visibly upset): I don't get it. Aren't you supposed to help? Isn't that your job?
>
> COUNSELOR: Wait a minute—I'm getting lost. A little while ago you were talking about friends and you said that friends help each other. Now you're talking about my job.
>
> INMATE (increasingly annoyed): Maybe I'm crazy, but I thought you people are supposed to help us.
>
> COUNSELOR: I think I get it now. When you said "friends" you weren't talking about the kind of friendship that works both ways. The kind you meant was where I help you, not where you do anything for me.
>
> INMATE: Well . . . I guess so. If you put it that way.
>
> COUNSELOR: Okay. (Relaxing noticeably from his previous tone of persistence.) Now, how do you feel I can help you?
>
> INMATE: Well you're supposed to help people get rehabilitated, aren't you?

> COUNSELOR: Wait. I'm lost again. You say I'm supposed to do some-
> thing for people. I thought you wanted me to do some-
> thing for you. So you want me to help you get rehabili-
> tated?
> INMATE: Sure.
> COUNSELOR: Fine. Rehabilitated from what?
> INMATE: Well, so I won't get in trouble anymore.
> COUNSELOR: What trouble?

At this point the inmate launched into a vehement recital of the abuses to which he had been subjected from his first contact with the juvenile authorities to his most recent difficulties with his probation officer immediately prior to the offense (stealing a car) leading to his present sentence. During the entire recital he never referred to any offense he had committed but, instead, laid exclusive emphasis on his mistreatment.

The counselor heard this account out with an expression of growing puzzlement which was not lost on the inmate, who continued with increasing vehemence as his listener appeared increasingly puzzled. At length the counselor, with a final gesture of bewilderment, broke in:

> COUNSELOR: Wait. . . . I don't understand. When you said you wanted
> me to help you stop getting into trouble I thought you
> meant the kind of trouble that got you in here. Your
> difficulties with the law, for example. You've talked
> about your troubles with different people and how they
> get you angry but you haven't talked about what got you
> into jail.
> INMATE (visibly trying to control himself): But I am talking about
> that! I'm talking about those bastards responsible for me
> being here.
> COUNSELOR: How do you mean?

The inmate again repeated his tirade, interspersing it with frequent remarks addressed to the counselor. ("What about this? Do you think that was right? Is that the way to treat a young guy?" etc.) The counselor once more looked puzzled, and broke in again.

> COUNSELOR: I still don't see it. We'd better get more specific. Now take
> your last trouble—the one that got you into the reforma-
> tory. This car you stole . . .
> INMATE (excitedly): It was that——P.O. [probation officer]. I
> asked him if I could get a job in New York. He said no.
> COUNSELOR: What job?
> (The inmate admitted that it wasn't a specific job.)
> COUNSELOR: But I still don't follow. The probation officer wouldn't let
> you work in New York. By the way—don't the regula-
> tions forbid probationers from leaving the state?
> INMATE: Well, he could've given me a break.

COUNSELOR: That may be—but I still don't follow you. He wouldn't let you work in New York, so you and a few other guys stole a car. How does that figure?

(Here the inmate "blew up" and started to denounce "bug doctors who don't help a guy but only cross-examine him.")

COUNSELOR: Wait a bit, now. You said before that you wanted me to help you. We've been trying to find out how. But so far you haven't been talking about anything the matter with you at all. All you've talked about are these other people and things wrong with them. Now are we supposed to rehabilitate you or rehabilitate them?

INMATE: I don't give a——who you rehabilitate. I've had about enough of this. If you don't mind, let's call the whole thing off.

COUNSELOR: But I do mind. Here you've been telling me that my job is to rehabilitate you and we haven't talked five minutes and now you want to call the whole thing off. Don't you want to be rehabilitated?

(Inmate is silent.)

COUNSELOR: Let's see if we can review this thing and put it in the right perspective. You said you wanted to be rehabilitated. I asked you from what and you said from getting into trouble. Then I asked you to talk about your troubles and you told me about this probation officer. He didn't give you what you wanted so you stole a car. Now as near as I can understand it, the way to keep you out of trouble is to get people to give you what you want.

INMATE: That's not true, dammit!

COUNSELOR: Well, let's see now. Have I given you what you wanted?

INMATE: Hell, no!

COUNSELOR: You're pretty mad at me right now, aren't you?

(Counselor smiles. Inmate is silent, looks away.)

COUNSELOR (in a half-kidding tone): Here, not ten minutes ago you were talking about what good friends we could be and now you're acting like I'm your worst enemy.

INMATE (very halfheartedly, trying not to look at the counselor's face): It's true, isn't it?

COUNSELOR: C'mon now. Now you're just trying to get mad. You won't even look at me because you're afraid you'll smile.

(Inmate cannot repress a smile. Counselor drops his kidding tone and gets businesslike again.)

COUNSELOR: Okay, Now that we've agreed to stop kidding, let's get down to cases. Why did you come to see me today?

(Inmate halfheartedly starts to talk about rehabilitation again, but the counselor cuts in.)

COUNSELOR: Come on, now. I thought we agreed to stop conning. Why did you come?

INMATE: Well . . . I heard you sometimes see guys . . . and . . .

COUNSELOR: And what?

INMATE: Help them.

COUNSELOR: How?

INMATE: Well, I tell you my story . . . and . . .

COUNSELOR: And then? What happens then?
(Inmate is silent.)

INMATE (finally): You tell them about it.

COUNSELOR: Who do I tell?

INMATE: You know—people who read them.

COUNSELOR: Should I write a report on this session?

INMATE: Hell, no!

COUNSELOR: What do you think we should do?

INMATE (looking away): Maybe I could . . . (Falls silent.)

COUNSELOR (quietly): Maybe you could come and to talk to me when we really have something to talk about?

INMATE: Yeah . . . Aw, hell . . . (Laughs.)

This interview illustrates the problems and possibilities inherent in the crucial first counseling session with a sociopathic offender of average intelligence who attempted to conceal his true feelings and his motive to manipulate the therapist under the disguise of a request for friendly help.

The special character of the delinquent's motivations concerning treatment requires a special counseling technique. The usual methods of permissiveness, nondirection, and acceptance require modification. To have permitted the delinquent to "define the relationship" would have been disastrous, since that definition would have left the counselor no alternative to the roles of dupe or oppressor ("sucker" or "S.O.B."). Similarly, to have encouraged this sociopathic delinquent to "solve his problems in his own way" would have been merely to collaborate with him in the continuation of his antisocial pattern: the manipulation of personal relationships for the purposes of self-aggrandizement and exploitation.[1]

Another element involved in the individual counseling of delinquents is related to their rationalizing away their delinquent behavior by projecting the blame onto the larger society. This manipulation was part of the described interaction between Dr. Korn as the "counselor" and the "inmate."

In this context, very often in treatment, I have noticed that offenders tend to exonerate or neutralize their delinquent behavior by blaming "the society" which shortchanged them and caused their delinquency. Poverty, abusive parents, broken homes, limited opportunities, all real causal variables, are cited by the delinquent as the problem, rather than accepting any

[1]From *Criminology and Penology*, by Richard R. Korn and Lloyd W. McCorkle, pp. 562–566. Copyright © 1959 by Holt, Rinehart and Winston, Inc. Reprinted by permission of Holt, Rinehart and Winston, Inc.

responsibility for their own deviance. Although these rationalizations (which do have a basis in reality) are more likely to be used by adult criminals, they are also part of the self-concept system of youthful offenders. In the face of these overwhelming variables, the delinquent asserts that he is not responsible for his delinquent behavior. Society is responsible for his plight, and he concludes that nothing can change these causal conditions, so why should he "even try to change?" Although the offender's defense may be true, if he is to change, the therapist must get him to accept responsibility for his behavior, and some awareness of his own power in the therapeutic process.

These described conceptions of "the offender as victim of society" were cogently formulated and propagated during the late 1960s, especially in the writings of two black authors, George Jackson and Eldridge Cleaver. Both men were criminals and spent a good part of their life in prisons. In the book *Soledad Brother* (Bantam, 1970) by Jackson and in *Soul on Ice* by Cleaver, they put society on trial for their plight and rationalized away their own culpability and responsibility for their extensive criminal behavior.

The neutralization or nonacceptance of a self-concept of delinquent status impedes the possibility of treatment since the offender denies he has done anything wrong. He clings to the rationalization that, "it's all society's fault." A parallel is found in the Alcoholics Anonymous philosophy, which posits that before an alcoholic can be helped he must, as a first step, admit he is an alcoholic. For a delinquent to be resocialized he must acknowledge that his drug abuse, violence, theft, or gang behavior is wrong, and he bears the responsibility for his behavior. If his self-concept is one of denial of responsibility, it is difficult to reach and rehabilitate the offender. In the individual session presented here, the counselor was effective in not being manipulated and in getting the client to accept responsibility for his behavior and the *reality* of his life situation.

REALITY THERAPY

In the context of therapies that attempt to get an offender to confront reality, Dr. William Glasser, a psychiatrist who has worked with delinquent girls at the Ventura School in California, has developed a treatment strategy that he calls "reality therapy." Dr. Glasser maintains that, from a treatment standpoint, both the theory and practice of reality therapy are incompatible with the prevalent concept of mental illness. He describes the task of the therapist as one of becoming involved with the patient and then inducing the patient to face reality. A major objective is to get the patient to decide to take the responsible path. Dr. Glasser feels that reality therapy differs from conventional therapy on six points related to involvement:

1. Because we do not accept the concept of mental illness, the patient cannot become involved with us as a mentally ill person who has no responsibility for his behavior.

2. Working in the present and toward the future, we do not get involved with the patient's history because we can neither change what happened to him nor accept that he is limited by his past.
3. We relate to patients as ourselves, not as transference figures.
4. We do not look for unconscious conflicts or the reasons for them. A patient cannot become involved with us by excusing his behavior on the basis of unconscious motivations.
5. We emphasize the morality of behavior. We face the issue of right and wrong which we believe solidifies the involvement, in contrast to conventional psychiatrists who do not make the distinction between right and wrong, feeling it would be detrimental to attaining the transference relationship they seek.
6. We teach patients better ways to fulfill their needs. The proper involvement will not be maintained unless the patient is helped to find more satisfactory patterns of behavior. Conventional therapists do not feel that teaching better behavior is a part of therapy.[2]

The case of Maria illustrates Dr. Glasser's application of reality therapy:

Apathetic and despondent, Maria, a seventeen-and-a-half-year-old girl, was a far different problem from Jeri. Jeri was at least capable of taking care of herself fairly well, albeit illegally. She had good intelligence and some sort of warped self-reliance. Maria, on the other hand, had almost nothing. In institutions since she was about twelve, before then in foster homes, with no family, few friends, not too much intelligence (although test results are misleadingly low on these deprived girls), she came to my attention after she was involved in a serious fight in her cottage. I was asked to see her in the discipline cottage because she seemed so hopeless. She had been sitting in her room, eating little, and making no effort to contact any of the cottage staff. There seemed to be little we could do for her because she had given up herself. The fight that brought her into discipline was the result of a building frustration caused by an older, smarter girl, Sonia, who, recognizing Maria's desperate need for affection, pretended to like her in order to get Maria to be a virtual slave. Maria had attacked another girl whom Sonia had openly preferred to her and who joined with Sonia in making fun of Maria.

When I sat with her in the day room of the discipline unit, she refused to speak, just sitting apathetically and staring at the floor. I asked her my routine getting-acquainted questions, such as, How long have you been at the school? What are you here for? What are your plans? Do you want to return to your cottage? Maria just sat and stared. Finally she asked me to leave her alone. She had seen plenty of psyches (as our girls call psychiatrists) before, but she never talked to them. It was a discouraging interview, if it could be called an interview at all. We were worlds apart. After about twenty very long minutes I said, "I will see you next week." Saying nothing, she walked quietly back to her room. I felt that I had made no impression whatsoever. None!

Each week for seven weeks the same scene was repeated, except for different questions, and few enough of them because I could not think of what to ask. My

[2]Pages 44–45, 80–81 from *Reality Therapy* by William Glasser. Copyright © 1965 by William Glasser, M.D. Reprinted by permission of Harper & Row, Publishers, Inc.

most frequent question was, "Don't you want to get out of here?" Her reply, on occasions when she did reply was, "What for?" My attempts to answer were met with silence. I did not have a good answer because she was obviously involved with no one and had no way to fulfill her needs—her isolated room was probably the most comfortable place for her. At least in a room by herself she did not have to see others doing and feeling what was not possible for her.

At the eighth visit I detected the first glimmer of hope. She said "Hi" in answer to my "Hi" and looked at me occasionally during the interview. I decided on a whim to ask her about her tattoos. Tattoos are the rule with our girls, nine girls out of ten have some. On her legs and arms Maria had twenty or thirty self-inflicted tattoos—dots, crosses, words, initials, and various marks, all common with our girls. I asked her if she would like a large, particularly ugly tattoo removed. Unexpectedly, she said she would; she would like them all out. Her request surprised me because girls like Maria are more apt to add tattoos rather than want them out. Lonely, isolated girls, particularly in juvenile halls, derive some sense of existence through the pain of pushing ink or dirt into their skin and by the mark produced by the act. It is a way they have, they tell me, of making sure they are still there. On the next visit we talked further about her tattoos and her feelings of hopelessness. In addition, she brought up her fear that her housemother, toward whom she had some warm feeling, would not take her back into the cottage because of what she had done. Although a housemother can refuse to take a girl back into the cottage when there are serious fights between girls, she rarely does so. I said I did not know whether or not her housemother would take her back, but that I would have her house-mother stop by and see her if Maria wished it. She said she would appreciate seeing her housemother very much.

Maria now started to make progress. Her housemother, who liked her and recognized the loneliness in her quiet, uncomplaining ways, visited her and told her she was welcome back in the cottage. Her housemother also said how much she missed Maria's help with the cottage housework. Maria had been a tireless worker in the cottage. I told Maria that I had discussed her problems with the girls in my therapy group and that they wanted her to join the group. My few interviews, together with the powerful effect of the housemother's visit, had already caused some change in Maria when she left discipline. The girls in my group therapy took a special interest in her, something which might have been resented by a more sophisticated girl, but was deeply appreciated by Maria. The technique of getting girls who are more responsible to become particularly interested in someone like Maria is strongly therapeutic for them because it directly leads to fulfilling their needs and helps them to identify with the staff, thereby helping to sever ties with their own delinquent group.

Taking more interest in school, Maria began to learn to read for the first time. In the group we talked at length about what she might do, and it was decided that a work home with small children, whom she could love and who might love her in return, would be best. Older girls who have no families do well in carefully selected homes where they are paid to do housework and child care. Although by then she was no problem, we kept her a few extra months so that some of her worst tattoos could be removed and to allow her to become more ac-customed to relating to people.

The case of Maria illustrates that the key to involvement is neither to give up nor to push too hard. No matter how lonely and isolated a girl may be, if the therapist adheres to the present and points to a hopeful future and, in cases like Maria's, expands her initial involvement into a series of involvements as soon as possible, great changes can take place. Here the need for group therapy was critical for there she could gain strength from relating to more responsible girls and could see how she might emulate their more responsible behavior. Through our persistence Maria, perhaps for the first time in her life, was able to fulfill her needs.

From her good relationship with her housemother, Maria was able to go to a work home where her hard work and love for children were deeply appreciated. Later she married and our assistant superintendent has several pictures of Maria's growing and successful family in her "grandchildren" picture gallery.[3]

GROUP THERAPY WITH OFFENDERS

Dr. J. L. Moreno, a pioneer psychiatrist, first introduced a form of group psychotherapy into the correctional process in 1931. Before this innovation, the only form of therapy employed in the corrections and mental health fields was individual therapy, that is, a therapist-patient relationship. The group therapy methodology was described by Moreno in an article published in 1932 by the National Committee on Prisons and Prison Labor. The historic article was based on his work at Sing Sing Prison in New York. Moreno's later research and action methods, used at the Hudson Training School for Girls, provided valuable material for his now classic work, *Who Shall Survive?*[4]

Virtually every correctional institution for delinquents now has some form of group therapy included in its program. Some programs are therapist-centered; that is, the therapist attempts to treat each member of the group individually or together but does not intentionally use the members of the group to help one another. Other programs are group-centered. In such groups, the therapist considers every member of the group to be a therapeutic agent for every other member. Guided group interaction, which will be discussed later, is a group-centered method. Here the group is treated as an interactional unit. Some groups are psychoanalytically oriented, with the therapist seeking to give individual members of the group insight into their problems from a psychoanalytic point of view. Others are spontaneous and free and encourage members of the group to develop spontaneity. Psychodrama and role training are action methods designed to develop spontaneity and to modify illegal behavior.

In individual therapy sessions, an offender can rationalize, distort, or simply lie about what is taking place. However, in group therapy he must necessarily be aware that his description of the group process is subject to a

[3]Ibid., pp. 80–82.
[4]J. L. Moreno, *Who Shall Survive?* Nervous and Mental Disease Monograph Series, no. 58 (New York, 1934). Reprinted by Beacon House.

wider commentary and audience. Group methods, therefore, usually have broader impact than individual methods. An interesting anecdote that partially illustrates this point, with special reference to social control, is described by Korn in an article on a group therapy program that he directed in Vermont. Two youths, both members of the same therapy group, found some money on the grounds of the institution. Both knew that if they kept the money, one or the other, or both, might discuss the find in the group session. If they accepted the need to tell the truth in their therapy, they were confronted with a role conflict, and one or both might "cop out," tell the truth on the other. The group process produces an open situation that tends to merge the prison underworld with its more formal structure.

In addition to blending the subculture of the institution with its upper world, group therapy also opens up the therapist's activity to wider inspection and more critical analysis, not only by his peers, but by his clients. What he does as a group therapist is much more open to discussion than what he does in the individual therapy situation. The process of group therapy, therefore, presents the possibility for much greater impact than individual therapy, not only upon offenders, but also upon staff and the total social system of the institution.

In dyadic therapeutic interaction (single therapist-single patient), two personalities who may be far apart in intellectual abilities attempt to communicate about one of the individual's problems (usually the offender's). Generally speaking, therapists tend to come from a different sociocultural milieu than criminals. Therapeutic communication may therefore be significantly impaired. This is not necessarily the case in group therapy. Delinquents in group therapy are (by definition) in interaction with others who have comparable levels of understanding and usually a similar set of difficulties.

In group therapy delinquents become co-therapists with each other, and this seems to increase the potentiality of group understanding. Often in group psychotherapy, offenders who have difficulty interpreting and diagnosing their own problems are experts vis-à-vis their fellows. In fact, many sociopaths, generally considered the most difficult type of delinquent to treat, are excellent diagnosticians and interpreters of the problems of other delinquents. Sociopaths can thus be enlisted as effective co-therapists, and this sometimes has a positive effect on their own behavior.

In comparing group therapy with individual therapy (formal psychoanalysis in particular), one finds that the average offender's educational background and intellectual abilities are more adaptively geared to the group process. In psychoanalysis with offenders, for example, the therapist may develop excellent and appropriate formulations about the offender's problem. However, the analyst may have considerable difficulty inducing the offender to understand himself in the same way that the psychoanalyst thinks he understands the criminal. In group psychotherapy, which tends to operate on a less sophisticated intellectual level, the offender, with other offenders as co-therapists, is more likely to develop insights and under-standing of his behavior beneficial to his treatment. The offender can thus relearn behavior patterns on an emotional and action level in the group process, rather than being required to attempt an intellectual analysis that may be foreign to his thought processes.

GUIDED GROUP INTERACTION

Guided group interaction is a form of group treatment developed by Dr. Lloyd McCorkle during World War II while on duty with the army at Fort Knox, Kentucky. The treatment gained prominence in the area of delin-quency when it was successfully applied by Dr. McCorkle at Highfields, an institution for delinquent boys in New Jersey. Little emphasis is placed on academic training as a prerequisite for group leadership of guided group interaction sessions, and for that reason it is widely used in halfway houses throughout the country.[5] Guided group interaction is based on the view that delinquent adolescents can realistically appraise their life situations and make decisions based on that appraisal. The leader encourages free discussion of the events of the day and of relationships within the group. It is a "here-and-now" approach to behavior and concentrates on developing concern for others and mutual concerns with others. Each individual is encouraged to recognize his shortcomings and deal with them. The follow-ing is a description of a guided group interaction session:

> A guided group interaction meeting usually runs for ninety minutes. Typically, ten or twelve boys file into the room promptly at the scheduled hour, dragging in their own chairs. The director may introduce a new boy to the others, explaining that he was there to help them with their problems, as the experienced mem-bers were to help him with his.
>
> Immediately after such an introduction, Harvey, one of the group members who has been at the center for some months now, becomes the focus of attention, describing, in a somewhat belligerent tone, a clash he has had that morning with his work supervisor. The latter had taken offense at a comment he had meant to be humorous, and had yelled at him. Harvey, in turn, had grabbed the employee's arm. The employee had then shouted, "Get your——hands off of me." Although the narrator was giving a version of the incident favorable to his point of view, the other boys were hesitant to credit it, one after another criticizing him for having deliberately aggravated the employee: "What's wrong with you, Harvey? The man was simply doing his job." Harvey replies that he felt he had been humiliated, or "put down" by the employee, to which the others retort: "You put yourself down." Harvey, now aroused, states that he would not have grabbed the employee's arm if he had not "hollered and cussed at me," at which, he said, he himself had become excited and scared.

[5]Oliver J. Keller, Jr., and Benedict S. Alper, *Halfway Houses: Community Centered Correc-tion* (Lexington, Mass.: Lexington Books, Heath, 1970), pp. 69–72.

At this point, the leader intervenes, for the first time in fifteen minutes, quietly asking the group why they thought Harvey had acted as he did. The boys are quick to reply that, although he had been at the center for five months, Harvey could still be expected to make "smart" remarks and wisecracks. Almost half the group now hurl questions at Harvey, many of them simultaneously, all accusing him of being a troublemaker, a faker, and a "bad mouth." [These are euphemisms for more profane language.] Harvey at this point admits that the employee with whom he had argued probably agreed with the group's opinion of himself.

One boy then asks, "What will it take to get you interested in people?" When all he gets back is a muttered reply, another boy comments, "It would be easy to talk Harvey into committing a crime if he was 'on the outside.'" Here again (ten minutes having elapsed since his last question), the leader quietly asks, "Why?" The boy replies: "It doesn't matter much to him. Harvey seems like a weak person." The comments that follow are not all so negative, the boys admitting that, "Harvey does not enjoy hurting people like he used to."

The significance of this remark can better be judged by the fact that Harvey had had a long history of violent assault. In his most recent act, the one resulting in his arrest and conviction, he had forced a grown man, at the point of a gun, to crawl, bare-chested, on a gravel road. After several hundred feet of such humiliation and torture, when the victim, his chest torn and bleeding, attempted to lift himself up from the road, he had been met with threats that his head would be blown off.

Harvey now voices his concern that he might get sent to the state training school. "Why do you enjoy wising off?" The leader asks this question, to which Harvey admits that he didn't think of the feelings of others. Then one of the group comments, "If Harvey doesn't like someone, he just messes over him. He doesn't care."

"Does Harvey intend to hurt people here, at this time?" the leader asks, to which one boy replies, "No, he didn't mean to. His smart remarks were more off the cuff."

The counselor cuts in: "Harvey is not really sorry about the employee. He is simply sorry because he knows the man will be riding him from here on. He's sorry for himself, not for what he did."

The conversation had now gone on for an hour, and Harvey was permitted to step down from the "hot seat." In his place came Stanley, a black boy who had hit another boy with a mop because, "He told me I was lying. I didn't want him lying on me."

"How did this affect you?" the group asked. "Why did it make you mad when the boy said you were lying?"

Stanley began to get angry. "I thought it was like a team here. I got attached to you guys, when I tell you what I've done, you give me hell even though I said I was sorry."

The boys, thoroughly aroused, all reject his statements. "How come no one in the group can talk to you, Stan? What are you going to do about it, Stan?"

Incensed, Stanley remarks that he is "a cool agent," who does not have to justify himself to anybody. The others better not "mess" with him.

Harvey, now a discussant rather than the target of the group's concern, comments, "You're not near as cool as you think you are, Stan."

Another asks, "What does this 'cool' mean, Stan? Suppose you tell us just what this 'being cool' means."

Stanley becomes thoroughly belligerent at this point: "Anything I feel like doing, I'll do it. Besides, Harvey'd better watch himself, 'cause I don't like him messing with me."

The intensity of the attacks now increases: "What is this threatening stuff, Stan? Let's face it, Stan, you do threaten people."

Above the loud and angry attacks Stanley is heard defending himself: "That still stands. Ain't no one going to mess over me."

Another member of the group, stung but undaunted by his threats, asks, "What are you, Stan, a giant superman?"

Stanley fights back, "You just——with me and you'll find out. I won't let little boys like you——over me. I can handle myself pretty well. I ain't been——up like I have been. I been trying."

Suddenly he seems to change his tactics and, although still furious, pretends complete agreement though in a low monotone, "I'll go by what the group says. If you say I don't know what I'm doing, I guess I don't."

The others are not so easily placated. One comments, "Now you're playing games, Stan. You're acting like a baby. Your threats aren't bothering anybody."

Quite subdued, now, Stanley: "I don't mean it as a threat. I've been saying that kind of stuff all my life." As if he suddenly realizes that he himself has let drop his guard, Stanley shouts back angrily, "But nobody better tangle with Stan!"

Suddenly the air is thick with obscenities. A third boy, Frank, as angry as Stanley, now remarks, "You don't scare me none. Go ahead and make your move."

A fight appearing imminent, the leader, who has been silent during all the foregoing, quietly asks, "What's the group doing now? Aren't you trying to force a challenge?"

The tension eases and one of the group says quietly, "We just want him to stop that kind of——."

Stanley rejoins, "I ain't going to like these boys, if they keep messing with me."

For the remaining quarter hour the leader now took over, giving a summary of what had taken place. He referred to Harvey's clash with the employee and his belief that progress had been made, because this was the first time that Harvey had admitted being afraid. He was confident of Harvey's ability to control himself even when other people shout at him. He pointed out that Harvey had acted belligerently because of his fear of being "put down" before the group. The leader then emphasized the boys' concern for one another by relating how, when Harvey had recently got himself into an embarrassing situation, it had been Stanley who had stepped forward and permitted Harvey to "save face."

He then referred to Stanley's attack with a mop on another boy, pointing out that Stanley had told the other boy he was sorry. "Stan says he's trying to change, and he complains that the group won't recognize this. The group, on the other hand, says it does care for Stan, but it's not afraid of him either. The group feels that Stan is trying to 'put them down' by making them afraid of Stan. But," he continued, "Stan is showing us some of his true feelings in contrast to Frank who has been playing it real 'cool' in keeping his feelings hidden."

Here Frank admitted that, "I've had these feelings for a long, long time," that he often felt angry, and that he tried to conceal it by "playing it cool."

The leader then criticized the group for not having stopped Frank at the point when he had challenged Stanley to "make his move."

"The group should have asked what was going on because Frank left the issue of helping Stan and simply got mad."

Frank, his head low, in an undertone: "I might as well let my anger out here, or I'll never get out of this place."

The leader assured him, "Don't worry about letting it out."

The meeting ended with Stanley, still appearing angry, remarking, "I don't know what to say."

With the other boys looking concerned, the director closed the meeting: "You boys recognize you've got problems, and you're doing something about them."[6]

TRANSACTIONAL ANALYSIS

Eric Berne, the psychiatrist who developed the treatment strategy called transactional analysis, based it on the assumption that every person has available a limited repertoire of three ego states.[7] These are:

1. *Parent:* ego state that resembles that of parental figures. Tells us how to do things and what we should and should not be doing.
2. *Adult:* ego state that is autonomously directed toward objective appraisal of reality. Examines and evaluates. Bases decisions on facts.
3. *Child:* still active ego state that is fixated in childhood. The "I-want-to" feelings and emotions.

The treatment in transactional analysis consists of efforts to get Parent, Adult, and Child to work together, to allow Adult to solve problems.

In transactional analysis terms, a stroke is a fundamental unit of social action. An exchange of strokes is a transaction. When interacting with others, transactions take the form of (1) rituals, (2) pasttimes, (3) games, (4) intimacy, and (5) activity. Each person, in interaction with others, seeks as many satisfactions as possible from his transactions. The most gratifying social contacts are games and intimacy. Most games are ways of avoiding intimacy. In transactional analysis, the focus is on finding out which ego states (Parent, Adult, or Child) implement the stimulus and which the response. To attain autonomy, the individual must become game-free. He must overcome the programming of the past. The transactional analysis

---

[6]Ibid., pp. 69–72. Reprinted by permission of the authors.
[7]Eric Berne, *Transactional Analysis in Psychotherapy* (New York: Grove, 1961). See also, Eric Berne, *Games People Play* (New York: Grove, 1964).

group is considered effective in analyzing transactions. When applied to delinquents, it has been found helpful in improving life positions, vocations, recreations, and interpersonal relationships.

THE ENCOUNTER-GROUP PROCESS FOR TREATING DELINQUENT DRUG ABUSERS[8]

The members of an encounter group are very direct, bordering on harshness, in encountering a delinquent. This "directness" is a significant element in the encounter approach that is used in therapeutic communities. Following is a description of the encounter approach as it has evolved in treating delinquent substance abusers in a therapeutic community. Although this discussion focuses on the "encounter method" in a "therapeutic community" setting, it should be noted that this approach has been increasingly used for delinquents in general as a group approach in training schools, reformatories, and mental hospitals and other institutions for delinquents. (In the analysis T.C. stands for "therapeutic community.")

Most encounter groups consist of eight to twelve participants. In a typical session, everyone in the group settles down, as comfortably as possible, in a circle, facing one another. There is usually a brief silence, a scanning appraisal as to who is present, a kind of sizing one another up, and then the group launches into an intense emotional discussion of the basic personal and emotional issues that relate to the group's problems. In most groups a different person is put on the "hot seat" and is confronted in a rotation fashion. Sometimes an individual may request the group to discuss his or her particular problem, but most of the time the person on the "hot seat" is picked by another group member who has observed something in the person's behavior that requires attention.

A person's T.C. status, high or low, is left outside of the encounter group. This makes the group process more democratic and enables lower-status people in the T.C. with less power to speak up about issues that are bothering them. This opportunity is not usually allowed in the group system in the larger society. It is a valuable situation for adjusting grievances—and generally gives the recovering delinquent a feeling of power that he probably never had in his former life situation.

A conscious dimension of the group process is the use of senior members as "role models," and this is a significant factor in encounter-group sessions. A "role model" is a person who has been in the situation of the newer person and has made progress to a higher level of life performance in the group's structure. The "role model" is a dynamic example of what the newcomer can become after he learns, grows, and develops in the T.C.

---

[8]The following analysis of encounter groups is derived from a paper delivered by Lewis Yablonsky at the 15th International Institute on the Prevention and Treatment of Drug Abuse, Noordijkerbout, The Netherlands, April, 1986. The overall concept of the "therapeutic community" for delinquents will be more fully developed in Chapter 15.

A person who is a "role model" in a T.C. has gone through three levels of valuable experience: He has (1) been a substance abuser; (2) gone through the complex emotional process of eliminating drugs from his life; and (3) developed skills for remaining substance-free and leading a responsible life. These experiences can be passed on to a recovering delinquent through the group process.

Role models in a T.C. encounter group are usually not appointed as leaders in the group. Different group leaders emerge in any given session. Leadership evolves in a spontaneous way as a result of length of time "clean," seniority in group experience, and the person's effective talent and ability to contribute to the group process.

The senior members of a T.C. who become role models for new-comers have logged more encounter-group time and are usually more so-phisticated in their encounter-group ability. For example, when they get together in a "senior-members group" (as often occurs), they throw up fewer "smokescreens" to defend self-deceptions and to obscure their prob-lems. They waste less time on irrelevance and quickly get to the subject under discussion.

Their verbal fighting style is more like a rapier than a bludgeon. When a point is made, the group does not dwell on it and savor its "great success"; they move into another problem area. At least one senior group person who has logged many hours is injected into every T.C. group in order to facilitate the interaction, pace, and productivity of the session.

Also necessary in an encounter group is an awareness of each group member's ability to examine his self-deception at that time about himself. The newcomer is often handled lightly (given a "pass") until he becomes trained in the method. More experienced, senior residents are considered fair game for all-out attack. When they are on the "hot seat," there is an assumption that their encounter-group experiences have toughened their emotional hides. They can defend more capably and are better prepared to handle the group's biting appraisal of their personal problems.

When newly arrived individuals dominate a group, the sessions are more apt to be cathartic sessions that involve excessive and wild verbal responses. As an individual grows and develops skills in the T.C. organiza-tion, he usually develops better control and has greater insight. Older mem-bers tend to be more intellectual and in most respects more capable in group sessions as facilitators of productive group interactions and role models. They are also usually more adept at summarizing insights that may emerge in the process.

Often the comment made by a senior-person role model in a group to a newcomer is, "I remember when I was like you when I was here X amount of time." He then shares why he feels he is no longer in imminent danger of returning to a delinquent lifestyle. This permits the newcomer to identify with someone who has experienced the same internal conflicts that he is currently facing and has resolved these issues. The role model is "listened to" and respected because he is a living example of the success that can be achieved by the newcomer. He is not a professional who had not lived the experience—the role model has "been there."

In addition to this, a "role model" provides some preliminary information about the problems that the newcomer can anticipate when he reaches a higher level of social functioning. A role model might comment to a newcomer, "I vividly remember telling a group exactly what you just said when I was here six months. I talked about how helpless I felt at the prospect of never drinking or using drugs again—and in the back of my mind I had this terrible urge to use. I too thought that after I'd been clean six months I could smoke and drink 'recreationally.' I've been there. I tried it two or three times, fell right on my ass, and went back to my old habit. Now that I've been clean two years, I know I can't use, even a little. I can't use at all. Maybe you can benefit from my experience with failure. Take my word for it. You are just like I was, and like me you can't use drugs 'recreationally.' It's a dumb idea."

This kind of open self-revelation by a senior patient-therapist in a T.C. is rarely found in professional group therapy. Professional group leaders seldom use their own problems as examples for their patient. In fact, it is counterindicated in most therapeutic methodologies. In a T.C., however, it is standard technique for the acting "doctor" to "cop-out" and identify himself with the "patient's" problem. In the encounter group, therefore, an individual has pointed out to him an achievable, positive goal, exemplified by a person who can guide his growth from the successful position of his own personal experience. The role-model concept is often discussed in T.C. encounter groups as a basic socialization process for developing a personality that will be "drug-free."

It is important to note that related to the senior role-model concept is the fact that both the senior patient and the junior patient comprise an interaction of value to both. It can be stated that "when delinquent A *helps* delinquent B, delinquent A is also helped." When the role model is explaining why the junior addict can't use again, he is reinforcing his own resolution to stay drug-free. Therefore, a delinquent in a T.C. playing the role of "therapist" is being helped personally by his role. And since all residents of a T.C., at varying times, play "therapist," in the group process, they are helping resolve their own problems in the process.

The dynamic that should be emphasized in this interaction is that the "junior patient" can perceive future possibilities through his role model, whose progress represents an achievable goal. The "senior patient" can see where he was in his earlier approach to life, and this constant reminder of the way he was as a newcomer is important in reinforcing his resolve to remain drug-free.

The characteristic of random group construction in a T.C. sets up a mathematical probability that no one specific group will meet intact more than once. This gives all people in the overall T.C. a chance to meet almost everyone else in the population on a personal, emotional basis. This positively affects the esprit de corps of the overall T.C., since everyone gets to know everyone else on a very personal basis in the encounter-group situation.

This random group factor also helps defeat the problem of the "therapeutic contract" that emerges in many professional therapy groups, where the same people meet regularly in the same group. The "therapeutic contract" problem emerges in usual group therapy in a conscious and unconscious reciprocal agreement between two or more people, after meeting in the same group for a period of time, not to expose one another's psychological Achilles' heel. The unstated contract might be, for example, "If you don't expose or attack my embarrassing and painful problem, I won't bring up the problem that you don't want to discuss." This type of "covert" contract, which often emerges in group-therapy situations, impedes personal growth in the group, since the group becomes constricted in its search for truth. In a T.C. the problem is avoided because of the randomization of group construction.

In a T.C. encounter group, general good behavior is demanded on the implicit assumption that it affects internal psychodynamic processes. Most T.C.s use an approach that is the reverse of that commonly used in traditional psychotherapy. In most traditional therapeutic practice, the starting point for treatment is the internal dynamics of the patient. Generally, in professional therapy, the assumption is made that if a person's inner problems are somehow resolved, he will stop "acting out" his "bad" behavior, such as using drugs. T.C.s start with an attack on the reality of overt bad behavior that takes place in the T.C. daily life situation. In the encounter group, and in their life situation in the T.C., the group demands positive work habits, truth telling, and nondeviant behavior. If the addict in a T.C. lives positively and constructively in this manner drug-free for one or two years, it is conceivable that this will positively change his inner emotional dynamics. This theme of demanding positive behavior is repetitively hammered home in the T.C. encounter group. Any deviant irresponsible (often labeled "dope fiend") behavior is always subject to verbal attack. The fact that it is a *verbal* attack is also a learning experience, since many former addicts using verbal violence in an encounter group are learning physical violence impulse control. Many of these people who would formerly act out physical violence to express their angry emotions have learned to express these raw feelings verbally in an encounter group.

A key issue in the acceptance of the T.C. approach to delinquency is related to the reaction to the encounter-group approach. Many professionals and people in general raise such questions as: "Isn't it harmful to verbally attack a young delinquent who already has a weak ego?" or "How do you know when one delinquent is ventilating their own hostility and has no concern for the person on the hot seat?" or the basic question, "How does this approach change the delinquent's self-destructive behavior?"

My main response to these controversial issues is to point out that in the verbal "attack" in an authentic encounter group, what is under attack is not the *person* or the *person's ego*, but their *deviant behavior* and *self-deception*.

In an effective encounter group the "attackers," through hyperbole and exaggeration, denounce the self-deception that fosters self-destructive drug-abuse behavior and delinquency.

Another key factor about encounter groups in T.C.s is their emphasis on extreme uncompromising candor in their necessary attack on self-deception. No holds or statements are barred from the group effort at truth seeking about problem-solving situations, feelings, and emotions of each and all members of the group. In the encounter process on a verbal level, "anything goes" that will help the subject and the group in their better understanding of a situation or in their search for the truth about themselves.

The "anything-goes-verbally" concept about the encounter group is the *one* point that most participants of the verbal mayhem find difficult to comprehend. Too often they interrupt what is being done as a "personal attack," when it is in fact an act of caring. The best way I know how to explain this point is to clearly state that the rules of regular society and social interaction are modified or suspended in the encounter-group processes for the purpose of exploring truth and understanding. When the encounter-group process ends, the people involved return to the rules of more civilized society. This concept is often made clear when people who have been viciously attacking or ridiculing each other in the group situation smile and hug each other after the group session ends.

The encounter group may, therefore, be perceived as an emotional battlefield where an individual's delusions, distorted self-images, and negative behavior are attacked by the group to help the person under verbal attack better understand the reality of his life—at least as perceived by other group members who share the same problem. The method often involves *at first* exaggerated statements, ridicule, and analogy; and after the person whose self-deceptions are being attacked begins to listen to other group members more rationally, the situation is discussed in more rational, intellectual, and philosophical terms.

The encounter, paradoxically, is an expression of love. As one delinquent told another at the end of a harsh group encounter, "If I didn't care about you and also feel that you could change, I wouldn't tell you the things I do. It would be foolish to attack someone who is hopeless or helpless."

The encounter group, in addition to exposing valuable truths, has the effect of emotionally "toughening up" the egos of delinquents who are usually, underneath it all, vulnerable, dependent, and overly sensitive people.

It helps delinquents to see themselves as relevant others do. The encounter often produces information and valid insights into a person's problems. If at the conclusion of a term on the "hot seat" an individual who has been under attack has been able to hang on to any of his defenses about his behavior, they are probably "valid defenses." The delinquent is forced to examine positive and negative aspects about himself, as well as some dimensions about his behavior he would never have considered on his own.

This often leaves him with a clearer knowledge of his inner and outer world. It should also be noted that a significant part of the process involves support and "picking up" a person at the end of or after an encounter-group session. Here the positive aspects of the groups members are reinforced with care and love.

PSYCHODRAMA AND ROLE TRAINING

Psychodrama was first created in 1910 by Dr. J. L. Moreno. The method has been used in a variety of institutional and community clinics for delinquents. I have employed the method with considerable success since 1983 in two psychiatric hospital programs for delinquents and in my work over the years with a variety of delinquents.

The psychodramatic method can be described in brief as follows.[9] Psychodrama is a natural and automatic process. Everyone at some time has an inner drama going on in his mind. In this confidential setting you are the star of your psychodrama session and play all of the roles. The others you encounter in your monodrama may be your parents, an employer, a God you love or one who has forsaken you, a wife, husband, or lover who has rejected you or demands more than you are willing to give. The others, or, as they are called in psychodrama, your "auxiliary egos," may not be actual human adversaries but some ideal someone or something you want but cannot have—an unfulfilled dream or perhaps an obsession for fame or wealth.

Many people are able to act out these internal psychodramas in the reality and activity of their external life. For such people, psychodrama is not a necessary vehicle, except as an interesting adjunct to their life experiences. But for most people, psychodrama can provide a unique opportunity for externalizing their internal world onto a theatrical stage of life; and, with the help of the people present at a session playing relevant auxiliary ego roles, emotional conflicts and problems can often be resolved.

Psychodrama produces peak experiences—or exciting modes of acting—that often result in individual and social change. In psychodrama a person is encountering his conflicts and psychic pain in a setting that more closely approximates his real-life situation than in most other therapeutic approaches, where one is mainly talking about one's problems to a therapist. In psychodrama, for example, a young man in conflict with a parent talks directly to a person who, as an auxiliary ego, plays his parent. His fantasy (or reality) of his hostility or love can be acted out on the spot. He can experience his pain (in one context, his primal emotions) not in an artificial setting but in direct relationship to the father, mother, or other person who helped build the pain into him, since his enactment takes place

---

[9]Derived from Lewis Yablonsky, *Psychodrama: Resolving Emotional Problems Through Role Playing* (New York: Basic Books, Harper & Row, 1976; New York: Gardner Press, 1980).

as closely as possible to the pertinent, specific core situations in his life. The resolution of his pain or conflict does not necessarily require an extensive analysis or discussion, because he is experiencing the emotions and resolving his problem in action. Often when someone has had a deep psychodramatic experience, there is no need for lengthy group discussion or analysis. The protagonist has unraveled the mystery of his problem in action.

In most psychodrama sessions, benefits can accrue to members of the group other than the central protagonist. Group participants other than the main subject of the session are encouraged to witness aspects of their own lives that became manifest in the session, as if watching a dramatic play that projects their own behavior onto the stage in front of them. This kind of personal participation either as a subject or member of a group in a live psychodrama produces maximum emotional impact and therapeutic benefits.

Psychodrama often emerges spontaneously in a regular discussion-group therapy session. A therapeutic community paraprofessional makes this point when he described the following incident as it occurred in a regular therapy group session. The example involved a 17-year-old female delinquent in a three-day marathon group session, who spontaneously became involved in a psychodrama.

When her defenses were low on the third day of the group meetings, she began talking about her unresolved hostility towards her father, who had sexually abused her. (A painful traumatic situation that accounts for the drug-abuse patterns of many women and men.) At a certain point in her monologue on her painful and hostile feelings towards her father she said, "It's weird but Dominic here [another addict] really reminds me of my father." At this point a senior member of the group, who had some experience with psychodrama said, "OK, Dominic will play the role of your father."

What followed was an intense, cathartic verbal outburst of hostility towards "the father" which verged on physical violence as she got into her feelings. The director of the session placed a pillow in front of Dominic, and the young woman, without too much encouragement, viciously rained blows on the pillow, as she expressed her venom about how her father's sexual abuse had caused her a life of pain, a low self-concept, and how she had used drugs to kill the pain. Her feelings were later shared by other people in the group. The psychodrama had developed into a valuable, cathartic, and analytic discussion on how early parental abuse had affected various individuals' drug and alcohol problems.

John G. Hill, a correctional counselor in a Los Angeles County probation camp for juveniles, describes the rationale for and the methodology of using psychodrama to reduce aggressive behavior in a juvenile institution.

One of the major problems faced by correctional counselors in the care and treatment of juvenile offenders in the institutional setting is that of the aggressive, assaultive ward. He presents unique difficulties in terms of control and adaptability especially in the group living situation, and as his behavior directly affects the behavior of his peers, his negative acting out exerts undue pressures upon the group as a whole. . . .

With these thoughts in mind the possibility of utilizing psychodrama as a treatment tool in dealing with the aggressive ward became readily apparent based on four major assumptions.

1. Aggressive and assaultive impulses could be channeled in a controlled monitored setting allowing full expression without the danger of physical injury.

2. Motives behind these impulses could be explored in a manner readily visible to the wards involved.

3. Immediate catharsis could be achieved, reducing the probability of uncontrolled aggression and pressure in the group living situation.

4. Precipitating problems could be alleviated, examined, and explored as they occurred by a restaging of the problem in a psychodramatic setting. . . .

An examination of the case of David M. will serve as an example of the process in action. David M. is a Mexican-American youth of seventeen years, committed to Camp Fenner for murder. He is a large heavsyset boy, intensively gang oriented. His case file reveals a record of seventeen arrests ranging from assaults and robberies to the committing offense.

David entered "A" dormitory reluctantly. His initial reaction to camp was negative in the extreme. Within three hours of entering the program he had managed to alienate virtually everyone in the dormitory, staff and peers alike. His answer to every reasonable request was a resounding obscenity. The consensus of opinion by staff was that David should be removed to a security or "lock up" facility as soon as possible. This would probably have been initiated in short order had he not become involved in an incident with the reigning chicano in the dorm, Leon, a member of a rival gang. Staff intervened before blows were struck and David and six other wards were taken to the office for counseling. . . .

It was felt that the psychodramatic approach might prove effective in this case and the transition from encounter group to psychodrama was made by setting the stage for a reenactment of the confrontation between David and Leon. Initially an auxiliary ego staff member played the part of Leon to alleviate the bad emotional climate.

David was seated in a chair facing Staff who assumed the role of the other, Leon.

> DAVID: You bastards (indicating the group as a whole) are always messin' with me.
>
> STAFF: Man, you come walking in here like *vato loco* trying to prove how tough you are, what do you expect?

David does a double take and demands to know who staff is. Is he to be a staff or is he supposed to be Leon? The ground rules are repeated, indicating that what we are trying to accomplish is to relive the incident so that we can see what the problem is.

> DAVID: How come that punk (indicating Leon) don't do it himself?

Leon becomes visibly agitated and starts to get out of his chair. He is waved back. Staff explains that because of the charged atmosphere and raw feelings a substitute for Leon is being used. David is to regard staff as Leon for purposes of the psychodrama and respond to him accordingly. The initial confrontation is reviewed with the wards explaining that David had challenged Leon and that Leon had reacted by questioning David's right to enter the dormitory as a new boy and throw his weight around. Staff, assuming the *role* of Leon, picked it up from there.

> STAFF: How come you think you're such a bad ass? You can't come walking in her talking all that crap and shoving people around. You better get your act together.
>
> DAVID: Screw you man! You don't tell Mad Dog what to do or not to do!
>
> STAFF: Mad dog? Mad dog? They usually put mad dogs to sleep. What does that mean Mad Dog? Everyone here knows where dogs come from.

Leon laughs from the sidelines as David balls up his fists and glares about him.

> DAVID: I'm going to waste you *puto!* (This is directed toward the vacant space halfway between Staff and Leon.)

The interchange continues for some minutes and is evidently a source of some satisfaction to David who begins to relax as he realizes that he can express himself verbally without fear of physical retaliation. Another ward, James, a black who has been in obvious delight over the exchange, is moved into position next to David to act as his *double*.

> STAFF: (Continuing) I don't know how a punk like you stayed alive on the outs. If I'd seen you out there I would have brought back your *cojones* in a paper bag.
>
> DAVID: (Reddening at this reflection on his manhood, struggles with himself for a moment before answering) At least I got *cojones.* You ain't nothing but a *viēja.* You ain't nothing at all unless you got your home-boys around.

At this point James, who has obviously been anxious to participate, interjects as David's *double*—helping David to present himself more effectively.

> JAMES (as David): Yeah, you think you runnin' this dorm, tellin' everybody what to do all the time. You think you cool but you ain't crap!

David is somewhat taken aback at the unexpected support he has found and warms to his role. He begins to reflect on his statements, picking up cues from James.

> DAVID: Yeah, how come when I come in here you all of a sudden start giving orders? You ain't no better than me even if you been here longer. . . .

Leon now enters the session to play himself. The interchange between the two boys was now taking place in fairly normal tones as Leon, having vented his personal feelings from the group, begins dealing with David on the level of a person of authority trying to reason with a recalcitrant underling. David was resisting this process by pointedly ignoring Leon's arguments and discussing his own feelings of right and justice. While he played the *role* of wronged party with obvious relish it was apparent that he had little or no insight at this point into his role in the problem.

Staff suggested that the wards physically exchange places and Leon play the *role* of David while David assume the *part* of Leon. Both boys initially balked at the idea of role reversal but at the urging of others in the group reluctantly exchanged seats. Leon was the first to begin the dialogue. He assumed an exaggerated stance of braggadocio, fists clenched and lips drawn back. He stared defiantly at David.

LEON: (As David) You *puto* you ain't gonna tell me what to do!

David was obviously struggling at this point, not sure of how he should react. Then, apparently remembering Leon's tirade against him, launched into a vituperative monologue which continued for some minutes despite Leon's attempts to interrupt. The other members of the group seemed to be enjoying the performance immensely.

When David finally ran out of words Staff asked him what he was feeling at that moment.

DAVID: I don't know man, but I really got pissed off when he called me a *puto* and started staring at me like that. It made me feel like just kicking him and going off on him.

STAFF: Do you want to go off on him now?

DAVID: Yeh, yeh I do!

STAFF: (Handing David a towel) Okay, hit the desk with this. Hit the desk like it was Leon.

David takes the towel and tentatively hits the desk; once, twice, three times. Then he knots the end and brings it crashing down a half a dozen times.

STAFF: Who are you hitting, David?

DAVID: Him, Leon, the Flores.

STAFF: (Turning to the *audience*) What's happening here?

JERRY: It seem to me that he's getting pissed off at Leon for doing the same thing to him that he did to Leon.

MIKE: I think he's pissed off at himself.

STAFF: (To David) What do you think about that?

DAVID: I don't know what you're talking about.

LEON: Look man, I was doing the same thing you were doing from the first minute you walked in here. So maybe you can see how you was coming off.

David struggles with the concept for a moment then crashes the towel violent against the desk.

DAVID: You guys don't know crap!

David does not say this too convincingly, however. The rest of the group have had a glimpse of the truth and immediately begin to belabor the point.

STEVE: Hey man, maybe you got angry because you know the way it really is. Maybe you better face it instead of copping out.

JERRY: (Changing allegiance) Yeah, don't seem like you can take what you was giving out.

CARLOS: That's the trouble with you man, you don't know what's coming down even when everyone else can see it! . . .

Suddenly David lashes out with the towel striking Leon across the face, then screams at the group.

DAVID: Damn it! Why don't you *putos* get off my back?

Leon has reacted by pulling the towel out of David's hands and is about to hit him with the knotted end when Staff intervenes and pushes both boys back into their chairs. The other boys have leaped up anticipating a fight.

> STAFF: Okay, okay, now just sit down and calm down.

Leon is rubbing his face, looking daggers at David who is sitting slumped in his chair breathing heavily. The other members of the group settle back as Staff asks them to explain what has just happened.

> JAMES: I think David knows what's happening and is afraid to face it. He can't admit he's wrong so he has to take it out on somebody.
> MIKE: Yeh, he acts just like my little brother when he doesn't get his way or what he wants. He has a tantrum.
> JERRY: Yeah, he acting like a kid.

The others all echo Jerry's sentiments as David sits in his chair fighting back tears. Leon, sensing that David has just passed through an emotional crisis, relaxes and begins to talk. He becomes quite reflective and adult.

> LEON: I don't know, sometimes it's hard to be real. I mean to really see yourself. (He reflects for a moment.) When I was on the outs . . . when I was a kid, I got into fights all the time. I guess I was a real *vato loco,* everybody thought I was crazy, even my parents. I was in the hospital maybe five or six times. When I was fifteen I got shot and everybody thought I was going to die. When I got back on the streets I was a big man. I was tough. Then I started thinking how weird it was that it took almost getting killed and having a hole in my side to make me a person of respect. Anyway, now I had my rep and didn't have to go around personally going off on people. Sure, I done some gang banging but most of the time since then I kept laid back out of sight. I got things I want to do. I got a *veija* and a kid. I guess I know what David feels like. I guess he still got to make his rep. He's just not going about it the right way. Going off on *vatos* in camp ain't gonna make it. That way somebody going to do him when he gets back on the street. We all got to get along here and do our time the best way we can. We got to stick together. When I was sitting here doing his trip I was getting next to how he was feeling. I guess because I been there myself.

Leon has appeared to have lost all his animosity, and during the course of his soliloquy David listened intently. David seemed surprised that Leon expressed empathy with his feeling, especially in view of the towel incident. He was having difficulty in controlling his tears.

> STAFF: (To David) Okay, how are you feeling now?
> DAVID: I don't know man. I don't know how I'm feeling. I feel all washed out. I feel like I don't give a damn about anything. I'm tired.
> LEON: You got to get with it. You were talking that everyone was down on you without giving you a chance. Well it seems to me that you were down on everybody without giving us a chance.
> DAVID: I don't know. With the *putos* on the street you got to get them before they get you, you know that, otherwise they walk all over you. I know you got homeboys here but no one is going to walk over me.

LEON: Okay, no one is going to walk over you here as long as you take care of business. There's too many dudes out there that want to see us firing on each other. You're just going to make it harder on yourself and the rest of us unless you're cool.

DAVID: (Shaking his head to indicate doubt, reflects for a moment then tentatively holds out his hand. He finds it hard to meet Leon's eye.) Okay, okay. I'm sorry about the towel, huh? I guess I was pretty pissed off.

Leon takes David's hand and shakes it firmly, making the comment that he can clearly see why they call him Mad Dog. At this point David has some recognition of responsibility to the group.

For David the psychodrama was both a catharsis and an initiation into the group living setting of "A" dormitory. While the session could not be considered a panacea for David's problems it did provide the initial step which allowed him to remain in the program instead of being transferred to maximum security prison. Perhaps most important, for the first time, it allowed him to see himself as others saw him; the beginnings of insight, and hopefully a positive change in behavior.[10]

The foregoing examples are cases handled in an institutional setting. In my work with gangs, I often used role playing in crisis situations. Gang life moves so fast that it is not possible to wait until gang members are apprehended and placed in an institution. To prevent crime, one must respond to emergencies. In the following account, the underlying theory and elements of a psychodramatic session (warm-up, action, and postdiscussion) are applied to (1) an immediate "live" problem (2) of an "emergency" nature, (3) in the "open community," and (4) often emerging unexpectedly.

A disturbed gang leader, accompanied by two friends, accosted me as I was walking down the street, pulled out a switchblade knife, and announced that he was on his way to kill a youth who lived in a nearby neighborhood on the upper west side of Manhattan. I moved into action armed with a psychodramatic approach.

First, I was prepared for this emergency-possibility, since on a continuing basis I had made sociometric tests which revealed the relationships of various gangs and gang networks in the area. I knew the gangs that were feuding and the leadership patterns of each group. More than that, the youth facing me already had had previous exposure to psychodrama; this was helpful, as we could move right into action. In short, the groundwork was set for this emergency use of psychodrama.

I asked myself: why did the youth stop me before he went to stab the other youth? I suspected the chances were good that he really did not want to commit this violence and wanted me to help him find a way out.

The "Ape," as this boy was called by the gang, was openly defiant and upset.

[10]John Hill, "Psychodrama With Gangs," an unpublished paper.

His opening remark was:

> "Man, I'm packin'; I got my blade (switch-blade knife) right here. I'm going to cut the s——out of those m—— f—— Dragons. I'm going up and get them now . . . once and for all."

In short, he had a knife and was going to stab any Dragon gang boys he met that day. It was also reasonable to assume that he would stab any youth who, in his hysterical judgment, was a Dragon.

The boys followed me to my nearby office and the session began with the use of another gang boy as an auxiliary ego in the role of the potential victim. A paper ruler replaced the knife (for obvious reasons), and the "killing" was acted out in my office under controlled psychodramatic conditions.

The psychodrama, in brief, had all of the elements of a real gang killing. The Ape (the subject) cursed, fumed, threatened, and shouted at the victim, who hurled threats and insults in return. Ape worked himself into a frenzy and then stabbed the auxiliary ego (the gang boy playing the part) with the paper knife. The psychodramatic victim fell dead on the floor.

The Ape was then confronted with the consequences of his act in all of its dimensions, including the effect on his family. He began to regret what he had done and was particularly remorseful when (psychodramatically) an auxiliary ego playing the role of a court judge sentenced him "to death in the electric chair."

The psychodrama accomplished at least two things for this very potential killer: (1) He no longer was motivated to kill, since he had already accomplished this psychodramatically. (2) He was confronted with the consequences of this rash act; this was an added dimension of consideration. Many gang boys are unable to think ahead in a situation to the outcome. These factors possibly served as a deterrent to the actual commission of a murder. Of course, this boy required and received further therapy, which sought to deal with his more basic personality problems. Moreover, considerably more work was attempted on the gang networks, so as to minimize their potential for violence. However, the emergency psychodrama, *in situ,* the immediate situation, did deter the possibility of Ape's committing a homicide, at least on that particular day.[11]

Group psychotherapy and psychodrama provide the opportunity for actual direct role training. Here offenders can view themselves and others by presenting their problems for group discussion and analysis. More than that, they are in a position to correct (or edit) their illegal actions in the presented situations. The offender can try out or practice legally conforming roles in the presence of criminal "experts," who quickly detect whether he is conning the group or playing it straight. In a role-playing session in which offenders were being trained for future employment, for example, one offender (who was soon to be released from prison) went through the

---

[11]Lewis Yablonsky, "Sociopathology of the Violent Gang and Its Treatment," in *Progress in Psychotherapy*, eds. Jules H. Masserman and J. L. Moreno (New York: Grune & Stratton, 1956–1960), vol. 5, *Reviews and Integrations* (1960), pp. 167–168. Reprinted by permission.

motions of getting a job with apparent disinterest. This fact was quickly and forcefully brought out in the open by other members of the group, producing a valuable discussion on the basic need of employment for going straight. In another session one of the authors observed a violent offender learn to control his assaultive impulse by talking about, rather than acting out, his wish to assault a member of the group. He learned to talk about violent impulses rather than assault first and discuss later.

A characteristic of group treatment, therefore, is that it provides an opportunity for violent offenders to talk or act out their illegal motivations in a controlled setting. After acting out their destructive impulses in the session, they may no longer have the need to carry them out in reality. The group also gives offenders and their peer co-therapists an opportunity to assess the meaning of violence through discussion. An empathic group can help the violent offender understand his compulsive emotions. Among other things, he learns he is not alone in his feelings.

Many offenders have difficulty controlling immediate compulsions for future goals. They tend to live in the moment and often lack the ability to relate the past to the present, the present to the future. The thought of future punishment or past experience doesn't usually enter their conscious deliberations to serve as a deterrent to illegal action. Training in understanding time dimensions is therefore often useful in crime prevention.

Psychodrama as a group process provides such time flexibility. The offender can act out the past, immediate, or expected problem situations that are disturbing him. The process is useful in working with criminals who manifest impulsive behavior. Psychodrama, in particular the "future-projection technique," by means of which a person propels himself into a future situation, provides an opportunity for the offender to plan for a legally conforming future. This technique has been used with offenders about to be released into the open community, to project them into relevant future social situations in which they will find themselves. These role-test situations include potential problems in the community, on the job, with the family, with supervising probation officers, and others.

The role-training process tends to build up the offender's resistance to efforts on the part of his delinquent friends to seduce him back into delinquent activity. Psychodrama, therefore, provides an opportunity for the immediate-situation-oriented delinquent to review some of his past and future behavior with its many implications for resisting delinquent activity. To the offender with con-man or sociopathic characteristics, words are cheap. Considerable research indicates that it is very difficult to lie in action during psychodrama. Because group pressures make distortion so difficult, the offender is forced to assess his behavior and its rationale closely. This, combined with opportunities to try out legally conforming behavior patterns before such severe judges as his peers, helps the offender to reexamine and reject his illegal behavior patterns and learn socially conforming practices. Individual therapy, group therapy, and psychodrama are widely used in a variety of community and institutional treatment settings.

SUMMARY: BASIC THEMES FOR CLASS DISCUSSION

1. There are special problems inherent in the individual counseling of most delinquents, especially sociopaths. They are often manipulative, recalcitrant, and self-deceptive. Consequently, the therapist must often deal with a tough facade and deceptive tactics in order to get through to the delinquent client. Once the therapist gets past the youth's delinquent mask and game playing, he can help by counseling the real person behind the facade.

2. In this context, "reality therapy," a method developed by Dr. William Glasser, is effective in helping delinquents confront the reality of their problems and to accept responsibility for their deviant behavior. His approach tends to deal with the "here and now" rather than dwell on the historical case history factors that caused the juvenile's delinquent behavior. In the process of reality therapy, the therapist also confronts morality issues and how bad behavior affects the delinquent, his future, his family, and his victims. The therapist attempts to help the client find a more satisfactory way of behaving to fullfil his or her needs.

3. Since Dr. J. L. Moreno introduced group therapy and psychodrama into correctional facilities in the early 1930s, the methods have flourished and have been utilized in almost every type of treatment approach for both criminals and delinquents. Group therapy facilitates the delinquent's confrontation with his or her behavior. Members of a group can sometimes see the flaws of rationalizing their delinquent behavior when they hear someone like themselves presenting a problem. They can also begin to see in a group that they are not alone and that their problems are very similar to other delinquents' in the group. In group therapy, not only is the professional leader helpful, but delinquents can become co-therapists to each other in the process of personal problem solving.

4. *Encounter-group therapy* helps delinquents confront the falaciousness of their self-deceptions and rationalizations about their delinquent behavior. When various self-deceptions are removed in the encounter-group process, delinquents can face the reality of their behavior, how it has hurt them, and how they can change. A key point in the method is that self-destructive behavior is challenged rather than one's self or ego. The process is basically involved with getting at the truth of a person's self-destructive behavior, and points out ways in which one's life can change in a positive direction, away from delinquent behavior. The process leaves members of the group with a clearer perception of their inner and outer world.

5. Psychodrama has become an important method in working with delinquents. It enables delinquents to examine and analyze situations and scenes in their lives which lead to their self-destructive delinquent behaviors. In particular, role-playing sessions related to better communication with parents and resolving family problems are very useful. Moreover, the acting out of the range of problems

felt by most delinquents in the safe group setting of a psychodrama enables a youth to better understand the source of his anger (usually towards his parents) and how he can control his violent tendencies. Acting out violent or deviant behavior in psychodrama often deters the delinquent involved in this therapeutic process from the necessity of acting out his violent proclivities in real life. In a psychodrama, under controlled conditions, the delinquent can learn more about the causes of his or her delinquent behavior, and develop skills and strategies to control negative, impulsive behavior patterns.

QUESTIONS

13.1. What factors should a therapist take into account in the process of individual counseling with a delinquent?

13.2. What are some of the goals of Glasser's "reality therapy"?

13.3. What are the advantages and disadvantages of group therapy with delinquents as compared to individual counseling?

13.4. Discuss the dynamics of encounter-group therapy. Select a negative behavioral pattern like alcohol or substance abuse and set up a modified encounter group in the classroom for discussing the subject using the "hot-seat" approach discussed in this chapter. At the end of the brief session have each student discuss their pro and con feelings about the encounter method and its efficacy.

13.5. What are the advantages of psychodrama over discussion-group therapy?

chapter 14

Community Treatment and Prevention Programs

A number of methods have evolved for treating juvenile offenders in the community. Dominant among these are probation and parole. Another strategy involves community delinquency-prevention programs in high-delinquency areas. Many of the individual- and group-treatment approaches described in the last chapters are utilized in these community settings.

All these varied approaches rest on the assumption that there are advantages to treating the offender or potential offender in the community. The general advantages of community-based programs are that they are less costly and have a better chance for success than institutional programs because the environment is more natural than the onerous and artificial milieu of the state reformatory. The prime disadvantage of treating the offender in the community is the fact that the individual is apt to be living within the same environmental set of causal factors that originally produced his crime or delinquency. These negative forces must be vitiated or overcome if the individual is to function as a law-abiding citizen, whether or not he spends time in a correctional instutition.

COMMUNITY CRIME AND DELINQUENCY PREVENTION

In addition to the standard approaches of probation and parole, a variety of other systems attempt to prevent crime. These include attacks on the problem at various levels in the social system.

Macrosociological programs, or efforts at large-scale social change, have been organized to provide opportunities for more people to achieve the culturally approved goals of the society without having to resort to illegal means. These include increased access to education, training, and employment for all members of the society, including those in the lowest socioeconomic categories.

On another level, neighborhood and community programs have been designed to reduce the incidence of criminality and delinquency in problem areas. These programs are based on the assumption that certain urban areas with high delinquency rates tend to foster crime and delinquency and that the development of indigenous anticriminal leadership and services in these areas would reduce the incidence of criminal and delinquent behavior.

Clinical treatment programs, largely psychological in orientation, have been developed on the assumption that delinquent behavior results from personal pathology. The programs developed include psychiatric casework, social group work, and combinations of these with services to individuals and families. Professional people, usually social workers, attempt to modify attitudes and behavior patterns of persons deemed likely to engage in delinquent behavior.

Child-Guidance Programs

Virtually every large city in the United States has one or more child-guidance clinics offering treatment to adolescents. These services are not limited to children considered delinquent or diagnosed as predelinquent, but they have been considered useful in preventing delinquent behavior. Problem children are referred to these clinics by social work agencies, schools, police, and at times juvenile courts. The first clinic of this type directed at delinquency prevention was established by Dr. William Healy in Chicago in 1909 as an adjunct of the Chicago juvenile court.

In an attempt to evaluate the effect of child guidance on delinquency in Boston, the Cambridge-Somerville Youth Study was instituted in 1936.[1] The program continued for nine years, through 1945. On the basis of interviews with teachers, psychiatric evaluations, and psychological tests, some 750 boys attending schools in Cambridge and Somerville, Massachusetts, were classified as to the likelihood of their becoming delinquent. By a random process 325 were assigned to an experimental group to receive preventive treatment and a matched group of 325 boys was studied as a control group. The experimental group was provided with family guidance, individual counseling, tutoring, camp and recreational facilities, correction of health defects, medical care, and when deemed necessary, financial assistance from community agencies. Services were provided for an average of five years. Surprisingly, follow-up studies made 5, 10, and 25

---

[1]Edwin Powers and Helen Witmer, *An Experiment in the Prevention of Delinquency: The Cambridge-Somerville Youth Study* (New York: Columbia University Press, 1951).

years later revealed no statistically significant difference between the treated and the untreated group with respect to number of criminal convictions or age at conviction. The treatment program had been relatively ineffective as a preventive of delinquency or criminality.[2]

Area Projects in Delinquency Prevention

In contrast to the child guidance or clinical approach, which attempts to work on the child, area programs try to change the social environment in which the child grows up. Such programs coordinate the activities of existing facilities and agencies and establish additional facilities if this seems advisable. Community organization experts attempt to activate or organize councils representing as many social-welfare agencies as will cooperate and sometimes seek to organize the people of the delinquency or problem area into neighborhood committees for action.

The Chicago Area Project   The first important program of this sort was initiated by Clifford R. Shaw in Chicago in 1933. The program was developed after the research of Shaw and his colleagues had clearly indicated that the slum areas of large cities were characterized by a disproportionately large number of delinquent children and criminals. The program was based on several assumptions that have become standard:

1. In high-delinquency areas, delinquency is symptomatic of deeper social ills. It is a product of the social milieu. The same blighted areas that have high delinquency rates also have high rates of economic dependency, illness, infant mortality, substandard housing, and poverty. (This is as true today as it was in the 1930s.)
2. Delinquency cannot be attributed to factors inherent in race or nationality groups.
3. Delinquency in deteriorated areas may frequently be regarded as conformity to the expectations, behavior patterns, and values of the groups of boys in the neighborhood.
4. Most delinquents in deteriorated areas are not inferior to children in the more privileged communities in any fundamental way. Delinquency is a part of the social tradition of the neighborhood; a large segment of the population tolerates, reinforces, and even encourages delinquent behavior.
5. Current practices in dealing with delinquency have been ineffective. It is not possible to save a boy apart from his family or community. A community with a new morale and new leadership directed in socially constructive channels is essential.
6. *The local neighborhood can be organized to deal effectively with its own*

---

[2]Joan McCord and William McCord, "A Follow-up Report on the Cambridge-Somerville Youth Study," *Annals of the American Academy of Political and Social Science* 322 (March 1959): 89–98.

problems. There exists in the neighborhood sufficient indigenous leadership to bring about changes in attitudes, sentiments, ideals, and loyalties for the construction of a more acceptable community lifestyle.

The Chicago Area Project organized community committees in six areas of Chicago: Hegewisch, Russell Square, South Side, Near North Side, Near West Side, and Near Northwest Side. Twenty-two neighborhood centers involving over 7,500 children developed in these areas. The community committees were organized with the aid of a staff member of the project, but the staff member did not exercise control. He was available to mobilize needed resources or as an adviser only if called upon by the committee. The neighborhood committee selected a qualified local resident as director, and that person was then employed as a staff member of the area project. Policy decisions were left to the neighborhood committee, whether the "experts" on the staff of the area project agreed or not. The residents of the neighborhood were in control.[3] Ten years after its inception, the Russell Square Community Committee, for example, had 125 active members and 700 contributing members. These included local businessmen and political leaders, bartenders, plumbers, carpenters, workers, and some former delinquents.

The projects encouraged the expansion of existing facilities for recreation and the construction of new ones. Efforts were made to improve school community relations and particularly to encourage teachers to remain in the schools. Clubwork, discussion groups, and hobby groups were used as tools for developing community spirit.

One of the most important aspects of the area-project program has been the preparation of offenders for return to the community. Offenders soon to be released are visited in their institutions, encouraged to participate in committee activities upon their return, and helped to establish contacts with employers and other local groups. These legitimate activities furnish the framework within which the offender returning from an institution can become accepted and can come to think of himself as a full member of the community.

The social climate of a community can be expected to improve as the people in it assume greater responsibility for its direction. A community administered by outsiders is less likely to develop esprit de corps. The Chicago Area Project demonstrated that people can be found in the deteriorated areas of our cities capable of supplying the leadership necessary to increase constructive action. While the effect of the Chicago Area Project on delinquency was not precisely measured, in all probability delinquency was substantially reduced as a consequence of the effort. The Chicago Area Project was the pioneer model for many comparable programs that have emerged in recent years.

[3]Solomon Kobrin, "The Chicago Area Project: A 25-Year Assessment," *Annals of the American Academy of Political and Social Science* 322 (March 1959): 19–29.

The Mid-City Project: Boston   The Mid-City Project was a delinquency-control program in a lower-class district of Boston, in operation between 1954 and 1957. It was in many ways similar to the Cambridge-Somerville Youth Study and the Chicago Area Project. A major objective of the project was to reduce the amount of illegal activity engaged in by resident adolescents. On the assumption that delinquent behavior by lower-class adolescents, whatever their personality characteristics, was to a significant extent influenced by characteristics of the community, the project initiated action programs directed at three of the societal units considered to exert important influence on delinquent behavior: the community, the family, and the gang.

The community program concentrated on developing and strengthening local citizens' groups so that they might deal with delinquency more effectively. An attempt was also made to secure the cooperation of professional agencies operating in the community, including settlement houses, churches, schools, the police, the court, and the probation department. One of the goals of the program was to increase cooperation among the assorted professional agencies and between those agencies and the citizens' groups. The long-range goal was to improve the processes of delinquency prevention and control.

The family program was based on the assumption that problem families contribute to delinquency. Families that had used public welfare services over a long period of time were located and subjected to an intensive program of psychiatrically oriented casework.

The gang program was modeled after the New York City Youth Board detached-worker program. Detached street workers were assigned to groups with instructions to contact, establish relationships with, and attempt to change the attitudes and behavior patterns of gangs in the area.

All workers were professionally trained, with degrees in group work, casework, or both. Each worker devoted primary attention to a single group, maintaining intensive contact with group members over an extended period. Psychiatric consultation was available on a regular basis.

Contact was maintained with 400 youngsters between the ages of 12 and 21, comprising the membership of 21 corner gangs. Seven of these, totaling 205 members, were subjected to intensive attention. Workers contacted these groups on an average of three and a half times a week. Contact periods averaged five or six hours. The total duration of the services was from 10 to 34 months. Four of the groups were white male, Catholic, largely Irish, with some Italian and French-Canadian membership. One was black male, one white female, and one black female. The average size of the male groups was 30; of the female, 9. The groups were indigenous, self-formed, and inheritors of a gang tradition that in some cases extended back almost 50 years.

In evaluating the results of the project, researchers concluded that there was no significant measurable inhibition of lawbreaking or morally disapproved behavior as a consequence of the project efforts. They found the program's impact was negligible in counteracting the thrust toward delinquent behavior that was reinforced by the general values of the community.[4]

The Key Program: Boston Another standard program found in many communities is the Key Program in Massachusetts. The program offers a wide range of counseling and advocacy services to delinquent and non-delinquent youth. Supervision and intensive counseling are used to intervene in the child's daily life and activity in the community to prevent delinquency. Counselors help children deal with educational and vocational planning, with the juvenile court, and with their personal lives. Advocacy programs exist in storefronts, and services also involve the use of foster-care facilities.

The program was recently evaluated to determine which Key Program services provided the most assistance to children. Recidivism studies found that about half the children who had been in juvenile court before they became involved with the program reappeared in the court within six months. On the other hand, the Key Program was able to reduce children's contacts with the court while they were actually in the program. Key Program services were most helpful to children who had committed property offenses or who had lost interest in school. They were less successful with those who had a serious criminal history.[5]

COPING WITH GANGS AND DELINQUENCY IN THE COMMUNITY

The following discussion, although focused on resolving the gang problem, has broader implications. Many of the programs described have usefulness in preventing delinquency in general. This analysis is based on my work with violent gangs in New York City over a five-year period.[6]

Levels of Attack

Whatever specific factors determine the emergence of a specific violent gang at a particular time and place, there is little reason to question the observation that the existence of violent gangs is a recurrent social phenomenon in many places and must ultimately be related to deeper, more general disruptions in the social fabric itself. If this consideration is relevant to a thorough assessment of the problem, it must be equally relevant to a thorough and effective attack upon it. Since the roots go deep, we cannot

---

[4]Walter B. Miller, "The Impact of a Total Community Delinquency Control Project," *Social Problems* 10 (Fall 1962): 168–191.

[5]Jonathan Katz, *An Evaluation of Community Based Services for Delinquent Youth: The Key Program* (Worcester, Mass.: Key, 1979).

[6]See Lewis Yablonsky, The Violent Gang (New York: Macmillan, 1962; New York: Penguin, 1966; New York: Irvington, 1980.)

expect the problem to disappear without recourse to remedies that go to the roots. All of which is to make the commonplace observation that a society that fails to find remedies for its own disorganization and for its own institutionalized inequities is likely to continue to suffer from their consequences—violent gangs among them.

Nothing in this perhaps overrepeated observation provides a valid argument for inaction. What is implied, however, is a working discrimination between the necessary strategy for broad social change and the practical tactics of local control.[7] If we cannot "immediately" eradicate the roots, there may well be something immediate and effective we can do about the branches and tendrils as they emerge in the social soil of our particular communities. Accordingly, the central emphasis of this discussion will be upon the treatment and control of the violent gang in its emergent form.

Reaching the Violent Gang

Community gang-prevention projects are usually subdivisions of larger delinquency-control programs. The only type of preventive project expressly designed for the violent gang is the detached-worker program. In this approach, a professional, usually a social worker, is assigned to a particular gang. The essential avowed goal of the youth worker is to redirect the gangs from destructive behavior patterns into "constructive" activities. Reaching the gang through detached youth workers entails pitfalls. Foremost among these potential problems is the possibility of inaccurately diagnosing gang structure. Distinctly different treatment methods are required for treating the *social,* the *delinquent,* and the *violent gang.* The blurring of these differentiations produces ineffectual approaches, even with a sincere and dedicated worker.

With reference to the violent gang in particular, the fact that differential levels of involvement (i.e., core group and various marginal categories) and participation dictate different treatment prescriptions is of crucial significance. The marginal gang member can generally be reached through the more conventional methods of recreation, providing a job, counseling, and so on, whereas the core violent gang leader and participants require a differential approach.

The diagnostic assumption that working through the violent gang leader will redirect the gang provides another problem. Often working through the leader of a violent gang solidifies its structure. Official sanction of the sociopathic leader by a worker may give status to an individual who was formerly considered a "character" by most of the marginal gang participants.

---

[7]On the broader societal front, governmental and private programs aimed at reducing social and economic inequalities, equalizing opportunities, facilitating the integration of new populations—each of these would work to ameliorate the background conditions that foster the gang problem.

Merely gaining access to violent gang participants is frequently mistaken for acceptance and rapport. Contrary to popular belief, getting in touch with the gang is not difficult for a detached worker. However, the meaning given to the relationship by gang members varies and is of major significance. If the gang worker appears as a "mark" to most members, a "do-gooder" who doesn't know the score, they will simply use him for money, cigarettes, or whatever favors they can obtain. The negative nature of this situation is not simply the gang worker's being duped, but his incorrect assumption of success. Many gang workers, rather than resocializing gang members, are themselves negatively affected by the gang. They may rationalize their personal motives toward "adventuresome" gang behavior as necessary to maintain their relationship. In fact, this behavior is not necessary. Becoming a "gang member" neutralizes their impact as an adequate adult role model.

When the detached gang worker is duped by the gang or misinterprets the meaning of a situation, he is reinforcing rather than modifying illegal behavior. In his capacity as gang worker he is, in effect, a carrier of the values and norms of the larger society. Initially the gang member resists the intrusion into the subculture he has created (to act out his problems). The gang will attempt to get what it can without changing and then seduce the detached worker into becoming part of the gang. The gang worker should be aware of the negative implication of compromising the relevant norms of the larger society in order to gain false acceptance and superficial approval. When he does this, he is fairly quickly eliminated as a force for changing the gang, since they begin to view him as a mark or sucker susceptible to manipulation. This defeats the objectives the worker is attempting to achieve.

The gang worker must have a realistic image of gang structure, or he is likely to be duped by the illusory conceptions of the gang described by its members. The worker's acceptance of the fantastic stories created by core gang participants produces a reinforcement of undesirable gang mythology.

The validity of such antisocial patterns as gang warfare, territory, and peace meetings should be challenged and discouraged rather than accepted and, in some cases, aggrandized and given legitimacy. The enlightened detached gang worker can sometimes operate effectively through the use of ridicule, disbelief, and criticism.

The worker is often presented with wild stories of gang activity, some believed and some not believed by the gang participants themselves. If he "buys" their story, the worker becomes a dupe who loses his potential for positive influence. On the other hand, if the worker pushes the "gang stories" of divisions and warfare to their illogical conclusion by sensitive caricaturing, he makes treatment progress. First, he achieves stature with the boys as an adult person who can't be "conned" or manipulated. This the gang members respect. Second, he turns the gang and its members back upon self-evaluation and assessment. This process causes them to begin to look at themselves and their gang as it exists in reality.

A Case in Point   The following is an actual report of a worker's handling of a problem.

Four marginal gang boys enter a gang worker's office; they are obviously nervous but attempting to give a "cool" appearance:[8]

FIRST GANG BOY: Well, that's it—we'll whip it on tonight at seven and then the whole city will rumble. I mean we're not going to sit still for that bullshit. The Dragons are through once and for all.

WORKER: Now, really, what is all this bullshit anyway? Wait a minute, I have to make a call. (Makes an inconsequential phone call, emphasizing disinterest in the mass rumble that is supposed to engulf the city, then turns to the boys with a look of disgust.) Now, what's all this rumble stuff about?

GANG BOY: Well, they're suppose to whip it on tonight. Duke says . . .

WORKER: Wait a minute now. Duke told you this? (In disbelief) He told you this and you believe him?

GANG BOY: Well, yeah—he and Pete met with Loco from the uptown Dragons, and he says that . . .

WORKER: (Interrupting): Just a minute. You mean to tell me those nuts Duke, Loco, and Pete cook up some nonsense about a rumble and you guys jump right into the fire. (In disbelief) How stupid can you get?

SECOND GANG BOY: I told them it was a lot of crap and . . .

WORKER: Don't tell them. Why didn't you tell Duke—right there? Besides, you guys don't really have anyone to fight for you anyway. (Refers at length to a previous meeting with twelve of the "gang" where they finally agreed they were the only twelve they could count on in a fight.)

THIRD GANG BOY: Well, Duke and Jerry say our ten divisions can . . .

FOURTH GANG BOY: (Interrupts): Oh, man you guys still dig all that bullshit. (Turns) I didn't believe none of it—but they all got excited.

WORKER: Maybe one of these days you guys will wise us. Let's talk about something important. Are you all set up for the game at the Columbia gym Sunday?

At the time the worker drops the gang-war subject, but he picks it up later with the police and another social agency to check it out further. If the worker had become involved and called a peace meeting with relevant gang leaders, he might have poured gasoline on the fire by reinforcing, joining, and helping develop a possible gang rumble. What occurred as a result of his not being drawn in was to destroy the potential support of many mar-

---

[8]Reprinted with permission of Macmillan Publishing Co., Inc. from *The Violent Gang* by Lewis Yablonsky. © Lewis Yablonsky 1962. Pp. 242–243.

ginals for a rumble, discredit the gang leader's fantasy, cause the youths to examine some of the mythology of their near-group structure, and change over to a positive subject. Another main goal in this type of ridiculing approach is to encourage the marginal members to confront the fantasy of the gang and the gang-war plans on their own at the source—the leader. In some cases they effectively mimic the worker's sarcastic and caustic comments with the provocative gang leader, vitiating the leader's negative impact toward violence. Castrating his fantasy through sarcasm and ridicule helps to minimize his negative effect, rather than support and reinforce the gang leader's potential impact.

The "conned" detached worker tends unwittingly to reward what is in fact sociopathic behavior. The misguided worker not only legitimizes the gang and its core but also provides them with a type of "social director." In this role he aids the violent gang leader in his nefarious activities by providing attractive activities, dances, athletic events, and so on for marginal members.

He may be incorporated into and become part of the gang's structure. Having a gang worker attached to one's gang becomes a status symbol of being a real "down," "bad," or tough gang. As one violent gang leader espressed it: "We're a real down club. We got a president, a war counselor, and a Youth Board man."

The incorrectly oriented detached worker may indirectly help to produce and articulate violent gang culture.

Some Guidelines for More Effective Use of the Detached-Worker Approach

Reaching the gang in its own milieu through the detached gang worker is a significant approach to the violent-gang problem. However, several issues require revision and redefinition if this approach is to modify rather than solidify or reinforce violent-gang structure and behavior. On the basis of the near-group conception of violent-gang organization and other factors that have emerged in the analysis, the following guidelines are suggested for a more effective approach to the violent-gang problem.

1. It is necessary for the detached gang worker to be trained to diagnose accurately several types of gang structure. Different approaches are required for the social, delinquent, and violent gangs.
2. The accurate diagnosis of the violent gang reveals different degrees of participation and involvement. One may work with marginal members through more conventional treatment approaches: core violent-gang participants and leaders require a different and more intense form of treatment.
3. A violent gang can be further integrated by working through the leaders. The detached gang worker should avoid giving the leader credence, since this may reinforce violent-gang structure. Providing the sociopathic leader with "official" status and activity oppor-

tunities for his gang tends to defeat rather than achieve sound corrective goals.

4. The detached gang worker, as an official representative of the more inclusive society, must avoid sanctioning or participating in deviance to gain what will turn out to be a false acceptance and rapport. He should serve as an adequate law-abiding adult role model. In this way, he may become a bridge or vehicle for bringing the larger society's constructive values and norms to the gang.

Violent gangs should not be treated by any official community program as a "legitimate" social structure. Giving credence to the violent gang by providing it with an official representative of society is giving tacit authorization to pathology and violence. For example, peace meetings that involve gang leaders and paid representatives of city government implicitly provide an illegal, pathological enterprise with official support.

These conclusions are not based upon moral or legal considerations but upon the nature of gang organization. An entity, such as the violent gang, cannot be treated as a unit. The type of detached-worker policies and the programs that have been employed in the past appear to solidify and legitimize the violent gang, reinforcing its pathological behavior rather than modifying its antisocial activity.

Rather than "redirecting" and implicitly reinforcing the violent gang as an institutionalized and legitimized pattern of illegal behavior, the focus should be upon eliminating it as an entity. This goal may be worked toward by a combination of modified detached gang work, police action, incarceration, group therapy, and a new "milieu-therapy" approach to sociopathic behavior. If these approaches are utilized, the violent gang may be dismembered and its participants resocialized and legally reconnected into the inclusive society.

Programs based on the foregoing principles have demonstrated their effectiveness in a number of large cities around the country. The following editorial in the *Los Angeles Times* hails the effectiveness of this approach:[9]

Winning Against Gangs

Among the many statistics compiled at the end of 1986, we noted with encouragement a small but significant number suggesting that the violence caused by youth gangs in Los Angeles can eventually be brought under control.

Spokesmen for the Los Angeles County Sheriff's Department report that in 1986 gang killings reached a 10-year low in unincorporated East Los Angeles, the heavily Latino community three miles east of downtown that is patrolled by sheriff's deputies. Only four homicides in the area were found to be gang-related in 1986—a dramatic decrease from a high of 24 in 1978. Department officials attribute the improvement to anti-gang programs run by local community groups, a coordinated campaign by law-enforcement

---

[9]Editorial, "Winning Against Gangs," *Los Angeles Times*, January 6, 1987. Copyright, (1987), Los Angeles Times.

agencies to monitor gang activity, and the innovative efforts of the Community Youth Gang Services Project, a county program created five years ago specifically to reduce gang violence.

Youth Gang Services was controversial when it was launched. The gang workers it employs are often former gang members themselves. Trained in crisis-intervention techniques, they patrol their old turf and try to stop violence before it breaks out. This approach was criticized in late 1981 by many who doubted that it could work, even though a similar program had helped reduce gang violence in Philadelphia a few years earlier. Back then, everyone agreed that the toughest test for Youth Gang Services workers would be the barrios of East Los Angeles, where about 70 gangs operate—many of them so entrenched that they date back to the 1940s.

The drop in gang killings in East Los Angeles is evidence that Youth Gang Services' approach can work, given enough time. It is also a good argument for continuing, and expanding, similar efforts that are under way in other parts of town where new gangs are growing even as the gang problem in East Los Angeles is being calmed. Among the problems that these new gangs have created is an upsurge in violence within the City of Los Angeles, where police recorded 180 gang-related homicides last year.

An area of special concern to gang specialists is South-Central Los Angeles, where several gangs that have emerged in recent years are now warring over the control of cocaine and other illegal drugs. Given the profits generated by the illicit drug trade, the new gangs could pose as formidable a challenge for Youth Gang Services and other agencies as the gangs of East Los Angeles did. But the fact that things improved in East Los Angeles is reason to think that they can improve elsewhere—with enough patience and community support.

HALFWAY HOUSES AND COMMUNITY TREATMENT

Most inmates of prisons and training schools were, prior to their incarceration, members of delinquent groups with subcultures deviating materially from that of the dominant culture in our society. While in these institutions, inmates are subjected to a continuous acculturation and assimilation of the delinquent value system. They tend to develop a vocabulary that reflects attitudes, beliefs, opinions, and orientations different from and often opposing those of the conventional person, if they did not have such attitudes when they arrived at the institution. The roles played by the inmate and the roles he is required to play upon his release are vastly different in most important aspects. This is obviously true of the important family roles. The inmate is living apart from his parents, his brothers and sisters, or any other relatives with whom he normally resides. We often forget that he is also away from his community roles and normal occupational roles.

In spite of the fact that most inmates do some work while at an institution, the attitudes attached to the role of worker differ materially from the attitudes required for satisfactory achievement in a work situation on the outside. Workers in the correctional labor system are encouraged to be nonproductive, dilatory, and contentious. Institutionally developed attitudes affect the individual's concept of the role of the job seeker. In reform school or prison, the inmate does not have to seek a job. It is considered to be the duty of the officials to provide him with work, and the inmate comes to feel that he has a right to a job. Foremen in prison are content with a limited amount of productivity, the standards being far lower than those set by employers outside the institution. Far more cooperation than the inmate is accustomed to give is expected of him by fellow workers, foremen, and employers when he works on the outside.[10]

As a result of his stay at a juvenile institution, a youth is disconnected from his ordinary occupational, family, and community roles. While inside, he adjusts to prison life, and upon his release he may be expected to have difficulty reestablishing occupational and family roles in the community. He needs time to adjust and to reconnect to society. Institutions organized to facilitate the necessary transition are called halfway houses, to symbolize their status as an establishment between a prison and the residence of a free citizen. The halfway house as now constituted is a temporary residence for released offenders, usually located in the community in which the inmates resided before they were incarcerated, or as near to that community as possible. At the halfway house, a building housing 20 to 50 youths under the supervision of a correctional authority, the released prisoner can look for a job, work on a job, meet with family and friends, and begin to assume the roles normally acceptable in his community.

"SCARED-STRAIGHT" DELINQUENTS

Another community-based program for delinquents that has emerged in recent years is the "scared-straight" approach. In 1978 a TV documentary called "Scared Straight" was seen by millions of viewers throughout the United States. The documentary revealed a program for delinquents that has some resemblance to the Synanon method, in that it makes use of adult ex-offenders as "therapists" to "scare juvenile delinquents straight."

The documentary was filmed at the Rahway State Prison in New Jersey, where alleged hard-core juvenile offenders, both young men and young women, were exposed to three hours of prison life with inmates serving life sentences. According to the warden, the exposure to the inmates was handled exlusively by the inmates, who went to some length to inform the juveniles that there would be no psychologists, social workers, or probation officers to turn to during their stay at the prison.

In raw language, the inmates yelled at, harassed, intimidated, and challenged the juveniles. The inmates took turns in detailing certain aspects of their lives, while at the same time mocking the youths and demanding their complete and unwavering attention. The juveniles were threatened

[10]Martin R. Haskell, "An Alternative to More and Larger Prisons: A Role Training Program for Social Reconnection," *Group Psychotherapy* 14 (March –June 1961): 30–38.

with physical and sexual assault by the convicts and were told of the horrors that would befall them if they ever wound up in prison.

The narrator (actor Peter Falk) discussed the value of this "scared-straight" approach—its low cost (since the inmates are not paid), its short duration (three hours), and its successes. Of the 17 juveniles involved in the documentary, it was claimed that only one had gotten into difficulty with the law in the six months following the prison experience. Since these juveniles were supposedly hard-core offenders and not status offenders, such a success rate would be remarkable indeed.

The reaction of the viewing audience was positive; none seemed to be bothered by the program's rather strong tactics. However, two sociologists, Jorja Manos and Jerome Rabow, had a different reaction:

> We were upset and angered with the program. Neither the language nor the paraprofessionals' control of the program were the issues for us. What we envisioned after the massive publicity to get similar programs started in states throughout the country was a movement spearheaded by the institutionalization of scare tactics.
>
> What we were angered about was the simplified approach to rehabilitation, its emphasis upon fear and repression as the factors of social control and, by direct implication, its rejection of rehabilitation and treatment. What was emphasized in the program were the physical and sexual abuses. . . . The program seemed to be another spike in the rehabilitation coffin. It implied that rehabilitation is dead and that we can now return to the warehousing and punishment orientation of yesteryear.[11]

The project, despite the conflicting conclusions on its effectiveness, deserves attention because of the enormous impact it has had on the general population. We tend to agree with Drs. Finckenauer, Storti, Rabow, and Manos that the "scared-straight" concept is relatively ineffectual in modifying delinquent behavior. Moreover, the program was widely accepted without scientific substantiation for several possible reasons: (1) It was dramatic, interesting entertainment. (2) Many adults watching the program vicariously enjoyed seeing "juvenile delinquents" getting yelled at; this satisfies some latent emotions in adults who felt that the delinquency problem was out of hand. (3) The simplistic nature of the approach was appealing because it added no great expense to the taxpayer's bill and gave recalcitrant offenders something to do, besides "time." (4) A basic problem with the project is that it depends on maintenance of the most brutal aspects of the prison system for the "training" of new "prisoner therapists." If correctional institutions were made humane, the "scared-straight" program would go out of existence because there would be no frustrated, vicious inmates to enact the role of "therapist."

---

[11]Jorja Manos and Jerome Rabow, "Social Scientists' Contribution to the Demise of Delinquency Rehabilitation," *Crime Prevention Review* (Attorney General's Office, State of California) 6 (July 1979): 33.

Despite these criticisms, some juveniles are changed by the "scared-straight" approach when they accept the horrendous endpoint of continuing their delinquent behavior. I have used the tape with adolescent delinquents in a treatment facility. My conclusion is that the "scared-straight" program per se, used alone, is not as effective as when it is used as an adjunct to other treatment methods. I have observed a number of juveniles in my work who responded in a positive way to my playing the documentary tape for them—followed by a discussion of its implications to them on a personal level. Some appeared to be "scared straight" as a result of this combination of methods.

PROBATION AND PAROLE

Probation represents a sentence imposed by a court in lieu of confinement. The delinquent sentenced to probation by a judge is relatively free as long as he conforms to the conditions imposed by the court. The juvenile is placed under the supervision of a probation officer, who is a peace officer charged with seeing that the court's conditions are met.

Parole is similar to probation in that the parolee is also relatively free in the community. He, too, is supervised by a peace officer, usually called a parole agent. The major difference between probation and parole is that the parolee has served at least part of his sentence in a correctional institution. He is released from the correctional institution prior to the expiration of his sentence and allowed to serve the remainder of his sentence in the community, provided he lives up to the conditions imposed by the releasing authority.

Probation

Probation is a treatment program in which the final action in an adjudicated offender's case is suspended, so that he remains at liberty, subject to conditions imposed by or for a court under the supervision and guidance of a probation officer. The correctional system provides for the treatment and supervision of offenders in the community by placing them on probation in lieu of confinement in a custodial institution. In most states, probationers serve the sentence of a court under the supervision of a probation officer assigned by the court. The judge has broad powers in this situation and sets the conditions of probation and the length of the supervision period. He maintains the power to order revocation of probation, usually for a violation of one of the conditions set by him or his agent or for the commission of another offense. The effect of revocation is to send a probationer to a custodial institution.[12]

[12]David Dressler, *Practice and Theory of Probation and Parole* (New York: Columbia University Press, 1969), pp. 16–36.

A few states have centralized probation systems, but most of the 3,068 counties in the United States exercise autonomy within limits set by state statutes. For example, the probation system in California is a centralized system that authorizes each county to provide facilities, services, and regulations. In many states, probation is an activity of the court—criminal, juvenile, or other—with the probation officer serving as an appointee of the judge. There is therefore considerable variation in the use of probation and the manner in which it is administered.[13]

In general, adult probation services are state functions, and juvenile probation services tend to be local functions. In 32 states, juvenile courts administer probation services. In 30 states, adult probation is combined with parole services.[14] In terms of the number of persons served and of total operating costs, the juvenile probation system has approximately twice as many resources per capita as the adult system.[15]

The average juvenile case load assigned to a probation officer is usually around 50 cases. The typical probation case load is usually a random mixture of cases requiring varying amounts of service and surveillance.

The probation officer sees that the probationer lives up to the conditions of the probation. He assists the probationer with problems at work or school, or with members of his family, and provides guidance. Dressler notes four central techniques used by the probation officer:

1. *Manipulative techniques.* The environment may be manipulated in the interests of the person seeking help. The end product is usually something material and tangible received by the individual under care, for example, financial aid rendered by the agency or an employer persuaded to rehire a discharged worker.
2. *Executive techniques.* The probation officer may refer the individual to other resources in the community for help that the correctional agency cannot render. For example, the probation officer may refer the individual to a legal aid society or secure public assistance for him.
3. *Guidance techniques.* The probation officer may give personal advice and guidance on problems not requiring complex psychological techniques. The advice is likely to be fairly direct and the guidance comparatively superficial. The end product is intangible, although it may facilitate the achievement of tangible goals. For example, the individual is advised how to budget his income or helped to explore the possibilities of training for a trade.
4. *Counseling techniques.* These are based largely upon psychological orientations and require considerable skill. The services are intangible, concerned with deep-seated problems in the emotional area—for example, aid in adjusting a marital situation or help in overcoming specific emotional conflicts.[16]

[13]Ibid., p. 27.
[14]President's Commission on Law Enforcement and Administration of Justice, *Task Force Report: Corrections* (Washington, D.C.: U.S. Government Printing Office, 1967), p. 35.
[15]Ibid., p. 27.
[16]Dressler, *Practice and Theory of Probation and Parole*, pp. 151–152.

It is obvious that a probation officer cannot possibly perform all these services for 50 people, the average case load. Authorities are agreed that there are far too few probation officers and that not all of them are adequately trained. Contacts are infrequent and services inadequate. Nevertheless, the success of probation, as measured by those who complete probation without revocation, has been surprisingly high.

Conditions of Probation

Because probation has always been regarded as a form of leniency through which the judge permits a convicted person to remain in the community instead of being sent to an institution, the power of the judge to impose conditions is seldom challenged. The courts have even upheld conditions of probation that restrict the constitutional rights of a probationer, where the restrictions have a clear-cut relationship to his rehabilitation. However, the limitations imposed on a probationer must not be capricious or impossible.

In an analysis of standards relating to probation, Carl H. Imlay and Charles R. Glasheen list the following questionable conditions of probation imposed by some courts across the country:

1. Must attend church.
2. Cannot marry without permission of the supervising officer.
3. Cannot smoke.
4. Total abstention from alcohol.
5. Cannot frequent places where liquor is served or sold.
6. Must not grow a beard or long hair or wear clothing not in conformance with the customs of the community.
7. Require the wife to report when the probationer is unable to.
8. Submit to search and seizure at the discretion of the probation officer, including home as well as person.
9. Pursue medical or psychiatric treatment.
10. Unrealistic fines and restitution.
11. Refrain from driving a car, especially where a car is needed in work.
12. Requirement as to how earnings are to be spent.
13. Refrain from associating with any person who has been convicted at one time or another.
14. Requirement to pursue employment that is contrary to probationer's interests.
15. Requirement to contribute to a charitable cause.
16. Requirement to do charitable work.
17. Cannot become pregnant during probation.
18. Unrealistic restrictions on travel (e.g., a weekend trip from Chicago to Milwaukee to visit family members).
19. Restrictions on dates.
20. Be at home at unrealistic evening hours.
21. Unrealistic reporting requirements (e.g., an invalid, a person living a considerable distance from the office or during hours of probationer's employment).

22. Requirement to attend school when past the compulsory attendance age.
23. Requirements to live in a special place of noninstitutional residence.[17]

The probation officer is now given greater discretion than heretofore in interpreting the condition imposed by the court, in favor of greater freedom for the probationer. For example, one condition imposed on a probationer is that he not associate with known offenders. For many years this provision interfered with the application of group therapy to offenders on probation; however, in recent years there has been a more logical attitude in place which allows for group therapy. The objectives of a probation program have been listed as follows:

1. To determine, after careful investigation and analysis, whether probation is the most appropriate treatment plan.
2. To help the individual, juvenile or adult, accept the reality of community rules and legal sanctions, and to work on such personality factors and environmental conditions as interfere with his acceptance of such limitations.
3. To help the probationer (an individual who according to a decision by society can be rehabilitated while continuing to live in the community) change his behavior to meet society's demands and to make a different use of himself—a use that is positive, constructive, and in conformance with the standards imposed by society. This process is referred to as probation casework.
4. To provide children who cannot be cared for in their own homes with foster homes or institutional care; to continuously evaluate the use of the placement with a view toward eventual return home; to work with the child's parents, as well as the child, toward termination of the separation from home.
5. To recommend termination of probation whenever it is recognized that this service is no longer needed or appropriate.[18]

Contact is generally established when, having been placed on probation by a court, a juvenile or adult appears for his first appointment. The probation officer to whom the person is assigned has usually received an advanced report from the probation officer who investigated the case.

During the initial interview, the ward's attitude is of primary concern and often determines the treatment program arranged for him. The resistant person is generally seen more frequently than one who relates easily. Priority for treatment is usually given to (1) those probationers the probation officers feel they can definitely aid, and (2) those probationers against whom the most complaints have been made.

The probation officer makes an effort to influence the parents as well as the probationer. The probation officer has the power to remove the probationer from the home and place him in a foster home or remove him from the community and place him in an institution. When dealing with

[17]Carl H. Imlay and Charles R. Glasheen, "See What Condition Your Conditions Are In," *Federal Probation* 35 (June 1971): 3–11. Reprinted by permission.
[18]The program described is that of the Los Angeles County Probation Department.

adults, the probation officer places most of the responsibility on the individual. Most adults are placed on probation at the request of the probation officer and as a result of court determinations.

Probation officers have two major problems: the amount of their paperwork and the size of their case loads. The vast amount of paperwork that is required is responsible for much of the ineffectiveness of the program, since it takes valuable time away from the vital human association between the probation officer and his client. (One probation officer indicated, for example, that he often found himself looking for ways to cut his interviews short to allow himself enough time to finish his paperwork.)

Nearly all probation officers are dissatisfied with the size of their case loads. One probation officer who had 226 individuals under his supervision met with approximately 90 wards a month. He obviously had little time to attempt rehabilitation or therapy of any kind. Even with the smaller case loads of juvenile probation officers, an individual is seldom seen more than twice a month.

According to one officer, for every 85 cases on probation, about 15 are placed in camps or special schools. About 35 clients are dismissed within six months, and the other 35 are visited rather informally in their homes to see how they are doing. When handled in this way, the actual case load is not too large. A juvenile probation officer with a case load of 75 may place his clients in three categories: (1) minimum services (seen once a month or less); (2) medium services (seen once a month); (3) maximum services (seen frequently). Normally, only about ten would fall into the third category and be seen once or possibly two to three times a week. Obviously, youths seen once a month or less do not receive the attention they require.

The probation officer's definition of his task and the style in which he functions are significant vectors in his degree of success. In a research article by Elaine Anderson and Graham Spanier, these issues were researched.[19] The fundamental research conclusion, based on 255 self-administered questionnaires, was that the officer who is treatment-service oriented is less likely to label juvenile acts as delinquent than the officer who responds to lawyer role models. Officers who make rehabilitative recommendations are less likely to label acts as delinquent than those who do not.

The results of this study indicate that life experiences and perceptions of work by the probation officers also may influence the interaction between the officers and the youth. The study illustrates the need for and importance of continued research concerning the decision making of juvenile probation officers.

Parole

Parole is a treatment program in which the offender, after serving part of a term in an institution, is conditionally released under the supervision and treatment of a

---

[19]Elaine Anderson and Graham Spanier, "Treatment of Delinquent Youth: The Influence of the Probation Officer's Perception of Self and Work," *Criminology* 174 (February 1980).

parole officer. There are basically three types of agencies that are empowered to grant parole: a board set up for the correctional institution; a central parole board for a state; and a group of officials, usually called a parole commission.

It is expected that while in the state institution, a youth will be provided with job training or some vocational skills that will better prepare him or her for life in the community. Recreational-, educational-, and vocational-training facilities are intended to help in rehabilitation. Medical, psychological, and counseling programs, group-therapy sessions, and other therapeutic processes are supposed to prepare the individual to reenter society.

A counseling program is one important aspect of a prerelease preparation program. The inmate may be deemed ready for release when he appears before a parole hearing officer. However, he may suffer anxieties and fears about the outside world. Whether or not the parolee leaves the institution with hostile attitudes will depend in part on the way the parole hearings are held and the way he has been treated in the institution.

Parole is in every sense a continuation of the correctional process. The goal is to help reestablish the parolee in the community as a law-abiding citizen. Parole supervision includes efforts to discover the strengths in the parolee's personality and his ways of dealing with emotional problems. The parole officer cannot permit the parolee to become dependent on him for all decisions and solutions to his problems. The individual on parole must learn to handle successfully difficult situations that may arise. However, the parole officer should be able to obtain help for the parolee when required.

The parole officer has three main functions in his relationship with the parolee. The first is to use his knowledge of community resources to help the parolee and his family adjust to society. The second is to provide or obtain treatment for the parolee when required. This includes dealing with psychological problems. The third function is supervision. The parole officer is supposed to do what he can to keep the parolee from violating the conditions of his parole. He may visit the parolee's home or work location to determine his progress. He may also interview family members and other important persons who can help the parole officer in determining the parolee's progress. The necessity of field visits depends on each individual case. Visits may occur as often as once a week or as seldom as once a month, depending on the parolee's adjustment.

The parolee is required to accept and sign the parole agreement. He is told that if he breaks any condition his parole will be revoked and he will have to go back to prison.

The period of parole varies from state to state and among individuals as well. It largely depends on the progress made by the parolee in the community.

Parole officers do not necessarily receive specific training in the role of a parole officer. At school they may have taken courses in one or more of the social sciences such as psychology, sociology, social welfare, or criminology. However, probation and parole authorities have consistently failed to agree upon a program of academic training and therefore have not set up specific academic requirements for appointment. The social science fields do teach things about parole but do not provide adequate training. Educators in schools of social work are in general agreement that a master's degree in social work is an excellent form of academic preparation for work in the parole and probations fields. However, few parole officers have such degrees.

There has been a tendency in recent years to combine probation and parole operations under one organization, and this is always done for those convicted in federal courts. Both probation and parole deal with adjudged criminals and delinquents outside institutions, and since the services they render are similar, it is logical that they should be placed under one administrative agency. If that agency also controls the confinement facilities, coordination and integration of the various correctional services and institutions are facilitated.

The Volunteer in Probation and Parole

Probation supervision in the United States began as a voluntary activity of interested citizens. For some years, however, the role of the probation officer has been professionalized and institutionalized. People occupying the position of probation officer have acquired skills and expertise and generally perform a valuable service in an effective manner. It is understandable, therefore, that the addition of volunteers to the staffs of probation departments is viewed as a threat to the security of the probation officer. Despite this fact, many probation departments throughout the country use volunteers to supplement the activities of probation officers. Considering the large case loads of the probation officers, the utilization of volunteers appears to be an excellent idea. The use of volunteers by the probation department of Royal Oak, Michigan, for example, appears to fulfill this need for extra personnel and to utilize the services of the volunteer in an effective manner.

The need for more staff, more resources, and greater community understanding paved the way for the use of the volunteer in Royal Oak. As with most program innovations, the involvement of the community in improving the correctional process generated much anxiety. The most important problem centered around the need to define the role of the volunteer while, at the same time, preserving the role and importance of the paid professional. If probation duties could be performed by an unpaid volunteer, this would constitute a threat to the security of the probation officer. A related problem is the traditional skepticism and suspicion toward any new concept or program on the part of correctional agencies.[20]

Because of these problems the role of the corrections volunteer had to

---

[20]Ira M. Schwartz, "Volunteers and Professionals: A Team in the Correctional Process," *Federal Probation* 35 (September 1971): 46–50.

be narrowly defined. Corrections literature clearly shows that no volunteers are seen as providing "professional" service. The role of the volunteer is limited to that of complementing or supplementing the work of the professional staff. The volunteer, therefore, has been looked upon as one who simply relieves the professional of routine, nonprofessional tasks so that the professional's time can be freed to allow him to devote his attention to where it is needed most. This implies that the services that volunteers offer to offenders are different from those that are made available by the probation officer.

The distinction between many of the services provided by probation officers, who in most instances lack advanced academic training themselves, and those provided by volunteers is more imagined than real. The work of the volunteer must be directed to the advantage of the probationers, and the probation officer has an important supervisory role. The role of the paid professional becomes even more important because it is he who must harness this valuable resource, provide adequate training and supervision, and assign responsibilities in ways that will yield the greatest benefits.

The typical volunteer is a sensitive and concerned person who has demonstrated maturity in his ability to solve his own problems and in adjusting to society. He is able to relate well to others and, primarily in an intuitive way, to implement basic social work principles and values that are important in the establishment of any helping relationship. Many volunteers would rather be referred to as "unpaid staff" because they have the credentials and experience that would qualify them for employment. Also, the average volunteer appears to be aware of society's ills (particularly in the area of juvenile delinquency and adult crime), desires to become involved in implementing change, and seeks the opportunity to participate and contribute.[21]

Court service volunteers are told during their screening interview that they will be expected to serve for at least a 12-month period and that they will be expected to see a probationer at least once a week. The professional staff runs the program, not the volunteer. A member of the staff observes the volunteer-probationer relationship through the eyes of the volunteer by way of the volunteer's written or oral reports. Thus, the staff knows where more intensive supervision is necessary.

Less than 5 percent of all court service volunteers have dropped out during their first year, and over 85 percent of those who have completed a full year of service have continued in the program.[22]

It is estimated that over 500 courts and nearly an equal number of parole and detention locales use volunteers. In addition, other social service agencies are thought to use a combined total of 60 million volunteers. These people are motivated by altruism, humanitarianism, the desire to continue personal growth and development, the need to form more mean-

[21]Ibid., p. 47.
[22]Ibid.

ingful interpersonal relationships, the need for a change of pace in their usual routine of activities, or combinations of these.[23] In general, middle-class people, who are in a position to pay their own expenses, volunteer for programs in greater numbers than minority groups, ex-offenders, offenders themselves, youth, and older people who need to have their expenses defrayed.[24] Frequently, it is difficult to establish relationships between middle-class volunteers and minority-group members on parole and probation.

One of the authors, Haskell, headed an aftercare program in New York City for several years. As part of that program, he established a "Big Brother Project" using volunteers. The volunteers, without exception, were middle-class Caucasians. The boys who asked for Big Brothers were, with one exception, black or Puerto Rican. While a few useful Big Brother relationships were established, for the most part, the needs of the boys were not met. The Big Brother project was abandoned, and two minority-group persons were hired to assist in the aftercare program, performing the functions previously assigned to the volunteers. Such persons are now called paraprofessionals.[25]

Most probation officers have two major problems: too much paperwork and too many probationers. The average supervising probation officer has a voluminous amount of paperwork, including maintaining a casework file, writing up all client and family contacts, dictating violation reports, writing up "work-determination" plans, and other tasks. Many probation officers complain that they hardly have time to see their probationers because of paperwork demands. Because of other tasks, a probation officer may actually utilize only about 10 percent of his total time in face-to-face meetings with his clients. It is not unusual for client to go many months without seeing his probation officer because he may "report" by mail.

Probation departments tend to place a very high priority on paperwork. It is a "measureable" way of evaluating the job the probation officer is doing. "Good casework management" usually means that all the casework planning and recording is up to date and that all "reports" have been filed on time; everything "looks good," and there is an obvious "product" that can be evaluated and converted into charts and graphs and statistics. However, these paper results tell very little if anything about the probation officer's interpersonal skills or professional knowledge; they reveal very little about his effectiveness in dealing with the problems of clients or in modifying delinquent behavior.

There has been some controversy in the field of probation related to the degree to which a probation officer should provide "treatment" or

[23]Ivan H. Scheier and Judith Lake Berry, *Guidelines and Standards for the Use of Volunteers in Correctional Programs* (Washington, D.C.: U.S. Government Printing Office, 1972).

[24]Alexander B. Smith and Louis Berlin, *Introduction to Probation and Parole* (St. Paul, Minn.: West, 1976), pp. 225–226.

[25]Martin R. Haskell, "The Berkshire Farm Aftercare Program," *Group Psychotherapy* (September 1959): 183.

"supervision" which protects the community. On this issue M. A. Schumacher states:

> The goal of probation supervision is the protection of the community, and that supervision should not singularly emphasize either rehabilitation or punishment. The focus should be on assessment and management of the offender in terms of risks and needs. The return on that investment will be a high level of community protection from those individuals who present the greatest risk of committing further law violations, good supervision and resocialization programs, and the ability to use [community] resources wisely.[26]

SUMMARY: BASIC THEMES FOR CLASS DISCUSSION

1. One of the major advantages of treating a juvenile in his or her community is that the negative forces which contribute to the youth's delinquency need to be dealt with in their real-life situation. In this regard, removing a juvenile from the community and sending them to an institution may not equip him to cope with the day-to-day life problems they confront in their home and neighborhood.

2. Community-based "area projects" attempt to work with delinquents in their difficult neighborhood situations. Some, like the Chicago Area Project and the Boston Mid-City Project, have been successful in resocializing some delinquents in their community. Essentially, these programs attempt to employ local citizens and neighborhood resources to help juveniles stay out of trouble, acquire jobs, receive counseling, and ensure that they attend school.

3. Reaching violent gangs and redirecting their negative activities in more constructive directions is a difficult process. One approach utilizes a "detached gang worker" who may be a professional or an ex-gang member. The worker goes into the neighborhood, develops a relationship with the gang and attempts to reconnect them with positive community resources. Effective detached gang workers can accurately diagnose the structure of the gang they are working with and effectively help various members move into more constructive law-abiding activities. Adult youth associations involving various positive activities can also be effective.

4. Halfway houses attempt to integrate youths who have been incarcerated back into the community where they live. An effective halfway house bridges the gap from institutionalization to a more normal way of life in the former offender's community.

5. Probation involves the supervision and treatment of a delinquent under the control of the court in the community in lieu of his being incarcerated. Parole involves substantially the same goals as probation carried out with youths released into the community after they

---

[26]M. A. Schumacher, "Implementation of a Client Classification and Case Management System," *Crime and Delinquency* 31 (November 1985).

have spent time in an institution. There are divergent views on how probation and parole officers should carry out their duties. One position is that they are in a sense primarily law enforcement officers, whose function is to supervise their wards in order to deter them from violating the law. Another position is that they should mainly be counselors who, through individual, family, and job counseling, facilitate law-abiding behavior in their clients. The most effective parole and probation approaches incorporate both supervision and treatment through the proper utilization of community resources for the client.

QUESTIONS

14.1. List and discuss the advantages and disadvantages of treating a juvenile delinquent in his or her community.

14.2. Specifically, what do "area projects" do to help delinquents become law-abiding citizens?

14.3. What are the functions and goals of the detached gang worker? What are some of the pitfalls and dangers inherent in this work?

14.4. Develop a plan for what you would consider to be an ideal probation or parole department. Be specific about the size of the officer's case load and the actual therapeutic methods and tasks performed by the officer in implementing this model program.

chapter **15**

Institutions and Therapeutic Communities for Delinquents

In most societies, recalcitrant delinquents who persistantly violate the law are removed from the community and placed in long-term institutions in an effort to change their behavior. This approach for dealing with delinquents is often a last resort after various counseling and community-based programs have been attempted and failed.

In this chapter I will analyze and assess the value of the variety of institutions and facilities currently available for the custodial treatment of delinquents from juvenile reformatories to the recent breakthrough developments in bona fide therapeutic communities.

LONG-TERM STATE INSTITUTIONS

Most juvenile delinquents, especially those who commit status offenses or are incorrigible, are diverted into various treatment programs. Some simply keep coming back to court, are held in detention for a brief period, and then sent back to their community. The recalcitrant youths who persistantly commit serious violent acts or other serious offenses are, however, placed in longer-term juvenile institutions. In these institutions they may spend one to three years, and in some cases they are incarcerated until they are 21.

When a juvenile has been found to be delinquent for a serious offense and is turned over to this type of institution, society has decided that his behavior will be closely supervised, that he is to be deprived of some or all of his liberty, that a significant change in his values, attitudes, and behavior is desirable, and that this experience within the system will result in less likelihood of his violating the law in the future. Thus we see that the juvenile institution has been assigned the functions of protecting society and rehabilitating the juvenile offender.

These institutions for juveniles, often referred to as "training schools" or "reformatories" when they were originally established, were patterned after adult prisons. Juvenile institutions have many of the same problems as prisons for adults. Juvenile institutions, however, place greater emphasis on rehabilitation, less on custody, and some attention to treatment. They have populations varying from 20 to 300 children and a diversity of educational, vocational, and therapeutic programs, including individual casework, group therapy, guided group interaction, encounter groups, psychodrama and role training, and milieu therapy. After leaving these institutions, children are usually assisted in their adjustment to the community by parole personnel of the institution or by social-work agencies in the communities in which they reside.

The state training school or reformatory is the "total institution" for juveniles and is the "backup" long-term institution found in most states. By backup, I mean most states have shorter-term, more therapeutic facilities; however, the juvenile in these other institutions knows that if he or she does not fit into the less confining institution, they will ultimately end up in the "total state institution." The security is not as severe as it is in the adult prison, and rehabilitation programs are more prevalent. Nevertheless, the social system of the state training school is very similar to that of an adult prison.

CALIFORNIA YOUTH AUTHORITY

The state training school reformatory system is typified by the California Youth Authority. Most states have a system that somewhat parallels the following description.

The California Youth Authority is administered by a director appointed by the governor, subject to confirmation by the state senate. The Youth Authority Board, consisting of eight members, is also appointed by the governor and given overall responsibility for the acceptance of cases, assignment of wards to institutions, releases to parole, revocations of parole, and final discharges of wards.

The California Youth Authority operates two reception centers, one at Norwalk, which receives all wards committed to the Authority by all courts in southern California, the other at Perkins, which receives all wards committed to the Authority by all courts in the rest of the state. It also operates five correctional schools for boys, two for girls, and four forestry camps.

The Norwalk Reception Center

The Norwalk Reception Center receives all wards committed to the Youth Authority by juvenile, superior, and municipal courts in southern California. Approximately 90 percent of these commitments are made by juvenile courts. The wards range in age from 8 to 21 years. Most of those received are between 15 and 17 years of age, with very few under 12 or over 19.

The Norwalk Center is a diagnostic center, not a correctional institution. There is no attempt made to provide academic or vocational training. The wards are held there for a standard period of 28 days. Occasionally, however, wards have been held as long as six months to a year. Legally a ward can be held until he turns 21. During the time he is there, achievement tests are administered to determine his academic level. He is observed, interviewed, and counseled by social workers and youth counselors, and sometimes by psychologists or psychiatrists. One the basis of these tests, interviews, and observations, a diagnostic report is submitted to the board, which decides on the disposition of his case.

For administrative purposes, the diagnostic division of the reception center consists of all employees, who are under the direct supervision of the assistant superintendent, who functions as the clinical director. This division includes psychiatry (two positions); psychology (four positions); social work, including parole agents (15 positions); group supervision (77 positions); educational diagnostic services, including recreation and physical education (12 positions); and chaplains' services (two positions).

The wards live in cottages, with 50 occupants to a cottage, selected according to age, sophistication, and past histories. Each ward has a room, or cell, of his own. The doors are locked at night, but unlocked at 5:45 in the morning, when the boys get up. During the day the boys are under the supervision of the youth counselor assigned to their cottage.

Five of the seven cottages are concerned only with the therapeutic diagnostic programs. The sixth is devoted to a 20-day program for youths ready for immediate release; the other is devoted to a 90-day program called the James Marshall Treatment Program, which allows a youth to be released into the community after a short institutional stay.

During the first week he is at the reception center, a ward undergoes complete medical and dental examinations. On the Monday of his first week at the institution, he reports to an assigned testing group in the school and is assigned to a social worker and a group supervisor. The latter performs a custodial function and also counsels him in his living unit. On the basis of reports from the medical officer, the living unit, the school, or the social workers, he may be referred to the psychological section for further evaluation. The final report consists of a confidential diagnostic summary that is presented to the Youth Authority Board as a recommendation for a proposed treatment program. The social worker assigned to the case makes the board presentation. Complete diagnostic summaries are prepared for all first commitments and for selected parole violators. The diagnostic summary is used by the Youth Authority Board as a basis for its judgment in the disposition of a case. The institituion to which the ward is sent uses it for planning his preliminary program. At a later time, the Division of Parole may use the summary as a basis for planning the ward's return to the community.

The board may dispose of a case in any of the following ways:

1. Transfer the ward to Fricot Ranch School for boys, Fred C. Nelles School for boys, Paso Robles School for boys, Preston School of Industry, or the Youth School. Older wards who are parole violators or recommitments are sometimes transferred to the Deuel Vocational Institution and very occasionally to Soledad, Department of Corrections institutions.
2. Transfer the ward to one of the four Youth Authority camps.
3. Refer the ward to immediate parole under regular parole supervision.
4. Return the ward to the commiting court as unfit for the Youth Authority program.
5. Transfer the ward to the Department of Mental Hygiene for a 90-day period of observation and/or treatment.
6. Transfer the ward for a short period to a county jail.
7. Direct that the ward remain at the receiving center for further diagnosis and/or treatment.
8. Direct that the ward remain at the clinic for inclusion in the Marshall Program.
9. Transfer the ward to the Narcotics Control Program.
10. Place the ward in a halfway house operated by the Parole Division.
11. Recommend that the ward be considered for placement in the psychiatric treatment program found in all Youth Authority institutions.

The James Marshall Treatment Program

The primary goal of the Norwalk Reception Center's Marshall Program is to prepare selected wards (males from ages 15 to 17½) to return to their home communities after successful completion of 90 days of treatment. It involves approximately 40 boys. The staff is composed of group supervisors, a school psychologist, a social caseworker, and clerical help.

The treatment program is based on the group method. All the boys in the program meet with all available staff members for one hour daily, five times a week, to discuss their living experiences and interpersonal difficulties. These group meetings are structured to provide a positive and constructive communication channel in which feelings about the impact of the institutional experience can be examined and resolved. The establishment of positive relationships between the wards and the staff also serves to reduce the problems of management of the ward population.

A 30-minute staff critique immediately follows each community meeting. This allows the staff, and especially the group supervisors, who are closest to the wards, constantly to evaluate these meetings with an eye to both content and group interaction.

Each ward is assigned to a small peer group—six to eight members—led by a group supervisor. Within this primary group the ward is given an intensive and dynamic experience. He is confronted with his own behavior as well as given an opportunity to examine that of his peers. The group supervisor's efforts are focused on motivating anxiety and stimulating stress situations, in which the individual and his peers assume major responsibility for examining behavior. The whole group thus becomes involved in the problem-solving process.

The boys have their own "government," and most decisions they reach are honored. They take part in the screening process that decides whether or not a ward should be allowed to enter the program. They check each other's progress toward rehabilitation. With the help of the group leaders, they may decide whether a boy is ready to be released to his parents and a probation or parole officer.

The idea of constant interaction is heavily stressed within the Marshall Program. Every effort is made to discourage boys from isolating themselves from their peers. Group games and projects are fostered whenever possible. Control of "outbursts" and verbalization of feelings are also encouraged.

Before any boy may be accepted into the program, his parents must be willing and able to give their full support and substantial time to work with the group worker in the adjustment and rehabilitation of their son. The group worker attempts to help them accept their son's problems and to provide a better environment for the boy after his release. The group worker also attempts to establish a relationship between the boy and his future probation or parole officer.

The Youth Training School: Ontario

The Youth Training School at Ontario was established in December 1959. It was the first specialized school and is now the largest operated by the California Youth Authority.[1] Youths sent to the school are wards of the court and have been certified to and accepted by the California Youth Authority for treatment and training. No youth may be committed who at the time of his offense was 21 years of age or older or under 16. Wards are sent to Ontario by California Youth Authority Board decisions based on classification and diagnostic studies made at the northern or southern reception center.

The boys at Ontario are considered to be past the age when they can be expected to return to school. They are therefore given vocational training to enable them to become self-supporting.

---

[1]*California Youth Training School* (Ontario: California Youth Training School, n.d.).

The average stay at Ontario is nine months, although the school budget provides for an average stay of eight months per ward.

The school is a medium-security correctional institution. The main security measure is a 16-foot fence encompassing the campus area. From the observation tower, located at the end of the administration building, it is possible to see and control almost every area of the campus. Wards may therefore go to and from classes and to work assignments without direct supervision. This is known throughout the school as "free movement."

The institution provides both lay and professional counseling. Lay counseling is by far the most used of the two. Every one of the 400 staff members, in theory at least, serves as a counselor to the wards. The use of professional counseling is very limited because of the general unavailability of professional personnel. Wards who are believed to be mentally ill are transferred out of Ontario to a more appropriate institution.

Individual counseling is available to the wards in their own living units. This counseling is given by the classification officer. His case load is about 100 wards. He works irregular hours, so he is available to the wards when they have free time at night. The classification officer also evaluates the wards, handles their personal business, and performs various other duties.

Controlled group sessions, with approximately 12 to 14 wards involved in each session, are held once a week for one hour. The entire program of group counseling is voluntary, but certain wards are particularly encouraged to attend. There are about 500 wards involved in the program. The academic teachers as well as the vocational teachers at times employ group counseling in the classroom.

Both the Protestant and the Catholic churches provide chaplains, who are available for counseling in the church at the wards' convenience. Approximately 240 wards attend church services. The chaplains also hold premarital and marriage classes for the wards. These have proved to be highly popular, since most of the wards contemplate marriage and tend to marry quite young. The personal counseling of the chaplains, like the other forms of counseling at the institution, is completely confidential.

The ward is allowed two visits of two hours each per month. These are held Saturdays, Sundays, and holidays, when there are no vocational training classes. The boys see their visitors in the visiting lounge, toward the front of the institution. The only factor that creates an institutional atmosphere is the control room with double-locked doors through which the visitor must pass upon entering the school. The school finds these visits an effective aid in securing cooperation as well as good for morale and institutional adjustment.

The school at Ontario is accredited by the state of California, and wards are encouraged to get their high school diplomas. There are 28 vocational education classes designed to give practical experience, and many are utilized in the maintenance of the facility. These include plumbing, electricity, painting, carpentry, furniture refinishing, masonry, nursery and gardening, building maintenance, and food services. The boys prepare all food served in the school and deliver it to the dining rooms in the housing units. Special meals and baked goods are prepared by the boys for guests at the school. Boys in the auto-repair and body-and-fender classes work on state-owned vehicles. Outside organizations such as the Salvation Army bring in used typewriters and office machines for rebuilding or repair, furniture to be refinished or reupholstered, or shoes to be repaired. These vocational activities give the boys an opportunity to participate in meaningful occupations and achieve a sense of success and accomplishment.

THE STATE REFORMATORY: AN INMATE'S VIEWPOINT

To provide a closer appraisal of the social-psychological impacts of a state reformatory system, we will here briefly describe an institution and then present one inmate's viewpoint. The ward who describes his viewpoint is Claude Brown, who was committed to Warwick by the Juvenile Courts of New York three times. Later in life, he achieved great literary success through a book, *Manchild in the Promised Land*, his account of his life on the streets of New York and the "time" he did at Warwick. Brown's account of reformatory life provides a different viewpoint than the one portrayed by the state's official manuals.

The Warwick School for Boys, a Division for Youth facility of the State of New York, is a total institution for juveniles, serving boys from 13 to 15 years of age committed by juvenile courts in New York City and the southeastern portion of New York State. Boys sent to the institution spend from 11 to 13 months at Warwick.

The Warwick School, situated in a suburban area of Warwick, includes 740 acres of landscaped countryside. Boys are housed in cottages, each with its own dining area. Total capacity is 260. There is a school on the grounds, which offers an academic program with emphasis on remedial reading and advanced reading to a basic skill level. Twenty-one teachers conduct ungraded classes under the direction of an educational director assisted by a vocational supervisor and an academic supervisor. The vocational education program includes courses in barbering, printing, carpentry, electrical work, and drafting. Boys, in addition to attending classes, work in the vocational program and perform housekeeping services in their cottages.

Recreational programs include intramural sports, films, recreational trips, and other sociocultural experiences. Recreational facilities include a baseball diamond, football field, and gymnasium, which includes a basketball court. The treatment program includes group counseling and individual casework provided by seven social workers under the supervision of a director of social services. The two full-time chaplains, one Catholic and one Protestant, offer family counseling. A psychologist conducts psychological testing and aptitude testing. Diagnostic and therapeutic services and staff training are provided by the five part-time psychiatrists. Medical and dental services are available at infirmary facilities on the grounds, and full-time nurses are on duty at the infirmary. Visiting by parents is encouraged; boys are permitted home visits on a regular basis and can earn incentive visits.[2] Here is Claude Brown's analysis of Warwick,[3]

I came out of the reception center on a Friday afternoon. They put me in cottage C2. There were mostly Puerto Rican fellows in there, a few Negroes, and a sprinkling of white cats. The cottage parents were Puerto Rican. I remember it well.

When they were bringing us all up the walk of the cottage area, a lot of cats started bowing their heads and saying, "Bye, Brown," in a whisper, as if they thought I as going to my funeral or something. . . .

Warwick was a funny kind of place. It was a jail in disguise. The windows in the cottage and in most of the buildings were divided into very small sections, and they had steel dividers that were painted to look like wood. The panes between the dividers were only about six square inches, and the windows were usually down from the top and up from the bottom. It would look like a normal house to anybody from the outside. But if any of the cats had tried to push a window up more from the bottom or pull it down more from the top, they would have found out that it had slats on the side, long wooden slats that wouldn't allow the window to go up or down any more than a couple of inches farther.

It was a pretty place. They had people walking around looking like they were free, but you had to have a pass to go anywhere and if you were gone too long, they had somebody out looking for you. They had what they called "area men," and the area men were like detectives up at Warwick. Anytime something happened—if something had been stolen or if someone had gotten stabbed—these were the cats who came around and investigated and found out who had done it. They were usually big cats, strong-arm boys. And they usually found out what it was they wanted to know.

The area men would come for you if you were gone from a place too long, and they would bring runners. Runners were like trusties. They would run after guys in the woods if they ran away, and they'd bring them back. The runners usually came from cottage A4 or one in the D group, where most of the big cats were. A4 was a crazy cottage. They had the nuts in there; they had the rapists, murderers, and perverts in there. These were the most brutal cats up there, and everybody knew it. A lot of times when people ran away, if they saw these cats behind them they would stop, because they knew they didn't have much chance of getting away. And if they gave the A4 guys a hard time, they'd catch hell when they were caught.

To someone passing by, Warwick looked just like a boys' camp. *But everybody was under guard, all the time,* and everybody had a job to do. You worked in the

[2]*A Division for Youth Facility: Warwick School for Boys* (Albany: New York State Division for Youth). This manual contains a description of the institution.
[3]Reprinted with permission of Macmillan Publishing Co., Inc., from *Manchild in the Promised Land* by Claude Brown. Copyright © Claude Brown, 1965. Emphasis added.

bakery or in an office or on the work gangs, and so on. Work gangs were a lot like chain gangs, minus the chains. In the summer, work gangs just busted rock and threw sledgehammers and picked onions and stuff like that. In the winter, the work gangs shoveled coal and shoveled snow. If you were a decent guy or if you could be trusted, you could get a job in one of the offices or in one of the buildings. That where most of the younger guys worked if they weren't hell raisers. Most of the older guys were runners. They'd take people back from offices, take them around whenever they had to go see their sponsors or social workers. That sort of business. Everybody had a place to fit into, so it seemed. . . .

One of the first guys I met up at Warwick was a guy I'd read about in the paper. Just about everybody had read about him, I suppose. He had been blamed for shooting somebody in the Polo Grounds in the summer of 1950. It was a jive tip, but there were a whole lot of cats up there on humbles. He was a damn nice guy, but they had him in A4, the crazy cottage. Just about all the guys under sixteen who were up there for murder were in A4.

This guy was on Mrs. Washington's gang with me, and he was telling me one day how they sent him up there on a humble. He said when this guy had gotten shot in the Polo Grounds, they started looking in all the houses on Edgecombe Avenue, and that's where he lived. They started looking for guns and stuff. They had a house-to-house search for guns. And they found a .22 rifle in his house. The man had been shot with a .45, but they blamed it on him.

He turned out to be a real nice cat. It was a funny thing, but all the cats I met up there and all the cats I knew on the streets who had been accused of murder or who had actually killed somebody always seemed to be the nicest cats. . . .

There were a lot of real hip young criminals at Warwick. It wasn't like Wiltwyck. For one thing, Wiltwyck only had about a hundred guys, and Warwick had five hundred. And Warwick had guys from all over New York City. They had cats from Brooklyn, the Bronx, Manhattan, Queens, and Richmond—everywhere. There were even cats from small towns upstate and from surburban areas of New York City. And Warwick had real criminals. Nobody at Wiltwyck was there for murder, and they didn't have any cats up there who knew how to steal a car without the keys. But it seemed like just about everybody at Warwick not only knew how to pick locks but knew how to cross wires in cars and get them started without keys. Just about everybody knew how to pick pockets and roll reefers, and a lot of cats knew how to cut drugs. They knew how much sugar to put with heroin to make a cap or a bag. There was so much to learn.

You learned something new from everybody you met. It seemed like just about all the Puerto Rican guys were up there for using drugs. They had a lot of colored cats up there for using drugs, but most of them were jive. Most of the guys were just using drugs to be down and to have a rep as a junkie. You could tell that these cats were jive by the way they went around saying, "Yeah, man, do you shoot stuff?" and all this sort of nonsense, as though they were bragging about it. They would start talking about how much stuff they used a day. I'd look at them and say, "Yeah, like, that's real nice," but they could never make me feel bad or anything, because all I had to do was say my name was Claude Brown. I didn't have to use drugs. I already had a reputation. I'd been other places. I knew people from here, I knew people from there.

Cats had heard about me when I was in Brooklyn gang fighting with K. B. and the Robins. And when I got shot, it was something that everybody seemed to respect me for. I'd only gotten shot with a .32, but the word was out that I'd gotten shot in the stomach with a .38. Cats didn't believe it. They'd come up to me and say, "Man, did you really git shot wit a .38?" and I'd either joke it off or act like they were being silly. I'd say, "Shit, people have gotten shot with .45's, so what?" They would go away marveling.

When we were in the dormitory getting ready to take a shower, the cool guys would say, "Hey, Brown, could I see your scar?" or they would just say, "Man, is that your scar?" I'd say, "Yeah, that's it." If they were hip cats, they might just say something like "Yeah, man, those bullets can really fuck you up." And I'd say something like, "Yeah, but you can keep gittin' up behind 'em."

Cats used to come up and offer me ins or reefers or horse or anything I wanted. I had two or three flunkies after I'd been there for a month. It was no sweat for me; I was ready to stay there for a long time and live real good. I knew how to get along there. I'd had a place waiting for me long before I came. If I'd known that Warwick was going to be as good as it turned out to be, I would never have been so afraid. As a matter of fact, I might have gotten there a whole lot sooner.

At Warwick, it all depended on you when you went home for a visit. The first time, you had to stay there twelve weeks before you could go home. After that, you could go home for a three-day visit, from Friday to Monday, every eight weeks. That's if you didn't lose any days for fucking up or fighting. This was pretty good, because some people were always going home, and they would see your fellows and bring messages back, and your fellows were always coming up every Friday. A new batch of guys would come up and drugs would come up. When you came back from a weekend home visit, you were searched everywhere. They'd even search in the crack of your ass. You had to go to the doctor and let him look for a dose of clap. But cats would always manage to bring back at least a cap of horse or at least one reefer. Everybody could always manage to smuggle in a little bit of something. . . .

We all came out of Warwick better criminals. Other guys were better for the things that I could teach them, and I was better for the things that they could teach me. Before I went to Warwick, I used to be real slow at rolling reefers and at dummying reefers, but when I came back from Warwick, I was a real pro at that, and I knew how to boost weak pot with embalming fluid. I even knew how to cut drugs, I had it told to me so many times, I learned a lot of things at Warwick. The good thing about Warwick was that when you went home on visits, you could do stuff, go back up to Warwick, and kind of hide out. If the cops were looking for you in the city, you'd be at Warwick. . . .

After about eight months at Warwick, they told me that I'd be going home in about a month. When K. B. heard about it, he panicked. He said, "I want to go home too, man. These people better let me outta here."

"Look, K. B., I been tellin' you ever since I came here, if you want to git outta this place, you got to stop fuckin' up. It's, like, you gotta stop all the beboppin' and you gotta stop all that fuckin' up with the area men, like, just goin' around tryin' to be bad. You can do that shit with the cats around here, but if you start screamin' on the area men like that, you can't possibly win, man. Because these are the cats who can keep you up here all your life if they want to."

"Look, Claude, you don't understand. I'm from Brooklyn. There's a whole lotta stuff goin' on up here that I can't stay out of. You know, like, when my fellas, the Robins or the Stompers, go to war, it's, like, I've got to git into it too, because cats gon be lookin' for me to kick my ass or stab me or some kinda shit like that even if I don't come right out and declare war, because they know, like, I'm in this clique, man. Just about everybody who comes up here from Brooklyn, they know who's in what gang."

I said, "Yeah, man, but that's not the main thing. The main thing is to stop screamin' on the area men. You can go and have your rumbles and shit if you want, but you know if you stab anybody and they find out about it, you're through. The only way you gon make it outta here is to cool it. Didn't I tell you I wasn't gon stay up here a year when I came? And now I'm walkin', right? So it must be somethin' to it."

K. B. said, "Yeah, Claude, it's, like, yeah, man; I should-a listened to you, 'cause I now you usually know what you're talkin' about. I'm gon change my whole way-a actin' up here. And I'm gon be gittin' outta here soon. I'm gon be gittin' outta here in about three months now, just you watch."

I left Warwick after staying up there for about nine months and three weeks. I came home and went to the High School of Commerce, down around Broadway and Sixty-fifth Street.

I didn't go for school too much. The cats there were really dressing, and I didn't have any money. The only way I could make some money was by not going to school. If I told Dad I needed about four or five pair of pants and some nice shirts, he would start talking all that nonsense again about, "I didn't have my first pair-a long pants till I was out workin'." That shit didn't make any sense, not to me. He had been living down on a farm, and this was New York City. People looked crazy going around in New York City with one pair of pants, but this was the way he saw it, and this was the way he talked. I think the nigger used to talk this nonsense because he didn't want to get up off any money to buy me some clothes. So I just said, "Fuck it, I'll buy my own."

The only way I could buy my own was by selling pot when I went to school. And I'd take some loaded craps down there, some bones, and I would beat the paddy boys out of all their money. They were the only ones who were dumb enought to shoot craps with bones.

After a while, I just got tired. I never went to any of the classes, and if I did go to one, I didn't know anything. I felt kind of dumb, so I stopped going there. The only time I went to school was when I wanted to make some money. I'd go there and stay a couple of hours. Maybe I'd take Turk with me. Turk would sell some pot, and I'd shoot some craps, and when we got enough money, we'd go uptown.

A JUVENILE DETENTION CAMP

A major change in reformatories since Claude Brown's time has been an increase in gang violence. In recent years interracial conflict has flared in juvenile reformatories. Some of these conflicts have been of such propor- tions as to be labeled "miniriots." The following article describes a pro- totypical riot that took place in a juvenile institution in California. This "anatomy of a riot," much like Claude Brown's "rap," reveals some of the underlying violent sociodynamics of a reformatory.

Juvenile Detention Camp: Anatomy of a Riot

Shortly before 11 P.M. May 2, the customary quiet of a walled camp in the San Dimas foothills was shattered by the sounds of boys screaming and glass breaking.

Youths rampaged through the camp's 94-bed open dorm, wielding table legs, forks, wooden stakes, ceramic ashtrays, belts, even beds, as weapons in a fever to do each other harm.

Some just ran—in fear for their lives.

In all, that night there were 80 youths—many of them street-sophisticated, muscular 17- and 18-year olds described as "hard-core" by their probation officers—and five probation officers on duty in the dorm of the county-run maximum security camp for juvenile offenders.

After it was over and the sheriffs, the deputies, the ambulances, the doctors, the paramedics and the injured had gone, it was determined that 15 young wards of the county and the five probation officers had been injured in the melee.

Nine inmates had escaped. Today, three of them are still at large. . . .

"There are always racial overtones in a camp setting," according to one staff officer.

"The degree of racial overtones varies, depending on how hot the day is, how lax the staff is, and what they allow in terms of racial comments."

Question: "Was there any indication the blacks felt shortchanged at the camp?"

"Only after the situation (riot) had taken place," one black camp officer told an investigator. "After we started talking to the individuals, things came out."

Among the things that "came out" was the apparent existence of resentment among black inmates over the "privilege" extended Mexican-American inmates to hold La Raza meetings in camp.

There was nothing equivalent to La Raza for the blacks at Camp Rockey.

"There is no actual group or togetherness among the blacks as there is amongst the Chicanos," a white camp officer said. "Chicanos, when incarcerated or contained in institutions, have been known to band together."

"Even though they might be enemies in the community, when they come to camp, La Raza sticks together. They do their best to support one another and to hang together. Here at Camp Rockey the La Raza movement has been a positive one."

"Now the blacks have never, during the present camp programming, indicated a real desire to get together," he said. "They are very much more fragmented and many are very much enemies with one another. . . "

On the Saturday evening before the riot on Sunday, the camp's weightlifting champion, a 5-foot-9, 185-pound, black 18-year-old, went out to the weight pit on the field to work out.

The pit was occupied by Chicano youths, holding a La Raza meeting.

The black left the field. The next morning at breakfast he punched two Mexican-Americans at a table that seats eight on each side. The punches followed an exchange of racial slurs.

On the witness stand in Juvenile Court, the black youth said he had "heard this Mexican-American at the end of the table say '(obscenity) niggers.' I say, 'Why you want to talk racial that way?' And then he said to '(obscenity) me.'"

Lawyer: "And what did you do then?"

"I said '(obscenity) all of you.'" After that, he was escorted out of the dining hall but reentered a few minutes later by another door.

"When I went by (a Chicano ward) he said, 'I'm gonna shank you'."

"What does that mean?"

"Cut me, stick me," he replied.

"What did you do then?"

"I hit him."

When that happened, "bedlam broke loose" in the dining hall, according to a probation officer who was there. The riot was yet to come that night. The breakfast disturbance was the prelude.

"Immediately all the wards stood up, picked up forks, spoons, started throwing pitchers of hot coffee, cups, trays," the officer said of the breakfast incident.

"The whole population of the dining hall polarized. The blacks came into one area, the Chicanos into another. I saw a young black standing up on a table swinging with both arms. The KPs came out of the kitchen. A lot of kids took off outside.

"They broke out, through the door, and, as it settled down, well it didn't settle down, but as it continued to develop, all the black kids went out of the dining hall and all the Chicanos stayed in.

"All the white kids—a few of them were kind of scattered around everywhere—most of them ran down to the administration building (for protection).

"The minority in Camp Rockey is the white youth so he didn't really know where to go."

Outside, "the black kids broke off some of the stakes holding up trees, they found pieces of pipe, pieces of chairs from the dining hall and they were trying to break windows and get into the dining hall. The Mexican-Americans were trying to get out. So a lot of windows were busted as a result."

It took "approximately two to four hours, I guess, before we finally got them all settled back down to where they could all actually be in the same building," he said.

A veteran of the rioting at Camp Rockey mused on the two-fold nature of his role as a camp officer—part cop, part counselor.

"There's a difference if the staff member is acquainted with juveniles and knows how to work with juveniles . . . to where you're not classed (by them) as a worker or 'the man,'" he said.

"We are the man as well as the friend of these guys. If he does something wrong, we're the ones that have to punish him, more or less. As well, we have to try to show him a better way to do it.

"So when you have new staff members staffing a maximum security institution, I do not feel that it's fair to the other guys working here."

In the present open-door arrangement, the officers know the wards, know they [the boys] have the edge in numbers.

"In other words," another officer said, "it's a security camp, and it isn't secure at all. It's a very insecure situation as far as I'm concerned . . . I've been in the county (employ) for seven years, and this is too much."

"In other words, you are pretty much at the mercy of the boys?" he was asked.

"Why, definitely, definitely. We've got nothing but the files, man. You know, we gotta play their game. They don't have to play our game.

"When the (trouble) comes down, we can't do anything about it. Just say 'No, don't do that, don't do this.' And if you give a man a zero you've got to write out a gram (report), have it approved by the supervisor and it's just not worth going through all the paperwork. Administrators don't give a damn anyway, so why should we?"[4]

CONFLICTING ATTITUDES ON JUVENILE INSTITUTIONAL TREATMENT

A common problem in long-term juvenile institutions like Warwick or the probation facility described in the riot article is conflict and mutual hostility between treatment personnel and those concerned with custody and discipline. This problem of value conflict between these authority figures often emerges most sharply in an institution changing over from a "juvenile prison" emphasizing custody to a rehabilitation approach.

George H. Weber carried out a penetrating study that reveals the conflict that occurs in a training school where two divergent systems of resocialization exist.[5] He analyzed a state training school that was shifting from a generally custodial-punitive approach to a psychiatric-social work approach entailing diagnosis, group therapy, and individual attention. The institution housed 150 boys between the ages of 12 and 16 in five cottages. The staff was composed of five social workers, two psychologists, one psychiatrist, and 46 cottage parents.

Weber noted the following areas of organizational changes:

The approach generally shifted from tight control of behavior to permissiveness that allowed acting out. This pattern was more congenial to members of the treatment staff, as they considered it helped them to see the child "as he really was." Therapeutic or counseling functions were substantially removed from cottage parents and given to the regular therapeutic staff. Cottage parents were explicitly instructed not to attempt any counseling and to "make sure they did not interfere with the child treatment program."

Several noticeable effects resulted from these organizational changes:

---

[4]Dorothy Townsend, "Juvenile Detention Camp: Anatomy of a Riot," *Los Angeles Times*, August 8, 1976. Copyright, 1976, *Los Angeles Times*. Reprinted by permission.

[5]George H. Weber, "Emotional and Defensive Reactions of Cottage Parents," in *The Prison*, ed. Donald R. Cressey (New York: Holt, Rinehart and Winston, 1961), pp. 189–228.

1. A degree of disciplinary power was taken away from the cottage parents. Instead of controlling a boy through fear of punishment, the cottage parent was forced to establish a relationship based on friendship.
2. The cottage parents were given a subordinate and confusing role in the organization. Their frustrations and anger were often displaced onto the boys.
3. Often the boys would play one authority figure (the cottage parent) against another (the therapist).

After a time the institution began to move more smoothly and positively toward its rehabilitative goal. The research revealed, however, the inherent conflicts that exist between a custodial emphasis and a rehabilitative approach in the institutional treatment of juveniles.

NEW YORK'S "RESIDENTIAL TREATMENT CENTERS"

"Residential treatment centers" are like long-term reformatories in many ways; however, there is more of an emphasis on therapy. New York State was one of the first to give financial support to this type of institution for juveniles. Some six institutions established by private charitable organizations and operated under private auspices have been officially classified as "residential treatment centers" by the State of New York and these served as models that were replicated in other states. The designation is made by the New York City Commission for the Foster Care of Children. Accreditation by this group leads to substantial financial benefits, and hence the evaluations are made with considerable care. The six institutions designated as residential treatment centers by the commission provide a combination of individual and milieu therapy based on a clinical study of each child.

A majority of the cases accepted by these institutions are referred by the children's court; others are referred by the New York City Department of Welfare, mental hospitals, child-guidance clinics, social agencies, and private psychiatrists. Because of intake policies and limits of capacity, the number of referrals is four or five times the number actually accepted. All the children accepted in the institutions are considered to be emotionally disturbed and in need of psychotherapeutic treatment.

Before a child is accepted, the intake study must indicate that he is amenable to treatment by the facilities available at the institution. Children with IQs below 70 are not considered acceptable. The ratio of staff (including all types of service, treatment, custodial, and managerial) to inmates varies between one to one and four to five. Psychiatrists are available as consultants to the psychiatric social workers. Psychologists, in the main, administer tests. Social workers, in addition to providing individual casework and group therapy, are often assigned the task of coordinating all the services. Each center has a school geared to the institutional approach. Insofar as practicable, the education of the child is coordinated with the activities of those directly involved in his therapy.

Most residential treatment centers of this type are located in countryside areas, a considerable distance from the cities from which virtually all the inmates come. Although distances are not very great by modern standards, transportation costs are prohibitive for most poor people. Contacts between children and their parents and relatives are therefore limited during the period of institutionalization. Contacts between staff members and the children and their families are likewise limited when the children are returned to their urban communities. Furthermore, the distances between the institutions and the family residences make it difficult for staff members to work with parents and institutionalized children in an effort to improve relationships between them. While no two residential treatment centers are identical, a description of one of them will serve to illustrate the basic ways in which these institutions function.

Wiltwyck School for Boys

Wiltwyck was established in 1937 by the New York Protestant Episcopal City Missions Society to house black Protestant boys. Boys between the ages of eight and twelve are referred to Wiltwyck by the children's court and the Welfare Department of New York City. It has become interracial and has a capacity of about 100 boys.

The typical boy at Wiltwyck is considered to be suffering from serious emotional disturbance or maladjustment as a result of parental neglect or mistreatment. The intake committee rejects boys believed too psychotic or unmanageable to be fitted into the minimum-custody open setting of the institution. The average length of stay is about two years.

The boys are divided into eight "living groups" or cottage groups, with ten to fourteen boys in each. Two counselors live and work with each group, and there are four relief counselors. Counselors have complete responsibility for the boys except when they are assigned to an activity or treatment under the supervision of another staff member. In the past, "cottage parents," who lived in the cottages with the boys and were to fulfill the roles of father and mother, performed the duties now assigned to counselors. The change was made because it was believed that the counselors not only would provide guidance, leadership, and advice for the boys but also would serve as young male role models, believed necessary for youths who usually did not have a functional father.

The philosophy of the institution is nonpunitive and permissive. Boys may freely express their feelings of antagonism and hostility but must bear the consequences of any misbehavior. "Consequences" may follow misbehavior, but they are not to be regarded as punishment. An effort is made to get the boy to distinguish between rejection of the misbehavior (harmful consequences follow) and rejection of himself. In this way the institution sets behavioral limits for the boy.

In addition to a therapeutic program, the institution provides indoor games, movies, television, arts and crafts, social dancing, hikes, camping, swimming, and other sports.

The professional treatment staff includes eleven caseworkers, two casework supervisors, one assistant casework supervisor, three psychiatrists, a psychologist engaged in testing, two group therapists, an art therapist, a drama therapist, a dance therapist, and three remedial reading therapists. Every boy sees a caseworker every week or two. The same caseworker sees the parents of the boys under his charge at least once a month, in an effort to prepare the boy and his family for home visits and for the eventual return home.

The school facility at Wiltwyck is a "600" school (a school for problem children) of the City of New York. There are seven ungraded classes. Besides regular academic subjects such as reading, arithmetic, and social studies, there are classes in shopwork, including ceramics, metalwork, and mechanical drawing. The school places strong emphasis on achievement. Ten teachers are assigned to the school, seven of whom have been certified as competent to teach in a 600 school.

Aftercare services are provided for at least six months after the child is returned to the community. Children receive aftercare supervision whether they return to their own homes, go to a group home supported by the institution, or are placed in foster homes. The principal aftercare service is an interview by a social caseworker once or twice a month.

A study of 65 boys five years after they left Wiltwyck showed that 70.8 percent had made a good or reasonably good adjustment after release from the school; 43.2 percent had not had any court appearances; 27.6 percent had appeared in court for one of three reasons: a request to return to Wiltwyck, running away from home, or truancy; 29.2 percent were failures, having appeared in court on serious charges. A carefully controlled study comparing Wiltwyck with a New England training school whose program was based on strict discipline and formal education showed that Wiltwyck exceeded the training school in developing improved attitudes. The improved attitudes and the low percentage of recidivists were believed by the researchers to be the result of the Wiltwyck experience.[6]

Removing the child from the urban scene and placing him in a residential treatment center not readily accessible to his old habitat to some extent protects society from the offender's potential for delinquency. Because most residential treatment centers provide minimum security, many young people run away. They are then placed in state training schools or prisons when these steps are deemed necessary to control the child and protect society.

[6]William McCord and Joan McCord, "Two Approaches to the Cure of Delinquents," *Journal of Criminal Law, Criminology and Police Science* 44 (December 1953): 442–467.

The Delinquent Subculture in a Residential Treatment Center

Howard W. Polsky carried out several years of significant research into a private cottage-type residential treatment center called Hawthorne-Cedar Knolls in New York.[7] Supported by the Jewish Board of Guardians, Hawthorne-Cedar Knolls School is essentially devoted to individual psychoanalytic treatment of emotionally disturbed delinquent children, as well as withdrawn, bizarrely acting, prepsychotic, and fragile children who are not able to live in the community.

The school provides academic and vocational courses and intensive remedial programs. A full range of clinical services is provided by psychiatrists, psychologists, and social workers. Treatment includes individual psychotherapy, group therapy, family therapy, and other services provided in accordance with the child's individual needs as seen by the staff. Social workers provide continuing contacts with parents of residents. There is an elaborate recreational program, and facilities include two gymnasiums, an outdoor swimming pool, ball fields, and recreation rooms in each cottage. Recreational trips are made outside the institution. While approximately half the students are Jewish, about 25 percent are Negro or Puerto Rican, and the remainder are from other ethnic groups.[8]

The focus of Polsky's study was on the cottage's subcultural values and the relationships between the socialization process in the cottage and the treatment program. He observed a definite hierarchy of status in the cottage he studied by participant observation. The stratification system was essentially based on power "toughness" and the ability to manipulate (precisely the behavioral patterns the institution was supposed to change).

As far as group processes and structure were concerned, Polsky came to the following conclusions:

1. The boys were highly conscious of each other's position in the rigid social hierarchy. It was this preoccupation with each other's relative strength that dominated and framed much of the boys' interactions, even apparently the most simple kinds, such as the passing of food at the dining table. He observed that "there was very little opportunity for the group to work together to dilute these crystallized roles based on toughness."

2. Another great imbalance appeared to exist around the issue of sharing. He observed, for example, that food was used as a tool to exert pressure and control. There was an individualistic and inequitable distribution of power: The top clique controlled choice items such as butter, and all boys at other tables had to go to them for it. Standing in line for food often becomes a testing ground as boys tried to step in front of each other and show their superiority. It became natural for the tougher, older boys in the cottage to

---

[7]Howard W. Polsky, *Cottage Six* (New York: Russell Sage Foundation, 1962).
[8]"Some Facts about the Hawthorne-Cedar Knolls School," mimeographed. This material was furnished by Frank Modica, assistant director of the school, on September 19, 1973.

control those of lower status. In the cottage there was a formalistic organization around authority. This was not worked out in rules or as a constitution, but as the accretion of experience—implicit recognition by all the boys of exactly where they stood vis-à-vis the others. When a high-status boy was challenged by someone of lower status, a very dramatic outbreak occurred, and generally the upstart was "put in his place."

3. Within this cottage there was very little tendency to make status contingent upon service to the cottage. Nor did status within the cottage seem to depend in any way on skills developed outside it. Status seemed to be determined solely by toughness and ability to control others. The constant hazing of a scapegoat by the group could become so oppressive that the scapegoat would have either to "stand up" or to leave. The consolidation of the group against one or several of its members was established procedure in the cottage. The soil in which scapegoating flourished was the pervasive "ranking" (a pattern of insults) and shaming, dominant characteristics of the pecking order.

4. Finally, there seemed to be a tendency within the cottage for some solidarity to form within subgroups on the basis of close association; there was little or no tendency toward overall cottage solidarity. In the course of time these cliques became increasingly crystallized. Clique loyalties predominated. In time, the top clique became quite effective in exerting control over the others, and the top clique's attitude toward the staff, whether defiance or cooperation, was established as the basic pattern for the entire cottage.

The cottage, according to Polsky, was therefore culturally and organizationally "delinquent-bound." There was little opportunity for the boys to offset the constant, overwhelming delinquent-expressive behavior with positive socioemotional interactions. Polsky found that the cottage was to a large extent a vacuum in which peer-group authoritarianism and toughness reigned supreme. The individuals tested their emotional problems upon each other and in fact moved very little together in meeting challenges placed before them as a cottage group. In the elaboration of their personality distortions, interpersonal cyclical movements were set up in which a preponderance of negative individual acting out resulted in a kind of group pathology. The negative delinquent cottage culture was thus a major source of resistance to treatment.

Polsky's research indicates the absolute necessity of extending individual and group therapy programs to encompass the entire pattern of living in juvenile institutions. The separation of treatment from the youth's day-to-day encounters and lifestyle in the cottage tends to sabotage the treatment program and render it relatively ineffectual.

In general, the programs of juvenile institutions are superior to adult correctional efforts; however, with some exceptions they suffer from similar problems. These include:

1. The existence of a criminogenic "crime school" atmosphere and value system.
2. An artificial "homosexual" environment.
3. A "doing time" atmosphere.
4. A schism between treatment program and delinquent subculture.

HIGHFIELDS

The prototype for a treatment-oriented small residential group center is the Highfields program, originated in 1950 by Lloyd W. McCorkle in New Jersey. The program was not designed for deeply disturbed or mentally deficient children. The Highfields approach limits the population to 20 boys, aged 16 and 17, assigned directly from the juvenile court. They are youths who have not previously been committed to a correctional institution. Highfields will be closely analyzed here since it is a popular institutional model that has been replicated recently in many states.

The boys who lived in the first experimental Highfields stayed there for an average of four months. During the day they worked at a nearby institution performing menial labor. There were few security measures and little or no authoritarian leadership. Every evening the boys were divided into two groups of ten each for a meeting built around the technique of guided group interaction.

Guided group interaction sessions are at the heart of the Highfields system. The method is cogently described as follows by McCorkle:

> Rehabilitation begins with changes in attitudes. But how can these be brought about? The boys entering Highfields have for years identified themselves as delinquents. Their close friends are delinquent. Group pressure has generally pushed and pulled them into delinquency and prevented their rehabilitation. Most delinquents feel rejected and discriminated against by their parents. They generally manifest strong emotional reactions, particularly against their fathers, but often against their mothers, brothers, and sisters. By the time they are confronted with law-enforcing agencies they have developed strong ego defenses. They do not take the responsibility for their delinquency. Instead, they tend to blame others—their parents, their associates, and society.

> The whole Highfields experience is directed toward piercing through these strong defenses against rehabilitation, toward undermining delinquent attitudes, and toward developing a self-conception favorable to reformation. The sessions on guided group interaction are especially directed to achieve this objective.

> Guided group interaction has the merit of combining the psychological and the sociological approaches to the control of human behavior. The psychological approach aims to change the self-conception of the boy from a delinquent to a nondelinquent. But this process involves changing the mood of the boy from impulses to be law breaking to impulses to be law abiding.[9]

[9]Lloyd W. McCorkle, *The Highfields Story* (New York: Holt, Rinehart and Winston, 1958), p. v.

At Highfields, emphasis was placed on normal social activities and values. This was accomplished by four devices intended "to help the boys to be like everybody else." (1) Family members and friends of boys were encouraged to visit them at Highfields, and see how they were getting along. (2) An effort was made to educate the surrounding community to accept the boys, rather than to show suspicion or reject them entirely. (3) Perhaps most important, the boys did useful work and were paid for it. (4) The stay at Highfields was limited to a maximum of four months. This time factor was considered an important device that contributed to successful rehabilitation.

Institutions modeled after the original Highfields have been developed around the country. Some are now located in central city areas. Much like the original, they house about 20 persons each, and custodial personnel are held to a minimum. Residents are permitted to receive visitors. Residents usually work outside the institution and participate in group therapy sessions on a regular basis.

The philosophy, operation, effect, and potentialities of the Highfields program have been summarized as follows:

1. Its thoroughgoing use of the group as an instrument of rehabilitation is social-psychologically sound and has been verified by experience.
2. The method of guided interaction directs group influences toward rehabilitation rather than, as in the large reformatory, to the reinforcement of attitudes of delinquency and hostility to authority.
3. In the guided group interaction sessions the youth achieves an understanding of himself and his motivations which enables him to make constructive plans for his future.
4. Highfields greatly reduces the time of treatment from the usual one to five years in training schools or reformatories to three or four months.
5. It requires a minimum of staff as compared with other methods of treatment.
6. Highfields has far lower per capita costs than other institutions for the treatment of delinquents.
7. There is every reason to believe that Highfields can be successfully established elsewhere provided the new projects incorporate its philosophy, its design of operation, and a specially trained staff.[10]

The Highfields experiment has been considered generally successful by several research evaluations. With some variations, it was successfully replicated in Provo, Utah.[11] While Highfields was originally designed for adolescents, a similar type of institutional approach is now used for adult probationers and parolees.

It is apparent from the foregoing that at least some state training

---

[10]H. Ashley Weeks, *Youthful Offenders at Highfields* (Ann Arbor: University of Michigan Press, 1958), pp. xvii–xviii. See also McCorkle, *The Highfields Story.*
[11]Lamar T. Empey and Jerome Rabow, "The Provo Experiment in Delinquency Rehabilitation," *American Sociological Review* 26 (October 1961): 679–695.

schools do not have as damaging an effect on juveniles as prisons. Furthermore, even in the best sort of residential treatment center a delinquent subculture develops to challenge administration norms. The small Highfields-type residence provides the best opportunity for staff members to challenge the leadership of the delinquent subculture. Nevertheless, the failure rate at Wiltwyck and other residential treatment centers is far lower than that of the state training schools. Scientific comparisons between the two types of institution are difficult if not impossible, however, because the populations are not really comparable. The admission committees of the residential treatment centers can refuse to take a boy if they feel their program does not suit his needs; the state training school must take every boy a court sends to it. This power to select gives the residential treatment center an advantage. The fact that residential treatment centers are privately operated and are able to spend more than state-run schools has enabled them to experiment with costly programs and make considerable progress in treatment.

COMMUNITY-BASED MENTAL HOSPITALS FOR JUVENILES: A NEW DIRECTION

In the 1980s there has been a proliferation of referrals of delinquents to psychiatric hospital programs. In this regard, according to a report by the 240-member National Association of Private Psychiatric Hospitals of America, teenage psychiatric admissions rose over 400 percent between 1980 and 1985, from roughly 10,800 in 1980 to more than 48,000 in 1985. This trend appears to be increasing in the late 1980s. More and more delinquents who would ordinarily go to juvenile detention or state training schools are now treated in mental hospitals.

The juveniles placed in these facilities are usually, but not always, more emotionally disturbed than the average state training school or residential treatment center client. They are more likely to be placed in a mental hospital if they exhibit bizarre behavior or are suicidal; however many standard sociopathic, substance-abusing, violent delinquent youths are placed in mental hospitals by their parents or the juvenile courts. An issue in the placement is whether or not their parents have health insurance. For this reason, the youth population in this type of institution is more likely to come from a middle- or upper-class background. Unfortunately, the youth's length of stay in the mental hospital is too often not based on the degree to which the treatment program is helping the child, but on the amount of time permitted by the family's health insurance.

Most hospital programs utilize a wide range of treatment approaches. The program is usually coordinated by the psychiatrist, psychologist, or social worker who has placed the child in the hospital. They have individual counseling sessions with the client and his or her family several times a week.

Following is a fairly typical list of treatment services that the patient and his or her family participate in on a weekly basis when the child is in the hospital.[12]

Community Meetings

This group brings patients and staff together to discuss issues and resolve problems that occur on the unit. Communication and leadership skills are encouraged in this process, as each patient takes a turn in assisting in the leading of these meetings.

Drug/Alcohol Abuse Groups

An important part of the process is counseling in the area of alcohol and drug abuse for those patients who can benefit from this additional service. The program provides Alcoholics Anonymous Meetings in the hospital on a regular basis. The emphasis is on drug awareness and education, sobriety, and related personal growth. In addition, the staff offers a transition to aftercare programs and support groups in the community.

Art Therapy

Art therapy is based on the principle that most fundamental thoughts and feelings reach expression in images rather than in words. Through the process of drawing, painting, sculpting, etc., combined with the art therapist's skill in helping the patient discover and release unconscious feelings and thoughts, the patient can then work to resolve conflicts and fears.

Educational Therapy Group

Educational therapy is a modular-activity group program. The modules have been developed to help patients explore, through educationally therapeutic activities, social, family, and intrapsychic dynamics. Also, patients explore their interrelationships with school and their environment in general.

Group Psychotherapy

Group psychotherapy sessions are held daily. These groups are designed to complement individual psychotherapy with an emphasis on mutual sharing as well as giving support and constructive feedback to one another. Group goals include encouraging self-exploration and self-expression, identifying current behavior patterns and alternative options, and expanding social skills. As a result, the individual goal is to generate new, more effective interpersonal skills.

[12]This list of treatment approaches is derived from the Manual of the Coldwater Canyon Hospital, "Adolescent and Child Mental Health Program," Los Angeles, California, 1987.

Movement Therapy

Movement therapy is a therapeutic use of movement to help improve the emotional and physical integration of an individual. In addition to helping patients find appropriate ways to release tension, movement therapy provides patients with the opportunity to express and deal with feelings which have defied words.

Multifamily Group

This is a weekly group designed for all parents and patients. The group provides a forum for the modeling and teaching of good communication skills between parents and their child. An important goal is to help strengthen the parent's ability to provide the son or daughter with limits and structure while still offering love and caring. Issues of the child's growing up and separating from the family are also addressed when relevant. In addition, the group provides an important support network for parents whose children are hospitalized.

Occupational Therapy

A registered Occupational Therapist (OTR) provides patients with the opportunity to learn and practice skills needed for a successful "occupation" of their time. The OTR evaluates the patient's strengths and weaknesses in the areas of self-care, social, emotional, mental, and physical and occupational functioning.

Psychodrama

Psychodrama groups meet on a weekly basis. The purpose is to provide an alternative expressive mode in which dramatic techniques are utilized to facilitate the exploring of painful emotional issues.

Recreational Therapy

The goal of recreational therapy (RT) at the Center for Personal Development is to provide patients with opportunities for learning and practicing social-recreational skills: skills which help individuals learn to use their time in more satisfying ways and to feel better about themselves.

School

The school program was provided by the school district. Teachers are trained in special education to meet the unique needs of hospitalized youth in the area.

One adolescent who was successfully treated in a program of this type in a psychiatric hospital was Jill. The following analysis reveals some of the reasons why Jill was helped by the processes in the program. A drug encounter group I directed was especially useful to her treatment in the hospital.

In Jill's overall treatment sessions she explored, and to a large extent, resolved her difficulties with her parents. In the drug encounter-group sessions she was confronted by me, the ex-addicts, and others in the group with the necessity of eliminating her self-destructive drug abuse. Here she was intensely verbally engaged about her drug abuse, and her general delinquent behavior.

In the adolescent drug group she regularly attended in the hospital, the several recovering ex-addicts from a total drug-addict therapeutic community were valuable in Jill's overall therapy. They were masters at encounter therapy. Of considerable importance was an ex-addict counselor named Renee from the therapeutic community (T.C.). Renee, 21, had a life experience that was very similar to Jill's. Renee at that time had been drug-free in her T.C. for two years. Renee became, for Jill, a friend, a role model, and a sponsor. In group, Renee made many comments like, "Jill I remember when I was your age I had the exact feelings you're talking about and I handled them." She would then delineate for Jill exactly how she handled her problems after she became drug-free.

In the conceptual scheme of the adolescent drug encounter group was the idea that when Addict A helps Addict B, Addict A is helped. In brief, it was not a one-way therapeutic contract between Renee and Jill; Renee's helping Jill in group and in many personal conversations was helpful to Renee in terms of reviewing the path she had traveled out of her own addiction. (Later on, Jill herself served as a role model with other younger people in the program.)

Two other teenagers who helped Jill immensely as role models for staying drug-free were Bill and Jane. They were both adolescent ex-addicts who had been in the hospital therapeutic community but now were living in the outside community. They had successfully traveled the track Jill was on and were able to help Jill through some difficult times in her social growth.

They were particularly helpful to Jill in a "slip" situation in the encounter group. Jill, on pass, went out with a young man on a date and had a few drinks and used some cocaine. She tearfully and fearfully copped out in the encounter group: "I have something to tell the group. I went out with this guy Jack and I like him a lot. I had a few drinks and when Jack offered me some coke I felt I couldn't say No. I mean I could say No—but I felt if I did he would think I was a jerk, and I'd never see him again. Anyway, I did take coke and I feel horrible. I thought I was cured."

Coming from a self-righteous position Bill blasted Jill. "I'm really pissed-off at you. You've been sitting in this group for four months and you haven't learned yet that this dick who offered you coke was not your friend. 'Friends' don't offer recovering addicts poison."

After some other verbal blasts from members of the group, including

Jill's sponsor Renee telling some stories about her slips, the group became very supportive of Jill's plight and talked about their own slips. It was valuable to hear from her peers about this. In fact, the group had become for Jill both a support and a control group. She commented, "When I did the coke I really didn't enjoy it like I used to. My first thought was shit I'm going to have to cop out to the group and I felt terrible." In a way the group had disabled her from going too far wrong, because they had inculcated her with an anti-drug attitude into her thought processes.

Another part of the program, in addition to the peer therapy that was of great significance in Jill's recovery, were the program directors and the adolescent ward psychiatric aides. On a nonschedule basis, either the adolescent ward director or a psychiatric aide with whom she had built a relationship would have a therapeutic session on the spot—at a time when it was often most vital for Jill to have someone to talk to. The aides and several residents in the program functioned as Jill's "caring circle of friends." Their caring and understanding treatment was vital to Jill's recovery process.

Along with the drug encounter group, the total process of the psychiatric individual and group counseling Jill received in the hospital program helped her to get along better with her family, and change her incorrigible delinquent behavior to a more acceptable law-abiding life situation.

In fact, most training schools produce the kind of negative experience described by Claude Brown. They tend to reinforce deviant values rather than resocialize the youth. These latter types of institutional programs appear to be more effective in treating delinquents than the long-term state facilities. These programs tend to reach the needs of the delinquent more effectively.

THE "THERAPEUTIC-COMMUNITY" CONCEPT APPLIED TO DELINQUENTS

An issue that has puzzled professionals in the field of treatment is: How do we *reach* recalcitrant teenagers like Claude Brown, and how do we incorporate some of their positive energy into the treatment process? A methodology that has emerged is the new "therapeutic community" movement.

The first therapeutic community, called Synanon, originated in 1958 with its founder Charles E. Dederich.[13] It employs a notable methodology that has had considerable impact on the treatment of juvenile delinquents, adult criminals, and drug addicts. The original organization has recently had internal problems that have incapacitated its work. The original Synanon method, however, has been replicated around the United States and Europe. Consequently, it is of value to delineate its approach, in some detail, in cross-comparison with the older reformatory systems described

---

[13]See Lewis Yablonsky, *Synanon: The Tunnel Back* (New York: Macmillan, 1965; Baltimore: Penguin, 1967).

here. The therapeutic-community concept has been adopted for the treatment of delinquents by a staff of former delinquents.[14]

CROSS-COMPARISONS OF THE SOCIAL STRUCTURE OF THERAPEUTIC COMMUNITIES AND TRADITIONAL CORRECTIONAL INSTITUTIONS: PRISONS, HOSPITALS, AND REFORMATORIES

In order to fully understand the structure of therapeutic communities for delinquents it is useful to cross-compare their organization with the traditional institutions devoted to resocializing deviants. Most traditional treatment structures have a two-tier caste system of organization. There are the "doctors" and the "patients"; the "correctional officers" and the "prisoners"; the "healers" and the "sick." This castelike division is based on the premise that if the patient follows his doctor-therapist's instructions, he will get well. Most reformatories reflect this type of medical model.

In a prison or a hospital, the assumption is that if the prisoner-patient follows the rules of the institution and properly interacts with his therapist, he will change and become a better citizen who can function more effectively in the larger society.

These castelike we-they medical model institutions have been dramatically changed by the therapeutic community approach. This point may be best made for our purposes by the following closer examination of the differences between the social structure of T.C.s and traditional institutions for deviant behavior change.

Most delinquents have a close familiarity with traditional "correctional" systems. The typical offender has learned how to do time in reformatories, prisons, jails, mental hospitals, or addict hospitals. Even at his first arrest, he is already equipped with a set of attitudes for handling encounters with society's law enforcers. He learns the proper set of attitudes and responses on the streets, and these are reinforced in the institution.

The "bad guys" are the cops, squares (nonaddicts), judges, jailers, and administrators. On the right side of the fence are "righteous dope fiends" and "stand-up guys." The offender learns quickly to trust the "right guys" and to hate and distrust the correctional officials.

In the traditional institution, if he's a right guy, he lives according to inmate rules. He believes "Thou shalt not squeal," engages in petty larceny, and gets some homosexual kicks from the prison punks. If he is a "solid" member of the inmate ingroup, he cons the staff members whenever he can. They are the enemy inside the walls, who represent the enemy (square society) outside the walls of the institution.

[14]The following analysis and discussion of therapeutic communities is derived from a paper by Lewis Yablonsky, presented at The Institute of The Eighth World Conference of Therapeutic Communities in Rome, Italy, in 1984. This paper is incorporated into Lewis Yablonsky, *The Therapeutic Community* (New York: Gardner Press, 1987).

Almost all members of hospital and prison officialdom are stereotyped by the inmate code—at best as inept, at worst as proper targets of extreme rebellious hatred. For most inmates they are objects to be manipulated for quick release, or they are tricks to beat for small scores to relieve the boredom and monotony of custody. In the chess game of manipulation, the institution's officials are pawns. This inmate code tends to confirm and reinforce criminal-addict ethics and behavior. The code reinforces lying, manipulation, and sociopathic behavior.

In contrast, the offender entering a T.C. is usually baffled by what he encounters in this different social system. Everyone is a "right guy," including the administrators, most of whom were in his position at one time. If he tries to play his usual institutional games, he is laughed at. He has difficulty hating the officials in a T.C., because they are people like himself or people who have experienced his delinquent lifestyle.

If he wants to break out (a common subject of conversation in most institutions), he is invited to get lost by the T.C. staff. At every turn he discovers new responses to old situations and, most important, other people who know how he feels and understand him. Instead of receiving a callous reaction, he is told, "I remember how I felt when I first got here," and this is often followed by a detailed description of the precise feeling he is experiencing at the time. This is often disconcerting and frightening, because it is a new and strange situation. Yet, at the same time, the sight of others like himself who "made it" gives him confidence. He has role models, people he can emulate, unlike the therapists he has known in most custodial situations.

In a T.C. he finds a new society. He encounters understanding and affection from people who have had life experiences similar to his own. He finds a community with which he can identify, people toward whom he can express the best human emotions that are in him, rather than the worst. He finds friends who will assist him when he begins to deviate or fall short of what he has set out to do: to develop and mature. In the new society of the T.C., he finds a vehicle for expressing his best human qualities and potential.

Caste and Stratification

The inmate subculture develops within any custodial institution, producing a "we-they" attitude between the professional administration and the inmates. The underground inmate society has norms, patterns of behavior, and goals different from and usually in conflict with those of the overall institution. This is partly due to the fact that inmates cannot rise in the status system and become staff.

The inmates and officialdom are divided into two segregated strata. The inmates may, in one context, be viewed as a caste of untouchables. They are restricted to an inferior position in the hierarchy, and in prison there is no possibility of their moving up. It is conceded by most correctional administrators that this inmate-administration conflict situation contradicts and impedes therapeutic progress for the inmate.

The inmate subsystem helps the patient or inmate cope with the new set of problems that he finds in most institutions. He feels rejected by the larger society and tries to compensate for this rejection. One way he does this is to reject and rebel against the *administrators* of society's rejection—the custodial staff.

A true T.C. does not have a "we-they" caste system. It provides an open-ended stratification situation. Upward mobility is distinctly possible in the organization, and in fact, upward movement in the system is encouraged. As one T.C. leader told a newcomer during an indoctrination session: "In a couple of years, you just might be a big shot around here and have my job." Not only is upward social mobility possible in a T.C., but healthy status-seeking is encouraged. This type of upward mobility is not possible in a traditional institution.

A T.C. organization assumes, with some supportive evidence, that a person's position in its hierarchy is a correlate of social maturity, "mental health," increased work ability, and a clear understanding of the organization. Another assumption is that the social skills learned in a T.C. structure are useful within the larger society. The reverse appears to be true of the "skills" learned in custodial institutions. The "we-they" problem does not exist in a true T.C. structure, since the administration and the "inmates" are one and the same; and upward mobility is encouraged in this open-ended stratification system.

PERSONALITY CHANGE IN A THERAPEUTIC COMMUNITY: ELIMINATING THE "CRIMINAL MASK"

Most delinquents who enter a T.C. for treatment have a tough facade or a "criminal mask" that they developed in their deviant lifestyle to survive on the streets. A postulate in a T.C. is that this face must be changed and a new one developed. This involves a 180-degree turn from the offender's past patterns of behavior. In a T.C., criminal language, jargon, and values are viewed with disdain and extreme disapproval. The newcomer may hang on to his past destructive mold for a brief time. In short order, however, new words and behavior patterns are ruthlessly demanded in an effective T.C.

Charles E. Dederich, the founder of Synanon, the first T.C., made the following cogent remarks on this issue to describe part of Synanon's resocialization process:

> First you remove the chemical. You stop him from using drugs and you do this by telling him to do it. He doesn't know he can do it himself, so you tell him to do it. We tell him he can stay and he can have a little job. We tell him we have a lot of fun and might get his name in the newspapers. We say, "People come down and you can show off and have a fine time as long as you don't shoot dope. You

want to shoot dope, fine, but someplace else, not here." Then you start working on secondary aspects of the syndrome. Addicts live by the discipline of narcotics; therefore, they talk about this all the time. They discuss petty theft and short con; none of them is well enough for big con. Addicts never pull any big scores; they can't—they're sick people. They talk about this.

The next thing you do is attack the language. Eliminating their criminal language is very important. We get them off drugs by telling them, "Live here without using drugs and you can have all this." We get them off the negative language by initially giving them another. Since there is some vague connection between their personality problem and the social sciences, we encourage them to use this language. The language of psychology and sociology is great stuff. Whether or not the recovering addict knows what he's talking about is exquisitely unimportant at this time.

Very quickly, in a matter of about ninety days, they turn into junior psychiatrists and sociologists. They become familiar with the use of a dozen or twenty words and misuse them. Who cares! It doesn't make any difference. Now they're talking about "the unconscious," "transferences," "displacement," "primary and secondary groups." This is all coming out, and they're not saying drugs, "fix, fix, fix" all the time. "I used $100 a day." "Joe went to jail behind this broad." "Where did you do time?" and all that. They get off that, and they talk about ids, superegos, and group structure. They make another set of noises, and their criminal facades drop away.[15]

Language is, of course, the vehicle of culture and behavior; and in a T.C., it is instrumental in shifting the behavior patterns that the addict has used in the past. He begins to use a new, still undeveloped set of social-emotional muscles.

T.C. members are not identified as wards, prisoners, or patients, and this also makes a big difference in their self-identity and outlook. The person can identify himself with the constructive goals of the organization for which he works. He automatically becomes an employee in the T.C. organization, at first on a menial level. Later on, he is encouraged to take part in the T.C.'s management and development.

In the traditional institution, the inmate feels helpless and hopeless about his destiny. He has limited power in the institution, since it is run by administrators who are indifferent to his opinions about its management. Moreover, as I have noted, institution officials are seen as representatives of society's rejection, and this sets up additional blockades to his progression in the custodial institution. Inmates have a clear authority object for their frustrations and hatreds: the custodial staff. In a T.C., there is no such split, since the administration consists of co-workers and colleagues. There is no "they" to hate within the organization.

Involvement in a T.C. helps to foster empathy in a youth whose basic problem is alienation from society. Identification with the T.C. involves feelings of concern for the other members and for the destiny of the totality

[15]Lewis Yablonsky, *Synanon: The Tunnel Back* (New York: Macmillan, 1965), p. 86.

of the organization. The development of these empathic qualities reverses the delinquent's past lack of social concern, and has a real impact on positive personality change. Vital to this personality change are various group processes directed by former delinquents.

GROUP PSYCHOTHERAPY IN CORRECTIONAL INSTITUTIONS AND IN A THERAPEUTIC COMMUNITY

All T.C.s have some form of regular group process built into their social structure. One significant major difference between T.C. group therapy and the usual institutional forms of group psychotherapy is that the T.C. sessions are not usually directed by professional therapists. There is considerable evidence that inmates participate in group psychotherapy with an eye on the gate leading out of the institution. Consciously and unconsciously, the inmate may verbalize "insights," seemingly indicating therapeutic progress, in an effort to convince the therapist and custodial officials that he has changed and is ready for release. At a group-therapy session I observed in a California institution, several inmates made a great show of getting wonderful insights, and as one fellow put it, "This program really makes me see life more clearly." But several inmates admitted in private, "Of course, I want to look good to get out of this joint."

T.C. sessions are more closely related to the real-life and work problems that confront the members. Given the lack of caste division, lines of communication are open throughout the organization. This, plus a goldfish-bowl atmosphere, is conducive to a more extensive examination of underlying problems. T.C. group sessions make intense efforts to surface all possible data about a member, since this is vital to the protection and growth of both the person and the T.C. organization. Since all T.C. members work for the organization, many real on-the-job problems are funneled into the T.C.'s group psychotherapy. All of these factors give a T.C.'s group process a reality not found in the closed-off social systems of most custodial institutions.

In summary, the following elements reflect the significant differences between the social structure and organization of effective T.C.s and traditional correctional institutions for delinquents:

1. There is a qualitative difference between indoctrination in T.C.s and other settings. The contractual arrangements for therapy and the prospect's expectation of success are different. The indoctrination of the delinquent by people who have themselves been in his shoes and succeeded appears to be a significant element, providing the newcomer with a role model of what he can become. Also, the "indoctrinator" sees where he was when he looks at the newcomer, and this is valuable for reinforcing his personal growth.
2. T.C.s provide the possibility of upward mobility, whereas most institutions are caste systems. Becoming a T.C. member is an incentive for changing one's delinquent motivation to antidelinquent motivation. The T.C. resident can actually achieve any role in the

organization. In contrast, in the traditional institution, an inmate or patient is locked into the inmate position.

3. There is a qualitative difference between the T.C. and the form of group therapy carried on in prisons and hospitals. This is partly a function of the described differences in the overall social-system context. The T.C. resident, as a voluntary participant, has little to gain from faking progress, whereas in other institutions, the appearance of being "rehabilitated" may be rewarded by an earlier release from custody. The T.C. resident is encouraged to reveal and deal with his problems honestly by others who have traveled the established T.C. route to recovery.

4. The T.C. subculture is integrated into the larger societal structure in a way that traditional institutions never are. The flow of members of the community through a T.C. and the participation of T.C. members in the larger society place it closer to the real-life situations of the outer world than the artificial communities of the traditional institutions that attempt personality change.

5. The work assigned in a T.C. is real work, unlike the often contrived jobs in most institutions. All work serves the real needs of the organization. This includes the functions of the procuring of food, an office staff, maintenance and service crews, automotive crews, and the coordinating staff. Everyone in a T.C. usually has meaningful work to do.

There have been attempts at self-government in reformatories and hospitals. In these settings, however, the inmates recognize that final decisions on important matters remain with the administration. In a T.C., perhaps for the first time in his life, a delinquent assumes a significant role in controlling his future. Leadership in a constructive situation is a new experience for him, and it appears to develop personal responsibility. The residents of a T.C., unlike patients and inmates, are involved with the growth and development of their own organization. Because there is a generally held belief by the residents that "the T.C. saved our lives," the esprit de corps in the organization is quite powerful. Few inmates would give three cheers for Warwick or Wyltwych, but in a T.C., youths seem to enjoy praising the organization that saved their life at every opportunity. They work hard for its growth and development.

PRINCIPAL SOCIAL FORCES AT WORK IN AN EFFECTIVE THERAPEUTIC COMMUNITY

The following elements comprise the essential social-psychological forces at work in an ideal therapeutic community for delinquents.

Involvement

Initially the T.C. society is able to involve and control the newcomer by providing an interesting social setting comprised of understanding associ-

ates who will not be outmaneuvered by manipulative behavior. The indoc-
trinators understand the newcomer because they were once in his position.

Achieveable Success Goals

Within the contest of this system, the delinquent can (perhaps for the first
time) see a realistic possibility for legitimate achievement and prestige. A
T.C. provides a rational opportunity structure for the newcomer. He is not
restricted to inmate or patient status, since there is no inmate-staff division
and all residents are immediately staff members.

New Social Role

Being a T.C. person is a new social role. It can be temporarily or indefinitely occupied in the process of social growth and development of new
projects. T.C.-trained staff are increasingly in demand.

Social Growth

In the process of acquiring legitimate social status in a T.C., the former
offender necessarily, as a side effect, develops the ability to relate, communicate, and work with others. The values of truth, honesty, and industry
become necessary means to this goal of status achievement. With enough
practice and time, the individual socialized in this way reacts according to
these values—naturally. This is a most effective system for people who,
upon entrance into a T.C., had an egocentric-sociopathic posture towards
life.

Social Control

The control of deviance is a byproduct of the individual's status seeking.
Conformity to the norms is necessary for achievement in a T.C. Anomie,
the dislocation of goals and means, is minimal. The norms are valid and
adhered to within the social system, since the means are available for legitimate goal attainment.

   Another form of control is embodied in the threat of ostracism. This,
too, becomes a binding force. The relative newcomer in a T.C. usually does
not feel adequate for participation in the larger society. After a sufficient
period of T.C. social living, the resident no longer fears banishment and is
adequately prepared for life outside (if this is his choice). However, he may
remain voluntarily because he feels a T.C. is a valid way of life for him. In a
T.C. he has learned and acquired a gratifying social role that enables him to
help others who can benefit from the approach.

   Another form of social control is the group process. Here the individual is required to tell the truth. This helps to regulate his behavior. Trans-
gressions are often prevented by the knowledge that his deviance will

rapidly and necessarily be brought to the attention of his pals in a group session. He is living in a community where others know about and, perhaps more important, care about his behavior.

Empathy and Self-Identity

The constant self-assessment required in daily life and in the group sessions fosters the consolidation of self-identity and empathy. The individual's self-estimation is under constant assessment by relevant others, who become sensitive to and concerned about him. The process provides the opportunity for the individual to see himself as others see him. He is also compelled, as part of this process, to develop the ability to identify with and understand others, if only to acquire higher status in the system. A side effect is personal growth, greater social awareness, an improved ability to communicate, and greater empathy. When these socialization processes take hold in the T.C., the participant learns how to function more effectively in both the T.C.'s social structure and, consequently, he is better prepared for life in the larger society. This is due to the fact that life in a T.C., unlike life in most correctional institutions, parallels the realities of life in the larger society.

Frankie: Delinquent to Artist

The delinquent's point of view and case history tend to best illuminate the T.C. process. The transition of Frankie, an 18-year-old former New York street gang member, reveals the therapeutic community process. The following summary of Frankie's odyssey from delinquent to artist is based on a number of interviews I had with Frankie and observations I made of him over the three-year period he resided in Synanon in California.

Frankie's first reaction to the T.C. was confusion: "The first thing they hit me with flipped me. This tough-looking cat says to me, 'There are two things you can't do here, shoot drugs or fight'." Frankie said, scratching his head, "I was all mixed up—these were the only two things I knew how to do."

Despite his confusion, he found the environment interesting and exciting and quite different from places where he had "done time." There were, for him, "lots of hip people." Among this group, was Jimmy, who at 48 had been an addict, a criminal, and a con man for more than 30 years. He was assigned as Frankie's sponsor. Jimmie ran the kitchen at that time. Frankie got his first job scouring pots and pans and mopping floors. According to Frankie, Jimmy could not be "conned" or manipulated out of position like the officers and therapists that Frankie had encountered in various New York institutions for juveniles. Jimmy, of course, knew the score: To him Frankie, with all his exploits, was a "young punk," who could give him no trouble. "I've met kids like this all my life—in and out of the joint," he said.

According to Frankie, "At first, I hated this bastard. I used to sometimes sit and plan ways to kill him." When Frankie wanted to fight Jimmy over a disagreement about work, Jimmy laughed and told him that if he wanted a fight, he would be thrown out of the place, get sent back to New York and a long prison term.

The usual institutional situation was reversed, and this confused Frankie. In other insitutions if Frankie got in trouble, confinement became increasingly severe, with the "hole" (solitary confinement) as an end point. In the Bellevue Hospital psychiatric ward, where Frankie had also spent time, it was a straitjacket. What made Frankie behave in order to stay in the T.C.? It wasn't only the potential threat of prison. In another setting his low impulse control would propel him out the door.

The fact that Frankie was exported from New York to Los Angeles was a significant initial force in keeping him in the T.C. As he commented: "At times I felt like splitting, then I thought it would be hard to make it back to New York. I didn't know Los Angeles and was afraid to go downtown where the drugs were, because I didn't know the people. Where I was was better than anything else I could do—at the time.

What was also of importance for Frankie was that there were others who understood him, had made the same "scenes," intuitively knew his problems and how to handle him. Although he would not grudgingly admit it, he respected people he could not "con." He belonged and was now part of a "family" he could accept.

Frankie could also make a "rep" in the T.C. without getting punished or locked up. In other institutions the highest he could achieve in terms of the values of the other inmates was to become "king" in the inmate world, acquire a "stash" of cigarettes, obtain some unsatisfactory homosexual favors, and land in the "hole." In the T.C., he felt he could acquire any role he was "big enough or man enough to achieve," and "growing up" carried the highest approval of his fellows. He could actually become a director in this organization. For the first time in his life, Frankie was receiving status, in gang terms a "rep," for being "clean" and nondelinquent.

Of course, when he first arrived, Frankie attempted to gain a "rep" by conniving and making deals, in accord with his old mode of relating. When he did, he was laughed at, ridiculed and given severe "haircuts" by other "old-time con men" in group session. They were, he learned, ferociously loyal to the organization, which had literally saved their lives and given them a new life status. He began to develop an esprit de corp for the T.C. As he once put it, "I never would give three cheers for Warwick reformatory. But I'm part of this place. It's a home to me."

Frankie found that "rep" was acquired in this social system (unlike the ones he had known) by truth, honesty, and industry. The values of his other life required reversal if he was to gain a "rep" in the T.C. These values were not goals per se that someone moralized about in a meaningless vacuum: They were means to the end of acquiring prestige in this tough social system with which he increasingly identified.

In the encounter groups, three nights a week, Frankie participated in a new kind of group psychotherapy, unlike the kind he had "fooled around with" in the reformatory. Here the truth was viciously demanded. Any rationalizations about past or current experiences were brutally demolished by the group. There was an intensive search for self-identity. He found that, in the process, he learned something of what went on beneath the surface of his thoughts. Frankie admitted that for the first time in his life he had found other people who had some idea of his underlying thoughts. He had had individual and group therapy in prison, but there he could "con" the therapist, and, most important, "I said what I thought they wanted to hear so I could get out sooner."

Frankie, who at first had followed his usual pattern of self-centered manipulation of others, now began to care about what happened to others, who were real friends to him. He began to identify with the organization and learned on a "gut level" that if any other member failed, in some measure he, too, failed.

Frankie began to gain some comprehension of what others thought in a social situation. The concept of empathy, or identifying with the thoughts and feelings of others, became a significant reality.

In the status system, Frankie's rise in the hierarchy was neither quick nor easy. He first moved from the "dishpan" to serving food at the kitchen counter. After several months, he began to work outside on a pickup truck that acquired food and other donations.

Here he had his first "slip"—no doubt, in part, to test the waters. With two other individuals who worked with him on the truck, a group decision was made one day that "smoking a joint might be fun." They acquired some grass from a connection known to one of the group.

When they arrived back from work, their slightly "loaded' appearance immediately became apparent to the group. ("They spotted us right away.") They were hauled into the main office and viciously (verbally) attacked and ordered to "cop out" (tell) or "get lost." A general meeting was called, and they were forced to reveal "all" before the entire group in a fireplace scene. That night Frankie was back washing dishes.

Frankie learned the hard way that the norms of the T.C. were the reverse of the criminal code he knew. In another slip situation Frankie, with two other members, went for a walk into town. One individual suggested buying some drugs from someone he knew in town. Frankie and the other member rejected the proposal. However, no one revealed the incident until two days later, when it came up in group. The group jumped hardest on Frankie and the other individual, who had vetoed the idea, rather than the one who had suggested buying the coke. Frankie and the other "witnesses" were expected to report such slips immediately, since the group's life depended on keeping one another straight. For the first time in his life, Frankie was censured for *not* being a snitch. The maxim "thou shalt not squeal," basic to the existence of the usual underworld delinquent gang culture, was reversed and ferociously upheld.

In another challenge for this former violent gang member, the no-physical-violence rule was at first difficult for Frank to grasp and believe, since his usual response to a difficult situation was to leap, fists first, past verbal means of communication into assault. As a result of the groups and other new patterns of interaction, Frankie's increasing ability to communicate began to minimize his assaultive impulses. Although at first he was kept from committing violence by the fear of ostracism, he later had no need to use violence, since he then had some ability to interact effectively. He learned to express himself in what was for him a new form of communication, on a nonviolent, verbal level. On occasion, Frankie would regress and have the motivation for assault, but the system had taken hold. In one session I heard him say, "I was so fucking mad yesterday, I wished I was back in the joint. I really wanted to hit that bastard Jimmy in the mouth."

Frankie had a sketchy almost nonexistent work record. Most of his time was taken up with gang fighting, pimping, armed robbery, or dealing drugs. Aside from some forced labor in the institution, he was seldom engaged in anything resembling formal work. His theme had been "work was uncool." He learned how to work in the T.C. as a side effect of his desire to rise in the status system. He also learned, as a side effect of working, the startling new fact that "talking to someone in the right way made them do more things than threatening them."

As a consequence of living in this new social system, Frankie's social learning and ability continued to increase. His destructive pattern of relating to others withered away. It was no longer functional for him in this new way of life. The T.C. experience increasingly developed his empathic ability. It produced an attachment to different, more socially acceptable values and reconnected him to the larger society in which the T.C. functioned as a valid organization.

The T.C. process unearthed a diamond in the rough. Frankie always had a proclivity for art. As he later described it to me, "When I was a kid I always liked to draw—but no one paid any attention to my sketches. The only thing I got was that I was teased by the other kids. I did some secret art work in the joint but tore it up. One day in a group discussion, they asked me what I really liked to do 'when I grew up.' I was scared to say it—but I said, 'I want to be an artist.' It was amazing for the first time in my life no one laughed. They even encouraged me to go to art school."

The T.C. truly worked for Frankie and the society. It converted a potential gang-killer into an artist. Frankie to date has been crime- and drug-free for over five years, works as a lithographer, has created many interesting works of art, and has given up the delinquent life he seemed destined to live.

AFTERWORD

The total array of indidivual and group processes described in this section, including reality therapy, transactional analysis, guided group interaction, encounter groups, psychodrama, role playing, and role training, constitute a significant body of treatment methods that can help change delinquents into law-abiding citizens. These methodologies can effectively be incorporated into the various institutional and community-based programs described. They have a special relevance and effectiveness for resocializing delinquents when they are properly utilized in the correct setting.

Most delinquents, in my view, are amenable to becoming law-abiding, productive citizens if they are helped through their difficult adolescent years by caring, empathetic adult role models who use the variety of methodologies and institutional systems that have been developed over the years in an effective way. In my work, I have seen extremely recalcitrant delinquents respond to treatment when they are treated with intelligence, love, and respect in a truly therapeutic community.

SUMMARY: BASIC THEMES FOR CLASS DISCUSSION

1. Incarceration in a state or county institution for a long period of time, usually over a year, is the endpoint for delinquents who are persistent law violators. These are "total institutions" in the sense that they attempt to administer to the total range of social and psychological needs of the juvenile. They are prisons in the sense that a youth is controlled and deprived of his or her freedom; however, an attempt is made to rehabilitate youths through educational, occupational, and emotional treatment programs.

2. In these long-term institutions, an inmate social system often emerges which is in conflict with treatment and resocialization goals. In the deviant subculture of the institution, "toughness" and negative values demonstrating antisocial behavior are too often the norm. Claude Brown describes in great detail the underground culture of the institution and its deviant norms, which tend to reinforce "street-smarts" and a continuation of delinquency when a ward is released from custody. In effect, many long-term state reformatories are "schools for delinquency."

3. To counteract this "training-schools-for-delinquency" problem, many states have developed smaller residential treatment institutions which emphasize more individualized treatment, positive values, and various types of group therapy. This type of institution appears to have a higher success rate than the traditional state reformatory system.

4. A major development in recent years has been the burgeoning use of psychiatric and mental hospitals for juvenile delinquents. In these settings, various treatment approaches are emphasized. Prototypically, the treatment includes individual and family counseling, group therapy and psychodrama, special education for learning-disabled youths, and special groups for treating alcohol and substance abuse problems.

5. A significant development and breakthrough in the treatment field is the concept of the therapeutic community. Although these pro-

grams utilize some standard treatment modalities, a great emphasis is given to the utilization of ex-criminals, ex-delinquents, and re-covering, drug-free substance abusers in the process. In the hier-archy of the therapeutic community paraprofessionals who have had problems themselves are utilized in the treatment process.

In brief, in the therapeutic community, in addition to stan-dard mental health professionals, treatment energy is drawn from people who were former addicts or delinquents. These paraprofes-sionals have four significant areas of expertise:

a. They are familiar with the substance-abuse delinquent problem from their own experience.

b. They have gone through the recovery process and are familiar with the pitfalls, the process, and the value changes required for rehabilitation.

c. They know something about the difficulties and pressures re-lated to remaining delinquency- or drug-free in the open com-munity.

d. They are highly motivated to help others. This provides them with a worthwhile occupation that is personally beneficial and rewarding and in addition helps others become resocialized into productive, law-abiding citizens.

QUESTIONS

15.1. Cross-compare the relative merits and problems of total state reformatories as compared to smaller residential treatment centers.

15.2. Delineate and discuss the divergent perspectives of the administrators of in-stitutions for juveniles, and the subculture and viewpoint of the inmate of the institution.

15.3. Can a residential treatment institution function without the potential threat for a ward of being sent to the larger, more onerous state reformatory if he misbehaves?

15.4. Why are some state institutions for delinquents characterized as "crime schools?"

15.5. What are some of the background differences between youths sent to state reformatories in contrast with youths placed in mental hospitals? Why don't we send all delinquents to mental hospitals?

15.6. Discuss the structure and process of the therapeutic community. What are some of the advantages and problems inherent in the therapeutic-community approach, compared to other modalities, for resocializing delinquents?

Name Index

Subject Index